CATALOGUE OF THE BABYLONIAN TABLETS IN THE BRITISH MUSEUM

VOLUME VIII: TABLETS FROM SIPPAR 3

by

ERLE LEICHTY

J.J. FINKELSTEIN

and

C.B.F. WALKER

PUBLISHED BY BRITISH MUSEUM PUBLICATIONS FOR
THE TRUSTEES OF THE BRITISH MUSEUM
1988

Published by the British Museum Publications Ltd.
46 Bloomsbury St. London WC1B 3QQ

British Library Cataloguing in Publication Data

British Museum

Catalogue of the Babylonian tablets in the British Museum
Vol. VIII: Tablets from Sippar, 3.
1. Akkadian language—Texts—Catalogs
I. Title II. Leichty, Erle
III. Finkelstein, J.J.
IV. Walker, C.B.F.
492′.1′0216 PJ3701
ISBN 0-7141-1124-4

PRINTED IN GREAT BRITAIN

PREFACE

The publication of the present volume of the *Catalogue of the Babylonian Tablets in the British Museum* completes the series of three volumes (VI-VIII) which largely contain tablets excavated in the last century on behalf of the Trustees by Hormuzd Rassam at Abu Habbah, ancient Sippar. This volume also includes substantial collections from Sippar and Tell ed-Der acquired for the Trustees by E.A.W. Budge.

This volume, like its two predecessors, is in large part the work of Professor Erle V. Leichty, Professor of Assyriology at the University of Pennsylvania and Curator of Akkadian Language and Literature in The University Museum. He has made use of a manuscript catalogue of the Old Babylonian tablets in the Bu 88-5-12 and Bu 91-5-9 collections which had been prepared by the late Professor J.J. Finkelstein, formerly William M. Laffan Professor of Assyriology and Babylonian Literature at Yale University. Professor Finkelstein's contribution has been revised by Mr. C.B.F. Walker, Assistant Keeper in the Department, who has catalogued the remaining Old Babylonian tablets in this volume and has continued to act as coordinating editor of the series.

As with the two previous volumes Professor Leichty has arranged for the preparation of the camera-ready sheets in Philadelphia, the printing and binding being done in London. The completion of this volume marks the culmination of some fifteen years' work by Professor Leichty, and it is an appropriate occasion to record the gratitude of the Department for the dedication which has brought him year by year to the British Museum in order to devote so much of that precious commodity, his time, to the project. His contribution has not ended there because he has given up a considerable amount of time to it in Philadelphia, and has acted as a very effective link with The University Museum and its resources. All specialists owe him a great debt for this contribution to ancient near eastern studies.

T.C. MITCHELL
Keeper

DEPARTMENT OF WESTERN ASIATIC ANTIQUITIES
THE BRITISH MUSEUM
August 1987

To the Memory of

R.D. Barnett

who initiated the Sippar cataloguing project

CONTENTS

FOREWORD

This volume is the third and final volume comprising the catalogue of the "Sippar" tablets. The volume contains an introduction on the provenience and content of the pertinent collections and a catalogue of tablets numbered BM 74329-84999; 93043-93064; 99439-99999; 100701-101945. The introduction and index of Old Babylonian tablets were written by C.B.F. Walker. The other indices are the work of Pamela Gerardi. The catalogue of the Old Babylonian tablets was made by J.J. Finkelstein and revised by C.B.F. Walker. The rest of the catalogue is my work.

Entries are made by date number rather than by BM number because the date numbers have some bearing on provenience. BM numbers normally follow in the same sequence as date numbers but there are exceptions which are cross-indexed on pp. xxvii-xxxi. Date number and BM number are given for each entry. The third column of each entry contains chronological information. If there is no entry in this column, the tablet is Neo-Babylonian. The fourth column denotes preservation: C = complete, NC = nearly complete, and F = fragment. The final column contains a brief description of content. Bibliographical information is given minimally. Normally the reader is referred to the primary publication only and can expect to find further bibliographic information in Borger's *HKl*.

This volume catalogues a large number of Old Babylonian tablets. In legal texts the oaths by the king are used as evidence for dating, but are not individually specified. Thus a tablet dated in the catalogue simply as "Ha" may have a broken Hammurapi year formula or may have an oath by Hammurapi. Royal names appearing on seal inscriptions (e.g., "servant of Hammurapi") have not been used as dating evidence. The term "seals" simply means that a tablet is sealed without reference to the number of seal impressions that appear on a tablet; there may be impressions of several seals, multiple impressions of a single seal, or a single impression of a single seal. It is assumed that students of seals will re-examine all sealed tablets themselves to verify the facts. In cases where a case tablet has been wholly or partially broken open the fact of its being a case tablet is obvious; but occasionally there may be room for doubt whether a tablet is really an unopened case tablet. Therefore we distinguish between "tablet in case" (where the inner tablet is visible) and "case unopened" (where the inner tablet is not visible). The Old Babylonian tablets are indexed separately on pp. 427-432.

We have been fortunate in receiving help from Assyriological colleagues throughout the world. The list of all those who helped us is far too long to print here, and we hope those slighted will forgive us. A few colleagues who were of extraordinary helpfulness are singled out below.

Special thanks for help with the Sumerian tablets goes to S.N. Kramer, P. Michalowski, and H. Behrens. Literary and bilingual texts were shown to I.L. Finkel, M. Geller, and W.G. Lambert. F. Köcher aided us with the medical texts, and the late D.A. Kennedy with the late texts.

The typesetting of the volume was done by Michael Arnush. We received considerable help from Pamela Gerardi who also prepared the mechanicals. I.L. Finkel and C.B.F. Walker read proofs and offered numerous improvements.

We are indebted to the Trustees of the British Museum and a succession of Keepers of Western Asiatic Antiquities, the late R.D. Barnett, E. Sollberger, and T.C. Mitchell. The friendly support and generous help of the staff of Western Asiatic Antiquities contributed greatly to the completion of this catalogue.

We would like to take this opportunity to dedicate this volume to the memory of Richard D. Barnett, who renewed the cataloguing of western asiatic antiquities in the British Museum and initiated the "Sippar" catalogue.

Erle Leichty,
December, 1987

INTRODUCTION

by

C.B.F. Walker

The present volume contains a catalogue of those tablets in the Museum's collections which fall between the BM numbers 74329 and 84999, together with a few groups of tablets belonging to the 83-1-21 collection which have higher BM numbers. All the tablets here catalogued were acquired or registered in the collections between September 1882 and October 1895. They include the final part of the tablets excavated by Hormuzd Rassam at Sippar, Babylon, etc., major Old Babylonian archives, which if Budge's informants are to be believed came largely from Sippar and Tell ed-Der, and some smaller collections purchased from dealers. Other tablets acquired by the Museum in the 1890s onwards are numbered in the series BM 12230-29999 and 85000ff. In particular three collections of tablets acquired from Selim Homsy & Co and supposedly deriving from Tell ed-Der are numbered BM 16465-17596 and 22509-22714.

Rassam's excavations have been discussed in Dr J. E. Reade's introduction to volume VI of this Catalogue. The catalogue of the AH 82-9-18A and 83-1-21 collections given here completes the catalogue of the registered collections from Rassam's excavations at Sippar and elsewhere.

The evidence for Budge's major purchases in Baghdad and his excavation at Tell ed-Der is given here in quotation from published and unpublished sources. It will be apparent from this evidence that it is not possible to give a reliable account of the origins of any part of these collections. The three relevant collections (Bu 88-5-12, Bu 89-4-26 and Bu 91-5-9) plainly contain parts of major archives of the Old Babylonian period which Budge, relying on the statements of the dealers and the visible evidence of excavations at the sites, believed to come from Sippar and Tell ed-Der. He also believed that the 89-10-14 collection, purchased from Selim Homsy & Co, came from Tell ed-Der.

Most of the remaining tablets catalogued here were purchased from the dealers Spartali & Co, and J. M. Shemtob. It is evident from Budge's reports and correspondence that he believed these dealers to be receiving their tablets directly or indirectly from the watchmen appointed by the Museum to guard its excavations at Babylon and Sippar. Official correspondence demonstrates clearly that Selim Homsy & Co also represented the interests of several Baghdad families.

Budge's reports and correspondence include a considerable amount of information on the activities of the Museum's watchmen, on the illegal excavations, and on the affairs of the various antiquities dealers and their families in Baghdad and London. The whole subject would be material for an informative and entertaining monograph, but the present discussion is restricted to what can be learned about the origins of the Museum's collections.

In the following discussion of the individual collections note that in quotations from original records and published sources some editorial comments are presented in square brackets. The copies of the Trustees Minutes and Reports to the Trustees preserved in the Department of Western Asiatic Antiquities are referred to simply as TM and TR. Trustees Minutes are referred to by the date of the relevant Trustees' meeting and page number.

It will be readily apparent that in most cases it is not possible to be specific about the provenance of either individual tablets or whole collections. One chronological remark may however be useful. It appears both from the previous two volumes of the catalogue and from the material here catalogued that only a very small proportion of the later Babylonian tablets in these "Sippar" collections are datable after the reign of Artaxerxes (probably Artaxerxes I). Given the evidence for the inclusion of tablets from Babylon and Borsippa in these collections, and the existence of many Hellenistic and Seleucid period tablets in the "Babylon" collections, it seems quite probable that the Sippar archives in fact came to an end in the time of Artaxerxes and that all later tablets included in the "Sippar" collections and catalogued in volumes VI-VIII of this catalogue come from Babylon or its vicinity.

82-9-18A, 45-408 (74329-74683 etc.)

From Rassam's excavations; largely from Abu Habba (Sippar).

For comment on this collection see *Catalogue of the Babylonian Tablets* VI xxxiii, and for the original inventory of the 82-9-18 collection, with which this group certainly belongs, see *Catalogue of Babylonian Tablets* VII xvii.

The collection includes 44 inscribed and uninscribed objects, and tablets numbered 45-408. Of these 5 are Old Babylonian (139, 140, 141, 220, 220A); the remainder are Neo-Babylonian, dated from Nabopolassar to Xerxes, except for 219 (Esarhaddon) and 377 (Šamaš-šumukin). The majority of tablets for which this catalogue records a provenance come from Sippar; others are from Babylon or its environs, and one (320) comes from Uruk.

AH 83-1-18, 1-2600A (74684-77218 etc.)

From Rassam's excavations at Abu Habba (Sippar), Babylon, Borsippa, and Nineveh (76091, 77023).

For comment on this collection see *Catalogue of the Babylonian Tablets* VI xxxiv.

Hormuzd Rassam's report to the Museum of 18th October 1882 (P 5206, 16 Nov 1882) describes the material which should comprise the 1883-1-18 and AH 1883-1-18 collections as follows:

Case 1, from Kuyunjik, contains 91 whole, and 822 fragments of inscribed terracottas, 8 pieces of clay seals, 5 heads of terracotta figures, 7 pieces of broken arms of statues, 10 pieces of inscribed stone, 2 pieces of alabaster bowls with figures on them, a kite of marble with a gold ring on its head, 3 glass bottles, an iron hatchet, a copper bell, 12 pieces of old iron objects, 4 copper hooks, 3 pieces of broken glass and a terracotta lamp.

Case 2 contains bricks from Kuyunjik and Nimroud.

Case 3 contains sculptured and inscribed stones from Kuyunjik.

Case 4 contains 17 whole and 1177 fragments of inscribed clay tablets from Birs Nimroud; 850 very small pieces of inscribed clay, broken bowls inscribed with Hebrew characters, and a small stone duck from Aboo-habba, 2 whole and 116 pieces of inscribed clay, 5 ivory pens, a unique inscribed stone tablet, 4 terracotta figures, and a piece of silver bullion from Babylon.

Case 5 contains inscribed bricks from Aboo-habba, a piece of wood from Birs Nimroud, and a piece of black basalt with a rude bas-relief from the mound of Jirjib on the Haboor.

This is the last collection from the explorations in Assyria and Babylonia.

In the AH 83-1-18 collection as catalogued items 2478 and 2589-2596 are uninscribed. The remainder of the collection consists mainly of Neo-Babylonian economic texts dated between Nebuchadnezzar II and Artaxerxes (except for 1337 Sargon, 1131 and 2555 Kandalanu, 1847 Philip [literary], 2583 Antiochus, 2340 and 2344 Seleucus/Antiochus from Borsippa); 1456 and 2398 are Neo-Assyrian.

The majority of tablets for which this catalogue records a provenance come from Sippar; a few are from Babylon or its environs, and two (2340, 2344) come from Borsippa.

Fragments in this collection have been joined to fragments from the K, 81-11-3, 82-3-23, 82-7-

14, 82-9-18, and 83-1-21 collections.

83-1-18, 704 (91036)

From Rassam's excavations.

Cone of Kadashman-Enlil, *BBSt* no. 1; see *Tell ed-Der* III 106-7.

For comment on this collection see *Catalogue of the Babylonian Tablets* VI xxxiv, and for its inventory see on the AH 83-1-18 collection above.

83-1-21, 1-3606 (82838-84525, 84910-84999, 94043-93064, 99439-99999, 100701-101945)

From Rassam's excavations.

For comment on this collection see *Catalogue of the Babylonian Tablets* VI xxxiv.

The tablets in this collection until recently only bore BM numbers (with a few exceptions: 70, 72-3, 1974-2117, 2137-40, 2143-5) and were described as "AH unnumbered." They mostly represent the better part of those tablets from Rassam's excavations in Babylonia which had been unpacked in the 19th century but not fully registered. The majority of the tablets here catalogued are Neo-Babylonian economic (from Nabopolassar to Artaxerxes) and literary texts of a character similar to those already catalogued from Rassam's excavations at Babylon, Sippar and elsewhere. A few are dated at Babylon, Borsippa, and Sippar. Only detailed study will reveal the provenance of individual tablets. The collection includes 1 Old Akkadian tablet, 59 Old Babylonian tablets and 1 Kassite(?) tablet. The Old Babylonian tablets are likely to have come from Sippar or its vicinity.

There is some evidence that a few original groups of tablets have been kept together despite everything, e.g. a large group of NB letters, 1689-1778, a group of literary and lexical texts, 1779-1800, and a large group of tablets marked 84-2-1 mostly being astronomical texts, 1974-2117. The mark 84-2-1 also appears on nos. 70, 72, 73; nos. 2137-2140 and 2145 are marked 82-9-18, and nos. 2143-2144 are marked AH 82-9-18.

Fragments in this collection have been joined to fragments from the 82-5-22, 82-7-14, AH 82-9-18, 83-1-18, K and Sp III collections.

83-4-5, 1-2 (77219-77220)

Purchased from J. M. Shemtob, London.

Two Neo-Babylonian literary texts and one uninscribed object.

83-6-30, 1-29 (77221-77249)

Purchased from J. M. Shemtob, London.

Neo-Babylonian tablets, including many astronomical texts which probably come from Babylon. Fragments in this collection have been joined to fragments from the Rm, Sp and Sp III collections.

SH 83-9-28, 1-42 (77250-77274 and 82820-82836)

Purchased from J. M. Shemtob, London.

Neo-Babylonian tablets including many astronomical texts which probably come from Babylon. Fragments in this collection have been joined to fragments from the Sp, Sp II, Sp III, 81-2-1, and SH 83-9-28 collections.

83-12-31, 1 (82837)

Presented by W. Boyd Dawkins.

1 Neo-Babylonian economic text.

84-2-11, 1-557, 595 (77275-77808, etc.)

Purchased from Spartali & Co, London.

The collection is reported by Birch (TR 1882-84, 227) as coming from "Sippara Babylon Cuthah and Dilbat or Dailma."

According to Budge the Spartali company failed in 1884 (TR 1888-89, 155).

Neo-Babylonian tablets, mostly economic (from Kandalanu to Darius), and one Old Babylonian tablet.

Fragments in this collection have been joined to fragments from the Sp II, and 82-5-22 collections.

84-11-12, 1-5 (77809-77813)

Presented by W. M. Ramsay.

Five Old Assyrian tablets and one uninscribed object. This was one of the first groups of Old Assyrian tablets to arrive in western Europe. See T. G. Pinches, *PSBA* 4 (1882) 11-19 and A. H. Sayce, *PSBA* 6 (1883) 17-25.

85-4-30, 1-257 (77815-78063, etc.)

Purchased from J. M. Shemtob, London.

This collection was apparently a selection from a group of 874 tablets first offered in July 1884.

Neo-Babylonian tablets, mostly economic

(from Šamaššumukin to Artaxerxes), and 4 Old Babylonian tablets.

One fragment in this collection has been joined to a fragment from the 82-9-18 collection.

85-11-27, 1-12 (78064-78075)
Purchased from J. M. Shemtob, London.
Neo-Babylonian tablets, mostly economic.

86-5-12, 1-9 (78076-78083)
Purchased from J. M. Shemtob, London.
Neo-Babylonian economic, literary and scientific texts.

86-5-20, 1 (78084)
Purchased from J. M. Shemtob, London.
Neo-Babylonian mathematical text.

86-6-17, 1-15 (78085-78099)
Purchased from J. M. Shemtob, London.
Neo-Babylonian tablets, mostly economic (Šamaššumukin to Xerxes).

86-7-20, 1-46 (78100-78141, etc.)
Purchased from J. M. Shemtob, London.
According to TR 1885-86, 89 this was "a careful selection from a large collection."
Neo-Babylonian tablets, mostly economic (Šamaššumukin to Darius) and lexical.

87-1-14, 1-2 (78142-78143)
Vendor/donor unknown.
Two Achaemenid economic texts (from Babylon and Sippar) and two cylinder seals.

87-7-25, 1-6 (78144-78148, etc.)
Purchased from J. M. Shemtob, London.
Neo-Babylonian tablets (Nabopolassar to Darius).

88-4-19, 1-26 (78149-78170, etc.)
Vendor/donor unknown.
Neo-Babylonian tablets, mainly economic (Tiglath-pileser III to Darius).

Bu 88-5-12, 1-769 (78172-78814, etc.)
Budge purchase.

Discussion of this collection should begin with a warning. The British Museum has two separate collections, Bu 88-5-12 (collected by Budge) and 88-5-12 (purchased from J. M. Shemtob). The distinction between the two collections may not always have been fully observed in published or unpublished records.

The Bu 88-5-12 collection was acquired by the Museum as a result of E. A. W. Budge's second mission, to Egypt and Mesopotamia in 1887-88; the mission was primarily intended to investigate the "leakage" of tablets from sites supposedly guarded on behalf of the British Museum.

The earliest, albeit brief, account of this mission is given in the Trustees Minutes (relevant extracts are here quoted from the manuscript copy in the Department of Western Asiatic Antiquities). In a letter dated 18th February 1888 Budge reported that since his arrival on 13th February he had purchased about 300 tablets in Baghdad (TM 1888-4-14/2234). In a letter written at Baghdad on 29th February, "on returning from inspection of Hillah, Gimgimah, Babil, and Abu Habbah," he reported that he had purchased 450 tablets from "the late large find of Tablets" made at Gimgimah [part of Babylon]; he knew where the remainder of the tablets were and they would be consigned to him in London (TM 1888-4-14/2238 and 2263). A letter dated Suez, 2 April (1888) reported that he had "bought about 500 tablets which are on the road to England; and another 380 are also on their way" (TM 1888-4-14/2243 and 2265). The summary report made to the Trustees on 12 May 1888 lists Budge's Babylonian purchases as: 1 Stone weight with bilingual Persian and Babylonian inscription. 10 fragments of Babylonian historical cylinders. Porcelain figure of an animal. About 780 inscribed case and other tablets, dating from B.C. 2500 to the time of Darius (about 150 of these have not yet arrived). In addition 9 Babylonian contract tablets were received as gifts. (TM 1888-5-12/2257, 2259; TR 1887-89, 81-82, May 19th 1888). [Do the 150 later arriving tablets represent the "remainder" of the tablets found at Gimgimah?]

Budge gives a lengthy personal account of the mission in *By Nile and Tigris* (London, 1920) I 123-338 (written 30 years after the events narrated). Specific reference to the finding and acquisition of tablets is made on pages 227-28, 233-41, 268-74, 311-323, 338. The first part of the collection was purchased by Budge directly from several dealers in Baghdad (pp. 235-36) and reportedly included tablets from Abu Habbah (p. 235). In view of the facts that the collections acquired by Rassam from Babylon, Sippar etc. were overwhelmingly Late Babylonian, and that the Bu 88-5-12 collection is mostly Old Babylonian, it is curious that Budge should claim (p. 239): "I saw for myself and was firmly convinced that more than nine-tenths of the tablets came from sites which the Trustees had spent some thousands of pounds excavating. Moreover, I saw that they belonged to the same sets as tablets in the British Museum."

Having despatched these to London, Budge subsequently visited Cutha, Babylon, Hillah and Borsippa (pp. 249-58, 268-74, 311-14). In Hillah he purchased the basalt weight of Darius I [Bu 88-5-12, 257 = BM 91117; p. 268]. At Babylon he purchased "several old Babylonian contract tablets [not at present identifiable] for a few piastres each, and several large pieces of cylinders of Esarhaddon [Bu 88-5-12, 74-80 and 101-3; registered as coming from Hillah] for a majîdî (dollar) each" (p. 273) and "several contract tablets of the Persian and later periods" (p. 311). Budge completed his tour with visits to Abu Habbah [Sippar] and Dêr [Tell ed-Der] (pp. 315-21). He subsequently purchased in Baghdad a collection of tablets [from Jumjumah?] and cylinder seals [Bu 88-5-12, 770-780?] belonging to the watchman at Abu Habbah (pp. 317-19). At Dêr he was shown a collection of Old Babylonian case tablets (p. 320). In Baghdad he purchased "the tablets which I had reason to believe came from Dêr, namely, a small collection of very fine and perfect case-tablets, which dated from about B.C. 2000."

In total Budge gave himself credit for "saving for scientific investigation some thousands of valuable tablets" (p. 329). On the same expedition he also acquired for the Museum 81 Amarna tablets in Egypt [Bu 88-10-13, 1-81 = BM E.29784-29828, 29830-29865] (pp. 128-29, 139-43, 338) and a Parthian stone coffin [presented by T. J. Malcolm; 88-7-14, 1 = BM 91933; TR 1888-89, 91] (p. 332).

Budge summarises his acquisitions of tablets on this mission as "About 750 Babylonian tablets, purchased in Baghdâd and Hillah, and about 1520 tablets which I selected from collections offered to me at Baṣrah, and for which I arranged that payment should be made in London" (p. 338). The 750 tablets plainly correspond to the Bu 88-5-12 collection (though see the cautionary remarks made below on the size of this collection). The 1520 tablets cannot be accounted for; it may be noted that his own narrative makes no reference to seeing tablets at Baṣrah, but even if Baghdad be intended rather than Basrah it is not clear what subsequently purchased collections (if any) he had in mind. Apart from the 88-5-12 collection (126 items purchased from J. M. Shemtob) all later purchased collections arrived in the British Museum after Budge's 1889 mission.

Budge's description of the same mission in *The Rise and Progress of Assyriology* (London, 1925), pp. 138-40, adds details of his purchases and his visit to Dêr:

"Within a week I found that the exportation of tablets was an important and profitable business in Baghdâd and Baṣrah. Mr. Dawud Thômâ, Rassam's overseer, and his brother ᶜAbd al-Karîm and ᶜAbd al-Aḥad possessed very large collections from Abû Habbah; and when I had acquired these, Dawud Thômâ took me to the houses of his friends, where I found other large collections of tablets from Abû Habbah and some sites near the Birs-i-Nimrûd. Rassam's overseer and some of his watchmen sold me several collections of valuable tablets. . . . [All this presumably relates to the purchase of the first 300 tablets; Abdulkerim and Daud Thoma subsequently sold the Museum several collections of tablets, often using Selim Homsy & Co as intermediary.] From Baghdâd I visited all the sites where Rassam had carried on excavations, Abû Habbah, Tall Ibrâhîm, Birs-i-Nimrûd, Ibrâhîm al-Khalîl, Jumjumah and other places near Babylon, and Dailem. . . . At every place I visited I purchased good tablets . . ."

"Whilst I was wandering about Musayyib one evening, a native brought me several fine "case-tablets," i.e. inscribed tablets encased in clay envelopes, inscribed with a duplicate of the text on the tablet, and bearing impressions of many seal-cylinders, which he wanted to sell. They were the finest of their kind that I had ever seen; and with difficulty I drew from him the fact that they came from Dêr, a site about twenty miles south of Baghdâd. He said there were ruins of walls there in which the openings where gates had been could be seen, and that in one corner there were several chambers full of such tablets. This seemed incredible; but I rode to the ruins the following day, and I saw enough to convince me that the site was worth excavating. At a depth of three feet from the surface the natives with me showed me fine solid walls built of large rectangular Babylonian bricks about 16 inches square; but when I pressed to see the chambers about which the native had told me the previous day, they said that men were watching them from a distance, and they were afraid of getting into trouble with the authorities in Baghdâd."

He also comments on his visit to Abu Habbah (p. 133): "I visited the site in 1888 and 1891 and found the natives digging in the chambers which Rassam had left untouched, under the excuse that they were digging for bricks, and carrying away the dust to spread over their fields for top-dressing. On going through the chambers I saw the remains of great numbers of large jars, which resembled the *zîr*, or waterpot; and the natives told me that when they opened them, they found them full of soft unbaked inscribed tablets. In other chambers they discovered small sealed pots, which contained large inscribed baked tablets about 4 inches long. In one chamber they found rows of larger tablets arranged on stone shelves; and to these dockets or seals were attached by means of cord made of some kind of vegetable fibre."

It will be readily apparent that the figures given by these three sources are fully reconcilable neither with each other nor with the Museum's actual collections. The major problems are the 450 tablets reported as acquired from the find at Gimgimah (Babylon) and the missing collection of 1520 tablets selected for purchase at Baṣrah(?). The major part of the Bu 88-5-12 collection are Old Babylonian tablets, and study of these over the years has indicated that by and large they come from Sippar or its vicinity; there is no obvious large collection of OB tablets from Babylon. The Late Babylonian tablets in this collection amount to about 80, and even if almost all came from Babylon there is a significant discrepancy with the reported figure of 450. In any case "provenances" derived essentially from the claims of dealers have doubtful value as evidence.

In the face of the discrepancies between the various accounts and the presently ascertainable facts one has to conclude that the most useful evidence about the provenance of this collection (apart from a few specific items) is the internal evidence yielded by the content of the tablets themselves.

Examination of the handwriting in the register of this collection shows that the entries for several numbers were at first left blank, and only completed later. A whole series of numbers were added later at the end of the first series registered. The numbers in question are: 59, 75-80, 101-13, 135, 135A, 257, 625, 651-54, 665, 667A, 668, 711-14, 717, 731-81 and 731A-42A. Plainly some objects were on exhibition at the time when the register was first compiled. Those objects added to the register in the 1970s and later (135, 770-81 and 731A-42A) were added because they were found to have the Bu 88-5-12 number already on them although not previously included in the register; this also explains the duplicate numbering from 731A onwards). These remarks serve only to show how difficult it would have been even when Budge was writing his accounts in the 1920s to establish the precise nature and size of this collection. Items 74-80, 101-3, 135A, 257, 651-54 are specifically registered as coming from Hillah, but it will be noted that these items are all among the later additions to the register; the register entry may derive from Budge's publications or oral information. A succession of ditto-marks may also suggest that items 81-94 and 104-13 also come from Hillah, but experience suggests that ditto-marks in the Museum's registers are to be treated with considerable caution.

The large majority of tablets in this collection are Old Babylonian, ranging in date from Sumulael and Immerum to Samsu-ditana but mostly (about 90%) from the time of Hammurapi or later.

Over nearly a century of study Assyriologists have concluded that the bulk of the Old Babylonian tablets come from the city of Sippar or its vicinity. It is not feasible to document that statement in detail; see in general R. Harris, *Ancient Sippar* (Leiden, 1975). Apart from legal texts which contain oaths by the city of Sippar (not detailed in the catalogue; mostly from the reign of Hammurapi or earlier), numerous references to the city of Sippar and its dependencies Sippar-amnānum and Sippar-iaḫrurum occur in legal and administrative documents and letters. Few of these references are alluded to in the necessarily brief format of this catalogue, but for examples see the entries for Bu 88-5-12, 15, 133, 233, 251, 262, 271, 348 and 628. Many tablets concern commercial or legal transactions involving the Šamaš temple, *naditu*'s of Šamaš and the *gagûm*.

Any more detailed statement of the provenance of the OB tablets must await the detailed study which can only follow the complete publication of the collection. It is not at present possible to identify with confidence which tablets came from Tell ed-Der. A recent unpublished study at the University of California at Los Angeles suggested on grounds of prosopography that some Old Babylonian tablets from the British Museum's published "Sippar" collections might come from Dilbat (note Budge's reference to Dilbat quoted above).

Apart from Old Babylonian tablets the Bu 88-5-12 collection contains:

4 Gudea cones (651-4), presumably originally from Girsu (Tello) but registered as [acquired at] Hillah.

3 Neo-Assyrian tablets (11, 120, 335).

82 Neo-Babylonian tablets: apart from those specified all date from the time of Šamaš-šumukin to Artaxerxes—9, 23, 25, 26, 27*, 30*, 59*, 69, 70, 82, 83, 94-6, 98 (Alexander), 99, 107-108A, 112, 121, 124, 128, 129*, 131-2, 142, 146*, 149, 154, 156, 201, 226**, 236, 287**, 300, 311-2, 317, 319, 325, 326, 336-7, 343*, 388, 393*, 407, 427, 440, 446, 457, 490, 495, 497*, 508, 510*, 514 (Sel), 533*, 553-4, 556, 557*, 560*, 562 (Alexander), 570-1, 572 (Philip), 575, 582, 584, 588-9, 593*, 596*, 608, 619 (Alexander), 625*, 637, 639, 641, 643* [* = Babylon; ** = Sippar]. The large archives apparently from the Šamaš temple at Sippar catalogued in vols. VI and VII of this catalogue cover the same time span, and suggest that the few Hellenistic tablets in the Bu 88-5-12 collection come from Babylon rather than Sippar, which would be consistent with Budge's own comments on the tablets he purchased at Babylon (*By Nile and Tigris* I 31).

10 Esarhaddon prism fragments: 74-80, 101-3 (Babylon/Hillah).

5 Nebuchadnezzar II bricks: 731A-734A & 781.

1 basalt weight of Darius: 257 (Hillah).

1 Sassanian object: 135A (Hillah).

11 cylinder seals, Old Akkadian to Old Babylonian periods: 770-780 (from Sippar? see above).

A few uninscribed objects: 735Aff.

Four fragments from this collection have now been joined to fragments from other collections: 5 + 1985-10-6, 5(BM 13968); 79 + 1958-4-12, 28 (BM 132294); 440 + 1985-10-6, 9 (BM 139972); 592 + 1985-10-6, 6 (BM 139969). The 1958-4-12 collection was purchased from the executor of the late Mr. E. W. B. Chappelow, who had inherited the collection from his former teacher T. G. Pinches [TM 1958-4-12/212]. The 1985-10-6 collection was purchased at the sale of the collection of the late Lord Amherst of Hackney, a collection originally formed in the 1890s.

The nine Babylonian contract tablets which were reported as having been presented were in fact presented by Dr H. Martyn Suton of the Church Missionary Society, Baghdad (TR 1888-89, 92); they are not separately registered, and one must suppose that they were included in this or another registered collection.

88-5-12, 1-126 (78815-78940)

Purchased from J. M. Shemtob, London.

The collection is listed in TR 1887-89, 60-66. It had apparently been in the Museum already for two years at the time of purchase (TR 1887-89, 78).

The collection contains both Old Babylonian tablets (probably from Sippar and its vicinity) and Neo-Babylonian tablets (Šamaššumukin to Darius), together with a cone of Eannatum I of Lagash and two tablets dated to the reign of Antiochus.

Bu 88-10-13, 1-81 (E.29784-29865)

El-Amarna letters purchased by E. A. W. Budge on his second mission, to Egypt and Mesopotamia in 1887-88; the circumstances of the purchase are described in *By Nile and Tigris* (London, 1920) I 128-129, 139-143. A further tablet was purchased in 1891 (see below on the Bu 91-5-9 collection), but is erroneously included by Budge in his total for the collection acquired in 1888 (*By Nile and Tigris* I 236, 241, 338).

Bu 89-4-26, 234-755 (78941-79458, etc.)

Budge purchase. From Der, Abu Habba, etc.

The Bu 89-4-26 collection was acquired as a result of Budge's third mission, to Mesopotamia in 1889.

The fullest account of Budge's purchases in Baghdad is given in *By Nile and Tigris* II 121-7:

"In many houses we found boxes of fragments of sun-dried contract-tablets and business documents from Abû Habbah, which were useless. During Mr H. Rassam's excavations on that site his workmen discovered various chambers filled with sun dried tablets, in number 'between forty and fifty thousand.' Had these tablets been taken out and dried slowly in the sun all might have been brought unbroken to England, but the natives baked them in the fire with the terrible result that they either cracked in pieces or their inscribed surfaces flaked off. Several natives bought large quantities of these fragments at Abû Habbah, and hoped to sell them, and were greatly disappointed when they found they could not do so. In one house I found a large collection containing many valuable tablets, which was offered to me on behalf of a highly placed Baghdâd official. Most of the larger tablets were found in a chamber near the wall at Abû Habbah, in which Rassam discovered the famous 'Sun-God Tablet,' and the inscriptions upon them were of a miscellaneous character. Besides these there was an odd object of baked clay, the like of which I had never seen [BM 92668]. . . . I bought the whole collection and made arrangements to take it with me to London."

"In another house I examined a second fine collection of early Babylonian tablets, which came from the same place and were of the same period as those I bought in 1888. These I also bought at a reasonable price. . . ."

"Having acquired all the tablets I had money to pay for, I made a little journey to the mounds on the Dîyâlâ river where the natives had found some tablets and several small terracotta figures and bronzes, all of which were in a poor state of preservation. I acquired a selection from the 'find,' and took the objects to Baghdâd and arranged for them to be sent to London, where they would be paid for."

The results of this mission as claimed by Budge (p. 137) included 210 tablets and fragments, and miscellaneous objects from Kuyûnjik, and 1500 tablets, 49 cylinder seals, etc., from Abû Habbah and Dêr.

Budge's brief account of this mission in *The Rise and Progress of Assyriology* pp. 140-41 only summarises his Babylonian acquisitions, "having acquired several collections of Babylonian tablets"; he also incorrectly gives the number of Assyrian tablets as 310 (no doubt a misprint for 210).

Budge on his return from Baghdad presented a full report of this mission (TR 1888-89, 140-161). His purchases of tablets are briefly described (pp. 151-52): "While at Baghdad I found among the dealers in antiquities between four and five hundred Babylonian clay tablets which had been discovered at Hillah and Dêr. It was from this latter place that the greater number of the tablets which I bought last year came and from what I have seen and heard of the place it seems to have been a very important town. The name which a part of it bore in the days of old was Shakhrinu and the evidences for the importance of the ancient city which we can glean from the tablets support Sir Henry Rawlinson's view that the district called Agade was situated here. After some days bargaining I bought these tablets. . . . If the Trustees are able to obtain a generous firman from the Turkish Government . . . it would be well worth their while to dig at Dêr."

TM 1889-5-11/2421 records the Keeper's report on Budge's results: "Mr Budge brought home 200 tablets from Kouyunjik and 550 tablets and fragments from Dêr, Abu Habbah, and other places." TR 1888-89, 139 lists the sources of tablets as "Dêr, Abu Habbah, Birs Nimrud and a new place on the Diala river."

There is nothing in any of these reports to indicate that Budge visited any Babylonian sites other than on the Diyala, nor any evidence apart from Budge's claims that the tablets necessarily came from Abu Habbah and Der. There are obvious discrepancies between the first report and the published statement about the number of tablets acquired from these two sites. The objects from the Diyala area are not identifiable from the Museum's registers.

The registered collection is as follows:

1-177 and 209 Kuyunjik tablets (and 250, 255, 299, 310, 403).

178-208 and 210 Kuyunjik objects.

211-233 Babylonian objects.

234-482 Babylonian tablets originally registered (including 5 Neo-Assyrian tablets); the recorded provenance of all these is simply "Babylonia."

483-755 Babylonian tablets (including one Neo-Assyrian tablet) registered in the hand of C. J. Gadd (presumably having been originally numbered but not registered); the register makes no comment on provenance.

Plainly none of the reported or published figures of the contents of the collection are reliable.

The collection contains both Old Babylonian tablets (probably from Sippar and its vicinity) and Neo-Babylonian tablets (Šamaššumukin to Artaxerxes), together with one Old Akkadian tablet, one Middle-Babylonian, 6 Neo-Assyrian, 10 Hellenistic (probably from Babylon), and one tablet dated to the reign of Tammaritu of Elam.

89-9-30, 1 (79459)

Presented by W. J. Loftie.

A Seleucid economic tablet.

89-10-14, 1-691 (79460-80148 etc.)

Purchased from Selim Homsy & Co, London.

The collection was reported as coming from Tell ed-Der, but in addition to Old Babylonian tablets there are a considerable number of Neo-Babylonian tablets (Nebuchadnezzar II to Xerxes), some of which are dated at Sippar or Babylon, and one Neo-Assyrian tablet.

Bu 91-5-9, 82 (E.29829)

This tablet is part of a collection of Egyptian antiquities acquired by E. A. W. Budge on his fourth mission, to Egypt and Mesopotamia in 1890-91 (*By Nile and Tigris* I 291); the collection is registered in the Department of Egyptian Antiquities and is distinct from the Bu 91-5-9 collection registered in the Department of Western Asiatic Antiquities. The tablet is part of the archive found in 1882 at El-Amarna.

Bu 91-5-9, 262-2551 (80149-82541, etc.)

Budge's excavations at Tell ed-Der and purchases in Baghdad and elsewhere.

The Bu 91-5-9 collection was acquired by the Museum as a result of E. A. W. Budge's fourth mission, to Egypt and Mesopotamia in 1890-91. The mission was primarily intended to excavate at Dêr (now known as Tell ed-Der) and neighbouring sites (*By Nile and Tigris* II 143-7).

A brief account of this mission is given in the Trustees Minutes. Budge was sent to Mesopotamia to excavate at Kouyunjik, and at Dêr when the permit for the latter should arrive (TM 1890-10-11/2555). The permit for Dêr being granted he proceeded from Mosul to Baghdad (TM 1891-1-10/2572-5). There followed a curious succession of letters and telegrams, given here in the order in which they apparently reached the Museum:

Letter from the Foreign Office, 31 December, communicating telegram from Consul General at Baghdad that Mr Budge states that, during the summer, nearly half of the site at Der had been excavated by Arabs, and that, fearing that adequate results were now improbable, he desired the Trustees' instructions. (TM 1891-1-10/2576)

The Museum replied, "The Trustees of the British Museum are of the opinion that Mr Budge should prosecute excavations at Dêr as the Arab diggings cannot have been scientifically conducted." (TM 1891-1-10/2577)

Letters from Mr Budge, dated Baghdad 29 December and 3 January, stating that he . . . proceeded to Baghdad which he reached on 20th December. He proceeded to make preparations but met with opposition in collecting labour for the proposed excavations at Dêr from persons formerly employed by the Trustees . . . Mr Budge had ascertained that immediately on the Trustees' application [for a permit to excavate] being known, the local Commissioners for Crown Lands had at once set to work and had excavated the best part of the site, and had officially reported that nothing was found though Mr Budge thinks there were results. (TM 1891-2-14/2584-5)

Letter from Sir W. White, Constantinople, 29 January, forwarding copy of a telegram from Colonel Tweedie in reply to his enquiries how the excavations at Dêr were proceeding. Colonel Tweedie proposed to inspect the site [Dêr] on the following day (30th January) and added, "only difficulties known to me his (Mr Budge's) belief that others have dug before him." (TM 1891-2-14/2586-7).

Telegram from Mr Budge, 2 February, that the Consul General (Colonel Tweedie) had visited Dêr and was telegraphing to Sir W. White:- "The site systematically excavated already." Mr Budge added:- "Hitherto my excavations during past month yielded no results." (TM 1891-2-14/2587)

Telegram from the Museum through the Foreign Office to Colonel Tweedie for communication to Mr Budge:- "Mr Budge's letters of 29 December and 3 January, and telegram of 2 February, received. Abandonment of excavations apparently inevitable but must be left to his discretion." (TM 1891-2-14/2588)

Telegram sent by Colonel Tweedie, 2 February, sent through British Embassy at Constantinople, reporting visit to the site of excavations: "No difficulties exist but there is no doubt site has been opened and contents probably removed by others. Nothing has been discovered so far except useless fragments without value." (TM 1891-2-14/2589)

Further letter from Mr Budge, 10 January, giving an account of the commencement of work at Dêr and of difficulties with local Arabs; and commenting on the diggings previously carried on by the natives. (TM 1891-2-14/2589)

Letter from Mr Budge, dated Baghdad, 20 January, reporting endeavours to ascertain, by local enquiry, who was responsible for the excavation, before his arrival, of more than one half of the site at Dêr, and observing that excavations under the present rules, are practically impossible in Mesopotamia. (TM 1891-3-14/2600)

Telegram from Mr Budge, received in London on 18th February, that his excavations would cease on the 13th and that he would leave for Suez on the following Sunday. (TM 1891-3-14/2601)

Letter from Mr Budge, 31st January, giving details of his operations up to date; regretting that there are no results; describing endeavours of Baghdad to reclaim antiquities obtained by Arab diggers; reporting visit of the Consul General (Colonel Tweedie) to Dêr, resulting in an interview with the local Wali and a report to Sir W. White; and advising shipment from Basra of seven boxes of antiquities; one of the boxes containing 240 tablets from Kouyunjik excavated last year, and the others, about 1,400 tablets from Dêr and Abu Habbah. (TM 1891-3-14/2601)

Letters from Mr Budge, dated Baghdad, 9 and 20 February, reporting closing of the excavations at Dêr on the 12th February. . . . Mr Budge had had an interview with the Wali on the subject of the secret diggings at Dêr by the Arabs. The Wali named Abd-el-Kerîm Thoma, a relative of Mr Hormuzd Rassam and a former servant of the Trustees, as the person who found money for prosecuting the diggings. Mr Budge reports purchases of about 2,400 tablets and a number of cylinder seals: most of them are from Dêr. For these he had paid £1200 on account, and a sum of about £800 which can be met out of this year's purchase grant. By this purchase he had exceeded the allowance of £1500 for his expedition, but he believed that he had done right in securing the tablets. (TM 1891-4-11/2618-9)

The official report to the Trustees made by his Keeper after Budge's return specified as additions to the Museum's collections "261 tablets and fragments from Kouyunjik . . . Also 2393 tablets belonging to the ancient Babylonian Empire, discovered chiefly at Dêr . . . Also 25 Babylonian cylinder seals . . . The Kouyunjik tablets were excavated by Mr Budge. The tablets and seals from Dêr he purchased . . ." (TM 1891-5-9/2631-4; see also TR 1890-94, 56)

Memorandum, 11 July 1891. "The Principal Librarian has accepted a bill for £648.17.3, drawn by Messrs Lynch, of Baghdad, in payment of the balance due for the purchase of cuneiform tablets from Abdul Karim Toma (including Messrs Lynch's commission) as arranged by Mr Budge when in Baghdad and approved by the Trustees in May last. . . . The Principal Librarian has also, in completion of the purchase, paid to Mr Jusuf Svoboda the sum of £130 for a collection of twenty-five fine cylinder seals, secured by Mr Budge in Baghdad." (TM 1891-7-11/2646-7) Jusuf Svoboda was Clerk of Stephen Lynch Bros. (TR 1888-89, 75)

A rather fuller account of Budge's purchases of tablets and his excavations at Dêr is given in *By Nile and Tigris* II 256-91, and creates, no doubt intentionally, a quite different impression. Prior to his arrival at Baghdad unofficial excavations conducted at Dêr had resulted in the discovery of "Babylonian cylinder seals, several small hoards of coins in pots, and three chambers containing many thousands of Babylonian 'case-tablets'"; Budge was told that these had been kept for him to purchase (pp. 258-59). He gives a detailed description of the eventual purchase (pp. 261-62): "We therefore set out early in the evening, and I spent nearly three nights in examining the large collections to which he took me. There were dozens of collections to be seen, and Jews, Armenians, Muslims and Christians alike had invested their money in the tablets from Dêr, and were very anxious to sell to me. There was no doubt about the existence of the tablets, there they were before me; and there was no doubt about their provenance, for the material and the writing and the royal names showed that they were similar in every way to those which I had bought nearly two years before. Among them were hundreds of the largest, finest and oldest Babylonian contract tablets I had ever seen, and several large tablets inscribed with magical and other texts that were clearly unique; at all events, I remembered nothing like them in the British Museum. The supply of tablets was abundant, the demand for them was small, and their owners wished to sell; therefore I bought very cheaply. I selected about 2,500 tablets and other objects from among the different collections that were shown to me, and took possession of them and packed them in stout wooden boxes for transport to London. These represented the cream of the collections. I then went over the collections a second time, and made a further selection of about 7,000 tablets, and arranged with some friends to take charge of them until the 2,500 tablets were out of the country. When I had paid for the 2,500 tablets, and they had been sent down the river a few boxes at a time, I packed up the 7,000 tablets in boxes and arranged with their owners to send them to the British Museum after my departure from Baghdâd, and to receive payment for them then. This arrangement they carried out loyally, and the Trustees acquired the whole collection before the end of 1893." [It will be apparent from the list of the Museum's tablet collections that in fact apart from the 2551 items of the Bu 91-5-9 collection less than a hundred other tablets arrived before the end of 1893.]

Subsequent to this purchase Budge then undertook his own excavations at Dêr (pp. 262-68, 277-82). On arrival at Der, "I found that Hasan's report was correct, and that a great many parts of the largest mounds had been dug into, especially in the south-east portion of it, and the broken tablets which were lying about everywhere convinced me that a great 'find' had been made by those who dug there secretly. In some half dozen places it was easy to see that the excavations which they had made had been filled in again carefully, and I decided to clear these out first of all. In two places we found piles of large bricks of the

Sassanian period, and close to the east gateway we uncovered easily a part of a massive buttress made of burnt bricks, bearing the name and titles of Nebuchadnezzar II" (p. 265).

Excavations apparently began on January 9th, 1891, and within about two weeks there were some two hundred men employed. The excavations were conducted with the assistance of Nimrûd Rassam (pp. 251-54, 267). The official Delegate eventually advised Budge "that the men were finding more tablets than they admitted, and some cylinder seals, and that they were sending them into Baghdâd to the dealers" (p. 267). "I therefore rode into Baghdâd on several occasions and secured many tablets and small objects which I felt certain came from Dêr. When the workmen found that I did this regularly they thought they had beeter treat with me on the spot, and save the percentage they had been giving to the dealers, and in the end I paid each man a piastre or two for every object he found" (p. 267).

On his return from a visit to Al-Kûfah Budge records (p. 277): "A good deal of work had been done during the eight days of my absence, but only a limited number of tablets had been found, and the best of these came from the ruins of the private houses and business quarter of the ancient Babylonian city, or town, which had occupied the site. The chambers in which the great hoard of tablets were found had been uncovered, and thus there was no doubt that the contents of the mound had been rifled before the Porte gave the Trustees of the British Museum a permit to "inspect" the site. Large portions of thick walls made of burnt bricks, stamped with the name and titles of Nebuchadnezzar II, came to light in two or three places. . . . I did not want them for the British Museum . . . ."

Later he records (pp. 279-80): "I went . . . to Maḥmûdîyah, and tried to obtain from the Mudîr some information about the secret diggings at Dêr, but we failed. However, he offered to sell me some very good tablets, and among those which I bought from him were the List of Events by which the Babylonians reckoned their years during the reigns of Sumu-abu, Sumu-la-ilu, Zabum, Apil-Sin, Sin-muballiṭ, Khammurabi and Samsu-iluna, i.e. from B.C. 2300 to B.C. 2110 [Bu 91-5-9, 284 = BM 92702], and the four-sided block of clay inscribed with lists of names of stones, plants, fish, birds, garments, etc. [Bu 91-5-9, 285 = BM 92611]."

The excavations were closed on or after February 15th (p. 281), but shortly after he records (p. 282), "Whilst I was getting ready to break camp Hasan brought me news of another good collection of tablets which were at Abû Habbah. I went to see them, and found they were good . . . I agreed to take them." They were eventually smuggled into Baghdad (pp. 282-83).

This is the fullest available account of Budge's activities and purchases at Dêr and Abû Habbah, and one cannot help remarking that he leaves us without any useful information about what he had excavated, without one single plan of the excavations, and without the identification of one single object found at Dêr. One is reminded of the story told of Budge by Sir Leonard Woolley (*As I Seem to Remember* [London, 1962], 32-33): "The buying of antiquities can be a very difficult thing and it is not always a very safe thing. It was, of course, a very popular thing with Museum Directors. There was a Keeper of the Egyptian Department in the British Museum years ago who always maintained that he would far sooner buy an object than get it from an excavation, 'Because,' he said, 'if it comes from an excavation, the excavator gives me all sorts of information about it, information about its level and its date and its history and so on, which isn't very interesting. Whereas if I buy it from a dealer I can use my own imagination and say what it really is. So, I'd far sooner buy.'"

While at Dêr, however, Budge did obtain further information on the previous excavations at Dêr (pp. 267-8): "On one occasion Hasan brought to me two men who had been among the gang that had carried on excavations at Dêr secretly, and who seemed to be willing to give us information about the 'finds' they made there. According to them, there were many thousands of contract tablets and business documents in clay cases, stamped with impressions of the seals of witnesses. The biggest of these were deposited in large unbaked earthenware jars, which stood on the ground, and the smaller were stacked in heaps on slabs of stone laid flat on the earth. They tried to move the jars without emptying them, but the jars collapsed under the weight of their contents, and many tablets were broken by falling on the ground. The chambers in which these jars were found were 6 cubits long, 3 cubits wide, and 5 cubits deep. They had no doors, and the only access to them was through the roof. In one chamber they found rows of tablets lying on slabs, as if they had been arranged there in some special order. On the ground below them they picked up scores of pyramidal clay objects bearing seal-impressions; in the apex of each of these were the remains of a thin piece of fibrous wood, and it is probable that each pyramidal object was attached by means of the wood to a special tablet, and served as a label, but fell to the ground when the wood rotted. A considerable number of seal-cylinders were found whilst these men were digging at Dêr, and they gave me the name of a European gentleman in Baghdâd who was their chief customer. Later I entered into negotiations with him, and I acquired from him about thirty very fine cylinders of various periods, the oldest dating from about 2400 B.C. Among them were the cylinder-seal of Adda, the scribe, which is engraved with a remarkable mythological scene, not found elsewhere, and the cylinders engraved with a scene of the Sunrise, in which Shamash, the Sun-god, is depicted issuing from the portals of heaven."

These latter seals are identified by Budge (p. 268 n. 2) as BM 89115, 89110, 89531, 89548; their registration numbers (Bu 91-5-9, 2553; 1873-9-1, 1; 1846-5-23, 333; 1846-5-23, 3340) show just how misleading Budge's memory and published account can be.

The acquisitions resulting from the 1890-1 mission appear to have included "a batch of round tablets, about thirty-five in number" from a new site [probably Girsu-Tello] on the Hayy River (p. 269) which Budge purchased at Al-Kûfah together with several Babylonian letters and contracts (pp. 273-4). From Budge's description of these tablets as "like large, round buns" (p. 273) and from his inclusion in his book of a photograph of the field-survey text BM 19042 (plate facing p. 273) it seems likely that these "about 35" round tablets were all of this category. Curiously, although Budge describes repacking the tablets and taking them from Al-Kûfah himself, they appear never to have arrived in London. Three years later, in October 1894 he reported to the Trustees of the British Museum the discovery of the archives of Tello (TR 1894-96, 3441) and remarked on the special interest of "circular cake-like tablets," adding, "No similar tablets exist in the Museum collection, and their acquisition is much to be desired." Several such tablets were later acquired from Baghdad dealers and incorporated in the 94-10-16, 94-10-19, 95-10-12, 95-12-14, 96-3-28, 96-3-30, 96-4-7, 96-4-10 and other collections (see *CT* 1 and G. Pettinato, *Texte zur Verwaltung der Landwirtschaft in der Ur-III Zeit*).

The acquisitions made on this mission as reported by Budge (p. 291) included a total of 2552 Babylonian tablets and 25 Babylonian cylinder seals (the Bu 91-5-9 collection), 261 Assyrian tablets and fragments and miscellaneous antiquities from Kuyûnjik, and one Amarna tablet [BM E.29829 (E. Bu 91-5-9, 82), purchased in Egypt]. In practice the 91-5-9 collection as originally registered contains 2551 tablets, etc., *including* the 261 items from Kuyunjik (Bu 91-5-9, 1-261), and 48 other objects (Bu 91-5-9, 2552-2599).

The account given in *The Rise and Progress of Assyriology* pp. 141-2, is again different. "On my arrival there [at Baghdad], I found that, when it became known in Baghdâd some months before that the British Museum wanted to excavate Dêr, the Pâshâ had commissioned certain natives to go there and dig on his behalf. They did so, and found two chambers full of tablets, which they carried into Baghdâd; and they were sold there to the dealers. Most of them were 'case-tablets', and all belonged to the period of about 2000 B.C. But there was a third chamber at Dêr, built into a corner of a large room; and, though known to the native who was in charge of the Pâshâ's excavations, he did not reveal its existence to his subordinates, but kept it secret, in order that he might sell his knowledge to me. When the débris was cleared from the entrance, which was in the roof, we saw that the chamber contained many large jars, with coverings fixed in position with bitumen. Some jars were full of tablets, and others only half-full; and three were empty. Each jar contained the contracts and business documents probably of one family, like the modern black tin boxes seen in solicitors' offices. The jars broke when attempts were made to move them; but every tablet in them was secured unbroken. There were nearly 3000 tablets in that chamber, which was a comparatively small one; and judging by the size of the collections which I saw in Baghdâd, the total number of tablets found in the three chambers at Dêr cannot have been less than 15,000. I secured about 2300 of the largest and best of them, and shipped them to London in batches, as opportunity offered, before I left Baghdâd, and I arranged with the dealers to despatch the rest, a few hundred at a time, to the British Museum; and in due course all arrived there, and were purchased." That is the complete account of the 1891 mission given in *The Rise and Progress of Assyriology*; it could hardly be more inconsistent with the account given in *By Nile and Tigris*. Budge also comments on the identity of Tell ed-Der (pp. 142-3).

One must now turn to the actual contents of the Bu 91-5-9 collection.

The first 261 items in the collection are Assyrian and come from Nineveh; 1-240 are catalogued by Bezold, 241-61 are uninscribed items.

Items 2552-2599 are cylinder seals and uninscribed objects.

7 Old Akkadian tablets: 293, 588, 589, 590, 972, 1002, 1329.

1 Ur-Bau cone: 2546.

1 Ur-Nammu brick: 264.

13 Nuzi tablets: 295, 296, 297, 526, 527, 532, 592, 871, 1202, 1373, 1630, 1641, 2543. (These seem to be the earliest Nuzi tablets to reach European collections.)

21 Kassite tablets: 386, 518, 752, 793, 868, 963, 1165, 1229, 1237, 1261, 1281, 1313, 1334, 1341, 1420, 1496, 1507, 1734, 1790, 1818, 1910. (Probably from Nippur.)

1 Middle Elamite inscription: 870.

38 Late Babylonian tablets: 266, 637, 673, 678, 718, 745, 800, 808, 820, 849, 880, 893*, 897, 961, 1000, 1059**, 1130***, 1133 (Seleucus), 1140, 1215, 1228**, 1238, 1293**, 1297, 1360, 1378*, 1510, 1545, 1568, 1693 (Seleucid), 1737, 1830, 1836, 1935, 1943, 1957, 1977, 2545 [* = Babylon, ** = Sippar, *** = Borsippa].

2 Early Bronze jewelry moulds of Anatolian style: 2534, 2535.

There seems to be no compelling reason why any of these should be given a Der provenance. Apart from Budge's claimed purchase of tablets at Abu Habba (perhaps including the Late Babylonian tablets marked ** here) all of these could have been acquired through the Baghdad dealers.

The remainder of the collection (2254 items, excluding A and B numbers) are OB tablets, mostly from the time of Hammurapi onwards. As in the case of the Bu 88-5-12 collection Assyriologists have generally been content with the proposition that the bulk of the published tablets from this collection came from Sippar or its vicinity. Sippar or its subsidiary settlements are mentioned in the catalogue entries for the following items: 302, 326, 346, 412, 426, 435, 455, 471, 708, 776, 789, 809, 853, 882, 917, 998, 1045, 1050, 1064, 1185, 1392, 1399, 1531, 1605, 1644, 1653, 1698, 1773, 1825, 2347. It has not so far proved possible to separate those archives deriving from Sippar (Abu Habba) or other sites from those deriving from Tell ed-Der. In R. Harris' *Ancient Sippar* the documents from this collection are freely used as illustrative of the life and administration of Sippar. Since we are not able from Budge's record to identify any individual tablet as necessarily coming from Der, we are unable to prove her procedure incorrect. Given that Tell ed-Der is only 6 km from Sippar one would assume that the economic lives of the two settlements were closely interlinked. The comments made above about the need for further study of the Bu 88-5-12 collection apply with equal force to this collection.

Two items in this collection have so far been joined to items from other purchased collections: 1592 + 96-3-28, 416 (BM 13325), 1152 + 1958-4-12, 2 (BM 132268).

93-4-10, 1-12 (91037-91067 [in part])
Purchased from J. M. Shemtob, London.
Cones of Ur-Baba and Gudea.

93-5-13, 1-7 (82542-82548)
Purchased from J. M. Shemtob, London.
5 Old Babylonian and 2 Neo-Babylonian tablets, and one Old Persian royal inscription.

93-10-14, 1-50 (82549-82598)
Purchased from J. M. Shemtob, London.
Neo-Babylonian tablets (Šamaššumukin to Artaxerxes), together with one Old Akkadian, 3 Old Babylonian, and 2 Kassite tablets.

93-11-2, 1 (82599)
Vendor/owner unknown.
Aššurnaṣirpal II sculpture with standard inscription.

94-1-13, 1-13 (82600-82606, etc.)
1-7 purchased from Ibrahim Gejou, Paris; 8-13 purchased from J. M. Shemtob, London.
7 Old Babylonian tablets; 6 Gudea cones.

94-6-11, 1-49 (82607-82654, etc.)
Purchased from Kirkor Minassian, Constantinople.
The collection includes one Old Babylonian letter and one Nuzi contract; the remainder are Neo-Babylonian economic texts and contracts dating from Šamaššumukin to Xerxes, the majority dated at Borsippa, one dated at Uruk. The reported purchase, however, was of one bronze rhyton, ten cylinder seals, a letter "about B.C. 2300" [i.e. OB], a list of tithes due to Marduk, and 37 [Neo-Babylonian] contract tablets. Evidently 10 tablets have been added to this collection, perhaps from other collections offered by Minassian which were the subject of correspondence with Budge between September and November 1894. A letter to Budge dated 14 August 1894 indicates that Minassian was also using Sivadjian as a forwarding agent; see the next collection.

94-7-16, 1-28 (82655-82682)
Purchased from Mihran Sivadjian, Paris.
Three astronomical(?) texts and 25 Neo-Babylonian economic texts and contracts dating from Nebuchadnezzar II to Darius, the majority dated at Borsippa.

94-7-17, 1-134 (82683-82817, etc.)
Purchased from Malcolm Thaddeus, Baghdad.
The collection includes 15 Ur III tablets; one Old Babylonian tablet; 8 Kassite tablets; the remainder are Neo-Babylonian economic texts and contracts dating from Kandalanu to Xerxes, many dated at Borsippa. The reported purchase was of "3 Babylonian letters belonging to the period about B.C. 3000 [actually Kassite]; 17 contract tablets of the same period [the Ur III tablets + ?]; two lists of names, and one fine list of contributions to a temple(?); about 80 [Neo-Babylonian] tablets . . . ." Again additions appear to have been made to this collection. A letter from Thaddeus to Budge dated 10 May 1894 refers to "the 25 Niffer tablets"; this may be a clue to the origin of the Ur III and Kassite tablets in this collection.

95-10-22, 1-2 (82818-82819)
Purchased from Mrs Netherton, Liverpool, apparently acting on behalf of Captain Cowley (from whom the 96-4-7 and 97-5-14 collections were purchased).
Ur III tablets.

The chronological sequence of the Museum's tablet collections continues in volume I of this catalogue.

LOCATION OF BM NUMBERS
(out of sequence)

22452	AH 82-9-18A, 25
22463	85-4-30, 5
E29784-29865	Bu 88-10-13, 1-81
E29829	Bu 91-5-9, 82
77218	83-1-18, 2600
82820-82836	SH 83-9-28, 26-42
82837	83-12-31, 1
89106	84-2-11, 490
89304	87-1-14, 4
89306	87-1-14, 3
89571	84-2-11, 489
89572	84-2-11, 491
90109	Bu 88-5-12, 734A
90319	Bu 88-5-12, 731A
90822	Bu 88-5-12, 732A
90823	Bu 88-5-12, 733A
91011	83-1-18, 1856
91021	AH 82-9-18A, 37
91036	83-1-18, 704
91037	93-4-10, 9
91038	93-4-10, 7
91039	93-4-10, 11
91040	Bu 88-5-12, 651
91041	Bu 88-5-12, 652
91042	Bu 88-5-12, 654
91044	93-4-10, 5
91045	94-1-13, 8
91046	94-1-13, 10
91047	94-1-13, 9
91048	94-1-13, 11
91049	93-4-10, 4
91050	94-1-13, 12
91051	93-4-10, 8
91052	93-4-10, 6
91053	Bu 88-5-12, 653
91054	94-1-13, 13
91055	93-4-10, 10
91062	93-4-10, 2
91064	93-4-10, 1
91066	93-4-10, 3
91067	93-4-10, 12
91076	85-4-30, 3
91077	Bu 91-5-9, 2548
91078	Bu 91-5-9, 2549
91079	Bu 91-5-9, 2550
91080	Bu 91-5-9, 2551
91089	86-7-20, 1
91090	86-7-20, 1
91117	Bu 88-5-12, 257
91142	85-4-30, 1
91143	85-4-30, 2
91154	Bu 88-5-12, 111
92090	Bu 88-5-12, 135A
92501	82-9-18A, 220
92501A	82-9-18A, 220A
92502	84-2-11, 356
92503	Bu 88-5-12, 6
92504	Bu 88-5-12, 7
92505	Bu 88-5-12, 8
92506	Bu 88-5-12, 12
92507	Bu 88-5-12, 21
92508	Bu 88-5-12, 22
92509	Bu 88-5-12, 31

92510	Bu 88-5-12, 37
92511	Bu 88-5-12, 43
92512	Bu 88-5-12, 45
92513	Bu 88-5-12, 46
92514	Bu 88-5-12, 47
92515	Bu 88-5-12, 48
92516	Bu 88-5-12, 49
92517	Bu 88-5-12, 50
92518	Bu 88-5-12, 51
92519	Bu 88-5-12, 48A
92520	Bu 88-5-12, 57
92521	Bu 88-5-12, 58
92522	Bu 88-5-12, 60
92523	Bu 88-5-12, 135
92524	Bu 88-5-12, 143
92525	Bu 88-5-12, 147
92526	Bu 88-5-12, 150
92527	Bu 88-5-12, 153
92528	Bu 88-5-12, 155
92529	Bu 88-5-12, 157
92530	Bu 88-5-12, 158
92531	Bu 88-5-12, 159
92532	Bu 88-5-12, 172
92533	Bu 88-5-12, 175
92534	Bu 88-5-12, 176
92535	Bu 88-5-12, 179
92536	Bu 88-5-12, 185
92537	Bu 88-5-12, 186
92538	Bu 88-5-12, 194
92539	Bu 88-5-12, 203
92540	Bu 88-5-12, 205
92541	Bu 88-5-12, 206
92542	Bu 88-5-12, 210
92543	Bu 88-5-12, 211
92544	Bu 88-5-12, 213
92545	Bu 88-5-12, 214
92546	Bu 88-5-12, 216
92547	Bu 88-5-12, 215
92548	Bu 88-5-12, 222
92549	Bu 88-5-12, 227
92550	Bu 88-5-12, 229
92551	Bu 88-5-12, 234
92552	Bu 88-5-12, 244
92553	Bu 88-5-12, 258
92554	Bu 88-5-12, 264
92555	Bu 88-5-12, 269
92556	Bu 88-5-12, 274
92557	Bu 88-5-12, 281
92558	Bu 88-5-12, 283
92559	Bu 88-5-12, 285
92560	Bu 88-5-12, 290
92561	Bu 88-5-12, 291
92562	Bu 88-5-12, 292
92563	Bu 88-5-12, 302
92564	Bu 88-5-12, 305
92565	Bu 88-5-12, 330
92566	Bu 88-5-12, 332
92567	Bu 88-5-12, 346
92568	Bu 88-5-12, 404
92569	Bu 88-5-12, 419
92570	Bu 88-5-12, 435
92571	Bu 88-5-12, 454
92572	Bu 88-5-12, 458
92573	Bu 88-5-12, 488
92573A	Bu 88-5-12, 488A
92574	Bu 88-5-12, 616
92575	Bu 88-5-12, 645
92575A	Bu 88-5-12, 646
92576	Bu 88-5-12, 673
92576A	Bu 88-5-12, 674
92577	Bu 88-5-12, 677
92577A	Bu 88-5-12, 678
92578	Bu 88-5-12, 683
92578A	Bu 88-5-12, 684
92579	Bu 88-5-12, 685
92579A	Bu 88-5-12, 686
92580	Bu 88-5-12, 693
92580A	Bu 88-5-12, 694
92581	Bu 88-5-12, 703
92581A	Bu 88-5-12, 704

92582	Bu 88-5-12, 705
92582A	Bu 88-5-12, 706
92583	Bu 88-5-12, 711
92583A	Bu 88-5-12, 712
92584	Bu 88-5-12, 713
92584A	Bu 88-5-12, 714
92585	Bu 88-5-12, 719
92585A	Bu 88-5-12, 720
92586	Bu 88-5-12, 721
92586A	Bu 88-5-12, 722
92587	Bu 88-5-12, 723
92587A	Bu 88-5-12, 724
92588	Bu 88-5-12, 725
92588A	Bu 88-5-12, 726
92589	Bu 88-5-12, 741
92589A	Bu 88-5-12, 742
92590	Bu 88-5-12, 745
92590A	Bu 88-5-12, 746
92591	Bu 88-5-12, 751
92591A	Bu 88-5-12, 752
92592	Bu 88-5-12, 753
92592A	Bu 88-5-12, 754
92593	Bu 88-5-12, 769
92593A	Bu 88-5-12, 769A
92594	Bu 88-5-12, 743
92594A	Bu 88-5-12, 744
92595	Bu 89-4-26, 241
92595A	Bu 89-4-26, 241A
92596	89-10-14, 36
92597	89-10-14, 40
92598	89-10-14, 41
92599	89-10-14, 45
92600	89-10-14, 46
92601	89-10-14, 49
92602	89-10-14, 50
92602A	89-10-14, 50A
92603	89-10-14, 52
92604	89-10-14, 53
92605	89-10-14, 312
92606	89-10-14, 489
92607	89-10-14, 510
92608	Bu 91-5-9, 269
92609	Bu 91-5-9, 274
92610	Bu 91-5-9, 275
92611	Bu 91-5-9, 285
92612	Bu 91-5-9, 289
92613	Bu 91-5-9, 303
92614	Bu 91-5-9, 317
92615	Bu 91-5-9, 318
92616	Bu 91-5-9, 331
92617	Bu 91-5-9, 332
92618	Bu 91-5-9, 338
92619	Bu 91-5-9, 351
92620	Bu 91-5-9, 357
92621	Bu 91-5-9, 362
92622	Bu 91-5-9, 367
92623	Bu 91-5-9, 377
92624	Bu 91-5-9, 387
92625	Bu 91-5-9, 450
92626	Bu 91-5-9, 340
92627	Bu 91-5-9, 476
92628	Bu 91-5-9, 503
92630	Bu 91-5-9, 705
92631	Bu 91-5-9, 712
92633	Bu 91-5-9, 938
92634	Bu 91-5-9, 1081
92635	Bu 91-5-9, 1387
92636	Bu 91-5-9, 2172A
92636A	Bu 91-5-9, 2172B
92637	Bu 91-5-9, 2173A
92637A	Bu 91-5-9, 2173B
92638	Bu 91-5-9, 2174A
92638A	Bu 91-5-9, 2174B
92639	Bu 91-5-9, 2176A
92639A	Bu 91-5-9, 2176B
92640	Bu 91-5-9, 2177A
92640A	Bu 91-5-9, 2177B
92641	Bu 91-5-9, 2191
92642	Bu 91-5-9, 2192
92643	Bu 91-5-9, 2193

92644	Bu 91-5-9, 2196
92644A	Bu 91-5-9, 2196A
92645	Bu 91-5-9, 2421
92645A	Bu 91-5-9, 2421A
92646	Bu 91-5-9, 2424
92646A	Bu 91-5-9, 2424A
92647	Bu 91-5-9, 2427
92647A	Bu 91-5-9, 2427A
92648	Bu 91-5-9, 2428
92648A	Bu 91-5-9, 2428A
92649	Bu 91-5-9, 2439
92649A	Bu 91-5-9, 2439A
92650	Bu 91-5-9, 2440
92650A	Bu 91-5-9, 2440A
92651	Bu 91-5-9, 2441
92651A	Bu 91-5-9, 2441A
92652	Bu 91-5-9, 1018
92653	Bu 91-5-9, 2443
92653A	Bu 91-5-9, 2443A
92654	Bu 91-5-9, 2451
92654A	Bu 91-5-9, 2451A
92655	Bu 91-5-9, 2455
92656	Bu 91-5-9, 2463
92656A	Bu 91-5-9, 2463A
92657	Bu 91-5-9, 2468
92657A	Bu 91-5-9, 2468A
92658	Bu 91-5-9, 2470
92658A	Bu 91-5-9, 2470A
92659	Bu 91-5-9, 2485
92659A	Bu 91-5-9, 2485A
92660	Bu 91-5-9, 2498
92660A	Bu 91-5-9, 2498A
92661	Bu 91-5-9, 2502
92661A	Bu 91-5-9, 2502A
92662	Bu 91-5-9, 2503
92662A	Bu 91-5-9, 2503A
92663	Bu 91-5-9, 2518
92663A	Bu 91-5-9, 2518A
92664	Bu 91-5-9, 2519
92664A	Bu 91-5-9, 2519A
92665	Bu 91-5-9, 2534
92666	Bu 91-5-9, 2535
92667	Bu 91-5-9, 2444
92667A	Bu 91-5-9, 2444A
92668	Bu 89-4-26, 238
92669	Bu 88-5-12, 41
92670	Bu 88-5-12, 72
92671	Bu 88-5-12, 209
92672	Bu 91-5-9, 324
92673	Bu 91-5-9, 399
92674	Bu 88-5-12, 252
92675	Bu 91-5-9, 2512
92675A	Bu 91-5-9, 2512A
92676	Bu 91-5-9, 2459
92676A	Bu 91-5-9, 2459A
92677	Bu 91-5-9, 329
92678	Bu 91-5-9, 325
92679	Bu 91-5-9, 606
92689	88-4-19, 17
92691	83-1-18, 1330
92692	83-1-18, 1331
92693	83-1-18, 1336
92694	83-1-18, 1341
92702	Bu 91-5-9, 284
92722	82-9-18A, 49
92723	82-9-18A, 50
92724	82-9-18A, 57
92725	82-9-18A, 63
92728	82-9-18A, 191
92729	82-9-18A, 194
92733	82-9-18A, 310
92734	82-9-18A, 335
92749	83-1-18, 41
92750	83-1-18, 69
92751	83-1-18, 78
92752	83-1-18, 200
92753	83-1-18, 254
92754	83-1-18, 280
92755	83-1-18, 305
92756	83-1-18, 327

92757	83-1-18, 410
92758	83-1-18, 425
92759	83-1-18, 528
92760	83-1-18, 532
92761	83-1-18, 533
92762	83-1-18, 537
92763	83-1-18, 545
92764	83-1-18, 609
92765	83-1-18, 690
92766	83-1-18, 748
92767	83-1-18, 831
92768	83-1-18, 833
92769	83-1-18, 836
92770	83-1-18, 837
92771	83-1-18, 838
92772	83-1-18, 839
92773	83-1-18, 845
92774	83-1-18, 855
92775	83-1-18, 861
92776	83-1-18, 863
92777	83-1-18, 867
92778	83-1-18, 876
92779	83-1-18, 891
92780	83-1-18, 900
92781	83-1-18, 964
92782	83-1-18, 1127
92783	83-1-18, 1128
92784	83-1-18, 1143
92785	83-1-18, 1148
92786	83-1-18, 1169
92787	83-1-18, 1325
92788	84-2-11, 11
92789	84-2-11, 12
92790	84-2-11, 24
92791	84-2-11, 33
92792	84-2-11, 57
92793	84-2-11, 61
92794	84-2-11, 64
92795	84-2-11, 94
92796	84-2-11, 103
92797	84-2-11, 133
92798	84-2-11, 155
92799	84-2-11, 158
92990	84-2-11, 163
92991	84-2-11, 243
92992	85-4-30, 37
92993	85-4-30, 67
92994	86-5-12, 6
92995	86-7-20, 3
92996	87-7-25, 1
92997	88-4-19, 26
92998	Bu 88-5-12, 59
92999	Bu 88-5-12, 343
93000	94-6-11, 36
93001	94-7-17, 32
93006	84-2-11, 1
93017	88-4-19, 13
93018	Bu 91-5-9, 2508
93018A	Bu 91-5-9, 2508A
93032	83-1-18, 2359
93035	83-1-18, 1332
93042	85-4-30, 6
93043-93064	83-1-21, 1779-1800
93074	85-4-30, 229
93081	83-1-18, 1905
93084	83-1-18, 1391
93085	86-7-20, 17
99439-99999	83-1-21, 1801-2361
100692	Bu 88-5-12, 781
100701-101945	83-1-21, 2362-3606
116624	83-1-18, 2598
116664	88-4-19, 5
118767	86-7-20, 47

ABBREVIATIONS

Aa	lexical series á A = *nâqu*
AbB	*Altbabylonische Briefe in Umschrift und Übersetzung*
ABC	J.H. Stevenson, *Assyrian and Babylonian contracts with Aramaic reference notes*
ACT	O. Neugebauer, *Astronomical Cuneiform Texts*
ActaSum	*Acta Sumerologica*
Ad	Ammi-ditana
Ae	Abi-ešuḫ
Afk	*Archiv für Keilschriftforschung*
AfO	*Archiv für Orientforschung*
AH	tablets in the collections of the British Museum
AJSL	*American Journal of Semitic Languages and Literatures*
Am	Amel-Marduk
Am	B.T.A. Evetts, *Inscriptions of the reigns of Evil-Merodach, Neriglissar and Laborosoarchod*
AnSt	*Anatolian Studies*
Antig	Antigonus
Ant	Antiochus
AOAT	*Alter Orient und Altes Testament*
AOATS	*Alter Orient und Altes Testament-Sonderriehe*
AOS	*American Oriental Series*
Art	Artaxerxes
Aṣ	Ammi-ṣaduqa
AS	Apil-Sin
AS	*Assyriological Studies*
ASKT	P. Haupt, *Akkadische und sumerische Keilschrifttexte . . .*
Assyrian Royal Inscriptions	F.M. Fales, ed., *Assyrian Royal Inscriptions: New Horizons in literary, ideological, and historical analysis*
BA	*Beiträge zur Assyriologie . . .*
Bar	Barzia
BASOR	*Bulletin of the American Schools of Oriental Research*

Bezold, *Amarna*	C. Bezold, *The Tell-El-Amarna Tablets in the British Museum*
Bezold, *Cat.*	C. Bezold, *Catalogue of the Cuneiform Tablets in the Kouyunjik Collection of the British Museum*
Birot *Fs*	J. Durand and J.R. Kupper, eds., *Miscellanea Babylonica: Mélanges offerts à Maurice Birot*
BL	S. Langdon, *Babylonian Liturgies*
BM	tablets in the collections of the British Museum
BMQ	*The British Museum Quarterly*
Brinkman, *MSKH*	J.A. Brinkman, *Materials and Studies for Kassite History*
BSOAS	*Bulletin of the School of Oriental and African Studies*
Bu	tablets in the collections of the British Museum
Cam	Cambyses
Cam	J. Strassmaier, *Inschriften von Cambyses*
CCT	*Cuneiform Texts from Cappadocian Tablets*
CT	*Cuneiform Texts from Babylonian Tablets*
Cyr	Cyrus
Cyr	J.N. Strassmaier, *Inschriften von Cyrus*
Dar	Darius
Dar	J.N. Strassmaier, *Inschriften von Darius*
Delaporte, *Épigraphes Araméens*	L. Delaporte, *Étude des textes araméens gravés ou écrits sur des tablettes cunéiformes*
Ea	lexical series ea A = *nâqu* (pub. *MSL* 14)
EB	Early Bronze
ED	Early Dynastic
En el	*Enūma eliš*
Esar	Esarhaddon
Farber, *Atti Ištar*	*Beschwörungsrituale an Ištar und Dumuzi: Attī Ištar ša ḫarmaša Dumuzi*
Gaster, *AV*	*Occident and Orient* (Studies in Honour of M. Gaster)
Geller, *Forerunners*	M.J. Geller, *Forerunners to* UDUG.ḪUL: *Sumerian Exorcistic Incantations*
Gilg.	*Gilgameš* epic
Gudea	inscriptions of Gudea, numbered according to the forthcoming edition by H. Steible
Guide 1922	British Museum, *A Guide to the Babylonian and Assyrian Antiquities* (1922)
Ha	*Hammurapi*
Ḫg	lexical series ḪAR = *gud*
Ḫḫ	lexical series ḪAR.ra = *ḫubullu*
JCS	*Journal of Cuneiform Studies*

JESHO	*Journal of the Economic and Social History of the Orient*
JNES	*Journal of Near Eastern Studies*
K.	tablets in the collections of the British Museum
Kan	Kandalanu
KAR	*Keilschrifttexte aus Assur religiösen Inhalts*
KAV	*Keilschrifttexte aus Assur verschiedenen Inhalts*
KB	*Keilschriftliche Bibliothek*
Kent, *Old Persian Grammar*	R.G. Kent, *Old Persian Grammar, Texts, Lexicon* (=*AOS* 33)
King, *BBSt*	L.W. King, *Babylonian Boundary Stones*
King, *Chronicles*	L.W. King, *Chronicles Concerning Early Babylonian Kings . . .*
Knudtzon, *El-Amarna*	J.A. Knudtzon *et al.*, *Die El-Amarna-Tafeln* (=*VAB* 2)
Köcher, *BAM*	F. Köcher, *Die babylonisch-assyrische Medizin in Texten und Untersuchungen*
Kohler u. Peiser, *Rechtsleben*	M. Kohler and F.E. Peiser, *Aus dem babylonischen Rechtsleben*
Kraus, *Edikt*	F.R. Kraus, *Ein Edikt des Königs Ammiṣaduqa von Babylon* (=*Studia et Documenta ad iura orientis antiqui pertinentia* 5)
Kraus *Fs*	G. VanDriel *et al.*, eds., *Zikir Šumim: Assyriological Studies Presented to F.R. Kraus*
Kraus, *Königliche Verfügungen*	F.R. Kraus, *Königliche Verfügungen in altbabylonische Zeit*
Kraus, *Texte*	F.R. Kraus, *Texte zur babylonischen Physiognomatik* (=*AfO Beiheft* 3)
Kugler, *SSB*	F.X. Kugler, *Sternkunde und Sterndienst in Babel*
Lambert, *BWL*	W.G. Lambert, *Babylonian Wisdom Literature*
Lambert-Millard, *Atraḫasis*	W.G. Lambert and A.R. Millard, *Atra-ḫasīs: The Babylonian Story of the Flood*
LBAT	T.G. Pinches, *Late Babylonian Astronomical and Related Texts*
LIH	L.W. King, *The Letters and Inscriptions of Hammurabi*
Lišan Mitḫurti	*lišan mitḫurti: Festschrift Wolfram Freiherr von Soden* (=*AOAT 1*)
LKA	E. Ebeling, *Literarische Keilschrifttexte aus Assur*
LKU	A. Falkenstein, *Literarische Keilschrifttexte aus Uruk*
Lm	Labaši-Marduk
Lm	B.T.A. Evetts, *Inscriptions of the Reigns of Evil-Merodach, Neriglissar and Laborosoarchod*
Lu	Lexical series lú = *ša* (pub. *MSL* 12 87-147)
Lugale	J. van Dijk, LUGAL UD ME-LÁM-bi NIR-ĞÁL
Malku	synonym list ***malku*** = ***šarru*** (Malku I, pub. A.D. Kilmer, *JAOS* 83 42ff.; Malku II, pub. W. von Soden, ZA 43 235ff.
MB	Middle Babylonian
MDOG	*Mitteilungen der Deutschen Orient Gesellschaft*

Meissner, *BAP*	B. Meissner, *Beiträge zum altbabylonischen Privatrecht*
MSL	*Materialen zum sumerischen Lexikon; Materials for the Sumerian Lexicon*
MKT	O. Neugebauer, *Mathematische Keilschrifttexte*
NA	Neo-Assyrian
NB	Neo-Babylonian
Nbk	Nebuchadnezzar
Nbk	J.N. Strassmaier, *Inschriften von Nabuchodonosor* . . .
Nbn	Nabonidus
Nbn	J.N. Strassmaier, *Inschriften von Nabonidus* . . .
Ner	Neriglissar
Ner	B.T.A. Evetts, *Inscriptions of the Reigns of Evil-Merodach, Neriglissar and Laborosoarchod*
Npl	Nabopolassar
Npl	J.N. Strassmaier, *Inschriften von Nabopolassar* . . .
OB	Old Babylonian
Oppenheim, *Dreambook*	A.L. Oppenheim, *The Interpretation of Dreams in the Ancient Near East* (=*TAPS* 46/3)
*Or*NS	*Orientalia* Nova Series
OrAnt	*Oriens Antiquus*
Parker-Dubberstein	R.A. Parker and W.H. Dubberstein, *Babylonian Chronology 626 B.C.-A.D. 75*
PEF Quarterly	*Quarterly Statement of the Palestine Exploration Fund*
Peiser	F.E. Peiser, *Aus dem babylonischen Rechtsleben*
Pinckert, *Nebo*	J. Pinckert, *Hymnen und Gebete an Nebo*
PSBA	*Proceedings of the Society of Biblical Archaeology*
R	H.C. Rawlinson, *The Cuneiform Inscriptions of Western Asia*
RA	*Revue d'assyriologie et d'archéologie orientale*
RT	*Receuil de travaux relatifs à la philologie et à l'archéologie égyptiennes et assyriennes*
S^a	lexical series *Syllabary A* (pub. *MSL* 3 3-45)
S^b	lexical series *Syllabary B* (pub. *MSL* 3 96-128 and 132-53)
Sachs *Fs*	*Occasional Publications of the S.N. Kramer Fund*, 9
SAKI	F. Thureau-Dangin, *Die sumerischen und akkadischen Königsinschriften* (=*VAB* 1)
San Nicolò, *BR 8/7*	M. San Nicolò, *Babylonische Rechtsurkunden des ausgehenden 8. und des 7. Jahrhunderts v. Chr.*
SANE	*Sources from the Ancient Near East*
SBH	G.A. Reisner, *Sumerisch-babylonische Hymnen nach Thontafeln griechischer Zeit*
Sd	Samsu-ditana

SE	Seleucid Era
Sel	Seleucus
Schmidt, *Persepolis 2*	E. Schmidt, *Persepolis 2, Oriental Institute Publications* 69
SH	tablets in the collections of the British Museum
Si	Samsu-iluna
Sm	Sin-muballiṭ
Sollberger, *Corpus*	E. Sollberger, *Corpus des inscriptions "royales" présargoniques de Lagaš*
Sp	tablets in the collections of the British Museum
Speiser *Fs*	*Essays in Memory of E.A. Speiser* (*AOS* 53)
StOr	*Studia Orientalia*
St. Pohl	*Studia Pohl*
Strassmaier, *8th Cong.*	*Actes du huitième congrès international des Orientalistes*
Streck, *Asb.*	M. Streck, *Assurbanipal* . . . (=*VAB* 7)
STT	O.R. Gurney, J.J. Finkelstein, and P. Hulin, *The Sultantepe Tablets*
Symb. Koschaker	*Symbolae P. Koschaker dedicatae* (=*Studia et documenta ad iura orientis antiqui pertinentia* 2)
Ššu	Šamaš-šum-ukin
TAPS	*Transactions of the American Philosophical Society*
TCS	*Texts from Cuneiform Sources*
TDP	R. Labat, *Traité akkadien de diagnostics et pronostics médicaux*
UE	*Ur Excavations*
Ur-Baba	inscriptions of Ur-Baba, numbered according to the forthcoming edition by H. Steible
VAB	*Vorderasiatische Bibliothek*
VAS	*Vorderasiatische Schriftdenkmäler*
Walker, *Bricks*	C.B.F. Walker, *Cuneiform Brick Inscriptions in the British Museum* . . .
Walker, *Tell ed-Der*	C.B.F. Walker, in L. de Meyer, *Tell el-Der* III
Waterman, *BusDoc*	L. Waterman, *Business Documents of the Hammurapi Period* (also pub. in *AJSL* 29 and 30)
Weidner, *Handbuch*	E. Weidner, *Handbuch der babylonischen Astronomie*
Weissbach, *VAB 3*	Weissbach, *Die Keilinschriften der Achameniden* (=*VAB* 3)
Weitemeyer, *Workers*	M. Weitemeyer, *Some Aspects of the Hiring of Workers in the Sippar Region at the Time of Hammurabi*
Winckler, *Untersuchen*	H. Winckler, *Untersuchen zur altorientalischen Geschichte*
WO	*Die Welt des Orients*
Xer	Xerxes
ZA	*Zeitschrift für Assyriologie*
ZDMG	*Zeitschrift der Deutschen Morgenländischen Gesellschaft*

CATALOGUE

AH 82-9-18A,

1-19				Uninscribed objects; Walker, *Tell ed-Der* 3 139
20		Pre-Sargonic	F	Inscribed alabaster vase; Walker, *Tell ed-Der* 3 pl. 27
21-24				Uninscribed objects; Walker, *Tell ed-Der* 3 139
25	22452	OAkk	F	Inscribed alabaster vase; *CT* 7 3
26		Joined to 82-7-14, 1013 (= BM 91019)		
27-36				Uninscribed objects; Walker, *Tell ed-Der* 3 139
37	91021 (= 12163)		F	Inscribed marble disk; Walker, *Tell ed-Der* 3 pl. 27
38-43				Uninscribed objects; Walker, *Tell ed-Der* 3 139
44		Joined to 82-7-14, 1018 (= BM 90902)		
45	74329		F	Myth of Dunnu; *CT* 46 43; *Kadmos* 4 (1966) 64f.; *SANE* 2/3
46	74330	Dar 6/12b/32	F	Apprenticeship contract
47	74331	Bar 26/3/-	NC	Contract for dates
48	74332	Nbn 9/7/16	C	House rental
49	92722	Dar 4/7/17	C	House rental; Sippar; Aramaic docket; Delaporte, *Épigraphes Araméens* 101; *ABC* 37
50	92723	Nbn -/10/8	F	Account of house rentals; Aramaic docket; *ABC* 30
51	74333	Dar 16/11/19	C	Purchase of sesame; Aramaic docket; *ABC* 38
52	74334		C	Letter; *CT* 22 105
53	74335	Nbn 28/4/14	C	Receipt for barley; *Nbn* 773
54	74336	Nbn 9/8/14	C	List of workmen; *Nbn* 804
55	74337	Nbn 1/3/16	C	Loan of silver; *Nbn* 959
56	74338	Nbn 15/5/10	C	Account of beeswax; *Nbn* 429

AH 82-9-18A,

57	92724	Nbn 15/9/5	C	Account of house rents; *Nbn* 201
58	74339	Nbn 14/5/8	NC	Receipt for emmer; *Nbn* 298
59	74340	Nbn 14/5/-	NC	Account of barley fodder; *Nbn* 1085
60	74341	Nbn 28/12/2	NC	Receipt for silver; *Nbn* 88
61	74342	Nbn -/1/17	C	Receipt for silver income; *Nbn* 1029
62	74343	Nbn 21/9/3	C	Account of royal silver for expenditures; *Nbn* 119
63	92725	Nbn 24/9/15	C	Account of dates; *Nbn* 911
64	74344	Nbn 23/10/16	C	Receipt for emmer and barley; *Nbn* 1001
65	74345	Nbn 27/1/16	NC	Receipt for oil; *Nbn* 957
66	74346	Nbn 16/12/8	NC	Account of dowry; *Nbn* 313
67	74347	Nbn 4/3/8	C	Receipt for barley for flour; *Nbn* 292
68	74348	Nbn 12/3/14	C	Receipt for flour for the *šalam biti*; *Nbn* 767
69	74349	Nbn 6/11/10	C	Receipt for bronze and tin; *Nbn* 471
70	74350	Nbn 9/12/11	NC	Letter; *CT* 22 165; *Nbn* 574
71	74351	Nbn 27/4/12	C	Receipt for purchase of dates; *Nbn* 612
72	74352	Nbn 26/7/12	C	Account of barley; *Nbn* 629
73	74353	Nbn 8/9/9	C	Purchase of sheep; *Nbn* 368
74	74354	Nbn 26/3/acc	C	Receipt for sheep; *Nbn* 2
75	74355	Nbn 10/9/15	C	Receipt for dates; *Nbn* 910
76	74356	Nbn 22/5/4	C	Account of garments of gods; *Nbn* 159
77	74357	Nbn 7/9/16	C	House rental; *Nbn* 996
78	74358	Nbn 25/7/-	C	Account of jewelry; *Nbn* 1097
79	74359	Nbn 7/3/4	C	Receipt for gold; *Nbn* 150
80	74360	Nbn -/5/11	NC	Barley for bird feed; *Nbn* 528
81	74361	Nb(-) 13/2/2	C	Receipt for various purchases; *Nbn* 61
82	74362	Nbn 4/2/9	C	Receipt for sheep; *Nbn* 328
83	74363	Nbn 14/2/3+	C	Account of silver income; *Nbn* 333
84	74364	Nbn 11/8/9	C	Account of barley; *Nbn* 361
85	74365	Nbn 9/1/9	C	Receipt for silver income; *Nbn* 321
86	74366	Nbn 20/1/14	C	Receipt for oil; two seals; *Nbn* 798
87	74367	Nbn 5/9/15	C	Receipt for date tithes; *Nbn* 902
88	74368	Nbn 9/12/10	C	Receipt for bitumen; *Nbn* 478

AH 82-9-18A,

89	74369	Nbn 9/4/7	C	Receipt
90	74370	Nbn 5/12/15	C	Contract for dates; *Nbn* 932
91	74371	Nbn 1/3/15	C	Receipt for salt; *Nbn* 850
92	74372	Nbn 24/12/8	C	Contract for barley; *Nbn* 315
93	74373	Nbn 23/8/12	C	Contract for wool; *Nbn* 637
94	74374	Nbn 9/2/3	C	Receipt for gold; *Nbn* 98
95	74375	Nbn 8/2/3	C	Receipt for gold for working; *Nbn* 96
96	74376	Nbn 29/11/16	C	Receipt for barley; drawing; *Nbn* 1009
97	74377	Cyr 24/8/acc	C	Receipt for barley provisions; *Cyr* 2
98	74378	Cyr 24/9/5	C	Letter; *CT* 22 233; *Cyr* 209
99	74379	Nbn 21/11/3	C	Exchange of garments and sesame
100	74380	Nbn 13/4/14	C	Receipt for sale of sheep
101	74381	Nbn 9/3/10	NC	Receipt for barley
102	74382	Nbn 15/9/3	NC	Receipt for bronze
103	74383	Nbn 8/3/17	F	Account of dates
104	74384	Nbn 9/1/16	C	Receipt for barley
105	74385	Nbn 21/-/-	F	Receipt for purchase of doors
106	74386	Nbn 25/-/9	NC	Receipt for date provisions
107	74387	Nbn 16/11/13	C	Account of dates
108	74388	Nbn 7/9/12	C	Receipt for cassia tithe
109	74389	Nbn 9/-/12?	NC	Receipt for flour
110	74390	Nbn 17/1/10	C	House rental
111	74391	Nbn 10/-/10	NC	Receipt for silver income
112	74392	Nbn 4/3/9	NC	Account of garments of gods
113	74393	Nbn 4/4/6	C	Receipt for beer
114	74394	Cyr 28/12/6	NC	Account of provisions
115	74395	Nbn -/10/3	NC	Receipt for barley provisions
116	74396	Nbn 13/2/3	NC	Receipt for flour
117	74397	2/-/15	NC	Account of silver
118	74398	Nbn 9/10/13	C	Receipt for garments
119	74399	Nbn 5/3/5	C	Receipt for silver
120	74400	Nbn 21/12/6	C	Receipt for sheep
121	74401	Nbn 17/11/6	C	Receipt for a cow
122	74402	Nbn 23/1/3	F	Economic
123	74403	Nbn 2/2/9	C	Receipt for oil
124	74404	Nbn 3/5/10	NC	Account of dates
125	74405	Nbn 10+/5/11	C	Receipt for gold
126	74406	Nbn -/-/12	NC	Receipt for flour
127	74407	Nbn 2/9/12	NC	Receipt

AH 82-9-18A,

128	74408	Nbn 10/11/12	C	Receipt for silver
129	74409	Nbn 18/6/5	C	Account of various purchases
130	74410	Nbn 13/2/12	F	Receipt for flour
131	74411	Nbn 30/2/12	NC	Account of purchases
132	74412	Cam 3/5/1	C	Sale of sheep
133	74413	Nbk 2/10/31	NC	Receipt for dates
134	74414	8/12/-	C	Three names
135	74415	Nbk 6/12/12	C	Receipt for flour
136	74416	Nbk -/8/27	F	Account of provisions
137	74417		C	Account of barley
138	74418	Bar 6/6/1	C	Receipt for bronze
139	74419	OB -/4/mu ma-da ...	C	Field rental; seal; tablet in case
140	74420	OB	C	Field rental; seal; tablet in case
141	74421	Ha -/1/38	C	Field rental; tablet in case
142	74422	Cam 19/6/1	C	Account of dates
143	74423		F	Ledger
144	74424		F	Account of oxen
145	74425	Nbn 6/4/12	C	Rental of an orchard
146	74426	Nbn 15/9/3	C	Exchange of wool and sesame
147	74427	Nbn 13/8/15	F	Account of flour
148	74428	Nbn 6/2/10	C	Receipt for vessels
149	74429	Nbn 29/3/14?	C	Receipt for silver for provisions
150	74430	Nbn 3/4/11	NC	Receipt for silver income
151	74431	Nbn 9/6/13	C	Receipt for wool
152	74432	Nbn 12/2/13	C	Receipt for gold for garments of gods
153	74433	Nbk 2/9/35	C	Receipt for sinews
154	74434	Nbk 1/3/20+	C	Receipt for silver for garments of gods
155	74435	Nbn 16/12/10	C	Receipt for sesame
156	74436	Nbn 24/7/16	C	Account of barley fodder
157	74437	Nbn 28/1/12	C	Account of sesame
158	74438	Nbn 15/11/15	NC	Account of silver
159	74439	Nbn 26/12/16	C	Rental of a field
160	74440	Nbn 12/12/10	C	Account of garments of gods for cleaning
161	74441	Nbk 6/-/16	C	Receipt for emmer
162	74442	Nbn 22/10/4	C	Receipt for garments; *Nbn* 174
163	74443	Nbn 5/1/14	C	Receipt for wool for garments of gods; *Nbn* 751
164	74444	Nbn 30/5/16	NC	Account of dates

AH 82-9-18A,

165	74445	Cyr -/9/5	NC	Letter; *CT* 22 219; *Cyr* 207
166	74446	Nbk 2+/8/20+	NC	House rental
167	74447	Nbk -/11/-	NC	Receipt for barley
168	74448	Nbn 25/-/-	NC	Receipt for silver
169	74449	Nbn 6/10/3?	NC	Receipt for beer
170	74450	Nbn 19/12b/1	C	Receipt for iron
171	74451	8/3/8	NC	Receipt for sheep
172	74452	Nbn 19/8/2	C	Receipt for gold
173	74453	Nbn 26/11/12	C	Receipt for silver for working
174	74454	Nbn 21/1/12	C	Receipt for sesame
175	74455	Nbn 5/3/12	C	Receipt for dates
176	74456	Cam 26/11/7	C	Receipt for dates
177	74457	Cam 26/10/7	NC	Sale of a donkey
178	74458	Cyr 5/9/3	NC	Account of dates
179	74459	Cam 10/-/1	F	Account of wool
180	74460	Cam 6/5/2	C	Loan of silver
181	74461	Cam 1/9/2	C	Receipt for sesame
182	74462	Cyr 16/1/3	C	Receipt for dates
183	74463	Cyr 4/12/3	C	Receipt for barley
184	74464	Cyr -/4/3	F	Account of oxen
185	74465	Nbk 21/5/acc	NC	Receipt for dates or grain
186	74466	Cam 28/3/1	F	Contract for dates
187	74467	Cam 27/8/1	C	Receipt for dates
188	74468	Cam 28/12/4	C	Account of dates or grain
189	74469	Cam -/6b/3	C	Receipt for dates
190	74470	Cam 17/7/6	C	Contract for dates
191	92728	Npl 12/2/10	C	Witnesses; Babylon; ZA 4 138
192	74471	Am 26/3/2	C	Receipt for silver
193	74472	Cam 10+/7/1	C	Receipt for dates; *Cam* 65
194	92729	Bar 15/6/1	C	Legal deposition; Zazanna; *ZA* 4 150
195	74473	Dar 10/2/3	C	Loan of silver
196	74474	Dar 19/11/8	C	Loan of barley
197	74475	Dar 5/5/29	C	Transfer of a woman in property division; Sippar
198	74476	Xer 18/2/1	C	House rental
199	74477	Dar 6/4/27	C	Contract for barley
200	74478	Nbn 18/12/11	C	Account of sheep
201	74479	Nbn 20/8/10	C	Account of wool
202	74480	Cam 8/2/1	C	Account of barley provisions

AH 82-9-18A,

203	74481	Cam 14/3/4	C	Receipt for barley
204	74482	Cam 13/5/5	C	Receipt for an ox
205	74483	Cam 15/11/1	C	Contract; Sippar
206	74484	Cam 3/1/4	C	Account of wool
207	74485	Cam 8/6/6	C	Account of aromatics
208	74486	Cam 9/8/1	NC	Receipt for silver for working
209	74487	Cam 25/1/7	NC	Contract for seed
210	74488	Cam 17/7/4	C	Receipt for barley
211	74489	Cam 11+/6b/3	NC	Account of garments of gods
212	74490	Cam 7/9/1	C	Receipt for sesame
213	74491	Cam 5/9/1	C	Account of dates
214	74492	Cam 23/8/1	NC	Receipt
215	74493	Nbk 1/5/8	C	Loan of silver
216	74494	Nbk 28/8/1	C	Loan of silver
217	74495	Ner 27/11/2	NC	Contract for barley; Sippar
218	74496	Nbk 3/2/-	C	Loan of silver
219	74497	Esar 23/12b/3	NC	Legal; dispute over income; Babylon; Strassmaier, *8th Cong.* 4
220	92501	Ha -/9/12	C	House sale; Meissner, *BAP* 30
220A	92501A	OB	F	Envelope to 82-9-18A, 220 (= BM 92501); seals
221	74498	Am 26/1/2	NC	Sale of land; Bit-bari; *AOATS* 4 57
222	74499	Nbk 8/2/36	C	Sale of a field; Alu-ša-Šamaš
223	74500	Cyr 10/6/8	NC	House rental
224	74501	Cyr 14/8/2	C	Account of dates
225	74502	Cyr 24/5/5	F	Deposit of a money bag; Sippar
226	74503	Cam 1/8/6	C	Receipt for dates
227	74504	Xer 9/4/2	C	Account of prebends; Sippar
228	74505	Nbn 9/4/13	C	Receipt for iron daggers
229	74506	Cyr 15/10/acc	C	Receipt for dates
230	74507	Cam 25/12b/5	C	Loan of silver
231	74508	Cam 22/2/6	C	Loan of silver; Sippar
232	74509	Nbk 20/5/42	NC	Receipt for sheep
233	74510	Cam 28/11/3	C	Receipt for barley
234	74511	Ner 6/7/1	F	Contract for barley
235	74512	Dar 17/9/-	NC	Receipt for gold temple paraphernalia
236	74513	Dar 19/4/13	NC	Receipt for barley
237	74514	Dar 9/6/-	F	Account of silver
238	74515	Dar 25/4/5	C	Deposition; Sippar

AH 82-9-18A,

239	74516	Dar 18/7/28	C	Loan of silver
240	74517	Dar 20/7/24	C	Promissory note for silver; Babylon
241	74518	Dar 24/12a/20+	C	Promissory note for barley
242	74519	Dar 4/1/2+	NC	Legal deposition
243	74520	Dar 27/3/-	NC	Legal; transfer of responsibility
244	74521	Dar 5/9/24	NC	Settlement of a loan
245	74522	Dar 16/2/24	C	Loan of silver; Sippar
246	74523	Dar 10/5/25	NC	Deposition concerning slaves; Babylon
247	74524		C	Account of dates
248	74525	Dar 21/3/35	C	House rental; Sippar
249	74526	Dar -/-/1	NC	Purchase of vessels; Sippar
250	74527	Dar 13/2/8	C	Loan of silver; Sippar
251	74528		F	Bilingual incantation
252	74529	Dar 15/12/25	C	Account of garments; Babylon
253	74530	Dar 26/6/25	C	Contract for dates
254	74531	Dar 2/1/25	C	Receipt for cassia
255	74532	Dar 8/12b/24	C	Loan of silver; Šuanna
256	74533	Dar 30/5/-	NC	Contract for barley; Sippar
257	74534	Dar 10/2/24	NC	Loan of silver; Ṣibti
258	74535	Dar 14/8/8	C	Contract for barley; Alu-ša-Belšunu
259	74536	Dar 15/11/24	C	Contract for dates; Sippar
260	74537	Dar -/9/15+	F	Receipt for bronze for vessels
261	74538	Dar 12/8/24	NC	Legal deposition; Bit-Šamaš-iddin
262	74539	Dar 4/12?/24+	NC	Contract for dates
263	74540	Dar 24/4/24	C	Contract for dates
264	74541	Dar 19/4/25	NC	House rental; Babylon
265	74542	Dar 24/-/-	F	Contract for barley; Šušanna
266	74543	Cyr 24/1/8	NC	House sale; Sippar
267	74544	Dar 25/7/2	F	Contract; Sippar
268	74545	Dar 6/2/15	C	House rental; Sippar
269	74546	Dar 24/1/-	F	Account of sheep
270	74547	Dar 26/5/29	C	Sale of sheep
271	74548	Dar 5/1/31	C	Loan of silver
272	74549	Dar 4/12/34	NC	Account of barley
273	74550	Dar 12/6/33	C	Account of offerings; Babylon
274	74551	Dar 24/6/27	C	Loan of silver; Babylon
275	74552	Dar 3/9/35	C	Loan of silver; Sippar
276	74553	Dar 11/7/33	C	Receipt for date provisions; Sippar
277	74554	Dar 24/6/36	C	Receipt for barley; Babylon

AH 82-9-18A,

278	74555	Dar 26/8/32	C	Letter; seal
279	74556	Dar 2/3/31	C	Loan of silver
280	74557	Dar 16/3/34	F	Contract for dates or grain; Sippar
281	74558	Dar -/10/28	NC	Legal deposition; Sippar
282	74559	Dar 26/8/33	C	Contract for provisions; Sippar
283	74560	Dar 16/7/26	C	Settlement of debts of barley; Sippar
284	74561	-/-/1	NC	Account of gold for a *makkasu* bowl; picture of the bowl
285	74562	Dar 16/9/29	NC	Receipt
286	74563	Dar 27/4/29	C	Loan of silver; Sippar
287	74564	Dar 10/4/26	C	Account of dates; Babylon
288	74565	Dar 29/4/28	C	Loan of silver; Sippar
289	74566	Nbn 19/5/12	NC	Receipt for barley
290	74567	Dar -/5/2	NC	Account of dates
291	74568	Dar 17/10/35	F	Debt of dates; Sippar
292	74569	Dar 6/10/34	NC	Account of dates
293	74570	Dar 29/7/35	C	Account of offerings in Sippar; Babylon
294	74571	Dar 1/1/34	NC	Debt of dates; Sippar
295	74572	Dar 11/12/-	C	Account of various purchases; Aramaic docket; *ABC* 39
296	74573	Dar 22/12/35	C	Contract for barley
297	74574	Cam 29/5/1	C	Receipt for silver
298	74575	Dar 5/3/16	C	Receipt for house rent; Sippar
299	74576	Dar -/2/20	NC	Loan of silver
300	74577	Dar 11/11/18	C	Account of garments of gods; Sippar
301	74578	Dar 12/3/3	C	Account of flour
302	74579	Dar 12/9/3	C	Account of wool and garments
303	74580	Dar 26/4/9	C	Loan of silver; Babylon
304	74581	Dar 4/-/9	NC	Loan of silver; Sippar
305	74582	Dar 18/8/10	C	Loan of silver; Sippar
306	74583	Dar 23/12b/16	NC	Contract for barley; Sippar
307	74584	Dar 25/6/10	C	Loan of silver; Babylon
308	74585	Dar 22/8/23	F	Accounts
309	74586	Dar 4/7/11	C	Loan of silver; Babylon
310	92733	Dar 18/6/10+	C	Receipt for silver; Aramaic docket; *ABC* 36
311	74587	Dar 4/7/10	NC	Loan of silver; Babylon
312	74588	Dar 28/3/10	C	Legal deposition; Sippar
313	74589	Dar 22+/3/12	C	Sale of a slave girl; Babylon
314	74590	Dar 15/6/23	C	Receipt for dates

AH 82-9-18A,

315	74591	Dar 6/11/20	C	Promissory note for silver; Sippar
316	74592	Dar 18/-/12	C	Contract for dates
317	74593	Dar 9/4/22	C	Loan of silver; Sippar
318	74594	Dar 21/6/23	C	Contract for dates; Sippar
319	74595	Dar 24/1/12	C	Loan of dates and barley; Zazanna
320	74596	Dar 26/2/29	C	Dowry list; Uruk
321	74597	Dar 17/7/4	NC	Loan of silver; Sippar
322	74598	Dar 2/6?/6	NC	Receipt for purchase of emmer
323	74599	Dar 14/1/6	NC	Receipt for figs
324	74600	Dar 2+/4/6	C	Receipt for dates or grain
325	74601	Dar 24/3/6	C	Receipt for toll; Babylon
326	74602	Dar 13/9/4	NC	Receipt for dates
327	74603	Dar 4/10/7	C	Loan of silver; Sippar; seal
328	74604	Dar 12/6b/19	C	Contract for dates; URU.LAM.KUR.RU; seal
329	74605	Dar 18/7/6	C	Loan of silver; Sippar
330	74606	Dar 20/12/12	NC	Contract for dates; Sippar
331	74607	Dar 4/11/10	NC	Loan of silver; Babylon
332	74608	Dar 25/2/9	NC	Receipt for barley
333	74609	Dar 2/12b/35	C	Contract for barley and dates; Sippar
334	74610	Dar -/8/34	C	Sale of a slave; Ṣibtum-šanummu
335	92734	Dar 18/10/3	C	Loan of silver; Sippar; Aramaic docket; *ABC* 33
336	74611	Nbn 4/4/14	NC	Contract; Bab-Nar-Šamaš
337	74612	Cam 6/12/5	C	Account of lambs
337A	74612A		F	Envelope to 82-9-18A, 337 (=BM 74612); seals
338	74613	Dar 10/4/4	C	Contract for barley
339	74614	Dar -/2/13	NC	Letter; seals
340	74615	Dar 6/6/14	C	Contract for dates; URU.BÀD-É-su
341	74616	Dar 18/8/5	NC	Receipt for aromatics
342	74617	Dar 2/7/5	C	Receipt for silver
343	74618	Dar 26/4?/13	NC	Loan of silver; Sippar
344	74619	Dar 17/9/2	C	Receipt for silver
345	74620	Dar 20/7/7	C	Loan of silver; Babylon
346	74621	Dar -/-/13	NC	Contract for purchase of barley; Zazanna
347	74622	Dar 26/5/14?	C	Sale of land; distinctive format; URU ba-x-ḫu-in-ni
348	74623	-/-/14	NC	Contract for barley; Zazannu

AH 82-9-18A,

349	74624	Dar 30/1/4	F	Rental of oxen
350	74625	Dar 8/7/4	C	Contract for dates
351	74626	Dar 5/8/19	C	Contract for dates
352	74627	Dar 2/4/7	C	Receipt for sheep and oxen
353	74628	Dar -/3/10	NC	Rental of a house(?); Sippar
354	74629	Dar 10/12/5	NC	Legal; transfer of responsibility
355	74630	Dar 20/8/33	NC	House rental; Sippar
356	74631	Dar 24/1/30	NC	Loan of silver; Sippar
357	74632	Dar 3/1/30	C	Loan of silver; Šušan
358	74633	Dar 22/11/30	NC	Loan of silver; Šušan; seals
359	74634	Dar 4/11/15	C	Receipt for silver
360	74635	Tar-zi-ia 11/8/1	F	Receipt; see *AJSL* 58 315
361	74636	Dar 2/4/31	C	Loan of silver; Upiya
362	74637	Dar 19/4/-	F	Loan of silver
363	74638	Dar -/-/4	F	Account of silver; Babylon
364	74639	Dar 23/6b/19	NC	Receipt for silver; Aramaic docket
365	74640	Dar 2/9/[21]	NC	Contract for dates; Sippar
366	74641		NC	Account of dates
367	74642	30/8/35	NC	Receipt for iron for spades
368	74643	Dar 24/4?/26	F	Loan of silver; Alu-ša-me-Bit-Bel-kaṣir
369	74644	Dar 7/9/30	C	Receipt for dates
370	74645	Dar 10/3/30	F	Dowry list; Sippar
371	74646	Dar 18?/6/20+	C	Account of temple lands
372	74647		F	Account of sheep
373	74648		C	Account of dates
374	74649		F	Account of hired men
375	74650	Nbn 12/3?/12?	NC	Receipt for sesame; drawing on reverse
376	74651	Nbn 5/2/-	F	Account of jewelry
377	74652	Ššu 20/3/-	F	Legal; "siege document"; *AfO* 16 37, *Iraq* 17 77
378	74653	21/-/4	NC	Account of wool
379	74654		C	Account of silver
380	74655	Nbn -/-/16	NC	Account of dates
381	74656		C	Account of dates or grain
382	74657	Cam 2/3/-	F	Contract for barley
383	74658	Dar 17/12/3	C	Legal deposition
384	74659	Cyr 19/11/8	C	Legal deposition; Sippar
385	74660	Cyr -/6/4	C	Account of dates
386	74661	Dar 13/8/6	C	Contract for delivery of sheep; Sippar

AH 82-9-18A,

387	74662	Dar 15/6/2	C	Contract for animals; Sippar
388	74663	Cyr 17/10/5	C	Receipt for wool
389	74664	Cam 7/8/1	C	Receipt for silver for purchases
390	74665		C	Letter
391	74666	Cyr 7/2/4	C	Account of oxen
392	74667	Dar 10/7/2	C	Legal deposition; Sippar
393	74668		C	Account of dates
394	74669	Cyr 20/8/9	C	Receipt for barley
395	74670	Cyr 18/1/8	C	Account of cloth and dyes for gods
396	74671	Cyr 30/9/6	C	Receipt for sesame
397	74672	Dar -/-/24	C	Audit of dates
398	74673	Dar 9/8/3	C	Account of silver and vats; Sippar
399	74674	Cam	C	Receipt for garments and grain
400	74675	Cam 12/8/1	C	Receipt for bronze
401	74676	Cam 19/5/3	C	Receipt for sesame
402	74677	Cam 3/9/3	NC	Receipt for flour
403	74678	Cam 10/2/3	C	Account of dates or grain
404	74679	Dar 25/2/29	C	Land sale; Sippar
405	74680	Dar 5/6/7	C	Contract for dates; Du-si-su
406	74681	Bar 6/19/1	C	Legal deposition; Sippar
407	74682	Cyr 5/9/5	C	Receipt for iron for tools
408	74683	Dar 3/9/8	C	Loan of silver; Sippar

AH 83-1-18,

1	74684	Nbn 10/5/11	C	Receipt for sale of gold; *Nbn* 522
2	74685	30/3/-	C	Receipt for barley
3	74686	Nbn 27/3/17	C	Receipt for reed mats; *Nbn* 1036
4	74687	Nbn 6/2/3	C	Receipt for a garment; *Nbn* 93
5	74688	Nbn 1/11/12	C	Receipt for a cloth *Nbn* 660
6	74689	Nbk 25/8/24	C	Receipt for dates or grain; *Nbk* 144
7	74690	Cyr 21/9/5	C	Receipt for silver; *Cyr* 208
8	74691	Cyr 28/1/8	C	Receipt for oil; *Cyr* 299
9	74692	Nbn 25/3/6	C	Receipt; *Nbn* 227
10	74693	Ner 25/6/acc	C	Receipt for wool
11	74694	Nbk 28/2/42	C	Receipt for sesame; *Nbk* 395
12	74695	Cam 2/1/1	C	Receipt for house rent; *Cam* 27
13	74696	Nbn 7/8/6	C	Receipt for bronze; *Nbn* 241
14	74697	Cam 1/9/2	C	Receipt for silver; *Cam* 128
15	74698	Cam 8/2/5	C	Receipt for sesame; *Cam* 275
16	74699	Nbn 12/8/14	C	Receipt for a garment; *Nbn* 805
17	74700	Cam 3/1/1	C	Receipt for house rent; *Cam* 29
18	74701	Nbk 30/10/34	C	Receipt for dates; *Nbk* 274
19	74702	28/4/15	C	Account of fruit; *Nbn* 869
20	74703	Nbn 9/12b/15	C	Receipt for iron; *Nbn* 939
21	74704	Nbn 18/4/15	C	Receipt for oxen; *Nbn* 867
22	74705	Nbn 27/11/16	C	Receipt for silver for working; *Nbn* 1007
23	74706	Cam 9/9/-	C	Receipt for emmer; *Cam* 424
24	74707	Nbk -/2/42	C	Sale of sheep; *Nbk* 396
25	74708		C	Account of dates or grain
26	74709	Am 15/4/2	C	Receipt for wool
27	74710	Dar 27/11/acc	C	Account of barley; *Dar* 3
28	74711	Dar 19/2/2	C	Receipt for sesame; *Dar* 32
29	74712	Cyr 3/8/2	C	Receipt for sesame; *Cyr* 67

AH 83-1-18,

30	74713	Nbn 4/6/11	C	Receipt for iron for tools; *Nbn* 530
31	74714	Nbk 5/9/25	C	Receipt for ducks; *Nbk* 154
32	missing	Nbk 5/7/acc	F	Account of garments of gods; *Nbk* 2
33	74715	Cam 23/2/3	F	Sale of beer; *Cam* 160
34	74716	Cyr 9/8/7	C	Receipt for bronze for vessels; *Cyr* 269
35	74717	Dar 4/8/25	C	Receipt for dates
36	74718	15/6/-	C	Receipt for sesame; *Nbn* 1093
37	74719	Cyr 17/8/2	C	Receipt for sesame; *Cyr* 70
38	74720	Cyr 30/7/2	C	Receipt for sesame; *Cyr* 66
39	74721	Nbn 16/5/15	C	Sale of oxen; *Nbn* 873
40	74722	Cyr 21/8/2	C	Receipt for barley; *Cyr* 71
41	92749	Nbk 5/8/37	F	Receipt for bricks; *Nbk* 321
42	74723	Nbk 1/2/27	C	Receipt for shoes; *Nbk* 173
43	74724	Cyr 9/2/3	C	Receipt for garments of gods; *Cyr* 104
43A	74725	Nbn 20/10/15	C	Sale of an ox; *Nbn* 923
44	74726	Bar 23/4/-	NC	Receipt for dates or grain; *ZA* 4, 150 no. 5
45	74727	Nbk 8/2/36	C	Receipt for dates or grain; *Nbk* 292
46	74728	Nbk 16/6/34	C	Account of dates; *Nbk* 267
47	74729	Nbn -/4/16	C	Receipt for dates: *Nbn* 968
48	74730	13/12/-	C	Letter; *CT* 22 207; *Nbn* 1134
49	74731	Nbk 6/1/26	C	Receipt for ducks; *Nbk* 159
50	74732	Nbn 4/3/15	NC	Receipt for sesame; *Nbn* 852
51	74733	Nbn 1/3/10	C	Receipt for fodder; *Nbn* 414
52	74734	Nbn 24/11/12	C	Receipt for sesame; *Nbn* 667
53	74735	Nbn 21/8/15	C	Account of barley; *Nbn* 899
54	74736	5/10/2	C	Purchase of dates; *Cyr* 75
55	74737	Dar 17/5/3	C	Receipt for barley; *Dar* 74
56	74738	Cam 20/11/6	C	Account of sesame; *Cam* 342
57	74739	Cyr 18/10/5	NC	Contract for barley; Sippar; *Cyr* 211
58	74740	Cam 13/11/1	C	Receipt for aromatics; *Cam* 91
59	74741		C	Letter; seal; *CT* 22 140; *Cyr* 371
60	74742	Cyr 5/1/8	C	Receipt for oil; *Cyr* 290
61	74743	Nbn 11/9/14	C	Receipt for iron for tools; *Nbn* 810
62	74744	Nbk 19/3/36	C	Purchase of reeds; *Nbk* 297
63	74745	Nbk 6/7/30	C	Receipt for barley; *Nbk* 215
64	74746	Nbn 1/11/3	C	Receipt for garments of gods; *Nbn* 125
65	74747	14/3/1	C	Receipt for barley for flour; *Nbn* 29
66	74748	Nbk 23/6/1	C	Receipt for wool and sesame; *Nbk* 14

AH 83-1-18,

67	74749	Nbk -/4/42	C	Sale of an ox; *Nbk* 399
68	74750	Cam 4/1/8	F	Deposition; Sippar; *Cam* 407
69	92750	Nbn 10/5/10	C	Account of house rentals; *Nbn* 428
70	74751	Nbn 27/8/12	C	Receipt for sesame tithe; *Nbn* 640
71	74752	Nbn 17/12/15	NC	Account of garlic; *Nbn* 933
72	74753	Nbn 17/10/9	C	Account of dates; *Nbn* 374
73	74754	2/5/4	C	Silver for dates; *Nbn* 156
74	74755	Cyr 26/11/1	C	Barley for wages; *Cyr* 24
75	74756	Nbn 7/5/8	C	Contract for dates; *Nbn* 297
76	74757		C	Receipt for dates or grain
77	74758		C	Account of dates and barley
78	92751	Cyr 3/10/2	C	Account of dates; *Cyr* 74
79	74759	23/2/1	C	Receipt for barley for goldsmiths; *Nbn* 25
80	74760	Nbn 22/2/8	C	Receipt for wool; *Nbn* 285
81	74761	Cyr 28/12/8	C	Deposition; Sippar; *Cyr* 328
82	74762		F	Account of dates or grain
83	74763		NC	Legal text concerning silver
84	74764	Cyr 17/8/8	C	Silver for a vessel; *Cyr* 319
85	74765	Nbn 15/2/10	C	Account of garments of gods; *Nbn* 410
86	74766	Nbn 7/5/16	C	Purchase of sesame; *Nbn* 971
87	74767	Nbn 15/8/9	C	Receipt for sesame tithe; *Nbn* 362
88	74768	Cyr -/-/8	C	Account of dates for tax; *Cyr* 333
89	74769		C	Receipt for dates or grain; reverse has description of a relief
90	74770	Nbn 7/4/17	C	Receipt for barley provisions; *Nbn* 1040
91	74771	Nbn 8/3/16	C	Receipt for lime; *Nbn* 961
92	74772	Nbn 29/5/15	C	Account of bitumen; *Nbn* 876
93	74773	Nbn 5/1/14	C	Receipt for silver for purchase of tools; *Nbn* 752
94	74774	30/6/39	C	Receipt for purchase of sesame; *Nbk* 349
95	74775		C	Receipt for barley
96	74776		C	Account of offerings; *Cyr* 383
97	74777	Nbn 24/5/-	F	Receipt for flour; *Nbn* 1086
98	74778	Nbn 27/2/1	C	Account of silver expended; *Nbn* 27
99	74779	Cam 22/1/4	C	Receipt for garments of gods; *Cam* 230
100	74780	Nbk 23/5/40	C	Receipt for sale of garlic; *Nbk* 362
101	74781	Nbn 19/1/12	NC	Receipt for sesame; *Nbn* 586

AH 83-1-18,

102	74782	Nbn 18/10/10	C	Receipt for work on garments of gods; *Nbn* 465
103	74783	12/3/5	C	Account of temple paraphernalia; *Dar* 160
104	74784		C	Receipt for sheep
105	74785	Nbn 29/6/11	NC	Account of jewelry; *Nbn* 537
106	74786	27/2/-	NC	Account of sheep(?)
107	74787	Nbn 2/12/9	NC	Account of bear skins; *Nbn* 386
108	74788	2/7/6	C	Receipt for date leaves; *Nbn* 240
109	74789		NC	Receipt for dates
110	74790	Cam 15/3/2	C	Receipt for dates or grain; *Cam* 108
111	74791	Cam 4/2/7	C	Receipt for garments of gods; *Cam* 363
112	74792	5/-/2	F	Loan; *Nbk* 21
113	74793	Cyr 22/4/7	C	Account of barley; Sippar; *Cyr* 260
114	74794	Nbk 14/2/42	C	Receipt for silver tithe; *Nbk* 393
115	74795	Nbn 8/6/16	C	Receipt for iron for tools; *Nbn* 980
116	74796	Nbn 8/11/13	F	Account of dates; *Nbn* 736
117	74797	Cyr 12/1/8	C	Account of barley; *Cyr* 295
118	74798	15/2/15	C	Receipt for barley provisions; *Nbn* 840
119	74799	Cyr 10/2/3	C	Purchase of oxen; *Cyr* 105
120	74800	Nbk 17/1/-	C	Receipt for iron tools; *Nbk* 418
121	74801	Nbn 26/9/15	C	Account of dates and sesame; *Nbn* 912
122	74802	Bar 6/5/1	C	Receipt for dates; *ZA* 4, 150 no. 6
123	74803	Cam 7/2/3	C	Receipt for flour for goldsmiths; *Cam* 157
124	74804		NC	Account of emmer
125	74805	1/8/-	C	Receipt for barley; *Nbn* 1105
126	74806	Nbn 19/6/11	C	Receipt for sesame; *Nbn* 535
127	74807		C	Receipt for dates or grain
128	74808	9/11/5	C	Receipt for a sheep; *Nbn* 208
129	74809	Cam 13/12/3	C	Receipt for dates; *Cam* 221
130	74810		C	Account of dates or grain; *Cam* 441
131	74811	30/1/2	C	Receipt for sesame; *Nbn* 57
132	74812	Nbn 8/12/16	C	Bronze for temple paraphernalia; *Nbn* 1012
133	74813	Nbn 13/11/11	C	Receipt for sesame; *Nbn* 569
134	74814	Cyr 20/6/3	C	Receipt for barley delivery to Babylon; *Cyr* 121
135	74815	Nbn 29/7/15	C	Receipt for a garment for repair; *Nbn* 896

AH 83-1-18,

136	74816	Cam 2/6/3	NC	Purchase of an ass; *Cam* 169
137	74817	Cam 29/4/1	C	Receipt for sesame; *Cam* 47
138	74818	Nbn 17/8/10	C	Receipt for bronze for temple paraphernalia; *Nbn* 447
139	74819	Nbn 9/5/14	C	Receipt for grain and wool; *Nbn* 775
140	74820	29/7/-	C	Receipt for dates or grain
141	74821	Nbk 27/11/30	NC	Legal dispute over silver; *Nbk* 227
142	74822	Nbn 16/9/15	C	Receipt for dates; *Nbn* 908
143	74823		C	Account of barley; *Nbk* 459
144	74824	Nbn 21/6/14	C	Receipt for wool for garments of gods; *Nbn* 788
145	74825	Nbn 7/2/10	C	Account for gold for jewelry; *Nbn* 406
146	74826	Cam -/-/acc	C	Receipt for dates; *Cam* 26
147	74827	Nbn 5/5/12	NC	Receipt for ox hides; *Nbn* 617
148	74828	Dar 14/9/2	NC	Receipt for dates; Sippar; *Dar* 50
149	74829		C	Receipt for wool; *Nbk* 455
150	74830		NC	Account of dates or grain; *Nbk* 456
151	74831	Am 9/5/2	C	Receipt for garments and jewelry
152	74832	Nbn 26/12/5	C	Receipt for silver; *Nbn* 215
153	74833	Cam 5/10/3	NC	Receipt for dates or grain; *Cam* 205
154	74834	Cam 16/6/3	C	Receipt for dates; *Cam* 171
155	74835	Nbn 6/12b/15	C	Receipt for alum for dyeing; *Nbn* 938
156	74836	Cyr 17/1/8	C	Receipt for silver, barley and dates; *Cyr* 296
157	74837	Nbn -/2/10	C	Receipt for myrrh; *Nbn* 413
158	74838	Nbn 23/12/16	C	Receipt for wine; *Nbn* 1016
159	74839	Nbn 19/6/17	C	Receipt for dates; *Nbn* 1051
160	74840	6/4/7	C	Receipt for purchase of garments; *Cyr* 258
161	74841	Nbn	NC	Receipt for purchase of dates
162	74842		C	Measurements of a field
163	74843	Dar 13/12/5	NC	Receipt for dates; *Dar* 216
164	74844	Nbn 16/6/-	C	Receipt for sesame; *Nbn* 1094
165	74845	Nbn 16/10/15	C	Receipt for purchase of dates; *Nbn* 921
166	74846	Cyr 9/6b/2	C	Receipt for sesame; *Cyr* 56
167	74847	Nbk 16/2/36	C	Purchase of oil, iron, and reeds; *Nbk* 294
168	74848	Cyr 21/3/2	C	Receipt for barley; *Cyr* 39
169	74849	Nbn 8/8/12	C	Receipt for sesame; *Nbn* 631
170	74850	Xer 20/6/1	NC	Receipt for dates

AH 83-1-18,

171	74851	Cyr 2/11/5	C	Receipt for purchase of leather; *Cyr* 214
172	74852	Nbn 20/8/10	C	Exchange of barley and dates; Alu-ša-Nabu; *Nbn* 448
173	74853	Nbn 28/7/11	C	Contract for barley; Sippar; *Nbn* 542
174	74854	Cam 8/8/4	C	Memorandum concerning various items
175	74855	Nbn 8/4/8	C	Receipt for animals; *Nbn* 296
176	74856	Nbn 25/1/17	C	Receipt for bitumen; *Nbn* 1026
177	74857	Nbn 5/11/9	C	Receipt for silver; *Nbn* 376
178	74858		C	Receipt for silver
179	74859	Cyr 28/8/7	C	Contract for pomegranates; *Cyr* 272
180	74860	Dar 11/3/28	NC	Sales receipt
181	74861	Nbn 8/5/11	C	Receipt for barley tithe; *Nbn* 521
182	74862	Nbn 10/6/8	C	Receipt for silver; *Nbn* 302
183	74863	Nbn 6/12b/12	F	Receipt for sesame; *Nbn* 683
184	74864	Nbn 8/2/3	NC	Receipt for tithes; *Nbn* 97
185	74865	Nbn 4/5/15	C	Receipt for dates; *Nbn* 871
186	74866	Nbn 6/12/5	NC	Receipt for linen; *Nbn* 213
187	74867	Cyr 26/8/2	C	Receipt for dates; *Cyr* 72
188	74868	Dar 26/8/4	C	Receipt for barley; *Dar* 135
189	74869	Dar -/6/2	NC	Account of barley; *Dar* 42
190	74870	Nbn 12/7/15	C	Account of sesame; *Nbn* 893
191	74871	Nbn 6/7/11	C	Purchase of dye; *Nbn* 538
192	74872	Dar 1/1/4	C	Receipt for dates; *Dar* 103
193	74873	Cam 19/12/acc	C	Receipt for garment; *Cam* 21
194	74874	Cyr 19/12/7	C	Receipt for silver; *Cyr* 283
195	74875	Cam 4/8/4	C	Receipt for linen; *Cam* 250
196	74876	Nbk 4/11/7	NC	Receipt for silver
197	74877	Nbn 20/4/13	C	Receipt for figs and pomegranates; *Nbn* 709
198	74878	Cam 19/6/acc	NC	Receipt for garments of gods; *Cam* 4
199	74879	Cam 7/3/1	C	Receipt for barley for fullers; *Cam* 40
200	92752	Cyr 14/10/2	NC	Account of barley; *Cyr* 77
201	74880	Nbn 17/2/2	C	Purchase of flour; *Nbn* 62
202	74881		NC	Letter; *CT* 22 54; *Cyr* 370
203	74882	Nbn 24/4/12	C	Receipt for sesame; *Nbn* 614
204	74883	21/9/-	C	Receipt for barley and date provisions
205	74884	Nbn 2/9/15	C	Receipt for sesame; *Nbn* 901
206	74885	Cyr 4/5/2	C	Account of barley; *Cyr* 46
207	74886	Cam 9/2/1	NC	Account of wool and other materials; *Cam* 36

AH 83-1-18,

208	74887	27/12/34	C	Purchase of sesame; *Nbk* 277
209	74888	Cam 12/12/5	C	Receipt for tools for a smith; *Cam* 297
210	74889	Nbn 28/11/9	C	Account of date products; *Nbn* 385
211	74890	Nbk 17/9/42	C	Receipt for bird feed; *Nbk* 405
212	74891	Nbk 2/7/41	C	Purchase of leather; *Nbk* 383
213	74892	Cyr 10/-/4	F	Marriage document; Sippar; *Cyr* 183
214	74893	Nbn 3/6/4	NC	Purchase of emmer; *Nbn* 161
215	74894	Dar 24/12/13	F	Receipt for purchase of barley; *Dar* 365
216	74895	Cyr 15/1/7	C	Receipt for a bucket; *Cyr* 246
217	74896	Nbn 13/9/15	NC	Receipt for barley; *Nbn* 906
218	74897	Cam 26/9/2	C	Receipt for dates; *Cam* 133
219	74898	Nbn 22/1/15	C	Receipt for barley provisions; *Nbn* 834
220	74899	Nbn 17/9/12	C	Receipt for dates or grain; *Nbn* 649
221	74900	Dar 24/7/25	NC	Receipt for barley
222	74901	Nbn 7/5/12	C	Receipt for wheat; *Nbn* 618
223	74902		NC	Account of provisions(?)
224	74903	Nbn 25/11/8	NC	Receipt for animals; *Nbn* 312
225	74904	Nbn 12/10/13	NC	Purchase of sheep; *Nbn* 734
226	74905	Nbn 6/2/4	C	Account of garments; *Nbn* 143
227	74906	Nbn 9/9/15	NC	Purchase of an ox; *Nbn* 904
228	74907	Ner 16/10/2	C	Receipt for iron
229	74908	Dar 18/12/1	NC	Receipt for barley; *Dar* 27!
230	74909	Cyr 20/1/4	C	Contract for barley tithe; *Cyr* 158
231	74910	Cyr -/2/8	F	Contract for service; Sippar; *Cyr* 304
232	74911	Nbn 17/9/10	C	Account of dates; *Nbn* 457
233	74912	Dar 30/10/6	C	Receipt for sesame
234	74913	Cyr 10/7/2	NC	Receipt for oil; *Cyr* 62
235	74914	Cam 7/8/2	NC	Account of wheat for flour; *Cam* 123
236	74915	Nbn 12/9/9	C	Receipt for linen and dates; *Nbn* 370
237	74916	Nbn 29/3/15	C	Receipt for sesame; *Nbn* 859
238	74917	Cyr 21/10/2	C	Account of dates; *Cyr* 78
239	74918		C	Account of gold; *Nbk* 454
240	74919	29/9/21	NC	Sales receipt
241	74920	Nbn 23/10/15	C	Account of bronze for working; *Nbn* 924
242	74921	-/-/8	C	Account of house rentals; *Nbn* 319
243	74922	Nbk 22/-/-	F	Account of barley and dates; *Nbk* 443
244	74923	Cyr 3/4/8	NC	Legal agreement concerning slavery; Sippar; *Cyr* 307

AH 83-1-18,

245	74924	Cam 2/7/1	C	Receipt for sesame; *Cam* 61
246	74925	Nbn 30/8/16	NC	Receipt for dates or grain; *Nbn* 994
247	74926	Ner 15/2/2	C	Account of purchase for silver
248	74927	Nbn 3/9/10	NC	Account of various payments; *Nbn* 452
249	74928	Nbn 4/6b/10	NC	Contract for rescheduling of debt; *Nbn* 436
250	74929	Dar 12/1/4	C	Wool for garments of gods; *Dar* 107
251	74930	Cam 7/10/3	C	Receipt for dates; *Cam* 207
252	74931	Cyr 3/10/8	F	Sale of a slave girl; *Cyr* 324
253	74932	Ner 9/6/1	C	Receipt for silver
254	92753	Nbn 29/8/11	NC	Account of fodder; *Nbn* 546
255	74933	Nbn 14/11/13	C	Account of sesame; *Nbn* 737
256	74934	Nbn 29/11/16	C	Account of barley and dates; *Nbn* 1010
257	74935	Dar 24/7/4	C	Receipt for sesame *Dar* 130
258	74936	Cyr 21/8/7	F	Deposition; *Cyr* 271
259	74937	Ner 3/10/1	C	Legal disclaimer
260	74938	Ner 17/2/1	C	Contract for beer
261	74939	Nbn 8/-/7	NC	Account of provisions; *Nbn* 278
262	74940	Cyr 10/1/8	NC	Deposition; *Cyr* 293
263	74941	Cam 5/12/acc	C	Account of tools; *Cam* 18
264	74942	Nbn 20/12/15	C	Contract for barley; Sippar; *Nbn* 934
265	74943	Nbn 11/11/9	C	Account of barley; *Nbn* 379
266	74944	Cam 9/8/6	C	Account of barley; *Cam* 324
267	74945	Cam 5/6/3	C	Account of barley; *Cam* 170
268	74946	Nbn 19/6/5	C	Receipt for gold jewelry; *Nbn* 190
269	74947	Cam 21/6/4	C	Purchase of garments; *Cam* 243
270	74948	Cam 21/3/4	NC	Receipt for barley and wool; *Cam* 234
271	74949	Dar 22/9/-	NC	Contract for sale of slave
272	74950	Dar 15/11/27	C	Letter
273	74951	Nbn -/9/17	C	Account of barley; *Nbn* 1055
274	74952	8/6b/-	NC	Account of wool and barley; *Nbn* 1099
275	74953	Ner 25/5/acc	C	Receipt for barley
276	74954	Nbk 19/9/29	NC	Contract for barley; *Nbk* 205
277	74955	Cyr 20/3/7	C	Contract for bricks; *Cyr* 255
278	74956	Nbn 19/11/9	C	Purchase of dates; *Nbn* 382
279	74957	Nbn 25/12/16	NC	Account of shipment of commodities; *Nbn* 1017
280	92754	Nbk 25/6/27	NC	Sale of a slave girl; *Nbk* 175
281	74958		C	Letter; *CT* 22 89; *Cyr* 372

AH 83-1-18,

282	74959	Cam 21/1/5	NC	Deposition; *Cam* 273
283	74960	Cam -/10/acc	NC	Assessment of liability for tax; *Cam* 13
284	74961	Dar 3/8/5	C	Account of dates; *Dar* 179
285	74962	Cyr 4/5/3	C	Loan; *Cyr* 119
286	74963	Dar 15/12/3	NC	Letter; seals
287	74964		C	Receipt for barley and silver
288	74965	Dar 21/9/21	C	Letter; seal; *Dar* 528
289	74966	Nbn 24/5/14	NC	Account of wine; *Nbn* 779
290	74967	Cam 12/11/2	NC	Account of wool; *Cam* 140
291	74968	Cam 30/10/7	C	Receipt for dates; *Cam* 392
292	74969	Nbn 21/7/7	NC	Receipt for purchase of wool; *Nbn* 262
293	74970	Nbk 3/6/31	F	Sale of a slave; *Nbk* 236
294	74971	Cyr 22/6/3	C	Sale of sheep; *Cyr* 122
295	74972	Nbn 10/8/17	C	Expenditure of silver and barley; *Nbn* 1054
296	74973	Cam 10/10/acc	C	Receipt for dates; *Cam* 10
297	74974	Cam 27/11/8	F	Contract; Sippar; *Cam* 412
298	74975	Nbn 10/10/10	C	Contract for dates; Alu-ša-Šamaš; *Nbn* 463
299	74976	Nbk 12/1/38	NC	Contract for barley; *Nbk* 330
300	74977	Dar -/-/26	F	Contract for wool
301	74978	Dar 24/12/acc	NC	Account of barley; *Dar* 7
302	74979	Nbn 26/-/14	NC	Account of date provisions; *Nbn* 824
303	74980	Cam 17/6/1	C	Account of dates; *Cam* 58
304	74981	Dar 21/12/acc	NC	Account of purchases; *Dar* 4
305	92755	Cyr 4/10/-	NC	Account of dates; *Cyr* 180
306	74982	Nbn 20/7/5	NC	Sale of a slave girl; *Nbn* 196
307	74983	Ner 28/-/1	NC	Receipt for silver
308	74984	Nbn 25/9/11	NC	Account of dates or grain; *Nbn* 556
309	74985	Cam 2/12/5	C	Receipt for dates; *Cam* 294
310	74986	Nbk 14/9/39	C	Receipt for sesame tithe; *Nbk* 354
311	74987	Nbn 10+/12/11	NC	Account of silver; *Nbn* 579
312	74988	Nbn 25/11/5	NC	Sale of slaves; Babylon; *Nbn* 212
313	74989	8/9/20	C	Receipt for dates or grain; *Dar* 508
314	74990	Cyr 23/3/7	C	Receipt for a house; *Cyr* 257
315	74991	Nbn 6/1/-	NC	Account of sesame; *Nbn* 1060
316	74992	Nbn 28/5/10	C	Account of gold for working; *Nbn* 431
317	74993	Dar 20/10/25	C	Receipt for sale of sheep
318	74994	Nbn 21/10/-	NC	Account of temple paraphernalia; *Nbn* 1121

AH 83-1-18,

319	74995	Dar 27/-/24	NC	Receipt for dates or grain
320	74996		NC	Letter
321	74997	Nbn 14/9/10	NC	Account of dates; *Nbn* 455
322	74998	Dar 5/8/5	NC	Account of sheep; *Dar* 180
323	74999	20/9/2	NC	Receipt for sesame; *Nbn* 81
324	75000	Nbn 12/12/12	NC	Account of dates; *Nbn* 676
325	75001	Nbn 15/2/11	NC	Contract for barley tithes; Sippar; *Nbn* 505
326	75002	Nbn 30/9/15	NC	Account of barley; *Nbn* 915
327	92756	Cam 22/1/7	C	Account of barley and dates; *Cam* 359
328	75003	Nbn 28/12/15	NC	Contract for silver, barley, and dates; Sippar; *Nbn* 936
329	75004	Nbn 23/-/12	NC	Contract for dates; *Nbn* 638
330	75005		C	Account
331	75006	Cyr 7/8/2	NC	Account of dates; *Cyr* 68
332	75007	Nbn 21/6/4	NC	Account of garments; *Nbn* 164
333	75008	12/5/-	C	Account of sheep
334	75009	Nbn 14/12/13	NC	Account of wool, dates, and wine; *Nbn* 743
335	75010	Nbn 11/11/12	NC	Receipt for wool; *Nbn* 664
336	75011		C	Receipt for dates and grain provisions
337	75012	Dar 4/10/30	NC	Receipt for dates
338	75013	Cyr -/-/3	F	Purchase of birds; *Cyr* 156
339	75014	Cam -/-/1	NC	Account of wool(?); *Cam* 99
340	75015	Dar 26/11/acc	NC	Account of dates; *Dar* 2
341	75016	Nbn 23/6/16	C	Receipt for barley tithe; *Nbn* 985
342	75017	Cam 22/1/7	C	Receipt for barley
343	75018	Dar 21/6/22	NC	Letter; seals; *Dar* 547
344	75019	Am 14/3/2	C	Receipt for barley
345	75020	10/2/8	NC	Account of oil for use in temple; *Nbn* 283
346	75021	Dar -/-/29	NC	Account of oxen
347	75022	Dar 5/2/-	C	Receipt for barley
348	75023	Dar 23/1/29	NC	Receipt for bird fodder
349	75024	Nbn 21/6/5	NC	Contract for dates; *Nbn* 191
350	75025	Nbk 24/10/30	NC	Receipt for iron; *Nbk* 223
351	75026	25/1/-	NC	Receipt for oil; *Nbn* 1064
352	75027	Cam 1/5/2	F	Receipt; *Cam* 111
353	75028	Dar 3/1/4	NC	Account of flour and barley; *Dar* 104
354	75029	10/7/32	NC	Receipt for wool(?)

AH 83-1-18,

355	75030	Nbk 14/2/36	F	Receipt for wine; *Nbk* 293
356	75031	Nbn 11/9/10	F	Receipt for purchase of wheat; *Nbn* 453
357	75032	Nbn 30/-/-	NC	Receipt for dates
358	75033	Nbk 2/-/30	NC	Contract for dates, cassia, and beer; *Nbk* 233
359	75034	Nbk 7/11/34	C	Receipt for sheep; *Nbk* 275
360	75035	2/3/9	F	Receipt; *Nbn* 338
361	75036		F	Letter; seals
362	75037		C	Account of provisions(?)
363	75038	Dar 2/10/30	F	Sales receipt
364	75039		NC	Account of garments
365	75040	Nbk 7/-/-	F	Receipt for bricks; *Nbk* 442
366	75041	18/1/25	NC	Account of sheep
367	75042	Nbk 22/9/39	NC	Sale of dates; *Nbk* 355
368	75043	Cyr 20/12b/3	F	Purchase of sheep; *Cyr* 152
369	75044	Dar 3/2/33	F	Receipt for silver
370	75045	Dar 21/6/22	NC	Receipt for silver; *Dar* 548
371	75046	Dar 14/9/20+	F	Receipt for dates
372	75047	Nbk 20/12/30	C	Receipt for bronze; *Nbk* 229
373	75048	Dar 13/4/2	C	Receipt for sesame; *Dar* 324
374	75049	Nbn 12/6/3	F	Receipt for dates; *Nbn* 114
375	75050	Nbn 1/2/5	NC	Receipt for wool; *Nbn* 186
376	75051		C	Account of provisions(?)
377	75052	Nbn 10/4/15	C	Receipt for dates; *Nbn* 864
378	75053	Nbn 2/1/11	NC	Account of gold for temple paraphernalia; *Nbn* 489
379	75054	10+/2/25	NC	Receipt for silver
380	75055	Nbn 12/8/1	C	Receipt for sesame; *Nbn* 38
381	75056	Nbn 10/2/2	C	Receipt for beer; *Nbn* 60
382	75057	9/11/11	NC	Account of barley and emmer; *Nbn* 567
383	75058	25/8/acc	NC	Receipt for dates
384	75059	6/6/-	NC	Receipt for dates; *Nbn* 1089
385	75060	Nbn 23/-/5	F	Account of fruit; *Nbn* 218
386	75061	-/1/-	NC	Account of workmen
387	75062	Dar 29/2/-	F	Receipt for barley
388	75063	21/12/35	NC	Receipt for emmer; *Nbk* 288
389	75064	Nbn 15/2/12	C	Receipt for sesame; *Nbn* 595
390	75065		F	Account of workmen
391	75066	Cyr 6/-/6	F	Deposition; *Cyr* 243

AH 83-1-18,

392	75067	Nbk 24/2/30	F	Receipt; *Nbk* 211
393	75068	Nbn -/2/-	F	Receipt for an ox as tithe; *Nbn* 1071
394	75069	Cyr 21/4/8	F	Contract; *Cyr* 309
395	75070	Xer 7/10/acc	NC	Letter; seals
396	75071	Nbk 10/2/38	NC	Receipt for bird feed; *Nbk* 331
397	75072		F	Sales receipt
398	75073	Cyr 16/2/5	F	Receipt for dates or grain; *Cyr* 193
399	75074		C	Receipt for dates or grain; *Cam* 440
400	75075	Cam 1/-/7	F	Contract for barley; *Cam* 401
401	75076		NC	Receipt for dates or grain
402	75077	5/12/1	F	Account of dates; *Nbn* 49
403	75078	Dar 10/3/33	NC	Receipt for bitumen
404	75079	Dar 22/12/1	F	Receipt for wool(?); *Dar* 29
405	75080		F	Receipt
406	75081	Nbn 13/2/11	NC	Receipt for a bronze vessel; *Nbn* 503
407	75082	Nbn 6/8/3	C	Receipt for linen for gods; *Nbn* 117
408	75083	Nbn 9/1/11	NC	Receipt for barley and dates; *Nbn* 493
409	75084	Cam 11/3/1	NC	Receipt for gold
410	92757	Cam 18/8/2	C	Receipt for aromatics for temple use; *Cam* 126
411	75085	Nbn 2/2/1	NC	Account of barley for flour; *Nbn* 23
412	75086	26/8/acc	F	Account of barley
413	75087	25/11/2	NC	Receipt for dates; *Cyr* 82
414	75088	Nbn 21/5/12	NC	Receipt for sesame(?) for cakes; *Nbn* 620
415	75089	Nbn -/11/-	F	Account of sheep; *Nbn* 1130
416	75090	-/-/25	F	Receipt for gold; *Nbk* 158
417	75091	Cam 2/4/4	NC	Receipt for barley; *Cam* 238
418	75092	Cam 9/11/6	C	Purchase of garments; *Cam* 340
419	75093	Cam -/12/2	NC	Purchase of sheep; *Cam* 146
420	75094	Dar 13/2/16	C	Receipt for flour; *Dar* 420
421	75095	Cyr 15/3/3	F	Account of barley; *Cyr* 112
422	75096	Cam 14/-/7	F	Account of barley; *Cam* 389
423	75097	Cam 6/11/3	C	Purchase of sheep; *Cam* 211
424	75098	Nbk 2/2/33	NC	Receipt for barley; *Nbk* 253
425	92758	Nbk 15/3/36	C	Receipt for boat rental; *Nbk* 296
426	75099		F	Account of workmen
427	75100	Cyr 20/12/8	NC	Receipt for grain and oil; *Cyr* 327
428	75101	Nbk -/5/30	F	Account of furnishings; *Nbk* 224

AH 83-1-18,

429	75102	22/10/-	F	Receipt for dates; *Nbn* 1122
430	75103	26/1/1	F	Account of dates; *Nbn* 20
431	75104	Cam 17/3/3	NC	Purchase of beer; *Cam* 163
432	75105		C	Receipt for dates or grain
433	75106	Am 8/7/2	C	Receipt for sheep
434	75107	Cam 27/7/1	C	Receipt for dates; *Cam* 67
435	75108	Nbk 21/8/36	F	Receipt for silver for jewelry; *Nbk* 306
436	75109	3/10/30	F	Receipt for oxen; *Nbk* 221
437	75110	Nbn 17/1/15	F	Receipt for silver for working; *Nbn* 831
437A	75111	Nbk 17/1/26	F	Receipt; *Nbk* 160
438	75112	Cam 3/7/acc	C	Receipt for barley bird feed; *Cam* 7
439	75113	Nbn 28/12b/15	F	Receipt for barley; *Nbn* 944
440	75114		NC	Account of dates or grain
441	75115	Cam 30/11/2	C	Receipt for wool for garments of gods; *Cam* 137
442	75116	Cam -/-/7	F	Animal ledger; *Cam* 405
443	75117		F	Account
444	75118	Nbk 17/10/33	C	Receipt for barley and dates; *Nbk* 260
445	75119	Cyr 7/5/5	F	Deposition; Sippar; *Cyr* 199
446	75120	Cam 14/9/7	F	Receipt; Sippar; *Cam* 386
447	75121	Nbk 6/8/9	F	Receipt for a sheep; *Nbk* 80
448	75122		F	Adoption; *Cyr* 368
449	75123		NC	Economic
450	75124		C	List of men; *Nbk* 449
451	75125	Cam 16/-/4	NC	Receipt for wool for garments of gods; *Cam* 267
452	75126		F	Contract
453	75127	Am 8/5/2	F	Receipt
454	75128	Dar 7/12b/22	NC	Letter; seals; *Dar* 557
455	75129	Dar -/-/12	F	Receipt for silver(?); *Dar* 343
456	75130	Cam 14/9/6	C	Account of dates; *Cam* 332
457	75131	Nbk 5/11/24	C	Receipt for geese; *Nbk* 145
458	75132		NC	Account of barley and dates
459	75133	Dar	F	Account of dates
460	75134	Nbk 20/12/29	F	Account of silver for making objects; *Nbk* 208
461	75135		NC	Account
462	75136	Cam 4/6/4	NC	Loan of silver; *Cam* 240
463	75137		F	Account of dates and grain provisions(?)

AH 83-1-18,

464	75138	Nbn 2/1/13	NC	Receipt for sesame; *Nbn* 692
465	75139	Nbn -/2/16	F	Deposition; *Nbn* 958
466	75140	Cam -/5/6	NC	Account of silver; *Cam* 318
467	75141		F	Receipt for dates
468	75142		C	Receipt for dates or grain
469	75143		F	Promissory note for dates
470	75144		F	*Ḫḫ* III; *Tintir* II; topographical(?)
471	75145	Dar 25/5/27	NC	Promissory note for barley
472	75146	Dar 8/2/12	NC	Receipt for a garment; *Dar* 322
473	75147	Dar -/2/14	F	Account of silver; *Dar* 373
474	75148		F	Account of silver
475	75149	OB	F	Contract; oath by Shamash and Il[umaʾila]; list of witnesses
476	75150	Nbk 8/5/-	C	Receipt for garments; *Nbk* 427
477	75151	22/1/9	F	Account of purchases of sheep; *Nbn* 324
478	75152	Am 17/9/acc	NC	Receipt for silver
479	75153	Nbn 29/3/6	NC	House rentals; *Nbn* 228
480	75154	Nbn 10/4/3	NC	Account of purchases; *Nbn* 108
481	75155	Nbk 20/12/35	C	Purchase of sesame; *Nbk* 287
482	75156	Nbn 12/9/16	C	Purchase of dates; *Nbn* 997
483	75157	Dar 20/12/1	F	Account of dates or grain; *Dar* 28
484	75158	-/7/34	F	Purchase of emmer; *Nbk* 270
485	75159	Cyr 5/8/6	NC	House rentals; *Cyr* 234
486	75160	-/5/-	F	Receipt for tools; *Cyr* 354
487	75161	Cyr -/-/5	F	List of workmen; *Cyr* 221
488	75162	Nbk 15/8/-	F	Receipt for dates or grain; *Nbk* 434
489	75163	Nbn 10/8/11	C	Account of bronze for objects; *Nbn* 545
490	75164	Cam 10/1/4	NC	Receipt for wool; *Cam* 227
491	75165	Cam 10+/6b/3	NC	Account of sesame; *Cam* 178
492	75166	Lm 13/2/acc	C	Receipt for baskets and spades
493	75167	Dar 22/11/20	F	Receipt for silver; *Dar* 512
494	75168	Nbn 17/12/4	NC	Account of linen; *Nbn* 179
495	75169	6/1/16	NC	Account of flour; *Nbn* 951
496	75170	Cam 7/6/4	NC	Receipt for dates or grain; *Cam* 241
497	75171	Nbn 2/4/15	C	Receipt for silver for working; *Nbn* 860
498	75172	Dar 15/8/3	F	Purchase of sesame; *Dar* 87
499	75173	Dar 11/2/25	NC	Receipt for barley for provisions
500	75174		F	Account of barley
501	75175		NC	Receipt

AH 83-1-18,

502	75176	Nbk 15/12b/33	NC	Receipt for silver; *Nbk* 262
503	75177	23/8/2	NC	Receipt for provisions(?)
504	75178	Nbn 6/4/15	C	Rental of boats; *Nbn* 862
505	75179		F	Receipt for sheep
506	75180	-/-/acc	F	Account of barley
507	75181	Ner 27/5/acc	NC	Receipt for hides (*gildu*)
508	75182		F	Account of dates
509	75183	Am 14/4/1	NC	Receipt for silver
510	75184	Nbk 2/9/30	F	Purchase of wool; *Nbk* 218
511	75185	Dar 6/5/11	F	Receipt for wool; *Dar* 303
512	75186	Dar 20+/2/28	NC	Receipt for silver
513	75187	Nbk 23/5/28	F	Receipt for barley; *Nbk* 186
514	75188	6/11/25	NC	Receipt for sale; *Nbk* 155
515	75189	Nbk	F	House rentals; *Nbk* 445
516	75190	28/2/41	NC	Receipt for wool and sesame; *Nbk* 375
517	75191	Dar 19/4/24	NC	Receipt for barley
518	75192	Dar	F	Account of dates
519	75193	Ner 2/6/acc	NC	Receipt for barley
520	75194	Nbk 10/10/-	F	Loan of barley; *Nbk* 438
521	75195		F	Accounts
522	75196		F	Account of dates
523	75197	Cyr -/-/8	F	Legal text concerning a dowry; *Cyr* 332
524	75198		C	Account of dates or grain
525	75199		F	Receipt for dates or grain
526	75200	Cyr 6/3/4	F	Account of various commodities; *Cyr* 162
527	75201	Cyr 3/2/9	F	Account of barley; *Cyr* 336
528	92759	Nbn -/-/11	F	Account of barley; *Nbn* 583
529	75202	Cyr 3/6/5	NC	Account of garments of gods; *Cyr* 201
530	75203	Cyr 8/-/2	NC	Account of barley; *Cyr* 90
531	75204	Nbn 24/1/15	C	Account of barley; *Nbn* 835
532	92760	Cyr 8/2/6	C	Account of barley; *Cyr* 225
533	92761	Cyr 26/4/3	NC	Account of oxen; *Cyr* 117
534	75205	Dar 6/1/6	C	Account of barley; *Dar* 198
535	75206	Cam 10/9/2	F	Account of dates and barley; *Cam* 130
536	75207		NC	Receipt for barley
537	92762	Nbk 11/8/31	NC	Account of dates; *Nbk* 239
538	75208		NC	Account of house rents
539	75209		F	*Izbu* V; *TCS* 4 238

AH 83-1-18,

540	75210	-/-/33	NC	Account of sheep
541	75211		C	Account of dates
542	75212		F	Account
543	75213	Nbn -/7/16	C	Account of barley; *Nbn* 988
544	75214	Nbn 18/3/acc	F	Account of garments; *Nbn* 1
545	92763	Nbn 21/9/11	NC	Account of dates; *Nbn* 554
546	75215		NC	Ritual for a sick man
547	75216	Cam -/6/3	NC	Account of wool, etc.; *Cam* 175
548	75217	Dar -/-/35	F	Account of dates
549	75218	Nbn 13/9/12	F	Account of oxen; *Nbn* 646
550	75219	Nbk 28/11/38	NC	Account of purchases of various commodities; *Nbk* 337
551	75220	Dar 21/3/20	NC	Loan of dates
552	75221	Dar 18/8/10	NC	Account of flour; *Dar* 281
553	75222	Art -/-/20	NC	Legal; contract for care of person; Borsippa; ZA 3 158
554	75223		F	Animal ledger
555	75224		F	*pan takaltim* XV; cf. *RA* 60 90; *JCS* 29 159f.
556	75225	20/8/16	NC	Payments to men; *Nbn* 991
557	75226		F	Incantation; dupl. AH 83-1-18, 568 (= BM 75237); dupl. Borger, *Lišan Mitḫurti* 10
558	75227	Nbn 9/4/-	F	Purchase of barley; *Nbn* 1078
559	75228		NC	Commentary on *Enuma Anu Enlil* (Dilbat)
560	75229	Nbn 19/5/6	F	Purchase of dates; *Nbn* 233
561	75230	30/5/20+	F	Account of barley
562	75231		F	Account of workmen
563	75232	Dar 25/3/32	NC	Receipt for repayment of loan
564	75233	Cyr 15/3/4	F	Deposition; *Cyr* 164
565	75234	Nbn 2/6/14	NC	Account of sheep; *Nbn* 780
566	75235		NC	Note concerning silver
567	75236	Cam 13/12/4	F	Account of barley; *Cam* 266
568	75237		F	Incantation; dupl. AH 83-1-18, 557 (= BM 75226)
569	75238	-/1/4	F	Account of barley; *Nbn* 136
570	75239	Nbn 25/8/12	F	Purchase of oxen; Babylon; *Nbn* 639
571	75240	Nbn -/8/acc	F	Account of dates
572	75241		C	List of workmen; *Nbk* 458

AH 83-1-18,

573	75242	Cyr 4/1/-	F	Receipt for barley; *Cyr* 347
574	75243	12/1/-	NC	Account of dates
575	75244	Cam 9/11/1	F	Account of wool; *Cam* 90
576	75245	Dar 5/10/22	NC	Receipt for dates or grain; *Dar* 553
577	75246	Ner 23/8/1	NC	Receipt for bitumen
578	75247		F	Account of dates or grain
579	75248		F	Account of dates
580	75249	Nbn 4/1/15	C	Receipt for lime; *Nbn* 825
581	75250	Dar 10/1/22	F	Receipt for barley; *Dar* 535
582	75251	Dar -/8/2	F	Receipt for seed; *Dar* 49
583	75252	Dar	F	Letter; seal
584	75253	Nbk 12/1/39	F	Receipt for silver; *Nbk* 340
585	75254	Cyr 15/12b/3	NC	Purchase of dates; *Cyr* 150
586	75255	-/-/26	NC	Receipt for dates or grain
587	75256	Nbn 29/1/2	C	Letter order; *Nbn* 56
588	75257	Nbk 3/1/36	F	Receipt; *Nbk* 289
589	75258	Cyr 21/1/3	F	Receipt for wool for garments of gods; *Cyr* 100
590	75259	Dar 25/9?/27	C	Sale receipt
591	75260	Nbk 13/2/-	F	Account of oxen; *Nbk* 421
592	75261	Dar 8/9/5	C	Receipt for dates; *Dar* 183
593	75262	Nbn 26/12/15	NC	Account of dates; *Nbn* 935
594	75263	Dar 30/1/21	NC	Receipt for dates or grain; *Dar* 521
595	75264	Cyr 21/12/-	NC	Receipt for oil; *Cyr* 363
596	75265	2/12/2	C	Receipt for flour for a bronzesmith; *Nbn* 86
597	75266	Nbn 7/10/13	F	Purchase of sheep; *Nbn* 733
598	75267	28/4/4	C	Receipt for dates or grain; *Nbn* 155
599	75268	Nbk 2/4/36	C	Purchase of dates; *Nbk* 298
600	75269	Nbk 21/12/30	F	Receipt for reed mats; *Nbk* 230
601	75270	Nbn 11/6/15	F	Receipt for linen; *Nbn* 879
602	75271	Nbn 24/2/3	F	Receipt for barley; *Nbn* 101
603	75272	Dar 20/1/9	NC	Receipt for barley; *Dar* 250
604	75273	Dar 24/8/26	NC	Receipt for barley
605	75274	Cyr -/-/3	F	Memorandum; *Cyr* 139
606	75275	Cyr 14/3/8	NC	Receipt for dates; *Cyr* 306
607	75276	Cyr 13/7/2	C	Receipt for sesame; *Cyr* 63
608	75277	Nbn 12/9/15	C	Purchase of dates; *Nbn* 905
609	92764	Nbk 22/5/33	C	Receipt for silver; *Nbk* 257

AH 83-1-18,

610	75278	13/5/35	C	Receipt for an ornament(?)
611	75279	Dar 20/-/14	F	Receipt for silver(?); *Dar* 394
612	75280	5/12/acc	NC	Account of garments; *Cyr* 6
613	75281	Dar 28/1/27	NC	Receipt for bronze
614	75282	Cyr 15/9/6	NC	Receipt for sesame; *Cyr* 238
615	75283	Dar 4/1/2	NC	Receipt for dates or grain; *Dar* 59
616	75284	10/3/9	F	Receipt; *Nbn* 341
617	75285	Ner 4/1/1	C	Receipt for silver
618	75286	Nbn 19/3/13	NC	Receipt for iron for daggers; *Nbn* 707
619	75287		C	List of commodities and utensils; *Nbk* 457
620	75288	Dar 1/11/25	NC	Receipt for barley
621	75289	Dar 21/9/-	NC	Receipt for purchase of wool
622	75290	Cyr 18/8/4	C	Receipt for sesame; *Cyr* 179
623	75291	Dar 17/6/23	NC	Receipt for silver for provisions
624	75292	Dar 19/6/26	NC	Receipt for dates or grain
625	75293	Nbk 3/6/2	C	Receipt for cassia; *Nbk* 25
626	75294		NC	List of silver objects; *Nbk* 451
627	75295	Nbk 12/4/35	C	Purchase of an ass; *Nbk* 282
628	75296	25/3/39	NC	Receipt for barley for birds
629	75297	Cam 22/6/3	C	Receipt; *Cam* 172
630	75298	Cam 13/4/6	NC	Account of barley; *Cam* 313
631	75299	8/10/-	NC	Receipt for sesame
632	75300	Nbn 6/2/3	NC	Letter order; *Nbn* 94
633	75301	Dar 21/7/3	NC	Receipt for dates or grain; *Dar* 83
634	75302	Nbn 22/6/12	F	Receipt for garments; *Nbn* 624
635	75303	Cyr 9/2/2	C	Account of barley; *Cyr* 36
636	75304	7/-/5	F	Account of garments; *Cam* 302
637		Temporarily missing		
638	75305	Nbn 15/5/13	C	Receipt for silver; *Nbn* 712
639	75306	Cam 11/5/3	F	Receipt; *Cam* 168
640	75307	Nbk 21/1/42	C	Purchase of alum; *Nbk* 392
641	75308	Nbn 3/9/3	NC	Receipt for gold and silver for working; *Nbn* 121
642	75309	Dar 20+/6/23	NC	Receipt for garments; *Dar* 567
643	75310	Nbn 10/6/4	C	Receipt for barley and dates; *Nbn* 162
644	75311	13/8/39	C	Receipt for sesame; *Nbk* 352
645	75312	Cam 17/4/6	C	Receipt for barley; *Cam* 314

AH 83-1-18,

646	75313	Dar 10/10/23	NC	Sales receipt; *Dar* 565
647	75314	Nbk 15/2/34	NC	Receipt for barley; *Nbk* 263
648	75315	Cam 24/12/5	NC	Receipt for sesame; *Cam* 299
649	75316	Nbn 9/5/1	C	Receipt for birds; *Nbn* 32
650	75317	Nbn -/6/1	C	Loan of barley; *Nbn* 35
651	75318	Bar 23/3/1	C	Receipt for dates; *ZA* 4, 149 no. 3
652	75319	16/11/30	C	Receipt for iron for tools; *Nbk* 226
653	75320	Nbk 29/4/28	F	Promissory note; *Nbk* 184
654	75321	Nbk 14/7/acc	C	Receipt for sesame; *Nbk* 1; Nbk III according to Parker-Dubberstein, 13
655	75322	Am 20/5/acc	C	Sales receipt
656	75323	Nbn 14/4/12	C	Receipt for silver; *Nbn* 607
657		Nothing registered		
658	75324		C	Receipt for flour
659	75325	Nbk 6/3/36	C	Receipt for wool; *Nbk* 295
660	75326	9/12/2	F	Receipt for dates or grain; *Nbn* 87
661	75327	Cam 26/12/3	C	Receipt for barley; *Cam* 224
662	75328	Ner 8/5/2	NC	Receipt for wool
663	75329	Nbn 11/2/1	C	Receipt for flour and beer; *Nbn* 24
664	75330	30/7/35	C	Receipt for barley; *Nbk* 284
665	75331		F	Receipt for gold
666	75332	Nbn 1/2/2	C	Receipt for beer; *Nbn* 58
667	75333	Nbk 7/4/36	F	Receipt for barley; *Nbk* 299
668	75334	15/9/30	C	Receipt for flour; *Nbk* 219
669	75335	17/9/-	F	Receipt for barley and dates; *Cyr* 359
670	75336	Nbn 2/12/14	NC	Receipt for wool for garments of gods; *Nbn* 818
671	75337	Ner	NC	Receipt for various products
672	75338	Cam 28/10/3	F	Account of barley; *Cam* 210
673	75339	Dar -/-/15	NC	Account of barley; *Dar* 414
674	75340	Nbn 11/12b/15	C	Deposition; *Nbn* 854
675	75341	Dar 17/5/2	C	Account of barley; *Dar* 36
676	75342	Cyr 6/11/1	C	Account of barley fodder; *Cyr* 22
677	75343	Nbk 17/11/25	C	Measurement of property; *Nbk* 156
678	75344	Nbn 10/12b/12	NC	Purchase of oxen; *Nbn* 940
679	75345	Nbn 16/7/13	C	Receipt for bronze and tin for working; *Nbn* 721
680	75346	Dar 15/1/27	NC	Receipt
681	75347	Nbn -/5/9	F	Loan of barley; *Nbn* 352

AH 83-1-18,

682	75348	Cam 19/8/4	C	Purchase of an ox; *Cam* 254
683	75349	Nbn 28/-/7	F	Receipt for barley and wine; *Nbn* 279
684	75350	Nbn 16/1/7	NC	Purchase of oxen; *Nbn* 250
685	75351	Nbn 16/4/16	C	Receipt for wool; *Nbn* 963
686	75352	Nbn 21/7/11	C	Receipt for emmer; *Nbn* 540
687	75353	Nbn 17/11/9	F	List of people; *Nbn* 381
688	75354	Nbn -/-/15	NC	Account of bitumen; *Nbn* 947
689	75355	Nbn 18/3/15	F	Loan; Sippar; *Nbn* 855
690	92765	Nbk 27/11/30	C	Sale of a slave; Sippar; *Nbk* 228
691	75356	20/10/22	NC	Account of barley; *Dar* 549
692	75357		NC	Letter
693	75358	Nbn -/8/5	NC	Contract for barley; Sippar; *Nbn* 197
694	75359	Nbk 4/12/36	C	Receipt for dates or grain; *Nbk* 310
695	75360	Nbn 1/7/3	NC	Account of linen; *Nbn* 115
696	75361	Nbk 9/7/42	C	Receipt for barley; *Nbk* 404
697	75362	Nbk 10/9/29	F	Receipt for iron for tools; *Nbk* 204
698	75363	Nbk 22/2/38	F	Receipt for weapons; *Nbk* 332
699	75364	24/2/32	NC	Receipt for sheep
700	75365	Dar 2/2/26	C	Receipt for sheep and oxen
701	75366	Nbn 21/6/4	C	Account of linen; *Nbn* 163
702	75367	Nbn 7/7/4	F	Receipt for sesame; *Nbn* 166
703	75368	Cam 30/6/4	F	Receipt for a garment; *Cam* 244
704	75369	Nbk 14/8/36	C	Receipt for garments; *Nbk* 305
705	75370	-/-/41	F	Receipt for sesame; *Nbk* 391
706	75371	Nbk 2/11/-	F	Receipt for ducks; *Nbk* 440
707	75372	Nbk -/4/25	F	Receipt for birds; *Nbk* 151
708	75373	Ner 14/11/2	NC	Receipt for barley
709	75374	Nbn 20/2/15	F	Receipt for barley; *Nbn* 842
710	75375	13/8/35	C	Receipt for iron for tools; *Nbk* 285
711	75376	Nbn 12/1/8	F	Receipt for silver for working; *Nbn* 281
712	75377		NC	Account of workmen
713	75378	Cam 15/6b/3	F	Receipt for dates; *Cam* 180
714	75379	Dar 9/12/-	F	Receipt for wool
715	75380	15/2/3	C	Receipt for provisions for goldsmiths; *Nbn* 99
716	75381		NC	Receipt for barley
717	75382		NC	Legal; promissory note

AH 83-1-18,

718	75383	Dar 7/12b/acc	C	Account of barley; *Dar* 8
719	75384	Cam 3/8/8?	F	Receipt for silver; *Cam* 411
720	75385	8/8/7	NC	Receipt for dates or grain; *Dar* 239
721	75386		F	Account of bird fodder
722	75387	Nbk 3/11/30	NC	Receipt for tools; *Nbk* 225
723	75388	Nbn 2/7/14	F	Receipt for silver; *Nbn* 792
724	75389	Dar 23/4/9	F	Only date formula preserved; *Dar* 251
725	75390	Nbk 14/11/24	C	Receipt for iron; *Nbk* 146
726	75391	Nbn 1/8/11	F	Receipt for sesame; *Nbn* 543
727	75392		NC	Receipt(?) for silver
728	75393	30/1/1	C	Receipt for flour; *Nbn* 21
729	75394	Dar 14/6/22	NC	Receipt for dates or grain; *Dar* 546
730	75395	21/8/-	NC	Receipt for dates or grain
731	75396	Xer 28/11/acc	C	Letter; seals
732	75397		NC	Account of garments
733	75398	24/1/-	F	Account; *Nbn* 1062
734	75399		F	Receipt for sale of sheep
735	75400	Am -/1/1	NC	Receipt for flour
735A	75401	Nbn 22/9/4	NC	Receipt for silver payment; *Nbn* 170
736	75402		F	Receipt
737	75403	Cam -/-/1	F	Account of fruit; *Cam* 101
738	75404		NC	Account of dates or grain
739	75405	Cyr 10/3/1	C	Receipt for barley; *Cyr* 16
740	75406	5/9/-	C	Receipt for iron and silver
741	75407	Nbk 17/1/25	C	List of provisions; *Nbk* 148
742	75408	Cyr 24/6/7	C	Receipt for garments; *Cyr* 266
743	75409	Nbn 10/6/14	NC	Boat rental; *Nbn* 782
744	75410	Nbk 25/12/27	C	Receipt for dyes; *Nbk* 180
745	75411	Nbk 1/2/25	NC	Receipt for dates; *Nbk* 149
746	75412	Ner 6/2/3	NC	Receipt for sesame
747	75413	Nbk 7/9/27	NC	Account of animals(?); *Nbk* 176
748	92766	Cam -/-/3	NC	Account of dates; *Cam* 225
749	75414	Cyr 4/5/3	C	Account of emmer; *Cyr* 118
750	75415		NC	Receipt for sheep
751	75416	Cam 23/12/5	C	Receipt for dates; *Cam* 298
752	75417	-/-/31	F	Receipt for tools; *Nbk* 245
753	75418	Nbn -/7/15	F	Contract for bitumen; Sippar; *Nbn* 897
754	75419	Nbn 26/8/9	NC	Receipt for fodder; *Nbn* 364

AH 83-1-18,

755	75420	Nbk 7/12/40	NC	Receipt for sheep; *Nbk* 372
756	75421	Cyr -/8/2	F	Receipt for barley; *Cyr* 73
757	75422	Nbk 7/9/33	F	Economic; *Nbk* 259
758	75423	8/2/-	C	Receipt for dates or grain
759	75424	Nbk -/5/24	F	Receipt for dates or grain; *Nbk* 143
760	75425	Nbk 9/6/42	F	Receipt for metal for daggers; *Nbk* 401
761	75426	Dar -/-/3	NC	Receipt for iron
762	75427		NC	Receipt for wool(?) for gods
763	75428	Dar 20/11/acc	F	Account of sheep; *Dar* 1
764	75429		C	School exercise
765	75430	Bar 26/3/1	C	Receipt for dates or grain; *ZA* 4, 149 no. 4
766	75431	Ner -/-/acc	NC	Receipt for dates
767	75432	27/2/8	C	Receipt for garments; *Nbn* 290
768	75433	Cam 3/1/1	C	House rentals; *Cam* 28
769	75434	Nbn 18/2/10	F	Receipt for a sheep
770	75435	Cam 15/9/1	NC	Receipt for dates and barley; *Cam* 80
771	75436	Cam 21/11/2	C	Account of dates; *Cam* 141
772	75437	Nbn 21/3/15	C	Purchase of a boat; *Nbn* 856
773	75438	Nbn 29/1/15	F	Receipt for dyes; *Nbn* 836
774	75439	Cam 16/5/7	NC	Receipt for dates; *Cam* 378
775	75440	Nbn -/-/10	F	Receipt for bronze; *Nbn* 484
776	75441	Cyr 11/8/2	C	Receipt for sesame; *Cyr* 69
777	75442		C	Date provisions for workmen
778	75443	Nbk	F	Receipt; *Nbk* 446
779	75444	-/-/6	F	House rentals; *Nbn* 247
780	75445	Nbn 21/7/1	C	Receipt for silver; *Nbn* 37
781	75446		F	Letter; *CT* 22 212
782	75447	5/3/-	C	Receipt for silver and barley; archaic ḪA sign; *Cyr* 382
783	75448	Nbn 6/10/15	C	Receipt for sesame; *Nbn* 918
784	75449	Am 7/4/2	NC	Receipt for *irbu*
785	75450	Dar 27/1/1	C	Receipt for silver for rings; *Dar* 11
786	75451	Nbk 28/5/32	NC	Receipt for dates; *Nbk* 248
787	75452	9/10/30	C	Receipt for wool; *Nbk* 222
788	75453	Nbn 5/6/6	F	Receipt for barley; *Nbn* 235
789	75454	Cyr 24/1/3	NC	Receipt for dates or grain; *Cyr* 101
790	75455	Nbn 28/-/-	NC	Receipt for dates

AH 83-1-18,

791	75456	Nbn 28/10/-	NC	Receipt for silver for hired men; *Nbn* 1124
792	75457	Dar 5/5/4	C	Receipt for barley
793	75458	Dar 21/12/1	C	Account of barley
794	75459	Nbn 8/8/10	C	Exchange of barley for dates
795	75460	-/-/7	F	Receipt for dates and barley; *Cyr* 288
796	75461	Nbn 3/2/12	NC	Receipt for sheep; *Nbn* 589
797	75462	Nbk 9/9/27	NC	Purchase of wool; *Nbk* 177
798	75463	Cam 15/2/4	C	Receipt for wool for payment for an ox; *Cam* 231
799	75464	Nbn 6/11/16	NC	Account of bitumen; *Nbn* 1003
800	75465		C	Account of dates or grain
801	75466	Nbn 14/5/10	C	Receipt for dates; *Nbn* 430
802	75467	Cyr 7/2/8	F	Account of jewelry of gods; *Cyr* 300
803	75468	Cam 14/5/-	NC	Receipt for silver; *Cam* 418
804	75469	Nbn 3/7/15	C	Receipt for purchase of dates; *Nbn* 887
805	75470	Nbn 4/4/1	NC	Purchase of ducks; *Nbn* 31
806	75471	Nbn 5/2/14	C	Receipt for barley; *Nbn* 762
807	75472	Cam 5/8/4	NC	Account of wine; *Cam* 252
808	75473	Nbk 20/12/26	F	Receipt for birds(?); *Nbk* 171
809	75474	Cyr 14/1/4	F	Receipt for metal for working; *Cyr* 344
810	75475	Nbk 29/6/34	C	Receipt for silver; *Nbk* 268
811	75476	Nbn 28/9/15	C	Receipt for sesame; *Nbn* 914
812	75477	Dar 25/11/4	C	Receipt for sesame; *Dar* 143
813	75478	Cyr 10/4/7	C	Account of wool for garments of gods; *Cyr* 259
814	75479	Cam 2/7/1	C	Receipt for dates; *Cam* 60
815	75480	Nbn 29/12/5	F	Receipt for wool for garments of gods; *Nbn* 217
816	75481	6/7/-	C	Receipt for barley; *Nbn* 1100
817	75482	Nbk 13/6/36	C	Receipt for dates; *Nbk* 303
818	75483	Nbn 17/10/15	C	Letter; *Nbn* 922
819	75484	Nbn 21/8/2	C	Letter order; *Nbn* 80
820	75485	Cam 10/9/3	C	Receipt for barley; *Cam* 198
821	75486	Cam -/11/4	NC	Receipt for dates, emmer, and sesame; *Cam* 265
822	75487	Dar 8/12/4	C	Receipt for barley tithe; *Dar* 148
823	75488	Nbn 27/2/12	C	Receipt for silver for working; *Nbn* 598
824	75489	Ner 1/2/acc	NC	Receipt for purchase of provisions
825	75490	Nbn 11/6/17	NC	Account of barley; *Nbn* 1049

AH 83-1-18,

826	75491	Dar 8/2/3	NC	Account of wool for garments of gods; *Dar* 62
827	75492	Cam 13/12/6	C	Letter; *CT* 22 88; *Cam* 347
828	75493	Nbn 8/6/2	C	Letter order; *Nbn* 73
829	75494	17/12/-	C	Receipt for sheep
830	75495	Nbk 27/8/30	F	Receipt; *Nbk* 217
831	92767	Nbn 18/12/13	C	Receipt for iron; *Nbn* 745
832	75496	Cyr	F	Receipt for barley; *Cyr* 367
833	92768	Cyr 12/12/6	C	Account of garments of gods; *Cyr* 241
834	75497		C	Field measurements; *Nbk* 450
835	75498	Cyr 24/6/4	C	Account of seed; *Cyr* 174
836	92769	Nbn 21/11/1	C	House rental; Sippar; *Nbn* 48
837	92770	Nbn 15/6/14	NC	Account of barley; *Nbn* 786
838	92771	Nbn 12/5/11	NC	Account of barley; *Nbn* 525
839	92772	Cyr 10/12/acc	NC	Account of garments of gods; *Cyr* 7
840	75499	Cam 19/5/5	C	Account of dates; *Cam* 281
841	75500	Dar 7/5/3	NC	Account of dates or grain; *Dar* 72
842	75501	Nbn 20/1/16	C	Receipt for wool for garments of gods; *Nbn* 952
843	75502	Nbn -/-/12	C	Account of barley tithes
844	75503	Cam 11/3/1	C	Animal ledger
845	92773	Cyr 17/6b/2	C	Account of barley; *Cyr* 59
846	75504	Cam -/-/2	C	Receipt for barley; *Cam* 151
847	75505	-/-/8	C	Ledger of barley and dates exchange
848	75506		NC	Account of date provisions
849	75507	Cyr 3/5/8	NC	Sale of a boat; Sippar; *Cyr* 310
850	75508		NC	Receipt for gold
851	75509	Ner 20/5/2	NC	Sale of a house
852	75510	21/5/-	F	Receipt
853	75511	20/12/5	NC	Account of expenditures for dyes, oxen, etc.; *Nbn* 214
854	75512		NC	Receipt for barley
855	92774	Cam 6/2/5	F	Account of dates; *Cam* 274
856	75513	Nbn 20/6/15	F	Account of sesame; *Nbn* 883
857	75514	Nbn 24/10/12	NC	Account of flour; *Nbn* 658
858	75515	-/1/3	C	Account of barley
859	75516	Dar 19/12/5	NC	Purchase of sheep; *Dar* 190
860	75517	Cam 26/11/1	C	Legal deposition
861	92775	Cyr 27/1/5	NC	Account of barley; *Cyr* 189
862	75518	Dar 11/8/2	F	Account; Alu-ša-Šamaš; *Dar* 47

AH 83-1-18,

863	92776	Nbn 5/1/9	NC	Account of garments of gods; *Nbn* 320
864	75519	Cyr 24/6/4	C	Field measurements; *Cyr* 173
865	75520	Dar 17/6/2	F	Account of dates; *Dar* 40
866	75521	Dar -/-/acc	F	Account of barley; *Dar* 10
867	92777	Cyr 29/6/3	C	Field measurements; *Cyr* 124
868	75522	Nbk 25/-/3	NC	Account of dates; *Nbk* 36
869	75523	6/4/7	C	Account of oxen; *Dar* 222
870	75524		F	Account of dates or grain
871	75525	-/2/3	F	Account of garments of gods; *Cyr* 109
872	75526	Nbn -/-/10	C	Account of barley
873	75527	Cam 13/9/4	C	Account of sheep; *Cam* 256
874	75528		F	Account of silver
875	75529	Cam 7/10/2	C	Sales receipt for wool
876	92778	Cyr 15/6b/2	C	Account of sheep; *Cyr* 57
877	75530	Dar 25/8/35	NC	Receipt for wool
878	75531	5/2/13?	NC	Account of garments of gods; *Nbn* 694
879	75532	Cyr 25/5/8	NC	Apprenticeship contract; Sippar; *Cyr* 313
880	75533	-/1/-	NC	Receipt for dates and wool
881	75534	Cyr 8/7/3	F	Cultivation contract; *Cyr* 126
882	75535	Cam 13/9/2	C	Exchange of barley and dates; *Cam* 131
883	75536	12/5/1	NC	Contract; Sippar; *Cam* 49
884	75537		NC	Account of oxen
885	75538	Cam 13/12/1	C	Contract for weapons; Sippar; *Cam* 93
886	75539	Dar 24/9/3	C	Account of dates; *Dar* 89; *KB* 4 307
887	75540	Cyr 12/2/6	C	Field measurements; *Cyr* 226
888	75541	Nbn 9/2/13	C	Account of garments of gods; *Nbn* 696
889	75542	25/-/5	NC	Legal deposition
890	75543	Cam 24/12b/5	C	Account of barley; *Cam* 300
891	92779	Nbk 28/11/25	NC	Account of dates; *Nbk* 157
892	75544		F	Account of provisions(?)
893	75545	Nbn 15/9/15	NC	Exchange of dates and barley; *Nbn* 907
894	75546	Nbn 28/12/14	C	Account of oil; *Nbn* 821
895	75547	Cyr 3/7/4	C	Purchase contract; Sippar; *Cyr* 175
896	75548	Dar 14/12/-	F	Receipt for barley
897	75549	-/10/4	F	Contract; *Nbn* 172
898	75550	Nbn 11/5/2	F	Deposition; Sippar; *Nbn* 72
899	75551	Cam 15/9/7	F	Account of dates; *Cam* 387
900	92780	Nbn 26/5/9	C	Account of dates; *Nbn* 351

AH 83-1-18,

901	75552		NC	Account of garments of gods
902	75553	Cam -/-/1	C	Account of sheep; *Cam* 100
903	75554	Cyr 18/7/6	F	Account of dates; *Cyr* 233
904	75555	-/1/6	F	Account of dates; *Nbn* 219
905	75556	Cam 7/8/1	F	Account of hides; *Cam* 71
906	75557	Cam 12/12/1	C	Barley and dates exchange
907	75558	Nbn 7/10/15	C	Receipt for dates; *Nbn* 919
908	75559	Cyr 8/1/8	C	List of lost workmen; *Cyr* 292
909	75560	Nbn 2/7/13	F	Account of barley; *Nbn* 718
910	75561	Dar 22/11/4	C	Purchase of animals; *Dar* 141
911	75562	Nbn 21/4/10	C	Receipt for silver; *Nbn* 424
912	75563	Cam 9/9/acc	NC	Account of barley; *Cam* 9
913	75564	Nbk 15/6/26	C	Receipt for barley
914	75565	Cam 8/6b/acc	C	Receipt for barley; *Cam* 5
915	75566	Nbn 21/8/15	C	Receipt for wool; *Nbn* 898
916	75567	Dar 22/1/25	NC	Receipt for silver tithe
917	75568	Cyr 9/11/2	C	Account of barley; *Cyr* 80
918	75569	Ner 2/4/1	NC	Receipt for oxen
919	75570	Dar 3/12/4	C	Receipt for barley; *Dar* 146
920	75571	Xer 21/2/acc	C	Receipt for beams
921	75572	Nbk 19/9/30	C	Account of barley; *Nbk* 220
922	75573		C	Letter; seal
923	75574	Dar 4/4/4	C	Receipt for vinegar; *Dar* 115
924	75575	Cyr +5/12/4	NC	Receipt for dates; *Cyr* 181
925	75576	11/2/12	F	Account of sheep offerings; *Nbn* 594
926	75577	-/-/6	NC	Account of barley income
927	75578	Nbk 12/2/43	NC	Receipt for iron tools; *Nbk* 413
928	75579	Nbn 12/2/9	C	Account of oxen and sheep offerings; *Nbn* 332
929	75580	Ner 13/-/1	NC	Receipt for sheep
930	75581	Nbn 4/3/14	F	Account of fodder; *Nbn* 766
931	75582	Nbn 28/8/10	F	Account of dates; *Nbn* 450
932	75583	Nbk 15/9/28	NC	Receipt for dates; *Nbk* 192
933	75584	Nbn 20/6b/10	C	Receipt for house rentals; *Nbn* 439
934	75585		F	Letter; *CT* 22 161
935	75586	Cam 9/2/7	NC	Receipt for oil; *Cam* 366
936	75587	Nbn 11/9/14	NC	Receipt for beer; *Nbn* 811
937	75588	Nbk 9/12/36	NC	Account of garments of gods; *Nbk* 312
938	75589	Cam 19/7/6	NC	Receipt for barley; *Cam* 323

AH 83-1-18,

939	75590	20/7/-	F	Receipt for barley
940	75591	Dar 19/12/2	NC	Receipt for sheep; *Dar* 55
941	75592	Nbn 3/9/8	C	Receipt for silver
942	75593	Dar 12/6/4	C	Receipt for sesame; *Dar* 125
943	75594	-/9/36	NC	Account of dates or grain
944	75595	Nbn 17/1/3	C	Receipt for iron; *Nbn* 89
945	75596	Am 29/3/1	F	Account of barley provisions
946	75597	Am 12/-/1	NC	Sales receipt
947	75598		C	Letter; *CT* 22 42
948	75599	Nbk 15/12b/26	F	Receipt for barley; *Nbk* 170
949	75600	Nbk 22/7/36	NC	Receipt for purchase of oxen; *Nbk* 304!
950	75601		F	Account of workmen
951	75602	Cam	F	Account of wool(?); *Cam* 437
952	75603	Nbn -/2/3	NC	Legal text concerning purchase of dates; Sippar; *Nbn* 95
953	75604	Nbn 7/2/11	C	Receipt for garments of gods; *Nbn* 502!
954	75605	Am 12/11/acc	C	Receipt for silver; seal
955	75606	Nbk 3/6/3	F	Account of sesame; *Nbk* 30
956	75607	Nbn 8/5/9	C	Receipt for lapis; *Nbn* 349
957	75608	Cyr 26/4/2	F	Deposition concerning oxen; *Cyr* 44!
958	75609	Nbk 27/7/1	F	Account of barley; *Nbk* 18
959	75610		NC	Letter; *CT* 22 230
960	75611		F	Receipt for barley
961	75612	Cam 21/9/1	C	Receipt for dates; *Cam* 83
962	75613		F	Receipt for silver
963	75614		F	Account of dates or grain; *Nbk* 437
964	92781	Nbk 20/3/30	NC	Account of oxen; *Nbk* 213
965	75615	Nbn -/1/9	F	Field measurements; *Nbn* 327
966	75616		NC	Letter
967	75617		C	Account of silver
968	75618	Nbn 27/12b/6	C	Purchase contract; *Nbn* 245
969	75619	Nbn 3/3/17	C	Receipt for leather harnesses; *Nbn* 1034
970	75620	Cam 6/5/1	F	Receipt for fruit; *Cam* 48
971	75621	Dar 5/8/3	C	Receipt for barley; *Dar* 86
972	75622	Nbn 15/12/13	C	Purchase of sheep; *Nbn* 744
973	75623	Cam 2/1/8	C	Receipt for dates; *Cam* 406
974	75624	Cam 3/12/7	C	Receipt for silver; *Cam* 396
975	75625	Nbn 2/7/13	NC	Receipt for silver; *Nbn* 717

AH 83-1-18,

976	75626	Cam -/8/6	F	Receipt for dates for iron smiths; *Cam* 327
977	75627	Nbn 2/3/9	NC	Receipt for bronze; *Nbn* 339
978	75628	Cam -/7/4	C	Receipt for sesame; *Cam* 249
979	75629	Cyr -/1/2	C	Purchase of dates; *Cyr* 35
980	75630	Cyr 24/6/7	NC	Receipt for a garment; *Cyr* 265
981	75631	Nbn 10/9/11	C	Receipt for an ox; *Nbn* 548
982	75632	Cam 18/8/1	C	Receipt for dates; *Cam* 75
983	75633	Cyr 12/10/7	NC	Receipt for iron; *Cyr* 276
984	75634	Cam 15/3/5	NC	Receipt for dates; *Cam* 278
985	75635	-/3/17	C	Letter; seal; *CT* 22 50; *Nbn* 1038
986	75636	Nbn 12/11/7	C	Receipt for an ox; *Nbn* 272
987	75637	Nbk 10/12/31	C	Loan; *Nbk* 242
988	75638	Cam 11/5/2	NC	Receipt for wages; *Cam* 115
989	75639	Cam 9/2/2	NC	Receipt for dates; *Cam* 103
990	75640		NC	Letter; *CT* 22 115; *Cyr* 373
991	75641	Dar 14/3/1	NC	Receipt for sesame; *Dar* 13
992	75642	Nbn 13/6/14	C	Receipt for iron tools; *Nbn* 784
993	75643	Dar 25/7/2	C	Receipt for dates; *Dar* 46
994	75644	Nbn 16/12/12	C	Receipt for gold for working; *Nbn* 677
995	75645	Cam 25/6b/3	C	Receipt for wool; *Cam* 183
996	75646	Nbn 28/1/14	C	Receipt for gold for working; *Nbn* 758
997	75647	Cyr 11/5/-	NC	Purchase of garments; *Cyr* 352
998	75648		C	List of workmen
999	75649	Nbn 7/3/10	C	Receipt for wool; *Nbn* 415
1000	75650	Nbn 13/10/15	C	Receipt for dates; *Nbn* 920
1001	75651	Cyr 14/12/7	C	Receipt for emmer and sesame; *Cyr* 282
1002	75652	Cam 19/10/3	NC	Receipt for bird feed; *Cam* 209
1003	75653	Cam 17/7/3	C	Receipt for emmer; *Cam* 188
1004	75654	7/8/4	C	Purchase of dates; *Cyr* 178
1005	75655	Nbn 3/7/15	C	Receipt for dates; *Nbn* 888
1006	75656	Cam 24/11/6	C	Receipt for dates; *Cam* 345
1007	75657	28/11/3	C	Receipt for an *ippatu*; *Nbn* 129
1008	75658	9/2/7	C	Receipt for garments of gods; *Nbn* 252
1009	75659	Nbn 17/2/6	C	Receipt for bronze; *Nbn* 223
1010	75660	Cam 12/10/acc	C	Purchase of dyes; *Cam* 11
1011	75661	Cyr 20/4/3	C	Receipt for jewelry; *Cyr* 116
1012	75662	Nbn 19/12b/15	C	Receipt for barley; *Nbn* 942
1013	75663	Nbn 20/7/14	C	Receipt for an ox; *Nbn* 797

AH 83-1-18,

1014	75664	Cyr 7/6/2	C	Purchase of dates or grain and a sheep; *Cyr* 53
1015	75665	Nbn 4/5/16	C	Receipt for dates; *Nbn* 969
1016	75666		C	Account of bitumen
1017	75667	Dar 18/5/1	C	Receipt for barley; *Dar* 18
1018	75668	Nbn 28/1/17	C	Receipt for dates; *Nbn* 1027
1019	75669	Nbn 14/11/16	C	Receipt for bitumen; *Nbn* 1004
1020	75670	Cyr 1/1/2	C	Purchase of sheep; *Cyr* 32!
1021	75671	Nbn 11/6/14	C	Receipt for silver and barley; *Nbn* 783
1022	75672	Nbn 13/11/11	NC	Receipt for silver; *Nbn* 568
1023	75673	Cam 14/12/1	C	Receipt for fodder; *Cam* 94
1024	75674	Cam 22/9/3	NC	Receipt for flour; *Cam* 203
1025	75675	Cam 19/12/1	NC	Receipt for emmer; *Cam* 95
1026	75676	Dar 3/-/27	NC	Receipt for wool
1027	75677	Nbn 2/1/16	NC	Purchase of dates or grain; *Nbn* 950
1028	75678	Cyr 28/8/3	C	Receipt for flour; *Cyr* 131
1029	75679	Nbn 21/5/14	NC	Receipt for bronze objects; *Nbn* 778
1030	75680	Nbn 16/12b/15	NC	Receipt for dates; *Nbn* 941
1031	75681	Nbn 28/11/15	C	Receipt for dates; *Nbn* 930
1032	75682	Cyr 27/11/7	NC	Receipt for dates; *Cyr* 280
1033	75683	Nbn 1/3/8	C	Receipt for linen; *Nbn* 291
1034	75684	Cam 20/10/1	C	House rentals; *Cam* 89
1035	75685	Dar 24/11/3	C	Account of barley; *Dar* 94
1036	75686	Nbn 1/10/13	C	Receipt for barley fodder; *Nbn* 732
1037	75687	Dar 17/8/3	C	Account of emmer; *Dar* 88
1038	75688	Nbn 6/1/11	C	Receipt for linen; *Nbn* 492
1039	75689	Nbn 15/9/11	C	Receipt for dates; *Nbn* 551
1040	75690	Cam 13/7/1	C	Receipt for dates; *Cam* 62
1041	75691	Nbn 22/2/4	C	Account of garments; *Nbn* 146
1042	75692	Nbn 4/10/11	C	Receipt for dates; *Nbn* 559
1043	75693	Dar 21/-/23	C	Receipt for barley
1044	75694	Cam 18/12/3	C	Receipt for emmer; *Cam* 222
1045	75695		NC	Letter; *CT* 22 117; *Cyr* 369
1046	75696	Dar 20/5/4	C	Receipt for barley; *Dar* 121
1047	75697	Nbn 25/7/7	C	House rentals; *Nbn* 264
1048	75698	Cam 26/7/3	NC	Receipt for linen; *Cam* 191
1049	75699	Nbn 21/6/15	C	Receipt for barley; *Nbn* 885
1050	75700	2/2/4	NC	Receipt for dates; *Nbn* 142
1051	75701	Nbn 3/8/16	F	Receipt; *Nbn* 989

AH 83-1-18,

1052	75702	Cyr 13/6/2	C	Receipt for barley; *Cyr* 342
1053	75703	26/1/5	F	Receipt for oil; *Nbn* 185
1054	75704	Nbk 11/2/2	F	Loan; *Nbk* 22
1055	75705	Cyr 24/-/7	F	Account of silver; *Cyr* 287
1056	75706	Cyr 23/11/7	NC	Purchase of oil; *Cyr* 279
1057	75707	Nbn 11/6/15	F	Receipt for iron for tools; *Nbn* 878
1058	75708	Dar 27/1/28	C	Receipt for sheep
1059	75709	Cam 19/5/7	F	Receipt for barley; *Cam* 380
1060	75710	Cyr 30/8/5	NC	Account of cassia; *Cyr* 204
1061	75711	Cam 9/7/7	C	Purchase of an ox; *Cam* 381
1062	75712	30/12/-	C	Receipt for barley
1063	75713	23/9/acc	C	Promissory note for animals
1064	75714	Nbn 2/1/11	NC	Receipt for sheep; *Nbn* 490
1065	75715	Cam 23/7/4	F	Receipt for sesame; *Cam* 247
1066	75716	Nbn 15/2/17	NC	Receipt; *Nbn* 1033
1067	75717	20/-/14	NC	Receipt for jewelry of gods; *Nbn* 823
1068	75718	Nbn 6/10/15	C	Receipt for dates; *Nbn* 917
1069	75719	Nbn 15/12/10	F	Receipt for silver; *Nbn* 481
1070	75720	Cam 14/5/1	F	Account of barley; *Cam* 50
1071	75721	Cam 8/3/7	NC	Receipt for barley; *Cam* 371
1072	75722	Cam 16/5/1	C	Purchase of figs and salt; *Cam* 52
1073	75723	Nbn 11/8/10	NC	Exchange of barley and dates; Alu-ša-Nabu; *Nbn* 446
1074	75724	Nbn -/2/3	C	Receipt for linen; *Nbn* 91
1075	75725	Nbn 4/3/16	C	Receipt for iron for working; *Nbn* 960
1076	75726	Cyr 19/12/4	NC	Receipt for sesame; *Cyr* 182
1077	75727	Cyr 28/9/3	C	Letter; seal; *CT* 22 179; *Cyr* 133
1078	75728	Nbn 25/6/16	C	Receipt for barley; *Nbn* 986
1079	75729	Cam 2/5/2	C	Receipt for date flour; *Cam* 112
1080	75730	2/4/35	NC	Purchase of barley and wine
1081	75731	Nbn 26/8/10	F	Account of dates or grain; *Nbn* 449
1082	75732	Cam 14/1/7	NC	Account of dates; *Cam* 357
1083	75733	Nbn 2/6/-	NC	Purchase of garments and wine; *Nbn* 1088
1084	75734	Nbn 18/9/15	C	Letter; seals; *CT* 22 51; *Nbn* 909
1085	75735	Cyr 18/12/1	C	Receipt for iron for working; *Cyr* 30
1086	75736	Dar 27/6/4	C	Deposition; *Dar* 128
1087	75737	1/2/1	NC	Account of gold; *Cam* 34
1088	75738	-/-/3	C	Letter; *Dar* 101

AH 83-1-18,

1089	75739	Dar 26/11/5	F	Receipt; *Dar* 188
1090	75740	Nbn 10/8/13	C	Receipt for sesame; *Nbn* 725
1091	75741	Nbn 2/3/9	C	Receipt for wool; *Nbn* 337
1092	75742		C	Receipt for dates
1093	75743	Nbn 24/12/9	C	Receipt for gold; *Nbn* 394
1094	75744	Cyr 22/9/7	C	Receipt for sheep; *Cyr* 273
1095	75745	-/-/12	C	Account of dates; *Nbn* 691
1096	75746	Cyr 26/11/7	C	Receipt for sesame
1097	75747	Cyr 7/12/2	C	Receipt for dates; *Cyr* 85
1098	75748	Cam -/10/-	NC	Purchase of wool; *Cam* 430
1099	75749	Nbn 11/9/13	C	House rentals; *Nbn* 728
1100	75750		C	Three personal names; *Nbk* 448
1101	75751	Cam 14/11/3	C	Receipt for barley and dates
1102	75752	Nbn 14/3/6	C	Receipt for sesame; *Nbn* 226
1103	75753	Cyr 29/9/3	C	Receipt for dates; *Cyr* 134
1104	75754	Dar 2/5/3	C	Account of barley; *Dar* 71
1105	75755	Nbn 13/9/11	C	Receipt for iron for working; *Nbn* 549
1106	75756	OB -/iti *e-lu-li*/-	C	Field rental
1107	75757	Ner -/7/acc	C	Loan of silver
1108	75758	Cam 7/2/3	C	Receipt for materials for dyeing; *Cam* 156
1109	75759	Cyr 21/7/2	C	Account of dates or grain
1110	75760	Nbn 1/3/12	C	Contract for dates; *Nbn* 599
1111	75761	Nbn 17/1/4	C	Account of garments; *Nbn* 137
1112	75762		F	Letter; *CT* 22 11
1113	75763	Cam 25/3/4	C	Receipt for dye; *Cam* 235
1114	75764		C	Letter; *CT* 22 76
1115	75765		NC	Letter; *CT* 22 245
1116	75766	Dar 16/1/4	C	Receipt for silver; *Dar* 109
1117	75767	Nbn 6/7/10	C	Receipt for garments of gods
1118	75768	Nbn 7/7/5	C	Receipt for gold jewelry of gods; *Nbn* 195
1119	75769	Cam 4/3/2	NC	Receipt for silver and iron; *Cam* 106
1120	75770	Cam 12/1/4	NC	Account of sheep; *Cam* 228
1121	75771	Cam 21/9/6	C	Receipt for dates; *Cam* 333
1122	75772	Cam 5/5/2	F	Receipt for dates or grain; *Cam* 113
1123	75773	Nbn 28/10/15	F	Receipt for iron for tools; *Nbn* 926
1124	75774		NC	Receipt for aromatics
1125	75775		C	Receipt for sale of birds

AH 83-1-18,

1126	75776	Nbn 7/12b/12	F	Receipt for iron; *Nbn* 684
1127	92782	Nbn 17/6/3	C	Promissory note; Sippar; *Nbn* 113
1128	92783	Nbn -/-/9	F	Account of barley; *Nbn* 398
1129	75777	Cam 8/8/2	NC	Receipt for fodder for oxen; *Cam* 124
1130	75778	Ner 11/11/2	C	Loan of gold; *Ner* 49
1131	75779	Kan 14/12/20	C	Receipt for purchase of reeds
1132	75780	Nbn 8/10/12	C	Contract for grain; *Nbn* 656
1133	75781	Cam 12/12/5	C	Account of barley; *Cam* 296
1134	75782	Dar 13/12/2	C	Receipt for dates; *Dar* 54
1135	75783	Nbn 24/10/11	C	Receipt for sesame; *Nbn* 565
1136	75784	Nbn 18/2/15	F	Account of barley; *Nbn* 841
1137	75785	Nbn 3/9/11	NC	Receipt for wool; *Nbn* 547
1138	75786	Cam 27/10/4	C	Account of dates; *Cam* 258
1139	75787	Nbn 24/8/16	C	Account of dates
1140	75788		NC	Receipt for silver
1141	75789	25/12/34	NC	Receipt for purchase of barley
1142	75790		F	Account of animal fodder
1143	92784	Nbk 15/8/32	F	Account of dates or grain; *Nbk* 249
1144	75791	Cyr 10/5/7	NC	Account of barley; *Cyr* 262
1145	75792	Cam 21/9/3	C	Account of barley; *Cam* 201
1146	75793	Nbn 25/-/1	F	Animal ledger; *Nbn* 54
1147	75794	Cam 11/3/-	C	Account of garments; *Cam* 415
1148	92785	Cyr 20/-/7	NC	Account of barley; *Cyr* 285
1149	75795		NC	Account of garments of gods
1150	75796	Cyr -/-/2	F	Account of dates; *Cyr* 92
1151	75797	Nbn 13/11/15	C	Receipt for hides; *Nbn* 928
1152	75798	Cam 30/11/7	NC	Receipt for dates or grain; *Cam* 395
1153	75799	19/3/1	C	Receipt for dates; *Dar* 14
1154	75800	-/1/8	C	Receipt for bird fodder
1155	75801	Dar 27/6/16	NC	Receipt for rental(?) of a field; *Dar* 427
1156	75802	Cyr 6/7/5	NC	Account of wool; *Cyr* 202
1157	75803	Nbn 24/10/2	F	Account of gold; *Nbn* 84
1158	75804	Nbn 27/7/7	C	Account of sheep offerings
1159	75805	Cyr -/5/5	NC	Cultivation contract; *Cyr* 200
1160	75806	Cyr 21/4/5	F	Account of fruit; *Cyr* 197
1161	75807	Nbn 5/3/17	C	Account of barley and dates; *Nbn* 1035
1162	75808	Cyr 7/1/5	F	Account of garments of gods; *Cyr* 186
1163	75809	17/12b/6	NC	Account of dates or grain
1164	75810	Nbn 17/8/2	C	Sale of property; Sippar; *Nbn* 79

AH 83-1-18,

1165	75811	Cam 22/7/2	C	Account of dates; *Cam* 121
1166	75812	Dar 27/12/4	F	Account of barley; *Dar* 150
1167	75813	Cyr 11/11/acc	F	Account of barley; *Cyr* 5
1168	75814	Nbn 12/4/12	C	Account of fruit; *Nbn* 606
1169	92786	Nbk 27/2/1	C	Account of dates; *Nbk* 11
1170	75815	Cam 18/8/3	C	Contract for birds; *Cam* 194
1171	75816	Nbn 19/2/11	C	Account of garments; *Nbn* 507
1172	75817	Nbn 24/10/13	F	Account of dates or grain; *Nbn* 746
1173	75818	Cam 25/12/7	C	Contract for garments; Sippar; *Cam* 398
1174	75819	-/7/3	C	Receipt for various purchases from *telitu* tax
1175	75820	Nbn 29/4/10	C	Receipt for iron; *Nbn* 425
1176	75821	Nbk 2/7/13	C	Sale of a girl; *Nbk* 100
1177	75822	Cam -/1/1	F	Account of barley; *Cam* 33
1178	75823	Dar -/12b/acc?	F	Account of dates or grain
1179	75824	Cyr 26/6/8	F	Deposition; *Cyr* 318
1180	75825	Cam 28/11/4	C	Receipt for dates; *Cam* 264
1181	75826	22/6/6	F	Account of dates and barley; *Nbn* 237
1182	75827	Dar -/-/13	F	Account of dates or grain; *Dar* 368
1183	75828		F	Account of dates or grain
1184	75829		F	Account of dates
1185	75830		F	List of workmen(?); *Nbk* 452
1186	75831	-/1/14	F	Account of dates or grain; two columns; *Dar* 370
1187	75832		F	Account of barley provisions
1188	75833	Cyr 17/1/2	F	Account of barley; *Cyr* 34
1189	75834		F	Account; only personal names preserved
1190	75835	30/12/8	F	Deposition; *Cyr* 329
1191	75836	-/5/-	F	Ledger
1192	75837		F	Account of sale of animals
1193	75838		F	Field measurements; *Nbk* 453
1194	75839	Dar -/-/21	F	Account; *Dar* 532
1195	75840		F	Dates or grain ledger
1196	75841		F	Account of dates or grain provisions
1197	75842		F	Animal ledger (audit)
1198	75843		F	Account of dates or grain
1199	75844	Nbk	F	Field measurements; *Nbk* 444
1200	75845		F	Account of sesame

AH 83-1-18,

1201	75846	Cam -/2/-	F	Account of garments of gods; *Cam* 414
1202	75847	Cyr -/-/2	F	Account of barley; *Cyr* 93
1203	75848		NC	Account of hired men
1204	75849	Dar 21/10/17	F	Legal deposition; *Dar* 451
1205	75850	Am 18/9/acc	NC	Deposition; *AOATS* 4 76
1206	75851	Dar 18/8/25	F	Account of barley
1207	75852	Nbn 24/5/7	F	Account of silver; *Nbn* 259
1208	75853	Dar -/7/1	F	Account of jewelry; *Dar* 20
1209	75854	Cam 28/12/6	F	Account of barley; *Cam* 350
1210	75855	Cam -/-/2	F	Account of barley; *Cam* 150; *RA* 63, 79
1211	75856	Cam 23/12/1	F	Account of dates; *Cam* 96
1212	75857	Cam 7/12/acc	F	Irrigation contract; Sippar; *Cam* 19
1213	75858		F	Account of sheep(?)
1214	75859		F	Account of dates and barley
1215	75860	Cam -/2/2	F	Account of bitumen; *Cam* 105
1216	75861	Cyr -/3/-	F	Deposition; Sippar; *Cyr* 349
1217	75862	Nbn -/11/11	F	Account of iron for tools; *Nbn* 571
1218	75863	Cyr -/-/1	F	Account of barley, dates and emmer; *Cyr* 31
1219	75864		F	Account of temple furnishings
1220	75865	Nbn 14/5/1	F	Receipt for silver, barley and dates; *Nbn* 33
1221	75866	Dar 20+/12/33	F	Receipt
1222	75867	Nbn 2/7/14	NC	Account of sesame; *Nbn* 791
1223	75868	Cam 6/5/-	NC	Receipt for reeds; *Cam* 417
1224	75869	Nbn 1/9/3	F	Receipt for silver; *Nbn* 120
1225	75870		F	Account of wool
1226	75871	Cam 24/8/1	NC	Receipt for barley tithe; drawing on reverse; *Cam* 76
1227	75872	Dar 16/11/2	F	Account of barley; *Dar* 52
1228	75873	Nbn 21/9/-	F	Account of silver; *Nbn* 1117
1229	75874	Nbn 26/9/1	F	Cultivation contract; *Nbn* 43
1230	75875	Cam -/-/7	F	Account of dates; *Cam* 402
1231	75876	Dar	F	Receipt for temple furnishings
1232	75877	Dar? 25/-/14	F	Receipt for barley; *Dar* 397
1233	75878	Dar 26/2/27	F	Receipt for dates or grain
1234	75879	Nbn 23/3/5	F	Contract; *Nbn* 188
1235	75880	Dar 7/3/25	F	Receipt for barley
1236	75881	Cyr 3/1/3	NC	Loan; *Cyr* 96

AH 83-1-18,

1237	75882		F	Account of various purchases
1238	75883	Dar 25/1/-	NC	Receipt for temple furnishings
1239	75884	-/-/11	F	Account of dates; *Nbn* 582
1240	75885		NC	Dates or grain ledger
1241	75886	Ner 5/-/-	F	Receipt
1242	75887		NC	Receipt for tools
1243	75888	29/1/-	F	Account of flour provisions for goldsmiths; *Nbn* 1065
1244	75889		NC	Receipt for garments
1245	75890		F	Account of dates or grain
1246	75891	Cyr 12/5/-	F	Account of barley; *Cyr* 353
1247	75892	Cyr 27/4/9	F	Contract; *Cyr* 341
1248	75893	Dar 5/-/10	NC	Letter; seal; *Dar* 291
1249	75894	2/4/6	C	Receipt for barley
1250	75895		F	Letter; *CT* 22 72
1251	75896	Dar 26/2/22	F	Receipt for barley; *Dar* 540
1252	75897		NC	List of workmen(?)
1253	75898	Cyr -/-/4	F	Account of dates; *Cyr* 159
1254	75899	Dar 22/4/17	NC	Receipt for wool provisions; *Dar* 442
1255	75900	14/3/6	C	Account of silver; *Nbn* 225
1256	75901	Dar 27/-/10	F	Receipt for silver; *Dar* 292
1257	75902	Nbn 22/4/9	F	Receipt for silver; *Nbn* 347
1258	75903	Nbn -/-/15	F	Account of wool; *Nbn* 948
1259	75904	Dar 1/6/1	F	Receipt for silver; *Dar* 19
1260	75905	Nbn 22/-/13	F	Account of silver; *Nbn* 749
1261	75906	Nbn -/-/6	F	Contract for dates; Sippar; *Nbn* 246
1262	75907	15/11/5	F	Account of emmer; *Nbn* 209
1263	75908	Nbn 4/7/-	NC	Account of silver; *Nbn* 1101
1264	75909	Cyr 12/11/2	F	Letter order; *Cyr* 81
1265	75910	Nbn 15/6/11	F	Purchase of a garment; *Nbn* 532
1266	75911	Dar 3/9/6	C	Letter; seals; *Dar* 209
1267	75912		F	Letter
1268	75913	Dar 20/1/4	NC	Contract for barley; *Dar* 111
1269	missing	Cyr 23/4/-	F	Receipt for barley tithe; *Cyr* 350
1270	75914	14/3/16	NC	Receipt for silver; *Dar* 422
1271	75915	30/4/14	F	Account of dates and barley; *Nbn* 774
1272	75916		NC	Receipt for alum
1273	75917	Dar 10/6/21	NC	Receipt for dates; *Dar* 525
1274	75918	Nbn 30/2/1	F	Account of barley and sesame; *Nbn* 28

AH 83-1-18,

1275	75919		C	Letter; *CT* 22 77
1276	75920	Cyr 16/2/5	NC	Account; *Cyr* 192
1277	75921	Nbn 15/7/12	C	Receipt for sesame; *Nbn* 628
1278	75922	Nbn -/3/3	NC	Account of garments; *Nbn* 104
1279	75923	Dar 18/1/4	F	Contract for barley tithe; *Dar* 110
1280	75924	Nbn 10/6/16	F	Receipt for silver; *Nbn* 981
1281	75925	Dar 22/1/-	F	Receipt for a sheep
1282	75926	Dar 18/6/25	C	Receipt for barley
1283	75927	10/2/4	C	Receipt for sesame; *Nbn* 144
1284	75928		F	Receipt for wool
1285	75929	-/9/1	F	Receipt for wool; *Nbn* 41
1286	75930	19/6b/15?	C	Receipt for bronze; Kugler *SSB* 2 418; Parker-Dubberstein 4 n. 8
1287	75931	Cam 22/9/-	F	Contract; Babylon; *Cam* 425
1288	75932	14/-/10	F	Receipt for bronze; *Nbn* 487
1289	75933	8/7/2	NC	Account of dates or grain; *Cyr* 61
1290	75934	Nbn -/8/12	F	Contract for bricks; *Nbn* 643
1291	75935	Dar 1/12/34	NC	Sales receipt
1292	75936	11/1/3	F	Account of wool; *Cyr* 98
1293	75937	Dar 29/7/15	NC	Receipt for barley; *Dar* 408
1294	75938	Cyr 8/12/8	NC	Account of garments; *Cyr* 326
1295	75939		NC	Legal deposition
1296	75940	Dar 30/-/5	NC	Receipt for sesame; *Dar* 197
1297	75941	Dar 15/2/34	F	Receipt for sale of dates or grain
1298	75942	Nbn -/8/7	F	Account of sheep sacrifices; *Nbn* 265
1299	75943	Dar 3/3/16	C	Account of dates or grain for temples; *Dar* 421
1300	75944	25/5/-	NC	Receipt for aromatics
1301	75945	17/9/10	NC	Account of barley; *Nbn* 458
1302	75946		NC	Receipt for barley
1303	75947	Nbn 28/4/11	C	Receipt for gold; *Nbn* 519
1304	75948	Dar 11/10/31	NC	Receipt for aromatics
1305	75949		NC	Account of workmen
1306	75950	-/-/12	NC	Letter; seal; *Dar* 344
1307	75951	Dar -/-/22	F	Receipt for animals; *Dar* 558
1308	75952	-/5/6	NC	Contract for bricks; *Nbn* 231
1309	75953		F	Account of wool(?)
1310	75954	Nbn 8/2/9	NC	Receipt for oil; *Nbn* 329
1311	missing	Nbn 8/6/16	NC	Receipt for wool; *Nbn* 979

AH 83-1-18,

1312	75955	Dar 28/1/24	NC	Receipt for dates or grain
1313	75956	Cyr 7/11/1	F	Contract for boats; *Cyr* 23
1314	75957	Nbn 7/7/15	F	Receipt for flour; *Nbn* 890
1315	75958	Cam 9/9/3	C	Receipt for barley; *Cam* 197
1316	75959	Dar 23/10/24	F	Receipt for sheep
1317	75960	Dar 30/10/8	C	Receipt for silver; seal; *Dar* 241
1318	75961	Nbn 9/4/11	C	Receipt for wool; *Nbn* 514
1319	75962	Cam 8/12/3	F	Receipt for dates; *Cam* 220
1320	75963		F	Receipt for barley
1321	75964	Nbn -/5/3	C	Receipt for silver; *Nbn* 110
1322	75965	Nbn 1/2/3	C	Receipt for flour; *Nbn* 92
1323	75966	Nbn 22/3/8	C	Receipt for oil; *Nbn* 295
1324	75967	Nbn 11/12/16	NC	Account of garments of gods; *Nbn* 1015
1325	92787	Cyr 7/7/6	F	Account of garments of gods; *Cyr* 232
1326	75968	Ner 18/-/1	NC	Loan of silver
1327	75969	12/7/-	F	Receipt
1328	75970	Nbn 9/6/-	NC	Account of garments; *Nbn* 1090
1329	75971	Nbn 4/1/7	C	Purchase of flour; *Nbn* 249
1330	92691		C	*Aa* VIII/1; *CT* 12 10; *MSL* 14 489
1331	92692	Art -/12b/10	F	*Aa* III/4; *CT* 12 8; *MSL* 14 339
1332	93035		F	*Aa* II/6; *CT* 12 4; *MSL* 14 289
1332A	75972		F	Account of barley
1333	75973		F	Incantation and ritual
1334	75974		NC	Hymn to a goddess; dupls. 82-9-18, 8610 (= BM 68611), 82-9-18, 8067 (= BM 68069), Sp III 654 (= BM 36106) and *KAR* 109
1335		Joined to 81-11-3, 465 (= BM 47760)		
1336	92693	Art -/12b/10	C	*Aa* I/4; *CT* 12 1; *MSL* 14 280
1337	75975	Sar 12/5/3	F	Deposition; Babylon; Strassmaier, *8th Cong.* 2
1338	75976		F	Babylonian Chronicle, *TCS* 5 69, pl. 14
1339	75977		F	Babylonian Chronicle, *TCS* 5 69, pl. 14
1340	75978	Joined to 82-3-23, 1687 (= BM 50695)		
1341	92694		C	Diagnostic omens; *TDP* 2 52-56; 1 XXXV
1342	75979	Nbn 29/-/13	F	Account of workmen
1343	75980		F	Dates or grain ledger
1344	75981		F	School exercise
1345	75982		F	Account of dates or grain provisions (?)

AH 83-1-18,

1346	75983		F	Only personal names preserved
1347	75984	-/3/-	F	Account of dates or grain
1348	75985		F	Sumerian; *aluzinnu*
1349	75986	Dar	F	Ledger
1350	75987	Cyr 14/9/3	NC	Measurements of fields
1351	75988	Nbk -/-/40	F	Account
1352	75989		F	Account
1353	75990		F	*Ḫḫ* IV
1354	75991	OB	F	Sumerian incantation
1355	75992		F	Account of dates or grain
1356	75993		F	Account of garments of gods
1357	75994	Dar 8/5/28	F	Account of wool
1358	75995		F	Account of fodder and provisions
1359	75996		F	School exercise
1360	75997		F	Account
1361	75998		F	Economic
1362	75999	-/-/5	F	Account
1363	76000		F	Account
1364	76001		F	Ledger
1365	76002		F	Account of aromatics
1366	76003	Ner 10/1/-	F	Receipt for silver
1367	76004		F	Account of dates or grain
1368	76005		F	Account of barley
1369	76006		F	Account
1370	76007		F	Only personal names preserved
1371	76008		F	Account of dates or grain
1372	76009	Joined to 82-9-18, 6876 (= BM 66882)		
1373	76010		F	Account of dates or grain
1374	76011		F	Account of work on metals (?)
1375	76012		F	*Ḫḫ* II
1376	76013		F	*Ḫḫ* V
1377	76014		F	Dates or grain ledger
1378	76015	Nbn -/-/2	F	Account of dates or grain
1379	76016		F	Only personal names preserved
1380	76017	6/2/-	F	Account of garments(?) of gods
1381	76018	Npl 28/5/19	F	Receipt for sale of dates
1382	76019		F	Letter
1383	76020	Nbn -/10/14	F	Receipt for silver for dates
1384	76021		F	*Ḫḫ* VIII; literary extracts

AH 83-1-18,

1385	76022		F	*Enuma ana bit marṣi* II; *TDP*, p. 6ff., pl. 1-3
1386+ 83-1-21, 172	76023+ 83009		F	Medical prescription and incantation
1387	76024		F	*Ḫg*; *MSL* 9 185
1388	76025		F	*Ḫḫ* III
1389	76026		F	School exercise; Sumerian
1390	76027	Nbn 10/7/2	F	Receipt; *Nbn* 76
1391	93084		NC	Stone list; similar to *RA* 59 154ff.; *CT* 14 16
1392	76028		NC	Stone list; similar to *RA* 59 154ff.
1393	76029	Art -/2/32	F	Marriage contract
1394	76030		F	Account of silver
1395	76031		NC	Account
1396	76032		F	Ledger
1397	76033		F	Account of dates or grain
1398	76034		F	Legal; dialogue contract
1399	76035		F	Contract
1400	76036	Dar 10+/11/-	F	Animal ledger
1401	76037		F	Account of silver
1402	76038	25/2/-	F	Legal deposition
1403	76039		F	Account of barley
1404	76040		F	Account of silver
1405	76041		F	Account of dates or grain
1406	76042		F	School exercise; personal names
1407	76043	Dar 10+/1/25	NC	Account of garments
1408	76044		F	Account of barley
1409	76045		F	Account of dates or grain provisions(?)
1410	76046		NC	Account of date provisions for workmen
1411	76047	25/1/-	F	Barley ledger
1412	76048	(Dar) 28/-/26	F	Account of dates or grain provisions
1413	76049		F	Account of barley
1414	76050		F	Account of dates or grain
1415	76051		F	Religious text concerning Marduk
1416	76052	Dar	F	Account of house rents
1417	76053		F	Ritual
1418	76054		F	Account of grain
1419	76055	Dar -/8/-	NC	Account of dates or grain
1420	76056		F	Account

AH 83-1-18,

1421	76057		F	Lexical; reverse ruled prior to inscription; cf. AH 83-1-18, 1436 (= BM 76072)
1422	76058		F	*Ḫḫ* VI; literary extract
1423	76059		F	Account of dates or grain
1424	76060		F	Account of various purchases
1425	76061		F	School exercise
1426	76062		F	Bilingual
1427+ 1570	76063+ 76205		F	Literary; *En el*; commentary and unidentified extract
1428	76064	20/-/29	F	Receipt
1429	76065		F	Account
1430	76066	Joined to 82-9-18, 6950 (= BM 66956)		
1431	76067	Dar 15/2/28	F	Only personal names preserved
1432	76068		F	Receipt for oxen
1433	76069		F	Ledger
1434	76070		F	Account of dates or grain
1435	76071		F	Account of sheep
1436	76072		F	Lexical text; reverse ruled prior to inscription; same tablet as AH 83-1-18, 1421 (= BM 76057)
1437	76073	5/-/-	F	Account
1438		Joined to 82-9-18, 6876 (= BM 66882)		
1439	76074		F	Account of oxen(?)
1440	76075		F	Omens; *Šumma alu* XVII
1441	76076		F	Only witnesses preserved
1442	76077		F	Dates or grain ledger
1443	76078		F	Account of dates or grain
1444	76079	8/-/21	F	Receipt
1445	76080		F	Ritual; medical(?)
1446	76081		F	Account of garments(?) of gods
1447	76082	17/-/+7	F	Account of dates or grain provisions
1448	76083		F	Account
1449	76084		F	Letter(?)
1450	76085		F	Receipt
1451	76086	Nb(k) -/6/26	F	Contract for dates(?)
1452	76087		F	Only personal names preserved
1453	76088	28/1/18	F	Account of barley provisions
1454	76089		F	List of workmen(?)
1455	76090	19/3/-	F	Contract

AH 83-1-18,

1456	76091	NA	F	Economic or legal
1457	76092		F	Account
1458	76093	Dar 27/6/-	F	Rental(?) of a field
1459	76094	Nbk 20/1/20	F	Account of dates or grain
1460	76095		F	*Ḫḫ* IV
1461	76096		F	Account of dates or grain
1462	76097		F	Account
1463	76098		F	List of workmen(?)
1464	76099	Joined to 82-9-18, 4356 (= BM 64377)		
1465	76100	Nbn	F	Account
1466	76101		F	School exercise; Sumerian
1467	76102		F	Account
1468	76103	Nbn 6/8/6	F	Account of provisions
1469	76104	Nbn	F	Account of silver
1470	76105		F	Account
1471	76106		F	Dates or grain ledger
1472	76107		F	Account of jewelry of gods(?)
1473	76108	Joined to 82-9-18, 7137 (= BM 67141)		
1474	76109	Nbn 10+/12b/3	F	Receipt for fruit
1475	76110		F	Account
1476	76111		F	Account of dates or grain
1477	76112	20/12/30+	F	Account of workmen
1478	76113		F	Receipt
1479	76114		F	Account of dates or grain
1480	76115		F	School exercise
1481	76116		F	Ledger
1482	76117		F	Account
1483	76118		F	Account
1484	76119		F	Wool(?) ledger
1485	76120		F	Account of dates or grain
1486	76121		F	God list; dupl. *AfK* 2 9ff.
1487	76122		F	Account of dates or grain
1488	76123	Nbk 16/-/-	F	Receipt for tools
1489	76124		F	Account of dates or grain provisions(?)
1490	76125		F	Lexical and bilingual literary extracts
1491	76126		F	*Ḫḫ* I
1492	76127		F	Lexical
1493	76128		F	Letter
1494	76129	12/9/-	F	Account of garments of gods

AH 83-1-18,

1495	76130		F	*Ḫb* I
1496	76131		F	Account of dates
1497	76132		F	Account of barley
1498	76133	-/11/14	F	Ledger
1499	76134		F	Receipt
1500	76135		F	Account of dates or grain
1501	76136		F	Account of garments
1502	76137		F	Ritual
1503	76138		F	Account
1504	76139		F	Letter(?)
1505	76140		F	School exercise
1506	76141	10/9/1	F	Account of silver
1507	76142		F	School exercise
1508	76143	Nbn 30/5/-	F	Receipt for oxen
1509	76144		F	Bilingual and lexical
1510	76145		F	Account of barley
1511	76146		F	School exercise
1512	76147	11/-/17	F	Account of animals
1513	76148		F	Dates or grain ledger
1514	76149		F	Only personal names preserved
1515	76150		F	Receipt for dates or grain
1516	76151		F	Receipt for provisions
1517	76152		F	Account
1518	76153	Dar -/7/-	F	Account of dates
1519	76154		F	Receipt for purchase of salt
1520	76155	17/-/1	F	Account of garments
1521	76156		F	Account of purchase
1522	76157		F	Account of provisions(?)
1523	76158		F	Astronomical(?); cryptic numbers(?)
1524	76159		F	Dates or grain ledger
1525	76160		F	School exercise
1526	76161		F	Account of dates or grain
1527	76162		F	Literary
1528	76163		F	Economic(?)
1529	76164	Cyr	F	Receipt for barley
1530	76165		F	Account
1531	76166	-/3/13	F	Account of silver
1532	76167		F	Account of workmen
1533	76168		F	Account of purchases

AH 83-1-18,

1534	76169		F	Bilingual incantation; cf. 82-9-18, 5445 (= BM 65458)
1535	76170	19/9/11	F	Account of dates
1536	76171		F	Astronomical
1537	76172		F	Economic(?)
1538	76173		F	Ledger
1539	76174		F	*Ḫḫ* IV
1540	76175		F	Account of provisions
1541	76176		F	Lexical; literary extract
1542	76177		F	Lexical; cf. *Ḫḫ* IX
1543	76178		F	Account of barley and flour
1544	76179		F	Account
1545	76180		F	Barley ledger
1546	76181		F	Account of silver
1547	76182		F	Account of silver
1548	76183		F	Economic
1549	76184	Nbk -/-/22	F	Receipt for silver
1550	76185	Nbn 7/3/2	F	Account of fodder and provisions
1551	76186		F	School exercise
1552	76187		F	Account of provisions(?)
1553	76188		F	Account
1554	76189		F	Account of dates or grain
1555	76190		F	Letter; seal
1556	76191		F	Account
1557	76192		F	Ledger
1558	76193		F	Bilingual
1559	76194	Nbk 14/2/43	F	Receipt
1560	76195		F	Account of dates
1561	76196		F	School exercise; personal names
1562	76197	21/12/-	F	Account of workmen
1563	76198		F	Astronomical
1564	76199	Joined to 82-9-18, 1597 (= BM 61625)		
1565	76200		F	Account; only personal names preserved
1566	76201		F	Lexical
1567	76202		F	Marriage contract
1568	76203		F	Lexical
1569	76204		F	Account
1570	76205	Joined to AH 83-1-18, 1427 (= BM 76063)		

AH 83-1-18,

1571+	76206+		F	Literary; ritual
AH 83-1-18,				
1654+	76286+			
83-1-21, 83+	82920+			
83-1-21, 125+	82962+			
83-1-21, 136	82973			
1572	76207	-/3/-	F	Economic
1573	76208	Dar 7/6/28	F	Receipt for wool(?)
1574	76209		F	Account of dates
1575	76210		F	Account of workmen
1576+	76211+		F	Literary; *Šurpu* VIII
1581+				
1586+				
83-1-21, 153+	82990+			
83-1-21, 206	83043			
1577	76212	Ha 10/2/42	F	Contract or receipt
1578	76213	Ner -/11/-	F	Receipt for sale of barley
1579	76214		F	Animal ledger
1580	76215		F	Account of silver
1581		Joined to AH 83-1-18, 1576 (= BM 76211)		
1582	76216		F	Account of flour
1583	76217		F	Lexical
1584	76218	-/-/acc	F	Receipt
1585	76219		F	Account of purchases
1586		Joined to AH 83-1-18, 1576 (= BM 76211)		
1587	76220		F	Account of workmen and women
1588	76221	Dar 23/11/27	F	Account of dates or grain
1589	76222	Dar 9/4/-	F	Letter; seals
1590	76223		F	Account of provisions(?)
1591	76224	Joined to 82-9-18, 4163 (= BM 64188)		
1592	76225		F	Account of wool
1593	76226		F	Medical
1594	76227		F	Account of dates or grain provisions
1595	76228	Nbk 4/3/-	F	Receipt
1596	76229		F	Account of dates
1597	76230		F	Literary
1598	76231	Dar -/-/12	F	Account of dates or grain
1599	76232		F	Account of dates or grain
1600	76233		F	Account
1601	76234		F	Economic
1602	76235		F	Lexical

AH 83-1-18,

1603	76236	Nbn 13/4/-	F	Receipt
1604	76237		F	*Marduk's Address to the Demons*
1605	76238		F	God list; dupl. *AfK* 2 9ff.
1606	76239	Nbn -/12b/12	F	Receipt for dates or grain
1607	76240	8/-/41	F	Receipt for barley provisions
1608	76241		F	Account of wool(?)
1609	76242		F	School exercise
1610	76243		F	Account
1611	76244		F	Literary
1612	76245		F	Receipt for dates or grain
1613	76246		F	Economic
1614	76247		F	Literary
1615	76248	6/5/-	F	Receipt
1616	76249		F	Economic; inscription obliterated
1617	76250		F	Account
1618	76251		F	School exercise; personal names
1619	76252		F	Account
1620	76253		F	Account of provisions(?)
1621	76254	Nbn 13/2/13	F	Offering ledger
1622	76255		F	Account of bread
1623	76256		F	Literary
1624	76257		F	Literary
1625	76258	Nbk -/-/27	F	Receipt for silver
1626	76259		F	Account of barley
1627	76260	Cyr 13/-/2	F	Receipt for dates
1628	76261		F	Account of workmen
1629	76262		F	Account
1630	76263	25/-/-	F	Dates or grain ledger
1631	76264	23/-/-	F	Offering(?) ledger
1632	76265	29/2/39	F	Receipt
1633	76266		F	Economic
1634	76267	Dar	F	Account
1635	76268		F	Account
1636	76269		F	Account of garments of gods
1637	76270	Dar -/5/36	F	Letter; seals
1638	76271		F	Receipt for dates or grain
1639+ 1640	76272		F	Account of dates or grain
1640		Joined to AH 83-1-18, 1639 (= BM 76272)		

AH 83-1-18,

1641	76273		F	Economic
1642	76274		F	Literary
1643	76275		F	Receipt for barley provisions
1644	76276		F	Account of garments of gods
1645	76277	Nbn 23/5/2	NC	Receipt for a shovel
1646	76278		F	Account
1647	76279		F	School exercise
1648	76280		F	God list
1649	76281		F	Account
1650	76282	Cam 21/12/5	F	Receipt for purchase of wool
1651	76283	Ad -/-/14	F	Receipt; seal
1652	76284		F	Lexical; literary extract
1653	76285		F	Account of emmer
1654	76286	Joined to AH 83-1-18, 1571 (= BM 76206)		
1655	76287		F	Account of bitumen
1656	76288		F	Account
1657	76289		F	School exercise
1658	76290		F	Account of sheep(?)
1659	76291	Nbn -/-/7	F	Account of garments of gods(?)
1660	76292		F	Account
1661	76293		F	Account
1662	76294	Joined to 82-9-18, 5459 (= BM 65472)		
1663	76295		F	Account of silver(?)
1664	76296		F	School exercise
1665+ 1827	76297+ 76459		F	*Tintir* V
1666	76298		F	Account
1667	76299	Joined to 82-9-18, 6132 (= BM 66141)		
1668	76300		F	Receipt for silver
1669	76301	Joined to 82-9-18, 7135 (= BM 67139)		
1670	76302		F	Receipt
1671	76303		F	Literary
1672	76304		F	Ledger
1673	76305		F	Bilingual and lexical; school exercise
1674	76306		F	Account of workmen
1675	76307		F	Account of dates or grain
1676	76308		F	Account
1677	76309		F	Account
1678	76310		F	Lexical

AH 83-1-18,

1679	76311		F	Literary
1680	76312		F	Gate lists of Esagil
1681	76313	Nbk -/12/22	F	Receipt
1682	76314		F	School exercise
1683	76315	3/1/2	F	Account of barley
1684	76316		F	Animal ledger
1685	76317		F	Literary extract; hymn
1686	76318		F	Offering ledger
1687	76319		F	Literary
1688	76320		C	Label; receipt
1689	76321		F	Account of tithes
1690	76322		F	Account of dates or grain
1691	76323		F	Lexical
1692	76324	Cyr 9/2/4	F	Sales receipt
1693	76325		F	Literary
1694	76326		F	*Ḫḫ* III
1695	76327		F	Lexical
1696	76328		F	Receipt for dates or grain
1697	76329		F	Receipt
1698	76330		F	Ledger
1699	76331		F	Economic
1700	76332		F	Economic
1701	76333	Dar 20/1/-	F	Account of dates or grain
1702	76334	Dar 25/8/-	F	Receipt for wool
1703	76335	Nbk 6/-/41	F	Receipt for sheep as tithe
1704	76336	Nbn 24/6/9	F	Receipt for barley
1705	76337	Nbk -/3/21	F	Animal ledger
1706	76338		F	Receipt for iron
1707	76339		F	Account of barley
1708	76340		F	Account of dates or grain
1709	76341		F	Account
1710	76342	23/9/14	F	Account of workmen
1711	76343		F	Account of workmen
1712	76344		F	Dates or grain ledger
1713	76345	Nbn -/-/4	F	Receipt for dates or grain
1714	76346		F	Account of dates or grain
1715	76347	17/1/28 Dar	F	Account of wool
1716	76348	Joined to K.11151		
1717	76349		F	School exercise

AH 83-1-18,

1718	76350		F	Animal ledger
1719	76351		F	Account of dates or grain
1720	76352		F	Ritual
1721	76353		F	Receipt
1722	76354		F	Economic
1723	76355		F	Account of dates
1724	76356	Nbk 3/3/17	F	Account of garments of gods
1725	76357		F	Account of workmen
1726	76358	Nbn -/-/8	F	Receipt
1727	76359	16/-/13	F	Account of silver for temple work
1728	76360	30/-/-	F	Account of barley
1729	76361		F	Ledger
1730	76362	Nbk 8/-/-	F	Receipt for bitumen
1731	76363	Nbn 15/3/-	F	Receipt for oxen
1732	76364		F	Account of dates or grain
1733	76365		F	Dates or grain ledger
1734	76366		F	Account of silver
1735	76367	(Nbk) 9/-/42	F	Receipt for silver income
1736	76368		F	List of people
1737	76369		F	Receipt for oxen
1738	76370		F	Ledger
1739	76371		F	Dates or grain ledger
1740	76372	22/8/-	F	Account of provisions
1741	76373		F	Account of dates
1742	76374	Joined to K.11151		
1743	76375	Nbk 8/2/17	F	Receipt
1744	76376		F	Account of dates(?)
1745	76377	Ner 20/10/-	F	Account of dates
1746	76378		F	Account of silver(?)
1747	76379		F	Account of aromatics
1748	76380		F	Lexical; literary extract
1749	76381		F	Account of garments(?)
1750	76382		F	Account of garments(?) of gods
1751+ 1791	76383+ 76423		F	School exercise; literary extract
1752	76384		F	Account
1753	76385		F	List of people
1754	76386	-/-/10	F	Account of dates or grain
1755	76387		F	*Ḫḫ* IV

AH 83-1-18,

1756	76388		F	Account of dates or grain
1757	76389		F	Account of wool(?)
1758	76390		F	Account of workmen
1759	76391		F	School exercise
1760	76392	25/-/-	F	Account of dates
1761	76393	12/4/15	F	Receipt for wool
1762	76394		F	Animal ledger
1763	76395	21/-/1	F	Dates or grain ledger
1764	76396		F	Account of oxen(?)
1765	76397	Ner -/3/1	F	Account of cows
1766	76398	4/7/-	F	Receipt
1767	76399		F	Account of wool
1768	76400		F	Astronomical omens
1769	76401		F	Account of dates or grain
1770	76402		F	Account of sheep
1771	76403		F	Contract
1772	76404	Nbn 7/2/-	F	Receipt for oxen
1773	76405		F	Account of grain for flour
1774	76406		F	Account of provisions
1775	76407	Nbk 17/1/19	F	Barley ledger
1776	76408		F	S^a
1777	76409		F	Account of dates or grain
1778	76410		F	Account of dates
1779	76411	Cam 10/-/7	F	Receipt for dates
1780	76412	-/8/-	F	Ledger
1781	76413	14/7/-	F	Account of *sattukku*
1782	76414	Nb(-) 10/3/-	F	Receipt for metal objects
1783	76415		F	Receipt
1784	76416	21/-/13	F	Account of wool
1785	76417		F	Accounts
1786	76418		F	Accounts
1787	76419		F	Letter
1788	76420	Nbn 8/9/8	F	Receipt for dates
1789	76421	Dar -/-/27	F	Account of dates or grain
1790	76422		F	Accounts
1791	76423	Joined to AH 83-1-18, 1751 (= BM 76383)		
1792	76424		F	Accounts
1793	76425		F	Account of dates or grain
1794	76426		F	*Ḫḫ* I

AH 83-1-18,

1795	76427		F	Economic
1796	76428		F	Economic
1797	76429	-/8/-	F	Animal ledger
1798	76430	-/2/-	F	Animal ledger
1799	76431		F	Account of barley
1800	76432		F	Account of dates or grain
1801	76433		F	Unidentified
1802	76434		F	Account of garments
1803	76435		F	School exercise
1804	76436		F	Barley ledger
1805	76437		F	School exercise
1806	76438		F	Only personal names preserved
1807	76439		F	Account of sheep(?)
1808	76440		F	Accounts
1809	76441		F	Letter(?)
1810	76442		F	Account of silver(?)
1811	76443		F	Contract for garments
1812	76444		F	Receipt
1813	76445		F	List of peoples
1814	76446		F	Only personal names preserved
1815	76447	Cyr 26/12/acc	F	Account of dates
1816	76448		F	List of people
1817	76449		F	Traces of three signs
1818	76450	Cam 1/9/3	F	Economic
1819	76451		F	Accounts
1820	76452		F	Seed ledger
1821	76453	Nbk 26/3/36	F	Loan of silver
1822	76454		F	Receipt for delivery of sheep
1823	76455	10+/3/-	F	Account of dates
1824	76456	Nbn 6/11/10	F	Receipt
1825	76457	9/1/31	F	Receipt for barley
1826	76458		F	Receipt
1827	76459	Joined to AH 83-1-18, 1665 (= BM 76297)		
1828	76460		F	Account of silver
1829	76461	-/-/2	F	Receipt for iron
1830	76462		F	No inscription remains
1831	76463		F	Accounts
1832	76464		F	Receipt for wool(?)
1833	76465		F	Sale(?) of sheep

AH 83-1-18,

1834	76466		F	Account of dates or grain
1835	76467		F	Account of barley
1836	76468		F	Account of garments of gods
1837	76469		F	Account of rentals
1838	76470	Dar	F	Loan of silver
1839	76471		F	Letter
1840	76472		F	Accounts
1841	76473		F	Only KAM sign remains
1842	76474		F	No longer inscribed
1843	76475		F	Economic
1844	76476		F	Economic
1845	76477		F	Sale of a house and furnishings
1846	76478		F	*Ḫḫ* I; *MSL* 5 6!
1847	76479	Philip I -/1/7	F	*Ḫḫ* I
1848	76480	Joined to 82-9-18, 1597 (= BM 61625)		
1849	76481		F	School exercise
1850	76482		F	*Ḫḫ* I
1851	76483		F	Medical
1852	76484		F	School exercise
1853	76485		F	Lexical
1854		Joined to 82-9-18, 5622 (= BM 93086)		
1855	76486		F	Dates or grain ledger
1856	91011		F	Incantation against SAG.GIG
1857	76487		F	Commentary; *CT* 41 45; rev. not copied
1858	76488		F	Astronomical procedures
1859	76489		F	Bird call text; dupl. of *AnSt* 20 112
1860	76490		F	Bilingual hymn; prayer; *Ḫḫ* V; dupl. Rm. 450; K.4982+ K.5050; Liverpool 63-188-4
1861	76491	Joined to 82-9-18, 5445 (= BM 65458)		
1862	76492		F	*Marduk prayer* 1; two columns; dupl. *AfO* 19 55ff.
1863+ 83-1-28, 188	76493+ 83025		F	Nippur temple list
1864	76494		F	*Ḫḫ* VIIA; *Tintir* IV; bilingual extract
1865	76495		F	Medical; two columns
1866	76496		F	School exercise; personal names; geographical names, etc.
1867	76497	Joined to 82-9-18, 5437 (= BM 65450)		
1868	76498	Joined to 82-9-18, 6950 (= BM 66956)		

AH 83-1-18,

1869	76499		F	Bilingual excerpt; *Ḫḫ* I
1870	76500		F	Literary extract and *Ḫḫ* IV; *MSL* 9 168
1871	76501		F	Bilingual; Nabu *Eršaḫunga*
1872	76502		F	Lexical; cf. *Ḫḫ* XI
1873	76503		F	School exercise
1874	76504		F	House or field plan and specifications
1875	76505		F	MUL.APIN I
1876	76506	Joined to 82-9-18, 6876 (= BM 66882)		
1877	76507		F	Account(?) of sacrifices(?)
1878	76508	Joined to 82-9-18, 6959 (= BM 66965)		
1879	76509		F	Literary extracts; *Ḫḫ* IV
1880	76510		F	Medical
1881	76511	Joined to 82-9-18, 1607 (= BM 61635)		
1882	76512	Dar	F	Contract
1883	76513		F	Account of dates or grain
1884	76514		F	School exercise
1885	76515		F	Medical
1886	76516	Joined to 82-7-14, 983 (= BM 56601)		
1887	76517		F	*Tintir* V
1888	76518		F	List of people
1889	76519		F	*Šumma alu* XL
1890	76520		F	*Ḫḫ* III
1891	76521		F	Literary
1892	76522		F	Lexical
1893	76523		F	Accounts
1894	76524		F	Account of dates or grain
1895	76525		F	Account of dates or grain
1896	76526		F	Animal ledger
1897	76527		F	*Ḫḫ* VI
1898	76528	29/6/-	F	School exercise
1899	76529		F	Account of dates or grain
1900	76530		F	Account of barley
1901+ 1945	76531+ 76574		F	Ritual
1902	76532		F	School exercise
1903	76533	-/-/3	F	Receipt for sale of wool
1904	76534	15/5/-	F	Receipt for silver
1905	93081		F	Bilingual incantation

AH 83-1-18,

1906	76535	Nbn -/7/9	F	Receipt for sheep given to finance a caravan
1907	76536	-/1/-	F	Account of house rentals
1908	76537		F	Lexical
1909	76538		F	Account of dates or grain
1910	76539		F	Account of barley
1911	76540		F	Account of dates
1912	76541		F	Bilingual; lexical
1913	76542		F	Accounts
1914	76543		F	Literary extract and lexical; dupl. *ZA* 30 189
1915	76544	Nbn	F	Royal inscription
1916	76545		F	Account of dates or grain
1917	76546	Temporarily missing		
1918	76547		F	Literary
1919	76548	-/1/-	F	Ledger
1920	76549	Art 25/6/-	F	Contract for dates; stamp seals
1921	76550		F	Account of dates or grain
1922+ 2158	76551+ 76786		F	Astrological
1923	76552		F	Incantations and prescriptions
1924	76553		F	*Ḫḫ* IX; literary extract
1925	76554		F	Dates or grain ledger
1926	76555		F	Accounts(?)
1927	76556	Nb(-) -/-/15	F	Receipt for barley
1928	76557		F	Medical (plants)
1929	76558	Nbn -/-/9	F	Account of dates
1930	76559		F	Account of dates or grain
1931	76560	11/10/-	F	Account of barley
1932	76561		F	Ledger
1933	76562		F	Account of birds
1934	76563		F	Lexical and literary extract
1935	76564		F	Lexical
1936	76565		F	Economic
1937	76566		F	*Ḫḫ* V
1938	76567		F	House sale
1939	76568		F	School exercise
1940	76569		F	Accounts
1941	76570		F	Literary
1942	76571		F	Economic

AH 83-1-18,

1943	76572		F	Account of dates or grain
1944+ 83-1-21, 206	76573+ 83037		F	Bilingual *Ḫulbazizi* incantation; extract
1945	76574	Joined to 83-1-18, 1901 (= BM 76531)		
1946	76575		F	School exercise; personal names
1947	76576		F	Ledger
1948	76577	Nbk 2/11/-	F	Accounts of various commodities
1949	76578		F	Literary
1950	76579	Cam	F	Account of dates or grain
1951	76580		F	Account of dates
1952	76581	Nbk?	F	Receipt for a pledge
1953	76582		F	Lexical
1954	76583		F	*Ḫḫ* IV
1955	76584		F	Account of workmen
1956	76585		F	*Ḫḫ* IV(?)
1957	76586		F	Omens(?)
1958	76587		F	Account of dates or grain
1959	76588		F	Receipt for bitumen
1960	76589		F	Account of barley
1961	76590		F	Account of garments of gods
1962	76591		F	Accounts of grain or dates
1963	76592	Nbn -/-/5	F	Receipt for purchases
1964	76593		F	Accounts
1965	76594		F	Account of silver
1966	76595		F	Dates or grain ledger
1967	76596		F	Account of dates or grain
1968	76597		F	Lexical
1969	76598		F	Account of dates or grain provisions
1970	76599		F	School exercise
1971+ 2393	76600+ 77018		F	Bilingual
1972	76601		F	Account of seed
1973	76602		F	*Ḫḫ* III
1974+ 2160	76603+ 76788		F	*Ḫḫ* I
1975	76604		F	Ledger
1976	76605		F	Astrological
1977	76606		F	List of names
1978	76607		F	School exercise

AH 83-1-18,

1979	76608		F	*Aluzinnu*; dupl. Bu 89-4-26, 268 (= BM 78973); 2 *R* 60
1980	76609		F	Account of vines
1981	76610		F	*Ḫḫ* XV; *MSL* 9 4
1982	76611		F	Account of sheep(?)
1983	76612		F	Ledger
1984	76613		F	Account of dates or grain
1985	76614		F	Ritual (medical?)
1986	76615		F	Only personal names preserved
1987	76616		F	Lexical
1988	76617		F	Economic; stamp seal
1989	76618		F	*Ḫḫ* IV
1990	76619		F	Accounts
1991	76620		F	Lexical
1992	76621		F	*Ḫḫ* VI
1993	76622		F	Ledger
1994	76623		F	Economic
1995	76624		F	Bilingual incantation to ^{d}SIG$_{4}$
1996	76625		F	*Ḫḫ* III
1997	76626	Cam 8/8/acc	F	Deposition
1998	76627		F	Contract
1999	76628		F	Bilingual(?); two columns
2000	76629		F	Lexical
2001	76630	Cyr -/-/3	F	Audit report
2002	76631	Art	F	Legal; stamp seals
2003	76632		F	Contract for dates
2004	76633		F	Account of sheep
2005	76634		F	Dates or grain ledger
2006	76635		F	*Ḫḫ* VIII(?); literary extracts
2007	76636		F	School exercise
2008	76637		F	Contract
2009	76638		F	Account of dates or grain
2010	76639		F	Offering ledger
2011	76640		F	Literary
2012	76641		F	Ledger
2013+ 83-1-21, 1789	76642+ 93053		F	*Lamaštu*; cf. 83-1-21, 154 (= BM 82991)
2014	76643		F	Astronomical omens
2015	76644	Nbk -/-/2	F	Receipt for sheep

AH 83-1-18,

2016	76645		F	Economic
2017	76646		F	Accounts
2018	76647		F	Ritual
2019	76648		F	Economic
2020	76649		F	Account of provisions
2021	76650		F	Ledger
2022	76651		F	Offering ledger
2023	76652		F	Accounts
2024	76653		F	*Izbu* X
2025	76654		F	Accounts
2026	76655		F	Lexical(?)
2027	76656		F	Economic
2028	76657	Nbk -/-/41	F	Account of garments of gods
2029	76658		F	Dates or grain ledger
2030	76659	Dar -/-/23	F	Account of garments of gods
2031	76660		F	Account of workmen
2032	76661		F	Commentary(?)
2033	76662		F	*Ḫḫ* III
2034	76663	Joined to 82-9-18, 8032 (= BM 68034)		
2035	76664		F	School exercise
2036	76665		F	Accounts
2037	76666		F	Precepts; dupl. Lambert, *BWL* 99f.
2038	76667		F	Accounts
2039	76668		F	Economic
2040	76669		F	Account of silver
2041	76670		F	Account of dates
2042	76671		F	Rituals of the *zabbu* priest; *AfO* 29/30 6, 13
2043	76672	Joined to Rm IV 411 (= BM 33851)		
2044	76673		F	Account of dates or grain
2045	76674		F	School exercise
2046	76675		F	Bilingual incantation(?)
2047	76676		F	Account of dates
2048	76677		F	Bilingual
2049	76678		F	Accounts
2050	76679	Joined to 82-9-18, 6132 (= BM 66141)		
2051	76680		F	School exercise
2052	76681		F	Economic
2053	76682		F	Account of silver
2054	76683		F	Omens

AH 83-1-18,

2055+ 83-1-21, 143	76684+ 82980		F	Bilingual incantation
2056	76685		F	Account of wool
2057	76686		F	Account of silver(?)
2058	76687		F	Literary
2059	76688		F	Accounts
2060	76689		F	Lexical(?)
2061	76690		F	Account of dates or grain
2062	76691		F	School exercise
2063	76692		F	Literary
2064	76693		F	School exercise
2065	76694		F	Lexical and literary; extract
2066	76695		F	Commentary
2067	76696		F	Accounts
2068	76697		F	Accounts of provisions(?)
2069	76698		F	Lexical and bilingual extract
2070	76699		F	Accounts
2071	76700		F	Ledger
2072	76701	Dar -/-/5	F	Letter; stamp seal; *CT* 22 108
2073+ 83-1-21, 81	76702+ 82918		F	Bilingual incantation
2074	76703		F	Astronomical procedure; *ACT* type
2075	76704		F	Account of garments of gods
2076	76705		F	Account of dates
2077	76706		F	Account of barley
2078	76707	Nb(-) -/-/2	F	Account of grain and fruit
2079	76708		F	School exercise
2080	76709		F	School exercise
2081	76710		F	School exercise
2082	76711		F	Account of silver for objects
2083	76712		F	Ledger
2084	76713		F	School exercise; personal names
2085	76714	-/-/16+	F	Receipt for a sale
2086	76715		F	Ledger
2087	76716		F	Contract
2088	76717		F	Account of silver
2089	76718		F	Bilingual
2090	76719		F	Literary
2091	76720		F	Ledger
2092	76721		F	Accounts

AH 83-1-18,

2093	76722		F	Exchange of dates and emmer
2094	76723		F	Ledger
2095	76724		F	Account of dates or grain
2096	76725	17/5/10	F	Receipt
2097	76726		F	Probably accounts
2098	76727	Cyr 28/1/-	F	Receipt for dates or grain as wages
2099+ 83-1-21, 182	76728+ 83019		F	Prayer
2100	76729		F	Economic
2101	76730		F	School exercise
2102	76731		F	*Ḫḫ* VI
2103	76732		F	School exercise; literary extract
2104	76733		F	Account of dates or grain
2105	76734		F	Account of jewelry mountings
2106	76735		F	Contract
2107	76736		F	Ledger
2108	76737		F	Accounts
2109+ 2185	76738+ 76813		F	Astronomical; collection of observations of Saturn, Kandalanu years 1-14
2110	76739	-/5/-	F	Accounts
2111	76740		F	Astronomical omens(?)
2112+ 83-1-21, 34	76741+ 82871		F	*Ḫḫ* XV; *MSL* 9 4
2113	76742		F	Unidentified
2114	76743		F	*Ḫḫ* II
2115	76744		F	Accounts
2116		Joined to 82-9-18, 5448 (= BM 65461)		
2117	76745		F	Lexical(?) extract
2118	76746		F	Lexical; literary extract; mythological
2119	76747	Cam 5/10/2	F	Account of wool
2120	76748		F	God list
2121	76749		F	Bilingual incantation
2122	76750	4/8/-	F	Account of workmen
2123	76751		F	Account of dates or grain
2124	76752	22/9/-	F	Receipt for barley
2125	76753		F	Lexical
2126	76754	Cyr -/5/1	F	Account of barley
2127	76755		F	Account of barley
2128	76756		F	*Ḫḫ* III; *MSL* 9 159
2129	76757		F	Accounts

AH 83-1-18,

2130	76758		F	Receipt
2131	76759		F	Receipt for barley
2132	76760	22/-/-	F	Ledger
2133	76761		F	Account of dates or grain
2134	76762		F	Literary; dupl. *STT* 1 71
2135	76763	Nbk -/3/20	F	Contract for purchase of oxen, barley, etc.
2136	76764		F	Offering ledger
2137	76765		F	Account of sheep
2138	76766	27/6/14	F	Account of workmen
2139	76767		F	Accounts
2140	76768		F	Ledger
2141	76769		F	Lexical and literary extract
2142	76770		F	Accounts of wool
2143	76771		NC	Account of garments of gods
2144	76772	-/10/9	F	Receipt for metal object
2145	76773	Nbk 14/5/33	NC	Receipt for bitumen(?)
2146	76774	Dar 26/2/35	F	Receipt
2147	76775		F	Literary
2148	76776		F	Account of dates or grain
2149	76777		F	Account of dates or grain
2150	76778		F	Account of garments of gods
2151	76779		F	Accounts
2152	76780		F	Account of dates
2153	76781		F	Ledger
2154	76782		F	Accounts
2155	76783		F	Ritual(?)
2156	76784	2/-/1	NC	Receipt for sheep
2157	76785	Nbk -/6/33	F	Letter
2158	76786	Joined to AH 83-1-18, 1922 (= BM 76551)		
2159	76787		F	Account of dates or grain
2160	76788	Joined to AH 83-1-18, 1974 (= BM 76603)		
2161	76789		F	Accounts
2162	76790	Nbn -/2/9	F	Account of dates and wool
2163	76791		F	Accounts
2164	76792		F	Contract(?)
2165	76793		F	School exercise
2166	76794		F	Account of bricks
2167	76795		F	Animal ledger

AH 83-1-18,

2168	76796	15/-/-	F	Account of dates or grain
2169	76797		F	School exercise
2170	76798	16/10/-	F	Accounts
2171	76799		F	Unidentified
2172	76800		F	Contract(?)
2173	76801		F	Loan of silver
2174	76802		F	Uninscribed
2175	76803		F	Omens
2176	76804		F	Lexical
2177	76805	Nbn 26/6/-	F	Receipt
2178	76806		F	Accounts
2179	76807	30/5/1	F	Receipt
2180	76808		F	Literary; two columns
2181	76809		F	Account
2182	76810		F	Account of barley provisions
2183	76811	Ner 1/-/3	F	Receipt
2184	76812		F	Account of dates
2185	76813	Joined to AH 83-1-18, 2109 (= BM 76738)		
2186	76814		F	Unidentified
2187	76815		F	Account of sheep(?)
2188	76816		F	Offering ledger
2189	76817		F	Unidentified
2190	76818		F	School exercise
2191	76819		F	Account of oxen
2192	76820		F	Account of dates or grain
2193	76821		F	Account of dates or grain
2194	76822		F	*Ḫḫ* II
2195	76823		F	Lexical
2196	76824		F	Literary
2197	76825		F	Royal inscription; NB
2198	76826		F	Letter
2199	76827		F	Dates or grain ledger
2200	76828		F	Accounts; only personal names preserved
2201	76829		F	List of zodiac constellations
2202	76830		F	Accounts
2203	76831	1/3/35	F	Accounts
2204	76832	Joined to 82-9-18, 6876 (= BM 66882)		
2205	76833		F	School exercise

AH 83-1-18,

2206	76834	-/-/2	F	Account of pomegranates
2207	76835	Nb(-) 14/-/-	F	Receipt
2208	76836	18/12/7	F	Account of garments of gods
2209	76837	-/12/5	F	Account of barley
2210	76838		F	Account of stones
2211	76839	Ner	F	Receipt for dates
2212	76840	22/7/-	F	Account of barley
2213	76841		F	Literary; hymn(?); dupl. to K.6461
2214	76842		F	Accounts
2215	76843	Cyr 19/3/2	F	Barley contract
2216	76844		F	School exercise
2217	76845		F	Unidentified
2218	76846		F	Unidentified
2219	76847		F	*Ḫḫ* IV
2220	76848		F	Account of barley
2221	76849		F	Plants, stones and trees
2222	76850		F	Dates or grain ledger
2223	76851	Nbn 28/11/15	F	Account
2224	76852		F	Account of sheep
2225	76853		F	Uninscribed
2226	76854		F	School exercise
2227	76855	Nbn 11/5/-	F	Receipt
2228	76856		F	Account of dates or grain
2229	76857		F	Lexical
2230	76858		F	God list
2231	76859		F	Lexical
2232	76860	Ner	F	Receipt for barley provisions
2233	76861		F	Receipt
2234	76862		F	Accounts
2235	76863		F	Bilingual(?)
2236	76864	21/3/-	F	Receipt for barley
2237	76865		F	*Ḫḫ* I
2238	76866		F	Account of dates or grain
2239	76867		F	Account of dates or grain
2240	76868		F	Account of garments of gods
2241	76869	Dar 4/12/acc	F	Account of barley
2242	76870	Dar -/-/15	F	Receipt
2243	76871		F	School exercise
2244	76872		F	Account of dates or grain

AH 83-1-18,

2245	76873		F	Account of garments of gods
2246	76874	-/10/-	F	Receipt for dates or grain
2247	76875		F	Literary; two columns
2248	76876		F	Literary extract(?)
2249	76877		F	Omens
2250	76878	6/-/15	F	Receipt for wool
2251	76879	7/5/-	F	Account of barley
2252	76880		F	List of people
2253	76881		F	School exercise
2254	76882		F	School exercise; personal names
2255	76883		F	Account of garments of gods
2256	76884		F	*Tintir* IV; traces
2257	76885		F	Accounts by day
2258	76886	8/7/-	F	Account of sheep
2259	76887		F	Topographical
2260	76888		F	Lexical
2261	76889		F	Only personal names preserved
2262	76890		F	School exercise
2263	76891		F	Bilingual
2264	76892		F	Lexical (GIŠ)
2265	76893	Nb(-) 9/1/26	F	Receipt
2266	76894	30/4/-	F	Account of sheep
2267	76895		F	School exercise
2268	76896		F	Animal ledger
2269	76897		F	Account of dates
2270	76898		F	Lexical
2271	76899		F	Omens; cf. AH 83-1-18, 2276 (= BM 76904)
2272	76900	Nbn -/-/7	F	Receipt for garments
2273	76901		F	Account of dates or grain
2274	76902	14/-/2	F	Account of dates or grain
2275	76903		F	Lexical
2276	76904		F	Omens; cf. AH 83-1-18, 2271 (= BM 76899)
2277	76905	Nb(-) -/10/6	F	Receipt
2278	76906		F	Account of workmen
2279	76907		F	Only personal names preserved
2280	76908		F	Literary
2281	76909		F	Receipt for barley
2282	76910		F	Receipt

AH 83-1-18,

2283	76911	Nbn 24/11/10	F	Receipt for purchase of dates
2284	76912		F	Account of sheep(?)
2285	76913		F	Economic
2286	76914		F	Incantation
2287	76915		F	Only personal names preserved
2288	76916		C	Account of silver(?)
2289	76917		F	Astronomical
2290	76918		F	School exercise; personal names
2291	76919		F	Accounts
2292	76920		F	Economic
2293	76921		F	Account of dates
2294	76922		F	Omens
2295	76923	Nb(-) -/7/3	F	Receipt for silver(?)
2296	76924		F	Receipt for iron for spades
2297	76925	Joined to 82-9-18, 862 (= BM 60886)		
2298	76926		F	Account of silver for jewelry
2299	76927		F	Account of barley
2300	76928	Nbn -/9/9	F	Receipt for barley
2301	76929		F	Lexical
2302	76930		F	Receipt
2303	76931		F	Receipt
2304	76932		F	Lexical
2305	76933		F	Bilingual(?)
2306	76934		F	Account of dates
2307	76935		F	Bilingual(?); extracts
2308	76936	Dar	F	Sales receipt
2309	76937	Nbn -/11/-	F	Accounts
2310	76938		F	Lexical(?)
2311	76939	Nbk? 7/6/36	F	Receipt for sesame
2312	76940	-/1/10	F	Receipt for oxen
2313	76941		F	Accounts
2314	76942		F	Accounts
2315	76943	Dar 10/6/10	F	Receipt
2316	76944		F	Sales receipt
2317	76945		F	Accounts
2318	76946	Joined to 82-9-18, 5984 (= BM 65992)		
2319	76947		F	Account of dates or grain
2320	76948	Nbn 11/-/10	F	Receipt for silver
2321	76949		F	School exercise

AH 83-1-18,

2322	76950		F	Receipt for silver(?)
2323	76951		F	Receipt
2324	76952	Nbn	F	Receipt for barley
2325	76953		F	Accounts
2326	76954		F	Lexical
2327	76955		F	Account of seed and oxen
2328	76956		F	School exercise
2329	76957		F	Contract(?)
2330	76958		F	Accounts
2331	76959		F	Account of garments of gods
2332	76960		F	Prayer
2333	76961		F	Lexical
2334	76962		F	Lexical
2335	76963	Nbn	F	Account of garments of gods
2336	76964	Nbk 28/10/16	F	List of workmen
2337	76965		F	Account of dates or grain
2338	76966		F	Lexical(?)
2339	76967		F	Sumerian
2340+ 2361+ 2463	76968+ 77085	Sel/Ant	NC	Marriage document; stamp seals; Borsippa; dupl. AH 83-1-18, 2344 (= BM 76972)
2341	76969		F	*Ḫḫ* III; *MSL* 9 159
2342	76970		C	Astronomical omens
2343	76971		F	Legal; division of a field(?)
2344+ 2469+ 2522	76972	Sel/Ant 27/11/108	F	Marriage document; stamp seals; Borsippa; dupl. AH 83-1-18, 2340 (= BM 76968)
2345+ 2408+ 2411	76973+ 77033		F	Astronomical
2346	76974		F	*Ḫḫ* X(?); Sumerian incantation
2347	76975		F	School exercise
2348	76976		F	Incantation; Farber, *Atti Ištar* 127, pls. 15-16
2349	76977		F	School exercise
2350	76978		C	School exercise
2351	76979		F	School exercise
2352+ 2367	76980		F	*Ḫḫ* I and literary extract
2353	76981		F	Sale of a field
2354	76982		F	School exercise

AH 83-1-18,

2355	76983		F	School exercise
2356+ 2468	76984+ 77090		F	Mathematical table
2357	76985		F	Commentary
2358	76986		F	Literary; dupl. *KAR* 165
2359	93032		F	S^b; *CT* 11 26
2360	76987		NC	Economic
2361		Joined to AH 83-1-18, 2340 (= BM 76968)		
2362	76988		F	Account of wool(?)
2363	76989		F	Incantation
2364	76990		F	Astronomical
2365	76991		F	*Ḫḫ* III
2366	76992		F	Accounts
2367		Joined to AH 83-1-18, 2352 (= BM 76980)		
2368	76993		F	Economic
2369	76994		F	School exercise
2370	76995		F	Accounts
2371	76996		F	Literary
2372	76997		F	Sales contract
2373	76998	Dar 27/12a/20+	F	Sale of a house
2374	76999	Cyr 2/2/acc	NC	Contract
2375	77000		F	Legal deposition
2376	77001		F	School exercise
2377	77002		F	Bilingual(?)
2378	77003	9/-/-	F	Accounts
2379	77004		F	*Ḫḫ* II; literary extract
2380	77005		F	School exercise
2381	77006		F	School exercise
2382	77007	Dar 28/10/9	C	Loan of silver
2383	77008		F	Uninscribed
2384	77009		F	Loan of silver
2385	77010		F	Contract for slaves
2386	77011		F	School exercise
2387	77012		F	Literary
2388+ 2435	77013		F	*Tintir* IV
2389	77014		F	Literary
2390	77015		F	Economic
2391	77016		F	Lexical(?)
2392	77017		F	School exercise

AH 83-1-18,

2393	77018	Joined to AH 83-1-18, 1971 (= BM 76600)		
2394	77019		F	Loan of silver
2395	77020		F	Contract
2396	77021		F	Incantation
2397	77022		F	Geographical list
2398	77023	NA	F	Inscribed bullae
2399	77024		F	Economic
2400	77025		F	School exercise
2401	77026		F	Lexical
2402	77027		F	School exercise
2403	77028		F	Akkadian Marduk hymn; tablet 25 of ÉŠ.GÀR ᵈEN ⌜x⌝
2404	77029		F	*Tintir* V
2405+ 2518	77030+ 77139		F	Astronomical omens
2406	77031		F	Literary
2407	77032		F	School exercise
2408	77033	Joined to AH 83-1-18, 2345 (= BM 76973)		
2409	77034		F	Literary
2410	77035	Nbk 17/4/-	F	Rental(?) of a house
2411		Joined to AH 83-1-18, 2345 (= BM 76973)		
2412	77036		F	School exercise
2413	77037		F	School exercise
2414	77038		F	School exercise
2415	77039		F	Only personal names preserved
2416	77040		F	School exercise
2417	77041		F	Prescription against Antašubba
2418	77042		F	School exercise
2419	77043		F	Bilingual incantation
2420	77044		F	Astronomical omens
2421	77045		F	Accounts
2422	77046		F	Omens derived from spitting
2423	77047	Cam -/-/22	F	Loan of silver
2424	77048		F	School exercise
2425	77049		F	Incantations against fever
2426	77050		F	Contract; Borsippa
2427	77051		F	Astronomical; numbers only
2428	77052		F	School exercise
2429	77053		F	School exercise
2430	77054		F	MUL.APIN

AH 83-1-18,

2431	77055		F	School exercise
2432	77056		F	Incantation and ritual
2433	77057		F	School exercise
2434	77058		NC	Dreams concerning stars; Pinches, *RT* 19 101-104
2435		Joined to AH 83-1-18, 2388 (= BM 77013)		
2436	77059		F	School exercise
2437	77060		F	Ritual
2438	77061		F	Sale of reeds
2439+ 2442	77062+ 77065		F	Prayer(?)
2440	77063		F	School exercise
2441	77064		F	School exercise
2442	77065	Joined to AH 83-1-18, 2439 (= BM 77062)		
2443	77066		F	Incantation against ghosts
2444	77067		F	Letter
2445	77068		F	School exercise
2446	77069		F	School exercise
2447	77070		F	Lexical
2448	77071		F	School exercise
2449	77072	22/12/-	F	School exercise
2450	77073		F	School exercise
2451	77074		F	School exercise
2452	77075		F	School exercise
2453	77076		F	*Ḫḫ* I
2454	77077		F	*Ḫḫ* III
2455	77078	8/10/-	F	Letter
2456	77079		F	School exercise
2457	77080		F	School exercise; Sumerian
2458	77081		F	Lexical
2459	77082		F	School exercise; wedges
2460	77083		F	Account of dates
2461	77084		F	Sale of house(?)
2462	77085		F	School exercise
2463		Joined to AH 83-1-18, 2340 (= BM 76968)		
2464	77086		F	*Tintir* I
2465	77087		F	Unidentified
2466	77088		F	Bilingual(?)
2467	77089		F	Lexical(?)
2468	77090	Joined to AH 83-1-18, 2356 (= BM 76984)		

AH 83-1-18,

2469		Joined to AH 83-1-18, 2344 (= BM 76972)		
2470	77091		F	Literary(?)
2471	77092		F	School exercise
2472	77093		F	Prayer
2473	77094		F	Letter; *CT* 22 244
2474	77095		F	Literary(?)
2475	77096		F	*Ḫḫ* VIIB
2476	77097		F	School exercise
2477	77098		NC	List of plants
2478+ 2481	77099+ 77102		C	Uninscribed bulla; 8 stamp seals
2479	77100		F	School exercise
2480	77101	Nb(-)	F	Receipt for dates or grain; seal
2481	77102	Joined to AH 83-1-18, 2478 (= BM 77099)		
2482	77103		C	Lid for jar of aromatics(?) with pious inscription
2483	77104		F	Lexical
2484	77105		F	Lexical and bilingual extract
2485	77106		F	Account of plants
2486	77107		F	Only personal names preserved
2487	77108		F	School exercise
2488	77109	Dar 25/-/9	F	Receipt
2489	77110		F	Economic
2490	77111		F	Lexical
2491	77112		F	Literary(?)
2492	77113		F	Literary
2493	77114		F	School exercise
2494	77115	Cam 4/6/2	NC	Loan of silver
2495	77116		F	School exercise
2496	77117		F	Unfinished god list
2497	77118		F	Lexical; literary extract
2498	77119		F	Lexical
2499	77120		F	Unidentified
2500+ 2501	77121+ 77122		F	Commentary on astrological omens
2501	77122	Joined to AH 83-1-18, 2500 (= BM 77121)		
2502	77123		F	Lexical
2503	77124		F	Literary
2504	77125		F	Sumerian; *Ḫulbazizi*
2505	77126		F	Economic

AH 83-1-18,

2506	77127		F	School exercise
2507	77128		F	Medical
2508	77129		F	Letter order
2509	77130		F	School exercise
2510	77131		F	*Ḫḫ* XVI
2511	77132		F	Only personal names preserved
2512	77133		F	Literary
2513	77134		F	School exercise
2514	77135		F	Literary
2515	77136		F	Lexical(?)
2516	77137		F	Literary
2517	77138		F	Astronomical(?)
2518	77139	Joined to AH 83-1-18, 2405 (= BM 77030)		
2519	77140		F	Literary
2520	77141		F	Only personal names preserved
2521	77142		F	Economic
2522		Joined to AH 83-1-18, 2344 (= BM 76972)		
2523	77143		F	Lexical
2524+ 2550	77144+ 77170		F	*Malku* II; same tablet as 82-9-18, 12193 (= BM 72188)
2525	77145		F	Accounts
2526	77146		F	School exercise
2527	77147		F	School exercise
2528	77148		F	Fragment of colophon
2529	77149	Art	F	Economic
2530	77150		F	Literary
2531	77151		F	*Ḫḫ* IV
2532	77152		F	Only personal names preserved
2533	77153		F	Prayer(?)
2534	77154		F	Economic
2535	77155		F	Economic
2536	77156		F	School exercise
2537	77157		F	*Ḫḫ* I
2538	77158		F	Lexical
2539	77159		F	School exercise; letter
2540	77160		F	Lexical
2541	77161		F	Ritual and incantations against *bušanu*, related to Köcher, *BAM* 1 29 etc.
2542	77162		C	Four personal names
2543	77163		F	School exercise

AH 83-1-18,

2544	77164		F	Accounts
2545	77165		F	Literary
2546	77166		F	School exercise
2547	77167		F	Letter
2548	77168		F	Literary
2549	77169		F	Economic
2550	77170	Joined to AH 83-1-18, 2524 (= BM 77144)		
2551	77171		F	School exercise
2552	77172	Nbk 25/3/-	F	Legal deposition
2553	77173		F	Unidentified
2554	77174		F	Economic
2555	77175	Kan 7/-/14?	F	Sale(?) of a field; Babylon
2556	77176		F	School exercise
2557	77177		F	Sale(?) of a house
2558	77178		F	Accounts
2559	77179		F	Account of bricks
2560	77180		F	Economic
2561	77181		F	Literary
2562	77182		F	School exercise
2563	77183		F	Account of aromatics
2564	77184		F	Contract
2565	77185		F	Contract(?)
2566	77186		F	*Ḫḫ* I
2567	77187		F	Lexical; Sumerian
2568	77188		F	Accounts
2569	77189		F	Literary extract
2570	77190		F	Lexical extract
2571	77191		F	*Ḫḫ* I
2572	77192		F	School exercise
2573	77193		F	School exercise
2574	77194		F	Lexical
2575	77195		F	Unidentified
2576	77196		F	Commentary
2577	77197		C	Letter
2578	77198		F	School exercise
2579	77199		F	Literary
2580	77200		F	School exercise
2581	77201		F	Lexical
2582	77202		F	Lexical and literary extract

AH 83-1-18,

2583	77203	Antig 1/1/4	C	Loan of silver; stamp seals; Babylon
2584	77204		F	Accounts
2585	77205		F	Lexical
2586	77206		F	Contract
2587	77207		F	Sale of a house(?)
2588	77208		F	Contract
2589	77209		F	Uninscribed bulla; 6 stamp seals
2590	77210		F	Uninscribed bulla; 5 stamp seals
2591	77211		F	Uninscribed bulla; 3 stamp seals
2592	77212		F	Fragment of a prism(?) with stamped impression; cf. *CT* 44 pl. 4
2593	77213		F	Uninscribed tag; seal impression
2594	77214		F	Uninscribed ball; stamp seal
2595	77215			Terracotta head
2596				Bronze
2597	77216	Ššu 24/5/19	NC	Sale of a slave girl; Babylon; *Iraq* 17 77 n. 26
2598	116624			Head of Huwawa; *AAA* 11 107ff.
2599	77216A		F	Lexical
2600	77218		F	Letter(?)
2600A	77217	Npl 29/7/18	C	Contract for barley

83-1-18,

1-703				Bezold *Cat.* pp. 1854ff.; 1950; 1952
704	91036	Kadašman-Enlil	F	Kudurru; King, *BBSt* no. 1; Walker, *Tell ed-Der* 3 106f. no. 107
705-900				Bezold *Cat.* pp. 1905ff.; 1950-1952

83-1-21, See below p. 323

83-4-5,

1	77219	F	Religious; bilingual; Sumerian *CT* 42 31
2	77220	F	Bilingual Hymn; *CT* 42 30
3			Lion's head

83-6-30,

1	77221		F	God list; dupl. *KAV* 154
2	77222		F	Astronomical
3	77223		F	Cylinder; NB royal inscription
4	77224		F	Astronomical(?)
5	77225		F	Astronomical almanac
6	77226		F	Astronomical diary
7	77227		F	Astronomical(?) omens
8	77228		F	Astronomical diary
9	77229		F	S^b; Akkadian and Greek
10	77230		F	Astronomical diary
11	77231		F	Physiognomic omens
12	77232		F	Astronomical diary(?)
13	77233		F	List of signs with equivalent number
14	77234	-/-/1	F	Loan of silver
15	77235	Joined to Sp II 770 (= BM 35212)		
16	77236		F	Location of cultic daises in Babylon
17	77237		F	Astronomical; *ACT* 15
18	77238		F	Astronomical; *ACT* 61a
19	77239	Joined to Sp 166 (= BM 34070)		
20	77240	Joined to Sp II 631 (= BM 35093)		
21	77241		F	Astronomical diary
22	77242		F	Astronomical; cosmography(?)
23	77243		F	List of workmen
24	77244	Joined to Rm.767		
25	77245	Joined to Sp II 134 (= BM 34651)		
26	77246		F	Astronomical diary
27	77247		F	Astronomical diary
28	77248		F	Only personal names preserved
29	77249		F	Astronomical diary

SH 83-9-28,

1	77250		F	Astronomical procedure
2	77251	Joined to Sp III 64 (= BM 35557)		
3	77252		F	Akkadian incantation
4	77253		F	*Ludlul*
5	77254	Joined to Sp 166 (= BM 34070)		
6	77255	Joined to 81-2-1, 63 (= BM 40098)		
7	77256		F	Astronomical procedure text
8	77257		F	Astronomical almanac for SE 234
9	77258		F	Omens
10	77259		F	Sumerian and bilingual cultic incantations
11	77260		F	Astronomical diary
12	77261		F	Physiognomic omens; dupl. Kraus, *Texte* no. 22 col. i
13	77262		F	Astronomical diary
14	77263		F	Incantation; Egalkurra
15	77264		F	Literary
16	77265		F	Astronomical; *LBAT* 1471*
17	77266		F	Literary
18	77267		F	Astronomical diary
19	77268		F	Astronomical diary
20	77269	Joined to Sp II 397 (= BM 35457)		
21	77270		F	Literary; bilingual
22	77271	Art	F	Contract
23	77272		F	Astronomical diary
24	77273		F	Astronomical diary
25	77274		F	Astronomical
26	82820		F	Astronomical
27	82821	6/1/20	F	Sale of dates
28	82822		F	Astronomical; eclipse omens

SH 83-9-28,

29	82823		F	Astronomical
30	82824		F	Astronomical
31	82825		F	Astronomical diary
32	82826		F	Lexical
33	82827		F	Economic
34	82828	Nbk -/-/27	F	Marriage text
35	82829		F	Astronomical
36+ 42	82830+ 82836	Cyr 10+/5/7	F	Contract for dates; Babylon
37	82831	5/12/-	F	Receipt for seed
38	82832		F	Astronomical
39+ 41	82833+ 82835	SE 11/12/217	F	Loan(?) of silver
40	82834		F	Contract
41	82835	Joined to SH 83-9-28, 39 (= BM 82833)		
42	82836	Joined to SH 83-9-28, 36 (= BM 82830)		

83-12-31,

1	82837	Nbn 3/10/11	C	Receipt for dates

84-2-11,

1	93006	Kan 13/2/14	C	Receipt for oil; *AfO* 16, pl. V, p. 41
2	77275	Npl 13/5/12	C	Receipt for purchase with wool of oxen; *ZA* 4 140ff.
3	77276	Npl 5/1/7	C	Account of garments of gods; *ZA* 4 137
4	77277	Npl 13/2/11	C	Offering ledger; *ZA* 4 139
5	77278	Npl 20/3/16	C	Account of dates or grain; *ZA* 4 142f.
6	77279	Npl 11/5/19	C	Receipt for wool; *ZA* 4 145
7	77280	Nbk 20/11/8	C	Contract for barley; Babylon; *Nbk* 71
8	77281	Nbk 27/9/-	C	Contract for dates; *Nbk* 436
9	77282	Nbk 8/6b/41	C	Contract for dates; *Nbk* 382
10	77283	Nbk 7/12/5	NC	Account of sheep; *Nbk* 49
11	92788	Nbk 28/7/5	C	Loan of silver; *Nbk* 45; *KB* 4 182
12	92789	Nbk 22/2/10	C	Receipt for bitumen; drawing on back; *Nbk* 84
13	77284	Nbk 5/8/11	C	Receipt for iron objects; *Nbk* 92
14	77285	Nbk 12/9/12	C	Sale of a slave girl; *Nbk* 97
15	77286	Nbk -/-/4	C	Receipt for barley; *Nbk* 104
16	77287	Nbk 2/8/14	NC	Loan of barley; Babylon; *Nbk* 105
17	77288	Nbk 8/4/24	C	Receipt for sheep
18	77289	Nbk 20/10/26	C	Receipt for grapes; *Nbk* 169
19	77290	Nbk 8/7/26	C	Receipt for doves; *Nbk* 162
20	77291	Nbk 7/5/26	C	Receipt for shoes; *Nbk* 165
21	77292	Nbk 7/8/28	C	Receipt for provisions; *Nbk* 190
22	77293	Nbk 17/1/29	C	Rental of workmen(?); *Nbk* 197
23	77294	Nbk 29/4/32	C	Sworn agreement to produce meat offerings regularly for the gods; *Nbk* 247
24	92790	Nbk 22/10/34	C	Contract for barley; Babylon; *Nbk* 273
25	77295	Nbk 24/10/40	C	Receipt for barley; *Nbk* 370
26	77296	Nbk 16/4/40	C	Sale of a donkey; Kurṣubaʾ; *Nbk* 360

84-2-11,

27	77297	Nbk 28/6/-	NC	Account of provisions; *Nbk* 433
28	77298	Nbk 5/5/10	NC	Account of garments; *Nbk* 87
29	77299	Nbk 8/1/28	C	Receipt for dates and barley
30	77300	Am 2/10/acc	NC	Statement of slave ownership; *AOATS* 4 88
31	77301	Am 15/12/acc	C	Receipt for *kasu*; *AOATS* 4 40
32	77302	Am 4/8/1	F	Receipt for sheep; *AOATS* 4 41
33	92791	Ner 12/6/acc	C	Sale of slaves; *Ner* 1; *KB* 4 202
34	77303	Ner -/-/1	C	Contract for dates; *Ner* 31
35	77304	Ner 7/9/2	NC	Loan of silver; Babylon; *Ner* 44
36	77305	Nbn 12/11/1	F	Obverse destroyed; Babylon; *Nbn* 46
37	77306	Nbn 27/-/2	C	Receipt for silver
38	77307	Nbn 26/4/3	C	Receipt for wool; *Nbn* 109
39	77308	Nbn 11/8/3	C	Receipt for silver; *Nbn* 118
40	77309	Nbn 25/11/3	C	Receipt for purchase of oxen; *Nbn* 127
41	77310	Nbn 6/6/4	C	Receipt for barley
42	77311	Nbn 20/1/4	C	Loan of silver; Babylon; *Nbn* 139
43	77312	Nbn 4/3/4	NC	Contract for dates; Babylon; *Nbn* 149
44	77313	Nbn 19/10/4	C	Account of provision purchases; *Nbn* 173
45	77314	Nbn 24/10/4	C	Receipt for dates; *Nbn* 175
46	77315	Nbn 24/5/5	C	Receipt for barley; *Nbn* 189
47	77316	Nbn 3/12/6	C	Receipt for wool; *Nbn* 242
48	77317	Nbn 5/2/6	C	Receipt for oil; *Nbn* 221
49	77318	Nbn 9/4/6	C	Receipt for sheep; *Nbn* 229
50	77319	Nbn 14/6/6	C	Account of barley; *Nbn* 236
51	77320	Nbn 11/11/7	C	Account of date palm products; *Nbn* 271
52	77321	Nbn 19/6/8	C	Receipt for purchase of sheep carcasses; *Nbn* 304
53	77322	Nbn 19/2/10	C	Loan of silver; *Nbn* 412
54	77323	Nbn 17/9/10	C	Receipt for silver; drawing; *Nbn* 456
55	77324	Nbn 19/9/11	C	Loan of silver; *Nbn* 553
56	77325	Nb(n) 7/11/12	C	Account of silver; *Nbn* 661
57	92792	Nbn 16/8/12	C	Division of the *isqu* of the *erib biti* officials; *Guide* 1922, p. 152
58	77326	Nbn 26/9/12	NC	Loan of silver; *Nbn* 650
59	77327	Nbn 5/8/14	NC	Loan of silver; *Nbn* 803
60	77328	Nbn 20/9/14	C	Receipt for silver; *Nbn* 812
61	92793	Nbn 16/4/14	C	Division of an inheritance; *Guide* 1922, p. 153

84-2-11,

62	77329	Nbn 5/5/16	C	Receipt for sesame; *Nbn* 970
63	77330	Nbn 21/8/16	C	Loan of silver; *Nbn* 992
64	92794	Nbn 13/8/16	NC	Marriage text; Babylon; *Nbn* 990; *KB* 4 252
65	77331	Nbn 3/6/17	NC	Receipt for bronze; nail marks; *Nbn* 1046
66	77332	Nbn 5/12/-	NC	Division of silver
67	77333	Nbn 19/2/13+	C	Receipt for barley; *Nbn* 844
68	77334	Nbn -/12/-	NC	Receipt for silver
69	77335	Nbn 30/6/-	NC	Sale of a slave girl; Babylon; *Nbn* 1098
70	77336	Nbn 27/2/-	NC	Contract for barley; *Nbn* 1070
71	77337	Nbn -/2/+6	C	Receipt for iron tools; *Nbn* 220
72	77338	Nbn 22/8/14	NC	Sale of a slave; *Nbn* 806
73	77339	Nbn	NC	Receipt for exchange of gold and silver
74	77340	Nbn 8/2/-	NC	Receipt for gold; *Nbn* 1067
75	77341	Npl 22/-/9	C	Receipt for iron tools; ZA 4 137ff.
76	77342	Cyr 22/3/2	C	Account of barley; *Cyr* 40
77	77343	Cyr 18/4/2	NC	Receipt; *Cyr* 43
78	77344	Cyr 10/8/3	NC	Adoption of a child; Babylon
79	77345	Cyr 6/11/3	C	Contract for dowry; Kohler u. Peiser, *Rechtsleben* 2 13ff.
80	77346	Cyr 9/5/6	NC	Contract for a field; *Cyr* 230
81	77347	Cyr 19/11/5	C	Receipt for sheep; *Cyr* 216
82	77348	Cyr 23/11/7	C	Rental of a house; *Cyr* 278
83	77349	Cyr 21/1/8	NC	Loan of silver; *Cyr* 297
84	77350	Cyr 22/6/-	C	Contract for *kasu*; *Cyr* 355
85	77351	Cam 17/11/acc.	C	Contract for dates and barley; *Cam* 14
86	77352	Cam 12/6/acc	C	Sale of a donkey; *Cam* 1
87	77353	Cam 6/6/1	C	Contract for dates; *Cam* 55
88	77354	Cam 23/4/1	C	Loan of silver; *Cam* 45
89	77355	Cam 6/6/1	C	Contract for dates; *Cam* 56
90	77356	Cam 13/12/2	C	Letter
91	77357	Cam 10/12/2	NC	Contract for a field; *Cam* 142
92	77358	Cam 29/12/2	C	Loan of silver; *Cam* 145
93	77359	Cam 21/2/3	NC	Receipt for silver; *Cam* 159
94	92795	Cam 13/8/3	C	Gift of dowry; *Cam* 193
95	77360	Cam 8/11/4	C	Receipt for silver (sale of property); *Cam* 260
96	77361	Cam 5/6/4	C	Contract for dates
97	77362	Cam 23/4/6	NC	Account of rentals; *Cam* 316

84-2-11,

98	77363	Dar 8/2/1	NC	Loan of silver; Babylon
99	77364	Dar 5/6/2	NC	Contract for dates; *Dar* 38
100	77365	Dar 25/6/2	C	Loan of silver; Babylon
101	77366	Dar 13/5/4	C	Contract for dates; Babylon; *Dar* 120
102	77367	Dar 15/4/5	C	House rental; Babylon; *Dar* 163
103	92796	Dar 19/5/2	C	Sale of a house; Babylon; *Dar* 37
104	77368	Dar 18/2/3	C	Loan of silver; *Dar* 67
105	77369	Dar 21/2/3	C	Loan of silver; Babylon; *Dar* 68
106	77370	Dar 23/2/3	C	Loan of silver; Babylon; *Dar* 69
107	77371	Dar 16/7/3	C	Loan of silver; Babylon; *Dar* 82
108	77372	Dar 16/5/3	C	Distribution of share of silver; Babylon; *Dar* 73
109	77373	Dar 18/2/3	C	Loan of silver; dupl. 84-2-11, 104 (= BM 77368); *Dar* 67a
110	77374	Dar 24/7/3	C	Receipt for silver and property; Babylon; *Dar* 84
111	77375	Dar -/7/4	C	Loan of silver; Kish; *Dar* 133
112	77376	Dar 25/4/4	C	Loan of silver; Babylon; *Dar* 117
113	77377	Dar 23/4/4	NC	Receipt for dates as rent; Sippar; *Dar* 116
114	77378	Dar 11/6/5	C	Contract for dates; *Dar* 169
115	77379	Dar 16/8/5	C	Loan of silver Ḫursagkalamma; *Dar* 181
116	77380	Dar -/1/6	C	Receipt for silver; *Dar* 199
117	77381	Dar 22/6/7	C	Contract for dates; *Dar* 226
118	77382	Dar 5/6/7	C	Contract for dates; *Dar* 224
119	77383	Dar 9/9/8	C	Receipt for tin; *Dar* 240
120	77384	Dar 11/1/8	C	Receipt for silver; *Dar* 234
121	77385	Dar 20/7/9	C	Loan of silver for purchase of garments; Babylon
122	77386	Dar 6/9/10	C	Loan of silver; Babylon
123	77387	Dar 18/6/10	C	House rental; Babylon; *Dar* 275
124	77388	Dar 19/6/11	C	Contract for dates; *Dar* 304
125	77389	Dar -/1/14	C	Account of oxen
126	77390	Dar 18/5/14	C	Contracts for dates; *Dar* 377
127	77391	Dar 25/3/15	NC	Loan of silver; Babylon
128	77392	Dar 5/10/17	C	Contract for dates and barley; Babylon
129	77393	Dar 3/1/18	C	Account of *isqu* shares; Babylon
130	77394	Dar 27/1/28	NC	Loan of silver; Babylon
131	77395	Dar 24/8/19	NC	Receipt for payment; Babylon
132	77396	Dar 22/[6]a/19	C	Receipt for beer

84-2-11,

133	92797	Dar 16/12/20	C	Sale of a slave; *PSBA* 6 102
134	77397	Dar 20/9/20	C	Receipt for barley
135	77398	Dar 10/6/21	C	Gift of a dowry; Babylon
136+ 478	77399+ 77731	Dar 10/11/21	C	Account of dowry given; Babylon; *Dar* 530
137	77400	Dar 5/3/21	NC	Gift of dowry; Babylon; *Dar* 522
138	77401	Dar 18/9/22	NC	Sale of slaves; stamp seals; Babylon; *Dar* 551
139	77402	Dar 19/12/22	C	Receipt for silver; *Dar* 555
140	77403	Dar 6/11/23	C	Loan of silver; Babylon; *Dar* 579 (part only)
141	77404	Dar 29/7/23	C	Gift of dowry; Babylon; *Dar* 568
142	77405	Dar 8/6/24	C	Loan of silver; Babylon
143	77406	Dar 29/6/25	C	Receipt for barley
144	77407	Dar 10/12/25	C	Loan of silver; Babylon
145	77408	Dar 20/-/25	F	Loan of silver
146	77409	Dar 15/12/25	NC	Loan of silver; Babylon
147	77410	Dar 9/4/25	C	Loan of silver; Babylon
148	77411	Dar 26/3/26	C	Transfer of responsibility for a slave; Dilbat
149	77412	Dar -/3/26	C	Loan of silver; Babylon
150	77413	Dar 25/7/26	NC	Loan of silver; Babylon
151	77414	Dar 4/3/27	C	Loan of silver; Babylon
152	77415	Dar 24/4/28	C	Receipt for silver
153	77416	Dar 21/7/28	C	Loan of silver; Babylon
154	77417	Dar 14/4/28	NC	Account of *isqu* payments; Babylon
155	92798	Dar 2/9/29	NC	Sale of fields
156	77418	Dar 19/5/33	C	Contract for barley provisions
157	77419	Dar 11/9/34	NC	Receipt for purchase of sesame
158	92799	Dar 6/12/33	NC	Sale of a house; nail marks
159	77420	Dar 2/12/1	NC	House rental; *Dar* 25
160	77421	Dar 4/7/29	NC	House rental; Babylon
161	77422		NC	List of workmen
162	77423		C	Receipt
163	92990		F	Sale of a field
164	77424	Dar 2/-/26	NC	Legal; division of *isqu* payments
165	77425		F	Legal deposition concerning a dispute over a contract
166	77426	Dar 2/9/29	NC	Sale of a field; Dilbat
167	77427		C	Receipt for bronze

84-2-11,

168	77428		C	Contract for bricks
169	77429		C	List of aromatics
170	77430		C	Account of stones
171	77431		C	Account of sheep
172	77432		F	Loan of silver; stamp seal
173	77433		NC	Disposal of income in temples
174	77434	24/-/4	NC	Loan of silver; Babylon
175	77435	Nbn -/3/9	NC	Sale of a slave girl; *Nbn* 343
176	77436	Bar -/5/1	C	Receipt for interest on a loan
177	77437	4/6/-	C	Contract
178	77438		F	School text(?); copy of an inscription of Gaddaš; bilingual lamentation; Winckler, *Untersuchungen* 156 no. 6; Brinkman, *MSKH* 1 127-128
179	77439		C	Receipt for dates or grain
180	77440		C	Account
181	77441	14/-/16	NC	Receipt for silver
182	77442		NC	Loan of silver
183	77443		C	Account of donkeys
184	77444		NC	Receipt for silver
185	77445		C	Account of interest payments
186	77446	-/-/27	NC	Loan of silver
187	77447	24/5/8	C	Account of dates or grain
188	77448		NC	Letter; *CT* 22 145
189	77449	OB	C	Administrative; late period; round type
190	77450	Nb(-) 30/-/6	NC	Sale of a slave girl; Babylon; *Nbn* 248
191	77451		C	Receipt for dates
192	77452		C	Accounts
193	77453		C	Receipt for purchase of provisions
194	77454	3/3/7	F	Receipt for barley
195	77455	24/2/8	C	Receipt for silver for purchase of a spade
196	77456		NC	Receipt
197	77457	6/6/3	F	Contract
198	77458		F	Account of jewelry
199	77459		F	Account of dates or grain
200	77460		NC	Account of sheep(?)
201	77461	Nbk 13/10/-	F	Legal text concerning the adoption of a child; *Nbk* 439; *BASOR* 91 36-37
202	77462	Kan 8/5/16	NC	Animal ledger
203	77463		F	School exercise

84-2-11,

204	77464	Nb(-) -/4/17	F	Account of barley provisions
205	77465		F	Account of oxen
206	77466		F	Account of bricks
207	77467	-/-/14	F	Account of dates or grain
208	77468	Joined to 82-3-23, 1513 (= BM 50522)		
209	77469		F	Account of sheep
210	77470	-/1/16	F	Account of barley provisions
211	77471	Nbn -/2/-	F	Contract; Babylon
212	77472	-/9/-	F	Sale of a slave girl; Dilbat
213	77473	-/6/-	F	Account of barley
214	77474		F	Division of an inheritance
215	77475		F	Astronomical diary; SE 153; *LBAT* 387
216+ 448	77476+ 77702	Dar 17/1/34	F	Loan of silver; stamp seals
217	77477		F	Field sale
218	77478		F	Contract
219	77479	15/4/5	F	Account of sheep
220+ 412+ 440+ 446+ 467+ 498	77480+ 77669+ 77694+ 77700+ 77721+ 77748	Cam	F	Astronomical omens
221	77481	20+/12/27	NC	Receipt for dates and barley
222+ 519	77482+ 77769		F	*Šaziga*
223	77483	Nbk 1/2/30	NC	Contract for barley; *Nbk* 210
224	77484	-/-/3	NC	Sale of a field
225	77485	Nbk -/7/41	F	Sale of a slave; *Nbk* 381
226	77486		F	Account of archers
227	77487		F	Letter
228	77488		F	Oxen ledger
229	77489	-/3/-	F	Sale of a slave girl(?)
230	77490	28/8/17	F	Account of dates or grain
231	77491	4/-/1	NC	Contract for dates
232	77492		F	Inheritance(?) text
233	77493	Nbn 27/-/15	F	Loan of silver; *Nbn* 946
234	77494		F	Account
235	77495		F	Sale of a slave(?)
236	77496	Nb(-) 21/-/14	F	Receipt for barley
237	77497	Cyr 11/3/3	F	Account of dowry; *Cyr* 111

84-2-11,

238	77498	Dar 13/7/-	F	Memorandum; drawing of winged solar disk
239	77499		F	Accounts of barley
240	77500		F	Account of sheep
241	77501		F	Sale(?) of a field
242	77502	Dar 13/1/11	F	Sale of a field; *Dar* 295
243	92991	Cam -/-/7	F	Sale of a field; Cutha; nail marks; *Cam* 403
244	77503		F	Offering ledger
245	77504		F	Account of garments of gods
246+ 424+ 449	77505+ 77678+ 77703		F	Astronomical omens
247	77506		F	Astronomical omens
248	77507		F	Administrative text describing areas for shepherding
249+ 469	77508+ 77723	Dar 19/3/29	NC	Sale of a field; Dilbat
250	77509	-/-/16	F	Account of dates
251	77510		F	Astronomical omens
252+ 445	77511+ 77699		F	Astronomical omens
253+ 499	77512+ 77749		F	Astronomical omens
254	77513	Dar -/-/26	C	Sale of a field; stamp seals; nail marks; Babylon
255	77514		F	Astronomical omens
256+ 361+ 430+ 473+ 506	77515+ 77618+ 77684+ 77726+ 77756		F	Astronomical omens
257+ 503	77516+ 77753	Cam 12/12/-	F	Sale of a field; Cutha(?); *Cam* 432 (part only)
258	77517	Nbk -/-/4	F	Sale of a field; *Nbk* 40
259	77518	Nbn 28/8/8	NC	Loan of grain; *Nbn* 307
260	77519		F	Liturgy; *uru amirrabi*; cf. *Aula Orientalis* 1 45ff.
261	77520	8/2/-	C	Receipt for oil
262	77521	Dar 2/6/-	F	Sale of a slave girl; Babylon
263	77522	Nbn -/12/-	F	Sale of a slave girl; Babylon
264	77523		F	Account of wool(?)
265	77524	4/7/7	F	Account of dates

84-2-11,

266	77525	Nbk -/5/9	NC	Account of barley; *Nbk* 77
267	77526		F	Receipt for silver
268	77527		F	Contract
269	77528	8/5/16	F	Sheep ledger
270	77529	Nbk 9/1/-	F	Sale of slaves(?); Babylon; *Nbk* 416
271	77530		F	Account
272	77531	Nbk 3/-/3	F	Receipt for purchase of dates; *Nbk* 35
273	77532		F	Receipt
274	77533	Dar 18/-/5	F	Contract for dates; Babylon; *Dar* 196
275	77534	-/9/-	F	Receipt for axes
276	77535	Dar 18/1/7	NC	Rental of a house; *Dar* 219
277	77536	Dar 20/12a/22	NC	Loan of silver; *Dar* 556
278	77537		NC	Contract for dates
279+ 436	77538+ 77690		F	Contract; stamp seals
280	77539	Cyr 7/12/-	F	Sale of a household; Uruk; *Cyr* 361
281	77540	Nbk	NC	Animal ledger
282	77541		F	Legal deposition concerning silver
283	77542	26/7/21	NC	Loan of silver; Babylon; *Dar* 520
284	77543	Dar -/3/-	F	Loan(?)
285	77544	Dar -/-/24	NC	Loan of silver
286	77545	Dar 15/1/16	NC	Contract for a field(?); *Dar* 419
287	77546	Dar 26/7/3	F	Loan of a silver cup; *Dar* 85
288	77547	Nbn -/10/5	F	Sale of slave girls
289	77548	Nbn 5/2/10	NC	Contract for barley; *Nbn* 405
290	77549	23/12/10	NC	Receipt for bitumen; archaic sign for fish
291	77550		F	Sale(?) of land
292+ 554	77551+ 77804	10/8/15	F	Sale of a slave; Babylon
293	77552		F	Accounts
294	77553		F	Account of silver
295	77554	Nbn -/7/12	F	Sale of slaves; Babylon; *Nbn* 615
296+ 330	77555	Nbk -/-/32	F	Oath concerning temple supplies; Babylon
297	77556		F	Letter
298	77557		C	Receipt for barley
299	77558	-/-/38	F	Loan of silver
300	77559		F	Economic
301	77560	Nbn 25/-/11	F	Transfer of a slave as collateral
302	77561		C	Receipt for oil

84-2-11,

303	77562		F	Account of sesame
304	77563	(Dar) 12/-/30	F	Receipt for oxen and sheep
305	77564		F	Contract
306	77565		F	Sale of a slave girl
307	77566	Nbn -/-/14	NC	Account of oxen sales
308	77567		F	Contract
309	77568	Joined to 82-5-22, 466 (= BM 54314)		
310	77569		F	Account of silver(?)
311	77570		F	Gift of dowry; dupl. 84-2-11, 136 (= BM 77399)
312	77571	Nbn -/2/15	NC	Contract for silver and barley; *Nbn* 849
313	77572	Dar 27/10/-	F	Account of dates or grain
314	77573		F	Account of barley
315	77574		F	Letter
316	77575	Nbn 2/8/5	NC	Loan of silver; *Nbn* 198
317	77576	Nbn 18/-/2	NC	Contract for dates; *Nbn* 70
318	77577	Dar 21+/3/27	F	Contract for provisions
319	77578	Dar 18/-/11	F	Account of barley; *Dar* 317
320	77579	Nbn 28/4/acc	F	Loan of silver(?); *Nbn* 3
321	77580	Nbk -/-/38	F	Receipt for dates and barley; *Nbk* 338
322	77581	Dar 26/-/19	F	Sale of a slave girl(?); *Dar* 496
323	77582		F	Contract
324	77583	Cyr 14/4/3	F	Court case; *Cyr* 127
325	77584	Nbk 11/12/-	F	Account of garments of gods(?)
326	77585		F	Only personal names preserved
327	77586	Ner 14/5/3	F	Account of dates or grain
328	77587	Nbn -/3/3	F	Contract(?); *Nbn* 105
329+ 441	77588+ 77695		F	Contract
330		Joined to 84-2-11, 296 (= BM 77555)		
331	77589		F	Sale of land; stamp seal
332	77590	Ner -/-/acc	F	Receipt for barley; drawing; *Ner* 11
333	77591	-/-/2	F	Loan of silver
334	77592	Dar 19/7/15	F	Contract; *Dar* 407
335	77593	Nbn 7/7/15	F	House rental; *Nbn* 891
336	77594	(-)-uṣur	F	Account of dates
337	77595		F	Contract
338	77596	Dar 4/6/28	F	Loan of silver
339	77597	-/12b/36	F	Receipt for dates or grain

84-2-11,

340	77598	-/1/35	F	Accounts; drawing
341	77599	Dar 12/3/24	F	Loan; Babylon
342	77600	-/-/29	F	Land sale
343	77601	Nbk -/-/30+	F	Loan of silver; *Nbk* 232
344	77602		F	Court case
345	77603		NC	Receipt for silver
346	77604		C	Legal deposition; *Cyr* 381
347	77605		F	Loan
348	77606	Nbn 26/11/-	C	Gift of dowry; *Nbn* 817
349	77607	Cam 10+/8/3	NC	Sale of house and field; *Cam* 192
350	77608	22/2/16	F	Account of barley
351	77609		F	Text concerning priests
352	77610		F	Sale of land
353	77611		F	Text concerning a temple prebend; probably of the time of Šamaš-šum-ukin; mentioning Aššur-nadin-šumi, with modelled imitation of Babylonian royal seal; cf. *OrNS* 41 248; *Assyrian Royal Inscriptions*, pl. 7 fig. 17
354	77612		F	Same tablet as 84-2-11, 353 (= BM 77611)
355	77613		F	School exercise; literary extract
356	92502	Dar +6/-/22	C	Chronicle; *TCS* 5 no. 1, pp. 70ff.
357	77614		F	Contract concerning temple supplies
358	77615		F	School exercise; personal names
359+ 428+ 474	77616+ 77682+ 77727		F	Astronomical omens
360	77617	Joined to Sp II 280 (= BM 34788)		
361	77618	Joined to 84-2-11, 256 (= BM 77515)		
362	77619	Joined to Sp II 624 (= BM 35086)		
363	77620		F	Astronomical procedure text; cf. 80-6-17, 165 (= BM 36438)
364	77621		F	Royal inscription(?)
365	77622	Dar 28/1/-	F	Account of purchase of wool
366	77623		F	Account of date products
367	77624		F	House rental
368	77625	-/-/12	F	House rental
369	77626	Ner 19/9/acc	NC	Gift of dowry
370	77627		F	Contract for dates
371	77628	26/9/20+	F	Contract; Babylon
372	77629	Am -/3/-	F	Loan of silver; Babylon; *AOATS* 4 82

84-2-11,

373	77630		F	Letter
374	77631		F	Economic
375	77632	Am 11/3/-	F	Economic
376	77633	Nbn -/1/-	F	Account of dates or grain
377	77634		F	Accounts
378	77635		F	Sale(?) of land
379	77636	Dar -/8/-	F	Rental of a house
380	77637	Ner 21/5/-	F	Loan of silver
381	77638	Dar 25/3/7	F	Loan of silver; *Dar* 221
382	77639		F	Contract
383	77640	11/-/1	F	Economic
384	77641	Dar	F	Account of barley
385	77642	-/-/14	F	Account of barley and dates; Babylon
386+ 540	77643+ 77790	Nbn 16/4/-	F	Division of *isqu* shares; Babylon
387	77644	-/4/-	F	Receipt for wool
388	77645		F	Loan(?) of silver
389	77646		F	*Šurpu* VIII
390	77647		F	Legal; stamp seals
391	77648		F	School exercise
392	77649		F	Sale(?) of a field
393	77650	-/-/9	F	Rental(?); Babylon
394+ 470	77651+ 77724		F	Contract
395	77652	Nbk	F	Dates or grain ledger
396	77653		F	Economic
397	77654		F	Economic
398	77655		F	Business contract
399	77656	19/11/-	F	Account of barley
400	77657		F	Economic
401	77658		F	Silver ledger
402	77659		F	Sales document
403	77660		F	Loan(?) of silver
404	77661	-/-/22	F	Account of dates
405	77662		F	Astronomical omens
406+ 507+ 555	77663+ 77757+ 77805		F	Astronomical omens
407	77664		F	School exercise
408	77665		F	School exercise

84-2-11,

409+ 415+ 416+ 417	77666		F	School exercise; literary extract
410	77667		F	Account of workmen
411+ 516	77668+ 77766		F	Astronomical omens
412	77669	Joined to 84-2-11, 220 (= BM 77480)		
413	77670		F	Astronomical diary
414	77671		F	School exercise
415		Joined to 84-2-11, 409 (= BM 77666)		
416		Joined to 84-2-11, 409 (= BM 77666)		
417		Joined to 84-2-11, 409 (= BM 77666)		
418	77672		F	School exercise; literary extract
419	77673		F	Only personal names preserved
420	77674		F	School exercise
421	77675		F	Contract; stamp seal
422	77676		F	Lexical
423	77677	10/6/17	F	House rental
424	77678	Joined to 84-2-11, 246 (= BM 77505)		
425	77679		F	Economic
426	77680		F	Contract
427	77681		F	Sales document
428	77682	Joined to 84-2-11, 359 (= BM 77616)		
429	77683		F	Contract for wool; stamp seal and nail marks
430	77684	Joined to 84-2-11, 256 (= BM 77515)		
431	77685		F	Economic
432	77686		F	Sale(?) of slaves
433	77687	Ner -/5/-	F	Account of dates
434	77688		F	Account of sheep
435	77689	Kan	F	Contract; Babylon
436	77690	Joined to 84-2-11, 279 (= BM 77538)		
437	77691		F	Astronomical(?) omens
438	77692	Dar	F	Contract
439	77693		F	Land sale(?)
440	77694	Joined to 84-2-11, 220 (= BM 77480)		
441	77695	Joined to 84-2-11, 329 (= BM 77588)		
442	77696	-/-/34	F	Account of sheep
443	77697		F	Field sale

84-2-11,

444	77698	Nbk 21/8/-	F	Loan(?)
445	77699	Joined to 84-2-11, 252 (= BM 77511)		
446	77700	Joined to 84-2-11, 220 (= BM 77480)		
447	77701	-/10/-	F	Receipt for purchase of dates
448	77702	Joined to 84-2-11, 216 (= BM 77476)		
449	77703	Joined to 84-2-11, 246 (= BM 77505)		
450	77704	Cam 14/11/-	F	Only personal names and date formula preserved
451	77705		F	Receipt for dates or grain
452	77706		F	School exercise
453	77707		F	School exercise
454	77708		F	Accounts
455	77709		F	School exercise
456	77710		F	*Ḫḫ* I and literary extract
457	77711		F	School exercise
458	77712		F	School exercise
459	77713		F	Literary extract
460	77714		F	School exercise
461	77715		F	School exercise
462	77716		F	School exercise
463	77717		F	School exercise
464	77718	Dar 4/5/-	F	Contract for oxen
465	77719		F	Economic
466	77720		F	Barrel-shaped fragment with one side badly defaced; unidentified inscription
467	77721	Joined to 84-2-11, 220 (= BM 77480)		
468	77722	Dar 8/-/-	F	Economic
469	77723	Joined to 84-2-11, 249 (= BM 77508)		
470	77724	Joined to 84-2-11, 394 (= BM 77651)		
471		Temporarily missing		
472	77725		F	Contract; nail marks
473	77726	Joined to 84-2-11, 256 (= BM 77515)		
474	77727	Joined to 84-2-11, 359 (= BM 77616)		
475+ 487	77728+ 77740		F	Bilingual incantation; cf. *CT* 17 47c
476	77729	Nbn	F	Receipt for barley
477	77730	Dar 15/10/28	F	Contract; Dilbat
478	77731	Joined to 84-2-11, 136 (= BM 77399)		
479	77732		F	Astronomical diary

84-2-11,

480	77733		F	Unidentified
481	77734		F	Economic
482	77735		F	Astronomical diary
483	77736		F	Astronomical
484	77737		F	School exercise; bilingual(?)
485	77738		F	Literary
486	77739		F	Omens; *Šumma alu*(?)
487	77740	Joined to 84-2-11, 475 (= BM 77728)		
488	77741	Nbk	C	Royal inscription; *VAB* 4 190; *Nbk* 23
489	89571			Cylinder seal
490	89106			Cylinder seal
491	89572			Cylinder seal
492	77742		F	Contract
493	77743		F	Loan of silver; seal
494	77744	-/6/-	F	Sale of a field; seals; Borsippa
495	77745	-/4/-	F	Sale of a field(?)
496	77746		F	Astronomical omen commentary
497	77747		F	Loan of silver
498	77748	Joined to 84-2-11, 220 (= BM 77480)		
499	77749	Joined to 84-2-11, 253 (= BM 77512)		
500	77750		F	Account of silver
501	77751		F	Sales contract
502	77752		F	Economic
503	77753	Joined to 84-2-11, 257 (= BM 77516)		
504	77754	Dar	F	Field sale; Babylon
505+ 527	77755+ 77777		F	Astronomical omens
506	77756	Joined to 84-2-11, 256 (= BM 77515)		
507	77757	Joined to 84-2-11, 406 (= BM 77663)		
508	77758		F	Account of dates or grain
509	77759		F	Receipt for barley
510	77760		F	Contract
511	77761	Nbk 5/7/42	F	Receipt for dates or grain
512	77762		F	Loan(?) of silver
513	77763	Nbn 19/12/4	F	Receipt for barley; Babylon
514	77764		F	Contract for barley
515	77765	13/-/-	F	Loan of silver
516	77766	Joined to 84-2-11, 411 (= BM 77668)		
517	77767	15/3/-	F	Receipt for barley

84-2-11,

518	77768		F	Astronomical omens
519	77769	Joined to 84-2-11, 222 (= BM 77482)		
520	77770	Nbk -/10/16	F	Contract; Babylon
521	77771		F	Sale of a field
522	77772		F	Economic
523	77773		F	Loan of silver
524	77774		F	Letter
525	77775		F	Contract
526	77776	Cyr 30/3/5	F	Loan of silver; Babylon; *Cyr* 195
527	77777	Joined to 84-2-11, 505 (= BM 77755)		
528	77778		F	Omens
529	77779	Npl 22/12/6	F	Loan of silver; *ZA* 4 137
530	77780		F	Lexical
531	77781		F	School exercise
532	77782		F	School exercise
533	77783	Nbn 20+/5/-	F	Loan of silver
534	77784	Cam	F	Receipt for barley
535	77785	-/-/17	F	Contract for barley
536	77786		F	Contract
537	77787	7/-/-	F	Account of dowry
538	77788		F	Receipt for dates or grain
539	77789	-/-/7	F	Account
540	77790	Joined to 84-2-11, 386 (= BM 77643)		
541	77791		F	Receipt for dates or grain
542	77792		F	Contract for meat
543	77793		F	Receipt for date provisions
544	77794		F	Contract for dates
545	77795		F	Loan of silver
546	77796		F	Contract
547	77797	26/2/2	F	Economic
548	77798	Nbk 26/6/-	F	Contract
549	77799	-/-/38	F	Loan of silver
550	77800	-/-/25	F	Loan of silver
551	77801		F	Loan
552	77802		F	Contract for dates
553	77803	4/7/-	F	Division of property; Babylon
554	77804	Joined to 84-2-11, 292 (= BM 77551)		
555	77805	Joined to 84-2-11, 406 (= BM 77663)		
556	77806		F	*Abnu šikinšu*

84-2-11,

557	77807	Joined to Sp II 1048 (= BM 35458)		
558-594				Clay figurines
595	77808		F	Commentary on *Izbu* I

84-11-12,

1	77809	OA	F	Account of loans; *CCT* 5 44; first 8 lines of obverse not copied
2	77810	OA	F	Account of tin; *CCT* 5 44; *Or NS* 21 271 n. 4; *JCS* 7 109
3	77811	OA	F	Loan; *CCT* 5 45
4	77812	OA	F	Letter; *CCT* 5 45
5	77813	OA	F	Account; *CCT* 5 50
6	77814			Uninscribed object

85-4-30,

1	91142	Nbk	C	Royal inscription; cylinder; *VAB* 4 112; *Nbk* 14
2	91143	Nbn	C	Royal inscription; cylinder; *VAB* 4 234; *Nbn* 3
3	91076 (= 12219)	Ha	C	Stone building inscription of Hammurapi; *CT* 21 45-6; *LIH* 3 180ff.
4	77815	Nbk 1/6/26+	NC	Field sale; seals; Babylon
5	22463	Nbn -/7/8	C	NB copy of Kurigalzu building inscription; *CT* 9 3 (published under wrong number, BM 22457)
6	93042		F	*Ea* IV; *CT* 12 27; *MSL* 14 353
7	77816		F	Account of barley and gold for jewelry
8	77817		C	Cultic inventory(?); cf. 82-7-14, 3728 (= BM 59319); 82-7-14, 4014 (= BM 59604); 82-7-14, 4015 (= BM 59605); 82-7-14, 4016 (= BM 59606); 85-4-30, 227 (= BM 78034)
9	77818	Nbk -/-/6	NC	Offering ledger
10+ 95	77819+ 77902		F	Astronomical omens
11	77820		C	Receipt for silver
12	77821	Dar 19/8/16	C	Contract for dates; Sippar; *Dar* 433
13	77822	Dar 2/6/25	C	Receipt for silver
14	77823	Nbk 26/6/11	C	Sale of a house; *Nbk* 90
15	77824		C	List of signs of the zodiac; Weidner, *Handbuch* 121; Kugler, *SSB* 1 228ff.; *AfO* 16 219
16	77825	Ner 28/4/2	C	Loan of silver; Babylon; *Ner* 36
17	77826	Dar 27/3/33+	C	House rental; Sippar
18	77827	-/1/4	C	Statement of responsibility for workmen
19	77828	Npl 7/8/11	NC	Account of barley; *ZA* 4 140
20	77829	Dar 23/9/29	C	Contract for barley

85-4-30,

21	77830		F	Receipt for purchases of barley
22	77831	Dar 28/11/11	C	Loan of silver; Babylon; *Dar* 312
23	77832	Dar 17/12/16	C	Sworn deposition; Babylon; *Dar* 434
24	77833		C	Account of silver(?)
25	77834		C	Accounts of deliveries to the temple
26	77835	Nbk	NC	Account of temple deliveries
27	77836		C	Letter
28	77837	28/8/-	NC	Account
29	77838	Dar 30/3/25	C	Contract for barley; Babylon
30	77839	Dar 2/8/34	C	Account of dates
31	77840	Dar 7/7/16	C	Loan of silver; Babylon; *Dar* 431
32	77841	Nbn -/-/2	NC	Account of dates or grain
33	77842	Nbn 17/1/7	C	Receipt for purchases
34	77843	Dar 12+/7/-	C	Contract for dates; Sippar
35	77844	11/12/10	C	Account of barley
36	77845	Nbn 21/9/acc	C	Account of garments; *Nbn* 10
37	92992	Nbk 18/1/22	F	Account of barley; *Nbk* 131
38	77846	Dar 10/9/34	C	Contract for dates; Sippar
39	77847		C	Account of wool
40	77848	Dar 7/10/6	C	Loan of silver; Babylon; *Dar* 213
41	77849	26/2/9	C	Audit of animals
42	77850	Dar 15/8/36	C	Letter; stamp seals
43	77851	Cyr 6/8/8	C	Receipt for dates
44	77852	Ha 14/2/17	C	Rental of a field
45	77853		C	Account of wool
46	77854	OB	NC	Disposition of an inheritance; Sabium oath
47	77855	Dar 21/6/32	C	Contract for dates
48	77856		F	Adoption; *Nbn* 380
49	77857	Nbn 29/5/10	C	Receipt for iron; *Nbn* 432
50	77858	Nbn 16/2/6	C	Receipt for wool; *Nbn* 222
51	77859		NC	Receipt for purchase of oxen
52	77860	Nbn 1+/10/11	C	Receipt for linen; *Nbn* 460
53	77861		C	Receipt
54	77862	Dar 10/12/3	C	Contract for barley; Babylon; *Dar* 96
55	77863	Cyr 13/5/7	C	Receipt; *Cyr* 263
56	77864	Nbk 5/11/38	NC	Account of barley and dates; *Nbk* 336
57	77865	Nbn 10/12/12	C	Account of silver; *Nbn* 673
58	77866	Nbk 1/3/33	C	Receipt for dates or grain; *Nbk* 255

85-4-30,

59	77867	Cyr 5/5/2	NC	Receipt; *Cyr* 47
60	77868	Nbk 8/4/35	C	Receipt for jewelry of gods; *Nbk* 280
61	77869	Nbk 2/-/39	F	Loan of silver; *Nbk* 357
62	77870	Dar 6/1/28	C	Receipt for flour
63	77871	28/7/-	C	Receipt for barley
64	77872	-/-/7	C	Receipt for dates or grain
65	77873	Nbn 25/5/3	C	Contract for barley and dates; *Nbn* 111
66	77874		NC	Receipt for goats
67	92993	Nbk 20/8/23	C	Receipt for silver; *Nbk* 139
68	77875	Nbk 10/8/31	C	Receipt for dates; *Nbk* 238
69	77876	10/7/30	C	Receipt for barley
70	77877	Cyr 6/1/3	C	Receipt for gold for jewelry; *Cyr* 97
71	77878		F	Field(?) sale; nail marks
72	77879		NC	Letter
73	77880	Nbk 2/-/31	NC	Account of dates; *Nbk* 243
74	77881		NC	Receipt for dates
75	77882	(Nbk) 2/2/43	NC	Account of *telitu* tax
76	77883	Nbk 19/12/35	C	Account of garments of gods; *Nbk* 286
77	77884	Npl 25/1/18	C	Contract for millet; Sippar; ZA 4 144
78	77885	14/8/-	C	Account of sheep(?)
79	77886	OB 26/2/-	C	Wool; tag
80	77887	Nb(-) 20/12b/12	NC	Account of barley
81	77888	Nbk -/-/2	C	Account of sheep
82	77889		NC	Ledger
83	77890	Nbk 7/7/41	C	Account of dates; *Nbk* 398
84	77891	Nbk 19/2/42	C	Receipt for an ass; *Nbk* 394
85	77892		C	Account of workmen
86	77893	1/2/41	C	Receipt for purchase
87	77894		NC	Contract
88	77895		F	Land sale; nail marks
89	77896		F	School exercise; literary extract
90	77897		F	Akkadian literary
91	77898		F	Account of silver
92	77899		F	Only personal names preserved
93	77900		F	Ledger
94	77901		F	Account of dates or grain
95	77902	Joined to 85-4-30, 10 (= BM 77819)		
96	77903		F	Account of sheep(?)
97	77904	Nbk 1/3/2	F	Animal ledger

85-4-30,

98	77905	-/-/15	F	Sworn deposition
99	77906	Dar 4/5?/12	F	Loan of silver; *Dar* 327
100	77907	Ššu [15]/1/1	C	Boat rental
101	77908	4/6/-	NC	Receipt for dates or grain
102	77909		F	Account of purchase of barley and dates
103	77910	Nbn 7/3/15	F	Loan of silver; *Nbn* 853
104	77911		F	Field plan; *St. Pohl* 11 253-255A, 516, no. 67
105	77912	Cyr 2/3/2	F	Account of dates or grain; *Cyr* 38
106	77913	Nbk 10/7/28	NC	Receipt for iron; *Nbk* 187
107	77914	11/12/41	C	Receipt for silver
108	77915	Cyr -/5/-	F	Account of dates or grain
109	77916	5/-/4	F	Sale of slaves
110	77917	Art 4/6/9	NC	Contract for dates
111	77918	Nbk 5/3/-	F	Receipt for dates
112	77919	19/6/22	NC	Receipt for dates or grain
113	77920		F	Receipt for garments
114	77921	Cyr 11/4/3	F	Loan of silver; *Cyr* 115
115	77922		F	Account of dates or grain
116	77923		F	Account of sheep
117	77924	2/2/42	F	Receipt for silver
118	77925	-/-/3	NC	Receipt for barley
119	77926	14/11/24	NC	Receipt
120	77927	Nbk 20+/7/4	NC	Receipt for barley
121	77928		C	Account of dates or grain
122	77929	Dar 17/9/16	C	Contract
123	77930		F	Animal ledger
124	77931		C	Receipt for silver
125	77932	Nbn 13/-/4	NC	Loan
126	77933		NC	Receipt
127	77934		F	Receipt
128	77935		NC	Receipt for barley
129	77936	-/-/28	F	Account of provisions
130	77937		NC	House rental
131	77938	Nbn -/7/10	C	Receipt for barley
132	77939		C	Account of dates
133	77940	13/4/5	NC	Offering ledger
134	77941	Nbk -/-/6	NC	Receipt for sheep(?)
135	77942	Ššu 9/1/-	F	Purchase of sheep

85-4-30,

136	77943	Nbn 5/3/-	NC	Receipt for iron tools
137	77944	Cyr 29/2/5	C	Receipt for oxen
138	77945	23+/-/19	F	Legal; concerning silver
139	77946	20/6/31	F	Sale receipt
140	77947	Npl 12/3/17	C	Account of sheep and goats
141	77948		C	Accounts
142	77949	Nbk 26/8/20+	F	Date ledger
143	77950		F	Offering ledger
144	77951		NC	Mathematical; standard table of reciprocals
145	77952		F	Hymn; *Emesal*; *CT* 42 44
146	77953		F	School exercise
147	77954		F	School exercise
148	77955		F	School exercise
149	77956		F	School exercise
150	77957		F	School exercise
151	77958		F	Account of purchases for silver
152	77959		F	Ledger
153	77960	Npl 14/12/10	F	List of *erib biti*
154	77961		F	List of people; perhaps same tablet as 85-4-30, 153 (= BM 77960)
155	77962		F	Accounts
156	77963		F	Account of dates or grain
157	77964		F	Accounts
158	77965		F	Account of dates or grain
159	77966		F	Accounts
160	77967		F	Ledger
161	77968	-/-/35	F	Account of garments of gods
162	77969		F	Account of dates or grain
163	77970		F	Account of dates or grain
164	77971		F	Medical astrology; cf. AH 83-1-18, 1851 (= BM 76483)
165	77972		F	Ledger
166	77973		F	Accounts
167	77974		F	Account of dates and barley
168	77975		F	Contract for beer(?)
169	77976	Dar 21/2/4	F	Accounts
170	77977	Nbk -/-/26	F	Receipt for barley
171	77978	Nbn 3/6/-	F	Receipt for barley
172	77979	Npl 9/-/2	F	Wool ledger; ZA 4 136

85-4-30,

173	77980		F	Ledger
174	77981		F	Ledger
175+ 199	77982+ 78006		F	Omens
176	77983		F	Accounts
177	77984		F	Ledger
178	77985		F	*Ikribu*
179	77986		F	Account of dates or grain
180	77987		F	Accounts
181	77988		F	Receipt
182	77989	13/-/8	F	Account of sheep and goats
183	77990		F	Account of dates or grain
184	77991	Nbk 19/12/22	F	Receipt for flour
185	77992		F	Account of dates or grain
186+ 189	77993+ 77996		F	Astronomical diary
187	77994	Joined to 82-9-18, 9324 (= BM 69327)		
188	77995		F	Literary
189	77996	Joined to 85-4-30, 186 (= BM 77993)		
190	77997		F	Astronomical almanac(?)
191	77998		F	Account of barley
192	77999		F	Economic
193	78000	Nbk 8/-/32	F	Economic
194	78001		F	Account of purchases
195	78002		F	Account of dates or grain
196	78003		F	Account of workmen
197	78004		F	Accounts
198	78005		F	Contract
199	78006	Joined to 85-4-30, 175 (= BM 77982)		
200	78007	Ner 21/5/2	F	Receipt
201	78008	Npl 1/-/-	F	Receipt for dates or grain
202	78009		F	Accounts
203	78010	Npl 4/8/-	F	Receipt for purchases
204	78011	-/5/19	F	Receipt for flour
205	78012	Npl -/-/12	F	Accounts
206	78013	26/2/-	F	Account of sheep
207	78014		F	Economic
208	78015		F	Account of barley
209	78016		F	Accounts
210	78017		F	Account

85-4-30,

211	78018		F	Account of barley
212	78019		F	Accounts
213	78020		F	Account of dates or grain
214	78021		F	*Šumma alu*
215	78022		F	School exercise
216	78023		F	School exercise
217	78024		F	School exercise
218	78025		F	Account of dates
219	78026		F	*Ḫḫ* XIV
220	78027		F	Account of sheep(?)
221	78028		F	Accounts
222	78029		F	Accounts
223	78030		F	Account of silver(?)
224	78031		F	Accounts
225	78032	Nbn 3/12/15	C	Letter
226	78033		NC	Receipt for dates
227	78034		NC	Cultic inventory(?); cf. 85-4-30, 8 (= BM 77817)
228	78035		F	Astronomical omens
229	93074		F	*Ḫḫ* XVIII; *CT* 14 12 (published under wrong number); *MSL* 8/2 95
230	78036	-/8/7	F	Accounts
231	78037		F	Ledger
232	78038		F	School exercise
233	78039		F	Legal text concerning scribe's honorarium
234	78040		F	Receipt for dates or grain
235	78041		F	Account
236	78042	Dar -/-/28	C	Receipt for oil
237	78043		F	Account of dates or grain
238	78044		F	Account of garments of gods
239	78045	Nb(-) -/11/-	F	Contract
240	78046	Ner	F	Account of dates or grain
241	78047	19/12/17	C	Receipt for iron objects
242	78048	Npl 16/4/11	C	Receipt for a pot
243	78049	Nbn 8/3/-	C	Receipt for sesame
244	78050	Npl 1/4/7	C	Account of animal deliveries to the temple
245	78051		F	School exercise
246	78052		F	School exercise

85-4-30,

247	78053		F	School exercise
248	78054		F	Ledger
249	78055	-/-/28	F	Loan(?)
250	78056	8/10/-	F	Receipt for silver
251	78057	Nbk -/9/29	F	Receipt for dates
252	78058	Nbn 5/3/2	F	Receipt for barley
253	78059		F	Ledger
254	78060		F	Account of dates or grain
255	78061	Dar 6/8/-	F	Account of dates
256	78062		F	Account of dates or grain
257	78063		F	Account of dates

85-11-27,

1	78064	Nbk 11/3/27	C	Field sale
2	78065	26/-/-	F	Receipt for lumps of metal
3	78066		F	Account of dates
4	78067		F	Account of dates or grain
5	78068	Npl	F	Ledger
6	78069		F	Account of seed
7	78070		F	Temple accounts
8	78071		F	Only personal names preserved
9	78072	Ner	F	Economic
10	78073		F	Hemerology
11	78074	Joined to 82-3-23, 2209 (= BM 51213)		
12	78075		F	Lexical

86-5-12,

1	78076	Dar 10/8/13	F	Ritual for festival of Bau in Kislimu; Babylon
2	78077		F	Akkadian literary with repeated refrain: *e-a mu-ri-ia mu-ri-ia* . . .
3	78078		F	Literary
4	78079		F	Mathematical tables(?)
5	78080		F	Astronomical; *JCS* 20 5-7, 28
6	92994	Nbk 15/2/35	NC	Land sale
7	78081	Nbk 5/10/15	NC	Division of an inheritance
8	78082	Dar 7/5/6	NC	Loan of silver; Borsippa
9	78083	Nbk 2/5/37	NC	Sale of a slave; Babylon

86-5-20,

1	78084	C	Mathematical problem text

86-6-17,

1	78085	Ššu	F	Sale of land; nail marks
2	78086	Ššu 2/8/6	NC	Sale of land; nail marks; Babylon
3	78087	Nbk -/8/-	F	Sworn deposition concerning land; Babylon
4	78088	Dar 25/-/-	NC	Contract for dates
5	78089		C	Horoscope for a new-born baby
6	78090	Xer 14/3/2	NC	Receipt
7	78091	10/12b/14	F	Account of seed
8	78092	Nbk -/-/2	F	Account of oxen
9	78093	Nbk 29/2/30	F	Sale of land
10	78094		F	Letter; *CT* 22 49
11	78095		F	Bilingual
12	78096		F	*Utukki lemnuti*; dupl. *CT* 16 12
13	78097		F	Sale of land
14	78098		F	Literary
15	78099		F	Incantation to Ištar and ritual

86-7-20,

1	91089+ 91090	Npl	NC	Clay cone and clay core; *VAB* 4, Npl 1; *ZA* 4 129ff.; *BA* 3 525ff.
2	78100		C	Letter
2A	78100A		NC	Envelope to 86-7-20, 2 (= BM 78100); stamp seals
3	92995	Dar 21/7/9	C	Sale of a slave girl; Babylon
4	78101	Dar 6/8/-	NC	Loan of silver; Babylon
5	78102	Dar 2/7/23	C	Loan of silver; Babylon
6	78103	Cam 21/6b/3	C	Contract for collateral; Babylon
7	78104	Cam -/-/6	NC	Contract for dates
8	78105		C	Memorandum requesting a message
9	78106		NC	Lenticular tablet with incised Aramaic
10	78107	Ššu 12/3/19	F	Land sale; nail marks; Babylon
11	78108		F	Legal; concerning slaves; two columns
12	78109		NC	Field given as dowry
13	78110		C	School exercise(?); lexical extract
14	78111		C	*Ḫḫ* VIII; *MSL* 9 173
15	78112		NC	*Ḫḫ* XIII
16	78113		NC	School exercise; incantation and lexical extracts
17	93085		F	Lexical; *CT* 14 49
18	78114		F	*Ḫḫ* III
19	78115		F	School exercise; left column list of animals and objects; right column list of pots
20	78116		F	Lexical (GIŠ)
21+ 32	78117		F	*Ḫḫ* III
22	78118		F	Letter(?)
23	78119		F	*Ḫḫ* III

86-7-20,

24	78120		F	School exercise; lexical and god list
25	78121	22/7/-	F	School text; lexical extract
26	78122		F	*Ḫḫ* IV
27	78123		F	Lexical
28	78124		F	Lexical
29	78125		F	School extract; literary and lexical
30	78126	27/[6]b/-	F	*Ḫḫ* II
31	78127		F	*Ḫḫ* VIII and IX
32		Joined to 86-7-20, 21 (= BM 78117)		
33	78128		F	Lexical
34	78129	17/7/-	F	Lexical; literary extract
35	78130		F	*Ḫḫ* V
36	78131		F	*Ḫḫ* VI
37	78132		F	Lexical (GIŠ)
38	78133		F	Lexical
39	78134		F	Lexical
40	78135		F	*Ḫḫ* XXIV
41	78136	29/7/-	F	Lexical (GIŠ)
42	78137		F	*Ḫḫ* IV
43	78138		F	Lexical
44	78139		F	Lexical
45	78140		F	Sumerian; Emesal litany
46	78141		F	Note of ownership(?); clay stopper; stamp seals
47	118767			Uninscribed bas relief

87-1-14,

1	78142	Cyr 24/-/6	C	Contract for dates; Babylon
2	78143	Dar 7/8/12	C	Account of deliveries to Ebabbar; lower edge hatched to prevent additions; Sippar
3	89306			Cylinder seal
4	89304			Cylinder seal

87-7-25,

1	92996	Npl 26/-/7	C	Copy of a land sale; nail marks; Babylon
2	78144	Nbk 2/5/20	NC	Account of dates
3	78145	Nbn 24/12a/1	C	Contract concerning access; Babylon
4	78146	Dar 7/9/5	C	Sworn deposition; Sippar
5	78147		C	Letter
6	78148	Nbk 26/9/36	NC	Field plan; *St. Pohl* 11 25-29, 462-463, text 1

88-4-19,

1	78149	Nbn -/11/5	NC	Receipt for purchase of provisions
2	78150		F	Receipt for bronze objects
3	78151	Nbn 16/9/7	C	Receipt for silver
4	78152		F	Lexical
5	116664			Stone head; *BMQ* 7 5
6	78153	Dar 26/-/acc	F	Account of dates
7	78154		F	Lexical
8	78155		F	Account of silver(?)
9	78156	TP III 25/4/2	C	Legal; dispute over inheritance; nail marks; Babylon
10	78157	14/24/7	C	Account of barley
11	78158		C	Copy of broken medical text, the original in 2nd mill. script with earlier colophon and colophon to whole
12	78159	Ššu 7/3/12	C	Purchase of sheep and goats; Kiš
13	93017		F	*En el* III 47-105; *CT* 13 10-11
	78160	Nothing registered		
14	78161		C	Astronomical; Sachs *Fs*
15	78162		C	Account of deliveries
16	78163		F	Ritual; cf. 82-9-18, 7552 (= BM 67554)
17	92689	Joined to 80-6-17, 442 (= BM 36710)		
18	78164		F	Bilingual hymn to Enki
19	78165	Dar 23/3/30	F	Distribution of *isqu* shares; Sippar
20	78166		F	Bilingual; dupl. *SBH* 4
21	78167	Ššu 19/-/1	F	Sale of land
22	78168		F	Rental of a boat
23	78169		F	Lexical
24	78170		F	Account of silver(?)
25	78171	Šši	NC	Ledger; animals
26	92997	Kan 26/5/15	C	Sale of slaves; *AfO* 16 pl. 5; Babylon

Bu 88-5-12,

1	78172	OB	NC	Inventory of equipment; *CT* 45 34 no. 75
2	78173	OB	NC	Sumerian *eršemma*; *CT* 44 12 no. 15; dupl. *CT* 42 7 and *VAS* 2 94
3	78174	Sm	F	Division of an estate; envelope; seals; *CT* 8 1
4	78175	OB	NC	Emesal hymn to Mullil; *CT* 44 11 no. 12; *JNES* 26 206-08
5+ 1985-10-6, 5	78176+ 139968	OB	C	Letter; *CT* 4 1-2; *AbB* 2 88
6	92503	OB	NC	Sumerian incantation; *CT* 4 3
7	92504	OB	NC	Sumerian incantation; *CT* 4 4; Geller, *Forerunners* pls. 19-20
8	92505	OB	C	Sumerian incantations; *CT* 44 20 no. 27
9	78177	NB	F	List of workmen(?) including Egyptians; *CT* 44 50 no. 89
10	78178	Ad 26/12/34	C	List of the dowry of a *naditu* of Marduk; seals; *CT* 8 2a
11	78179	NA	NC	Hemerology; *CT* 4 5-6
12	92506	Aş 23/6b/11	NC	Division of an estate; seals; *CT* 8 3a
13	78180	Sm 11+/diri-ga/-	C	Adoption agreement; part of case adhering; *CT* 45 9 no. 16; *RA* 73 93-94
14	78181	Sm	NC	Division of an estate; *CT* 8 4
15	78182	Ad 30/4/14	NC	Administrative; rations for chariotry and infantry in Sippar-amnanum; *CT* 45 23 no. 48
16	78183	OB	C	Širnamšubba or Ur-Nammu to Nanna in Emesal; *CT* 44 13 no. 16; *JAOS* 95 592ff.
17	78184	OB	C	Record of three law suits; *CT* 29 41-43
18	78185	OB	NC	Sumerian incantations; *CT* 44 22 no. 31; Geller, *Forerunners* pls. 15-16

Bu 88-5-12,

19	78186	Aṣ?	C	Legal protocol concerning the property of a *naditu*; *CT* 2 1; cf. Bu 88-5-12, 163 (= BM 78298)
20	78187	Ad -/-/3?	C	Administrative text concerning fields; *CT* 45 25 no. 52
21	92507	OB	NC	Marriage contract; Meissner, *BAP* no. 89
22	92508	OB	NC	Sumerian incantation; *CT* 44 21 no. 30
23	78188	NB	C	Account of barley provisions; *CT* 44 49 no. 85
24	78189	OB	F	Akkadian literary; *CT* 44 17 no. 23
25	78190	Dar 2/12/14	C	Contract for purchase of a field; *ša ḫarrani*; seals; ZA 3 223 no. 1; *Dar* 393
26	78191	Dar -/2/19	C	Deposition; *CT* 2 2
27	78192	Dar 8/12/25	C	Loan of silver; Babylon; *ZA* 3 224 no. 2
28	78193	OB	F	Sumerian hymn to Dumuzi; *CT* 44 11 no. 13
29	78194	OB	C	Ration list; two columns; *CT* 45 35 no. 77
30	78195	Art 1/9/4	C	Sale of slaves; seals; Babylon; *CT* 44 45 no. 77
31	92509	Sm -/-/13	C	Division of an estate; Meissner, *BAP* no. 103
32	78196	Ae 20/12/"k"	C	Administrative account; *CT* 45 20 no. 40
33	78197	Ha -/-/2	C	Heritage agreement for a *kulmašitu*; *CT* 8 50a
34	78198	OB	NC	Sumerian prayer; *CT* 44 12 no. 14
35	78199	OB	NC	Sumerian incantation for a sick man; *CT* 44 26 no. 34
36	78200	OB	C	Dowry (of a *naditu*?); approximately time of AS or Sm; *CT* 45 36 no. 79
37	92510	Si 5/10/2	C	Lawsuit over a wife's inheritance; Meissner, *BAP* no. 100
38	78201	AS -/-/13	C	Protocol concerning real estate sale; *CT* 4 7a
39	78202	Ha 11/6/41	C	Adoption contract; *CT* 8 5a
40	78203	AS	C	Claim for balance of purchase price of a field; *CT* 8 17a
41	92669	OB	C	Sumerian incantation; drawing; *CT* 44 19 no. 25
42	78204	Si 1/11/23	NC	Exchange of slaves; *CT* 8 6a
43	92511	Sabium -/*ti-ru-um*/14	C	Real estate sale; *CT* 2 3
44	78205	OB	NC	Exchange of real estate; *CT* 45 36 no. 80

Bu 88-5-12,

45	92512	AS	C	Real estate sale; Meissner, *BAP* no. 36
46	92513	Sm -/-/13	C	Division of an estate; Meissner, *BAP* no. 104
47	92514	Aṣ 6/4/14	C	Lawsuit concerning real estate; Meissner *BAP* no. 42; ZA 3 229 no. 6
48	92515	OB	C	Dedicatory inscription of Gimil-Marduk to Šamaš for the life of Aṣ; *Iraq* 31 90-92; (previously registered as Bu 88-5-12, 54)
48A	92519	OB	C	Adoption contract; Meissner, *BAP* no. 97 (under wrong number Bu 88-5-12, 54); (originally registered as Bu 88-5-12, 48)
49	92516	Ad 5/2/32	C	Field rental for three years; seals; *CT* 8 7a
50	92517	Sm?	NC	Purchase of threshing floor by a woman; *CT* 45 10 no. 19
51	92518	OB	NC	Bilingual incantation; *CT* 4 8
52	78206	OB	F	Lexical; *CT* 44 34 no. 47
53	78207	Ha	C	Lawsuit over division of an estate; *CT* 4 9a
54		See Bu 88-5-12, 48 (= BM 92515)		
55	78208	Aṣ 18/7/3	NC	Field rental; seals; *CT* 8 3b
56	78209	OB	C	Administrative account; late period; 45 48 no. 110
57	92520	Aṣ 30/1/16	C	Division of an estate; seals; Meissner, *BAP* no. 107
58	92521	Immerum	C	Real estate sale; Meissner, *BAP* no. 35
59	92998	Cyr 10/1/5	C	Sale of a field and orchard; Babylon; seals; nail- and finger-impressions; *Cyr* 188; ZA 3 226 no. 4
60	92522	Sm -/-/13	C	Division of an estate; *CT* 2 4
61	78210	Ad 20/12/13	C	Ration list; *CT* 4 8b
62	78211	OB	C	Ration list for temple officials; late period; *CT* 45 38 no. 85
63	78212	OB	NC	Ration account of oil and bread; *CT* 45 37 no. 81
64	78213	OB	F	Sale of temple office(?) (*parṣum*) involving *naditus*; Aṣ? oath; *CT* 45 29 no. 62
65	78214	OB	C	Letter; *CT* 29 33-34; *AbB* 2 162
66	78215	OB	NC	Real estate sale, involving *naditus*; early period; *CT*45 31 no. 64

Bu 88-5-12,

67	78216	OB	NC	Letter
68	78217	OB	C	Legal process between a husband and wife; Ha or older; *CT* 45 39 no. 86
69	78218	NB	C	List of workmen(?); *CT* 44 50 no. 87
70	78219	NB	F	Incantation; *Bit rimki* III; *CT* 44 27 no. 35
71	78220	OB	NC	Real estate purchase by a *naditu*, early period; *CT* 45 37 no. 82
72	92670	OB	NC	Sumerian incantation; drawing; *CT* 44 19 no. 26
73		Nothing registered		
74+ 75+ 76	78221+ 78222	Esar	F	Prism; Hillah; Budge, *By Nile and Tigris* I 273; *CT* 44 5-7 no. 5
75	78222	Joined to Bu 88-5-12, 74 (= BM 78221)		
76		Joined to Bu 88-5-12, 74 (= BM 78221)		
77+ 78	78223	Esar	F	Prism; Hillah; *CT* 44 2-4 no. 3
78		Joined to Bu 88-5-12, 77 (= BM 78223)		
79+ 1958-4-12, 28	78224+ 132294	Esar	F	Prism; Hillah; *CT* 44 4 no. 4
80	78225	Esar	F	Prism; Hillah; *CT* 44 8 no. 6
81	78226	OB	F	Lexical; *CT* 44 34 no. 46
82	78227	Cam 7/2/1	C	Account of garments for cleaning; *CT* 44 44 no. 73
83	78228	Art -/6/4	C	Sale of a house; seals; *CT* 44 46 no. 78
84	78229	OB 12/7/-	C	Bulla for a hired hand; seals; *CT* 45 33 no. 67
85	78230	OB 6/9/-	C	Bulla for a hired hand; seals; *CT* 45 33 no. 68
86	78231	OB 23/9/-	C	Bulla for a hired hand; seals; *CT* 45 33 no. 69
87	78232	OB 4/8/-	C	Bulla for a hired hand; seals; *CT* 45 33 no. 70
88	78233	Si 11/4/2	C	Bulla for a builder; seals; *CT* 45 33 no. 71
89	78234	OB 16/9/-	C	Bulla for a hired hand; seals; *CT* 45 33 no. 72
90	78235	OB 6/6/-	C	Bulla for a hired hand; seals; *CT* 45 33 no. 73
91	78236	OB 1/9/-	C	Bulla for a hired hand; seals; *CT* 45 33 no. 74

Bu 88-5-12,

92	78237	OB	NC	Pay list mentioning cities of Uruk, Ur and others; three columns; cf. Bu 88-5-12, 29 (= BM 78194); *CT* 45 40 no. 89
93	78238	OB	F	Summary of land belonging to various persons; *CT* 45 42 no. 94
94	78239	NB	F	Sumerian liturgical text; *elum didara* III; *CT* 44 14 no. 17
95	78240	NB	F	Akkadian incantation and ritual; *RA* 26 39-42; dupl. *KAR* no. 80
96	78241	NB	F	Extispicy; *CT* 44 28 no. 37
97	78242	Ae -/-/"s"	F	igi-sá imports in silver and spices(?); *CT* 45 21 no. 41
98	78243	Alex 8/7/12	C	Contract for barley; seals; *CT* 44 48 no. 83
99	78244	NB -/8/17	F	Account of date or grain provisions; seals; *CT* 44 47 no. 80
100	78245	OB	F	Akkadian hymn(?); *CT* 44 35 no. 49
101	78246	Esar	F	Prism; Hillah; *CT* 44 8 no. 8
102	78247	Esar	F	Prism; Hillah; *CT* 44 9 no. 9
103	78248	Esar	F	Prism; Hillah; *CT* 44 9 no. 7
104	78249	OB	F	Sumerian incantations; *CT* 44 23-24 no. 32; dupl. *ASKT* 11 and *LKA* 77; cf. Bu 88-5-12, 108 (= BM 78253) and 108A (= BM 78253A)
105	78250	OB	F	Bilingual penitential prayer; *CT* 44 18 no. 24
106	78251	OB	F	Economic; four columns; check marks
107	78252	NB	F	Account of date or grain provisions; *CT* 44 49 no. 86
108	78253	NB	F	Sumerian and Akkadian incantations; *CT* 44 25 no. 33; cf. Bu 88-5-12, 104 (= BM 78249)
108A	78253A	NB	F	Sumerian and Akkadian incantations; *CT* 44 25 no. 33; cf. Bu 88-5-12, 104 (= BM 78249)
109	78254	Ae -/-/"o"	F	Collection of real estate transactions
110	78255	Ha 21/1/1	C	Rental of a journey of the weapon of Šamaš; *CT* 8 8c; *AS* 16 220
110A	78255A	OB	F	Case of previous
111	91154	Ha	C	Cone with Sumerian inscription of Ha; dupl. *LIH* 1 102-105 no. 58 and 3 177-179

Bu 88-5-12,

112	78256	Art -/-/16	C	Contract for delivery of dates; *CT* 44 46 no. 79
113	78257	OB	F	*Atraḫasis* I; *CT* 44 16 no. 20
114	78258	Si 10/2/9	F	Case of Bu 88-5-12, 155 (= BM 92528); seals; *CT* 45 17 no. 33
115	78259	OB	F	*Edict of Ammiṣaduqa*; *Symb. Koschaker* 102-105; Kraus, *Edikt* 26-43 (Duplikat B); Kraus, *Königliche Verfügungen* 129 ff., 163 and pl. 7
116	78260	OB	C	School exercise; lenticular; *CT* 44 33 no. 43
117	78261	OB	C	School exercise; lenticular; *CT* 44 33 no. 44
118	78262	OB	C	School exercise; lenticular; *CT* 44 33 no. 45
119	78263	OB	F	Ration(?) list for women (*naditu*?); two columns; *CT* 45 41 no. 92
120	78264	Asb	F	Cylinder; Streck, *Asb* 228-233
121	78265	NB	NC	Tablet case; seals
122	78266	OB	F	Case; real estate sale; seals; *CT* 45 43 no. 98
123	78267	OB	NC	Multiplication tables; *CT* 44 30 no. 41
124	78268	Art 14/3/-	NC	Rental of a house; seals; *CT* 44 47 no. 81
125	78269	OB	F	Large economic tablet; mentions copper quantities
126	78270	AS	F	Case; sale of a field; seals; *CT* 45 4 no. 7
127	78271	OB	F	Case, with seal impressions and witnesses; early period; *CT* 45 34 no. 76
128	78272	Art 27/5/36	C	Contract for dates; *CT* 44 47 no. 82
129	78273	Art 10/-/1	C	Rental of a field; seals; Babylon; *CT* 44 45 no. 76
130	78274	OB	F	Sumerian literary; *CT* 44 15 no. 19
131	78275	NB	F	Akkadian prayer; *CT* 44 17 no. 22
132	78276	NB	F	Sumerian; dialogue between Inanna and Ningal; *CT* 44 10 no. 11
133	78277	OB	F	igi-sá imports of Sippar; mentions Si 37; cf. Bu 88-5-12, 97 (= BM 78242); *CT* 45 20 no. 38
134	78278	OB	F	Akkadian prayer to Marduk; *CT* 44 16 no. 21
135	92523	Si 8/11/30	NC	Real estate sale; *CT* 8 9b

Bu 88-5-12,

135A	92090	Sassanian	C	Glazed rhyton in the form of a hare; Hillah; Pope, *Survey of Persian Art* 4 184B; *BMQ* 7 5 and pl. VI/2
136	78279	OB	NC	Sumerian lexical text; obv. *Proto-Izi* I; rev. *Proto-Izi* II (with many variants); twelve columns (first and last columns missing)
137	78280	Ha 9 or 33	F	Case, real estate sale; seals; *CT* 45 11 no. 20; case of Bu 88-5-12, 176 (= BM 92534)
138	78281	Ad 1/4/14	NC	Account; (disbursements?) of barley and silver; *CT* 45 24 no. 49
139	78282	Ad 27/6/-	C	Settlement of a claim involving purchase of three asses; seals; *CT* 45 26 no. 53
140	78283	OB	C	Letter; *CT* 44 36 no. 51; *AbB* 1 127
141	78284	OB	NC	Ration list(?) for temple personnel of Ṣarpanitum; late period; *CT* 45 38 no. 84
142	78285	Dar -/-/35	C	Account of dates; *CT* 44 44 no. 74
143	92524	Ha 20+/7/24	C	Lawsuit over an inheritance; part of case adhering; Meissner, *BAP* no. 80
144	78286	OB	C	Letter; *CT* 43 4 no. 9; *AbB* 1 9
145	78287	Sm	NC	Purchase by a *naditu* with her ring; part of case adhering; *CT* 45 9 no. 17
146	78288	Ššu	NC	Sale of a field; nail marks; Babylon; *CT* 44 43 no. 70
147	92525	Ha 30/11/33	NC	Real estate sale; *CT* 45 13 no. 26
148	78289	Si 10+/8/-	NC	Exchange of real estate; *CT* 45 20 no. 39
149	78290	NB	F	Copy of a Maništusu inscription; *CT* 44 1 no. 1
150	92526	Si	NC	Marriage contract; Meissner, *BAP* no. 90
151	78291	Ha 15/*e-lu-li*/26	NC	Division of an estate; *CT* 45 12 no. 24
152	78292	OB	F	Rental of a field; late period; seals; *CT* 45 54 no. 120
153	92527	Si 22/4/15	NC	Real estate sale; *CT* 45 19 no. 35
154	78293	Nbk 20/12/-	C	Offering ledger; *CT* 44 43 no. 71
155	92528	Si 26/7/9	C	Real estate sale; *CT* 2 5; for case see Bu 88-5-12, 114 (= BM 78258)
156	78294	Nbk 12/9/6	C	Account of sheep; *CT* 44 43 no. 72
157	92529	Sm -/-/19	C	Divorce contract; Meissner, *BAP* no. 91
158	92530	Aṣ 1/2/10	C	Field rental; seals; *CT* 8 10b

Bu 88-5-12,

159	92531	Aṣ 1/10/14	C	Administrative list of issues of silver; *CT* 8 11a
160	78295	Ha	C	Lawsuit concerning inheritance claimed by a *naditu*; *CT* 8 12b
161	78296	Ad 14/7?/nun-maš-sù igi-gál-la dingir KIN-a	C	Marriage contract; seals; *CT* 48 24 no. 50; *Iraq* 42 57-8
162	78297	OB	NC	List of women; *CT* 45 35 no. 78
163	78298	Aṣ?	C	Legal protocol concerning the property of a *naditu*; *CT* 2 6; cf. Bu 88-5-12, 19 (= BM 78186)
164	78299	AS	F	Division of an estate?; *CT* 45 5 no. 8
165	78300	OB	C	List of provisions, chariot equipment, staples, and vessels required for the ki-sì-ga edin-na; late period; *CT* 45 44 no. 99
166	78301	Ha 20/1/35	NC	List of animals and slaves; seals; *CT* 45 14 no. 27
167	78302	OB	NC	Text relating to sale of real estate, involving inherited land; late period; *CT* 45 45 no. 102
168	78303	OB	C	Account with names of persons; *CT* 45 44 no. 100
169	78304	Ha -/-/14	F	Real estate sale; *CT* 8 13a
170	78305	OB	NC	Sale of a field by two brothers and their mother; early period; *CT* 45 52 no. 117
171	78306	Ad 9/3?/5	F	Ration account; obv. lost
172	92532	Ha -/11/40	C	Exchange of real estate; Meissner, *BAP* no. 50
173	78307	OB	F	Letter; late period; *CT* 52 no. 86; *AbB* 7 86
174	78308	OB	NC	Letter; *CT* 44 38 no. 57; *AbB* 1 133
175	92533	Ha -/-/9 or 33	C	Real estate sale; *CT* 2 7
176	92534	Ha -/-/9 or 33	C	Exchange of real estate; Meissner, *BAP* no. 48; for case see Bu 88-5-12, 137 (= BM 78280)
177	78309	OB	C	Allocation of foodstuffs including beer; seals
178	78310	OB	C	Letter; *CT* 52 no. 114; *AbB* 7 114
179	92535	Aṣ 3?/1/13	C	Field rental; seals; Meissner, *BAP* no. 74
180	78311	AS -/-/1	C	Legal protocol concerning the property of a *naditu*; *CT* 4 10
181	78312	OB	C	Economic
182	78313	Si 6/12/1	C	Lawsuit over division of an estate; *CT* 8 9a

Bu 88-5-12,

183	78314	Si 10/6/28	C	Agreement concerning an inheritance; *CT* 4 11a
184	78315	OB	C	Letter; *CT* 4 12; *AbB* 2 89
185	92536	Ha 1/8/23	C	Real estate sale; *CT* 8 13b; Meissner, *BAP* no. 31
186	92537	Aṣ 20/5/16	C	Field rental; seals; *CT* 2 8
187	78316	Ha -/-/31?	C	Duplicate text of a lost testament of bequest by a woman (a *naditu*?); *CT* 45 13 no. 25
188	78317	OB 10/11/mu i_7 nu-ḫu-uš ni-ši	C	Lawsuit over rights to temple offerings; *CT* 4 13a
189	78318	Aṣ 25/2/14	C	Ration list; *CT* 8 14b
190	78319	OB	C	Account of ration allocation; late period
191	78320	Si	C	Contract
192	78321	OB	C	List of personnel; seals; *CT* 4 15
193	78322	Ad 2/11/11	C	Marriage contract; seals; *CT* 8 7b
194	92538	Si -/6/14	NC	Real estate sale; *CT* 8 15b
195	78323	Sm	NC	Real estate sale; *CT* 8 4b
196	78324	Sabium	NC	Real estate contract
197	78325	Ad 14/12/2	NC	Sale of 2(?) slaves; seals; *CT* 45 21 no. 44
198	78326	OB 21/2/-	NC	List of recipients of beer rations; *CT* 45 47 no. 106
199	78327	Ha -/-/17	C	Lawsuit over real estate and movable property; *CT* 2 9
200	78328	OB	C	Letter; *CT* 2 10a; *AbB* 2 80
201	78329	NB 11/10/14	C	Account of dates; *CT* 2 10b
202	78330	OB	NC	Letter; *CT* 52 no. 88; *AbB* 7 88
203	92539	Sumula'el	NC	House sale; *JCS* 30 235-236
204	78331	OB	C	Ration(?) list; some names same as Bu 88-5-12, 168 (= BM 78303); *CT* 45 47 no. 108
205	92540	AS	NC	Division of an estate
206	92541	Ad	NC	Real estate sale
207	78332	OB	C	Letter; *CT* 2 11; *AbB* 2 81
208	78333	OB	F	Letter; *CT* 44 39 no. 61; *AbB* 1 137
209	92671	OB	C	Sumerian incantation; *CT* 44 20 no. 28; Geller, *Forerunners* pl. 17
210	92542	Ha	NC	Adoption contract; Meissner, *BAP* no. 95
211	92543	Ha 22/7/24	NC	Division of an estate; *CT* 45 12 no. 23
212	78334	OB	C	Letter; *CT* 2 12; *AbB* 2 82

Bu 88-5-12,

213	92544	Sabium	NC	Real estate sale; *CT* 45 3 no. 5
214	92545	Sm	NC	Real estate sale; *CT* 8 16b
215	92547	Aş 6/5/10	C	Receipt for oil to be traded for slaves; seals; Meissner, *BAP* no. 4
216	92546	Aş 8/4/3	C	Field rental; seals; *CT* 4 14a
217	78335	OB	C	Receipt for payment of a nurse; *CT* 4 13b
218	78336	Ad 13/5/3	C	Receipt for silver; seals; *CT* 4 15a
219	78337	Ae 2/1/"k"	C	Field rental; seals; *CT* 8 17b
220	78338	Ha 13/10/3	C	Real estate sale; *CT* 8 12a
221	78339	Ha	C	Bequest by father to daughter; *CT* 45 15 no. 29
222	92548	Sm	NC	Real estate sale; Meissner, *BAP* no. 37
223	78340	Aş 1/2/10	C	Field rental; seals; *CT* 8 14a
224	78341	OB	C	Letter; *CT* 44 41 no. 66; *AbB* 1 142
225	78342	Si 27/10/16	C	Sale of a field; *CT* 2 13
226	78343	Xer 24/8/-	NC	Loan of silver; Sippar; *CT* 44 45 no. 75
227	92549	Ha 11/11/14	C	Lawsuit over division of an estate; *CT* 8 18c
228	78344	Ae 10/11/-	F	Administrative text; obverse destroyed; seals; *CT* 45 21 no. 42; *Iraq* 42 59-60
229	92550	Ha -/-/39	NC	Gift of real estate and movable property to a daughter; Meissner, *BAP* no. 7
230	78345	Ae 2/4/"o"+1	NC	Administrative; seals
231	78346	OB	C	Administrative
232	78347	Ad 25/4/34	F	Contract; seals
233	78348	Ad 16/11/12	NC	Administrative; loan from the *natbaku*; Sippar; seals
234	92551	Aş 3/7/3	C	Sale of a slave girl; seals; Meissner, *BAP* no. 3
235	78349	OB	NC	Ration account; *CT* 45 47 no. 107
236	78350	NB	NC	Account of dates or grain; *CT* 44 50 no. 88
237	78351	OB	C	Ration list for various persons of barley and seed corn; *CT* 45 42 no. 95
238	78352	Aş 26/3/5	C	Field rental; seals; *CT* 8 19c
239	78353	OB	C	Pay list for harvest labourers
240	78354	Aş -/-/14	NC	Rental of a field; seals
241	78355	Aş 28/3/5	C	Rental of a field from a *naditu*; seals; *CT* 45 28 no. 57
242	78356	Ad 6/3?/35	NC	Legal proceeding concerning death of a principal to a contract; mentions year of Ae and year 35 of Ad; seals

Bu 88-5-12,

243	78357	OB	NC	Letter; *CT* 44 39 no. 60; *AbB* 1 136
244	92552	Sm	NC	Real estate sale; *CT* 8 20b
245	78358	OB	C	Ration list of various foodstuffs
246	78359	OB	F	Sale of a field; early period; *CT* 45 41 no. 93
247	78360	Aṣ 2/3/5	C	Issue of rations of barley; *CT* 8 21d
248	78361	OB	NC	Letter; *CT* 44 37 no. 55; *AbB* 1 131
249	78362	19/2/mu Ì-si-in-na šu-ni sá bí-in x	C	Contract about a partition wall; *CT* 48 50 no. 118
250	78363	OB	F	Roster of names; two columns
251	78364	OB	F	Letter about women in Sippar and the *gagum*; *CT* 52 no. 111; *AbB* 7 111
252	92674	Aṣ -/4?/11	NC	Field rental; seals
253	78365	OB	C	Letter; late period; *CT* 52 no. 167; *AbB* 7 167
254	78366	Si	F	Real estate contract between *naditus*
255	78367	OB	C	Administrative; list of erin-meš; late period; cf. Bu 88-5-12, 272 (=BM 78380)
256	78368	Sm -/-/7	NC	Gift of real estate; *CT* 4 16b
257	91117	Dar	C	Basalt weight of Darius I with trilingual inscription in Old Persian, Elamite and Babylonian; said to have come from Hillah; *PBSA* 10, 464-466; *VAB* 3 xxii and 104-105 (Dar.Pond. a); Kent, *Old Persian Grammar*, 114 Wa; Schmidt, *Persepolis* 2 105; Budge, *By Nile and Tigris* 1 268
258	92553	Si -/-/20?	NC	Purchase of an é ki-x by a *naditu* with silver ring
259	78369	Aṣ 1/2/11	C	Rental of a field
260	78370	OB	NC	(Beer?) ration list
261	78371	Ad 13/4/14	C	Adoption of a girl to be married; seals; *CT* 33 34
262	78372	OB	NC	Real estate contract, not completed; Sippar-amnanum
263	78373	Ad 16/10/4	C	Receipt for silver; seals; *CT* 33 27
264	92554	Ae 3/2/28	NC	Sale of an ox; seals; Meissner, *BAP* no. 2
265	78374	AS	C	Real estate sale; *CT* 4 16a
266	78375	OB	NC	Sumerian incantation; *CT* 44 21 no. 29; Geller, *Forerunners* pl. 18
267	78376	Ha -/8/-	NC	Exchange of real estate; *CT* 8 22a
268	78377	OB	F	Purchase of a field from the king by a *naditu*; no oath; *CT* 45 54 no. 121

Bu 88-5-12,

269	92555	Aș 20/8/9	C	Field rental; *CT* 4 17a
270	78378	Sd 30/6?/11	NC	Loan for a trading journey; seals
271	78379	Ad -/6/2	NC	Assignment of impost (igi-sá) in Kar Sippar; seals; *CT* 45 21 no. 43
272	78380	Aș 22/1/7	NC	List of erin-meš; cf. Bu 88-5-12, 255 (= BM 78367)
273	78381	Si 1/šu-níg-gi-na/2	C	Summaries of small cattle under the charge of various herdsmen; seals; *CT* 45 16 no. 31
274	92556	Si -/10/31	NC	Real estate sale; *CT* 4 18a
275	78382	OB	C	Declaration of items given to a *naditu*; *CT* 4 18b
276	78383	Aș 1/10/5?	C	Hire of a boat from the king's daughter; (same var. year formula as in Bu 88-5-12, 241 = BM 78355); seals; *CT* 45 28 no. 58
277	78384	OB	C	Mathematical; catalogue of quadratic equations; *CT* 44 29 no. 38; *JCS* 33, 57-64
278	78385	OB	C	Letter; *CT* 4 19; *AbB* 2 90
279	78386	Aș 1/10/5	C	House rental; seals; *CT* 45 28 no. 56
280	78387	Sabium	NC	Real estate sale; *CT* 8 23a
281	92557	Ad 1/6/2	C	House rental; seals; Meissner, *BAP* no. 68
282	78388	Si 10/9/?	C	Real estate sale; *CT* 4 19b
283	92558	Aș 10/2/10	NC	Field rental; seals; *CT* 45 29 no. 59
284	78389	Aș 12/1/11	NC	Rental of house from a *naditu* Šamaš and Aya witness; seals
285	92559	Sm -/-/15	C	Real estate sale; *CT* 4 20a
286	78390	OB	F	Loan of silver (trading journey?); seals
287	78391	Dar 5/1/19	C	Contract for rent; Sippar; *CT* 4 21
288	78392	Ad 26/4/3	C	Harvest loan; sealed
289	78393	OB	F	Loan of silver for a journey of the weapon of Šamaš; seals
290	92560	Sm -/-/17	NC	Real estate sale; Meissner, *BAP* no. 32
291	92561	Ha -/-/11	C	Real estate sale; *CT* 2 14
292	92562	Ad 12/11/34	C	House rental; seals; Meissner, *BAP* no.69
293	78394	OB	C	Ration list; rev. uninscribed
294	78395	OB -/-/ mu *ša lipit-ištar Amurrum iṭruduš*	C	Receipt for silver; *CT* 4 22c
295	78396	OB	C	Lawsuit concerning a debt; *CT* 4 23a
296	78397	Ae 7/12/-	C	Receipt for barley and silver to be credited to account; seals

Bu 88-5-12,

297	78398	Ha 21/9/16	NC	Contract for nursing an infant girl
298	78399	Ha 6/6/27	C	Division of an estate among heirs; *CT* 48 12 no. 22
299	78400	Si 5?/7?/7	F	Case; field rental; seals; envelope
300	78401	NB	F	Bilingual; liturgical text with musical annotations
301	78402	OB	F	Letter; late period; *CT* 52 no. 138; *AbB* 7 138
302	92563	Ad 22/4/33	NC	Field rental; seals; Meissner, *BAP* no. 76
303	78403	OB	C	Letter; *CT* 52 no. 30; *AbB* 7 30
304	78404	OB	NC	Letter; *CT* 52 no. 100; *AbB* 7 100
305	92564	Ad 13/7/32	NC	Harvest loan; seals; Meissner, *BAP* no. 25
306	78405	OB 19/7/-	C	Payment of a debt and voiding of duplicate of debt document after loss of the original
307	78406	OB	F	Envelope; names of witnesses; seals
308	78407	OB	F	Envelope; real estate contract; seals
309	78408	Aș 10/1/15	C	Field rental; seals; *CT* 4 23b
310	78409	OB	C	Administrative; list of names
311	78410	NB	C	Account of sheep; *CT* 4 24
312	78411	NB 6/8/7	NC	Account of *erib biti*
313	78412	Sd 23/1/5	C	Rental of a journey of the weapon of Šamaš; seals; *AS* 16 223; *CT* 4 23c
314	78413	Ae 25/12/28	C	Lawsuit concerning two slaves; seals; *CT* 8 17c
315	78414	OB	F	Letter; *CT* 52 18; *AbB* 7 18
316	78415	OB	C	Real estate contract; late period
317	78416	NB	C	Account of workdays of brewers
318	78417	Ha 10/ezen ᵈiškur/34	C	Real estate sale; *CT* 4 25a
319	78418	Dar 22/12/35	NC	Contract
320	78419	Ae 20/8/?	C	Hire of a harvest labourer; seals; *CT* 33 46a
321	78420	OB	F	Large tablet dealing with fields
322	78421	Ha -/-/14	F	Adoption contract; dupl. *VAS* 8 127; Meissner, *BAP* no. 94
323	78422	OB	C	Letter; *CT* 4 20b; *AbB* 2 91
324	78423	Aș 1/8/8	C	Rental of a journey of the weapon of Šamaš; seals; *AS* 16 221; *CT* 4 18c
325	78424	Dar 27/10/2	C	Receipt
326	78425	Art 19/3/11	C	Receipt for garments
327	78426	Aș 29/12/16	C	List of issues of silver; *CT* 4 26c

Bu 88-5-12,

328	78427	OB	F	Economic
329	78428	OB	C	Letter; *CT* 4 27; *AbB* 2 94
330	92565	Ad 25/6/4	C	Field rental; seals; *CT* 33 33
331	78429	OB	NC	Real estate contract; old period
332	92566	Si 10/1/3	C	Real estate sale; *CT* 2 15
333	78430	OB	C	Letter; *CT* 4 28; *AbB* 2 96
334	78431	OB	F	Letter; *CT* 44 36 no. 52; *AbB* 1 128
335	78432	NA	F	Prayer; *PSBA* 40 104-110
336	78433	Cam 4/7/5	C	Account of wool; *CT* 4 27c
337	78434	NB	C	Medical; *CT* 44 27 no. 36
338	78435	OB	F	Inheritance text
339	78436	Ha 23/5/8	NC	Administrative list; silver and date-palms; *CT* 4 31a
340	78437	Ad 28/8/31	C	Rental(?) of a field; seals
341	78438	Sm 19/5/13	C	Administrative list of wages paid in barley; *CT* 4 25c
342	78439	OB	C	Letter; *CT* 4 27d; *AbB* 2 95
343	92999	Ššu 14/7/14	C	Law suit concerning a field; Babylon; nail marks; ZA 3, 228 no. 5
344	78440	OB	C	Exercise tablet; bilingual; religious(?)
345	78441	Sm 6/1/17	C	Legal protocol concerning a wall; *CT* 4 14b
346	92567	OB	NC	Harvest loan; Meissner, *BAP* no. 10
347	78442	OB	C	Economic
348	78443	Aṣ 10$^{?}$/12/10	C	Administrative; concerning a garment of ^{d}*Annunitum šarrat Sippar*; seals
349	78444	Aṣ 1/2$^{?}$/14	C	Small administrative text; seals
350	78445	Ha 9$^{?}$/6$^{?}$/42	C	Small ration list; seals
351	78446	Ha 11/6/35	C	Small ration list
352	78447	Aṣ 16/5/11	C	Small administrative; seals
353	78448	Ad 4/7/11	NC	Small; temple loan; seals; *CT* 48 43 no. 96
354	78449	Si 14/2$^{?}$/19 or 21	C	Small; temple loan
355	78450	Si 25/6/29$^{?}$ mu gibil	NC	Small administrative; seals
356	78451	Ha 1/8/38	C	Small administrative
357	78452	OB	C	Small administrative; date encrusted
358	78453	Ha 15/6/35	C	Small administrative
359	78454	OB	C	Receipt for silver; seals; Meissner, *BAP* no. 86
360	78455	11/10/-	C	Small administrative; seals; year encrusted

Bu 88-5-12,

361	78456	OB	C	Small administrative; date encrusted
362	78457	Ha 22/7?/35	C	Small administrative; personal names
363	78458	Ha 5/6/35	C	Small administrative; names of hired hands; Meissner, *BAP* no. 52; Weitemeyer, *Workers*, pp. 22, 91
364	78459	Aş 30/12b/13 or "17+a"	C	Small administrative; seals
365	78460	OB	C	Small administrative; round type
366	78461	Aş 6/12b/13	C	Small administrative; seals
367	78462	Aş -/6/8	C	Small administrative; seals
368	78463	Si 2/11/4	C	Small administrative bulla; seals
369	78464	Ha -/-/22	C	Small administrative; round type; seals
370	78465	Ad 24/12b/10	C	Small administrative; round type
371	78466	Si 10/2/-	NC	Small; loan
372	78467	Aş 2/12/16	C	Small administrative; round type
373	78468	Si 21?/3/6	C	Small administrative; seals
374	78469	Ae 5/7/"e"	C	Small administrative
375	78470	Ha 11?/9/35	C	Small administrative
376	78471	OB	C	Small administrative
377	78472	Ha 3/12/3	C	Small administrative; seals
378	78473	OB	C	Small administrative
379	78474	Ha 28?/7/35	C	Small administrative
380	78475	Ha 27/4/38	C	Small administrative; seals
381	78476	Aş 10/3/14	C	Small administrative; round type
382	78477	OB	C	Small administrative
383	78478	Ha 23/6/35	C	Small administrative; Weitemeyer, *Workers* pp. 28, 93
384	78479	Ha 2/8/35	C	Small administrative; Weitemeyer, *Workers* pp. 31, 95
385	78480	Ha 22/4/42	C	Small administrative; seals; date by ductus
386	78481	Ha 27/6/35	C	Small administrative; Weitemeyer, *Workers* pp. 29, 94
387	78482	Aş 2/5/17	C	Small administrative; seals
388	78483	NB	C	Letter
389	78484	Ha 5/9/35	C	Small administrative
390	78485	Ha 2/5/38	NC	Small administrative; seals
391	78486	Ha 11/-/2	C	Small administrative; seals
392	78487	Ha 21/6/35	F	Small administrative; Weitemeyer, *Workers* pp. 27, 92
393	78488	Ner 22/7/2	C	Contract for rental; Babylon

Bu 88-5-12,

394	78489	Aş 3/2/11	F	Small administrative; round type
395	78490	Aş 29/9/6	C	Small administrative; seals
396	78491	Aş 14?/9/4	C	Small administrative
397	78492	Ha 28/4/35	C	Small administrative
398	78493	Ha 5?/9/28? mu é-dIškur-ra: not Sumula'el	C	Small administrative; seals
399	78494	Aş 4/2?/15	C	Small administrative; round type
400	78495	Ae 1/7/"k"	C	Small administrative; seals
401	78496	OB	C	Small administrative
402	78497	Aş 10?/5/7	NC	Small administrative; round type
403	78498	Si 16/3?/-	C	Small administrative; seals
404	92568	Sm -/-/13	C	Loan of silver; Meissner, *BAP* no. 14
405	78499	OB 21/11/-	C	Small administrative; seals; Meissner, *BAP* no. 84
406	78500	Ha 21/6/35	C	Small administrative
407	78501	Art 26/2/18	NC	Receipt for a loan of barley
408	78502	Ha 28/6/35	C	Small administrative; Weitemeyer, *Workers* pp. 29, 94
409	78503	Ad 3/4/2	C	Small administrative
410	78504	Ha 27/7/35	C	Small administrative; Weitemeyer, *Workers* pp. 31, 95
411	78505	Aş 1/1/?	C	House rental; seals; Meissner, *BAP* no. 63
412	78506	Aş 4?/1/11	C	Small administrative; seals
413	78507	OB	C	Small administrative
414	78508	OB	NC	Small administrative; seals
415	78509	Ha 21/5/23	C	Small administrative; seals
416	78510	Si 12/5/-	C	Small administrative
417	78511	Ad 18/2/2	C	Small administrative; seals
418	78512	Ha 10/6/35	C	Small administrative
419	92569	Si 14/12/2	C	Agreement to make a yearly payment of silver; seals; Meissner, *BAP* no. 6
420	78513	OB	C	Small administrative; design on rev.
421	78514	Ha 24/6/35	C	Small administrative; Weitemeyer, *Workers* pp. 28, 93
422	78515	Aş 23/9/8	C	Small administrative; seals
423	78516	OB	NC	Small administrative; seals
424	78517	Ha 22/6/35	C	Small administrative; Weitemeyer, *Workers* pp. 28, 93
425	78518	Aş 1/4/4	C	Small administrative; seals

Bu 88-5-12,

426	78519	Ha 11/1/39	C	Small; loan
427	78520	Xer 17/8/16	C	Letter
428	78521	Ha 7/9/35	C	Small administrative; Weitemeyer, *Workers* pp. 33, 95
429	78522	Ha 23/7/35	C	Small administrative
430	78523	Sd 12/9/12	C	Small administrative; round type; seals
431	78524	OB	C	Small administrative
432	78525	Ha 10/3/28?	C	Small administrative; seals; not Sumulaʾel, by script
433	78526	Ha 30/6/2	C	Small administrative; seals
434	78527	OB	C	Small administrative
435	92570	Ad 10/8/35	C	Loan of barley; Meissner, *BAP* no. 21
436	78528	Ha 12/6/35	C	Small administrative
437	78529	Aṣ 10?/10/17	F	Small administrative; seals
438	78530	OB	C	Small administrative
439	78531	Ad 12/9/10	C	Small; loan; seals
440+ 1985-10-6, 9	78532+ 139972	NB	F	Lexical; dupl. *MSL* 4 202; see *St. Pohl* 12 149
441	78533	Si 22/12/14	C	Small administrative; seals
442	78534	OB	C	Bulla
443	78535	OB	C	Bulla
444	78536	OB	C	Bulla
445	78537	OB	C	Bulla
446	78538	Dar -/4/36	C	Account of barley deliveries
447	78539	Aṣ 28?/6/16	C	Bulla; seals
448	78540	OB	C	Small administrative
449	78541	Aṣ 26/9/11	C	Small administrative; seals
450	78542	OB	NC	Small; loan
451	78543	OB	C	Letter; round type; *CT* 52 no. 174; *AbB* 7 174
452	78544	Aṣ 1/7/12	C	Small; hire of a boat(?)
453	78545	Aṣ 25/4/4	C	Loan; seals
454	92571	Aṣ 22/12b/13 or "17+a"	C	Loan of silver; Meissner, *BAP* no. 9
455	78546	Aṣ 10/4/ᵈLama Lama didli-a é-babbar-ra-šè in-tu ...	C	Administrative; seals
456	78547	OB	NC	Administrative
457	78548	Nbn 28/5/2	C	Receipt for barley and sesame
458	92572	OB 30/2/?	C	Loan of barley; Meissner, *BAP* no. 20

Bu 88-5-12,

459	78549	OB	F	Loan
460	78550	Ha 7/6/35	C	Administrative; Weitemeyer, *Workers* pp. 23, 91
461	78551	Ae 18/10/"bb" ᵈSin sag-dù-ga-ni-im	C	Administrative; loan
462	78552	Ha 1/6/35	C	Small administrative; Weitemeyer, *Workers* pp. 22, 91
463	78553	Ha 26/7/35	C	Small administrative; Weitemeyer, *Workers* pp. 30, 94
464	78554	Aṣ 1/1/-x-x *a-na* é ᵈSin *ú-še-lu-ú*	C	Hire of a female worker; seals; *CT* 48 49 no. 116
465	78555	OB	C	Small; round type; economic
466	78556	OB	C	Field rental
467	78557	Ad 14/1/16 or 35	C	Administrative; farm implements; seals
468	78558	OB	F	Administrative
469	78559	OB	C	Administrative
470	78560	Aṣ 14?/12/9	C	Loan; seals
471	78561	Ha 1?/9/37	C	House rental; seals; Meissner, *BAP* no. 64
472	78562	Aṣ 25/6/11	C	Loan; seals
473	78563	Si -/1/2	C	Field rental
474	78564	OB 5/5/-	C	Divination report; *JCS* 21, 222-223
475	78565	Aṣ 12/6/15	C	Administrative; seals
476	78566	Aṣ 4/7/16	C	Administrative; round type
477	78567	OB	C	Letter; *CT* 52 no. 166; *AbB* 7 166
478	78568	Sd 10/6/19	C	Administrative; seals
479	78569	OB	C	Economic
480	78570	Aṣ 1/1/14	C	House rental; seals
481	78571	Aṣ 25?/3/"17+b"	C	Loan; seals
482	78572	Ha 16/6/35	C	Administrative; Weitemeyer, *Workers* pp. 25, 92
483	78573	Ha 23/8/42	NC	Administrative
484	78574	OB	C	Letter; round type; seals; *CT* 52 no. 89; *AbB* 7 89
485	78575	Ha 24/11/39	C	Payment of rental fee
486	78576	OB	C	Letter; round type; *CT* 52 no. 132; *AbB* 7 132
487	78577	Aṣ 9/10/9	C	Temple administration (Šamaš, Marduk witnesses); seals
488	92573	Ha -/-/16	C	Harvest loan
488A	92573A	Ha -/-/16	C	Case of previous; seals; Meissner, *BAP* no. 11

Bu 88-5-12,

489	78578	OB	C	Economic
490	78579	Art 21/6/26	C	Receipt for barley
491	78580	OB	F	Economic; large tablet
492	78581	OB	F	Letter; *CT* 52 no. 139; *AbB* 7 139
493	78582	OB	C	Administrative
494	78583	Aṣ 10/2/"17+b"	C	Administrative; loan; seals
495	78584	Nbn 22/9/13	C	Receipt for delivery
496	78585	OB	C	Economic; round type
497	78586	Nbn 9/-/acc	C	Loan of silver; Babylon
498	78587	OB	NC	Administrative
499	78588	Ad 20/9/10	F	Contract
500	78589	Ad 6/8/36	C	Administrative; seals
501	78590	Sd 10/3/17	C	Administrative(?); seals
502	78591	OB	C	Loan
503	78592	Ae 30/5/28	F	Loan(?)
504	78593	Aṣ 28/8/5	C	Administrative; round type; *CT* 4 29b
505	78594	OB	C	Letter; round type; *CT* 4 29c; *AbB* 2 97
506	78595	Aṣ	C	Administrative(?); seals
507	78596	Aṣ 27/2/"17+e" (dEn-líl ì-maḫ-a)	C	Rental of a journey of the weapon of Šamaš; seals; *CT* 4 29a; *AS* 16 222
508	78597	NB -/8/3	C	Receipt for barley
509	78598	Aṣ 5/9/12	C	Administrative; round type; *CT* 4 30a
510	78599	Ššu 13/12/15	C	Loan of silver; Babylon
511	78600	Ad 3/1/19	C	Contract about doors; seals
512	78601	Aṣ 15/4/11	NC	Administrative (*isiḫtu*); seals
513	78602	OB	NC	Debt record, strange script and format; seals
514	78603	Sel 3/1/8	NC	Purchase of a horse; *CT* 4 29d
515	78604	Aṣ 18/7/-	NC	Administrative; *Iltani*, a *naditu*, *marat šarrim*; seals
516	78605	Aṣ 1/4/-	C	Economic; round type
517	78606	Sd -/10/12	C	Free loan
518	78607	Aṣ -/-/13 or 17 (urudu-ki-lugal ...)	NC	Economic
519	78608	Aṣ 20/8/1	C	Rental record; seals
520	78609	Ad 30/12/32	C	Temple loan; seals
521	78610	OB	C	Economic; round type; check marks
522	78611	Ad 27/11/27	C	Administrative (*isiḫtu*); seals; *CT* 4 31b; *AfO* 25 80
523	78612	OB	C	Administrative; round type; list of names; house plan on reverse

Bu 88-5-12,

524	78613	OB	C	Amulet; Akkadian text; design on reverse
525	78614	OB	F	Bilingual; literary; mentions the steeds of Utu; cf. *OrAnt* 8 14
526	78615	Aş	C	House rental; seals
527	78616	OB	NC	Letter; *CT* 52 no. 119; *AbB* 7 119
528	78617	Si 5/11/3 or 4	NC	House rental(?); seals
529	78618	OB	C	Practice tablet; round type
530	78619	OB	C	Administrative; round type
531	78620	Ad -/4?/2	C	Loan; seals
532	78621	Aş 10/1/16	C	House rental; seals; *CT* 4 31a
533	78622	Šsu 8/8/15	C	Loan of silver; Babylon; *CT* 4 31c
534	78623	OB	NC	Loan
535	78624	OB	NC	Real estate sale; *CT* 4 43c
536	78625	OB 1/12/-	NC	Hire of a workman; seals
537	78626	Aş 1-9/8/17	NC	Administrative; round type
538	78627	Ae 10/10/28	C	Temple administrative (*šik mešeqim biruyaum*); seals
539	78628	Aş 19/3/13	NC	Administrative; round type; seals
540	78629	OB ...-ditana 23/4/-	C	Loan; seals
541	78630	Aş 14/6/12	C	House rental; seals; *CT* 48 26 no. 54
542	78631	Ad 13/12/16?	C	Loan; seals
543	78632	OB	NC	Administrative
544	78633	Aş 2/8/4	C	Administrative; loan; seals
545	78634	Aş 22/9?/14	C	Administrative; loan; seals
546	78635	Ha 22/6/35	C	Administrative
547	78636	Aş 1/5/14	C	Administrative
548	78637	Aş 18/4/15	C	Administrative; seals
549	78638	Aş 10/4/"17+b"	C	Loan agreement; seals; *CT* 4 30d
550	78639	Aş 25/5/"17+b"	NC	Loan; seals; *CT* 48 42 no. 92
551	78640	Aş 30/12/1	C	House rental; seals
552	78641	OB	NC	Administrative; earlier period; seals
553	78642	Nbk 4/9/5	C	Offering ledger
554	78643	Npl 11/12/18	C	Account of wool; *CT* 4 14d
555	78644	Aş 10/2/3	C	Administrative; shepherding contract; seals
556	78645	Nbk 14/4/10	C	Receipt for bitumen; *CT* 4 14c
557	78646	Dar 13/11/20	C	Sale of a slavegirl; Sippar; *CT* 4 32a
558	78647	OB	C	Economic
559	78648	OB	C	Letter; *CT* 52 no. 140; *AbB* 7 140

Bu 88-5-12,

560	78649	Nbn 6/9/12	C	Loan of silver; Babylon; *CT* 4 30b
561	78650	Ha 10/10/43	C	Economic
562	78651	Alex 5/12/9	C	Account of silver payments; *CT* 49 1 no. 5
563	78652	OB	C	Economic
564	78653	OB 11/6/-	C	House rental; *CT* 4 30c
565	78654	OB	F	"Sammeltafel" of contracts; four columns
566	78655	Aş 24?/5/"17+b"	NC	Extispicy report; drawing; *JCS* 21, 223-224
567	78656	Aş 25?/1?/5	C	Administrative; seals
568	78657	OB	C	Letter; *CT* 4 33a; *AbB* 2 99
569	78658	OB	NC	Economic; round type
570	78659	NB 29/11/16	C	Purchase of baked bricks
571	78660	Dar -/-/16	NC	Contract
572	78661	Philip 7/12/3	C	Receipt for purchase of provisions; *CT* 49 3 no. 10
573	78662	Sd -/-/4	NC	Temple office (*parşu*) contract; seals; *AfO* 25 78; *CT* 48 22 no. 45
574	78663	Sd 25/4/dInanna nin-Babiliki-ma	C	Loan for commission; seals; *AfO* 25 82; *CT* 48 19 no. 40
575	78664	Dar 27/9/19	C	Contract for bales of straw
576	78665	OB	F	Completely obliterated surface
577	78666	OB	F	Literary; bilingual hymn to Šamaš as the "pure *baru*"
578	78667	Ae -/9/-	NC	House rental
579	78668	Ad 6/12b/32	C	Loan of barley; seals
580	78669	AS	C	Real estate sale; *CT* 4 33b
581	78670	OB	C	Letter; round type; *CT* 4 35b; *AbB* 2 100
582	78671	Dar 24/6/30	NC	Receipt for bread and beer
583	78672	OB	NC	Administrative; round type
584	78673	NB	F	Literary; bilingual incantations on behalf of the king
585	78674	OB	C	Bequest of a field; *CT* 4 34a
586	78675	OB	C	Description of a field; round type; late period; *CT* 4 34c
587	78676	Sabium	NC	Real estate sale; *CT* 4 35a
588	78677	NB	F	Literary; bilingual litany
589	78678	Dar 11/8/-	C	Contract
590	78679	Ha 1/2/3	C	Field rental
591	78680	OB	C	Extispicy report; *CT* 4 34b

Bu 88-5-12,

592+ 1985-10-6, 6	78681+ 139969	OB	C	Copy of royal inscriptions; *CT* 44 1 no. 2
593	78682	Xer 24/8/10	C	Contract for dates; Babylon; *CT* 4 34d
594	78683	OB	NC	Contract; oath
595	78684	Aṣ -/2/ᵈEn-líl ...	F	Economic; round type
596	78685	Nbn 25/9/10	NC	Contract for dates; Babylon
597	78686	OB	F	Round type; disintegrated
598	78687	OB	C	Letter; round type; *CT* 4 32b; *AbB* 2 98
599	78688	OB	C	Administrative; round type
600	78689	OB	C	Sale of house(?); early period
601	78690	Ad 10/1/12	C	List of the property of a *qadištu*; *CT* 4 40b
602	78691	OB	C	Letter; round type; *CT* 4 36a; *AbB* 2 101
603	78692	Ae 10/6/d?	C	Field rental; seals; *CT* 4 40c
604	78693	OB 4/2/-	C	Field rental; *CT* 4 39b
605	78694	OB	F	Round type; disintegrated
606	78695	OB	C	Rental contract
607	78696	OB	NC	Letter; *CT* 4 37a; *AbB* 2 102
608	78697	Nbk 9/2/13	C	Account of garments of gods; *CT* 4 38a
609	78698	Si	C	Memorandum on transfers of real estate between *naditus* in Si 18 and 20; round type; *CT* 4 37c
610	78699	OB	F	House sale; early period
611	78700	Si -/3/28	C	Administrative(?) seals
612	78701	OB	C	Administrative; summary of fields
613	78702	OB	NC	Real estate contract
614	78703	OB	NC	Administrative
615	78704	Ad 30/8/4	C	Agreement to replace lost fowl; seals; *CT* 33 47b
616	92574	Sabium	C	Real estate sale; *CT* 2 16
617	78705	Si 15/7/30	NC	Marriage contract; *CT* 4 39a
618	78706	Ad 28/11/4	NC	Loan of bran; seals; *CT* 4 37b
619	78707	Alex 6/11/9	C	Receipt for payment of silver; Aramaic docket; *CT* 4 39c; *CT* 49 2 no. 6
620	78708	Aṣ -/7/6	NC	Economic
621	78709	OB	C	Letter; round type; *CT* 4 39d; *AbB* 2 104
622	78710	OB	C	School exercise(?)
623	78711	OB	C	Administrative; receipt of silver; *CT* 4 36c
624	78712	Ha -/-/29	C	Real estate sale; *CT* 4 40a

Bu 88-5-12,

625	78713	Dar 26/4/19	C	Contract for dates; Babylon; *ZA* 3, 225; *Dar* 484
626	78714	OB	C	Agreement over a party wall; *CT* 4 37d
627	78715	OB	C	Memorandum of real estate sales; round type; *CT* 4 41a
628	78716	OB	C	Memorandum about delivery(?) of two large groups of asses to Sippar and KÁ ᵈUTU; *CT* 45 37 no. 83
629	78717	Aṣ 21/3/3	F	Field sale or rental
630	78718	OB	F	Administrative; late period
631	78719	Ad 30/12/36	F	Loan of barley; seals
632	78720	Aṣ 8/8/4	C	Economic; tabular
633	78721	OB	C	Letter; *CT* 52 no. 62; *AbB* 7 62
634	78722	Aṣ 10/8?/11	F	Herding contract; seals
635	78723	Ad 5/9/8	C	Loan of barley; seals; *CT* 4 36b
636	78724	Ha 1/2/42	C	Receipt for hire payment; seals; *CT* 4 42b
637	78725	Dar 26/2/29	C	Loan of silver; *CT* 4 41b
638	78726	OB	C	Letter; *CT* 4 38b; *AbB* 2 103
639	78727	Dar 5/1?/25	C	Sale of a slavegirl; *CT* 4 43a
640	78728	OB	F	Gift of real estate to a *naditu*; now disintegrated; *CT* 4 43b
641	78729	Nbn 28/2/8	C	Account of barley; seals; *CT* 4 41
642	78730	Sd 12/10/16	C	Loan of onions; *CT* 6 23c
643	78731	Dar 22/12b/24	C	Rental of a field; Babylon; *CT* 4 44a
644	78732	OB	C	Administrative
645	92575	Ha 1/10/25	C	*CT* 4 38c
646	92575A	Ha 1/10/25	C	Case of previous; seals
647	78733	Aṣ 1/7/3	C	Loan of barley; seals; unopened case
648	78734	Ha -/-/40	C	House rental; seals; part of case adhering
649	78735	Si 15/8/7	C	Administrative; seals
650	78736	OB	C	Loan; seals; part of case adhering
651	91040 (= 12183)	Gudea	C	Cone; *Gudea* no. 51; said to come from Hillah
652	91041 (= 12184)	Gudea	C	Cone; *Gudea* no. 51; said to come from Hillah
653	91053 (= 12196)	Gudea	C	Cone; *Gudea* no. 51; said to come from Hillah
654	91042 (= 12185)	Gudea	C	Cone; *Gudea* no. 51; said to come from Hillah
655	78737	OB -/6/?	C	Harvest loan; *CT* 4 46c

Bu 88-5-12,

656	78738	OB -/6/?	F	Case of previous; seals
657	78739	Ha or Si; mu ugnim	C	Loan
658	78740	OB	F	Case of previous; seals
659	78741	OB 1/1/mu gibil	C	Rental of *rugbum*; Meissner, *BAP* no. 65
660	78742	OB 1/1/mu gibil	NC	Case of previous; seals; Meissner, *BAP* no. 65
661	78743	Ha -/-/4?	C	Administrative; cultic
662	78744	OB	F	Case of previous; seals
663	78745	OB	C	Field rental; early period
664	78746	OB	F	Case of previous; seals
665	78747	OB	C	Administrative; part of case adhering; no date or date not visible; *sissiktu* impression
666	78748	Si 1/8/14	C	Loan of silver
667	78749	OB	F	Case of previous; seals
667A	78750	Aş 5?/5/11	C	Administrative, involving wool; seals
668	78750A	Aş 5?/5/11	F	Case of previous; seals
669	78751	OB	C	Free loan of barley; date obscured by adhering case
670	78752	OB	NC	Case of previous; seals
671	78753	Ha -/-/3?	NC	Hire of a slavewoman
672	78754	Ha -/-/3? mu giš-gu-za ^{d}nanna uri^{ki}	F	Case of previous; seals
673	92576	Sabium	C	Sale of a field; *CT* 8 23c
674	92576A	OB	F	Case of previous; seals
675	78755	Ha	C	Gift of real estate, etc.; *CT* 4 1b
676	78756	Ha	F	Case of previous; seals
677	92577	Sm	NC	Real estate sale; *CT* 4 44b
678	92577A	Sm	F	Case of previous; seals
679	78757	Si 1/1/7	C	Field rental; *CT* 4 44c
680	78758	Si 1/1/7	C	Case of previous; seals
681	78759	Sabium	C	Real estate sale; *CT* 4 45a
682	78760	Sabium	F	Case of previous; seals
683	92578	OB	C	Real estate sale; *CT* 45 6 no. 10
684	92578A	AS	F	Case of previous; seals; *CT* 45 6 no. 10
685	92579	Si 5/10/22	C	Real estate sale; *CT* 8 15a
686	92579A	Si 5/10/22	NC	Case of previous; seals
687	78761	Si -/9/22	NC	Real estate sale; *CT* 4 17b
688	78762	OB	F	Case of a sale contract; seals
689	78763	OB	NC	Real estate sale; *CT* 4 45b

Bu 88-5-12,

690	78764	Sm	F	Case of previous; seals
691	78765	Ha	NC	Settlement of an estate
692	78766	OB	F	Case of previous; seals
693	92580	Ha -/-/35?	C	Settlement of an estate; *CT* 4 46b
694	92580A	Ha	NC	Case of previous; seals
695	78767	OB	NC	Administrative; issue of rations to Kassites; refers to Ae year "h"; seals
696	78768	OB	F	Case; real estate sale
697	78769	Ha	C	Agreement for maintenance of an adoptive parent; *CT* 4 45c
698	78770	Ha -/-/6 mu bára guškin dnin-pirìg	F	Case; contract concerning a field; Ha oath; seals
699	78771	Si 24/11/22	C	Real estate sale; *CT* 4 7b
700	78772	Si 24/11/22	F	Case of previous; seals
701	78773	Si 7/11/9	C	Real estate sale; *CT* 4 17c
702	78774	Si -/11/9	F	Case of previous; seals
703	92581	OB	C	Adoption contract; Meissner, *BAP* no. 96
704	92581A	OB	NC	Case of previous; seals
705	92582	Si 4/12/6	C	Real estate sale; *CT* 4 46a
706	92582A	Si 27/10/16	F	Case; real estate sale(?); seals
707	78775	Si 1/5/15	C	Designation of heir by a nu-maš; part of case adhering; *CT* 45 18 no. 34
708	78776	OB	F	Case of previous; seals; *CT* 45 18 no. 34
709	78777	OB	F	Real estate sale
710	78778	OB	F	Case of previous; seals; *sissiktu* impression
711	92583	AS 5/*e-lu-nim*/5	C	Lawsuit over the loss of a hired donkey; *CT* 4 47a
712	92583A	AS 5/*e-lu-nim*/5	NC	Case of pervious; seals; *AfO* 15 p. 77
713	92584	Ha -/-/15	NC	Real estate sale; *CT* 4 48a
714	92584A	Ha -/-/15	NC	Case of previous
715	78779	Si 1/12/10	C	Real estate sale; *CT* 8 24a
716	78780	OB	F	Case of previous; seals
717	78781	Sumula'el	NC	Real estate sale; *CT* 4 48b
718	78782	OB	F	Case of previous; seals
719	92585	Sm	NC	Division of an estate; *CT* 8 16a
720	92585A	OB	F	Case of previous; seals
721	92586	Sm 4/5/13	C	Real estate sale; *CT* 4 49b
722	92586A	OB	NC	Case of previous; seals
723	92587	OB -/7/mu ús-sa šu? an-na	C	Loan of silver

Bu 88-5-12,

724	92587A	OB -/7/mu ús-sa šu? an-na	F	Case of previous; seals
725	92588	AS	C	Real estate sale; *CT* 4 49a
726	92588A	OB	F	Case of previous; seals
727	78783	Si -/-/1	C	House rental
728	78784	Si -/-/1	F	Case of previous; seals
729	78785	OB	C	Loan of silver
730	78786	Ha -/-/18 or 26 (bára-maḫ guškin [d]En-líl-lá)	NC	Case of previous; seals
731	78787	Sm	C	Real estate sale; tablet in case; seals; *CT* 4 50b
731A	90319	NB	F	Nebuchadnezzar II brick; Walker, *Bricks* no. 102
732	78788	OB Ammi-...	C	Real estate purchase, *naditu* involved; part of case adhering; seals
732A	90822	NB	C	Nebuchadnezzar II brick; Walker, *Bricks* no. 102
733	78789	Si	F	Court proceeding; case adhering to tablet
733A	90823	NB	C	Nebuchadnezzar II brick; Walker, *Bricks* no. 102
733B	78789A	OB	F	Case of Bu 88-5-12, 733 (= BM 78789)
734	78790	OB	NC	Loan; tablet in case, date not visible; seals
734A	90109	NB	C	Nebuchadnezzar II brick; Walker, *Bricks* no. 102
735	78791	Si 15/11/2	C	Receipt for the produce of a field; seals
735A				Uninscribed object
736	78792	OB	C	Case of previous
736A				Uninscribed object
737	78793	OB	C	Loan from a *naditu*
737A				Uninscribed object
738	78794	Ha -/-/16	C	Case of previous; seals
738A				Uninscribed object
739	78795	Ha 3/12b/33	C	Loan from a *naditu*; see *LIH* 3, p. 13 no. 1
739A				Uninscribed object
740	78796	Ha 3/12b/33	C	Case of previous; seals
740A				Uninscribed object
741	92589	OB	C	Harvest loan repayable in the month Šaddutum

Bu 88-5-12,

741A				Uninscribed object
742	92589A	Ha 20/11/35	C	Case of previous; seals
742A				Uninscribed object
743	92594	OB	C	Hire of two workmen; Meissner, *BAP* no. 57
744	92594A	Ha -/-/3 or Si -/-/5	C	Case of previous; seals
745	92590	Ha 1/11/21	C	Loan of silver
746	92590A	Ha 1/11/21	NC	Case of previous; seals
747	78797	Ha 26?/4/18	C	Deposit of *siḫlu*
748	78798	Ha 26/5/18	C	Case of previous; seals
749	78799	OB	C	Loan of grain from a *naditu*
750	78800	Ha -/-/18	C	Case of previous; seals; *sissiktu* impression annotated
751	92591	Ha 10/8/-	C	House rental
752	92591A	Ha 10/8/43 (mu *e-pi-ri*)	C	Case of previous; seals
753	92592	Si -/8/6	C	Loan of bricks; Meissner, *BAP* no. 26
754	92592A	Si -/8/6	C	Case of previous
755	78801	OB	C	Rental of house; part of case adhering; seals
756	78802	Si 17/12/4	F	Case of previous; seals
757	78803	Ha 7/11/40	C	Loan of barley
758	78804	Ha 7/11/40	F	Case of previous; seals
759	78805	Sm	C	Purchase of field; Sm oath
760	78806	Sm -/-/7	C	Case of previous; seals
761	78807	Ad 13/10/15	C	Receipt for sheep
762	78808	Ad 13/10/15	C	Case of previous
763	78809	OB	C	House rental
764	78810	OB	C	Case of previous; seals
765	78811	Ha -/-/9 or 33	C	Adoption of a child from a *naditu*
766	78812	Ha -/-/9 or 33	C	Case of previous; seals
767	78813	OB	C	Loan of barley ḫar-ra máš at 100% from a *naditu*, to be repaid in the month of Šaddutum
768	78814	Sm -/-/7?	C	Case of previous; seals
769	92593	AS	C	Inner tablet of following
769A	92593A	AS	C	Real estate sale; *CT* 2 17; sealed
770				Cylinder seal
771				Cylinder seal
772				Cylinder seal

Bu 88-5-12,

773				Cylinder seal
774				Cylinder seal
775				Cylinder seal
776				Cylinder seal
777				Cylinder seal
778				Cylinder seal
779				Cylinder seal
780				Cylinder seal
781	100692	NB	C	Nebuchadnezzar II brick; Walker, *Bricks* no. 102

88-5-12,

1	78815		F	Account of dates
2	78816	Nbn -/-/2	NC	Receipt for beer
3	78817		F	Lexical (urudu)
4	78818	Nbk 11/2/-	NC	Receipt for silver
5	78819	Nb(-) -/-/2	NC	Receipt for beer
6	78820	Nbn 1/12/4	F	Receipt for silver for manufacture
7	78821		F	Letter
8	78822		C	Accounts of seed
9	78823	Dar 22/1/1	C	Contract for barley
10	78824	Nbk 1/9/6	C	Receipt for garments
11	78825	Joined to 81-7-6, 129 (= BM 45722)		
12	78826		C	Account of barley and dates
13	78827	Dar 10/12/11	NC	Contract
14	78828	Nbk 23/4/28	F	Account of provisions for a military expedition
15	78829	Joined to Sp II 125 (= BM 34642)		
16	78830		NC	Account of garments
17	78831	Joined to Sp II 44 (= BM 34572)		
18	78832		F	Economic
19	78833	18/12b/20	F	Contract
20	78834		F	Royal inscription(?)
21	78835	OB	F	Envelope with seal; early period
22	78836		C	Animal ledger
23	78837		NC	Account of weapons
24	78838	OB	F	Envelope of a letter with seal
25	78839	Ha -/9/16	F	Envelope; cf. 88-5-12, 726 (= BM 78940); seals
26	78840	OB	F	Envelope with seal
27	78841	OB	F	Envelope with seal

88-5-12,

28	78842	OB	F	Envelope with seal
29	78843	OB	F	Envelope with seal
30	78844	OB	F	Envelope with seal
31	78845	OB	F	Envelope with seal
32	78846	OB	F	Envelope with seal
33	78847	OB	F	Envelope with seal
34	78848	OB	F	Envelope; witnesses
35	78849	OB	F	Envelope
36	78850	OB	F	Envelope with seal
37	78851	OB	F	Envelope with seal
38	78852	OB	F	Envelope with seal; witnesses
39	78853	OB	F	Envelope with seal
40	78854	OB	F	Envelope
41	78855	OB	F	Envelope with seal
42	78856	OB	F	Envelope with seal
43	78857	OB	F	Envelope with seal; witnesses
44	78858	OB	F	Envelope; witnesses
45	78859	OB	F	Envelope with seal; witnesses
46	78860	OB	F	Envelope with seal
47+ 49	78861+ 78863	OB	F	Envelope with seal
48	78862	OB	F	Envelope with seal
49	78863	Joined to 88-5-12, 47 (= BM 78861)		
50A+ 50B	78864	OB	F	Envelope with seal
50B		Joined to 88-5-12, 50A (= BM 78864)		
51	78865	OB	F	Envelope with seal
52	78866	OB	F	Envelope with seal
53	78867	OB	F	Envelope of a letter(?) with seal
54	78868	OB	F	Envelope with seal; early period
55	78869	OB	F	Envelope with seal; witnesses
56	78870	OB	F	Envelope with seal
57	78871	OB	F	Envelope; field sale or rental
58	78872	OB	F	Envelope with seal
59	78873	OB	F	Envelope with seal
60	78874	OB	F	Envelope with seal
61	78875	OB	F	Envelope with seal
62	78876	OB	C	Tag with seal
63	78877	Antig -/7/-	F	Legal text; stamp seals; Babylon

88-5-12,

64	78878		F	Nabu liturgy; Sumerian; M. Gaster, *AV* 335-48
65	78879	OB	C	Account of silver
66	78880	OB	NC	Account
67	78881	Aṣ 4/8/"17+a"	C	Account of provisions
68	78882	OB	C	Account
69	78883	Si 15?/11/-	C	Legal; dispute concerning a field
70	78884	-/8/12	F	Barley ledger
71	78885	5/1/15	NC	Offering ledger; Sippar
72	78886		C	List of workmen(?)
73	78887		C	Receipt for bitumen
74	78888	Nbk 29/6/26	C	Receipt for bales
75	78889		C	Receipt for tools
76	78890	Npl 26/9/2	C	Account of dates or grain
77	78891	25/9/14	F	Memorandum concerning an ass
78	78892	Npl -/-/19	F	Animal ledger
79	78893	Nbn 4/7/4	F	Account of garments of gods
80	78894	Nbk 2/1/21	F	Offering ledger; Sippar
81	78895	(-)-uṣur	F	Receipt for bronze for tools
82	78896	Nbk 23/11/28	F	Receipt
83	78897	Nbn 25/-/-	F	Account of cattle
84	78898	Nbk 30/11/18	C	Receipt for hides for shoes; Uruk
85	78899	Nbk 4/-/7	C	Receipt for iron tools
86	78900	Npl 4/11/6	C	Receipt for hides for shoes
87	78901	20/12/17	C	Offering ledger
88	78902	Dar 12/10/22	NC	Letter; stamp seals
89	78903	Ššu 15/5/7	NC	Bilingual; hymn to Istar; Nippur; dupl. *BL* no. 8
90	78904	Nbk 27/3/8	C	Account of oxen
91	78905		C	Measurements of the shrines of Ebabbar; *PSBA* 33 155-7, pl. 21
92	78906	Kan 15/12/20	C	Contract for delivery of reeds; Sippar
93	78907		C	Account of boat rentals
94	78908	Npl -/8/11	NC	Account of cattle
95	78909	12/9/-	C	Account of bitumen
96	78910	Npl 28/10/16	NC	Account of sheep
97	78911	Npl 6/5/17	C	Apprenticeship contract; Babylon
98	78912	Ššu 20/6/14	C	Loan of silver
99	78913	Npl 11/12/18	C	Loan of silver

88-5-12,

100	78914	Nbk 20/8/5	C	Receipt for a bedspread
101	78915	Npl 13/3/17	C	Account of animals
102	78916	Nbn 28/1/2	C	Receipt for beer
103	78917	Nbk 2/9/13	C	Receipt for baskets
104	78918	Npl 29/9/20	C	Account of animals
105	78919		C	Receipt for dates or grain
106	78920	Nbk 28/8/12	C	Receipt for iron daggers; archaic sign for fish on reverse
107	78921	1/6/14	C	Receipt for hides; archaic sign for fish on reverse
108	78922		C	Receipt for bran; incised Aramaic docket; Pinches, *An Outline of Assyrian Grammar* p. 62 no. 1
109	78923	23/12/10	C	Receipt for bitumen; archaic sign for fish on reverse
110	78924		F	Inventory; nail marks
111	78925		F	Account of dates
112	78926		F	Account of garments of gods
113	78927	4/9/-	F	Account of barley
114	78928	Dar 2/11/35	C	Contract for barley
115	78929	11/8/-	F	Marriage contract; stamp seals; Babylon; *CT* 49 167
116	78930	Ant 9/12/-	F	Gift of dowry; Babylon; *CT* 49 165
117	78931	ED	F	Nail; Eannatum I of Lagaš; dupl. Sollberger, *Corpus*, En. I 10
118	78932		F	Incantation and ritual
119	78933	Nbk 24/6b/40+	C	Receipt for barley provisions
120	78934		F	Field sale
121	78935		F	Accounts
122	78936	Nbn 8/4/3	NC	Receipt
123	78937	Nbk 14/2/3	NC	Receipt
124	78938		F	Field sale
125	78939	Si -/-/5	C	Harvest loan
125A	78939A	Si -/-/5	NC	Case of previous; seals
126	78940	Ha -/9/16	C	Loan of fish; for case see 88-5-12, 25 (= BM 78839)

Bu 88-10-13,

1	E29784	MB	C	Amarna letter; Bezold, *Amarna* 71; Knudtzon, *El-Amarna* 1
2	E29785	MB	NC	Amarna letter; Bezold, *Amarna* 55; Knudtzon, *El-Amarna* 9
3	E29786	MB	NC	Amarna letter; Bezold, *Amarna* 40; Knudtzon, *El-Amarna* 10
4	E29787	MB	C	Amarna letter; Bezold, *Amarna* 74; Knudtzon, *El-Amarna* 5
5	E29788	MB	NC	Amarna letter; Bezold, *Amarna* 67; Knudtzon, *El-Amarna* 35
6	E29789	MB	C	Amarna letter; Bezold, *Amarna* 38; Knudtzon, *El-Amarna* 34
7	E29790	MB	C	Amarna letter; Bezold, *Amarna* 27; Knudtzon, *El-Amarna* 37
8	E29791	MB	C	Amarna letter; Bezold, *Amarna* 62; Knudtzon, *El-Amarna* 19
9	E29792	MB	NC	Amarna letter; Bezold, *Amarna* 72; Knudtzon, *El-Amarna* 17
10	E29793	MB	C	Amarna letter; Bezold, *Amarna* 56; Knudtzon, *El-Amarna* 23
11	E29794	MB	NC	Amarna letter; Bezold, *Amarna* 43; Knudtzon, *El-Amarna* 26
12	E29795	MB	NC	Amarna letter; Bezold, *Amarna* 45; Knudtzon, *El-Amarna* 74
13	E29796	MB	NC	Amarna letter; Bezold, *Amarna* 42; Knudtzon, *El-Amarna* 114
14	E29797	MB	C	Amarna letter; Bezold, *Amarna* 53; Knudtzon, *El-Amarna* 83
15	E29798	MB	C	Amarna letter; Bezold, *Amarna* 64; Knudtzon, *El-Amarna* 73
16	E29799	MB	C	Amarna letter; Bezold, *Amarna* 51; Knudtzon, *El-Amarna* 136
17	E29800	MB	C	Amarna letter; Bezold, *Amarna* 44; Knudtzon, *El-Amarna* 88

Bu 88-10-13,

18	E29801	MB	NC	Amarna letter; Bezold, *Amarna* 23; Knudtzon, *El-Amarna* 132
19	E29802	MB	C	Amarna letter; Bezold, *Amarna* 69; Knudtzon, *El-Amarna* 125
20	E29803	MB	NC	Amarna letter; Bezold, *Amarna* 32; Knudtzon, *El-Amarna* 123
21	E29804	MB	NC	Amarna letter; Bezold, *Amarna* 4; Knudtzon, *El-Amarna* 86
22	E29805	MB	C	Amarna letter; Bezold, *Amarna* 50; Knudtzon, *El-Amarna* 87
23	E29806	MB	C	Amarna letter; Bezold, *Amarna* 76; Knudtzon, *El-Amarna* 102
24	E29807	MB	NC	Amarna letter; Bezold, *Amarna* 80; Knudtzon, *El-Amarna* 131
25	E29808	MB	C	Amarna letter; Bezold, *Amarna* 70; Knudtzon, *El-Amarna* 118
26	E29809	MB	NC	Amarna letter; Bezold, *Amarna* 31; Knudtzon, *El-Amarna* 141
27	E29810	MB	NC	Amarna letter; Bezold, *Amarna* 47; Knudtzon, *El-Amarna* 142
28	E29811	MB	C	Amarna letter; Bezold, *Amarna* 81; Knudtzon, *El-Amarna* 149
29	E29812	MB	C	Amarna letter; Bezold, *Amarna* 59; Knudtzon, *El-Amarna* 147
30	E29813	MB	C	Amarna letter; Bezold, *Amarna* 79; Knudtzon, *El-Amarna* 151
31	E29814	MB	NC	Amarna letter; Bezold, *Amarna* 22; Knudtzon, *El-Amarna* 155
32	E29815	MB	NC	Amarna letter; Bezold, *Amarna* 25; Knudtzon, *El-Amarna* 235
33	E29816	MB	F	Amarna letter; Bezold, *Amarna* 73; Knudtzon, *El-Amarna* 64
34	E29817	MB	C	Amarna letter; Bezold, *Amarna* 60; Knudtzon, *El-Amarna* 63
35	E29818	MB	C	Amarna letter; Bezold, *Amarna* 78; Knudtzon, *El-Amarna* 161
36	E29819	MB	C	Amarna letter; Bezold, *Amarna* 65; Knudtzon, *El-Amarna* 55
37	E29820	MB	C	Amarna letter; Bezold, *Amarna* 5; Knudtzon, *El-Amarna* 53
38	E29821	MB	NC	Amarna letter; Bezold, *Amarna* 6; Knudtzon, *El-Amarna* 303
39	E29822	MB	F	Amarna letter; Bezold, *Amarna* 11; Knudtzon, *El-Amarna* 304

Bu 88-10-13,

40	E29823	MB	NC	Amarna letter; Bezold, *Amarna* 18; Knudtzon, *El-Amarna* 306
41	E29824	MB	C	Amarna letter; Bezold, *Amarna* 37; Knudtzon, *El-Amarna* 59
42	E29825	MB	NC	Amarna letter; Bezold, *Amarna* 24; Knudtzon, *El-Amarna* 100
43	E29826	MB	C	Amarna letter; Bezold, *Amarna* 1; Knudtzon, *El-Amarna* 197
44	E29827	MB	C	Amarna letter; Bezold, *Amarna* 19; Knudtzon, *El-Amarna* 101
45	E29828	MB	C	Amarna letter; Bezold, *Amarna* 49; Knudtzon, *El-Amarna* 139
46	E29830	MB	NC	Amarna letter; Bezold, *Amarna* 3; Knudtzon, *El-Amarna* 227
47	E29831	MB	NC	Amarna letter; Bezold, *Amarna* 17; Knudtzon, *El-Amarna* 228
48	E29832	MB	C	Amarna letter; Bezold, *Amarna* 7; Knudtzon, *El-Amarna* 299
49	E29833	MB	C	Amarna letter; Bezold, *Amarna* 33; Knudtzon, *El-Amarna* 298
50	E29834	MB	C	Amarna letter; Bezold, *Amarna* 63; Knudtzon, *El-Amarna* 297
51	E29835	MB	C	Amarna letter; Bezold, *Amarna* 29; Knudtzon, *El-Amarna* 325
52	E29836	MB	C	Amarna letter; Bezold, *Amarna* 39; Knudtzon, *El-Amarna* 323
53	E29837	MB	NC	Amarna letter; Bezold, *Amarna* 13; Knudtzon, *El-Amarna* 324
54	E29838	MB	C	Amarna letter; Bezold, *Amarna* 68; Knudtzon, *El-Amarna* 316
55	E29839	MB	NC	Amarna letter; Bezold, *Amarna* 36; Knudtzon, *El-Amarna* 315
56	E29840	MB	NC	Amarna letter; Bezold, *Amarna* 30; Knudtzon, *El-Amarna* 296
57	E29841	MB	C	Amarna letter; Bezold, *Amarna* 57; Knudtzon, *El-Amarna* 30
58	E29842	MB	C	Amarna letter; Bezold, *Amarna* 14; Knudtzon, *El-Amarna* 248
59	E29843	MB	C	Amarna letter; Bezold, *Amarna* 52; Knudtzon, *El-Amarna* 215
60	E29844	MB	NC	Amarna letter; Bezold, *Amarna* 28; Knudtzon, *El-Amarna* 252
61	E29845	MB	C	Amarna letter; Bezold, *Amarna* 66; Knudtzon, *El-Amarna* 270

Bu 88-10-13,

62	E29846	MB	C	Amarna letter; Bezold, *Amarna* 34; Knudtzon, *El-Amarna* 269
63	E29847	MB	NC	Amarna letter; Bezold, *Amarna* 21; Knudtzon, *El-Amarna* 256
64	E29848	MB	C	Amarna letter; Bezold, *Amarna* 58; Knudtzon, *El-Amarna* 330
65	E29849	MB	C	Amarna letter; Bezold, *Amarna* 48; Knudtzon, *El-Amarna* 224
66	E29850	MB	C	Amarna letter; Bezold, *Amarna* 75; Knudtzon, *El-Amarna* 284
67	E29851	MB	C	Amarna letter; Bezold, *Amarna* 77; Knudtzon, *El-Amarna* 282
68	E29852	MB	NC	Amarna letter; Bezold, *Amarna* 20; Knudtzon, *El-Amarna* 278
69	E29853	MB	F	Amarna letter; Bezold, *Amarna* 82; Knudtzon, *El-Amarna* 264
70	E29854	MB	C	Amarna letter; Bezold, *Amarna* 8; Knudtzon, *El-Amarna* 294
71	E29855	MB	C	Amarna letter; Bezold, *Amarna* 41; Knudtzon, *El-Amarna* 245
72	E29856	MB	C	Amarna letter; Bezold, *Amarna* 12; Knudtzon, *El-Amarna* 69
73	E29857	MB	C	Amarna letter; Bezold, *Amarna* 16; Knudtzon, *El-Amarna* 318
74	E29858	MB	C	Amarna letter; Bezold, *Amarna* 61; Knudtzon, *El-Amarna* 261
75	E29859	MB	C	Amarna letter; Bezold, *Amarna* 54; Knudtzon, *El-Amarna* 213
76	E29860	MB	C	Amarna letter; Bezold, *Amarna* 35; Knudtzon, *El-Amarna* 187
77	E29861	MB	C	Amarna letter; Bezold, *Amarna* 15; Knudtzon, *El-Amarna* 205
78	E29862	MB	C	Amarna letter; Bezold, *Amarna* 10; Knudtzon, *El-Amarna* 251
79	E29863	MB	C	Amarna letter; Bezold, *Amarna* 9; Knudtzon, *El-Amarna* 272
80	E29864	MB	C	Amarna letter; Bezold, *Amarna* 26; Knudtzon, *El-Amarna* 277
81	E29865	MB	C	Amarna letter; Bezold, *Amarna* 2; Knudtzon, *El-Amarna* 357

Bu 89-4-26,

1-233				Kuyunjik and uninscribed objects
234+ 236	78941+ 78943	OB	F	*Atraḫasis* I; *CT* 46 1ff.; Lambert-Millard, *Atraḫasis*, p. 40ff.
235+ 266+ Bu 91-5-9, 524	78942+ 78971+ 80385	OB	F	*Atraḫasis* III; *CT* 46 13ff.; Lambert-Millard, *Atraḫasis*, p. 40 ff.
236	78943	Joined to Bu 89-4-26, 234 (= BM 78941)		
237+ 274	78944+ 78979	OB	F	Hammurapi laws; *JCS* 21 39ff.
238	92668	OB	C	Liver model; *CT* 6 1
239	78945	Nbk -/9/36	NC	Account of dates or grain provisions
240	78946	Sm -/-/12	F	Sale of a field
240A	78946A	OB	F	Case of previous; seals
241	92595	Ha -/-/21	C	Field sale
241A	92595A	Ha 20?/9/21	C	Case of previous
242	78947	Joined to 82-5-22, 1056 (= BM 54728)		
243	78948	Alex	F	Account of barley provisions
244	78949	Alex	F	Account of barley provisions
245	78950	-/-/22	NC	Account of barley provisions
246	78951	OB	C	Field exchange
246A	78951A	Si 20/12/30	NC	Case of previous; seals
247	78952		F	Account of barley provisions
248	78953	Seleucid	NC	Contract; stamp seals
249	78954	NB	F	Royal inscription; cylinder
250	78955	NA	NC	Incantations and rituals against fear and nightmares
251	78956	Nbk 4/3/3	NC	Animal ledger
252	78957	Alex -/11/-	NC	Account of barley provisions
253	78958	Joined to Sp II 280 (= BM 34788)		

Bu 89-4-26,

254	78959		F	Accounts
255	78960	NA	F	*Šumma alu* (snakes)
256	78961	Nbn 28/10/8	NC	Account of sheep
257	78962	OB	NC	Akkadian literary; *AnSt* 33 145-152
258	78963		NC	Medical
259	78964	Art -/-/8	F	Account of barley
260	78965		F	Account
261	78966		NC	Contract
262	78967	Sel/Ant 2/9/-	NC	Loan of silver
263	78968		F	Accounts
264	78969	OB	C	School exercise; lenticular; literary extract concerning Samsuiluna
265	78970	OB	C	School exercise; lenticular
266	78971	Joined to Bu 89-4-26, 235 (= BM 78942)		
267	78972	Ha -/1/35	NC	Field sale(?)
267A	78972A	OB	F	Case of previous; seals
268	78973		F	Literary; dupl. 2*R* 60; *aluzinnu*
269	78974		F	Account of wool(?)
270	78975		F	Contract
271	78976	Art	F	Account of dates or grain
272	78977	Art	F	Sale of a slave girl; stamp seals
273	78978	Art 30/9/4	F	Contract for barley; stamp seals
274	78979	Joined to Bu 89-4-26, 237 (= BM 78944)		
275	78980	Ššu 20/9/19	NC	Land sale; nail marks; Babylon
276	78981		F	Ledger
277	78982		F	Receipt; stamp seals
278	78983	OB	F	Sumerian literary
279	78984	1/9/12	NC	Account of barley; turns wrong
280	78985		NC	Account
281	78986	OB 20/6b/-	NC	Five real estate transactions; late period
282	78987		F	Account of dates
283	78988	Ha -/6/9	F	Field sale
284	78989	Art -/1/4	F	Account of wool
285	78990	OB	F	Account; two columns; late period
286	78991		F	Account of barley
287	78992	OB	F	Sumerian literary
288	78993	Cyr 28/7/1	NC	Account of barley
289	78994		C	Account of barley and dates

Bu 89-4-26,

290	78995	27/-/-	NC	Contract; stamp seals
291	78996	Art	NC	Sale of a field; nail marks
292	78997	-/5/12	C	Account of barley or dates provisions
293	78998	Art -/7/16	C	Account of barley provisions
294	78999	Dar	NC	Account of dates or grain provisions
295	79000	Art 16/9/2	NC	Contract; stamp seals
296	79001	Art -/7/4	C	Receipt for dates or grain; stamp seals
297	79002	Art -/11/19	C	Receipt for oil
298	79003		F	Prayer against sorcery
299				Bezold, *Cat.* p. 1931
300	79004	Aş 21/12/5	C	Account
301	79005	Aş 8/3/5	C	Account in silver
302	79006	OB	C	Four real estate transactions; late period
303	79007	OB	F	Legal dispute concerning a field
304	79008	Aş -/2/?	NC	Field rental; seals
305	79009		F	Animal ledger
306	79010	Aş 6/12b/"17+a"	NC	Account; check marks
307	79011		F	Account of barley; stamp seals
308	79012	Philip 2/18/8	F	Receipt
309	79013	Tammaritu (Elam) 6/12b/acc	C	Deposition of property; Hidalu; *AnSt* 33 153ff.
310				Bezold, *Cat.* p. 1931
311	79014	Art	NC	Economic
312	79015		F	Contract; stamp seals
313	79016	-/9/-	F	Account of dates or grain; stamp seals
314	79017	Dar 27/6/5	NC	Sale of land
315	79018		F	Account of date or grain provisions
316	79019	14/-/-	F	House rental; stamp seals
317	79020	OB	F	Account; check marks
318	79021	Aş 6/11/?	C	Field rental; seals
319	79022	OB	F	Incantations to attract women; partial dupl. of Bu 89-4-46, 596 (= BM 79299)
320	79023		F	Division of property
321	79024		F	Account of barley
322	79025		F	Account
323	79026		F	Legal; stamp seals
324	79027		F	Loan of silver
325	79028	Sel/Ant -/8/27	NC	Contract for juniper

Bu 89-4-26,

326	79029	Art -/12/8	F	Account of barley provisions
327	79030	Art -/-/8	NC	Contract for temple deliveries; stamp seals
328	79031	-/-/9	F	Account of barley provisions
329	79032		F	School exercise; wedges
330	79033	Art 25/8/7	NC	Contract
331	79034	Sel/Ant -/-/31	F	Contract
332	79035	NA	F	Royal inscription; cylinder; mentions Esarhaddon
333	79036		NC	Account of dates or grain
334	79037	MB?	F	Sumerian literary; Emesal litanies
335	79038	Aṣ 4/2/14	NC	Account
336	79039		F	Account of dates or grain
337	79040		F	Account of dates or grain
338	79041	Npl 7/12/1	C	Account of dates
339	79042	Nbk 8/1/4	C	Offering ledger; Sippar
340	79043		F	Contract; stamp seals
341	79044	Ad 28/1/35	NC	Loan of silver; seals
342	79045	Art	F	Account of garments
343	79046	Dar 8/7/+6	C	Sale of slaves
344	79047	OB -/12/-	F	Accounts; ***ištu*** KASKAL Sippar
345	79048	Dar 7/4/6	C	Sale of slaves
346	79049	Nbn 11/12b/12	C	Loan of silver; stamp seals
347	79050	OB	C	School exercise; personal names; lenticular
348	79051	OB	C	School exercise; lenticular; literary extract concerning Hammurapi
349	79052	Nbn 16/6/7	NC	Account of barley tithes
350	79053		F	Astronomical omens (Sin)
351	79054	Nbn 10+/7/acc	NC	Account of house rentals
352	79055	Dar 17/3/25	C	Loan of silver
353	79056	OB	F	Contract; gift of an É ^{d}*Išḫara* by a man to his wife
354	79057		C	Accounts
355	79058	Npl 30/-/4	C	Account of dates
356	79059	3/11/8	C	Offering ledger
357	79060		F	*Namburbu* concerning braziers
358	79061		F	Ritual to ensure pregnancy
359	79062	OB	C	Sumerian; model contract
360	79063	Sd 15/11/?	NC	Field rental; seals

Bu 89-4-26,

361	79064	OB	F	Field rental; seals
362	79065	-/-/26	NC	Account of dates
363	79066	-/-/9	C	Field sale; Babylon; nail marks
364	79067	Ad 10/-/4	C	Field rental; seals
365	79068	OB	F	Letter
366	79069	Dar 8/5/18	F	Account of silver; drawing
367	79070	Dar 8/4/-	NC	Loan of silver
368	79071	Si 9/10/6	C	Contract for making bricks; seals; unopened case tablet
369	79072		C	Account
370	79073	Dar 11/9/35	C	Loan of silver
371	79074	Dar 28/4/36	C	Sale of slave girl
372	79075	Aş 14/2/13 or "17+a"	C	Account; round type
373	79076	Art 11/1/-	C	Contract for barley
374	79077	20+/-/-	F	Loan(?)
375	79078		F	Contract
376	79079	Nbn 3/3/2	C	Field sale
377	79080	Dar -/-/21	NC	Contract for oxen; Babylon
378	79081	OB	F	Account; check marks
379	79082	Cam	F	Contract
380	79083		NC	Account
381	79084	Nbk 3/11/3	C	Offering ledger
382	79085	Si 12/1/7	C	Loan for a trading journey
383	79086	OB	C	Legal deposition; round type; late period
384	79087	Xer 16/-/1	C	Loan
385	79088	OB	C	Account of oil
386	79089		NC	Account
387	79090	Nbk 20/2/8	NC	Offering ledger
388	79091	OB	NC	Account
389	79092	14/5/-	NC	Contract for seed
390	79093	OB	F	Contract; seals
391	79094		F	Receipt for provisions
392	79095	12/12/15	C	Receipt for dates or grain
393	79096	OB	NC	Account; round type; late period
394	79097		C	Account; stamp seals
395	79098	Nbn 8/3/-	NC	Contract for dates and barley
396	79099	NA	F	Letter
397	79100	Alex 1/10/11	NC	Loans; stamp seals

Bu 89-4-26,

398	79101	Ha -/5/40	C	Contract(?)
398A	79101A	OB	F	Case of previous; seals
399	79102	OB	F	Letter collection (Nanna-kiag); Sumerian
400	79103	Dar 7/12b/22	C	Contract for dates
401	79104	Si	C	Contract
402	79105	OB 29/3/-	NC	Account; round type; late period
403	79106	NA	F	Ritual; medical
404	79107	OB	F	Account; check marks
405	79108	OB	C	Letter; round type; late period
406	79109	(-)-uşur 25/2/10	F	Account of silver
407	79110	OB	NC	Receipt for oil; seals
408+ 89-10-14,612	79111+ 80065	OB	F	Literary; Akkadian
409	79112	1/10/-	C	Receipt
410	79113	Nbn 8/5/5	C	Account of dates
411	79114	OB	C	Field rental
411A	79114A	OB	F	Case of previous; seals
412	79115	Nbn 20/8/9	NC	Contract for dates or grain
413	79116	Dar 13/2/15	C	Loan of silver; Sippar
414	79117	Dar 16/1/17	C	Contract for barley
415	79118	OB	C	Harvest loan; part of case adhering; seals
416	79119	OB	F	Harvest loan; seals
417	79120		NC	Account of sheep
418	79121	Aş -/-/15	C	Year formula for Aş year 15
419	79122	Dar 15/11/6	C	Sale of a slave girl; Borsippa
420	79123		C	Account of dates or grain
421	79124		C	Account of wool
422	79125	OB	C	Incantation and ritual against dog-bite; cf. *VAS* 17 8, etc.; late period
423	79126	Aş 9/2/6	C	Account of garlic and onions; round type
424	79127	OB	NC	Letter; round type; late period; seals(?)
425	79128	Dar 2/4/16	C	Loan of dates; Sippar
426	79129	OB	F	Purchase of a field
427	79130	OB	F	Accounts
428	79131	-/12/acc	NC	Account of silver and gold
429	79132	Nbn 24/8/8	NC	Account of dates
430	79133		C	Sales receipt

Bu 89-4-26,

431	79134	Nbn 7/1/6	NC	Account of garments of gods
432	79135	Dar 15/6/20+	C	Loan of silver
433	79136	OB	C	Accounts; round type; late period
434	79137	29/12/-	C	Accounts of bitumen
435	79138	OB	C	Account; round type; late period
436	79139	Ha -/-/2	C	Hire of a slave; cf. Bu 89-4-26, 518 (= BM 79221)
436A	79139A	OB	C	Case of previous; seals
437	79140	Dar 21/7/7	C	Account of barley and emmer; Sippar
438	79141	Aṣ 1/8/14	NC	Account of barley; round type
439	79142		C	Letter
440	79143	OB	F	Account
441	79144		F	Accounts
442	79145		F	Receipt for dates or grain
443	79146		F	Literary; two columns
444	79147	OB	C	Letter; round type; late period
445	79148	OB	F	Account; round type; late period
446	79149	OB	C	Account of sheep; round type; late period
447	79150	OB	F	House rental
447A	79150A	Ha 26/12/43	F	Case of previous; seals
448	79151	Cyr 24/6/8	NC	Sale of land; Babylon
449	79152	Si 12/12/4	C	Boat rental; part of case adhering
449A	79152A	Si 12/12/4	F	Case of previous; seals
450	79153	Nbn 11/7/14	C	House rental
451	79154	Ha 9/6/35	C	Account of hired men
452	79155	Nbn 3/6/6	C	Contract for bricks
453	79156	Sd 24/7/15	C	Boat rental; seals
454	79157	Aṣ 24/9/16	C	Loan of silver; seals
455	79158	Kan 6/7/20	NC	Contract; Sippar
456	79159	Kan 1/10/17	C	Contract for barley
457	79160	Art -/4/36	F	Receipt
458	79161	Dar 8/7/10	F	Receipt for silver
459	79162	OB 1/5/-	C	Loan of silver; seals
460	79163	Npl 22/12/6	NC	Sale of a slave(?)
461	79164	Ha 1/8/35	C	Account of personnel
462	79165	Nbk 22/1/3	NC	Sale of bitumen
463	79166	Cam -/-/5	NC	Sale of a slave(?)
464	79167	Ššu -/7/1	F	Deposition; Babylon

Bu 89-4-26,

465	79168	OAkk	C	Account of commodities
466	79169		F	Receipt for wool
467	79170	Ha 15/?/5	C	Issue of aromatics for *telitu* of en Kašbaran[ki]; seals
468	79171		C	Account of oil
469	79172	Ad 10?/10/2	C	Receipt for barley
470	79173	Art 4/-/13	F	Receipt for barley
471	79174	Nbn 20/1/-	NC	Loan of silver; Babylon
472	79175	Dar 10/10/11	C	Receipt for dates or grain
473	79176	Aş 29/4/17+b	C	Loan of silver; seals
474	79177	1/1/-	C	Accounts of dates or grain
475	79178	19/-/-	C	Account of dates
476	79179	Aş 20/9/14	C	Account of barley; round type
477	79180		C	Receipt
478	79181	Nbn 15/7/16	F	Contract
479	79182		F	Receipt
480	79183	Am 13/4/1	C	Sale of a slave
481	79184	Dar 13/12/23	C	Loan of silver; Sippar
482	79185	Ad 29/1/30	NC	Account; round type
483	79186	OB	F	Letter
484	79187	Nbn 29/1/3	C	Contract for barley
485	79188	OB	C	Account
486	79189	Aş 3?/8/9	C	Harvest loan; seals
487	79190		F	Account of dates or grain
488	79191		C	Account of pots
489	79192	OB mu x ús-sa-bi gu-za	C	Harvest loan
490	79193	OB	C	Loan; seals
491	79194	Nbn 14/10/2	NC	Contract for dates or grain
492	79195	Npl 1/2/19	C	Receipt for silver and iron tools
493	79196	Cyr 3/7/5	C	Contract for dates
494	79197	Nbn 1/4/8	NC	Account of barley
495	79198	Ha 2/6/37	C	Issue of barley; seals
496	79199	OB	C	Account of meat deliveries (*zibiltum*)
497	79200	Ha -/-/42 or Ad -/-/11	NC	Loan of silver; part of case adhering
498	79201	Npl 16/12/14	C	Account of iron tools
499	79202	Nbn 23/1/16	C	Contract for delivery of silver; Sippar
500	79203	Nbn -/5/3	C	Account of dates or grain

Bu 89-4-26,

501	79204	Cyr 6/6/-	NC	Loan of silver
502	79205	Dar 22/4/24	C	Receipt for sheep
503	79206		NC	Loan
504	79207	Nbn 24/12/2	NC	Loan
505	79208	Xer 11/6/1	C	House rental; Sippar
506	79209	Dar 14/11/22	C	Receipt for silver and dates
507	79210	Cyr 23/8/acc	NC	Temple accounts
508	79211	Ad 1/5/18	C	Delivery of lambs to a diviner
509	79212		C	Measurements of land
510	79213	Sd 28/2/18	C	Account
511	79214	Aş 27/5/8	C	Receipt(?); seals
512	79215	OB	C	Legal deposition(?)
513	79216	Cyr 18/11/1	C	Sale of a slave girl; Babylon
514	79217	14/6/acc	C	Account of iron tools
515	79218	Cam 1/11/3	F	Contract for dates; Sippar
516	79219	Aş 11?/3/?	C	Loan of silver involving a princess; seals
517	79220	Aş 27/7/"17+a"	NC	Loan of silver
518	79221	OB	C	Hire of a slave; cf. Bu 89-4-26, 436 (= BM 79139)
519	79222	Nbn 4/-/6	C	Receipt for dye
520	79223	Npl -/2/20	C	Contract for barley
521	79224	Nb(-) -/1/11	NC	Contract for barley
522	79225	Cam 11/8/1	NC	Loan(?)
523	79226	OB	NC	Hire of a slave
524	79227	Ad 27/10/18	C	Receipt; seals
525	79228		NC	Receipt
526	79229	13/iti ezen ᵈiškur/ Ha 42 or Ad 11	NC	Harvest loan
527	79230		F	Loan of silver
528	79231	OB 20?/5/mu gibil	C	Loan for a trading journey
529	79232	-/-/5	C	Account of barley
530	79233		C	Account of cosmetics
531	79234	Sd 1/1/2	C	Harvest loan; seals
532	79235	Cam 2/2/8	C	Contract for dates
533	79236	Ha 24/7/35	C	Administrative; list of names
534	79237	Aş 17?/3/?	C	Administrative; list of names; round type
535	79238	Ad 18/11/18	C	Administrative; concerning sale or hire of cattle; seals
536	79239		F	Receipt for silver and barley

Bu 89-4-26,

537	79240	Npl 19/9/20	C	Receipt for sheep
538	79241	Si 1/7/4	C	Receipt; seals
539	79242	OB	C	Administrative; list of names
540	79243	Dar 23/11/14	C	Receipt for a duck
541	79244		C	Medical prescription; salve for spots
542	79245	Sd 10/5/1	C	Loan of barley; seals
543	79246	Aş 1/6/13	NC	Receipt for fodder; seals
544	79247	Ad 19/3/3	C	Receipt for barley
545	79248	OB -/-/?	C	Hire of labour
546	79249		F	Account of barley
547	79250	Nbn 27/1/16	C	Loan of silver
548	79251	OB	C	Memorandum; round type; late period
549	79252	Nbn 8/12/-	C	Sales receipt
550	79253	Npl 24/4/6	C	Contract for barley
551	79254	Nbn 17/7/13	C	Receipt for purchase of wool
552	79255	Ha 28/3/40	NC	Field rental
553	79256	Kan 6/8/18	C	Field rental; Babylon
554	79257		C	Account of silver
555	79258	24/4/14	C	Memorandum concerning work on Esagila; account of sheep
556	79259	Npl 19/5/18	C	Loan of silver and barley; Sippar
557	79260	Dar -/-/23	NC	Contract for dates or grain
558	79261	Ner 10/10/-	C	Contract for a vat
559	79262	Npl 21/2/9	C	Account of dates
560	79263	OB 15/7?/mu ki-lugal-gub-ba	C	Field rental
561	79264	OB	C	Letter
562	79265	Ha -/9/42	C	Harvest loan
563	79266	Si -/-/?	C	Field rental; seals
564	79267	Nbk 21/8/-	C	Receipt for barley
565	79268	OB	C	Memorandum concerning fields
566	79269	OB	C	Account of grain; round type; late period
567	79270	Nbn 6/5/acc	C	Receipt for barley
568	79271	Nbn 18/3/5	C	Loan of silver
569	79272	Cam 6/2/-	C	Loan of silver
570	79273	-/-/5	NC	Contract
571	79274	25/1/-	F	Receipt
572	79275	Si 14/3/4	C	Loan of silver

Bu 89-4-26,

573	79276	Aş 25/8/7	C	Round type; seals
574	79277	Nbk 15/6/38	C	Loan of silver; Babylon
575	79278	OB	C	Letter(?); round type; late period
576	79279	Nbk 10/7/1	NC	Contract for dates; Babylon
577	79280	Nbk -/12/40	C	Exchange of a pledge for unpaid debt
578	79281	Aş 10/1/16	C	Rental of a house; seals
579	79282	OB	NC	Letter; round type; late period
580	79283	Dar 14/4/29	NC	Loan of silver
581	79284	Art 26/3/38	C	Receipt for barley provisions
582	79285	OB 5?/9/?	C	Account of barley; round type
583	79286	Sd 10/1/19	C	Account of barley; round type
584	79287	Aş 30/4/14	C	Account of barley; round type
585	79288		C	Account of sheep
586	79289	Dar 2/11/18	NC	Loan of silver
587	79290	Dar 11/12/24	C	Contract for dates and barley
588	79291	Si 21?/11/3?	C	Issue of barley
589	79292	OB 21/3/-	C	Memorandum concerning the departure of three men
590	79293	Dar 15/6/27	C	Contract; stamp seal; Babylon
591	79294	Ha 15/8/43	C	List of personnel
592	79295	Art 27/8/34	C	Receipt for barley provisions
593	79296	Ha 10/12/42	C	Loan of silver; seals
594	79297	Xer 12/9/10	C	Contract for dates
595	79298	21/10/18	NC	Receipt for dates
596	79299	OB	C	Incantation; phonetic Sumerian; round type; partial dupl. of Bu 89-4-26, 319 (= BM 79022)
597	79300	Dar 27/11/30	NC	Receipt
598	79301	Dar 17/6/17	C	Receipt for sheep
599	79302	Sd 1/12/18	C	Loan of silver; seals
600	79303		C	Account of barley
601	79304	Aş 6/?/"17+a"	C	Loan(?); seals
602	79305	Dar -/3/1	F	Loans; Babylon
603	79306	Aş 13/12/14	NC	Harvest loan
604	79307	Dar 4/4/10	NC	Loan
605	79308		NC	Medical prescription
606	79309	Ha 10/iti ezen *ḫu-un-ṭi*/37 or 39	C	Hire of labour
607	79310	Aş 27/4/"17+b"	NC	Ration list
608	79311	Cyr 10/-/5	C	Loan

Bu 89-4-26,

609	79312	OB	C	Administrative; list of names; round type; late period
610	79313	Aş 18/3/14	C	Account; round type
611	79314	Npl 21/9/18	C	Account of sheep
612	79315	Nbn 28/9/2	C	Contract for bronze
613	79316	OB -/-/mu bád IGI^{ki}	C	Loan of barley
614	79317	Nbn -/12b/6	C	Receipt for oxen
615	79318	Nbk 28/3/37	C	Loans; Babylon
616	79319	Nbn	NC	Description of property
617	79320		C	School exercise; same text on each side; economic
618	79321	Ha 26/5/42	C	Receipt for bricks
619	79322	Ha 13$^{?}$/6/35	C	Administrative; note of builders
620	79323		NC	Letter; *CT* 22 36
621	79324	Ha ?/?/42	C	Receipt for bricks
622	79325		C	Receipt for vats
623	79326	Nbk 2/11/9	C	Receipt for garments
624	79327		C	Letter; *CT* 22 2
625	79328	20/8/-	NC	Receipt for dates
626	79329		C	Account
627	79330	Nbn 30/1/16	C	Receipt for wool
628	79331	Dar 18/6/9	C	Receipt for beer
629	79332	Am 27/2/1	NC	Contract for barley
630	79333		NC	Receipt for dates
631	79334		C	Memorandum concerning barley and dates; drawing of a bird
632	79335	Dar 27/3/-	NC	Contract for barley
633	79336	OB 17/12/mu gu-za bára-[...]	C	Docket; seals
634	79337	Ha 28/5/42	C	Receipt for bricks
635	79338	Sd -/3 or 11/-	C	Issue of barley; round type
636	79339	Nbn 5/7/11	C	Receipt for dates or grain
637	79340	Aş 26/2/16	C	Issue of barley
638	79341	Npl 12/12/15	C	Contract for bronze bowls; Sippar
639	79342	OB -/6/-	C	Administrative; list of names
640	79343	Nbn -/10/15	C	Loan of silver
641	79344	OB	C	Receipt for barley; seals
642	79345	Ha 4/9/35	C	Adminstrative; list of names
643	79346	Nbn 17/4/10	C	Receipt for garments
644	79347	OB	F	Letter

Bu 89-4-26,

645	79348	Nbn 27/3/-	C	Receipt for dyes
646	79349	-/5/16	C	Sale of a slave
647	79350		NC	Letter; *CT* 22 208
648	79351	Ha -/7/9	C	Note on field produce
649	79352	Nbn 16/1/4	C	Receipt for dyes
650	79353		C	Receipt for purchase of sheep
651	79354	(-)-uṣur -/8/1	NC	Receipt for barley
652	79355	OB	F	Contract; seal
653	79356	Nbk 18/5/-	C	Receipt for dates or grain
654	79357	Nbn 24/6/4	C	Receipt for iron
655	79358		NC	Letter; *CT* 22 66
656	79359	11/5/-	F	Receipt for linen
657	79360	26/10/9	C	Receipt for dates
658	79361	16/10/3	C	Receipt for sheep
659	79362	Dar 10/2/8	C	Receipt for silver
660	79363	Ner 25/11/3	NC	Loan of silver
661	79364	Npl 26/1/11	C	Contract for barley; Sippar
662	79365	Ha -/8/43	C	Harvest loan
663	79366	Aṣ 11/10?/14?	NC	Ration list; round type
664	79367	Npl 9/7/9	C	Receipt for dates
665	79368	Ha 7/8/35	C	Administrative; list of names
666	79369		C	Receipt for barley
667	79370	29/7/-	C	List of wages for hired men
668	79371		F	Contract
669	79372	OB	C	Note concerning a reed worker
670	79373	19/12b/14	C	Receipt for iron
671	79374	Ha 20/5/4 mu bàd *ga-gi-im*	C	Loan of silver
672	79375	OB	C	Docket; number 66 and seal
673	79376	12/8/-	NC	Receipt for emmer
674	79377	Ha 12/6/35	C	Note concerning two men
675	79378	Ha 6?/1/40	C	Order to release a boat from customs; seals; cf. Bu 89-4-26, 690 (= BM 79393)
676	79379	Aṣ 19/12/16	C	Record of agricultural(?) labour; seals; cf. Bu 89-4-26, 729, 732, 737, 749 (= BM 79432, 79435, 79440, 79452)
677	79380	Ha 28/7/35	C	Note concerning two men
678	79381	Nbk 1/10/1	C	Receipt for sheep
679	79382	Ha 19/6/35	C	Note concerning two builders

Bu 89-4-26,

680	79383	Nbn 2/8/7	C	Receipt for wool
681	79384		C	Account of provisions
682	79385	Cyr 21/6/15	NC	Contract for barley
683	79386	(-)-uṣur -/-/12	NC	Account of garments of gods
684	79387	Ha 5/8/35	C	Account of barley
685	79388	OB	C	Issue of bran; cf. Bu 89-4-26, 724, 731, 734 (= BM 79427, 79434, 79437); seals; docket
686	79389	Npl 26/5/20	C	Receipt for oxen
687	79390	Nbk 17/3/4	C	Account of sheep
688	79391	Si 26/12/3	C	Harvest loan; seals
689	79392	OB	C	Issue of barley and flour
690	79393	OB	C	Release of a boat-load of onions from customs; seals; cf. Bu 89-4-26, 675 (= BM 79378)
691	79394	Si 13/4/7	C	Harvest loan
692	79395		C	Letter; *CT* 22 44
693	79396	Ha 15/10/43	C	Identification of a workman; seals
694	79397		NC	Loan of silver
695	79398	29/9/-	C	Receipt for bitumen
696	79399	Ha -/5/38	C	Record of storage of barley belonging to a *naditu*
697	79400	23/5/4	C	Receipt for silver
698	79401		C	Astronomical omen report
699	79402	15/7/2	C	Contract for dates; Babylon
700	79403	21/9/-	C	Receipt for bitumen
701	79404	Nbn 8/5/10	NC	Receipt for provisions
702	79405		C	Sales receipt
703	79406	Dar -/1/14	NC	Receipt for bronze
704	79407		F	Contract(?) concerning gold daggers
705	79408	-/-/12	F	Economic
706	79409	Nbn 12/4/6	NC	Loan(?)
707	79410	Nbk 25/12b/14	C	Receipt for bales
708	79411	Npl -/7/11	C	Account of beams
709	79412		C	Memorandum concerning receipt of barley
710	79413	Nbn 6/12b/6	NC	Receipt for dates
711	79414		F	Economic
712	79415		F	Receipt for oil and barley; scratches on reverse

Bu 89-4-26,

713	79416	OB 6/8/?	C	Bulla; seals; inscribed with reapers
714	79417	OB	C	Bulla; seals; inscribed with reapers
715	79418	OB	C	Uninscribed bulla; seals
716	79419	OB	C	Inscribed bulla; seals
717	79420	OB	C	Inscribed bulla; seals
718	79421	OB	C	Uninscribed bulla; seals
719	79422	Nbn 21/5/1	C	Receipt for a sheep
720	79423	OB	C	Uninscribed bulla; seals
721	79424	OB	C	Uninscribed bulla; seal
722	79425	OB	C	Uninscribed bulla; seals
723	79426	OB 16/8/-	C	Inscribed bulla; seals
724	79427	OB	C	Issue of bran; inscribed bulla; seals
725	79428	Nbn 29/12/7	C	Contract for barley
726	79429	OB	C	Inscribed bulla
727	79430		C	Letter; *CT* 22 185
728	79431	Ha 30/5/42	C	Note concerning bricks
729	79432	Aş 13/11/16	C	Record of agricultural(?) labour; seals; cf. Bu 89-4-26, 676 (= BM 79379)
730	79433		C	Receipt for silver
731	79434	OB	C	Issue of bran; inscribed bulla; seals; cf. Bu 89-4-26, 685 (= BM 79388)
732	79435	Aş 6/12b/13	C	Record of agricultural labour; seals; cf. Bu 89-4-26, 676 (= BM 79379)
733	79436	OB	C	Issue of wooden beams; seals
734	79437	OB	C	Issue of bran; inscribed bulla; seals
735	79438	OB	C	Note concerning two men
736	79439	OB	C	Loan; seals
737	79440	Aş 7?/11/16	C	Record of agricultural labour; seals; cf. Bu 89-4-26, 676 (= BM 79379)
738	79441	OB 14/3/-	C	Receipt for rations
739	79442	OB 12?/7/?	C	Inscribed bulla; seals
740	79443		C	Account
741	79444	OB	C	Inscribed bulla
742	79445	OB	C	Administrative; list of names
743	79446		C	Letter; *CT* 22 75
744	79447	Ha 16/iti *tám-ḫi-ri-i*/42	C	Note on the future delivery of eight oxen(?); seals
745	79448	Ad 10/5/24?	C	Loan of barley(?); seals
746	79449	OB	C	Contract(?); seals
747	79450	Nbn 14/2/4	NC	Receipt

Bu 89-4-26,

748	79451		C	Receipt
749	79452	Aş 28/12/14	C	Record of agricultural labour; seals; cf. Bu 89-4-26, 676 (= BM 79379)
750	79453	OB 6/9/-	C	Inscribed bulla; seals
751	79454	NA	F	NA royal inscription(?)
752	79455		F	Unidentified
753	79456	OB 26/9/-	C	Inscribed bulla
754	79457	Nbk	C	Royal inscription; cylinder; *VAB* 4 84; *Nbk* 6
755	79458	OB	C	Erased; only two signs visible

89-9-30,

1	79459	Seleucid	F	Only personal names preserved

89-10-14,

1	79460	OB 29/1/-	C	Account; round type; late period
2	79461	Ha -/-/8 or 31	C	Rental of a field
3	79462	OB	C	Agreement concerning a wall
4	79463	OB	C	Letter
5	79464	Ha 21/7/35	C	Administrative; list of names
6	79465	Si 6/7/4	C	Receipt for silver; seals
7	79466	OB	C	Receipt for barley; round type; late period
8	79467	Si 15/6/4	C	Issue of barley
9	79468	OB 10/2/-	C	Receipt for barley
10	79469	Si 17/11/30	C	Account
11	79470	OB	C	Letter; round type; late period
12	79471	Sm -/-/8	C	Field rental
13	79472	OB	C	Letter
14	79473	OB	C	Account; round type; late period
15	79474	Aş 22/11/13	C	Harvest loan; seals
16	79475	OB	C	Loan of silver
17	79476	Aş 23/2/"17+b"	C	Loan of onion seed; seals
18	79477	OB 7/12/-	C	Record of workmen
19	79478	Si -/-/7	C	Rental of an *edakkum*; seals
20	79479	Aş 1/12/13 or "17+a"	C	Hire of a slave girl; *sissiktu* impression; seals
21	79480	Si 4/4/4	C	Transfer of a debt in barley; seals
22	79481	Si 10/7/6	C	Rental of an *edakkum*; seals
23	79482	Aş 8/11/15	C	Pay-list of harvesters; round type
24	79483	Ha 13/8/33	C	Loan of silver; part of case adhering
24A	79483A	OB	C	Case of previous; seals
25	79484	Si 27/7/6	C	Hire of an *edakkum*; seals
25A	79484A	Si 27/7/6	C	Case of previous; seals

89-10-14,

26	79485	Aş ?/?/"17+a"	C	Ration list; check marks
27	79486	Si -/-/15	C	Partition of a field
28	79487	OB	C	Letter; late period
29	79488	OB	C	Letter; round type; late period
30	79489	Si 16/6b/5	C	Administrative; list of names
31	79490	OB	C	List of workmen
32	79491	OB	C	Letter; round type; late period
33	79492	OB	C	Letter
34	79493	15/5/Ha 13 or Si 8	C	Loan for a trading journey
35	79494	OB	C	Account of barley; round type; late period
36	92596	Ha -/-/3	C	Division of an estate
37	79495	Aş 26/1/6	C	Rental of three fields
38	79496	Sm	C	Sale of an empty plot
39	79497	Sabium	C	House sale
40	92597	Si 18/-/30	C	Sale of a field
41	92598	Aş -/1/16	C	Field rental; seals
42	79498	OB	C	Letter
43	79499	Aş 10/2/"17+a"	NC	Field rental; seals
44	79500	OB	F	Administrative; list of names
45	92599	Si 12/12/30	C	Sale of a field
46	92600	Sabium	C	Sale of a field
47	79501	Sm	C	Agreement concerning the ownership of property
48	79502	AS	C	Agreement concerning an inheritance; unopened case; seals
49	92601	Ha	C	Sale of a field
50	92602	AS	C	Sale of a field
50A	92602A	OB	C	Case of previous; seals
51	79503	NA	C	Copy of a bilingual votive inscription of Adad-apal-iddina with colophon of the time of Esarhaddon; *StOr* 1 pp. 28-33
52	92603	OB	C	Copy of a field sale; Sm oath; late period
53	92604	Sabium	C	Field sale; Sabium oath
54	79504	OB	C	Account of rations for wives
55	79505	OB	C	Account of rations
56	79506	OB	C	Account of expenditure of silver
57	79507	OB	C	Field sales from years Ae k, Si 28, unidentified, and Ae d

89-10-14,

58	79508	27/5/-	C	List of provisions
59	79509	OB	C	Ration list
60	79510	OB	F	Sumerian literary
61	79511	Dar 22/5/17	C	House rental
62	79512	Dar 5/3/13	C	Contract for dates; stamp seals
63	79513	Dar -/8/9	C	Contract for dates
64	79514	Dar 20/9/26	C	Letter; seals
65	79515	Am 28/6/1	C	List of hired workmen
66	79516	Nbn 29/2/15	C	Receipt for dates
67	79517	Am 12/10/acc	C	Hire of oxen; Sippar
68	79518	Cam 10/-/1	NC	Receipt for barley
69	79519	-/2/23	NC	Account of Dilmun dates
70	79520	10/4/35	NC	Receipt for sheep and oil
71	79521	Am 22/10/acc	NC	Receipt for purchase of sesame
72	79522	Nbn 9/1/8	NC	Receipt for purchase of sheep
73	79523	Nbn 26/12b/1	C	Receipt for iron
74	79524	Xer -/4/1	C	Receipt for barley
75	79525	Cyr 26/2/6	NC	Account of date provisions
76	79526	Cam 17/4/5	NC	Receipt for cedar
77	79527	Dar 5/9/1	NC	Contract for barley
78	79528	Dar 21/12b/27	NC	Letter; stamp seals
79	79529	28/5/5	NC	Contract for dates; Sippar
80	79530	Am 8/2/1	NC	Receipt for iron tools; stamp seal
81	79531	Dar 10/1/23	NC	Receipt for silver
82	79532		C	Account of sheep and goats
83	79533	Dar 15/-/-	C	Receipt for barley
84	79534	Nbn 10/10/-	NC	Receipt for iron
85	79535	10/8/17	C	Receipt
86	79536	Dar 24/12/21	C	Loan of silver
87	79537	Dar 14/5/5	NC	Loan of silver
88	79538	Cam 10/10/3	C	Receipt for wool
89	79539	Xer 30/12/1	NC	Receipt for dates or grain
90	79540	Xer 13/9/acc	C	Contract for barley; Sippar
91	79541	Dar 19/-/7	F	Land sale
92	79542	Xer 8/7/1	NC	Contract for barley
93	79543	Nbk 6/12/30+	C	Land sale
94	79544	Nbk 7/11/41	NC	Account of ducks
95	79545	7/10/2	F	Account of dates
96	79546	5/4/20	NC	Receipt

89-10-14,

97	79547		F	Contract
98	79548		F	Receipt for barley
99	79549	-/-/4	F	Contract for barley; Sippar
100	79550	-/6/-	NC	Account of silver *isqu* payments
101	79551	Nbn 2/6/13	NC	Receipt for tin
102	79552	Cyr 23/3/8	NC	Receipt for sesame
103	79553	Dar 2/10/34	F	Account of dates
104	79554	1/12/16	NC	Receipt for sesame
105	79555	Nbk 14/12/35	NC	Receipt for silver
106	79556	Nbn 27/4/17	F	Receipt for silver(?)
107	79557	Nbk 10/8/33	NC	Receipt for bitumen(?)
108	79558	-/12/34	F	Account of dates or grain
109	79559	Dar 12/1/31	NC	Letter
110	79560	Cyr -/6/1	F	Account of wool and garments of gods
111	79561	Nbk 25/2/36	NC	Receipt for wool
112	79562		F	Account of dates or grain
113	79563	Nbn 5/2/6	C	Receipt for sesame
114	79564	Nbk 17/11/-	F	Receipt
115	79565	Dar -/5/27	NC	Letter
116	79566	9/2/-	F	Receipt for silver
117	79567	Nbk 22/-/-	NC	Receipt for vats
118	79568		F	Receipt for wool
119	79569	Ner 27/1/-	NC	Account of barley
120	79570	-/3/-	F	Contract
121	79571	Nbk 29/2/29	NC	Account of date and barley provisions
122	79572	Nbn 25/9/4	C	Receipt for an ox carcass
123	79573		NC	Account of spades
124	79574	Cam	NC	Receipt for wax and IM.GUL
125	79575		NC	Account of sheep
126	79576	Dar 23/6/11	NC	Contract for dates or grain
127	79577	30/8/40	NC	Receipt for silver
128	79578	Nbk 11/6/34	NC	Payment of silver
129	79579	Nbk 14/6/9	NC	Receipt for a slave
130	79580	18/3/-	C	Receipt for barley
131	79581	Dar -/8/17	NC	Contract for silver
132	79582		NC	Letter; *CT* 22 59
133	79583		F	Letter; *CT* 22 61
134	79584		F	Animal ledger
135	79585		F	Letter

89-10-14,

136	79586	Am -/-/-	F	Sale of a slave girl
137	79587	OB	NC	Letter
138	79588		F	Letter; *CT* 22 116
139	79589	-/7/-	F	Account of dates
140	79590	-/5/41	NC	Sale of horses
141	79591	-/5/18	F	Receipt for silver
142	79592	Nbn 4/8/12	NC	Receipt for cows
143	79593	Dar 27/1/14	NC	Contract for dates
144	79594	Am 17/12/1	NC	Receipt for silver
145	79595	27/2/3	F	Account of dates
146	79596	Nbn 17/-/-	F	Account of silver
147	79597		F	Account of dates
148	79598		F	Animal ledger
149	79599	Nbn 15/7/9	NC	Sale of oxen
150	79600		NC	Receipt for barley
151	79601	Cyr 16/5/3	NC	Receipt for birds
152	79602	Dar 14/9/2	NC	Receipt for sesame
153	79603	Cam -/-/7	NC	Account of linen
154	79604	Nbk -/2/8	NC	Receipt for garments
155	79605		F	Contract for dates
156	79606		F	Receipt for barley
157	79607	Nbk 14/1/32	NC	Receipt for barley
158	79608	Nbn 5/8/3	F	Account of dates
159	79609	-/3/38	F	Receipt for dates or grain
160	79610	-/-/1	F	Receipt for dates
161	79611	Nbn 28/3/17	NC	House rental
162	79612	Dar 5/-/-	NC	Receipt for iron
163	79613		F	Inscribed bulla or lid; stamp seal
164	79614	Nbn -/2/5	NC	Account of dates or grain
165	79615		NC	Account of sheep
166	79616	3/1/-	NC	Receipt for wool
167	79617	Ner 8/2/2	NC	Receipt for purchase of oxen
168	79618	Nbn 27/3/11	NC	Receipt for a sheep
169	79619	(-)-uṣur -/6/2	NC	Account of dates or grain
170	79620	Nbk 15/11/30	NC	Receipt for barley
171	79621		F	Account of barley
172	79622		F	Contract
173	79623	Nbn 13/12/10	NC	Receipt for iron
174	79624	17/5/42	F	Account of ducks

89-10-14,

175	79625		F	Account of garments of gods
176	79626	Cyr 17/7/2	C	Receipt for silver
177	79627	Nbn 17/-/-	F	Receipt for sesame
178	79628	-/-/37	F	Account of silver payments
179	79629	-/-/7	F	Loan of silver; Sippar
180	79630		F	Loan of silver
181	79631		F	Account of dates or grain
182	79632	Nbn 20/1/11	NC	Land sale; Sippar
183	79633	Dar 17/-/35	F	Receipt for wool
184	79634		F	Account of workmen
185	79635		F	Account
186	79636	Nbn -/2/6	NC	Receipt for garments
187	79637	Dar 20/6/8	F	Contract for dates
188	79638		F	Account of barley
189	79639	Cam 2/2/2	F	Adoption(?)
190	79640		F	Loan(?)
191	79641	Dar 20/6/3	NC	Loan of silver
192	79642	Nbn -/-/7	F	Account of dates or grain
193	79643	Sd 26/10/11	F	Sale of a house; referring to an earlier sale in Si 19
194	79644	Dar 24/12/24	C	Loan of silver
195	79645	Dar 16/10/5	C	Receipt for sheep
196	79646		C	Letter; stamp seal
197	79647	Nbk -/-/31	NC	Account of wool
198	79648		C	Letter
199	79649	Nbn 6/8/12	C	Receipt for grain and beer provisions
200	79650	Nbn 11/12/-	NC	Receipt for purchase of dates and wool
201	79651	Nbk 8/12/34	C	Account of bricks
202	79652	Nbk 9/12/11	C	Account of barley
203	79653	Nbn 6/-/-	NC	Receipt for purchase of provisions; drawing on reverse
204	79654	Nbn 15/1/17	C	Receipt for purchase of bitumen
205	79655	2/-/30	NC	Account of wool
206	79656		C	Letter
207	79657	Nbk 23/1/37	C	Rental of a boat
208	79658	Nbk 18/5/41	C	Account of garments
209	79659	OB	NC	Rental of a field
209A	79660	OB	F	Case of previous
210	79661	Nbk 22/4/38	C	Receipt for sesame

89-10-14,

211	79662	Nbk 13/5/36	C	Receipt for barley as rent
212	79663	Nbn 14/-/6	C	Receipt for wool
213	79664	Nbk 10/11/30	C	Receipt for purchases
214	79665	Nbk 28/10/36	C	Sale of oxen
215	79666	29/10/33	C	Receipt for purchase of emmer
216	79667	Nbn 12/5/16	C	Receipt for sesame
217	79668	Nbk 12/3/40	C	Receipt for wool
218	79669	Nbn 18/9/10	C	Receipt for linen garments
219	79670	Nbn 16/1/5	C	Receipt for purchase of provisions
220	79671		C	Letter
221	79672	Dar 22/6b/3	C	Loan of silver
222	79673	Nbn 30/6/2	C	Receipt for sesame
223	79674	13/2/36	C	Receipt for purchase of reeds
224	79675	Nbn 17/11/5	NC	Receipt for pots
225	79676	Dar 14/8/8	C	Contract for barley
226	79677	Dar 22/2/21	C	Receipt for purchase of sheep
227	79678	Nbk 14/8/25	C	Receipt for provisions
228	79679	Nbn 6/2/1	C	Contract for an ox
229	79680	Dar 18/12/33	C	Letter; stamp seal
230	79681	Nbk 14/8/24	C	Receipt for grain and an ox
231	79682	Nbk 26/8/35	C	Receipt for purchase of birds
232	79683	Dar 10/11/25	C	Loan
233	79684	Nbk 23/12b/33	C	Receipt for silver(?)
234	79685	Dar 28/6/24	C	Receipt for silver
235	79686	Nbk 21/12/35	C	Account of purchases of building materials
236	79687	Nbk 3/12/26	C	Receipt for barley
237	79688	Nbk 22/10/28	C	Receipt for barley
238	79689	Nbk 17/1/28	C	Receipt for purchase of a sheep
239	79690	Dar 23/12a/13	C	Contract
240	79691	Dar 10/2/20+	C	Loan of silver; Ṣibtu
241	79692	Nbn 22/12b/1	C	Sale of an ox
242	79693	Dar 8/4/28	C	Letter
243	79694	Nbk 11/7/15	C	Receipt for rental payment
244	79695	Dar 15/8/29	C	Receipt for garments of gods
245	79696	Nbn 10+/12/10	C	Receipt for iron
246	79697	Nbk 6/8/30	C	Receipt for tools
247	79698	Dar -/7/25	C	Contract for dates
248	79699	Cyr 1/3/1	C	Receipt for barley

89-10-14,

249	79700	Nbn 23/10/acc	C	Receipt for sesame
250	79701	Dar 10/1/33	C	Receipt for barley
251	79702	Dar 20/10/19	C	Contract for dates
252	79703	Dar 6/3/22	C	Receipt for sheep
253	79704	Dar 25/12/33	C	Account of dates
254	79705	Nbk 7/3/9	C	Account of barley
255	79706	Dar 26/5/17	C	Sale of a slave girl
256	79707	Dar 2/2/29	C	Contract for dates
257	79708	Dar 27/5/17	C	Loan of silver; Aramaic docket; *ABC* no. 34
258	79709	Dar 20/8/27	C	Receipt for barley
259	79710	Dar 5/12/12	C	Loan of silver
260	79711	Dar 13/8/28	C	Account of garments
261	79712	Dar 2/1/30	C	Offering ledger
262	79713	Dar 3/12/26	C	Receipt for purchase of dates
263	79714	Dar 18/7/8	C	Sippar; contract for purchase of vats
264	79715	Cyr 8/1/8	C	Receipt for payment
265	79716	Nbk 23/3/37	C	Receipt for a garment
266	79717	Dar 2/10/23	C	Letter
267	79718	Nbk 25/11/37	C	Receipt for iron(?)
268	79719	Nbk 19/5/36	C	Receipt for iron
269	79720	Nbn 23/5/8	C	Receipt for a sheep
270	79721	Nbk 10/4/17	C	Receipt for hides
271	79722		C	Account of dates and other produce
272	79723	Dar 10/1/18	C	Receipt for silver
273	79724	Nbn 24/-/6	C	Receipt for ducks
274	79725	Nbn 2/9/3	C	Receipt for iron
275	79726	Nbn 5/5/3	C	Receipt for aromatics
276	79727	Nbn 16/9/4	C	Receipt for bronze
277	79728	Cam 18/10/1	C	Receipt for barley
278	79729	Am 7/5/1	C	Receipt for gold rings
279	79730	Ner 6/3/2	C	Account of reeds
280	79731	11/12/19	C	Account of silver
281	79732		C	List of workmen; Sippar
282	79733	Nbn 30/8/12	C	Sale of a slave girl; Sippar
283	79734	Dar 1/9/10	C	Contract for dates
284	79735	Dar 24/1/29	C	Receipt for silver
285	79736	Cam 21/8/acc	C	Receipt for dates
286	79737	17/12/2	C	Receipt for dates or grain

89-10-14,

287	79738	Dar 3/10/35	C	Receipt for barley
288	79739	Cyr 8/5/6	C	Receipt for barley
289	79740	Nbk 11/7/36	C	Receipt for barley
290	79741		C	Account of dates and barley
291	79742	Ner -/6/3	C	Receipt for sheep
292	79743	Cyr 19/9/2	C	Receipt
293	79744	Xer 23/4/1	C	Contract for barley
294	79745	7/1/10	C	Account of garments of gods for cleaning
295	79746	Cyr 7/10/8	C	Land measurements
296	79747		C	Receipt for dates
297	79748	Dar 28/8/24	C	Receipt for barley
298	79749		C	Receipt for oxen
299	79750		C	Account of objects
300	79751	Nbk 18/1/35	C	Receipt for bales
301	79752	Si 20/5/15	C	List of services of ox-teams; copy of a tablet sent to the *abi ṣabi* in Babylon; round type
302	79753	OB	C	Harvest loan; part of case adhering
303	79754	Ha -/-/36	C	Sale
304	79755	OB	C	Field rental
304A	79756	OB	NC	Case of previous; seals
305	79757	Aṣ 16/2/?	C	Receipt for silver; seals
306	79758	-/-/27? mu nir guškin dingir-gal-gal	C	Rental of a field
306A	79759	-/-/27?mu nir guškin [dingir-gal-gal]	F	Case of previous; seals
307	79760	OB -/-/mu uś-sa é x x x giš-gu-za in-dù	C	Loan of silver for a partnership
308	79761	OB	NC	Account of barley; late period
309	79762	Ad 1/3/36	C	Account of barley
310	79763	AS	NC	Sale of a field
311	79764	OB	C	School exercise; lenticular
312	92605	Sabium -/-/13	C	Legal dispute concerning ownership of a field
313	79765	OB	F	Account; check marks
314	79766	OB	NC	Letter
315	79767	Ha 12/11/28	C	Rental of a field
316	79768	Si 23/8/7	C	Hire of a slave
317	79769	Dar 11/8/22	F	Contract for dates or grain

89-10-14,

318	79770	Aş 25/4/4	C	Agricultural partnership; seals
319	79771	Ner -/6/acc	NC	Account of gold(?)
320	79772		F	Loan
321	79773	Dar 26/6/16	NC	Contract for dates
322	79774	Si	F	Legal dispute concerning purchase of property; referring to events in the 13th, 17th, and 22nd years of Si
323	79775	OB	NC	Letter; round type; late period
324	79776	OB	F	Incantation; Sumerian
325	79777	Aş 25/1/7	C	List of workmen
326	79778	Nbk 11/8/41	NC	Loan of silver
327	79779	Nbk 25/12/35	F	Account of barley
328	79780	-/-/28	F	Account; Sippar
329	79781	-/10/-	NC	Receipt for baskets
330	79782	Dar 4/2/11	C	Contract for sheep; Babylon; dupl. *Dar* 297; *PEF Quarterly* 32 (1900) p. 267
331	79783	Dar 28/2/2	NC	Contract
332	79784	Nbn 13/-/13	C	Account of workmen
333	79785	Aş 2/4/"17+a"	F	Ration list; check marks
334	79786	OB	C	Account of wool
335	79787	Aş 13/2/6	C	Contract for a journey of the weapon of Šamaš; seals
336	79788	Aş 5/8/16	NC	Account
337	79789	OB	NC	Letter; round type; late period
338	79790	Dar 2/5/26	C	Contract for dates
339	79791	Nbn	NC	Receipt for barley
340	79792	Xer 23/10/1	C	House rental
341	79793		F	Account of garments of gods
342	79794	OB -/?/-	C	Hire of two slave girls; *sissiktu* impression on edge
343	79795	OB 8/12/-	C	Receipt for services of hired men; seals
344	79796	Si -/-/36?	C	Loan of barley; harvest loan(?)
345	79797	Aş 22/6/16	C	Administrative; list of names; seals
346	79798	Aş 6/10/?	C	Receipt for silver; seals
347	79799	Si ?/12/6	C	Harvest loan; seals
348	79800	Aş 21/11/?	C	Loan(?) of silver
349	79801	Aş 20?/8?/13	C	Loan of wool; priced in silver and repaid in barley at the harvest; seals
350	79802	Aş ?/6/?	C	Loan of wool; seals
351	79803	Ha -/-/24	C	Loan of barley

89-10-14,

352	79804	OB	C	Account
353	79805	OB	C	Letter; round type; late period
354	79806	OB	NC	Account(?); round type; late period
355	79807	Aş 13/1/10	C	Receipt for barley; seals
356	79808	OB 10/-/-	C	Account
357	79809	OB	C	Memorandum concerning barley
358	79810	Si ?/8/4	C	Loan of silver
359	79811	OB	C	Field rental
359A	79811A	OB	F	Case of previous
360	79812	Aş 21/9/6	C	Issue to a weaver; round type
361	79813	OB	C	Field rental
362	79814	OB	NC	Field rental
363	79815	Aş 11/5/12	C	Receipt for silver; seals
364	79816	OB	C	Account
365	79817	Ae 24?/6/"l"	C	Loan of barley; seals
366	79818	Ad 22/5/35	C	Note concerning a man's entry into service in a private house; round type
367	79819	Aş ?/3/16	C	Receipt for a poplar log by seven men to be returned *ina paṭar alalli*; seals
368	79820	Aş 15/8/16	C	Harvest loan; sesame; seals
369	79821	OB -/2/-	C	House rental
370	79822	OB	C	Letter; round type; late period
371	79823	OB	NC	Letter(?); late period
372	79824	OB	C	Note concerning two fields; round type; late period
373	79825	OB	C	Note concerning three issues of barley in months 8 and 9; round type; late period
374	79826	OB	C	Letter; round type; late period
375	79827	OB	C	Administrative; list of names; round type; late period
376	79828	OB	C	Administrative; list of names; round type; late period
377	79829	OB	C	Letter; round type; late period
378	79830	OB 20/8/-	C	Receipt; seals
379	79831	OB 5/6/mu giš-gu-za	C	Receipt for bran; seals
380	79832	OB 9/6/- and 29/6/-	C	Receipt
381	79833	OB -/8/-	C	Rations for one man
382	79834	OB	C	Memorandum concerning barley
383	79835	Si 4/9/3?	C	Harvest loan

89-10-14,

384	79836	Aş 15/3/13	C	Note that a miller has no work; round type
385	79837	Si 3/8/4	C	Receipt; seals
386	79838	Si 21/6/4	C	Record of bricks baked(?) for the *gagum*
387	79839	OB	C	Receipt for beer
388	79840	Aş 5/6/8	C	Receipt for fodder; round type
389	79841	Ad 24/12/1	C	Record of a man's assignment to work in a private house; round type
390	79842	Ad 29/-/16 or 35	F	Receipt for silver
391	79843	OB 13/8/-	C	House rental
392	79844	Si 25/10/6	C	Harvest loan; barley; seals
393	79845	Aş 15/3/13	C	Receipt for rations
394	79846	Ha 17/1/5	C	Receipt for reeds; seals
395	79847	Si 10/8/4	C	Harvest loan; barley; seals
396	79848	Si 24/10/6	C	Harvest loan; barley as the price for wool; seals
397	79849	Ha 15/6/42	C	Receipt for barley
398	79850	OB	C	Description of a field; incomplete contract
399	79851	OB 27/1/mu-bàd-3-kam-ma	C	Account of barley
400	79852	OB	NC	Field rental
401	79853	Ad 27/5/lugal-e alam [...]	C	Receipt; seals
402	79854	Aş -/-/16	C	Receipt; seals
403	79855	Ae 11/6/"h"	C	Issue of beer; seals
404	79856	Aş 10/4/?	C	Receipt(?); seals
405	79857	OB	C	Account; late period
406	79858	OB	C	Letter; round type; late period
407	79859	Aş 12/4/1	C	Receipt for silver in part payment for a house; seals; round type
408	79860	OB	C	Record of agricultural activities(?); round type; late period
409	79861	OB	NC	Field plan; late period
410	79862	OB 1/iti *sí-bu-tim*/-	C	Hire of a slave; seals
411	79863	OB -/-/?	C	Field sale
412	79864	OB	C	Letter; round type; late period
413	79865	Aş 16/11/10	C	Account of wool; round type
414	79866	Aş -/11/16	C	Account of bread; round type
415	79867	Si 11/9/30 mu gibil 2 kam-ma	NC	Sale of a field

89-10-14,

479	79931	OB	NC	Letter
480	79932	Ha 12/5/42	C	House sale
480A	79932A	OB	F	Case of previous
481	79933	OB	C	Account of barley
482	79934	Aş 5/1/mu Aş lugal-e bad-gal-la ḫur-sag-gim ki-a íb-ta-an-è ka i_7-buranun[ki]-ta bí-in-dù-a	C	Field rental; seals
483	79935	OB	F	Letter
484	79936	Ae 21/3/"p"	NC	Harvest contract; seals
485	79937	OB	C	Only numbers preserved; mathematical exercise; circular tablet
486	79938	OB	F	Incantation; Akkadian; round type; late period, dupl. Bu 89-4-26, 422 (= BM 79125)
487	79939	OB	F	Letter
488	79940	Ha 14/11/23	C	Account of silver and textiles
489	92606	Aş 30/4/3	C	Sale of a slave
490	79941	OB	F	Letter
491	79942	Aş 1/8/14	NC	Account of barley
492	79943	OB	F	Account of silver; late period
493	79944	OB -/4 or 10/-	F	Agricultural contract; seals
494	79945	OB	C	School exercise; with paradigm for LÁ; lenticular
495	79946	OB	NC	Year formula for Aş 17b; Sumerian on one side, Akkadian on the other
496	79947	Ha 25/1/42[?]	C	Legal renunciation of claim for silver; *CT* 48 no. 10
497	79948	OB 1/7/?	NC	Receipt for silver; seals
498	79949	OB	C	Incantation; phonetic Sumerian; snake(?)
499	79950	OB	C	Account of barley; late period
500	79951	Aş 1/8/14	C	Barley ledger
501	79952	Ae ?/?/"o"	NC	Contract; seals
502	79953	Ha 11/6/37	NC	House sale
503	79954	Ha -/-/31[?] mu ugnim larsa[ki] giš-tukul ba-sìg	NC	Legal process(?)
504	79955	OB	C	Account of barley rations; late period
505	79956	Aş 6/8/16	NC	Ledger of workmen
506	79957	OB	C	Rental of a house to be repaired
507	79958	Si 30/1/30[?]	F	Legal agreement concerning ownership of a slave girl

89-10-14,

508	79959	Aş 1/10/10	C	Account
509	79960	Ad 4/5/9	C	Field rental
510	92607	Si -/-/4	F	Field sale
511	79961	OB	F	Legal agreement concerning ownership of a field
512	79962	OB	C	Account of barley; late period
513	79963	Aş 21/5/"17+b"	NC	Account
514	79964	OB	C	Letter
515	79965	OB	NC	Account; late period
516	79966	Aş -/12/?	F	Literary; Sumerian; Emesal; cf. *RA* 76 96
517	79967	Aş 11/1/3	F	Account
518	79968	OB	F	Account; late period
519	79969	OB	F	Account of garments(?); two columns
520	79970	OB	F	Account of silver; late period
521	79971	OB	F	Sale of a house or field
522	79972	OB	F	Account; late period
523	79973	Ad 1/10/6	C	Harvest loan of barley; seals
524	79974	Ha -/10/14	C	Harvest loan of silver; seals
525	79975	OB	NC	Account; round type; late period
526	79976	OB	NC	Account; round type; late period
527	79977	OB	F	Account; late period
528	79978	Aş -/6/"17+b"	NC	Hire of a slave
529	79979	OB	F	Letter; late period
530	79980	OB	C	Letter
531	79981	Aş 1/9/14	C	Account
532	79982	Si 10/7/7	C	Hire of a boy from his mother; unopened case tablet; seals
533	79983	OB	F	Letter
534	79984	Ha -/-/18	C	Rental of a field; unopened case tablet; seals
535	79985	OB	F	Literary; Sumerian
536	79986	OB	F	*Ḫḫ* XIII; OB forerunner
537	79987	OB	F	"*Insurrection against Naram-Sin*"; *RA* 70 103-28
538	79988	OB	F	Literary(?); Sumerian
539	79989	OB	F	Letter(?); round type; late period
540	79990	OB -/11/?	F	Account; late period
541	79991	OB	F	Sale of field or house
542	79992	OB	F	Account of barley; late period

89-10-14,

543	79993	OB	F	Account of wooden objects(?); lenticular
544	79994	Si 1/6b/8	C	Hire of a boy from his mother
545	79995	OB	C	Inscribed bulla; seals
546	79996	OB	F	Account; lenticular
547	79997	OB	F	Account
548	79998	OB	F	Sale contract; si-bi clause; seals
549	79999	OB	F	List of workmen; late period
550	80000	OB	F	Inventory of fields; late period
551	80001	OB	F	Literary(?)
552A	80002	Si 15/3/1	NC	Hire of a boy from his mother
552B	80003	Si 15/3/1	F	Case of previous; seals
553A	80004	Ha 1/11/42	C	Harvest contract for labour; two boys hired from their father
553B	80005	Ha -/11/42	F	Case of previous; seals
554A	80006	Si 20/12/7	C	Loan of silver; seals
554B	80007	OB	F	Case of previous; seals
555	80008	OB	F	Account
556	80009	Aş 19/1/2	F	Administrative note concerning beer rations; seals; round type
557	80010	OB	F	Letter; late period
558	80011	OB	F	Account of silver; two columns; late period
559	80012	OB	F	List of witnesses
560	80013	OB 2/6/?	F	Administrative note; round type; late period
561	80014	OB	F	Letter; round type; late period
562	80015	OB 21/1/-	C	Issues of barley; late period
563	80016	OB	F	Copy of two field sale contracts; one dated Si -/-/15; late period
564	80017	OB	F	Account(?); late period
565	80018	Ad 15/10/?	F	Loan(?) or issue of barley
566	80019	OB	F	Accounts; late period
567	80020	OB	F	Letter; late period
568	80021		F	Account of sesame and wool
569	80022	OB 1/-/?	NC	Loan of barley
570	80023	OB	F	Letter; late period
571	80024	OB	F	Letter; late period
572	80025	Ad -/12/1	F	Harvest labour contract; seals
573	80026	Si 1/11/4	F	Receipt or account of animals; seals

89-10-14,

574	80027	OB	F	Accounts; check marks; late period
575	80028	OB	F	Dream incantations; Sumerian; late period
576	80029	OB	F	Letter; late period
577	80030	Aṣ 2/1/15	F	Receipt for bran; seals
578	80031	Ha	F	Contract
579	80032	Si -/-/28	F	Sale of a field with a *dimtu*; part of case adhering
580	80033	OB	F	Account of barley; late period
581	80034	OB	F	Letter; late period
582	80035	Ha -/-/23	F	House sale; É *ḫu-da-du-um*
583	80036	OB	F	List of names; two columns; late period
584	80037	OB	F	Date formula list; King, *Chronicles* 2 181-191; 97-109
585	80038	OB	F	Economic(?); late period
586	80039	OB	F	Letter; late period
587	80040	OB	F	Letter
588	80041	OB	F	Account
589	80042	OB 22/6/?	F	Sale of a house
590	80043	OB	F	Account
591	80044	OB	F	Account
592	80045	OB	F	Account of bread and beer
593	80046	OB -/6/-	F	Contract for the hire of female workers; seals
594	80047	OB	F	Letter
595	80048	OB	F	Account(?); late period
596	80049	OB	F	List of names; late period
597	80050	OB	F	Account
598	80051	OB	F	Account; late period
599	80052	OB	F	Account; late period
600	80053	OB	F	List of witnesses; seals
601	80054	OB	F	*Inanna's descent*; Sumerian; cf. 89-10-14, 641 (= BM 80094)
602	80055	OB	F	Contract; seals
603	80056	OB	F	Account; late period
604	80057	OB	F	School exercise; god names; lenticular
605	80058	OB	F	Account; late period
606	80059	OB	F	Account; late period
607	80060	OB	F	Field rental; seals
608	80061	OB	F	Account of flour

89-10-14,

609	80062	OB -/12b/mu *am-mi-*[...] mu gibil egir [...] KAL.KAL [...]	F	Receipt; seals
610	80063	OB	F	Account; check marks
611	80064	OB -/1/-	F	Administrative; rations for slave girls
612	80065	Joined to Bu 89-4-26, 408 (= BM 79111)		
613	80066	Aṣ 3/3/14	F	Account of rations for slaves and slave girls; check marks
614	80067	Aṣ 1/5/14	F	Account of rations; check marks
615	80068	OB	F	Division of inheritance; case; seals
616	80069	OB	F	Only witnesses preserved; case; seals
617	80070	OB	F	Only witnesses preserved; case
618	80071	OB	F	Case of a letter; seals
619	80072	OB	F	Case; seals; uninscribed
620	80073	OB	F	Case of a letter; seals
621	80074	OB	F	Ledger of rations for months 1-6
622	80075	OB	F	Lexical(?)
623	80076	OB	F	Contract(?)
624	80077		F	Lexical
625	80078	OB	F	Mathematical
626	80079	OB	F	Letter(?)
627	80080	OB	F	Lexical
628	80081	OB	F	Letter
629	80082	OB	F	Letter(?); late period
630	80083		F	House plans; *AnSt* 22 144f.
631	80084	Aṣ -/4/5	F	Receipt for barley; seals
632	80085	Ha 23/11/14	NC	Field sale
633	80086	OB	F	Contract; seals
634	80087	OB	F	Loan of barley and silver
635	80088	OB	F	Mathematical problem text; areas; cf. 92-5-16, 221 (= BM 16685), 92-5-16, 245 (= BM 16709), 92-5-16, 254 (= BM 16718); late period
636	80089	Si 30/10/22	F	Sale contract
637	80090	OB	F	Account of barley
638	80091	OB	F	Sumerian literary; two columns
639	80092	OB	F	Account
640	80093	OB	F	Account of rations; check marks; late period
641	80094	OB	F	*Inanna's Descent*; Sumerian; cf. 89-10-14, 601 (= BM 80054)

89-10-14,

642A	80095	OB	C	Field rental
642B	80096	OB	NC	Case of previous; seals
643A	80097	Ha	C	Legal; concerning ownership of a field given to women
643B	80098	OB	NC	Case of previous; seals
644A	80099	OB	C	Field rental
644B	80100	OB	F	Case of previous
645A	80101	Si 5/2/7	C	Hire of a boy from his father
645B	80102	Si 5/2/7	C	Case of previous; seals
646A	80103	Si 15/3/13	C	Field sale
646B	80104	Si 15/3/13	F	Case of previous; seals
647A	80105	AS 5/*ki-nu-ni*/6	C	Legal decision concerning ownership of a field
647B	80106	AS 5/*ki-nu-*[*ni*]/6	C	Case of previous; seals; *sissiktu* impression
648A	80107	Sabium -/diri/mu-ús-sa tug [d]*na-bi-um* [I]*sà-bi-um áš-še-pí-šu*	C	Settlement of a claim concerning a payment of gold
648B	80108	Sabium -/diri/mu-ús-sa tug [d]*na-bi-um sà-bi-um áš-še-pí-šu*	NC	Case of previous; seals
649A	80109	Immerum -/-/mu *im-me-ru-um* giš-gu-za *iṣ-ba-tu*	C	Field sale
649B	80110	Immerum	F	Case of previous; seals
650A	80111	Sabium	C	Purchase of one-third share in an estate by two brothers from their sister
650B	80112	OB	F	Case of previous; seals
651A	80113	Ha -/1/5	C	Payment of a redemption price in silver
651B	80114	Ha -/1/5	C	Case of previous; seals
652A	80115	Si 2/2/7	C	Rental of a *rugbum*
652B	80116	OB	F	Case of previous; seals
653A	80117	OB -/-/mu ḫur-sag i_7 mu-na-an-tum	C	Agreement to supply barley to a *naditu* during her lifetime
653B	80118	OB -/-/mu ḫur-sag i_7 mu-na-an-tum	NC	Case of previous; seals
654A	80119	Ha 20/6b/3	C	Hire of a boy from his mother
654B	80120	Ha -/6b/3	NC	Case of previous; seals
655A	80121	Si 5/2/4	C	Hire of a boy from his mother
655B	80122	Si 5/2/4	NC	Case of previous; seals
656A	80123	OB	C	Hire of a man from a *naditu*
656B	80124	OB	F	Case of previous; seals

89-10-14,

657A	80125	Si -/-/3	C	Rental of a *rugbum*
657B	80126	Si -/-/3	F	Case of previous; seals
658A	80127	Ha	NC	Settlement of estate; *CT* 48 no. 20
658B	80128	Ha	F	Case of previous; seals; *CT* 48 no. 21
659A	80129	Ha -/-/30	C	Litigation; *CT* 48 no. 2
659B	80130	Ha -/-/30	F	Case of previous; seals; *CT* 48 no. 2a
660A	80131	Si 10/6/1	C	Exchange of a slave girl
660B	80132	Si 10/6/1	F	Case of previous; seals
661A	80133	Ha -/8/27	C	House sale
661B	80134	Ha -/-/27	F	Case of previous; seals
662A	80135	Sabium	NC	Sale contract
662B	80136	OB	F	Case of previous; seals
663A	80137	Sm -/-/12	C	Litigation about family, property; *CT* 48 no. 1
663B	80138	Sm	F	Case of previous; seals; *CT* 48 no. 1
664A	80139	OB Buntaḫʾunila	NC	Litigation over real property; Buntaḫʾunila oath; *CT* 48 no. 42
664B	80140	OB	NC	Case of previous; seals; *CT* 48 no. 42A
665	80141	Ha	F	Cone; Sumerian; Birot *Fs* 263-64
666	80142	Ha	F	Cone; Sumerian; Birot *Fs* 263-64
667A	80143	Ha -/8/mu bára ᵈnin-pirig	C	Litigation about family property; *CT* 48 no. 3
667B	80144	OB	F	Case of previous; seals; *CT* 48 no. 3
668A	80145	OB	C	Rental of a *rugbum*
668B	80146	Si -/iti ezen ᵈiškur/5	F	Case of previous; seals
669	80147	OB	NC	Account of three or four field sales; Si oath; part of case adhering; seals
670	80148	Aṣ 1/1/-	NC	Sumerian literature
671-687				Cylinder seals and other uninscribed objects
688			C	Inscribed bulla
689		Si -/3/6	C	Inscribed bulla
690			C	Inscribed bulla
691		Temporarily missing		

Bu 91-5-9,

1				Uninscribed object
2-240				Bezold, *Cat.* pp. 1931ff.
241-261				Uninscribed objects from Nineveh
262	80149	OB	F	Sumerian literary (Ninurta?); three columns
263	80150	OB	NC	Mathematical; *CT* 44 31-32 no. 42; *MKT* p. 11 no. 12
264	80151	Ur III	F	Ur-Nammu brick; Walker, *Bricks* no. 13
265	80152	Si	F	Summary of deliveries of garments in different years of Si, from 15th to 26th years; *CT* 45 19 no. 36
266	80153	NB -/3/6	NC	Account of garments of weavers; *CT* 44 48 no. 84
267	80154	Si	F	Rations of barley; *CT* 6 4
268	80155	OB	F	Legal document listing property, probably intended as dowry for a *naditu*; late period; *CT* 45 53 no. 119
269	92608	OB	F	*Atraḫasis*; *CT* 46 22-23; *CT* 6 5; Lambert, *Atraḫasis* 40
270	80156	Aṣ 4/8/11	NC	Lawsuit concerning a sale of real estate; seals; *CT* 6 6
271	80157	OB	F	Rations of barley and beer for troops (including Kassites) stationed at Kar-^{d}Utu; seals; *CT* 45 27 no. 54
272	80158	Si 15/12/5	NC	Lawsuit over the inheritance of a *naditu*; seals; *CT* 6 7a
273	80159	Sabium 5/10/10?	NC	Barley rations; *CT* 45 31 no. 63
274	92609	OB	NC	Summary of various real estate sales; *CT* 45 50 no. 113
275	92610	Aṣ	NC	Designation of a *naditu* as heir by her mother, the *naditu's* heir to be one of her brothers; *CT* 45 6 no. 11

Bu 91-5-9,

276	80160	Aş 10/4/"17+c"	NC	Legal dispute over an exchange of fields; seals; *CT* 45 30 no. 60
277	80161	Ad 30/4/6	NC	Legal case before, or involving, the king, over collection of silver; tablet is cross-cancelled; seals; *CT* 45 22 no. 46
278	80162	Sm -/3/17	NC	Sale of a field; seals; *CT* 45 7 no. 13
279	80163	OB	C	Letter; *CT* 6 8; *AbB* 2 106
280	80164	Sm -/-/7	C	Adoption contract; *CT* 8 25a
281	80165	OB	NC	List of persons under different ugulas; late period; *CT* 45 50 no. 114
282	80166	Sm -/-/17	NC	Lawsuit and settlement involving a slave woman; seals; *CT* 45 17 no. 37
283	80167	Aş 30/12/15	C	Administrative; issues of barley; *CT* 2 18
284	92702	OB	F	Date list; *LIH* 2 no. 101; *CT* 6 9-10
285	92611	OB	NC	Prism; list of stones, plants, etc.; *CT* 6 11-14
286	80168	OB	F	List of personnel; *CT* 6 15-18
287	80169	Si 11/2/2	NC	Tally of work quotas for various types of bricks, for six days; mostly female names; *CT* 45 16 no. 32
288	80170	OB	F	Sumerian literary; *Enlil and the Pickaxe*; *CT* 44 10 no. 10
289	92612	Aş	NC	Designation of a daughter as heir by her mother; *CT* 45 7 no. 12
290	80171	OB	C	Letter; *CT* 2 19; *AbB* 2 83
291	80172	Sm -/-/17	NC	Sale(?) of a son by parents; *CT* 45 8 no. 14
292	80173	Ha -/-/20	NC	Legal text relating to silver; Amorite names; *CT* 45 12 no. 22
293	80174	OAkk	NC	Administrative; *CT* 44 35 no. 48
294	80175	OB	C	Letter; *CT* 2 20; *AbB* 2 84
295	80176	MB	F	*ṭuppi maruti* contract; seals; Nuzi
296	80177	MB	C	Field rental; seals; Nuzi; *CT* 2 21
297	80178	MB	C	Lawsuit in Takuwa; seals; Nuzi
298	80179	OB	NC	Bequest of a house by a woman, who retains possession till death; early period; *CT* 45 41 no. 91
299	80180	OB	C	Inheritance of real estate; uncompleted text; *CT* 45 46 no. 105
300	80181	Sabium	NC	Lawsuit over real estate; *CT* 45 2 no. 3

Bu 91-5-9,

301	80182	OB	C	Lawsuit over a dead man's share of partnership funds; *CT* 2 22
302	80183	OB	C	Agreement between a creditor and a guarantor over an obligation in tin; early period; witnesses from Sippar and Ur; *CT* 45 52 no. 118; *JESHO* 11 202
303	92613	Ha	NC	Purchase of é-ki-gál by a *naditu* with silver ring; *CT* 45 15 no. 30
304	80184	OB	F	Sumerian literary; mentions Abiešuḫ; *CT* 44 15 no. 18; *RA* 63 179; *ActaSum* 8 1-11
305	80185	Ad 5/-/34	NC	Administrative; seals; *CT* 45 25 no. 51
306	80186	OB	NC	Letter; *CT* 29 28-29; *AbB* 2 159
307	80187	AS	NC	Purchase of real estate by a *naditu*; *CT* 45 5 no. 9
308	80188	OB	F	Real estate sale; Waterman, *BusDoc* 26
309	80189	OB	F	Letter; *CT* 44 41 no. 65; *AbB* 1 141
310	80190	OB	F	Lawsuit; signs on copy often impressionistic; probably late period; seals; *CT* 45 48 no. 109
311	80191	OB	F	Roster of work groups of ten men, each under an ugula; *CT* 45 51 no. 115
311A	80191A	OB	F	Contract(?)
312	80192	OB	NC	Purchase of a field by a *naditu* with a silver ring; *CT* 45 3 no. 4
313	80193	Ha -/4/-	F	Real estate sale; *CT* 45 14 no. 28
314	80194	Sm	NC	Gift of real estate, etc., with provision for the maintenance of a *naditu*; *CT* 8 20a
315	80195	OB	C	Letter; *CT* 6 19b; *AbB* 2 107
316	80196	OB	NC	List of lawsuits; *CT* 8 26a
317	91614	Sabium	NC	Real estate sale; *CT* 6 19a
318	92615	Sumulael -/*na-ab-ri*/ mu li-li-ìz *a-a-bi* ᵈutu-ra mu-na-an-dím	C	Sale of real estate; oath by Immerum and Sumulael; *CT* 4 50a
319	80197	OB	NC	Letter; *CT* 44 40 no. 63; *AbB* 1 139
320	80198	Ae 6/1b/"m"		Sale of a slave-girl and her child; seals; *CT* 8 27a
321	80199	Aṣ -/-/mu-ús-sa aga? ᵈUtu	NC	Dowry given to a *naditu*; *CT* 45 4 no. 6
322	80200	OB	NC	Letter; *CT* 44 37 no. 54; *AbB* 1 130
323	80201	OB	F	Summary of fields and orchards bought by and from *naditus*; late period; *CT* 45 49 no. 111

Bu 91-5-9,

324	92672	OB	C	Gift of real estate, slaves and livestock; *CT* 2 23
325	92678	OB	C	Letter; *CT* 2 38; *LIH* 1 93 no. 55; 3 160
326	80202	Ae 9/12/"e"	NC	Issue of barley as rations at Sippar-yaḫrurum; seals; *CT* 8 27b
327	80203	Sumulael	NC	Lawsuit over real estate, etc.; *CT* 8 28b
328	80204	Ae 10/4/"t"	C	Gift of real estate with maintenance agreement; *CT* 2 24
329	92677	OB	F	Letter; *LIH* 1 91 no. 54; *AbB* 2 52
330	80205	Si 15/3/29	C	Real estate sale; *CT* 6 20a
331	92616	Ha 28/6/10	C	Sale of a slave-girl; *CT* 2 25
332	92617	Sm 8/12/19	C	Real estate sale; *CT* 2 26
333	80206	Si 2/9/27	C	Real estate sale; *CT* 2 27
334	80207	Ha 11/7/14	NC	Division of an estate; *CT* 8 13c
335	80208	OB	F	Legal text relating to inheritance; late period; *CT* 45 32 no. 65
336	80209	OB	NC	Mathematical; *CT* 44 29 no. 39; *JCS* 33, 57-64
337	80210	OB	C	Inventory of wooden and reed items; *CT* 6 20b
338	92618	Ha	C	Contract for the ending of a trading partnership; *CT* 2 28
339	80211	OB	NC	Tabulated text of large sums of silver, giving names of persons or families; late period; *CT* 45 51 no. 116
340	92626	OB	NC	Letter; *LIH* 1 95 no. 56; *AbB* 2 54
341	80212	OB	C	Account of silver; *CT* 6 21a
342	80213	OB	F	Designation of father as heir by a *naditu*; early period; *CT* 45 49 no. 112
343	80214	OB	NC	Legal deposition and complaint relating to persons of different cities; early period; *CT* 45 39 no. 87
344	80215	OB	NC	Field rental; late period; seals; *CT* 45 32 no. 66
345	80216	OB	NC	Account of barley, silver, dates and other products; *CT* 45 46 no. 104
346	80217	OB	NC	Administrative texts dealing with grain delivery *šik mešeqim*, at the gate of Aya in Sippar-yaḫrurum, mentioning kaskal Abiešuḫ; seals; *CT* 45 26 no. 55
347	80218	OB	NC	Letter; *CT* 44 40 no. 62; *AbB* 1 138
348	80219	OB	NC	Letter; *CT* 44 36 no. 50; *AbB* 1 126

Bu 91-5-9,

349	80220	AS -/-/1	NC	Manumission of a slave with maintenance contract; *CT* 8 29b
350	80221	OB	NC	Letter; *CT* 44 41 no. 64; *AbB* 1 140
351	92619	AS	NC	Gift of real estate and slaves; *CT* 8 29c
352	80222	Ad 2/10/9	NC	Loan from Shamash and Aya for trading purposes; seals; *CT* 45 23 no. 47
353	80223	Ad 10/2/24	NC	Rental of a field from a *naditu*; seals; *CT* 45 24 no. 50
354	80224	OB	C	Letter; *CT* 2 29; *AbB* 2 85
355	80225	Ad 24/7/1	NC	Receipt for the price of a field; seals; Waterman, *BusDoc* 29
356	80226	OB	C	List of fields; *CT* 2 30
357	92620	Ad 20/1/4	C	Sale of a slave-girl from Subartu; seals; *CT* 33 41
358	80227	Aṣ 11/1/15	C	Field rental; seals; *CT* 8 10a
359	80228	Ad 7/5/31	C	Receipt for silver; seals; *CT* 33 31
360	80229	Sm	C	Lawsuit over inheritance and maintenance obligation; *CT* 2 31
361	80230	Aṣ 3/2/17	C	Rental of a field by a partnership; seals; *CT* 2 32
362	92621	Ha -/-/33	NC	Division of an estate; *CT* 8 5b
363	80231	Ad -/-/3	C	Purchase of a slave-girl from Ḫaḫḫum by a *naditu*; seals; *CT* 45 22 no. 45
364	80232	Sumulael -/6/33	C	Legal process involving the weapon of Shamash; *AS* 16 217; *CT* 6 22a
365	80233	OB	C	Division of estate; incomplete; *CT* 6 22b
366	80234	Sumulael	C	Adoption contract; *CT* 2 33
367	92622	Sumulael	C	Lawsuit over a field; *CT* 2 34
368	80235	Sm	C	Adoption contract; *CT* 2 40a
369	80236	Ad 3/9/5	C	Account of silver; seals; *CT* 8 30c
370	80237	OB	C	Letter; *CT* 6 21b; *AbB* 2 108
371	80238	OB	NC	Gift of real estate, etc., to a *naditu*; *CT* 6 21c
372	80239	AS	NC	Real estate sale; *CT* 8 31a
373	80240	OB 8/11?/?	NC	Real estate sale; Waterman, *BusDoc* 28
374	80241	Ha 3/2/12	NC	Sale of a child as a slave; *CT* 8 22b
375	80242	Sumulael	C	Adoption contract; *CT* 2 35
376	80243	Ha -/-/8	F	Manumission of slave-woman for temple service; *CT* 48 22 no. 46
377	92623	Sm	C	Real estate sale; *CT* 2 36
378	80244	OB	NC	Letter

Bu 91-5-9,

379	80245	Aş 10/2/12	C	Field rental; seals
380	80246	OB	NC	Real estate sale; oath by Iluma'ila (of Sippar); *CT* 8 26b
381	80247	Sabium	C	Sale of a field; *CT* 2 37
382	80248	Ha?	C	Record of disbursements of sesame oil for the gods Sin, Dilbat, Marduk, Nusku, and for persons; *CT* 45 46 no. 103
383	80249	OB	C	Letter; *CT* 6 23a; *AbB* 2 109
384	80250	OB	C	Letter; *CT* 52 110; *AbB* 7 110
385	80251	Ha 30/4/37	C	Sale of two slaves; *CT* 48 32 no. 65
386	80252	Kassite 24/12/17	C	Account of issues of oil; *CT* 2 38b
387	92624	Sabium	C	Lawsuit concerning real estate; *CT* 2 39
388	80253	OB	NC	Letter; *CT* 52 116; *AbB* 7 116
389	80254	Ha 10/9/38	NC	Hire of a slave; *CT* 48 31 no. 64
390	80255	OB	NC	List of furnishings and possessions
391	80256	OB	NC	Letter; *CT* 52 60; *AbB* 7 60
392	80257	OB	NC	Letter; *CT* 52 44; *AbB* 7 44
393	80258	Ad 1/2/3	C	Field rental; seals; *CT* 33 30
394	80259	OB	C	Adoption contract; seals; *CT* 2 40b
395	80260	Ha 15/1/17	C	Disbursements of silver for various objects (*ša ana aḫitim nadu*); *CT* 45 11 no. 21
396	80261	Si 10/12/10	C	Agreement concerning a cancelled sale; seals; *CT* 8 32c
397	80262	Ad 7/5/1	C	Temple loan of wool; seals; *CT* 6 24a
398	80263	OB	C	Letter; *CT* 52 22; *AbB* 7 22
399	92673	OB	C	Inventory of slaves and household goods; *CT* 6 25b
400	80264	Aş 14/1/16	NC	Field rental (vicinity of *naditu*'s); seals
401	80265	Ae 15/1/"k"	C	Field rental; seals; *CT* 6 24b
402	80266	Aş 20/4/14	C	Field rental in partnership; seals; Waterman, *BusDoc* 15
403	80267	Aş -/5/5	NC	Field rental; seals
404	80268	OB	NC	Letter; *CT* 52 80; *AbB* 7 80
405	80269	OB	C	Issues of silver; *CT* 6 25a
406	80270	Ae 10/8/"d"	C	Receipt for hides; seals; *CT* 8 33c
407	80271	Immerum	NC	Adoption and marriage contract; *CT* 6 26a; *AnSt* 30 15
408	80272	OB	C	List of fields; *CT* 6 30b
409	80273	Ae 22/3/"s"	C	Lawsuit over agricultural equipment; seals; *CT* 48 21 no. 43; *AfO* 25 78-79

Bu 91-5-9,

410	80274	Ha 13/6/38	NC	Adoption and maintenance agreement; *CT* 2 41
411	80275	OB	NC	Mathematical; *CT* 44 30 no. 40
412	80276	Ad 2/9/19	C	Administrative; disposition of barley *šik mešeqim*; Sippar
413	80277	OB	C	Letter; *CT* 6 27a; *AbB* 2 110
414	80278	OB	NC	Division of an estate; *CT* 6 28a
415	80279	OB	F	Letter; *CT* 52 98; *AbB* 7 98
416	80280	Ha -/-/5	NC	Lawsuit; *CT* 48 7 no. 12
417	80281+ 80784	Sm	NC	Trial and public disgrace of a plaintiff who contested a *ṭuppi la ragamim* against a group of *naditus*; *CT* 45 10 no. 18
418	80282	OB	C	Letter; *CT* 6 27b; *AbB* 2 111
419	80283	Ad 25/4/1	C	Manumission of a Babylonian slave escaped from his foreign owner; seals; *CT* 6 29
420	80284	Aṣ 7/3/lugal-e	C	Tabular list of harvest labourers; *RA* 63 57 n. 2
421	80285	Sumulael	C	Adoption contract; *CT* 6 30
422	80286	OB	F	Contract; early period
423	80287	OB	C	Lawsuit over a ferry-boat; *CT* 8 34c
424	80288	OB	NC	Plan of houses or rooms of a building with legends of identity and dimensions; reverse gives the dimensions of the doors to various parts of the building
425	80289	OB	NC	Administrative record relating to the edict of Ammiṣaduqa, quoting sections of the edict; *RA* 63 45-61 and 189-190; Kraus, *Königliche Verfügungen* 129ff., 164 and pl. 2
426	80290	Ad -/12/21	NC	Administrative; disposition of grain *šik mešeqim natbak* Sippar; seals
427	80291	Ad	NC	Marriage contract; *Iraq* 42, 58-59; *CT* 48 27 no. 55
428	80292	Si 7/2/27	NC	Sale contract; seals
429	80293	Ha 25/10/40	NC	Sale of two slaves; *CT* 48 30 no. 62
430	80294	Si 24/4/18	NC	Administrative; seals
431	80295	OB	C	Exercise tablet; personal names
432	80296	OB	NC	Bequest
433	80297	OB	C	Administrative; tabular text
434	80298	OB	NC	Text giving dimensions of fields and personal names; early period

Bu 91-5-9,

435	80299	Ae 1/11/"k"	C	Administrative text dealing with harvest labour for temple fields; seals; Sippar
436	80300	Aṣ 18/2/lugal-e	F	Administrative; list of personal names
437	80301	Si?	F	Real estate sale; part of case adhering
438	80302	Aṣ 1/12/12	NC	Field rental; seals
439	80303	Si 7/7/5	C	House sale; *CT* 4 11b
440	80304	Aṣ 15/3/15	C	Field rental; seals
441	80305	Ha 21/10/35	C	Purchase of a slave and her child; seals; *CT* 8 22c
442	80306	OB	C	List of harvest labourers; *CT* 6 23b
443	80307	Ad 24/7/4?	C	Loan of barley; seals
444	80308	OB	NC	Letter; *CT* 52 38; *AbB* 7 38
445	80309	Aṣ 15?/5/4	C	Field rental; seals
446	80310	Ha -/-/13	C	Real estate sale; *CT* 8 35c
447	80311	Sm 13/2/17	C	Administrative; wood, animals and birds; *CT* 6 24c
448	80312	Ae 20/1/"n"	C	Sale of an ox; seals; *CT* 8 1b
449	80313	Ae 14/12/"c"	NC	Commission for purchase of a *nawirtum* slavewoman; cancellation crosses; seals; *CT* 48 23 no. 47
450	92625	Si 27/2/6	C	Field rental; seals; Waterman, *BusDoc* 1
451	80314	OB	F	Pay-list (silver against personal names)
452	80315	Ae 24/8/"o"	C	Settlement of a debt by a guarantor; seals; *CT* 8 33a
453	80316	OB	NC	Letter; *CT* 52 14; *AbB* 7 14
454	80317	Ha -/8/41?	F	Sale contract
455	80318	Si -/-/24	NC	Report on proceedings in Sippar in consequence of a royal *mišarum* act; *AS* 16 235; *AbB* 7 153
456	80319	Sumulael	NC	Legal dispute over money; *CT* 48 16 no. 30
457	80320	OB	NC	Letter; *CT* 52 104; *AbB* 7 104
458	80321	Sm -/-/19	C	Real estate sale; part of case adhering; seals; Waterman, *BusDoc* 27
459	80322	OB	NC	List of professional personal names summarized as é-ḫi-a, detailed for work KÍN? ᵈ*Šamaš*
460	80323	Aṣ 5/10/11	C	Field rental; seals; *CT* 8 19b
461	80324	OB	C	Letter; *CT* 52 9; *AbB* 7 9
462	80325	OB	NC	Administrative list of names
463	80326	OB	NC	Division of an estate
464	80327	Ad 6?/3/13	C	Administrative; disposition of barley *šik mešeqim ra*-x ...; seals

Bu 91-5-9,

465	80328	OB	NC	Genealogy of the Hammurapi dynasty; check-marks; *JCS* 20 95ff.; *JCS* 22 1-2; *Lišan Mitḫurti* 269-73; Speiser *Fs* 163ff.
466	80329	OB	C	Letter; *CT* 29 11a; *AbB* 2 140
467	80330	Aṣ 11/12/5	C	Loan of barley; seals; *CT* 8 21b
468	80331	OB	C	Letter; *CT* 6 28b; *AbB* 2 112
469	80332	Aṣ 15/5/14	C	Field rental in partnership; seals; Waterman, *BusDoc* 16
470	80333	Ad 1/6/16 or 35	C	Contract about udu-šu-gi-na; seals
471	80334	Ad 28/3/8	C	Receipt for sesame; Kar-Sippar-yaḫrurum; seals; *CT* 8 36c
472	80335	Aṣ 14?/2/9??	C	Field rental; seals
473	80336	Ad 30/12/1	C	Deliveries of oil; *CT* 6 26b
474	80337	OB	NC	Sale of a calf; seals; Waterman, *BusDoc* 33
475	80338	OB -/*ti-ri-um*/mu *I-zi-Su-mu-a-bu-um* ba-ug$_6$	NC	Gift of a field; seals; *CT* 4 47b
476	92627	AS	C	Real estate sale; *CT* 6 31a
477	80339	Ad -/-/28	C	Administrative; about the collection of sesame
478	80340	OB	C	Letter; *CT* 29 25; *AbB* 2 156
479	80341	OB	NC	Letter; *CT* 52 51; *AbB* 7 51
480	80342	Si 20/9/2	NC	Proceeding confirming *ugbabtu* status of a woman; seals; *CT* 48 21 no. 44
481	80343	Aṣ 26/2/9	NC	Field rental; seals
482	80344	Ae 13?/3/"n"	C	Payments in silver for persons on a (military?) mission to *za-ga-na*^{ki}; seals
483	80345	Ad 23/1/26	C	Loan of barley to a trading partnership; seals; *CT* 8 36d
484	80346	Aṣ 11?/1/11	NC	Hire of a person from father for milling grain; seals
485	80347	OB	C	Letter; *CT* 52 53; *AbB* 7 53
486	80348	Sd 15/2/4	C	Field rental; seals; *CT* 8 23b
487	80349	Ae 10/6/"p"	C	Loan of barley; seals; *CT* 8 33b
488	80350	Aṣ 1/3/?	C	Field rental; seals; *CT* 48 44 no. 98
489	80351	Ha -/-/16	C	Concubinage contract; *CT* 48 23 no. 48
490	80352	OB	C	Account; *CT* 8 50d
491	80353	OB	C	Letter; *CT* 52 56; *AbB* 7 56
492	80354	OB	C	Letter; *CT* 29 31-32; *AbB* 2 161
493	80355	Ha	C	Real estate sale; *CT* 8 37c

Bu 91-5-9,

494	80356	Aş 20/4/13	C	Loan of wool; seals; *CT* 8 21a
495	80357	OB	C	List of personal names *ša i-na*? ká? [d]*Nun-gal ur-du*
496	80358	Ad 22/6/26	C	Loan of wool; seals; *CT* 8 36a
497	80359	Ad 3/8?/3 or 4	F	Slave sale; seals
498	80360	OB	NC	Letter; *CT* 52 121; *AbB* 7 121
499	80361	OB	NC	Administrative account
500	80362	OB	NC	House sale
501	80363	OB	NC	Deposition before witnesses; early period; *AfO* 25 79; *CT* 48 no. 10
502	80364	OB	NC	Purchase contract *ina šewirim*
503	92628	Aş 10/9/5	C	Field rental; seals; *CT* 8 11b
504	80365	OB	NC	*qatatum* contract and *ṭuppi la ragamim*
505	80366	OB	NC	Purchase of real estate by a *naditu*
506	80367	Ha -/8/41	NC	Bequest by (a *naditu*?) Amat-Šamaš to another woman, entailing support
507	80368	OB	NC	House purchase by a woman (*naditu*?)
508	80369	Si 13/6b/8	NC	Transfer of a debt; *CT* 33 47a
509	80370	Ad 2/5/18	C	Contract for the farming of the estate of a *naditu*; seals; *CT* 8 30a
510	80371	Aş 24?/1/5	NC	Register of personal names and professions, preceded by numerals
511	80372	Si 10/11/2	NC	Lawsuit concerning a field; *CT* 6 32a
512	80373	OB	C	Letter; *CT* 52 3; *AbB* 7 3
513	80374	OB	NC	Letter; *CT* 52 4; *AbB* 7 4
514	80375	Ha 10/6/25	NC	Purchase of threshing-floor by a *naditu*
515	80376	OB	NC	Letter; *CT* 52 91; *AbB* 7 91
516	80377	Ha	NC	Legal proceedings over a real estate sale; *CT* 48 10 no. 19
517	80378	OB	C	Letter; *CT* 43 no. 3; *AbB* 1 3
518	80379	Kassite	C	Administrative account; horse text; *CT* 44 42 no. 69
519	80380	OB	F	Letter; *CT* 52 118; *AbB* 7 118
520	80381	OB	NC	Letter; *CT* 52 84; *AbB* 7 84
521	80382	OB	F	Lower half of tabular economic text listing personal names (by family); check-marks
522	80383	OB	C	Letter; *CT* 52 74; *AbB* 7 74
523	80384	OB	NC	Large account tablet of quantitites of barley with personal names
524	80385	Joined to Bu 89-4-26, 235 (= BM 78942)		
525	80386	Ae -/9/"p" or "u"	NC	Ration list(?)

Bu 91-5-9,

526	80387	MB	F	Real estate list; seals; Nuzi
527	80388	MB	F	Adoption and sale contract; Nuzi
528	80389	Ae 20/3/"r"	NC	Purchase by a *naditu* of cow and calf, with her ring; seals
529	80390	Sm	NC	Purchase (real estate?)
530	80391	OB	F	Letter; *CT* 52 141; *AbB* 7 141
531	80392	Si	NC	Real estate purchase
532	80393	MB	F	Seals and witnesses; Nuzi
533	80394	Si 8/1/8?	NC	Administrative; list of objects received, *piḫatam* é-gal *apalum*; seals
534	80395	OB	NC	Letter; *CT* 6 32b; *AbB* 2 113
535	80396	Sabium	NC	Real estate purchase
536	80397	Si -/10/1?	C	Purchase by a *naditu* of a slave, with her ring
537	80398	OB	F	Real estate contract
538	80399	OB	NC	Letter; *CT* 52 71; *AbB* 7 71
539	80400	OB	C	Letter; *CT* 52 16; *AbB* 7 16
540	80401	OB	NC	Letter; *CT* 52 112; *AbB* 7 112
541A	80402A	OB	F	Letter; *CT* 52 146; *AbB* 7 146
541B+ 1077	80402B+ 80940	OB	C	Letter; *CT* 52 83; *AbB* 7 83
542	80403	Ad 10/7/22	NC	Commission for purchase of two *namru* Subarian slaves from *Birit-narim*; seals; *CT* 48 37 no. 66
543	80404	Aş 30/12/17	NC	Deposit with a judge of money for the sale of real estate; seals; *CT* 48 36 no. 76
544	80405	OB	C	Gift of real estate; *CT* 8 34a
545	80406	Si 23/5/21	C	Relocation of a shepherd; seals; *CT* 8 32b
546	80407	Ad 17?/3/-	C	Loan for purchase of a field; seals
547	80408	Ad 20/5/27	NC	Purchase of a *tamšaru*(?) ox(?); seals
548	80409	OB	NC	Letter; *CT* 52 101; *AbB* 7 101
549	80410	OB	C	Letter; *CT* 29 27; *AbB* 2 158
550	80411	22/9/mu-ús-sa gu-za ^{d}utu	F	Lawsuit over cows; *CT* 48 7 no. 13
551	80412	OB	NC	Letter; *CT* 52 107; *AbB* 7 107
552	80413	Aş -/2/16	NC	Field rental; seals
553	80414	OB	NC	Letter; *CT* 52 78; *AbB* 7 78
554	80415	OB	C	Marriage-concubinage contract; *CT* 48 33 no. 67
555	80416	Si	F	Sale of a slave(?)

Bu 91-5-9,

556	80417	OB	NC	Letter; *CT* 52 39; *AbB* 7 39
557	80418	Si 18/11/18	NC	Sale of a slave-girl; Waterman, *BusDoc* 20
558	80419	OB	C	Sale of a field; *CT* 8 25b
559	80420	Aṣ -/12/-	NC	Purchase of a slave-woman(?)
560	80421	Ad 1/9/1	NC	Temporary deposit of money, the purchase price of a slave; seals; tablet curiously constructed
561	80422	Ad 25/6/5	C	Receipt for wool, to be repaid on demand of palace; seals
562	80423	OB	NC	Letter; *CT* 52 21; *AbB* 7 21
563	80424	OB	NC	Letter; *CT* 52 7; *AbB* 7 7
564	80425	Ad 8/12/34	NC	Contract concerning a field and barley
565	80426	Si -/4/8	NC	Adoption and maintenance contract; *CT* 6 33a
566	80427	Ha 25?/8/17	F	Contract; right half only
567	80428	Ha -/-/11	NC	Purchase of real estate by a woman, with her ring
568	80429	Si -/-/mu gibil-ús-sa	NC	Purchase of real estate
569	80430	Ae 20/4/"h"	C	Cancellation of a debt; *CT* 8 38c
570	80431	OB	NC	Letter; *CT* 52 19; *AbB* 7 19
571	80432	OB	NC	Tabulated account of disbursements, deliveries, and their difference, of sesame, for different persons; *CT* 45 43 no. 97
572	80433	OB	NC	Administrative receipt; seals
573	80434	Ae 20/11/"l"	C	Field rental; seals
574	80435	OB	F	Letter; *CT* 43 no. 28; *AbB* 1 28
575	80436	OB	F	Field rental; seals
576	80437	Ae -/-/"bb"	NC	Administrative text relating to a meeting with Kassite clans; seals
577	80438	Ad 11/5/13	NC	Receipt for silver for purchase of an udu-šu-gi-na for the Šamaš temple; seals
578	80439	OB	NC	Letter; *CT* 52 92; *AbB* 7 92
579A	80440	OB	C	Letter; *CT* 6 39; *AbB* 2 116
579B	80441	OB	F	Case of previous; seal impression as on Bu 91-5-9, 2422 (=BM 82366)
580	80442	OB	NC	Letter; *CT* 52 106; *AbB* 7 106
581	80443	Ad -/-/27?	C	Record of various real estate sales
582A	80444	OB	F	Letter; *CT* 52 142; *AbB* 7 142

Bu 91-5-9,

582B	80445	OB	F	Letter; *CT* 52 130; *AbB* 7 130
583	80446	OB	F	Letter; *CT* 52 65; *AbB* 7 65
584	80447	OB	NC	Letter; *CT* 52 37; *AbB* 7 37
585	80448	OB	C	Letter; *CT* 6 32c; *AbB* 2 114
586	80449	AS -/-/8	C	Lawsuit over the sale of a house; *CT* 6 33b
587	80450	OB	C	Letter; *CT* 6 34a; *AbB* 1 115
588	80451	OAkk	NC	Receipt for grain; *CT* 1 1b
589	80452	OAkk	F	Receipt for grain; *CT* 1 1a
590	80453	OAkk	C	Receipt for grain; *CT* 1 1c
591	80454	OB	C	Letter; *CT* 52 66; *AbB* 7 66
592	80455	MB	C	Contract concerning barley and sheep; seals; Nuzi
593	80456	OB	NC	Letter; *CT* 52 93; *AbB* 7 93
594	80457	OB	NC	Real estate sale; Waterman, *BusDoc* 43
595	80458	Aṣ -/11?/-	C	Field rental; seals
596	80459	Aṣ 12/3/1	NC	Loan of wool; duplicates Bu 91-5-9, 1491 (=BM 81355); seals; *CT* 8 11c
597	80460	OB	NC	Marriage contract; part of case adhering; *CT* 48 27 no. 56
597A	80460A	OB	F	Case of previous; *CT* 48 27 no. 56
598	80461	Ha 21?/3/9?	F	Real estate purchase with ring
599	80462	Aṣ 5/1/17	C	Field rental; seals
600	80463	Si 20/12/6	F	Real estate sale; Waterman, *BusDoc* 44
601	80464	OB	NC	Letter; *CT* 52 81; *AbB* 7 81
602	80465	Si 11/-/?	NC	Sale of a slave; Waterman, *BusDoc* 46
603	80466	OB	F	Letter; seals; *CT* 52 117; *AbB* 7 117
604	80467	OB	C	Protocol concerning a loan; *CT* 6 34b
605	80468	Sm -/*e-lu-li*/9	NC	Field rental; *CT* 8 39a
605A	80468A	OB	F	Content not apparent
606	92679	OB	NC	Letter; *LIH* 81; *AbB* 2 62
607	80469	OB	F	Letter
608	80470	Ad 15/1/36	C	Field rental; seals; Waterman, *BusDoc* 2
609	80471	OB	NC	Letter; *CT* 52 85; *AbB* 7 85
610	80472	Ad 28/4/6	NC	Field rental; seals
611	80473	Ae 10/8/"d"	NC	Receipt for hides; seals; *CT* 8 1c
612	80474	Ad 14/12/2	NC	Hire of three harvest labourers; seals; Waterman, *BusDoc* 47
613	80475	Ad 1/1/32	NC	Field rental; uncultivated land; seals; Waterman, *BusDoc* 48

Bu 91-5-9,

614	80476	OB	NC	Real estate sale; seals; Waterman, *BusDoc* 49
615	80477	Ha 4/4/4	NC	Memorandum concerning real estate; seals; Waterman, *BusDoc* 51
616	80478	Ad 23/11/6	NC	List of personnel; Waterman, *BusDoc* 50
617	80479	OB -/-/... gibil?	NC	Administrative; inventory of implements
618	80480	AS	NC	Real estate sale; Waterman, *BusDoc* 45
619	80481	OB 3/3/?	NC	Economic
620	80482	OB	NC	Bequest of an estate to a woman
621	80483	Sm	NC	Purchase of real estate by a *naditu*
622	80484	OB	NC	Letter; *CT* 29 12; *AbB* 2 142
623	80485	Si -/9/21	NC	Legal procedure over certain real estate of *naditus*; reference to Si years 11 and 21; seals; *CT* 48 4 no. 5
624	80486	OB	F	Contract
625	80487	Ha	F	Real estate sale
626	80488	OB	F	Real estate contract
627	80489	OB	NC	Administrative text concerning silver and sesame
628	80490	Ha -/-/17	NC	Field rental; Waterman, *BusDoc* 52
629	80491	OB	NC	Exercise tablet; model contract
630	80492	OB	F	Issues of silver; Waterman, *BusDoc* 53
631	80493	Ha -/12/35	NC	Contract for sale and adoption of a girl; Waterman, *BusDoc* 54
632	80494	OB	NC	Letter; *CT* 52 131; *AbB* 7 131
633	80495	OB	NC	Legal proceedings over a field; *CT* 48 13 no. 24
634	80496	OB	F	Court case at Dimat-Enlil involving a man, his wife and a third person; *CT* 48 4 no. 7
635	80497	OB	F	Bequest (probably a dowry to a *naditu*); late period; seals
636	80498	OB	F	Account of silver paid to or collected from personal names
637	80499	NB	F	Economic(?)
638	80500	OB	NC	Pay(?)-list (two columns of personal names on obverse only)
639	80501	AS	NC	Real estate sale; Waterman, *BusDoc* 55
640	80502	OB	F	Letter; *CT* 52 103; *AbB* 7 103
641	80503	OB	NC	Economic
642	80504	OB	F	List of names

Bu 91-5-9,

643	80505	OB	F	Real estate purchase by a *naditu*, with ring
644	80506	OB	F	Real estate sale
645	80507	OB Immerum	F	Sale or exchange contract
646	80508	OB	NC	Real estate purchase by a *naditu* with ring
647	80509	Ad 28/1/6	F	Summary of properties in Dimat-Enlil
648	80510	OB	NC	Letter; *CT* 44 38 no. 58; *AbB* 1 134
649	80511	OB	F	List of household equipment and jewelry, as part of a dowry(?); *CT* 48 19 no. 41
650	80512	Aṣ 18/5/5	NC	Lawsuit over a missing tablet concerning real estate; seals; *AS* 16 218; *CT* 8 19a
651	80513	Ad 30/8/24?	F	Administrative text concerning barley; seals
652	80514	Ad -/-/19	NC	Full year formula
653	80515	Ha -/2/40?	F	Memo giving the yield of two fields
654	80516	OB	C	Lawsuit; *CT* 8 50c
655	80517	Ha	F	Bequest of real estate; Waterman, *BusDoc* 66
656	80518	OB	F	Summary of land sales
657	80519	Ha 26/6/12	F	Real estate sale
658	80520	OB	F	Letter; *CT* 52 63; *AbB* 7 63
659+ 94-1-15, 417	80521+ 22615		F	Liver omens; *naplastum*; cf. Bu 91-5-9, 1046 (=BM 80906)
660	80522	OB	F	Purchase of a slavewoman; early period; *CT* 48 30 no. 61
661	80523	AS	F	Sale contract
662	80524	OB	F	Letter; *CT* 52 32; *AbB* 7 32
663	80525	Sabium	F	Division of an estate; Waterman, *BusDoc* 68
664	80526	Ha	F	Bequest of real estate; Waterman, *BusDoc* 65
665	80527	OB	NC	Letter; *CT* 44 38 no. 56; *AbB* 1 132
666	80528	OB -/-/[...]-*ta-na* lug[al-e]	F	Deposit(?); contract; seals
667	80529	OB	F	Legal process; testimony about Ḫalḫalla[ki] and an enemy; seals
668	80530	Aṣ 9/2/14	F	Roster of 45 men; part destroyed
669	80531	OB	NC	Summaries of the extents of various fields and personal names under an ugula; *CT* 45 42 no. 96

Bu 91-5-9,

670	80532	OB	F	Sumerian literary
671	80533	Ha -/-/28	NC	Bequest for an é-ki-gal to a *naditu*
672	80534	OB	F	Letter; *CT* 52 152; *AbB* 7 152
673	80535	Art -/-/18	NC	Contract for dates; seals
674	80536	OB	NC	Bequest of real estate with maintenance contract; Waterman, *BusDoc* 56
675	80537	OB	NC	Letter; *CT* 52 129; *AbB* 7 129
676	80538	OB	F	Economic
677	80539	OB	NC	Field rental; Waterman, *BusDoc* 58
678	80540	Art -/-/6?	NC	Contract; seals
679	80541	OB	F	Sumerian hymn
680	80542	OB	F	Ration list; check-marks
681	80543	OB	F	Administrative; mu-túm; seals
682	80544	Ha -/3/36	C	Field rental; seals; part of case adhering; Waterman, *BusDoc* 82
683	80545	OB	C	Acknowledgement for repayment of a debt; seals; case unopened
684	80546	Ad 10/5/15	C	Loan of wool; seals; *CT* 8 30b
685	80547	OB	C	Loan of silver; *CT* 4 22a
686	80548	Ha -/-/41	C	Adoption contract; *CT* 8 37d
687	80549	Aṣ 12/12/5	C	Loan of barley; seals; *CT* 8 10c
688	80550	OB	C	Field rental; *CT* 6 35a
689	80551	Sm	C	Agreement for the management of a woman's lands by her brothers; Waterman, *BusDoc* 70
690	80552	OB -/-/?	C	Deposit of barley; *CT* 6 35b
691	80553	Ha -/-/32	C	Agreement concerning a boundary wall; *CT* 4 22b
692	80554	OB	NC	Gift of real estate; Waterman, *BusDoc* 69
693	80555	Aṣ 2/6/"17+b"	NC	Administrative
694	80556	Ad 16/10/29	C	Hire of a labourer; seals; unusual *sissiktu* impression; Waterman, BusDoc 17
695	80557	OB	NC	Letter; *CT* 52 105; *AbB* 7 105
696	80558	OB	NC	Letter; *CT* 29 14; *AbB* 2 144
697	80559	Si -/7?/30	NC	Marriage contract; Waterman, *BusDoc* 72
698	80560	Si 1/1/3	NC	Economic; tabular
699	80561	OB	NC	Lawsuit over real estate; Waterman, *BusDoc* 64

Bu 91-5-9,

700	80562	OB 20/-/-	NC	Field rental; seals; Waterman, *BusDoc* 59
701	80563	Aş 1/1/2	C	Loan of wool; seals; *CT* 6 35c
702	80564	OB	NC	Field rental; late period; seals
703A	80565	OB	F	Contract; field rental(?)
703B	80566	OB	F	Field rental; seals
704	80567	Sumuel	C	Gift of real estate to the gods Ḫaniš and Šullat; *CT* 6 36a
705	92630	Ha -/-/4?	NC	Real estate sale; *CT* 6 36b
706	80568	Si? 4/6b/-	NC	Sale of slaves; Waterman, *BusDoc* 63
707	80569	OB	C	Adoption and marriage of a slave, with provision for maintenance of the adoptor; *CT* 6 37a
708	80570	Ae -/-/"k"	NC	Administrative; concerning barley *šik mešeqim* for Sippar-yaḫrurum
709	80571	OB	C	Gift of real estate; *CT* 6 37b
710	80572	Sm	NC	Real estate sale(?)
711	80573	Aş 27?/2/8	NC	Field rental; Šamaš and Aya witnesses; seals
712	92631	Ha -/11/9	C	Real estate sale; *CT* 4 25b
713	80574	OB	NC	Letter; *CT* 52 6; *AbB* 7 6
714	80575	Aş 16/2/9	NC	Roster of personal names
715	80576	OB	NC	Adoption and concubinage contract; early period; *CT* 48 28 no. 57
716	80577	OB	C	Letter; *CT* 52 155; *AbB* 7 155
717	80578	OB 20+?/4/?	NC	Receipt; seals
718	80579	NB 4/11/19	C	Receipt for gold and iron; *CT* 44 50 no. 90
719	80580	OB	C	Memorandum concerning a subtraction from a loan account; *CT* 45 40 no. 90
720	80581	OB	NC	Account of silver (edge: ... *an-nu-um qá-ta-tum* x ...); early period
721	80582	Ad 1/1/5	NC	House rental; seals
722	80583	OB	F	Sumerian literary
723	80584	OB	F	Lawsuit; oath sworn in KÁ *niš ilim*; seals; *CT* 48 4 no. 6
724	80585	OB	NC	Economic memo; neither side completed
725	80586	OB	NC	Tabulated account of fields
726	80587	OB	NC	Letter; *CT* 52 13; *AbB* 7 13
727	80588	Si 20/11/32	NC	Inheritance record, listing objects; seals; *CT* 48 28 no. 58

Bu 91-5-9,

728A	80589	OB	F	Contract; seals
728B+ 1624	80590+ 81492	OB	NC	Letter; *CT* 52 122; *AbB* 7 122
729	80591	Ae 20/12b/"q"	C	Gift of real estate; *CT* 6 38a
730	80592	OB	C	Letter; seals; *CT* 52 127; *AbB* 7 127
731	80593	Ha	NC	Real estate sale; Waterman, *BusDoc* 61
732	80594	OB	C	Letter; *CT* 33 8b; *AbB* 2 174
733	80595	OB	C	Real estate sale; *CT* 6 38b
734	80596	Ad 17/12b/26	C	Administrative; emmer; *CT* 6 39a
735	80597	Ad 5/1/11	C	Harvest loan; seals; Waterman, *BusDoc* 18
736	80598	Ad 26/6/29	NC	Loan of wool; seals; *CT* 6 37c
737	80599	OB	NC	Administrative; mu-túm *a-na* é-gal; seals
738	80600	OB	C	Letter; *CT* 52 26; *AbB* 7 26
739	80601	OB	NC	Letter; *CT* 52 72; *AbB* 7 72
740	80602	Aṣ -/1/11	NC	Field rental; seals; Waterman, *BusDoc* 60
741	80603	OB	NC	Letter; *CT* 44 39 no. 59; *AbB* 1 135
742	80604	Si 26/11/7	NC	Sale of two persons (slaves?); part of case adhering
743	80605	OB	NC	Economic; *namḫartu*
744	80606	Ad 1/1/5	NC	Field rental; seals; Waterman, *BusDoc* 3
745	80607	Cam -/9!/1	NC	Account of purchase of beer
746	80608	OB	F	Letter; *CT* 52 143; *AbB* 7 143
747	80609	Ad 20+?/4/34	NC	Account of receipts of silver; seals; *CT* 8 2b
748	80610	Sm -/-/13	C	Field rental; Waterman, *BusDoc* 4
749	80611	AS	NC	Bequest
750	80612	OB	C	Letter; *CT* 29 23; *AbB* 2 154
751	80613	OB	F	Sale of an ox; seals; Waterman, *BusDoc* 62
752	80614	Kassite 3/1/16	C	Tabulated account
753	80615	Aṣ 2/8/10	C	Receipt for silver; seals; *CT* 8 21c
754	80616	OB	C	Letter; *CT* 29 21; *AbB* 2 152
755	80617	OB	C	Account of oil; *CT* 8 38a
756	80618	Si 18/1/28	F	Real estate contract; seals
757	80619	AS	F	Real estate sale; Waterman, *BusDoc* 67
758	80620	Ae -/-/"g"?	NC	Loan of silver; seals
759	80621	Ad 8/2/2	NC	Hire of a slavewoman; seals
760	80622	OB	F	Letter; *CT* 43 16 no. 38; *AbB* 1 38

Bu 91-5-9,

761	80623	Ad -/-/2	NC	Administrative; subject not clear; seals
762	80624	OB	C	Administrative; barley rations to workers
763	80625	OB 20/3/mu gibil	C	Hire of a slave; seals; *CT* 33 46b
764	80626	Ad 10/2/32	C	Field rental; seals; *CT* 8 40d
765	80627	Aṣ 20/5/"17+b"	C	Tabulated ration list for a ten-day period under different ugula-mar-tu; *CT* 45 29 no. 61
766	80628	Ha -/-/30	C	Maintenance contract; *CT* 8 37a
767	80629	OB	C	Account
768	80630	Ad -/4/5?	C	Rental contract; seals; *CT* 8 8a
769	80631	OB	NC	House rental; seals; Waterman, *BusDoc* 71
770	80632	OB	F	Account of silver
771	80633	Ad 17/5/15?	C	Administrative; disbursement of barley *šik mešeqim*; seals; *CT* 8 8b
772	80634	Ad 1/4/-	F	Contract; seals
773	80635	Ha 16?/11/14	C	Real estate sale; *CT* 8 18a
774	80636	Ad 6?/4/23	NC	Administrative; loan of wool from palace, to be repaid in silver; seals
775	80637	Ad 6?/3/1	C	*namḫartu* receipt for money borrowed from Šamaš, Abiešuḫ 28; (cf. Bu 91-5-9, 807 = BM 80669)
776	80638	OB	NC	Lawsuit before judges of Sippar over a claim
777	80639	OB	NC	Administrative memo
778	80640	Si 16/11?/25	NC	Memo about shepherding
779	80641	OB	NC	Real estate (sale?); older period
780	80642	Ha 23/7/15	C	Field rental; Waterman, *BusDoc* 5
781	80643	Ad 21/6/29	C	Loan of wool; seals; Waterman, *BusDoc* 19
782	80644	Ad 3?/3/24	C	Administrative text relating to Elamite(?) wool(?) from the palace; seals
783	80645	Sabium	NC	Lawsuit over a claim on real estate that had been sold; *CT* 48 13 no. 25
784	80646	Ae 5/8/"b"	C	Receipt for silver; seals; *CT* 4 15b
785	80647	Ad 8/2/22	C	Temple loan of barley; Šamaš and Aya witnesses; seals
786	80648	OB	C	List of personnel; *CT* 8 40c
787	80649	OB	NC	Letter; *CT* 52 115; *AbB* 7 115; *WO* 9 209-211
788	80650	Sd 10/12/6	NC	Field rental; seals; Waterman, *BusDoc* 76; *JNES* 14, 160

Bu 91-5-9,

789	80651	Aṣ 28/1/5 or 21	NC	Roster of names; Sippar
790	80652	OB	C	Letter; *CT* 6 3c; *AbB* 2 105
791	80653	OB	F	Economic; tabular
792	80654	OB	NC	Real estate sale; Waterman, *BusDoc* 73
793	80655	Kassite	C	Letter; *CT* 44 42 no. 67
794	80656	OB	NC	Economic; tabular
795	80657	Ad 7/3/15	C	Administrative concerning two borrowed lambs; seals
796	80658	OB	F	Letter; *CT* 52 175; *AbB* 7 175
797	80659	Ha 15/*a-ia-ri*/38	C	Field rental; seals; unopened case; *CT* 8 40b
798	80660	OB	NC	Ration list
799	80661	OB	F	Administrative; šu-ti-a
800	80662	NB	NC	Letter
801	80663	OB 10/ezen *a-bi-i*/-	NC	Administrative
802	80664	OB	F	Letter; *CT* 52 12; *AbB* 7 12
803	80665	OB	F	Letter; *CT* 52 144; *AbB* 7 144
804	80666	Sm -/-/19 or Ha -/-/26 (mu bára ᵈiškur)	C	Field rental; part of case adhering
805	80667	OB	F	List of property, real estate and slaves; top half of tablet only; part of case adhering
806	80668	OB	NC	Field rental in partnership; seals; Waterman, *BusDoc* 75
807	80669	Ad 5/3/1	NC	Administrative; *namḫartu* for silver from Šamaš temple in Ae 28; cf. Bu 91-5-9, 775 (=BM 80637)
808	80670	NB	NC	Loan of barley
809	80671	Si -/-/8	NC	Loan of barley, to be repaid at *ka-ar* Sippar; Šamaš and Aya witnesses
810	80672	OB	NC	Pledge of a slave-girl as security for a loan; Waterman, *BusDoc* 74
811	80673	OB	F	Lexical; personal names; lenticular
812	80674	OB	C	Letter; *CT* 52 162; *AbB* 7 162
813	80675	Aṣ 2/12/15	C	List of disbursements of silver; round type; *CT* 8 14c
814	80676	OB	NC	Letter; *CT* 52 76; *AbB* 7 76
815	80677	Ha -/-/15	F	Field rental
816	80678	OB	F	Real estate contract; reverse not inscribed
817	80679	OB	NC	Loan of silver to buy barley; seals
818	80680	Sumulael	C	Legal protocol concerning payment of barley; *CT* 4 9b

Bu 91-5-9,

819	80681	Si 20/2/24	C	Administrative *namḫartu*; seals
820	80682	NB	F	Account of vats
821	80683	AS -/-/9?	NC	Administrative document concerning small cattle
822	80684	Si 9/6/23	F	Economic text
823	80685	OB	C	Letter; *CT* 29 13; *AbB* 2 143
824	80686	Ha 4/12/28	NC	Protocol concerning settlement of a lawsuit; *CT* 8 40a
825	80687	OB	NC	Administrative text concerning barley *šik mešeqim*, erín *Ka-aš-ši-i*; *CT* 48 37 no. 77
826	80688	4/11?/mu giš-gu-za a-r[a? ...]	F	Sale contract
827	80689	Sm -/3/19 or Ha -/3/26	NC	Field rental
828	80690	Ha -/5/30?	NC	Division of an estate; Waterman, *BusDoc* 78
829	80691	OB	NC	Letter; *CT* 52 73; *AbB* 7 73
830	80692	OB	NC	List of garments; round type
831	80693	Ha 10/7/11	C	Field rental; *CT* 8 41a
832	80694	OB	C	Letter; *CT* 52 64; *AbB* 7 64
833	80695	Ae 20/4/28	NC	Loan of silver; seals
834	80696	OB	F	Letter of Samsuiluna, mentions Ḫalab; *CT* 52 1; *AbB* 7 1
835	80697	OB	NC	Agreement concerning a party wall; Waterman, *BusDoc* 80
836	80698	OB	F	Field rental; seals
837	80699	Aṣ -/11/4	NC	Loan, for purchase of copper(?); seals
838	80700	OB -/5/?	C	Protocol concerning settlement of a debt; *CT* 4 6a
839	80701	OB	F	Administrative; beginning lost, ends: *ú-ul i-gi-ru-ú*; seals
840	80702	OB	C	Letter; *CT* 52 23; *AbB* 7 23
841	80703	OB	C	List of personnel; check-marks; *CT* 8 41b
842	80704	OB	NC	Letter; *CT* 52 126; *AbB* 7 126
843	80705	OB	NC	Memo about a real estate sale
844	80706	Ad -/9/26?	NC	Administrative (*šik mešeqim* for barley?)
845	80707	Ae 30/7/28	C	Administrative; wool; mentions Ae "k"; seals; *CT* 48 42 no. 93
846	80708	Si -/-/1	C	Sale of a slave; *CT* 6 3b
847	80709	Ha -/-/33	NC	Testimony of witnesses; *CT* 48 18 no. 36

Bu 91-5-9,

848	80710	OB	F	Sale contract; old period
849	80711	NB	C	Contract concerning temple staff; seals
850	80712	Ha -/-/29	F	Division of an estate, including *ilkum* duties
851	80713	Ad 24/10/27	NC	Field rental; seals; *CT* 8 36b
852	80714	Ad 1/8/29	C	Field rental; uncultivated land; seals; *CT* 33 36
853	80715	Sd 10/10/1	C	Administrative; mu-túm, *namḫartu*, silver and animal offerings to the Šamaš temple in Sippar-amnanum; seals; *CT* 48 18 no. 37
854	80716	OB	NC	Multiplication table for 12;30
855	80717	OB	NC	Field rental; tablet in case, date not visible; old period
856	80718	OB-/-/?	NC	Field rental; Waterman, *BusDoc* 6
857	80719	OB	C	Transfer of a debt; Waterman, *BusDoc* 21
858	80720	AS	C	Real estate sale; *CT* 8 31c
859	80721	Ha 2/11/40?	NC	Real estate sale; *CT* 8 35a
860	80722	OB	F	Sumerian proverbs; reverse deals with lion, fox, dog
861	80723	OB	C	Letter; *CT* 29 11b; *AbB* 2 141
862	80724	Ae -/8/"k"	F	Administrative
863	80725	Sumulael	C	Division of an estate; *CT* 8 28c
864	80726	Ad 16/2/35	C	Field rental; seals; Waterman, *BusDoc* 7
865	80727	OB	C	Harvest loan; *CT* 33 44a
866	80728	OB	C	Field rental; *CT* 33 45b
867	80729	Si 1/1/21	C	Field rental; *CT* 8 41c
868	80730	Kassite 10/5/17	C	Account
869	80731	OB	NC	School exercise
870	80732	MElamite	F	Limestone inscription; Elamite; *Iran* 18 79-80; fig 4
871	80733	MB	F	Contract(?); seals; Nuzi
872	80734	OB	F	Real estate sale; late period
873	80735	Ad 1/5/28	C	House rental; seals; Waterman, *BusDoc* 18
874	80736	Ae 1/12/"o"	NC	Loan of silver; seals; Waterman, *BusDoc* 79
875	80737	OB	F	Obverse destroyed; witnesses on reverse; old period
876	80738	OB	C	Lawsuit over payment for some real estate; late period; *CT* 45 39 no. 88

Bu 91-5-9,

877	80739	Iluma'ila	C	Real estate sale; oath by Iluma'ila (of Sippar); *CT* 8 41d
878	80740	OB	F	Real estate contract
879	80741	Aş 15?/8/15	F	Account of sheep, against personal names
880	80742	Cyr 30/6/5	NC	Loan of silver
881	80743	OB	NC	Letter; *CT* 52 133; *AbB* 7 133
882	80744	Aş -/7/11?	NC	Administrative text about palace implements brought from Babylon to Sippar-yaḫrurum *ana reši kullim*; seals
883	80745	OB	F	Contract (inheritance?)
884	80746	OB 30/1/?	NC	Administrative; release from *dikutu* duty of lú Šadlaš[ki]; sealed by the *rabianum* of Amnan-Šadlaš; *CT* 48 39 no. 83
885	80747	Aş -/-/9?	F	Field rental; seals
886	80748	OB	NC	Pay-list
887	80749	Si 6/10/7	NC	Barley loan, to be repaid by pressing (*maḫaṣu*) sesame oil
888	80750	Sabium	NC	Real estate sale
889	80751	OB	F	Contract; old period
890	80752	OB	NC	Letter; *CT* 52 124; *AbB* 7 124
891	80753	OB	NC	Field rental; Waterman, *BusDoc* 77
892	80754	OB	F	Letter; *CT* 48 37 no. 79; *RA* 68 111-120; *AbB* 7 188
893	80755	Cam -/-/4	NC	Loan of silver; Babylon
894	80756	OB	F	Account; tabular; check-marks on each line
895	80757	Ad 11/4/31	C	Hire of a slave as miller; seals; *CT* 33 32
896	80758	OB	F	Sumerian literary; syllabic Dumuzi lament; dupl. 1902-4-15, 13 (= BM 96692)
897	80759	NB	F	Deposition(?); seals
898	80760	OB	NC	School exercise; lenticular
899	80761	OB	NC	School exercise; lenticular; numbers at random
900	80762	OB	NC	School exercise; lenticular; random signs
901	80763	OB	NC	School exercise; lenticular; fish names
902	80764	OB	C	School exercise; lenticular; grammatical
903	80765	OB	C	School exercise; lenticular; arithmetical problem(?); drawing on reverse

Bu 91-5-9,

904	80766	OB	F	Legal (property settlement?); seals
905	80767	OB	F	Legal, concerning real estate
906	80768	Aş 18/4/15	C	Receipt for silver; seals; cross-cancelled; Waterman, *BusDoc* 30
907	80769	OB	C	House rental; seals; case unopened; Waterman, *BusDoc* 9
908	80770	OB	F	Letter; *CT* 52 43; *AbB* 7 43
909	80771	OB	F	Letter; *CT* 52 35; *AbB* 7 35
910	80772	Ha	F	Lawsuit; Waterman, *BusDoc* 81
911	80773	OB	F	Administrative, concerning money; late period; seals
912	80774	Si 1/8/14	NC	Administrative; concerning barley *šik mešeqim*; seals
913	80775	OB	NC	Letter; *CT* 52 69; *AbB* 7 69
914	80776	OB	F	Economic; tabular
915	80777	OB	F	Economic
916	80778	Si	F	Purchase with a ring
917+ 94-1-15, 439	80779+ 22637		F	Letter of Abiešuḫ to Sippar officials; *CT* 52 46; *AbB* 7 46
918	80780	OB	F	Letter; *CT* 52 10; *AbB* 7 10
919	80781	OB	F	Economic; concerning garments
920	80782	OB	F	Letter; *CT* 52 145; *AbB* 7 145
921	80783	Ha -/8/38	F	Economic
922	80784	Joined to Bu 91-5-9, 417 (= BM 80281)		
923	80785	OB	F	Rations of bread and beer; old period
924	80786	Si -/-/21	NC	Field rental
925	80787	OB	F	Field rental
926	80788	OB 2/*ma-mi-tim*/?	NC	Loan; part of case adhering
927	80789	OB	F	Field rental; approximately Si in date
928	80790	OB	F	Sumerian lexical; *Ḫḫ* forerunner, GIŠ
929	80791	Ha -/-/16?	F	Contract
929A	80791A	OB	F	Case of previous
930	80792	OB	F	Economic; late period
931	80793	OB	F	Contract
932	80794	OB	F	Contract
933	80795	OB	NC	Temple loan; gods as witnesses
934	80796	OB	NC	Letter; *CT* 52 75; *AbB* 7 75
935	80797	OB	C	Letter; *CT* 29 18a; *AbB* 2 148
936	80798	OB	C	Letter; round type; Waterman, *BusDoc* 32; *AbB* 1 102

Bu 91-5-9,

937	80799	Ha -/-/17	C	Renunciation of a claim; *CT* 48 38 no. 81
938	92633	Si -/-/1	C	Hire of a slave from ezen-ᵈiškur to Mamitum; seals; *CT* 6 40a
939	80800	OB	NC	Letter; *CT* 52 176; *AbB* 7 176
940	80801	OB	F	Field rental; late period; seals
941	80802	OB	C	Letter; *CT* 29 15; *AbB* 2 145
942	80803	Sm -/-/19 or Ha -/-/26	NC	Field rental
943	80804	Aṣ 30/6/6	NC	List of troops under ugula nam 70
944	80805	Ae 1?/12/?	C	Administrative; seals
945	80806	Ad 4/2/3	NC	Account of foodstuffs
946	80807	Ae 8?/12/"h"	C	Loan of silver for barley purchase; seals
947	80808	Ha -/1/38	NC	Field rental
948	80809	Aṣ 1/2!/12	C	Field rental, from a *naditu*; seals
949	80810	Si -/12!/1?	C	Hire of a person; seals
950	80811	OB	NC	List of witnesses; reverse uninscribed
951	80812	Ae 1/8/"e"	C	House rental, from a *naditu*; seals
952	80813	Ad 20/9/8	C	Arrangements concerning the *nudunnu* of a *šugetum*; seals; *CT* 48 39 no. 84
953	80814	Ad 9/12/4	C	Receipt for *ilkum* money; seals
954	80815	OB	C	Small list of furniture and house furnishings
955	80816	OB	C	Letter; round type; *CT* 29 40; *AbB* 2 172
956	80817	OB	C	Temple loan *ana* tab-ba; date obliterated, probably Si
957	80818	OB	NC	Loan of barley from granary; seals
958	80819	OB	C	Field rental; Waterman, *BusDoc* 57
959	80820	OB 1/12/?	C	Administrative; loan of grain to buy wool(?) and copper; seals
960	80821	OB	C	Letter; *CT* 52 59; *AbB* 7 59
961	80822	Cam 7/10/1	NC	Contract for dates
962	80823	Ad -/*sí-bu-tim*/2	C	Hire of two persons for work in the *gagum*; seals
963	80824	Kassite 16/3/16	C	Account of flour and beer
964	80825	OB	C	Field rental
965	80826	OB	C	List of witnesses present at some transaction; early period
966	80827	Ae 30/4/"c"	NC	Administrative text about sheep (carcasses?); seals
967	80828	OB -/1/mu gibil	C	Field rental; Waterman, *BusDoc* 10

Bu 91-5-9,

968	80829	OB	F	Pay-list
969	80830	Aş 28/2/17	C	List of eight hired men; round type
970	80831	OB	F	List of witnesses to payment of an obligation; old period
971	80832	OB	C	Letter; round type; late period; *CT* 45 54 no. 122; *AbB* 7 187
972	80833	OAkk	F	Economic; barley sag.gál
973	80834	Aş 1/7/11	NC	Barley loan(?); seals
974	80835	OB	C	Letter; late period; *CT* 52 177; *AbB* 7 177
975	80836	OB	C	Small economic; round type
976	80837	OB	C	Real estate sale; early period; *CT* 6 40b
977	80838	Ae 2/9/"k"	C	Administrative; loan of silver; seals
978	80839	OB	C	Ration list
979	80840	OB	C	Letter; *CT* 29 26; *AbB* 2 157
980	80841	Ha -/-/22?	C	Field rental
981	80842	Ha -/-/7	C	Field rental; seals
982	80843	OB	F	Letter; *CT* 52 87; *AbB* 7 87
983	80844	OB	F	Contract about an estate; late period
984	80845	OB	C	Economic memorandum
985	80846	OB	F	Letter; *CT* 52 178; *AbB* 7 178
986	80847	OB	C	Economic
987	80848	OB	C	Memorandum about location of fields; late period; round type
988	80849	OB	F	Letter; *CT* 52 128; *AbB* 7 128
989	80850	OB	NC	Letter; late period; *CT* 52 154; *AbB* 7 154
990	80851	OB	NC	Letter; *CT* 52 123; *AbB* 7 123
991	80852	OB	NC	Letter; *CT* 52 113; *AbB* 7 113
992	80853	OB	NC	Letter; *CT* 52 171; *AbB* 7 171
993	80854	OB	C	Field rental
994	80855	OB	C	Field rental
995	80856	OB	C	Letter; *CT* 52 120; *AbB* 7 120
996	80857	Si	NC	Contract(?); "vindication" clause
997	80858	OB	NC	Administrative; seals
998	80859	Si 11/-/34	F	Administrative; barley *šik mešeqim birum* in Sippar-amnanum; seals
999	80860	OB	F	Field rental; late period; seals
1000	80861	NB	NC	Loan of silver
1001	80862	OB	C	Economic memorandum
1002	80863	OAkk	F	Economic; left side only; *CT* 50 184

Bu 91-5-9,

1003	80864	OB	C	Field rental; Waterman, *BusDoc* 11
1004	80865	Ad -/1/3	NC	Loan of silver, free for 15 days and then for interest; seals; *CT* 48 39 no. 85
1005	80866	OB	NC	Letter(?); round type
1006	80867	Ha 14/2/34	F	Inheritance of a *naditu* from her father; *CT* 48 17 no. 33
1007	80868	OB 1/5/mu alan-a-ni ka? giš-gál	F	Real estate sale
1008	80869	OB	C	Short pay-list in silver; reverse uninscribed
1009	80870	OB	NC	Letter; *CT* 52 58; *AbB* 7 58
1010	80871	Aş -/-/5?	NC	Temple loan; gods as witnesses; *šalmu-balṭu* clause
1011	80872	Ha 29/12/36	C	Account of silver and barley
1012	80873	OB	NC	Ration account; round type; late period
1013	80874	Ad 15/10/26	C	Deposit of barley in a house, by a *naditu*; seals
1014	80875	Aş 26/11/lugal-e	C	Economic; account of silver; round type; seals
1015	80876	OB	NC	Purchase contract; practice text(?)
1016	80877	Si -/-/21	C	Hire of a slave; *CT* 8 15c
1017	80878	OB	C	Letter; *CT* 29 9a; *AbB* 2 135
1018	92652	OB	C	Letter; *LIH* 1 82 no. 48; *AbB* 2 46
1019	80879	OB	C	Account of rations for troops
1020	80880	OB 15/*ki-nu-nu*/-	C	Legal text concerning payment for a tin vessel and compensation for an injury; *JESHO* 11 204; *CT* 4 27b
1021	80881	Sm -/-/13	C	Agreement concerning a party wall; *CT* 33 44b
1022	80882	Ad 20+/12/37	C	Administrative text about part of the money allotted to buy slaves; seals
1023	80883	OB	NC	Location of field; round type; late period
1024	80884	Ha -/12/43	C	Field rental; *CT* 6 48c
1025	80885	OB	C	Letter; *CT* 29 41b; *AbB* 2 173
1026	80886	Sd 3/2/4	C	Temple loan; Šamaš and Aya witnesses; seals
1027	80887	Si?	NC	Memorandum concerning barley; seals
1028	80888	OB	NC	Memorandum concerning a sale; round type; late period
1029	80889	OB	NC	Letter; *CT* 52 102; *AbB* 7 102
1030	80890	Ad -/4/20	NC	Administrative mu-túm, *namḫartu* for silver; seals

Bu 91-5-9,

1031	80891	Ad 15/3/?	C	Field rental; seals; *CT* 8 8d
1032	80892	Ha 6/9/40	C	House rental; seals
1033	80893	OB	NC	Administrative; loan to buy sesame; seals
1034	80894	Ha	NC	Field rental(?); seals
1035	80895	OB	NC	Rental(?) of fig trees; seals
1036	80896	OB	C	Memorandum concerning things involved with specific numbers of days and months; round type; late period
1037	80897	OB	C	Letter; *CT* 29 19; *AbB* 2 150
1038	80898	OB	F	House sale; old period
1039	80899	Si 30/7/22?	F	Concerning a slave lú su-bir$_4$^{ki}; seals
1040	80900	OB	NC	Real estate sale; *CT* 33 48a
1041	80901	OB	NC	Letter; unusual format and ductus; *CT* 52 68; *AbB* 7 68
1042	80902	OB	F	Ration account
1043	80903	Si 4/8/3 or 4	NC	Division of proceeds of a partnership between a person and Šamaš (temple); drawing on left edge; *CT* 48 44 no. 99
1044	80904	Aṣ 22/2/13	C	Roster of personal names; round type
1045	80905	Ad 19/12/23 or 26	C	Administrative mu-túm of the ugula dam.qar of Sippar; seal inscription of long "Kassite" type as on Bu 91-5-9, 1109 (= BM 80971)
1046	80906	Si	F	Liver omen (igi-tab); cf. Bu 91-5-9, 659 (= BM 80521), possibly same tablet
1047	80907	Si -/-/14 and 17	F	Administrative; seals
1048	80908	OB	F	Administrative
1049A	80909	Aṣ 21/11/16	NC	Account; round type
1049B	80910	OB	F	Content not apparent; round type
1050	80911	Aṣ 11/5/16	C	Administrative; rations, *šik mešeqim* for personnel of Šamaš temple in Sippar
1051	80912	Si 2/ezen *a-bi*/6	C	Field rental; *CT* 8 42c
1052	80913	OB	C	Letter; *CT* 52 160; *AbB* 7 160
1053	80914	OB	C	Letter; round type; *CT* 43 3 no. 8; *AbB* 1 8
1054	80915	OB	C	List of witnesses; round type
1055	80916	OB	NC	Letter; *CT* 52 54; *AbB* 7 54
1056	80917	OB	C	Letter; *CT* 52 2; *AbB* 7 2
1057	80918	OB	C	Field rental; *CT* 6 41c

Bu 91-5-9,

1058	80919	Ha 14/11/1	C	Deposit of tin; *CT* 8 37b
1059	80920	Am 20/7/acc	F	Loan of silver; Sippar; *AOATS* 4 56
1059A	80921	OB	F	Letter; *CT* 52 168; *AbB* 7 168
1060	80922	OB	C	Letter; *CT* 48 33 no. 80; *AbB* 7 188
1061	80923	Aş 23/-/16	NC	Account of money expended; round type
1062	80924	OB	F	List of witnesses
1063	80925	OB	NC	Field rental; case adheres to reverse, date not visible
1064	80926	OB	NC	Administrative; loan to buy barley to be delivered in Sippar
1065	80927	OB	F	Field sale(?); seals
1066	80928	Si 6$^{?}$/12b/27	C	Memorandum about a land sale; round type
1067	80929	Aş 24/3/11	NC	House rental
1068	80930	OB	NC	Roster of names; round type
1069	80931	OB	NC	Letter; *CT* 52 163; *AbB* 7 163
1070	80932	Ha -/-/13	NC	House rental
1071	80933	Aş 10/11/12	C	Receipt of grain by a brewer to buy bran(?); seals
1072	80934	OB	F	Letter; *CT* 52 109; *AbB* 7 109
1073	80935	Ad 25/4/8	NC	Field rental; seals
1074A	80936	Aş 15/2/8	F	Probably field rental; seals
1074B	80937	OB	F	Contract
1075	80938	Si 15/7/8	NC	Bequest of land to a *naditu*
1076	80939	Aş 4/9/13	NC	Administrative transaction of silver, *muštapilti alim* for *nudunnu* and other purposes; seals
1077	80940	Joined to Bu 91-5-9, 541B (= BM 80402B)		
1078	80941	OB -/-/mu bàd URU$^{?}$ UL$^{?}$ ^{d}UTU-ke$_4$	NC	Hire of a person; seals; tablet in case
1079	80942	Si 8/2/7	F	Hire of a person
1080	80943	OB	C	Economic memorandum
1081	92634	Ha 1/*e-lu-li*/27$^{?}$	C	Hire of a slave; *CT* 6 41a
1082	80944	Ae 10/8/"m" or "r"	C	Administrative; loan of barley; seals
1083	80945	Ae 5/4/"v"	F	Contract; seals
1084	80946	OB	NC	List of personal names inscribed over an earlier text at right angles; drawing cancelled on reverse; round type; late period
1085	80947	OB	C	Letter, probably from Der (^{d}ištaran); round type; *CT* 29 38; *AbB* 2 170

Bu 91-5-9,

1086	80948	OB	C	Hire of a person
1087	80949	OB 10/11/-	C	Loan of barley; seals
1088	80950	Ad -/-/2	NC	Administrative transaction in silver in year 1 of Ad; seals
1089	80951	Ha -/-/43	C	Field rental; seals
1090	80952	Si 10/8/3	C	Temple (Šamaš) loan; Sin, Adad and Marduk as witnesses
1091	80953	OB	C	Field rental
1092	80954	OB	C	House rental
1093	80955	Ae 20/11/"m"	F	Administrative; seals
1094	80956	Aṣ 25?/9/17	C	Harvest labour loan; Šamaš and Aya as witnesses; seals
1095	80957	Ad 28?/-/36	NC	Loan of barley from granary; seals
1096	80958	OB	NC	Letter; *CT* 52 94; *AbB* 7 94
1097	80959	Ha -/-/9 or 33	C	Memorandum about *aplutu* money
1098	80960	OB	NC	Letter; *CT* 52 179; *AbB* 7 179
1099	80961	OB	C	Field rental; round type
1100	80962	Ad 2/2/mu x x zi-da An-dEn-líl?-na?	NC	Administrative; concerning silver; seals
1101	80963	Aṣ 21/9/17	C	Harvest labour loan; seals
1102	80964	Aṣ 3/8/"17+b"	C	Roster of troops under (*piḫat*) the *deku*; round type
1103	80965	OB	NC	Letter; *CT* 52 79; *AbB* 7 79
1104	80966	Aṣ 10?/6/14	C	Barley loan *ana usatim*; seals
1105	80967	OB	C	šu-ti-a for barley and oil; lenticular
1106	80968	OB	F	Memorandum about silver paid *ana asirim*
1107	80969	Aṣ -/10/alan-a-ni x ...	NC	Harvest labour loan; gods as witnesses; seals
1108	80970	Aṣ 8?/9/12	C	Harvest labour loan; seals
1109	80971	Ad 21/9/urudu-alan-a-ni-a-ni/KA-da-ab-bi-bi-e-ne-a	C	Administrative mu-túm; round type; "Kassite" seal as on Bu 91-5-9, 1045 (=BM 80905)
1110	80972	OB	NC	Letter; *CT* 52 173; *AbB* 7 173
1111	80973	OB	C	Mathematical(?)
1112	80974	OB	F	Letter; *CT* 52 147; *AbB* 7 147
1113	80975	AS?	C	Obligation for a sum of money
1114	80976	Aṣ 6/5/-	NC	Loan to buy bran(?); seals
1115	80977	Ad 17/12b/28	C	Hire of a worker, voluntarily; seals
1116	80978	Aṣ 4/6/"17+b"	C	Ration list; seals
1117	80979	Ad 5?/5/1?	C	Loan of silver; seals

Bu 91-5-9,

1118	80980	OB	C	Letter; *CT* 52 27; *AbB* 7 27
1119	80981	Si? 30/6b/8?	NC	Loan of silver
1120	80982	Ha -/-/37	NC	Legal procedure about documents relating to *meršum* land; *CT* 48 38 no. 82
1121	80983	OB	C	Uncompleted memo about location of a field; round type; late period
1122	80984	Aṣ 30/2/11	NC	Contract; seals
1123	80985	OB	C	Letter; *CT* 52 180; *AbB* 7 180
1124	80986	Ad 5?/12/19?	C	Harvest labour loan; seals
1125	80987	Aṣ -/9/5, 8 or 12	NC	Loan of barley, *ezub* previous loan of silver; seals
1126	80988	OB	C	Agreement about a wall; early period
1127	80989	Sd 1/9/4	NC	Rental of a house; seals
1128	80990	Aṣ 10/4/9	C	Administrative; loan to buy wool; seals
1129	80991	OB	C	List of recipients of rations
1130	80992	Nbn -/5/16	NC	Contract; Borsippa
1131	80993	OB	NC	Administrative; mu-túm; *namḫartum*; seals
1132	80994	Sd 11/4/11	C	Administrative; *pí-ḫu* rations; round type
1133	80995	Sel 23/1/15	NC	Loan of silver; *CT* 49 101
1134	80996	OB	NC	List of personal names; round type; late period
1135	80997	Ad 8/9/23	C	Administrative; loan for purchase of a heifer and sesame; seals
1136	80998	OB	C	Temple loan (Sin); seals; fabric impression (*sissiktu*?)
1137	80999	Ha -/6/42	C	Hire of a labourer; *CT* 6 41b
1138	81000	OB	C	Field rental; *CT* 33 42
1139	81001	OB	C	Account of ewes; round type; late period
1140	81002	Cam 1/6/5	NC	Contract for dates or grain
1141	81003	OB Ammiṣura	C	Division of an estate; oath by Šamaš and *Am-mi-ṣú-ra*; *CT* 48 41 no. 90
1142	81004	Aṣ 28?/8?/13	C	Administrative; loan of wool; seals
1143	81005	Ae 3/1/"s"	NC	Administrative; account of *piḫu* and other foodstuffs(?)
1144	81006	OB	NC	Letter; *CT* 52 77; *AbB* 7 77
1145	81007	OB	C	Letter; seals; *CT* 52 97; *AbB* 7 97
1146	81008	OB	NC	Ration list; late period
1147	81009	Ad 27/9/29	C	Loan from granary; seals

Bu 91-5-9,

1148	81010	OB	F	Dealing with real estate (parts of a single estate)
1149	81011	OB	F	Obverse of real estate text
1150	81012	Aṣ -/-/4?	F	Field rental; seals
1151	81013	Si	F	Court proceedings over real estate
1152+ 1958-4-12, 2	81014+ 132268	OB	F	Sumerian literary; cf. Bu 91-5-9, 896 (=BM 80758)
1153	81015	OB	F	Large real estate document
1154	81016	OB	C	Letter; *CT* 4 26a; *AbB* 2 93
1155	81017	Ha 21/2/32	C	Field rental; seals; *sissiktu* impression; unopened case; *CT* 33 48b
1156	81018	Ad 17/8/30	C	Entrustment (*paqadum*) of oxen; seals
1157	81019	OB	C	Issues of silver; *CT* 33 28
1158	81020	OB	NC	Letter; *CT* 52 181; *AbB* 7 181
1159	81021	OB	NC	Administrative; record of fields; tabular; round type; late period
1160	81022	OB	NC	Real estate contract; old period
1161	81023	Ad -/11/mu gi?-bíl? egir ...	NC	Harvest labour loan; seals; three *sissiktu* impressions, one annotated
1162	81024	Ha 1/-/41	NC	Payment receipt for real estate
1163	81025	OB	F	Real estate document
1164	81026	OB	F	Loan(?); old period
1165	81027	Šagarakti-Šuriaš 12/5/10	C	Account of tax; *CT* 44 42 no. 68
1166	81028	OB	F	Letter; seals; *CT* 52 148; *AbB* 7 148
1167	81029	OB	F	Letter; *CT* 52 95; *AbB* 7 95
1168	81030	OB	NC	Field rental; late period; seals
1169	81031	OB	F	Letter; *CT* 52 42; *AbB* 7 42
1170	81032	Si(?) 10/11/?	C	Real estate sale
1171	81033	Ae 2?/3/?	F	Field rental(?); seals
1172	81034	Ad 29?/11/37	C	Barley loan *ana usatim*; seals
1173	81035	OB	F	Punishment for raising an illegal claim; *CT* 48 3 no. 4
1174	81036	OB	F	Letter; *CT* 52 108; *AbB* 7 108
1175	81037	Ha 5/8/25	F	Exchange of fields
1176	81038	OB	NC	Letter; *CT* 52 161; *AbB* 7 161
1177	81039	OB	NC	Field rental(?); part of case adhering to tablet; seals
1178	81040	Sm 20/6/15 or 24 (mu bàd? kiš?ki-ši)	F	Loan(?) of silver; seals
1179	81041	OB	C	Letter; *CT* 52 172; *AbB* 7 172

Bu 91-5-9,

1180	81042	OB	C	Memorandum; round type
1181	81043	OB	NC	Letter; *CT* 52 17; *AbB* 7 17
1182	81044	OB	C	*ḫubuttatum* loan; *CT* 4 21b
1183	81045	OB	NC	Letter; *CT* 52 164; *AbB* 7 164
1184	81046	OB	C	Memorandum; round type; late period
1185	81047	Ad 7/12/32	NC	Agreement to deliver a sheep as offering in the Šamaš temple of Sippar; seals; *CT* 48 45 no. 101
1186	81048	Ha 24/2/23	C	Disbursement; account of barley
1187	81049	OB	F	Section from middle of tablet about some obligation; early period
1188	81050	OB	C	Account of *iniatum*; late period
1189	81051	Ha -/-/43$^{?}$	NC	Field rental; part of case adhering; seals
1190	81052	OB	F	Letter; *CT* 52 99; *AbB* 7 99
1191	81053	Ha 24/9/18	C	Sale of a slave girl; *CT* 8 43c
1192	81054	OB	C	Multiplication table for 16
1193	81055	Ad 26$^{?}$/11/12	C	Loan of silver for trading; seals
1194	81056	Ad 5/1/32	C	Harvest labour loan; seals
1195	81057	OB Ammi-. . .	NC	Account of silver and barley
1196	81058	Ae 3/8/"n"	NC	Loan from the granary; seals
1197	81059	Ad 21/2/28	NC	Shepherding contract; seals
1198+	81060+	OB	NC	Letter; *CT* 52 125; *AbB* 7 125
1900-10-13, 103	87323			
1199	81061	Si 20/1/24	F	Slave sale; Subarian slave; *CT* 48 30 no. 60
1200A	81062	OB	F	Contract; seals
1200B	81063	OB	F	Contract
1201	81064	OB	F	Administrative memorandum
1202	81065	MB	NC	List of animals; Nuzi
1203	81066	Ad 2/10/35	C	Contract for preparation of sesame oil; seals; *CT* 8 8e
1204	81067	OB	NC	Partnership agreement; seals
1205	81068	OB	NC	Administrative; memorandum about copper implements; seals
1206	81069	Si -/-/27	C	House rental; seals
1207	81070	Sm -/-/16	C	Field rental; *CT* 33 45a
1208	81071	OB	NC	Ration account
1209	81072	OB	NC	Field sale; old period
1210	81073	OB	C	Account of udu-šu-gi-na brought to the judges; late period; round type; drawing on reverse

Bu 91-5-9,

1211	81074	Aş 5/7/11	C	Administrative; record concerning seed-corn; seals
1212	81075	OB	C	Administrative; record of disposition of various amounts of barley; round type; late period; seals
1213	81076	OB	C	Letter; *CT* 52 182; *AbB* 7 182
1214	81077	OB	C	Pay-list(?) in silver for personal names listed; round type; late period
1215	81078	Nbk 15?/5/21	NC	Contract; mentions month 6b
1216	81079	Aş 30/3/"17+d"	NC	Ration account
1217	81080	OB -/-/mu bàd-gal kiš?ki?	NC	Field sale
1218	81081	OB	C	Memorandum giving location of a field; late period
1219	81082	Sm -/-/13	C	Field rental
1220	81083	OB	C	Field rental; parts of case adhering
1221	81084	OB	C	Memorandum; disposition of sesame; round type; late period; seals
1222	81085	OB -/-/9 mu *Na-ra-am-Sin*	C	Loan of silver and barley (Immerum a personal name in text)
1223	81086	OB	C	Field rental; *CT* 33 43
1224	81087	OB	NC	Loan of silver with land given as security; *CT* 33 29
1225	81088	Aş 5?/11/16?	C	Account of *ma-ka?-tum*; round type
1226	81089	Aş 20/9/17	NC	Harvest labour loan; seals
1227	81090	OB	C	Ration list; round type; late period
1228	81091	Nbn 7/7/17	C	Receipt for an iron spade; Sippar
1229	81092	Kurigalzu 3/8/2	C	Receipt for garments
1230	81093	Ha -/-/38	C	Field rental
1231	81094	OB -/-/mu íd ...	NC	Field rental
1232	81095	OB	C	Letter; round type; *CT* 29 39; *AbB* 2 171
1233	81096	Aş 30/12b/13 or "17+a"	NC	*pi-ḫu* account; round type
1234	81097	OB	C	Ration account; round type
1235	81098	Aş 26?/9/17	C	Harvest labour loan; seals
1236	81099	OB	C	Letter; *CT* 52 183; *AbB* 7 183
1237	81100	Kassite 21/3?/19	C	Receipt for flour
1238	81101	NB 4/7/16	C	Contract for silver
1239	81102	OB	C	Account of an ugula dam-gàr; round type; late period
1240	81103	OB	C	List of persons *ša ana* nu-banda *uš-bu*; round type; late period

Bu 91-5-9,

1241	81104	OB	NC	Ration account; round type; late period
1242	81105	Aş 30/8/12	C	Account of sheep; round type
1243	81106	OB	C	Account
1244	81107	OB	C	Field rental; old period
1245	81108	Aş 24?/9/17	C	Harvest labour loan; Šamaš and Aya as witnesses; seals
1246	81109	AS -/-/15? mu bàd an-na-ni gu-za ... dingir-ra[ki] *A-píl-Sin* mu-na-dím	NC	Loan of barley
1247	81110	OB -/-/mu gibil za-...	F	Loan(?); seals
1248	81111	OB	F	Memorandum about produce of a field; seals
1249	81112	Ha -/*ki-nu-ni*/16	C	Loan of silver to be repaid in barley
1250	81113	OB	F	Tablet largely disintegrated
1251	81114	OB, Buntaḫʾunila	F	Bequest to a woman; Buntaḫʾunila oath; *CT* 48 17 no. 34
1252	81115	OB	C	Short memorandum
1253	81116	OB	C	Agreement for field cultivation and delivery of barley; old period; *CT* 48 47 no. 107
1254	81117	OB	C	Economic(?); obverse written across long dimension and reverse across broad dimension
1255	81118	OB	C	Short memorandum about barley
1256	81119	OB	NC	Letter; *CT* 52 158; *AbB* 7 158
1257	81120	OB	C	Letter; *CT* 52 169; *AbB* 7 169
1258	81121	OB	NC	Field rental
1259	81122	Aş 12?/12/5	C	Barley loan, from granary; seals
1260	81123	Sd 14/7/12	F	Ration list(?)
1261	81124	Kassite 1/2/24	C	Receipt for beer
1262A	81125	Sabium	F	Contract
1262B	81126	OB	F	Contract
1263	81127	Aş 1/7/11	NC	Administrative; memorandum about bran for the taverner; round type
1264	81128	OB	C	Tag for the tablet container (gi-pisan *duppat*) of Halhalla and Merigat
1265	81129	Ad 15/1/1	C	Tag for harvest workers; seals; *RA* 63 57 n. 2
1266	81130	Aş -/6b/10	C	Memorandum about barley and oil; round type
1267	81131	Aş 11/10/11	C	šu-ti-a for barley
1268	81132	OB	NC	Pay-list(?)

Bu 91-5-9,

1269	81133	Aṣ 12/8/10	C	Small memorandum; round type
1270	81134	OB	C	Letter; *CT* 52 67; *AbB* 7 67
1271	81135	OB	NC	Administrative text about silver; late period
1272	81136	OB	C	Field sale; very old period; unique type of formulas; *CT* 48 41 no. 91
1273	81137	Si 4/1/9	C	Hire of a person to work in cloister
1274	81138	Ad 2/12/6	C	Loan of barley from granary
1275	81139	Aṣ 29/9/11	NC	Loan of seed-corn; seals
1276	81140	Ha -/-/42	NC	Field rental; year by ductus
1277	81141	Si -/12/19?	C	šu-ti-a receipt; seals
1278	81142	Ha 18/*si-bu-tim*/18	C	Hire of a person, pay at gate of cloister
1279	81143	OB	F	Cultic arrangement for ka-sì-ga *ša* é-gal *a-ki-tim*; late period; square tag; seals
1280	81144	Sd 15/8/3	C	Memorandum concerning rations; round type
1281	81145	Kassite -/1/13	C	Receipt for grain; seals
1282	81146	Sd 30/11/3	C	Administrative; receipt for silver; seals
1283	81147	Sd 4?/7/3	C	Administrative text dealing with silver; seals
1284	81148	OB	NC	Field rental; older period
1285	81149	OB 1/1/-	NC	List of personal names; Ae on seal impression
1286	81150	Ha 25/11/12	C	Loan of barley; interest
1287	81151	Ha 25/diri/26? mu bára-gal-gal guškin-ḫuš-a [d]utu [d]iškur	C	Loan of barley; *gagum*; seals
1288	81152	Aṣ 6/12/11	C	Disbursements of barley; round type
1289	81153	Aṣ 6/6/15	C	Pay-list; round type
1290	81154	OB	C	Memorandum concerning barley; round type; late period
1291	81155	Ad 18/9/12	NC	Barley rations, *šik mešeqim*, for different groups of persons; round type
1292	81156	OB	C	Account of silver and barley; round type; late period
1293	81157	Dar 25/12/acc	NC	Contract; Sippar
1294	81158	Aṣ -/5/11	NC	Loan of silver to buy barley; seals
1295	81159	Sm	F	Sale contract
1296	81160	Sm -/-/12	C	Barley loan; interest
1297	81161	NB	NC	Quantities of dates for professions
1298	81162	OB	C	Ration account

Bu 91-5-9,

1299	81163	Si 1/5/2	C	Administrative; concerning barley from the *rabianum* to persons of Eshnunna; seals
1300	81164	OB	C	Field rental
1301	81165	OB	NC	Hire of a person; *gagum*
1302	81166	OB	C	Administrative; barley loan(?); seals
1303	81167	Ad 1/10/35	C	Administrative; loan of sesame for pressing into oil; seals
1304	81168	OB	NC	Administrative; about materials brought to palace for washing(?); seals
1305	81169	OB	C	Memorandum concerning pay for harvest workers; round type; late period
1306	81170	Ha -/-/3	C	Field rental
1307	81171	Ad 21/7/16 or 35	NC	Administrative document concerning disbursements of barley
1308	81172	OB	NC	Free loan of barley
1309	81173	OB	NC	Memorandum concerning delivery of grain; seals
1310	81174	Si 20/1/1?	C	Hire of a slavewoman; seals
1311	81175	Ad 25/10/26	C	Loan from granary; seals
1312	81176	OB	C	Hire of a person
1313	81177	Kassite	C	Account of fruit
1314	81178	OB	NC	Account of silver(?)
1315	81179	Aṣ 5/4/16	C	Administrative; receipt; silver; seals
1316	81180	Ad 1?/8/5 or 30	C	Memorandum concerning an ass brought to Babylon; seals
1317	81181	OB	NC	Memorandum concerning month of Ayarum
1318	81182	Ad 1/11/29	NC	Harvest labour loan; seals
1319	81183	OB	NC	List of names
1320	81184	Ae 16?/8/"e"	NC	Administrative; receipt; seals
1321	81185	Ad 12?/12/35	NC	Loan(?); poor surface; seals
1322	81186	Sd 26/7?/3	NC	Account of silver and duḫ; seals; round type
1323	81187	OB	F	Letter; *CT* 52 149; *AbB* 7 149
1324	81188	OB	F	List of men; seals; late period
1325	81189	Aṣ 11/10/13?	NC	Harvester loan; seals
1326	81190	OB	C	Economic; products of field; round type
1327	81191	OB?	C	Economic; memorandum with names
1328	81192	OB	C	Letter; *CT* 52 184; *AbB* 7 184

Bu 91-5-9,

1329	81193	OAkk	C	Account of cereals; *CT* 50 164
1330	81194	Aş 20+/11/12	NC	Account of lambs; round type
1331	81195	Aş 15/4/15	F	Account; round type
1332	81196	Aş 8/3/9	NC	Administrative; transaction involving wool; seals
1332A	81196A	OB	F	Content unclear; seals
1333	81197	OB	F	Contract; seals
1334	81198	Kurigalzu -/7/13	C	Account of grain expenditures
1335	81199	OB	C	Account; seals
1336	81200	Ha -/-/27	NC	Field rental
1337	81201	OB	C	Protocol exempting a gardener from lawsuit about *girrum* (duty?); seals; *CT* 48 33 no. 69
1338	81202	Aş 24/9/16	C	Harvest labour loan; Šamaš and Aya witnesses; seals
1339	81203	Si -/*si-bu-tim*/2	C	Hire of a person; seals
1340	81204	OB	NC	Letter; *CT* 52 157; *AbB* 7 157
1341	81205	Kassite 15/1/18	C	Account of beer
1342	81206	Si 10?/6/2	C	Field rental; seals
1343	81207	OB	C	Memorandum about locations of fields; round type
1344	81208	OB	C	Field rental
1345	81209	OB	C	Memorandum; subject not clear
1346	81210	OB	C	Field sale; old period, older formulas; *CT* 48 41 no. 89
1347	81211	OB	C	Memorandum(?)
1348	81212	Si -/-/2	C	Hire of self by a person for one year; seals
1349	81213	OB	NC	Field rental
1350	81214	OB	F	Contract; obscure phrases
1351	81215	OB	C	Protocol about occupying a house before impending sale
1352	81216	Ha 4/1/25	C	Hire of self for labour
1353	81217	Ha -/-/38	C	Field rental; some unusual provisions; *CT* 48 48 no. 113
1354	81218	Aş 6?/8/11	NC	Account of silver; round type
1355	81219	Ad 6/12/4	C	Loan of barley from Šamaš and Aya; seals
1356	81220	Ha 15/12/30	C	Field rental; *gagum* payment
1356A	81220A	OB	F	Case of previous
1357	81221	Ae 30/12/"i"	NC	Administrative; receipt for silver; seals
1358	81222	Ha -/-/33	NC	Field rental

Bu 91-5-9,

1359	81223	Ha -/-/28	F	Administrative; receipt for ration for king's daughter
1360	81224	Nbn 7/2/17	NC	Receipt for barley; fabric impression
1361	81225	OB	C	Field rental
1362	81226	Ae 1/8/"c"	NC	Loan of silver
1363	81227	OB	NC	Account of ewes; round type; late period
1364	81228	OB	C	Memorandum concerning food rations for chariotry, infantry and horses; round type; late period
1365	81229	Aş 24/9/17	C	Harvest labour loan; seals
1366	81230	Aş 14/8?/9	NC	Administrative; loan of silver; seals
1367	81231	Aş 15/12/11	C	Administrative; receipt for silver; seals
1368	81232	OB	NC	Multiplication table for 25
1369	81233	Aş -/4?/?	NC	Administrative; loan; seals
1370	81234	Ae 17/10/"d"	NC	Loan of silver; seals
1371	81235	Si -/-/8	NC	Hire of a person
1372	81236	Aş 19/-/9	NC	Loan of silver to buy wool; seals
1373	81237	MB	C	List of issues of barley; seals; Nuzi
1374	81238	OB	NC	List of women *epišat* KIN?
1375	81239	OB -/6/mu-ús-sa MA? giš-bar dEŠ.DAR	C	Loan of silver
1376	81240	Sd 20/1/4	C	Loan of silver to buy barley; Šamaš and Aya witnesses; seals
1377	81241	Sd -/2?/9	NC	Loan to buy sheep(?); seals
1378	81242	Dar -/8/7	NC	Loan; Babylon
1379	81243	OB	NC	House rental
1380	81244	OB	C	Field rental
1381	81245	OB	NC	Memorandum concerning payment of food rations over a period of days
1382	81246	OB	C	Hire of a person; unusual month names; *CT* 48 48 no. 111
1383	81247	Ad 1/5/3	NC	Administrative; seals
1384	81248	OB	NC	Field rental
1385	81249	OB	NC	Administrative; loan
1386	81250	OB	F	Loan of silver; seals; late period
1387	92635	Si -/-/3? or 4?	C	Field rental; seals
1388	81251	Ad 21/4/25	C	Promissory note to pay a quantity of barley; seals
1389	81252	Aş 20/9/15	C	Harvest labour loan, Šamaš and Aya witnesses; seals

Bu 91-5-9,

1390	81253	OB	C	Letter; *CT* 52 61; *AbB* 7 61
1391	81254	Ad 1/4/25	C	Loan of silver; purpose unclear; seals
1392	81255	Sd 3/11/3	NC	Administrative; loan of barley from Sippar granary; seals
1393	81256	Si 21 or 11/*e-lu-nim*/6	C	Field rental, to be paid in *gagum*
1394	81257	OB	F	List of names
1395	81258	Ad -/11/28	C	Protocol cancelling some obligation; seals
1396	81259	Sm -/-/16	NC	House rental
1397	81260	Aş 8?/5/?	F	Account of objects; round type
1398	81261	Ad 20/1/24	NC	Hire of a person; seals
1399	81262	Sd 5/12/3	NC	Administrative; loan from Sippar granary; seals
1400	81263	OB	NC	Loan of silver; seals
1401	81264	Aş 11/11/7	NC	Administrative; loan of barley, níg-šu, personal name; seals
1402	81265	Ha -/7/43	C	Contract about wool; *marat šarrim*; unusual formulas; *WO* 9 209 n. 6; *CT* 48 47 no. 108; *AfO* 25 77-78
1403	81266	OB	NC	šu-ti-a memorandum; seals
1404	81267	Aş 6?/9/17	C	Loan of silver to buy barley; seals
1405	81268	OB	C	Field rental
1406	81269	OB	C	Letter; seals; *CT* 52 57; *AbB* 7 57
1407	81270	Ad 13/-/1?	NC	Special conditions for repayment of a debt of silver; seals
1408	81271	OB	C	Field rental
1409	81272	Ha 10/1/35	C	Field rental
1410	81273	Si 16?/1/38	C	Hire of a person; seals
1411	81274	OB	NC	Field rental(?)
1412	81275	OB	NC	Field rental (igi-3-gál); date not visible; seals; tablet in case
1413	81276	Ad 14/4/3	C	mu-túm, *namḫartu* receipt, *ilkum* money; seals
1414	81277	OB	NC	Šamaš loan; late period
1415	81278	OB	NC	Administrative(?); loan involving sesame; seals
1416	81279	Ae 28/4/"m"	F	Disappearance of two oxherds; seals
1417	81280	Sd 16?/9/2	C	mu-túm, *namḫartu*, for silver; seals
1418	81281	OB	C	Field rental; part of case adhering; seals
1419	81282	Ha -/-/9 or 33	C	Field rental
1420	81283	Kaštiliaš 28/7/acc	C	Receipt for sheep
1421	81284	Ha -/-/32	C	Loan of silver

Bu 91-5-9,

1422	81285	Ad 1/1/31	NC	Hire of a person for milling; seals
1423	81286	OB	NC	Contract for delivery of dates; case adheres; seals
1424	81287	Aṣ 28/5/14	C	Transfer of an obligation; seals
1425	81288	Si -/1/6	C	Field rental (?); seals; fabric impression (*sissiktu*?)
1426	81289	OB	C	Field rental
1427	81290	Si 1/2/7	C	Field rental
1428	81291	Ad 13?/4/28	NC	Loan(?); seals
1429	81292	Si -/-/8	C	Field rental
1430	81293	OB	F	Loan of silver
1431	81294	OB 25/3/-	F	Administrative
1432	81295	Aṣ 9/11/12	C	Memorandum concerning dead sheep; round type
1433	81296	OB	NC	Loan of silver
1434	81297	Aṣ 25?/9?/17	C	Harvest labour loan; seals
1435	81298	OB -/*du-mu-zi*/mu ki? lugal-DÙG-a-šè	C	House rental
1436	81299	OB	C	Letter; *CT* 52 185; *AbB* 7 185
1437	81300	Aṣ -/-/11	C	Harvest labour loan; seals
1438	81301	Ha -/-/26?	NC	Field rental; seals; tablet in case
1439	81302	OB -/2/?	NC	Cultic arrangements for Ayaru 15; seals
1440	81303	OB	C	List of persons; round type; late period; fabric impression
1441	81304	OB	C	Small account of barley and silver; round type; late period
1442	81305	Aṣ 13/10/8	NC	mu-túm, *namḫartu* of silver; seals
1443	81306	Ae 2/11/"k"	NC	Assignment of work for a basket-worker; seals
1444A	81307	Si 6/1/6?	F	Administrative text
1444B	81308	OB	F	Administrative text; seals
1445	81309	Ae -/-/"k"	C	Hire of an ox
1446	81310	Aṣ 2/1/17	C	Loan of silver, to be repaid in barley; seals
1447	81311	Ad 12/7/28	C	Commercial loan to buy kar.sum.sar; seals
1448	81312	Aṣ 14/12/17	C	Loan of silver to buy a field; seals
1449	81313	OB	C	Memorandum concerning distribution of barley; round type; late period
1450	81314	OB	NC	Harvest labour loan; seals
1451	81315	Aṣ 7/-/11	NC	Loan of silver, to be repaid in barley; seals

Bu 91-5-9,

1452	81316	OB	C	List of bronze vessels; early period
1453	81317	OB	C	Šamaš loan of silver; unusual formulas; seals; *CT* 48 46 no. 104
1454	81318	Ad 8/3/1	C	mu-túm, *namḫartu* for silver, in Ae 28; seals
1455	81319	Ad 1/9/5	NC	mu-túm, *namḫartu* for barley; seals
1456	81320	Ad or Sd 6/7?/-	C	Hire of a person; seals
1457	81321	Aṣ 8/5/9	C	Receipt for silver; seals
1458	81322	Ha -/-/22	C	Field rental
1459	81323	Ad -/2/4	NC	Administrative; mu-túm, *namḫartu* for silver; seals
1460	81324	OB	C	Brief summary of barley distributions
1461	81325	Ad 3 or 13/10/6	C	mu-túm, *namḫartu* for silver; seals
1462	81326	Ad 25/7/24	C	Loan to buy sesame; seals
1463	81327	Aṣ 25?/9/16	C	Harvest labour loan; seals
1464	81328	Aṣ 1/12/11	C	Šamaš and Aya loan of barley; seals
1465	81329	Ad 29/7/26	C	Loan of wool to be repaid in silver, *a-na it-ti il-i*-x; seals
1466	81330	Si 1/12/4	C	Receipt for copper *ana šiprim*; part of case adheres; seals
1467	81331	Ha -/-/24	NC	Hire of a person; part of case adheres
1468	81332	Ad 26/5/27	NC	Commercial loan of silver, šám SÍG, repayment to palace; seals
1469	81333	Ha -/-/42	NC	Receipt for copper; seals
1470	81334	Ad 17?/1/31	C	Administrative; loan of sesame, šám é-gal, níg-šu personal name; seals
1471	81335	Ad 26?/12/-	F	Text mostly destroyed; seals
1472	81336	Ad 15/5/18	C	Cultic memorandum; expenditure of a calf for the ki.se.ga offering of Ab; seals; *CT* 48 44 no. 100
1473	81337	Si 1/4/7	F	Contract; part of case adhering
1474	81338	Ad 18/7/-	NC	Memorandum concerning delivery of beams and boats
1475	81339	Ha -/-/34?	NC	Field rental
1476	81340	Aṣ 3?/4/"17+d"	C	Barley issue for rations; seals
1477	81341	OB	NC	List of families offering(?) udu-šu-gi-na; tablet reused
1478	81342	Ha -/-/25	NC	Field rental
1479	81343	Ad 4/8/31	C	Loan to buy wool; seals
1480	81344	Si -/-/2	NC	Field rental; seals
1481	81345	Si -/-/7	C	Field rental; seals
1482	81346	Aṣ -/5/-	NC	Ration list; seals

Bu 91-5-9,

1483	81347	Si 1/7/2	F	Contract concerning land
1484	81348	OB	C	Field rental
1485	81349	Aş 6?/3?/15	C	Loan or hire of a ram; seals
1486	81350	Aş 10/6b/11	C	Receipt for bran; seals
1487	81351	Si -/9/2	C	Loan of wool from king's daughter, to be repaid in silver
1488	81352	Si 27/4/7?	NC	Loan of barley; seals
1489	81353	OB	F	Administrative text
1490	81354	Ha -/-/11	C	Field rental
1491	81355	Aş 12/3/1	F	Administrative text concerning wool; dupl. Bu 91-5-9, 596 (=BM 80459); seals; *CT* 48 50 no. 119
1492	81356	OB	NC	Loan to be repaid in sesame; seals
1493	81357	OB	NC	Field rental
1494	81358	OB	NC	Letter; *CT* 52 41; *AbB* 7 41
1495	81359	Aş 4/2/-	NC	House rental; seals
1496	81360	Kassite	C	Account of dates or grain
1497	81361	Aş -/9/17	NC	Harvest labour loan
1498	81362	Ad 20/1/26	NC	List of names, including a lú *mu-ga-am-me-rum*; round type
1499	81363	OB	C	House rental; part of case adhering; seals
1500	81364	Aş 20/11/-	F	Extispicy report; round type; *JCS* 21 224
1501	81365	Ha 26/1/40	NC	Hire of a person
1502	81366	Ad -/7/-	NC	Memorandum concerning silver; round type
1503	81367	OB	C	Field rental; *ana šiknim*; seals
1504	81368	Ha 20/3/17	NC	Field rental
1504A	81368A	OB	F	Case of previous; seals
1505	81369	OB	C	Note concerning an interest-free loan; seals
1506	81370	Aş 10/11/"17+b"	C	Barley loan; *ana usatim*; seals; square tag
1507	81371	Kaštiliaš 8/5/1	C	Receipt for a sheep
1508A	81372	OB	C	Hire of a person
1508B	81373	Ad	F	Case of previous
1509	81374	OB	C	Withdrawal of silver (as partnership venture?) from Šamaš temple; seals; *CT* 48 46 no. 105
1510	81375	Cyr 11/9/6	C	Deposition
1511	81376	Ad 22/2/1	C	mu-túm, *namḫartu* for silver in Ae 28; seals

Bu 91-5-9,

1512	81377	Aṣ 10+?/6/8?	NC	Administrative; receipt for silver; some new phraseology; seals
1513	81378	Si -/-/3	C	Field rental; *ana šiknim*; seals
1514	81379	Aṣ 11/8/11	C	mu-túm, *namḫartu* for silver; seals
1515	81380	Si -/-/?	NC	Field rental
1516	81381	OB	C	Hire of a person
1517	81382	Sm 12/7/16	C	Administrative; completion of a mission to supply cloth(?) to the palace; *CT* 48 45 no. 103
1518	81383	OB	C	Administrative text concerning dates and other foodstuffs
1519	81384	Ha -/-/41?	C	House rental; part of case adhering
1520	81385	Ha -/-/30	C	Hire of a person(?)
1521	81386	OB	C	Administrative; seals
1522	81387	OB	C	Harvest labour loan; late period; seals
1523	81388	Si -/-/17	C	Administrative receipt; *namḫartu* for ewes by the su-si-ig; seals
1524	81389	Si -/5/1?	C	Issue of *ḫušu* copper to make a *ruqqu* for Šamaš; *CT* 48 47 no. 109
1525A	81390	OB	F	Ration list(?)
1525B	81391	OB	F	Case(?); seals
1526	81392	OB -/-/mu giš-gu-za ...	NC	Hire of a person
1527	81393	Sm -/-/19	C	Field rental; part of case adheres; seals
1528	81394	Aṣ 6/9/2	C	Receipt; šu-ti-a for bran; seals
1529	81395	OB -/-/mu *ba-ba-at ma-al-gi-im*?ki	C	House rental
1530	81396	Aṣ 12/12b/13	C	Earth removal contract to build a wall; cf. Bu 91-5-9, 1729 (= BM 81597); seals
1531	81397	Ae -/-/"i"	NC	Administrative; *namḫartu* of Ae "i" of a *na-qad* and su-si-ig of Sippar-amnanum; seals
1532	81398	Aṣ -/-/17	C	Administrative; loan to buy wool; seals; cross-cancelled
1533	81399	Si 6?/11/17	C	*namḫartu* for sheep; seals; square tag
1534	81400	OB	F	Administrative; *kanikšu iḫeppe* end; round type; late period
1535	81401	OB	F	Part of a will(?); earlier period
1536	81402	Si -/-/3 or 4	F	Interest free loan
1537	81403	Si -/-/3 or 4	F	Field rental
1538	81404	OB	F	Letter; *CT* 52 70; *AbB* 7 70
1539	81405	Ha 1/*a-ia-rum*/39	NC	Guarantor (*qatatum*?) agreement

Bu 91-5-9,

1540	81406	OB	NC	Economic; *pi-ḫu*; round type; late period
1541	81407	OB	F	Account of silver
1542	81408	OB	NC	Field rental
1543	81409	OB	C	Hire of a person
1544	81410	OB	F	Contract; seals
1545	81411	NB	F	Memorandum; mentions lú-nam *šá* uru *ú-ud-ri*
1546	81412	OB	F	Letter; *CT* 52 90; *AbB* 7 90
1547	81413	Aş 6/11/9	F	Economic; round type
1548	81414	OB 4/2/-	NC	Memorandum; round type; late period
1549	81415	OB	C	Loan of barley; part of case adheres; seals
1550	81416	OB	F	Economic
1551	81417	OB	F	Contract
1552	81418	OB	F	Subject not apparent; part of case adhering; seals
1553	81419	Sm	F	Sale contract
1554+ 92-5-16, 323	81420+ 16787			Letter; *CT* 52 134; *AbB* 7 134
1555	81421	Ha	F	Sale; *ina šewirim*
1556	81422	OB	NC	Administrative memorandum
1557	81423	OB	F	Legal proceedings(?); seals
1558	81424	Ad 15/3/alan *Sa-am-su-i-lu-na* ú alan nam-en-na-ni	NC	Hire of a person from his father *ana* gud šà-ga-*tum ana paṭar erešim*; seals
1559	81425	Ad -/-/21	F	mu-túm, *namḫartu*
1560	81426	Si -/-/7	NC	Partition wall agreement
1561	81427	OB	F	Pay list(?); late period
1562	81428	OB	F	Letter; *CT* 52 165; *AbB* 7 165
1563+ 1570	81429+ 81436	OB	F	Letter; *CT* 52 96; *AbB* 7 96
1564	81430	OB	F	Loan(?); part of case adhering
1565	81431	OB	F	Field rental
1566	81432	OB	NC	Field rental
1567	81433	Si 6?/8/20	F	Loan of silver; seals
1568	81434	NB 7/4/10	F	Legal text
1569	81435	OB	F	Subject not apparent
1570	81436	Joined to 91-5-9, 1563 (= BM 81429)		
1571	81437	OB	F	Protocol; seals
1572	81438	Ha -/-/34	NC	Hire of a slave

Bu 91-5-9,

1573	81439	OB	F	Loan of silver; seals
1574	81440	Sm -/-/13	NC	Loan of silver with interest
1575	81441	Si 16/10/7	NC	Economic memorandum; seals
1576	81442	OB	C	Acknowledgement of an obligation; seals
1577	81443	Aṣ 10/2/5	C	Administrative loan to process sesame for oil; seals
1578	81444	Ad 20/11/37	NC	Harvest labour loan; seals
1579	81445	Ad 11/12/31	C	Harvest labour loan; seals
1580	81446	Aṣ 20/9/17	C	Harvest labour loan; seals
1581	81447	OB	NC	Pay list(?)
1582	81448	OB	F	Field rental
1583	81449	OB	C	Memorandum concerning location of a field; round type; late period
1584	81450	Si 21?/10?/21	NC	House rental; seals
1585A	81451	Ha -/-/15	C	Field rental
1585B	81452	OB	F	Case of previous
1586A	81453	Ae 1/9/"k"	F	Sale of a slave; seals
1586B	81454	OB	F	Loan; seals
1587	81455	Ha -/-/20	NC	Partition wall agreement
1588	81456	OB	NC	Arrangement for payment of a debt incurred by purchase of an ox; seals
1589	81457	OB	C	Field rental
1590	81458	OB	C	Field rental
1591	81459	Ad 21/-/24 or 25	NC	Arrangement for payment of a debt incurred by purchase of a calf(?); seals
1592+ 96-3-28, 416	81460+ 13325		F	Letter; *CT* 52 82; *AbB* 7 82
1593	81461	Aṣ 25/9/17	C	Harvest labour loan; seals
1594	81462	Si 6?/6/7	C	Date processing contract; seals
1595	81463	Ha 26/2/25 or Si 26/2/16	C	Deposit agreement for barley; seals
1596	81464	Si 24/1/4	C	Memorandum concerning yield of a field
1597	81465	Ad 30/12/1	C	Memorandum concerning sheep given over for pasturing; seals; *sissiktu* impression annotated
1598	81466	Ad 10/9/23?	C	Provision for cancelling a debt; seals; *CT* 48 45 no. 102
1599	81467	Ad 2/4/1	C	mu-túm, *namḫartu* for silver
1600	81468	Ad 1/12/18	C	mu-túm, *namḫartu* for silver; seals

Bu 91-5-9,

1601	81469	Ha -/-/35	C	Field rental
1602	81470	OB	F	Economic
1603	81471	Ha -/-/31	C	Hire of a person
1604	81472	Ad 20/4/8	C	Loan; administrative for udu-šu-gi-na; seals
1605	81473	Sd 5/12/3	NC	Receipt for grain of granary of Sippar-yaḫrurum; seals
1606	81474	OB	F	Contract; seals
1607	81475	OB	F	Sumerian(?) literary(?); round type; late period
1608	81476	Aṣ 15/8/16	C	mu-túm, *namḫartu*; seals; round type
1609	81477	Aṣ 16?/11/-	NC	Harvest labour loan; seals
1610	81478	Si 10/3/4	C	Hire of a person
1611	81479	Ha -/-/16	C	Loan, from *naditu*, of silver and barley at interest
1612	81480	OB	F	Estate division; early period
1613	81481	Si -/-/11	C	Field rental; rent to be paid in *gagum*
1614	81482	Aṣ 7/7/10	C	Brief memorandum of rations; round type
1615	81483	Aṣ 5/1/14	C	Receipt for vessels in the house of a *sabitum*; seals; round type
1616	81484	OB	F	Field rental
1617	81485	OB . . .-*ditana*/11/9	F	Memorandum concerning issue of barley; round type
1618	81486	OB	C	Letter; *CT* 52 45; *AbB* 7 45
1619	81487	OB	NC	Field rental
1620	81488	OB	NC	Field rental
1621	81489	OB	F	Letter; *CT* 52 159; *AbB* 7 159
1622	81490	Si 1/1/4	C	Field rental; *ana ši-ki?-bi?-ru? nu-ka-ri-ib-bi*, to be paid in *gagum*; seals
1623	81491	OB -/-/mu ugnim ...	NC	Loan of silver
1624	81492	Joined to 91-5-9, 728B (= BM 80590)		
1625	81493	Ha -/-/42	C	Field rental; rent to be paid in *gagum*
1626	81494	Ad 10?/12/27	C	Harvest labour loan; seals
1627	81495	OB	C	Hire of a person
1628	81496	OB	NC	Loan of silver; interest
1629	81497	Ad -/1/13	F	Hire of a person(?); seals
1630	81498	MB	C	Receipt for sheep; Nuzi; seals
1631	81499	Si 7/*e-lu-li*/2	C	Memorandum concerning wages received
1632	81500	OB	NC	Hire of a slavewoman

Bu 91-5-9,

1633	81501	AS	F	Contract
1634	81502	Si 21/3/18	F	Sale(?) of an orchard; seals
1635	81503	OB	F	Legal text; *JCS* 30 235 and 243
1636	81504	OB	C	Loan; interest
1637	81505	Ha -/-/3	C	Field rental; seals
1638	81506	Aş 26?/3/10	NC	Memorandum; round type
1639	81507	OB	C	Receipt
1640	81508	OB	F	Hire of a person
1641	81509	MB	F	Subject not apparent; seals; Nuzi
1642	81510	OB	NC	Hire of a person; part of case adhering; seals
1643	81511	Si -/-/1?	C	Loan of barley; seals
1644	81512	Ae 6/6b/"i"	C	Receipt for carcass of a goat; su-si-ig of Sippar-amnanum; seals
1645	81513	OB	C	Memorandum concerning barley and oil; round type
1646	81514	Ha -/11/28	C	Loan with interest
1647	81515	OB	F	Part of a letter(?)
1648	81516	Ha -/-/19?	C	Memorandum concerning payment in barley of a rent
1649	81517	Ha -/-/29	C	Interest free loan
1650	81518	Si -/-/1?	C	Field rental; part of case adhering
1651	81519	Si 20/1/2	C	Field rental; seals
1652	81520	OB	C	Administrative; memorandum concerning foodstuffs(?)
1653	81521	OB	F	Administrative; Sippar-yaḫrurum; seals
1654	81522	Ae -/-/"k"?	NC	Memorandum concerning barley; seals
1655	81523	Aş 24?/9/17	C	Harvest labour loan
1656	81524	OB	C	Loan of silver with interest; seals; part of case adhering
1657	81525	Si -/-/2	NC	Receipt; object lost; *nebiḫ eqlim* from *naditu*
1658	81526	OB	C	Letter; strange names, gentilics; seal of an official of Ṣilli-Sin of Ešnunna; *CT* 52 29; *AbB* 7 29
1659	81527	OB	F	Letter; *CT* 52 150; *AbB* 7 150
1660	81528	OB	C	Letter; *CT* 52 15; *AbB* 7 15
1661	81529	Si -/-/2?	C	Loan of barley with interest; part of case adhering
1662	81530	OB	F	List of names; round type; late period
1663	81531	Si -/-/15?	C	Field rental
1664	81532	Ad 21/12/27	C	Obligation; *šalmu ù baltu* [d]*Šamaš ipal*

Bu 91-5-9,

1665	81533	Ha 8/5/43	C	Receipt for different items
1666	81534	Ha -/-/40	F	Hire of a person(?); tablet in case; seals
1667	81535	Sd 6/11/17?	C	Protocol about withdrawal of bran from house of a priest of Sin by a PA.PA; seals; round type
1668	81536	Ha 15/5/41	C	Hire of a person
1669	81537	Ha -/-/38	C	House rental(?)
1670	81538	Aṣ 25/9/17	C	Harvest labour loan; seals
1671	81539	OB	C	Field rental
1672	81540	Ha -/-/38	C	Field rental
1673	81541	OB	F	Administrative text concerning barley and sesame; seals
1674	81542	OB	F	Hire of a person; seals
1675	81543	OB	NC	Subject not apparent; seals
1676	81544	Si -/1/2	NC	Field rental; *ana šikni*
1677	81545	Si 24/8?/23	F	Contract; seals
1678	81546	OB	C	Letter; *CT* 52 25; *AbB* 7 25
1679	81547	Aṣ 5/10/1?	C	Memorandum concerning delivery of two oxen for deposit; seals; round type
1680	81548	OB	C	Field sale; very old period
1681	81549	Sumulael	F	Sale contract
1682	81550	OB	C	Receipt for sesame oil
1683	81551	Ad -/9/-	C	Administrative; loan of money *ana šám i-ki-im* to a gardener, which is to be given at harvest and the tablet is to be cancelled; seals
1684	81552	Si 9/11/17	NC	Receipt by a su-si-ig for ewes; square tag; seals
1685	81553	OB	C	Receipt for flour
1686	81554	OB	NC	Field rental
1687	81555	Ha 10/*Eluli*/42	C	Receipt for silver; seals
1688	81556	Si 22/9/17	C	Receipt by *šu-si-ik-ki* for dead goats; square tag; seals; *RA* 63 61 n. 4
1689	81557	Si 12/1/3	C	Receipt for rations at harvest work; seals; *RA* 63 57 n. 2
1690	81558	OB	NC	Loan of barley with interest
1691	81559	OB	C	Loan of barley with interest
1692	81560	OB	NC	Receipt; seals; round type; late period
1693	81561	Seleucid	NC	Horoscope; 172 Seleucid era
1694	81562	Si 14?/10/14	C	Receipt for dead goats by the su-si-ig é-bàd 30 ki; square tag; seal; *RA* 63 63 n. 1

Bu 91-5-9,

1695	81563	OB	C	Field rental; very early period
1696	81564	OB	F	Field rental
1697	81565	Aş 20/5/15	C	Short pay(?) list; round type
1698	81566	OB	F	Administrative; obverse lost; Kar-Sippar
1699	81567	Ad 12?/2/14	NC	Receipt by the maš-su-gíd-gíd of animals from herdsmen; seals
1700	81568	Ha -/ezen-an-na/26	C	Memorandum concerning payment of barley; seals, one of a servant of Išme-^{d}[. . .]
1701	81569	Ad 30/1 or 5/24	NC	Delivery of flour; seals
1702	81570	Ha 3/*si-bu-tim*/25?	C	Loan of silver with interest
1703	81571	OB	F	Memorandum concerning receipt of goats; late period; seals
1704	81572	Ha -/-/24	C	Field rental
1705	81573	Aş 15/6/-	C	Receipt for beer; seals; round type
1706	81574	Ha -/12/19	C	Deposition before witnesses about payment of a debt; *CT* 48 19 no. 39
1707	81575	OB	F	Dealing with some obligation
1708	81576	OB	NC	Loan with interest
1709	81577	OB	F	Obligation of some kind
1710	81578	Si -/-/3 or 4	F	Loan of barley; interest; seals
1711	81579	OB	F	Memorandum; round type; late period
1712	81580	Ad 18/9/27	C	Loan of silver; *muštapilti Babilim*; seals
1713	81581	Ha 2/2/38	NC	Obligation for delivery of yield of a field to a *naditu*; seals
1714	81582	Ad 1/8/26	C	Administrative; loan of wool from palace; seals
1715	81583	Ha -/-/4	C	Loan with interest from a *naditu*; *šalmukenu* (Sumerian); repayment in month Šaddutim
1716	81584	Ha -/-/9 or 33	C	Field rental with provisions for festivals
1717	81585	Ad 26/12/17	NC	Herding contract; *ḫaliqtum ù piṣṣatum izzaz*; seals
1718	81586	Aş 26/9/17	C	Harvest labour loan; seals
1719	81587	Aş 4+/5/11	NC	Account of cattle given over to shepherd(?)
1720	81588	Ad 10/12/25	C	Loan of silver, repayment in barley at current price; seals
1721	81589	OB	C	Loan; part of case adhering; seals
1722	81590	Sd 22/10/4	C	Delivery of silver; *ne-me-et* personal name; seals
1723	81591	Ad -/-/24?	NC	Administrative; loan of silver to buy wool, to be repaid in silver; seals

Bu 91-5-9,

1724	81592	Si 5/*ta-am-ḫi-ri*/4	NC	Temple loan; witnesses: Šamaš, Aya, Bunene; seals
1725	81593	Ad 23/2/14	C	Assignment (*paqadum*) of small cattle (to a shepherd?); seals
1726	81594	Ad 12/-/9	NC	Administrative; loan to buy an udu-šu-gi-na; seals
1727	81595	Si -/-/3 or 4	C	Field rental; a-šà *ši-ki-in mu-ša-ri*; Šamaš, Aya, Bunene witnesses; seals
1728	81596	Si 8/9/18?	C	Receipt by the su-si-ig for *pa-ag-ru*.ḫi-a; square tag; seals
1729	81597	Aṣ 26/12/13	C	Earth removal contract; cf. Bu 91-5-9, 1530 (= BM 81396); seals
1730	81598	Aṣ 6 or 7/1/"17+b"	C	Ration list; seals
1731	81599	Ad 10/-/5	C	Loan for purchase of sheep
1732	81600	Ad 15/2/13	C	Receipt for rations, *šik mešeqim* etc.; seals
1733	81601	Aṣ 9?/1/14	C	Issue of *piḫu*, to be repaid in barley; seals
1734	81602	Kassite 20/8/11	C	Receipt for oil; seals
1735	81603	OB 22?/8/mu amar? kin ú ri-eš (Si 2?)	C	Note of a debt for barley; unusual arrangement; *CT* 48 17 no. 35
1736	81604	Si 2/2/10	C	Names of two persons witnessing the *mayaru* of a quantity of earth; round type
1737	81605	Art 3/1/25	NC	Receipt for dates
1738	81606	Ha -/-/27 or Si -/-/7	NC	Loan of silver
1739	81607	OB	C	Note about the location of a field or house; round type; late period
1740	81608	OB	C	Bulla with seal; no writing
1741	81609	Ha -/-/34	C	Loan of silver
1742	81610	Aṣ -/9/1?	NC	Receipt for birds
1743	81611	OB -/8/-	C	Memorandum concerning barley; seals
1744	81612	OB	C	Letter; *CT* 52 55; *AbB* 7 55
1745	81613	Sd 27/3/13	NC	Memorandum concerning a debt of money; seals; round type
1746	81614	Aṣ 26/7/1 ("17+c")	C	Administrative; šu-ti-a PN; obverse damaged; round type
1747	81615	Ha 25/1/27	C	Administrative; memorandum concerning an account (*šutaḫruṣ-ma*); seals
1748	81616	OB	C	Letter; *CT* 52 40; *AbB* 7 40
1749	81617	Aṣ 10?/12/15	C	Administrative; transfer (*qati* PN *nasḫat*); Šamaš and Aya witnesses; seals

Bu 91-5-9,

1750	81618	Aş 10/7/13	NC	Administrative; receipt for silver; round type
1751	81619	OB	C	Field rental
1752	81620	Ha -/12/26	C	šu-ti-a for barley and silver
1753	81621	Ad?	C	Administrative; loan of silver to buy barley
1754	81622	Ha 28/6b/35	C	Administrative; disposition of quantities of barley; seals
1755	81623	Ad 26?/4/6	C	Tag; seals
1756	81624	Aş 30/5/"17+b"	NC	Memorandum concerning three Elamites(?) assigned to guard the Tigris together with Suteans; round type; *CT* 48 37 no. 78
1757	81625	Si 1/6/lugal	C	Hire of a person; seals
1758	81626	Si 1/12/3	C	Witnesses to the taking of a person as distrainee for 15 days of labour; tag shape; *CT* 48 18 no. 38
1759	81627	OB?	F	Economic
1760	81628	OB	NC	Ration account
1761	81629	Aş 15/10/14	C	šu-ti-a for barley; round type
1762	81630	Ad 3?/8/2	C	šu-ti-a for beer; seals
1763	81631	Ad 24/5/30	C	Administrative; protocol about beer; seals
1764	81632	OB 4/12/-	C	Hire of a person; seals
1765	81633	OB	NC	Memorandum concerning a debt; seals
1766	81634	OB	NC	Short economic text
1767	81635	Ha 15?/10/16	C	Loan of barley with interest
1768	81636	OB	C	Tag; for beer (*li-is-ti*); seals
1769	81637	Ae 18?/4/"e"	C	Loan of silver; seals
1770	81638	OB 30/12b/mu gibil	C	Loan of silver; seals
1771	81639	Si 4/9/6	C	šu-ti-a of barley for *gagum*, nig-šu *Ḫa-su-ub-te-eš-šu-ub*; seals
1772	81640	Ad 1/9/14	C	Memorandum concerning a bread ration; seals
1773	81641	OB	NC	Administrative; record about an unidentified subject; mentioning Sippar and Eshnunna; seals
1774	81642	OB	F	Loan; seals
1775	81643	OB	NC	Hire of a person; seals
1776	81644	Ae 20/3?/"t"	C	šu-ti-a memorandum; seals
1777	81645	Ha 10/5/43	C	Memorandum concerning *pi-ḫu* ration; seals
1778	81646	Aş 15/12/14	C	Loan of silver from Šamaš

Bu 91-5-9,

1779	81647	Aş 8?/5?/"17+b"	C	Ration account; seals
1780	81648	Aş 3/3/3? (mu gibil)	C	Ration protocol; round type
1781	81649	Aş 2/5/"17+b"	C	Ration list
1782	81650	Si -/8/6	C	Memorandum concerning two dead ewes; *šu-ši-ki*; square tag; seals; *RA* 63 61 n. 5
1783	81651	OB	C	Loan of silver, to be repaid in month Šadutim; seals
1784	81652	OB	C	Short administrative memorandum; seals
1785	81653	Ha -/ezen [d]iškur/28	C	šu-ti-a for barley; seals
1786	81654	Ad 10/1/6 var. [d]Utu en buru-na gu-zu guškin	C	Tag of three basketweavers (ad-kid) with holes; for date cf. Bu 91-5-9, 1799 (= BM 81667); seals
1787	81655	OB	C	Notation about amounts of barley and silver
1788	81656	OB	C	Small administrative text; mu-túm; ends: ugula *šu-i ìl-li-il*?; seals
1789	81657	OB	NC	Small administrative text; seals
1790	81658	Kassite 26/7/24	C	Account of beer
1791	81659	OB	C	Administrative; šu-ti-a; seals
1792	81660	Ha 16/*ki-nu-ni*/34	C	Deposition or oath before witnesses that swearer will pay the wages of and return a slavewoman to owner in five days; *CT* 48 13 no. 26
1793	81661	OB	C	Letter; *CT* 52 31; *AbB* 7 31
1794	81662	Ha 20?/11/24 ([id]ti-DI-[d]En-líl-lá)	C	Loan of silver with interest
1795	81663	OB 10/12b/-	NC	šu-ti-a for figs(?) and sesame oil
1796	81664	Aş 24?/4/"17+b"	C	Ration disbursement; zi-ga, níg-šu PN seals
1797	81665	Aş 22/6/15	C	Memorandum for beer ration; round type
1798	81666	OB	NC	Field rental
1799	81667	Ad 10/6/6	C	Tag with holes; basketweaver; seals
1800	81668	Aş 9/5/"17+b"	C	Memorandum for bread ration; *ma bar* PN *pa-ar-sa-at*; round type
1801	81669	Aş 23/4/"17+b"	C	Receipt for beer(?) from the lú-tín-na by the *rabi sikkatim*; unusual seal type; *CT* 48 42 no. 110
1802	81670	Ha -/-/3? or 14	NC	Memorandum appointing a person as a ka-bar; seals
1803	81671	OB	F	Field rental(?)
1804	81672	OB	C	Loan of barley with interest

Bu 91-5-9,

1805	81673	Ha 1/6/34	C	Hire of a person
1806	81674	Ha or Si -/-/mu urudu-ki-lugal-gub-ba	C	Receipt for wage payment
1807	81675	Ha 22/10/36	C	Memorandum concerning a dead infant of the nam-ra; seals
1808	81676	Ha 15/5/43?	C	Memorandum concerning brick production
1809	81677	Aṣ 12?/12/17	NC	Receipt for *piḫu*; seals
1810	81678	Si -/-/1 (mu-ús-sa saḫar Zimbir[ki])	C	Field rental
1811	81679	Ha 10?/5/43	NC	Memorandum concerning brick production; cf. Bu 91-5-9, 1808 (= BM 81676)
1812	81680	Ha -/12b/26	C	Guarantee, šu-du$_8$-a, for a loan
1813	81681	Aṣ 10?/1/14	NC	Administrative; loan of silver to buy barley; seals
1814	81682	Sd 10/10/2	C	Memorandum of silver, mu-túm, *namḫartu* for house purchase; seals
1815	81683	Ha -/-/24	C	Hire of a person
1816	81684	Ad -/-/25	F	Harvest labour loan; seals
1817	81685	OB	C	Pay list in silver; round type; late period
1818	81686	Šagarakti-Šuriyaš -/12/9	C	Receipt for sheep; seals
1819	81687	Si -/4/-	C	Field rental to be paid in *gagum*
1820	81688	OB	F	Pay list in silver; round type; late period
1821	81689	Si -/2/-	C	Field rental
1822	81690	OB	C	Memorandum of a loan of silver
1823	81691	Ad 2/6/33	NC	Pay list in silver; round type
1824	81692	Ha -/-/16	C	Loan of barley from a *naditu* out of the *našpakum*; seal on side
1825	81693	OB	C	Tag of a gi-pisan of Sippar
1826	81694	OB	C	Field rental
1827	81695	Si 23/9/7	C	Loan of barley to be repaid in month Šandutim
1828	81696	Ha -/4/30?	NC	Field rental
1829	81697	Ha -/-/35	C	Loan(?) of silver
1830	81698	NB 22/8/-	NC	Receipt for silver
1831	81699	Ha 6/5/38	NC	šu-ti-a for silver; seals
1832	81700	OB	C	Tag(?) for a Sumerian literary text: ù-mu-un-na ga-la-ra
1833	81701	Aṣ 18/1/16	C	mu-túm, *namḫartu* for oil; seals; round type

Bu 91-5-9,

1834	81702	Ad 23?/5/3	C	Memorandum concerning beer rations; seals
1835	81703	Ha -/-/11?	C	Loan of silver with interest
1836	81704	NB	NC	Letter
1837	81705	Sd 2/9/1	C	šu-ti-a for silver; seals; round type
1838	81706	OB	C	Memorandum concerning a dead ewe, su-si-ig; seals
1839	81707	Ha 16/1/2 (mu níg-si-sá ama-gi-kalam[ki])	C	Hire of a person; seals; *CT* 48 42 no. 94
1840	81708	Ha 24?/8/35?	NC	Memorandum concerning dates(?); seals
1841	81709	Ha -/-/1?	C	Field rental
1842	81710	Ha -/11/43	C	Loan of silver with interest
1843	81711	OB mu ugnim	C	Field rental
1844	81712	Ha -/-/41	C	House rental
1845	81713	OB	NC	Memorandum concerning silver to buy real estate; round type; late period
1846	81714	Aṣ 10+/3/"17+b"	F	Economic memorandum; round type
1847	81715	OB	NC	Field rental; early period
1848	81716	Aṣ 4?/5/"17+b"	C	mu-túm, *namḫartu*; round type; seals
1849	81717	Ha 16?/1/27	NC	Memorandum concerning a boatman; seals
1850	81718	OB	NC	Memorandum; obverse destroyed
1851	81719	OB	NC	Economic memorandum
1852	81720	Aṣ -/-/alan-a-ni ...	NC	Subject illegible; seals
1853	81721	Si -/-/7	C	Interest-free loan
1854	81722	Aṣ 16/4/"17+b"	C	Ration account; seals
1855	81723	OB	NC	Memorandum concerning small cattle
1856	81724	OB?	C	Short memorandum
1857	81725	OB	C	Economic memorandum
1858	81726	Si 1/1?/6	C	Field rental; seals
1859	81727	Ha 8/5?/27	C	šu-ti-a for silver; tag
1860	81728	Ha -/-/23	C	Memorandum concerning a garment
1861	81729	Ha 15/12/38	C	Memorandum concerning flour
1862	81730	OB	NC	mu-túm for silver(?); seals
1863	81731	OB	C	Memorandum concerning delivery of various minerals: na_4-im-ud-ud, esir ud-du, *u-ḫu-li*; seals
1864	81732	Ha 21/1/40	C	Repayment of a debt: *ṭuppum seḫtum, iliam ḫepe*; seals
1865	81733	Ad 26/6?/6?	C	Square docket; basketworker; seals
1866	81734	Ad 26/5/6	C	Square docket; basketworker; seals

Bu 91-5-9,

1867	81735	Sm 8/*ma-mi*/1	C	mu-túm of a-su-*il*, for ka igi *su-qí-ím*; seals
1868	81736	Ha -/6?/20	C	šu-ti-a for sesame(?); seals
1869	81737	Aş 25?/4/"17+b"	C	Issue of rations; seals
1870	81738	OB	NC	Loan for commission; seals
1871	81739	Ad 14/1/6	C	Square docket; four basketworkers; seals
1872	81740	Ae 2/4/"w"	NC	šu-ti-a for beer; seals
1873	81741	Ad 25/5/6	C	Docket for basketworker; seals
1874	81742	Ad 4/1/6	C	Docket for basketworker; seals
1875	81743	Ha 22/*e-lu-li*/40?	C	Interest-free temple loan of silver
1876	81744	Ad 4/1/6	C	Docket for basketworker; seals
1877	81745	Ad 20/5/6	C	Docket for basketworker; seals
1878	81746	Ad 26/5/6	C	Docket for basketworker; seals
1879	81747	Aş 4/12b/13	C	Administrative; record concerning earth removal work; seals
1880	81748	Ha -/9/28	C	Receipt for sesame oil; seals
1881	81749	Ad 26/5/6	C	Docket for basketworker; seals
1882	81750	Ha -/*sí-bu-tim*/13? (mu lugal urudu? GABA gub [...] a?-ki)	NC	Receipt for silver(?)
1883	81751	Aş 23/4/"17+b"	C	Ration account; seals
1884	81752	OB	C	Letter; *CT* 52 28; *AbB* 7 28
1885	81753	OB	C	Ration account; doodle design on reverse
1886	81754	Ha 21/11/40? (é-lam-mes!)	C	Receipt for sesame ; seals
1887	81755	Ha -/8/10?	NC	mu-túm, *namḫartu* for flour
1888	81756	Si 10/10/1?	C	Memorandum concerning grain paid to workers as wages; seals
1889	81757	OB	C	Payment of silver; seals
1890	81758	Si -/-/5 or Ha -/-/3	C	Loan of silver with interest; seals
1891	81759	Ae 29/3/"t"	C	Memorandum concerning return of a woman to her master's house; seals
1892	81760	Aş 28/4/"17+b"	C	Ration account; seals
1893	81761	Aş 27/12/16?	NC	Memorandum concerning sesame oil
1894	81762	OB	C	Issue of rations
1895	81763	Sm -/-/1?	C	mu-túm memorandum; seals
1896	81764	Ha -/-/39?	C	Loan of barley with interest
1897	81765	Ad 11/6/6	C	Docket for basketworker; seals
1898	81766	Si -/-/15	C	Loan of silver with interest

Bu 91-5-9,

1899	81767	Aş 8/5/-	C	Memorandum concerning some obligation; seals
1900	81768	OB	NC	Memorandum concerning reed objects; seals
1901	81769	Ha -/7/42	NC	Memorandum concerning flour; seals
1902	81770	OB	C	Memorandum concerning flour(?)
1903	81771	Si -/-/2	C	Economic docket; seals
1904	81772	Aş 6/7/16	C	Memorandum concerning reed objects; round type
1905	81773	Aş -/ezen. NE.NE/16	C	Receipt for barley
1906	81774	Si 10/8/7	C	Memorandum concerning barley
1907	81775	Ha -/12/43	F	Contract
1908	81776	Ha -/-/12	NC	Field rental
1909	81777	OB	C	Field rental; parts of case adhering
1910	81778	Kassite 4/10/4	C	Receipt for wool
1911	81779	OB	F	Memorandum
1912	81780	OB	NC	Memorandum concerning beer; seals
1913	81781	Aş 12/5/1 ("17+c")	NC	Memorandum concerning duḫ-a; seals
1914	81782	Aş 19/4/"17+b"	C	Memorandum concerning beer; seals
1915	81783	Aş 25?/4/"17+b"	C	Receipt for beer; seals
1916	81784	Aş -/-/13 or 15	NC	Harvest labour loan; seals
1917	81785	OB?	C	Memorandum or tag; seals
1918	81786	OB	C	Sale of an *atappum*
1919	81787	Aş 6/4/3?	C	mu-túm of barley; seals
1920	81788	Aş	F	Subject not apparent; seals
1921	81789	Ha 2?/2/36	C	Receipt for barley; seals
1922	81790	OB 18/12/-	C	Receipt for vegetables
1923	81791	OB	C	Economic memorandum
1924	81792	OB	C	Memorandum of a personal name
1925	81793	OB	NC	Memorandum concerning a field
1926	81794	OB 6/5/mu urudu-ki-lugal-gub	C	Square docket of a hired worker
1927	81795	OB	C	Memorandum concerning a deposit(?)
1928	81796	Si -/-/3 or 4	C	Field rental(?); parts of case adhering; seals
1929	81797	Ad 9?/6/6	NC	Docket for a basketworker; seals
1930	81798	Ad 2/6/6	C	Docket for a basketworker; seals
1931	81799	Aş -/10/15	NC	Memorandum concerning sheep; round type
1932	81800	Si	C	Sealed tag

Bu 91-5-9,

1933	81801	OB	C	Tag; seals only
1934	81802	Aş 19/4/"17+b"	C	Ration account; seals
1935	81803	NB	NC	Receipt
1936	81804	Si -/12b/20	F	Loan(?); seals
1937	81805	OB	F	mu-túm of garments and silver; seals; round type
1938	81806	Si -/-/2	C	Loan of silver
1939	81807	OB	C	Memorandum concerning a *maḫirtum* of bricks
1940	81808	Ha 24?/8/35	C	Two personal names
1941	81809	OB	C	Memorandum concerning flour and other things
1942	81810	Aş 18?/12/9	C	Memorandum concerning silver(?) for barley for the taverner; round type
1943	81811	NB	F	Receipt
1944	81812	OB	C	Memorandum concerning a deposit of stones; round type
1945	81813	Si -/-/2	C	Memorandum concerning silver
1946	81814	OB	C	Memorandum concerning *piḫu*
1947	81815	Aş 2/6/"17+b"	C	Memorandum concerning beer; seals; round type
1948	81816	OB	F	Loan(?) of silver for trading; seals
1949	81817	OB	NC	Receipt for barley; seals
1950	81818	Si -/-/9	C	Square tag; seals
1951	81819	Si -/-/9	C	Square tag; seals
1952	81820	Si -/-/23?	C	Receipt for gi-sa; seals
1953	81821	OB	C	Brief, one-line memorandum
1954	81822	OB	F	Subject not apparent
1955	81823	OB	NC	Memorandum
1956	81824	OB	C	Square tag; seals only
1957	81825	NB	NC	Receipt for dates or grain
1958	81826	OB	C	Memorandum
1959	81827	OB	C	Square tag; seals
1960	81828	Ha -/12/26?	C	Memorandum
1961	81829	OB	C	Tag; seals only
1962	81830	OB	C	Memorandum concerning copper
1963	81831	OB	C	Square tag concerning an ox; seals
1964	81832	Ha -/-/16	C	Receipt for barley
1965	81833	Aş 5/6?/-	NC	Receipt for beer; seals; round type
1966	81834	Ad -/-/24?	NC	Square tag; seals

Bu 91-5-9,

1967	81835	Aş 11/12b/13 or "17+ a" urudu-ki-lugal-gub	C	Earth removal contract to build a house; seals
1968	81836	OB	C	Square tag concerning an ox; seals
1969	81837	OB	C	Square tag concerning an ox; seals
1970	81838	Ha 16/8/35	C	Memorandum
1971	81839	Ha 6/ezen-an-na/12	C	Memorandum concerning a carpenter(?)
1972	81840	OB	C	Square tag concerning an ox; seals
1973	81841	OB	F	Square tag concerning duḫ(?); seals
1974	81842	OB	C	Square tag concerning an ox; seals
1975	81843	Aş 6/6/-	C	Memorandum concerning duḫ-a; seals; round type
1976	81844	OB -/5/-	F	Memorandum concerning brick-making
1977	81845	NB	NC	Receipt
1978	81846	OB	F	Memorandum
1979	81847	OB	C	Tag; seals only
1980	81848	Ad 28/5/6	C	Sealed tag; Weitemeyer, *Workers*, p. 59, 98
1981	81849	OB	C	Tag; seals only
1982	81850	OB	C	Tag; seals only
1983	81851	OB	C	Tag; seals only
1984	81852	OB	C	Tag; seals only
1985	81853	OB	C	Tag; seals only
1986	81854	OB	C	Tag; seals only
1987	81855	OB 4/11/-	C	Sealed tag; Weitemeyer, *Workers*, p. 60, 98
1988	81856	OB	C	Tag; seals only
1989	81857	OB	C	Tag; seals only
1990	81858	OB	C	Tag; seals only
1991	81859	OB	C	Tag; seals only
1992	81860	OB	C	Tag; seals only
1993	81861	OB	C	Tag; seals only
1994	81862	OB	C	Tag; seals only
1995	81863	Si 10/7/3 or 4	C	Sealed tag; Weitemeyer, *Workers*, p. 59, 98
1996	81864	Ha 3/2/31	C	Docket for a harvest worker; seals
1997	81865	OB	C	Tag; seals only
1998	81866	OB	C	Tag; seals only
1999	81867	OB	C	Tag; seals only
2000	81868	OB	F	Tag; seals only
2001	81869	OB	C	Tag; seals only

Bu 91-5-9,

2002	81870	OB	C	Tag; seals only
2003	81871	OB -/*e-lu-lí*/?	C	Hollow prism tag; seals
2004	81872	Aṣ 12?/7/9	C	Plum-shaped tag; barley
2005	81873	OB	C	Tag; seals only
2006	81874	OB 2/11/-	C	Sealed tag; Weitemeyer, *Workers*, p. 60, 98
2007	81875	OB	C	Tag; seals only
2008	81876	OB	C	Tag; seals only
2009	81877	OB	C	Tag; seals only
2010	81878	OB	C	Tag; seals only
2011	81879	OB	C	Tag; seals only
2012	81880	OB	C	Tag; seals only
2013	81881	OB	C	Tag; seals only
2014	81882	OB	NC	Tag; seals only
2015	81883	OB	C	Tag; seals only
2016	81884	OB	C	Tag; seals only
2017	81885	Ad 15/5/6	C	Sealed tag; Weitemeyer, *Workers*, p. 59, 98
2018	81886	OB	C	Tag; seals only
2019	81887	OB	C	Tag; seals only
2020	81888	OB	C	Tag; seals only
2021	81889	Si 10/12/2	C	Sealed tag; Weitemeyer, *Workers*, p. 59, 98
2022	81890	Si 10?/2/27	C	Docket for a harvest worker; *RA* 63 57 n. 2
2023	81891	OB	C	Tag; seals only
2024	81892	OB	C	Tag; seals only
2025	81893	OB	C	Tag; seals only
2026	81894	OB	C	Tag; seals only
2027	81895	Ha 2/2/8	C	Sealed tag; Weitemeyer, *Workers*, p. 58, 97
2028	81896	OB	C	Tag; seals only
2029	81897	OB	C	Tag; seals only
2030	81898	OB	C	Tag; seals only
2031	81899	OB	C	Tag; seals only
2032	81900	OB	C	Tag; seals only
2033	81901	OB	C	Tag; seals only
2034	81902	OB	C	Tag; seals only
2035	81903	OB	C	Tag; seals only
2036	81904	OB	C	Tag; seals only

Bu 91-5-9,

2037	81905	OB	C	Tag; seals only
2038	81906	OB	C	Tag; seals only
2039	81907	OB	C	Tag; seals only
2040	81908	OB	C	Tag; seals only
2041	81909	OB 28/6/-	C	Sealed tag; Weitemeyer, *Workers*, p. 14, 87
2042	81910	OB	C	Tag; seals only
2043	81911	OB	C	Tag; seals only
2044	81912	OB	C	Tag; seals only
2045	81913	OB 28/8/-	C	Sealed tag; Weitemeyer, *Workers*, p. 18, 90
2046	81914	OB	C	Tag; seals only
2047	81915	OB	C	Tag; seals only
2048	81916	OB 14/1/?	C	Sealed tag; Weitemeyer, *Workers*, p. 57, 97
2049	81917	OB	C	Tag; seals only
2050	81918	OB	C	Tag; seals only
2051	81919	OB	C	Tag; seals only
2052	81920	OB	C	Tag; seals only
2053	81921	OB	C	Tag; seals only
2054	81922	OB	C	Docket; five *ma-ka-tum*(?); seals
2055	81923	OB	C	Tag; seals only
2056	81924	OB	C	Tag; seals only
2057	81925	OB	C	Tag; seals only
2058	81926	OB	C	Tag; seals only
2059	81927	OB	C	Docket for a harvest worker; seals
2060	81928	OB	C	Tag; seals only
2061	81929	OB	C	Tag; seals only
2062	81930	OB 22/7/-	C	Sealed tag; Weitemeyer, *Workers*, p. 16, 88
2063	81931	OB	C	Tag; seals only
2064	81932	OB	C	Tag; seals only
2065	81933	OB	C	Tag; seals only
2066	81934	Ha 7/1/27	C	Sealed tag; Weitemeyer, *Workers*, p. 54, 96
2067	81935	Si 13/3/28	C	Harvest labour(?) docket; seals; *RA* 63 57 n. 2
2068	81936	OB	C	Tag; seals only
2069	81937	OB	C	Tag; seals only
2070	81938	OB	C	Tag; seals only

Bu 91-5-9,

2071	81939	OB 4/9/-	C	Sealed tag; Weitemeyer, *Workers*, p. 19, 90
2072	81940	OB	C	Tag; seals only
2073	81941	OB	NC	Tag; seals only
2074	81942	OB	NC	Tag; seals only
2075	81943	OB	C	Tag; seals only
2076	81944	OB	C	Tag; seals only
2077	81945	OB	C	Tag; seals only
2078	81946	OB 28?/8/-	C	Sealed tag; Weitemeyer, *Workers*, p. 18, 90
2079	81947	OB	C	Sealed tag; Weitemeyer, *Workers*, p. 71
2080	81948	OB	C	Sealed tag; Weitemeyer, *Workers*, p. 59, 98
2081	81949	OB	NC	Sealed tag; Weitemeyer, *Workers*, p. 69
2082	81950	OB	C	Sealed tag; Weitemeyer, *Workers*, p. 69
2083	81951	OB 1/7/-	C	Sealed tag; Weitemeyer, *Workers*, p. 14, 87
2084	81952	OB	C	Tag; seals only
2085	81953	Ha 19/1/35	C	Sealed tag; Weitemeyer, *Workers*, p. 58, 97
2086	81954	Ha 6/2/34	C	Sealed tag; Weitemeyer, *Workers*, p. 58, 98
2087	81955	OB	C	Tag; seals only
2088	81956	OB	F	Tag; seals only
2089	81957	OB	C	Tag; seals only
2090	81958	OB	C	Docket for harvest labour (*ḫa-mi-mu*); seals
2091	81959	OB	NC	Tag; seals only
2092	81960	OB	C	Docket for hired(?) labour; seals
2093	81961	Ad -/5/26	C	Square docket; basketworkers; seals
2094	81962	OB	C	Tag; seals only
2095	81963	OAss?	C	Tag; round; UD.DU Ì-*lí-sa-lik* ME. AN! TAM.ḪAR; seals
2096	81964	OB	C	Tag of éš.kar of five *ma-ka-tum* x; seals
2097	81965	OB	C	Tag; seals only
2098	81966	OB	C	Tag; seals only
2099	81967	OB	C	Tag; seals only
2100	81968	OB	C	Tag; seals only
2101	81969	OB	C	Tag; seals only
2102	81970	OB	C	Tag; seals and name ᵈSin-il; Weitemeyer, *Workers*, p. 60, 117

Bu 91-5-9,

2103	81971	OB 29/6/-	C	Sealed tag; Weitemeyer, *Workers*, p. 14, 87
2104	81972	OB	C	Tag; seals only
2105	81973	OB	C	Tag; seals only
2106	81974	OB 15/6/-	C	Sealed tag; Weitemeyer, *Workers*, p. 13, 86
2107	81975	OB	C	Tag; seals only
2108	81976	OB	C	Tag; seals only
2109	81977	Ha -/-/16	C	Docket; seals
2110	81978	OB	C	Tag; seals only
2111	81979	OB	F	Sealed tag; Weitemeyer, *Workers*, p. 19, 90
2112	81980	OB	C	Tag; seals only
2113	81981	OB	C	Tag of éš-kar of five *ma-ka-tum* x; seals
2114	81982	OB	C	Tag; seals only
2115	81983	OB	C	Tag; seals only
2116	81984	OB	C	Tag; seals only
2117	81985	OB 25/6/-	C	Sealed tag; Weitemeyer, *Workers*, p. 13, 86
2118	81986	OB	C	Tag; seals only
2119	81987	OB	C	Tag; seals only
2120	81988	OB	C	Tag; seals only
2121	81989	OB	C	Tag; seals only
2122	81990	OB	C	Tag; seals only
2123	81991	OB	C	Tag; seals only
2124	81992	OB	C	Tag; seals only
2125	81993	OB	C	Tag; seals only
2126	81994	OB	C	Tag; seals only
2127	81995	OB	C	Tag; seals only
2128	81996	OB	C	Tag; seals only
2129	81997	OB 4/9/-	C	Sealed tag; Weitemeyer, *Workers*, p. 18, 90
2130	81998	OB -/-/mu-ús-sa	C	Tag about oxen; seals
2131	81999	OB	C	Tag; seals only
2132	82000	OB 30/6/-	C	Sealed tag; Weitemeyer, *Workers*, p. 14, 87
2133	82001	Ha 11/7/36	C	Sealed tag; Weitemeyer, *Workers*, p. 54, 96
2134	82002	OB	C	Tag; seals only
2135	82003	OB 4?/1/?	C	Sealed tag; Weitemeyer, *Workers*, p. 56, 97

Bu 91-5-9,

2136	82004	OB	C	Tag; seals only
2137	82005	OB	C	Tag; seals only
2138	82006	OB	C	Tag; seals only
2139	82007	OB	C	Tag; seals only
2140	82008	OB	C	Tag; seals only
2141	82009	OB	C	Tag; seals only
2142	82010	OB	C	Tag; seals only
2143	82011	OB	C	Tag; seals only
2144	82012	OB 9/8/-	C	Sealed tag; Weitemeyer, *Workers*, p. 17, 89
2145	82013	OB 3/1/?	C	Sealed tag; Weitemeyer, *Workers*, p. 57, 97
2146	82014	OB	C	Tag; seals only
2147	82015	OB	C	Tag; seals only
2148	82016	OB	C	Tag; seals only
2149	82017	Ha -/-/16	C	Docket for boat(?) workers; cf. Bu 91-5-9, 2109 (=BM 81977); seals
2150	82018	OB 10/1/?	C	Sealed tag; Weitemeyer, *Workers*, p. 56, 97
2151	82019	OB	C	Docket for oxen; seals
2152	82020	OB	C	Tag; seals only
2153	82021	OB	C	Tag; seals only
2154	82022	OB	C	Tag; seals only
2155	82023	OB	C	Tag; seals only
2156	82024	OB	C	Tag; seals only
2157	82025	OB	C	Tag; seals only
2158	82026	OB	C	Tag; seals only
2159	82027	OB	C	Tag; seals only
2160	82028	OB	C	Tag; seals only
2161	82029	Ha 12/8/27	C	Tag for reed objects
2162	82030	Ha 13/8/27	C	Tag for reed objects
2163	82031	Ha 16 or 26/8/27	C	Tag for reed objects
2164	82032	Ha 22/8/27	C	Tag for reed objects
2165	82033	Ha 14/8/27	C	Tag for reed objects
2166	82034	Ha 20/8/27	C	Tag for reed objects
2167	82035	OB	C	Tag about sesame oil
2168	82036	Ha 19/8/27	C	Tag about reed objects
2169	82037	Ha 21/8/27	C	Tag about reed objects
2170	82038		C	Round lump; no inscriptions; no seals
2171	82039	OB	F	Content not apparent

Bu 91-5-9,

2172A	92636	Sumulael -/-/29?	C	Real estate sale; *CT* 8 44b
2172B	92636A	Sumulael	NC	Case of previous; seals
2173A	92637	Sm -/-/16?	C	Sale of a slave-girl; *CT* 8 45a
2173B	92637A	Sm	NC	Case of previous; seals
2174A	92638	Ha	C	Real estate sale; *CT* 2 42
2174B	92638A	Ha	F	Case of previous; seals
2175A	82040	Si 21/3/25	C	Lawsuit over responsibility for *igisu*-taxes; *CT* 2 43
2175B	82041	Si -/-/25	F	Case of previous
2176A	92639	OB	C	Marriage contract; *CT* 2 44
2176B	92639A	OB	NC	Case of previous
2177A	92640	Sumulael	C	Lawsuit over a real estate sale; *CT* 6 42a
2177B	92640A	Sumulael	F	Case of previous; seals
2178A	82042	Ha -/9/15	C	Lawsuit over a real estate sale; *CT* 2 45
2178B	82043	OB	NC	Case of previous; seals
2179	82044	Si -/4/2	NC	Bequest of the estate of a *naditu*; seals; case unopened; *CT* 8 46
2180	82045	Sm	C	Gift of real estate in the *gagum*; seals; case unopened; Waterman, *BusDoc* 24
2181	82046	Sm -/-/14?	C	Lawsuit between a dead man's family and his business partner; *CT* 2 46
2182	82047	OB	C	Lawsuit over the inheritance of an adopted daughter; *CT* 2 47
2183	82048	AS	C	Manumission of slaves with maintenance contract; seals; case unopened; *CT* 8 29a
2184	82049	OB -/-/mu NÍG Bu-un-taḫ-un-i-la	C	Lawsuit over real estate; oath by Sumulael and Buntaḫunila; Waterman, *BusDoc* 31
2184A	82050	OB -/-/mu NÍG Bu-un-taḫ-un-i-la	C	Case of previous; seals; *CT* 45 1 no. 1 Waterman, *BusDoc* pp. 134-135
2185	82051		C	Letter; *CT* 2 48; *AbB* 1 86
2186	82052	Sumulael	C	Lawsuit concerning real estate
2186A	82052A	Sumulael	C	Case of previous; seals; *CT* 8 28a
2187	82053	OB	C	Letter; *CT* 4 24; *AbB* 2 92
2188	82054	Sumulael	C	Adoption contract; *CT* 4 42a
2189	82055	Sabium -/*ti-ru-um*!/11	C	Lawsuit over a bequest; Waterman, *BusDoc* 22
2189A	82056	Sabium -/*ti-ru-um*!/11	C	Case of previous; seals; Waterman, *BusDoc* 23 and pp. 134-135
2190	82057	Sm	C	Lawsuit over a real estate sale

Bu 91-5-9,

2190A	82057A	Sm	NC	Case of previous; seals; *CT* 8 45b
2191	92641	AS	C	Real estate sale; *CT* 6 43
2192	92642	Ha 30/1/4	C	Real estate sale; *CT* 8 18b
2193	92643	Sabium -/6/14	C	Lawsuit over real estate; *CT* 8 42a
2194	82058	OB	C	Letter; *CT* 2 49; *AbB* 2 87
2195	82059	OB	C	Account of silver; *CT* 8 42d
2196	92644	Ha	C	Sale of a slave-girl and an ox; *CT* 8 35b
2196A	92644A	Ha	C	Case of previous; seals
2197	82060	OB	C	Letter; *CT* 52 5; *AbB* 7 5
2198	82061	Ha 11/11/14	C	Loan of silver with interest; seals; case unopened
2199	82062	Ha or Si 15/6/mu urudu-ki-lugal-gub-ba	C	Date culture contract; seals; case unopened; *CT* 48 49 no. 114
2200	82063	Ha 5/12/32	C	Field rental; seals; case unopened
2201	82064	Ha -/-/13	C	Voiding of a lost tablet in connection with a royal *ṣimdatum*; *CT* 48 8 no. 15; *AS* 16 244
2201A	82064A	Ha -/-/13	C	Case of previous; seals; *CT* 48 8 no. 15
2202	82065	Si 1/10/4	C	Rental of an é ganba; seals; case unopened
2203	82066	Si -/-/35?	NC	Loan of barley with interest; tablet in case; seals
2204	82067	OB	C	Letter; *CT* 52 33; *AbB* 7 33
2204A	82067A	OB	C	Case of previous; seals; *CT* 52 33; *AbB* 7 33
2205	82068	Ha -/-/17	C	Field rental; seals; case unopened
2206	82069	Si 16/1/7	C	Hire of a person; seals; case unopened
2207	82070	OB	C	Rental of a *miršum* and *ḫurpatum*, payment in silver and *buqlum* in month Kinunu
2207A	82070A	Ha -/-/14	C	Case of previous; seals
2208	82071	Si -/-/3	C	Field rental; seals; case unopened
2209	82072	Ad 13/11/mu alan-a-ni	C	Note of obligation for silver; seals
2210	82073	Ha -/-/40	C	Rental of a *rugbum*
2210A	82074	Ha -/-/40	C	Case of previous
2211	82075	Ha 28/11/34	C	Receipt for delivery of bricks; seals; case unopened
2212	82076	OB	F	Bequest
2213	82077	OB	C	Field rental; early period
2213A	82078	OB	NC	Case of previous; seals
2214	82079	OB	C	Field rental

Bu 91-5-9,

2214A	82080	OB	F	Case of previous; seals
2215	82081	OB	C	Loan of barley with interest
2215A	82082	Si -/-/31? (mu alan na_4 sìr x x x)	C	Case of previous; seals
2216	82083	Aṣ 1/10/11	C	Receipt for part of a wage; seals
2217	82084	Ha -/-/10 (mu ma-da ma-al-gi-a)	C	Field rental
2217A	82085	Ha -/-/10 (mu ma-da ma-al-gi-a)	C	Case of previous; seals
2218	82086	Si 20/3/4	C	Hire of a person
2218A	82087	Si -/3/-	NC	Case of previous; seals
2219	82088	Ha -/-/35	C	Field rental; seals; case unopened
2220	82089	OB	C	Field rental
2220A	82090	OB	F	Case of previous; seals
2221	82091	OB -/-/mu SI SI *Bu-ru-da*[ki]	C	Hire of a person; *CT* 48 35 no. 73
2221A	82091A	OB -/-/mu URUDU?-NIM?-tu	C	Case of previous; seals
2222	82092	Ha -/-/42	NC	Hire of a person; seals; tablet in case
2223	82093	Si -/-/6	C	Date culture contract; seals; case unopened
2224	82094	Ad 10/10/21? (mu en? x la ib gu-xxxxx)	C	Loan of grain for seed corn; seals
2225	82095	OB	C	Field rental
2225A	82095A	Ha -/-/10	NC	Case of previous; seals
2226	82096	Si 25/11/4	C	Hire of a person; seals; case unopened
2227	82097	Ha -/-/40	C	Field rental; seals; case unopened
2228	82098	OB 10/10/... guškin	C	Loan of silver with interest; seals; case unopened
2229	82099	Ha -/-/18	C	House rental
2229A	82100	OB	F	Case of previous; seals
2230	82101	Ha -/-/16	C	House rental
2230A	82102	Ha -/-/16	C	Case of previous; seals
2231	82103	OB	C	Letter; *CT* 43 14 no. 34; *AbB* 1 34; pierced vertically
2232	82104	OB	C	Field rental; part of case adhering; seals
2233	82105	Ha -/-/16	C	Loan of barley, from *naditu*; seals; case unopened
2234	82106	Ha -/-/40	C	Field rental
2234A	82107	OB	F	Case of previous; seals
2235	82108	Ha -/3/34	NC	Note concerning a debt of silver; seals
2236	82109	Si -/-/2	C	Field rental

Bu 91-5-9,

2236A	82110	Si -/-/2	F	Case of previous
2237	82111	Sm 16/4/6?	NC	Note of an obligation of barley; tablet in case; seals
2238	82112	Si 30/7/25	NC	Loan of barley with interest; seals
2239	82113	OB	C	Field rental; numbers on edge
2239A	82114	Ha -/8/33	F	Case of previous; seals
2240	82115	Si 27?/1?/mu Si lugal-e	C	Rental of *bit rugbum*; seals; case unopened
2241	82116	Si -/-/3 or 4	C	Field rental; seals; case unopened
2242	82117	OB	NC	Loan(?) of silver; seals
2243	82118	Ad 28/5?/?	C	Receipt for wooden objects, parts of harness equipment; seals
2244	82119	Ha -/-/10	C	Loan of silver with interest; seals; case unopened
2245	82120	Ha -/-/40	C	Hire of a worker from month Elunum; seals; case unopened
2246	82121	Ha -/-/40	C	Field rental; seals; case unopened
2247	82122	Ha 29/ezen ᵈiškur/16	NC	Loan of barley; seals; tablet in case
2248	82123	Ha -/-/17	NC	Field rental; seals; tablet in case
2249	82124	Ha 1/4/36	C	Hire of a person
2249A	82125	Ha 1/4/36	F	Case of previous; seals
2250	82126	Ha -/-/15? (mu alan-bi-6-àm)	C	Field rental; case unopened
2251	82127	Ha -/-/35	C	Promissory note(?) to repay a loan; seals; case unopened
2252	82128	Ha -/-/21? (mu bàd *ša ba?-ṣú-um*)	C	House rental; seals; case unopened
2253	82129	Ha 25/12b/26 (mu bára-gal-gal ᵈutu iškur an šu du . . .)	NC	Rental of *rugbum*; seals; tablet in case
2254	82130	Ha -/-/42	NC	Loan of barley; ḫar-*ra*; seals; tablet in case
2255	82131	Ha -/8/10	C	Loan of barley with interest; tablet in case; seals; *sissiktu* impression
2256	82132	Ha -/11/16	C	Loan of barley from *našpakum* (*ú-ta-ar*); month Šaddutum
2256A	82132A	OB -/11/-	F	Case of previous; seals
2257	82133	Ha 11/*si-bu-tim*/31	NC	Subject not apparent; seals; tablet in case
2258	82134	Si 30/4/3	C	Field rental; seals; case unopened
2259	82135	OB	NC	Field rental; seals; tablet in case
2260	82136	Si -/-/5 (mu giš-gu-za x-ga in-nu-gál)	C	Field rental; seals; case unopened

Bu 91-5-9,

2261	82137	Ha -/-/42	NC	Field rental; *ana šiknim*; seals; tablet in case
2262	82138	Ha 1/11/27	C	Loan of silver; seals; case unopened
2263	82139	Ha -/-/27	C	Field rental; seals; case unopened
2264	82140	Ha -/*i-si-in* diškur/17	C	Free loan of barley; seals; case unopened
2265	82141	Ha -/-/16	C	Loan of barley from *našpakum*; seals; case unopened
2266	82142	OB	C	Loan(?)
2266A	82143	OB -/-/mu giš-gu-za ...	F	Case of previous; seals
2267	82144	Ha -/-/33	C	Memorandum concerning an obligation for sesame oil
2268	82145	Ae 13/4/"k"	C	Deposition before judges about herdsmen; *CT* 48 17 no. 32
2269	82146	OB	C	Receipt for barley
2270	82147	-/-/x x x-ta dUtu-en x	C	Docket for a basket worker; seals
2271	82148	Ha -/-/9 or 33	C	Loan of silver with interest; seals; case unopened
2272	82149	OB	C	Ration account
2273	82150	OB	NC	Field rental
2273A	82151	OB	F	Case of previous; seals
2274	82152	Ha -/-/42	C	Hire of a person; extra formulas; seals
2275	82153	Ad 11/7/mu Ad lugal-e	C	Hire of a person for one month with provision for extension; seals; *CT* 48 43 no. 95
2276	82154	Si -/ezen *a-bi*/3 or 4	C	Field rental; seals; case unopened
2277	82155	Ha -/11/10	C	Receipt for barley; seals; case unopened
2278	82156	Ad 8/3?/1	NC	Administrative text concerning silver in year Ae 28
2279	82157	Ha -/-/43	C	Rental of a *rugbum*; seals; case unopened
2280	82158	OB	NC	Account of various items
2281	82159	Si 21/3/19?	C	Receipt for malt; seals
2282	82160	OB 4/1/?	C	Receipt; seals
2283	82161	Ad -/-/5	C	Square tag for basketworkers; seals
2284	82162	Ad -/5/6	C	Square tag for basketworkers; seals
2285	82163	Ad 2/1/5	C	Square tag for basketworkers; seals
2286	82164	Si 22/11/19	C	Receipt by a su-si-ig for dead ewes; square tag; seals
2287	82165	Aṣ -/8/"17+d"	C	Loan(?) of a door ba-zi-za(?); seals
2288	82166	OB	C	Administrative; receipt
2289	82167	OB	C	Administrative; receipt for silver and barley

Bu 91-5-9,

2290	82168	Ha -/-/16	C	Loan of barley
2290A	82169	Ha -/-/16	F	Case of previous; seals
2291	82170	Si 20?/3/19	C	Administrative; receipt
2292	82171	OB 25/6/-	NC	Receipt for pitch(?); seals
2293	82172	OB	C	House rental
2294	82173	Ad -/1/6 (mu dUtu en-sig$_5$)	C	Square tag for basketworker; seals
2295	82174	Ha -/-/43?	NC	Memorandum concerning a debt of silver
2296	82175	Si -/-/8	C	Square tag for an ox; seals
2297	82176	Ha -/5/42	C	Free loan of silver
2298	82177	Aṣ 9/7/"17+b"	C	Loan of sesame; seals
2299	82178	OB	C	Field rental
2299A	82179	OB	F	Case of previous; seals
2300	82180	OB	C	Hire of a person
2300A	82181	OB	F	Case of previous; seals
2301	82182	Ha -/3/14	C	Field rental
2301A	82183	Ha -/3/14	F	Case of previous; seals
2302	82184	Ha 18?/11/39?	C	Loan of barley; ḫar-ra
2302A	82185	OB	F	Case of previous; seals
2303	82186	OB	C	Hire of a person
2303A	82187	OB	F	Case of previous; seals
2304	82188	Ha -/-/40	C	Field rental
2304A	82189	OB	F	Case of previous; seals
2305	82190	OB	C	Letter; *CT* 52 11; *AbB* 7 11
2306	82191	-/10/mu-us-sa ...	C	Loan of barley; seals; *sissiktu* impression
2307	82192	Si 20+/8/24	NC	Receipt for barley; seals
2308	82193	Ae 27/6/"o"	NC	Commission from a *naditu, marat šarrim*, for purchase of two dug*al-lu-ḫa-aš-ša-tum*; seals; *CT* 45 48 no. 112
2309	82194	Ha -/9/29	C	Field rental
2309A	82195	Ha -/9/29	F	Case of previous; seals
2310	82196	Si 1/2/3 or 4	C	Rental of a *rugbum*
2311	82197	Ae 12/7/"k"	C	Receipt for wages; seals
2312	82198	Ha 3/11?/18	C	Loan of barley with interest; seals; case unopened
2313	82199	OB	C	Letter; *CT* 52 52; *AbB* 7 52
2313A	82199A	OB	C	Case of previous; seals; *CT* 52 52; *AbB* 7 52
2314	82200	Ha -/6b/40	C	Loan of barley; ḫar-ra; seals

Bu 91-5-9,

2315	82201	OB	NC	Field rental; seals; tablet in case
2316	82202	Ha -/-/10	NC	Hire of a person; seals; tablet in case
2317	82203	Si 25/1/6	C	Memorandum of an obligation involving *ilkum*; seals; case unopened; *CT* 48 5 no. 9
2318	82204	OB	C	Field rental
2318A	82205	OB	F	Case of previous; seals
2319	82206	OB	C	House rental
2319A	82207	OB	F	Case of previous; seals
2320	82208	OB	NC	Field rental; seals; tablet in case
2321	82209	Ha -/-/38	C	Hire of a person; seals; case unopened
2322	82210	Si -/-/7	C	Hire of a person; cf. Bu 91-5-9, 2321 (= BM 82209); seals; case unopened
2323	82211	Aṣ 2?/6/"17+a"	C	Loan of silver from *naditu*, to buy(?) barley; cf. Bu 91-5-9, 2337 (= BM 82227); seals
2324	82212	Ha 1/11/28	C	Hire of a person from a *naditu*; tablet in case; *CT* 48 49 no. 115
2324A	82212A	Ha 1/11/28	C	Case of previous; seals; *CT* 48 49 no. 115
2325	82213	OB	C	Field rental
2325A	82214	OB	F	Case of previous; seals
2326	82215	Ha 8/*a-ia-rum*/16	C	Loan of barley; tablet in case; seals
2327	82216	Ha 22/11/16	C	Loan of barley from *naditu*; seals; case unopened
2328	82217	OB	NC	Field rental; seals; tablet in case
2329	82218	OB 2?/2?/-	C	Administrative; receipt for barley; seals
2330	82219	Si 10/2/2	C	Accounts of barley from various sources; seals; case unopened
2331	82220	Si -/-/15	NC	Field rental; seals; tablet in case
2332	82221	Sd -/1/4	NC	Settlement of account by two persons with the *sabum*; seals; *CT* 48 46 no. 106
2333	82222	OB 20/5/-	NC	Hire of a person; unusual stipulations; seals; tablet in case
2334	82223	OB	NC	Field rental
2334A	82224	OB	F	Case of previous; seals
2335	82225	OB	NC	Field rental; seals; tablet in case
2336	82226	OB	C	Field rental from a *naditu*; seals; case unopened
2337	82227	Ha -/-/20	C	Loan contract; *CT* 4 20c
2337A	82227A	Ha -/-/20	C	Case of previous; seals

Bu 91-5-9,

2338	82228	Ha 1/8/20 (mu gu-za [d]Iškur-ra)	C	House rental
2338A	82229	Ha 1/8/20 (mu gu-za [d]Iškur-ra)	C	Case of previous; seals
2339	82230	Ha -/-/41	C	Field rental; seals; case unopened
2340	82231	Ha -/ezen [d]iškur/17	NC	Loan of silver with interest; seals; tablet in case
2341	82232	Ha -/-/16	C	Loan of barley; seals; case unopened; *CT* 4 12b
2342	82233	Ha -/2/42	NC	Field rental; seals; tablet in case
2343	82234	Ha 21[?]/7/24	NC	Contract concerning dates; seals; tablet in case
2344	82235	OB	C	Field rental
2344A	82236	OB	F	Case of previous; seals
2345	82237	OB	NC	Field rental; seals; tablet in case
2346	82238	OB	NC	Account of debts; ki Sin
2346A	82239	OB	F	Case of previous; seals
2347	82240	Ad 25/10/30	NC	Administrative; dealing with large quantity of silver of the palace of Sippar-yaḫrurum in Ad 24-25; seals; *CT* 48 35 no. 72
2347A	82241	Ad 25/10/30	F	Case of previous; seals; *CT* 48 35 no. 72
2348	82242	Ha -/-/16	NC	Field rental; seals; tablet in case
2349	82243	Si 1/8/3	C	Field rental
2349A	82244	OB	F	Case of previous; seals
2350	82245	OB	C	Bequest(?)
2350A	82246	OB	F	Case of previous
2351	82247	Aṣ 1/8/12	C	House rental; seals
2352	82248	Ha -/-/10	C	Field rental
2352A	82249	Ha -/-/10	F	Case of previous; seals
2353	82250	Ha -/-/36	C	Rental of a *rugbum*; seals; case unopened
2354	82251	OB -/-/mu *Sa-am-si-* AN	NC	Free loan; seals; tablet in case
2355	82252	Aṣ 9/7[?]/-	NC	Receipt for wool; seals
2356	82253	OB	NC	Letter; *CT* 52 24; *AbB* 7 24
2357	82254	Ha 5/12/26	NC	Field rental; seals; case unopened
2358	82255	Ha 5 or 6/*sí-bu-tim*/18	C	Field rental; seals; case unopened
2359	82256	Ha -/-/20	C	Rental of *iku malum ú ru*[?]*-bu*(?); seals; case unopened
2360	82257	Ha -/-/15	C	Field rental; seals; case unopened
2361	82258	OB	NC	Loan of barley; seals; tablet in case
2362	82259	OB	C	Field rental

Bu 91-5-9,

2362A	82260	Si -/-/3	F	Case of previous; seals
2363	82261	Ha 5/5/14	C	Field rental
2363A	82262	Ha 5/5/14	NC	Case of previous
2364	82263	Ha 6/11/21	C	Hire of a person
2364A	82264	Ha 6/11/21	NC	Case of previous; seals
2365	82265	OB	C	Court certification of legal ownership of real estate; *CT* 48 14 no. 27
2365A	82265A	Sabium	NC	Case of previous; seals; *CT* 48 14 no. 27
2366	82266	Ha 1/2/32	NC	House rental; seals; tablet in case
2367	82267	Ha 22/2/32	C	Field rental; seals; case unopened
2368	82268	Sm -/-/13	NC	Loan of silver(?) with interest; seals; tablet in case
2369	82269	Ha 1/2/43	C	Field rental; seals; case unopened; *CT* 6 44a
2370	82270	Ha -/ᵈdumu-zi/42	C	Field rental; seals; case unopened
2371	82271	OB	C	Rental of *miršum* and *urpatum*
2371A	82271A	Ha 15/ezen ᵈiškur/11	C	Case of previous; seals; *sissiktu* impression
2372	82272	OB -/3/mu AN [...] lá-bi	NC	Field rental; seals; tablet in case; not Sd
2373	82273	Ha -/-/13	NC	Field rental; seals; case unopened; Waterman, *BusDoc* 12
2374	82274	Sm -/-/9	C	Loan of barley and silver; *CT* 48 34 no. 71; *AS* 16 pp. 240 and 245
2374A	82275	OB	NC	Case of previous; seals; *CT* 48 34 no. 71
2375	82276	OB	NC	Inheritance text; real estate
2375A	82277	OB	F	Case of previous(?); seals
2376	82278	Ha -/3/41	C	Rental of a field, slaves and animals from a *naditu*; seals; case unopened
2377	82279	-/-/8? *Aš-ta-ba-la*ᵏⁱ *A-píl-*ᵈ*Sin aṣ-ba-tu*	C	Šamaš loan of silver; *CT* 48 50 no. 117
2377A	82279A	-/-/8? *Aš-ta-ba-la*ᵏⁱ *A-píl-*ᵈ*Sin aṣ-ba-tu*	NC	Case of previous; seals
2378	82280	Iluma'ila	C	Real estate sale; exceptional seals; case unopened; oath by Iluma'ila (of Sippar); *CT* 8 38b
2379	82281	OB	NC	House rental
2379A+B	82282	Si -/-/21	F	Case of previous; seals
2380	82283	Si -/-/3	C	Field rental
2380A	82284	Si -/4?/3	NC	Case of previous; seals
2381	82285	OB	F	House rental
2381A	82286	OB	F	Case of previous; seals

Bu 91-5-9,

2382	82287	OB	NC	Loan of barley with interest
2382A	82288	OB 26/11/-	F	Case of previous; seals
2383	82289	OB	C	Contract concerning partition wall
2383A	82290	OB	F	Case of previous; seals
2384	82291	Si -/-/1?	NC	Hire of a person
2384A	82292	OB	F	Case of previous; seals
2385	82293	Ha -/-/41	C	House rental
2385A	82294	OB	F	Case of previous; seals
2386	82295	Ha -/-/31	C	Loan of barley with interest; month Nabrum
2386A	82296	Ha -/-/31	C	Case of previous; seals
2387	82297	OB	C	Hire of a person
2387A	82298	OB	F	Case of previous; seals
2388	82299	-/-/mu É-gal-la-tum[ki]/Bu-ru-un-da	C	Loan of silver from a *naditu*; *CT* 48 36 no. 74
2388A	82300	-/-/mu É-gal-la-tum[ki]/Bu-ru-un-da	F	Case of previous; seals; *CT* 48 36 no. 74
2389	82301	OB	C	Hire of a person
2389A	82302	-/-/mu giš-⌜gu-za⌝ [...]	F	Case of previous; seals
2390	82303	OB	C	Hire of a person
2390A	82304	OB	F	Case of previous; seals
2391	82305	OB	C	Field rental
2391A	82306	-/-/mu giš-g[u ...]	F	Case of previous; seals
2392	82307	Sm -/-/11	C	Loan of barley and silver
2392A	82308	Sm -/-/11	F	Case of previous; seals
2393	82309	Si -/-/4	C	Field rental
2393A	82310	OB	F	Case of previous; seals
2394	82311	-/-/mu TUŠ [d]Utu [d]Aya	C	Loan of barley with interest
2394A	82312	-/-/mu TUŠ [d]Utu [d]Aya	F	Case of previous; seals
2395	82313	OB	C	Field rental
2395A	82314	OB	F	Case of previous; seals
2396	82315	Si -/*a-ia-rum*/mu-ús-sa	C	Field rental
2396A	82316	Si 8/*a-ia-rum*/1? (mu-ús-sa SAḪAR? Ḫ[I.A?])	F	Case of previous; seals
2397	82317	OB	C	Hire of a person
2397A	82318	OB	F	Case of previous; seals

Bu 91-5-9,

2398	82319	Ha -/-/35	C	Field rental
2398A	82320	OB	F	Case of previous; seals
2399	82321	Ha 20/1/40?	C	Field rental
2399A	82322	OB	F	Case of previous; seals
2400	82323	OB	C	Contract for growing dates
2400A	82324	OB	F	Case of previous; seals
2401	82325	Ha -/-/17	C	Field rental
2401A	82326	Ha -/-/17	F	Case of previous
2402	82327	OB	NC	Field rental
2402A	82328	OB	F	Case of previous; seals
2403	82329	OB	C	Field rental
2403A	82330	OB	F	Case of previous; seals
2404	82331	Ha 4/*a-ia-rum*/24	C	Loan of barley with interest
2404A	82332	Ha 4/*a-ia-rum*/24	F	Case of previous; seals; *sissiktu* impression
2405	82333	Ha -/*a-ia-rum*/16	C	Loan of barley from *našpakum* of a *naditu*
2405A	82334	Ha -/-/16	C	Case of previous; Šamaš, Aya and Adad as witnesses; seals
2406	82335	OB	C	Field rental(?)
2406A	82336	OB	F	Case of previous; seals
2407	82337	Ha -/-/40?	C	House rental
2407A	82338	OB	F	Case of previous; seals
2408	82339	Ha -/-/40	C	Field rental
2408A	82340	Ha -/-/40	F	Case of previous; seals
2409	82341	OB	C	Hire of a person
2409A	82342	OB	F	Case of previous
2410	82343	OB	C	Field rental
2410A	82344	OB	F	Case of previous
2411	82345	Ha 6/11/3	C	Loan of silver, KA x x, with interest; month Šandutim
2411A	82346	Ha 6/11/3	F	Case of previous; seals
2412	82347	Ha 14/7/24	C	Contract for date culture; *CT* 48 43 no. 97
2412A	82348	Ha 14/7/24	F	Case of previous; seals
2413	82349	OB	C	Bequest in favor of a *naditu*; lukur níg ^{d}Utu
2413A	82350	Sumulael	F	Case of previous; seals
2414	82351	Si 26/8/30	F	Sale of real estate
2414A	82352	OB	F	Case of previous; seals

Bu 91-5-9,

2415	82353	Ad 4/5/29	F	Record of real estate transaction of *naditu*'s going back at least to Si 19
2415A	82354	OB	F	Case of previous; seals
2416	82355	AS -/-/1	C	Sale of é *burubalum*; *CT* 48 33 no. 68
2416A	82356	OB	F	Case of previous; seals
2417+ 2417 A+B	82357+ 82358	Si	NC	Real estate(?) sale (*naditu*); payment with ring; part of case adhering
2417A+B	82358	Joined to Bu 91-5-9, 2417 (= BM 82357)		
2418	82359	OB	C	Bequest to a *naditu* and appointment of an heir
2418A	82360	OB	F	Case of previous; seals
2419	82361	Sm	NC	Bequest of land
2419A	82362	OB	F	Case of previous; seals
2420	82363	OB	C	Letter; *CT* 52 20; *AbB* 7 20
2420A	82364	OB	NC	Case of previous; *CT* 52 20; *AbB* 7 20
2421	92645	AS -/-/2	C	Harvest loan; *CT* 6 44b
2421A	92645A	AS -/-/2	C	Case of previous; seals
2422	82365	OB	C	Letter; *CT* 52 156; *AbB* 7 156
2422A+ 2422B	82366+ 82367	OB	F	Case of previous; seals; *CT* 52 156; *AbB* 7 156; cf. Bu 91-5-9, 5793 (= BM 80441)
2422B	82367	Joined to Bu 91-5-9, 2422A (= BM 82366)		
2423	82368	OB	C	Field rental
2423A	82369	OB	F	Case of previous; seals
2424	92646	Ha -/-/40	C	Hire of a person
2424A	92646A	Ha -/-/40	C	Case of previous
2425	82370	Ha 10/11/30	C	Loan to be repaid by harvest labour; *ṣimdat šarrim*; *CT* 6 44c
2425A	82371	Ha -/11/30	NC	Case of previous; seals
2426	82372	Ha -/-/16	C	Loan of silver and barley by Amat-Šamaš (probably a *naditu*)
2426A	82373	OB	F	Case of previous; seals
2427	92647	Ha 14/8/30	C	Field rental
2427A	92647A	Ha 14/8/30	C	Case of previous; seals
2428	92648	Si 27/1/6	C	Field rental
2428A	92648A	Si 27/1/6	F	Case of previous; seals
2429	82374	OB	NC	Field rental
2429A	82375	OB	F	Case of previous; seals
2430	82376	Ha -/9/14 or 17	NC	Field rental
2430A	82377	OB	F	Case (of previous?); seals
2431	82378	OB	C	Field rental

Bu 91-5-9,

2431A	82379	Si -/-/25? (mu alan é-sag-íl)	NC	Case of previous; seals
2432	82380	OB	F	Estate division(?); early period
2432A	82381	OB	F	Case of previous
2433	82382	OB	F	Real estate contract
2433A	82383	Si 1/1/12	F	Case of previous
2434	82384	Ha -/-/21? (mu bàd uru *ša*? *ba*?-*ṣum*ki)	C	Exchange(?) agreement
2434A	82385	OB	F	Case of previous; seals
2435	82386	OB	C	Field rental
2435A	82387	OB	F	Case of previous; seals
2436	82388	OB	C	Letter; *CT* 52 186; *AbB* 7 186
2436A	82389	OB	F	Case of previous; seals; *CT* 52 186; *AbB* 7 186
2437	82390	Ha -/2(gú-si)?/38	C	Field rental
2437A	82391	Ha 25?/2(gú-si)?/38	F	Case of previous; seals
2438A	82392	Sm	NC	Real estate sale; seals; tablet in case
2439	92649	Immerum	C	Real estate sale; *CT* 8 47
2439A	92649A	Immerum	C	Case of previous; seals
2440	92650	Ha 25/9/30	C	Sale of a field by and to a *naditu*
2440A	92650A	Ha 25/9/30	C	Case of previous; seals
2441	92651	AS	C	Sale of a field to a *naditu*
2441A	92651A	AS	F	Case of previous; seals
2442	82393	Ha -/-/9	C	Nursing contract for a *šilip remim* child; tablet in case; *CT* 48 34 no. 70
2442A	82393A	OB	NC	Case of previous; seals; *CT* 48 34 no. 70
2443	92653	Sm	C	Sale of a field to a *naditu*
2443A	92653A	Sm	NC	Case of previous; seals
2444	92667	Si 11/12/2	C	Lawsuit over real estate
2444A	92667A	Si 11/12/2	C	Case of previous; seals; *CT* 8 24b
2445A	82394	Sm	C	Bequest; seals; case unopened
2446	82395	Si 13/4/7	C	Marriage agreement involving a slave as bridegroom; tablet in case; *CT* 48 26 no. 53
2446A	82395A	OB	F	Case of previous; seals; *CT* 38 26 no. 53
2447A	82396	Si 5/10/7	C	Loan of barley from a *naditu*; seals; case unopened
2448	82397	OB	C	Marriage contract for a subordinate wife; Waterman, *BusDoc* 39
2448A	82398	OB	NC	Case of previous; seals; Waterman, *BusDoc* 39

Bu 91-5-9,

2449A	82399	Ha -/-/31	NC	Inheritance text; seals; tablet in case
2450A	82400	Sm -/-/6	C	Field rental; seals; case unopened
2451	92654	Sm	C	Purchase of a slave from a *naditu*
2451A	92654A	Sm	NC	Case of previous; seals
2452A	82401	Ha -/-/8	NC	Field sale; many buyers; seals; tablet in case
2453A	82402	Ha	C	Field sale(?); seals; case unopened
2454A	82403	OB	NC	Bequest of real estate; seals; tablet in case
2455	92655	Sm -/4/8	C	Contract for loan of silver and hire of slaves; *CT* 8 42b
2455A	92655A	Sm -/4/8	C	Case of previous; seals
2456	82404	OB	C	Lawsuit; Waterman, *BusDoc* 13
2456A	82405	OB	F	Case of previous
2457	82406	Si x+6/12/14	C	Marriage contract; *CT* 48 25 no. 51
2457A	82407	OB	F	Case of previous; seals
2458	82408	Si 6/1/3	C	Lawsuit over real estate; *CT* 8 6b
2458A	82409	OB	F	Case of previous; seals
2459	92676	Si 1/12/10	C	Purchase of a field by and from a *naditu*
2459A	92676A	OB	F	Case of previous; seals
2460	82410	Ha -/8/28	C	Contract for the maintenance of an adopted daughter; *CT* 8 12c
2460A	82411	Ha -/8/28	NC	Case of previous; seals
2461	82412	-/-/mu x gú [íd]Idigna [m]*A-píl-Sin* šu bi-in-zi	C	Adoption and designation as heir of a person (by a *naditu*?); *CT* 45 45 no. 101
2461A	82413	OB	NC	Case of previous; seals
2462	82414	AS	C	Real estate sale; *CT* 6 7b
2462A	82415	OB	F	Case of previous; seals
2463	92656	Sabium -/ezen-[d]iškur/12	C	Lawsuit over real estate; *CT* 2 50
2463A	92656A	Sabium -/-/12	C	Case of previous; seals
2464	82416	Ha -/-/9	NC	Real estate sale; *CT* 6 45
2464A	82417	Ha	F	Case of previous; seals
2465	82418	Ha -/-/41	C	Gift of a mill-stone; *CT* 8 43b
2465A	82419	Ha -/-/41	F	Case of previous; seals
2466	82420	Sm -/-/17	C	Declaration (by a debtor?) allowing no creditor to raise claim against deponent's family for debts contracted or to be contracted; *CT* 45 8 no. 15

Bu 91-5-9,

2466A	82421	Sm -/-/17	NC	Case of previous; seals
2467	82422	Ha 28/11/1	C	Field sale; *CT* 8 48b; for case see Bu 91-5-9, 2475A (= BM 82433)
2467A	82423	OB	F	Case of Bu 91-5-9, 2475 (= BM 82432); seals; *CT* 48 29 no. 59
2468	92657	Sm	C	Purchase of a house by a *naditu* from Šamaš and Aya
2468A	92657A	Sm	NC	Case of previous; enormous number of witnesses, at least 29; 20 seals
2469	82424	AS	C	Designation of an heir in return for support; *CT* 48 no. 29
2469A	82424A	OB	NC	Case of previous; seals
2470	92658	Sm	C	Inheritance of a field by a *naditu*; *CT* 6 42b
2470A	92658A	Sm	C	Case of previous; seals
2471	82425	OB	C	Real estate contract; inheritance(?)
2471A	82425A	OB	NC	Case of previous; seals
2472	82426	OB	NC	Sale of a field; oath, king's name lost
2472A	82427	Ha 28/7?/11	NC	Case of Bu 91-5-9, 2480 (=BM 82438); seals
2473	82428	Sabium	C	Lawsuit over real estate; *CT* 4 26b
2473A	82429	OB	NC	Case of previous; seals
2474	82430	Ha -/12/24	C	Lawsuit concerning a slave girl; *CT* 6 47b
2474A	82431	Ha 20/12/24	NC	Case of previous; seals; *sissiktu* impression
2475	82432	AS	C	Designation of heir in return for support; *CT* 48 29 no. 59; for case, see Bu 91-5-9, 2467A (= 82423)
2475A	82433	OB	F	Case of Bu 91-5-9, 2467 (= BM 82422)
2476	82434	Ha -/-/18	C	Legal proceeding in Ebabbar over the property inheritance of *naditu*s; tablet in case; seals; *CT* 48 5 no. 8
2476A	82434A	Ha -/-/18	NC	Case of previous; seals; *CT* 48 5 no. 8
2477A	82435	AS -/*a-ia-ri-im*/13?	NC	Real estate sale; seals; case unopened; *CT* 6 46
2478	82436	OB	C	Marriage contract; *CT* 48 25 no. 52
2478A	82436A	Ha -/-/4? (mu bád ši x [...][ki])	C	Case of previouis; seals; *CT* 48 25 no. 52
2479	82437	OB -/-/mu ká-gal [d]Suen-*ba-ni ú-di-šu-ú*	C C	Record of oath taken before the *šurin*(*n*)*um* of Šamaš before execution of a *kunuk la baqarim*; oath by Immerum and Su-mu-le-el; Kraus *Fs* 245-257

Bu 91-5-9,

2479A	82437A	OB -/-/mu ká-gal [d]Suen-*ba-ni Puzur-* [d]SAG.KUD *i-pu-šu-ú*	NC	Case of previous; seals; Kraus *Fs* 245-257
2480	82438	Ha-/-/11	C	Adoption contract; *CT* 8 48a; for case, see Bu 91-5-9, 2472A (= BM 82427)
2480A	82439	Sumulael	F	Case; cf. Bu 91-5-9, 2499 (= BM 82472); land sale; seals; *CT* 48 30 no. 31
2481	82440	OB	F	Large bequest to a woman Beltani (a *naditu*?) and appointment of her heir
2481A	82441	Ha	F	Case of previous; seals
2482	82442	Si 10/9/13	C	Purchase of a field by a *naditu*
2482A	82443	Si 10/9/13	NC	Case of previous
2483	82444	Sm	C	Lawsuit over real and movable property; Waterman, *BusDoc* 34
2483A	82445	Sm	F	Case of previous; seals; Waterman, *BusDoc* 35
2484	82446	AS -/-/mu *A-pil-Sin ú-ra-am-mi-ku*	C	Adoption contract; *CT* 8 49b
2484A	82447	AS -/-/mu *A-pil-Sin ú-ga-li-bu*	F	Case of previous; extraordinary seals
2485	92659	Si -/9/-	NC	Division of an estate; *CT* 6 31b
2485A	92659A	Si	F	Case of previous; seals
2486	82448	Sabium -/*ti-ri-im*/10	C	Lawsuit over a woman's inheritance; *CT* 6 47a
2486A	82449	Sabium 8/*ti-ru-um*/10	NC	Case of previous; seals
2487	82450	OB Immerum	NC	Division of an estate; Waterman, *BusDoc* 14
2487A	82451	OB	F	Case of previous; seals; Waterman, *BusDoc* 14
2488	82452	Si 14/7/8	F	Contract concerning large items of an estate
2488A	82453	OB	F	Case of previous; seals
2489	82454	AS	C	Adoption contract; *CT* 8 49a
2489A	82455	OB	F	Case of previous; seals
2490	82456	AS	C	Exchange of real estate; *CT* 8 31b
2490A	82457	OB	F	Case of previous; seals
2491	82458	Ha 20/4/2	NC	Marriage agreement stipulating support of mother-in-law by daughter-in-law; *CT* 48 24 no. 49
2491A	82459	OB	F	Case of previous; seals
2492	82460	Sm	C	Real estate sale; *CT* 8 39b
2492A	82461	Sm -/-/1[?] (mu Sm *a-na* é *a-bi-šu i-ru-bu*)	F	Case of previous; seals

Bu 91-5-9,

2493	82462	OB -/-/mu *ša* bàd *ga-gi-im im-me-ru-um i-pu-šu*	C	Loan of silver, with a field given as security, interest payable in barley; Waterman, *BusDoc* 37
2493A	82463	OB -/-/mu *ša* bàd *ga-gi-im im-me-ru-um i-pu-šu*	F	Case of previous; seals; Waterman, *BusDoc* 37
2494	82464	Si	NC	Sale of threshing floor
2494A	82465	OB	F	Case of previous; seals
2495	82466	OB	C	Bequest of real estate with maintenance contract; Waterman, *BusDoc* 25
2495A	82467	OB	F	Case of previous; seals
2496	82468	OB	F	Sale of a house in the *gagum*
2496A	82469	Ha	F	Case of previous; witnesses; Šamaš officials and *naditus*; seals
2497	82470	AS	C	Lawsuit, involving the emblem of Šamaš; Waterman, *BusDoc* 36
2497A	82471	OB	F	Case of previous; seals; Waterman, *BusDoc* 36
2498	92660	AS 29/*e-lu-nim*/1	C	Field rental; *CT* 6 48a
2498A	92660A	AS 29/*e-lu-nim*/1	NC	Case of previous; seals
2499	82472	Sumulael	C	Real estate sale; *CT* 8 44a; for case, see Bu 91-5-9, 2480A (= BM 82439)
2499A	82473	OB	F	Case, *not* of previous; of a sale contract
2500	82474	Sm	C	Real estate sale; Waterman, *BusDoc* 40
2500A	82475	OB	F	Case of previous; seals
2501	82476	Si 10/6/9	C	Sale of a slavewoman, described as a *kazirtum*; *CT* 48 14 no. 28
2501A	82477	Si 10/6/9	F	Case of previous; seals
2502	92661	Ha -/-/1	C	Lawsuit over a real estate sale; *CT* 6 49a
2502A	92661A	Ha 5/11/1	C	Case of previous; seals
2502B	82478	Ha -/-/43	F	Contract concerning brick making
2503	92662	Si -/12b/23	C	Real estate exchange; *CT* 8 32a
2503A	92662A	Si	F	Case of previous; seals
2504	82479	Sm 25/1/11	C	Gift of property by a man to his wife; *CT* 8 34b
2504A	82480	OB	NC	Case of previous; seals
2505	82481	OB	F	Sale of a threshing floor
2505A	82482	OB	F	Case of previous; seals
2506	82483	OB	C	Deposit of the property (house, slave, furniture, etc.) into the care of another, to be returned to the depositor on his return

Bu 91-5-9,

2506A	82484	OB	C	Case of previous; seals
2507	82485	Sabium 14/ezen *a-bi*/13	C	Legal proceeding over real estate; *CT* 48 8 no. 14
2507A	82486	Sabium 14/ezen *a-bi*/13	F	Case of previous; seals
2508	93018	OB	C	Letter; *CT* 44 37 no. 53; *AbB* 1 129
2508A	93018A	OB	C	Case of previous; *CT* 44 37 no. 53; *CT* 52 190; *AbB* 1 129; seals
2509	82487	OB	C	Division of an estate with maintenance contract; Waterman, *BusDoc* 41
2509A	82488	OB	F	Case of previous; seals; Waterman, *BusDoc* 41
2510	82489	Ha	F	Real estate sale
2510A	82490	Ha	F	Case of previous; seals
2511	82491	Sumulael	C	Purchase of orchards; principals and witnesses are female; *CT* 45 2 no. 2
2511A	82492	Sumulael	NC	Case of previous; seals
2512	92675	Ha 1/6/39?	NC	Real estate sale; *CT* 8 50
2512A	92675A	OB	F	Case of previous; seals
2512B	82493	OB	F	Subject not apparent
2513	82494	OB	F	Field rental
2513A	82495	OB	F	Case of previous; seals
2514	82496	Sumulael -/-/29	C	Division of an estate; *CT* 6 49b
2514A	82497	Sumulael -/-/29	C	Case of previous; seals
2515	82498	Ha -/-/11	C	Loan of silver with interest; seal(!); Waterman, *BusDoc* 38
2515A	82499	OB	F	Case of previous; seals; Waterman, *BusDoc* 38
2516	82500	Ha	C	Lawsuit over a slave pledged as security for a debt; *CT* 8 43a
2516A	82501	OB	F	Case of previous; seals
2517	82502	Ha	C	Gift made by a *naditu* in return for support during illness; Waterman, *BusDoc* 42
2517A	82503	OB	F	Case of previous; Waterman, *BusDoc* 42
2518	92663	Si -/-/12	C	Real estate sale; *CT* 6 49c
2518A	92663A	Si 20/7/12	NC	Case of previous; seals
2519	92664	Si 15/6/1	C	Loan of silver, with a field as security; *CT* 6 48b
2519A	92664A	OB	F	Case of previous; seals
2520	82504	OB	C	Manumission and adoption of a woman as an heiress; parts of case adhere

Bu 91-5-9,

2520A	82505	OB	F	Case of previous; seals
2521	82506	Ad	F	Exchange(?) of real estate(?) for slaves(?)
2521A	82507	OB	F	Case of previous; seals
2522	82508	Si	F	Sale; object lost
2522A	82509	OB	F	Case of previous; seals
2523	82510	Sm -/-/9	NC	Inheritance
2523A	82511	OB	F	Case of previous; seals
2524	82512	Sabium -/-/2	C	Harvest loan; *CT* 6 40c
2524A	82513	OB	NC	Case of previous
2525	82514	OB -/3/mu gibil x [...]	NC	Field rental
2525A	82515	OB 1?/3/mu alan [...]	F	Case of previous
2526	82516	Sumuabum	NC	Sale of a house
2526A	82517	OB	F	Case of previous
2527	82518	Immerum	C	Real estate sale; *CT* 8 47b
2527A	82519	Immerum	F	Case of previous; seals
2528	82520	Ha 28/5/22	C	Date production agreement; month Tamḫiri
2528A	82521	Ha 28/5/22	F	Case of previous; seals
2529	82522	OB	C	Field rental
2529A	82523	OB	F	Case of previous; seals
2530	82524	OB	NC	Loan of barley with interest
2530A	82525	Ha 14/11/34	F	Case of previous; seals
2531	82526	OB	C	Field rental
2531A	82527	OB	F	Case of previous; seals
2532	82528	Ha -/-/16	F	Field rental
2533	82529	OB	NC	Letter(?)
2534	92665	EB III	C	Steatite jewellery mould; *Guide* 1922 p. 189; *AfO* Beiheft 1 pl. 9: 21a-b
2535	92666	EB III	C	Steatite jewellery mould; *Guide* 1922 p. 189; *AfO* Beiheft 1 pl. 8: 15; K. Emre, *Anatolian Lead Figurines and Their Stone Moulds*, pl. XI:2
2536	82530	OB	F	Case; seals
2537	82531	OB	F	Tabulated account of real estate; late period
2538	82532	OB	F	Letter; *CT* 52 151; *AbB* 7 151
2539	82533	OB	F	Case; concerning a loan; seals
2540	82534	OB	F	Case; names of witnesses; seals
2541	82535	OB	F	Case; names of witnesses; month Ayaru
2542	82536	OB	F	Dealing with real estate

Bu 91-5-9,

2543	82537	MB	F	Uncertain content; seals; Nuzi
2544	82538	OB	F	Case; names of witnesses
2545	82539 (12046)	Nbn	F	Cylinder; *Nbn* 1; *VAB* 4 218ff.
2546	82540	Ur-Baba	C	Cone; *Ur-Baba* no. 7
2547	82541	Ur-Baba	F	Cone; *Ur-Baba* no. 7
2548	91077 (12220)	Ha	C	Cone; *LIH* 57D
2549	91078 (12221)	Ha	NC	Cone; *LIH* 57E
2550	91079 (12222)	Ha	C	Cone; *LIH* 58D
2551	91080 (12223)	Ha	C	Cone; *LIH* 57F
2552-2581				Cylinder seals
2582-2599				Uninscribed objects

(E) **Bu 91-5-9,**

82	E29829	MB	NC	Amarna letter; Bezold, *Amarna* 46; Knudtzon, *El-Amarna* 176

93-4-10,

1	91064 (= 12207)	Ur-Baba	Cone; *Ur-Baba* no. 7
2	91062 (= 12205)	Ur-Baba	Cone; *Ur-Baba* no. 7
3	91066 (= 12209)	Ur-Baba	Cone; *Ur-Baba* no. 7
4	91049 (= 12192)	Gudea	Cone; *Gudea* no. 48
5	91044 (= 12187)	Gudea	Cone; *Gudea* no. 48
6	91052 (= 12195)	Gudea	Cone; *Gudea* no. 48
7	91038 (= 12181)	Gudea	Cone; *Gudea* no. 48
8	91051 (= 12194)	Gudea	Cone; *Gudea* no. 48
9	91037 (= 12180)	Gudea	Cone; *Gudea* no. 48
10	91055 (= 12198)	Gudea	Cone; *Gudea* no. 48
11	91039 (= 12182)	Gudea	Cone; *Gudea* no. 48
12	91067 (= 12210)	Gudea	Cone; *Gudea* no. 48

Bu 93-5-13,

1	82542	OB	C	Adoption contract; early period
2	82543	OB -/4/-	C	Ledger
3	82544	Ae 16/4/"h"	NC	Field sale
3A	82544A	OB	F	Receipt
4	82545	Ha 8/1/11?	C	Repayment of a loan; witnesses include a *nagiru*; case unopened; seals; *sissiktu* impression(?)
5	82546	Dar 17/5/14	C	Loan receipt; Dilbat
6	82547	Early NB?	C	Medical prescription with exact quantities listed
7	82548	Dar	F	Royal inscription; Old Persian; Susa; *VAB* 3 xxix ff., 130 Inc B; *ZDMG* 91 82; *ZA* 44 151; *ZA* 25 394

Bu 93-10-14,

1	82549	Art 10/2/12	NC	Legal; seals; Babylon
2	82550		NC	Sale of a field
3	82551	-/3/14	F	Account of sheep
4	82552		NC	Animal ledger
5	82553	Art 9/10/26	F	Contract for dates; Dilbat
6	82554	Dar 5/2/9	NC	Contract for dates
7	82555		NC	Account of bird feed
8	82556	Dar 4/2/1	C	Letter; stamp seals
9	82557		NC	Account of barley
10	82558		C	Offering ledger
11	82559		C	Animal ledger
12	82560	27/8/11	C	Account of animals(?)
13	82561	Art 30/9/19	F	Contract for dates; Babylon
14	82562	Nbk 8/7/7	NC	Offering ledger; Sippar
15	82563	(S)šl -/-/acc	NC	Contract for purchase of sheep
16	82564	14/6/-	NC	Contract (loan?)
17	82565		C	List of weavers and apprentices
18	82566	Art 7/2/17	C	Loan of barley
19	82567	OB	NC	Letter; *CT* 52 8; *AbB* 7 8
20	82568	Dar 5/1/28	C	Receipt for wool and garments of gods
21	82569	7/11/-	NC	Loan
22	82570	Kassite 22-26/12/9	C	Administrative; beer(?); dated at Dur-Kurigalzu; case unopened; seals
23	82571		NC	Account of received items
24	82572		C	Receipt for dates
25	82573	Nbk 25/7/33	NC	Loan of dates
26	82574	24/11/-	NC	List of workmen
27	82575		C	Letter
28	82576	9/8/12	C	Account of barley for slaves

93-10-14,

29	82577	OB	F	Rental of a field
30	82578	Nbk 5/7/2	C	Account of garments
31	82579	Art -/-/2	NC	Loan
32	82580	Nbk 6/12b/28	C	Receipt for barley
33	82581	Nbk -/6/13	C	Account of garments of gods
34	82582	Kassite	NC	Letter; *CT* 43 60
35	82583	Nbk	NC	Receipt for purchases
36	82584	Nbk -/-/3	C	Account of sheep for offerings
37	82585		NC	List of workmen(?)
38	82586	Nbk 26/11/6	C	Receipt for wool for garments of gods
39	82587	Nbk 25/3/10	C	Receipt for clay
40	82588	Art 21/4/28	C	Receipt for juniper
41	82589	20/1/4	C	Receipt for a sheep
42	82590	18/11/13	C	Receipt for a ram
43	82591	-/-/15	NC	Receipt for silver
44	82592	OB 14/10/-	NC	Receipt for barley(?); seals
45	82593	Nbk 23/9/32	NC	Receipt for barley
46	82594	28/1/14	C	Receipt for gold for jewelry
47	82595		F	Account of garments(?)
48	82596	OAkk	C	List of workers; *CT* 50 97
49	82597	Art 2/2/-	NC	Marriage contract; stamp seals
50	82598	Ššu	F	Royal inscription; dupl. 82-7-14, 1000 (= BM 91107); ZA 8 392; Pinckert, *Nebo* Nr. 6

93-11-2,

1	82599	Asn II	F	"Standard inscription"; stone

94-1-13,

1	82600	OB	C	Plot of land located; round type; late period
2	82601	Aş 10/4/15	C	Field rental; seals
3	82602	Aş 26/4/12	C	List of workers
4	82603	Aş 10/12/-	C	Receipt for silver for grain; seals
5	82604	OB	C	Letter; *CT* 52 170; *AbB* 7 170
6	82605	Aş 9/5/4	C	Loan of silver; seals
7	82606	Aş 20/12/5	C	Account of silver and grain; seals
8	91045 (= 12188)	Gudea	C	Cone; *Gudea* no. 51
9	91047 (= 12190)	Gudea	C	Cone; *Gudea* no. 51
10	91046 (= 12189)	Gudea	C	Cone; *Gudea* no. 46
11	91048 (= 12191)	Gudea	C	Cone; *Gudea* no. 51
12	91050 (= 12193)	Gudea	C	Cone; *Gudea* no. 48
13	91054 (= 12197)	Gudea	C	Cone; *Gudea* no. 48

94-6-11,

1	82607	1/2/5	F	Dowry list; Borsippa
2	82608		F	Land sale
3	82609	Dar 19/11/1	NC	Dowry for a marriage; Borsippa
4	82610	Dar 5/2/-	F	Contract
5	82611		F	Sales contract
6	82612	Nbn 5/11/4	F	Sale of an orchard; Borsippa
7	82613	Dar -/-/22	F	Account of barley
8	82614	MB	F	Contract *ana šelluḫluti*; Nuzi
9	82615		F	Account of *maššartu* for 18th year
10	82616	OB	NC	Letter
11	82617	19/8/-	F	Contract
12	82618	-/-/6	F	Contract
13	82619	Dar 10/1/4	NC	Letter
14	82620	Dar 25/6/22	NC	House rental; Borsippa
15	82621		F	Account of silver(?)
16	82622	Dar -/-/14	F	Loan
17	82623	Ner 18/6/2	NC	Sale of a slave
18	82624	Dar 18/3/36	NC	Receipt for silver payment; Borsippa
19	82625	Dar -/5/-	NC	Rental of oxen; Borsippa
20	82626	Xer 18/1/2	NC	Loan of barley; Borsippa
21	82627	Dar 2/4/-	NC	Loan; Borsippa
22	82628	Cam 15/10/6	NC	Loan; Borsippa
23	82629	Lm 26/6/acc	NC	Marriage contract; Borsippa
24	82630	Dar 30/3/30	NC	Loan; Borsippa
25	82631	Cam 15/10/acc	C	Receipt for dates; Borsippa;
26	82632	Dar 8/9/1	C	Promissory note; Borsippa
27	82633	12/11/5	NC	Sale of a prebend; Borsippa
28	82634	Dar 29/8/7	C	Settlement of a debt; Borsippa
29	82635	Dar 20/3/8	C	Receipt for delivery of barley

94-6-11,

30	82636	Cyr -/12b/3+	NC	Loan; Borsippa
31	82637	Dar -/-/27	NC	Contract for bales (of straw)
32	82638	Nbn -/2/4	NC	Sale of a prebend
33	82639	Nbn 1/9/2	NC	Sale of a prebend; Borsippa
34	82640	Cyr 27/12/5	C	Sale of a slave girl; Borsippa
35	82641	Cam 1/7/7	NC	Receipt for barley; Borsippa
36	93000	Sši 12/10/7	C	Loan of silver; Uruk; *ZA* 9 398; San Nicolo, *BR* 8/7 no.71
37	82642	Dar 21/3/27	C	List of workmen(?); Borsippa
38	82643		NC	Loan of dates
39	82644	Dar 21/7/3 Dar	C	Loan; Borsippa
40	82645	Ššu 5/8/17	C	Promissory note; Borsippa
41	82646	Dar 22/3/5	NC	Account of meat; Borsippa
42	82647	Dar 19/-/-	NC	Loan
43	82648	Cam 5/6/4	C	Account of date payments; Borsippa
44	82649	Nbk -/4/18	F	Contract
45	82650	Dar 24/8/30	F	Obverse destroyed; Borsippa
46	82651	-/-/6	C	Receipt for aromatics
47	82652	22/6/5	F	Account of dates; Borsippa
48	82653	Dar 15/6/8	NC	Loan; Borsippa
49	82654	Dar 6/11/1	F	Contract; Borsippa

94-7-16,

1	82655	Nbk 6/11/-	NC	Adoption
2	82656	Dar 12/12/-	NC	Land sale
3	82657	Nbk 19/5/17	NC	Contract concerning business capital; Borsippa
4	82658		C	List of calendar dates; astronomical(?)
5	82659		C	List of calendar dates; astronomical(?)
6	82660	Cam 25/8/3	C	Field rental; Borsippa
7	82661	Dar 6/5/12	C	Loan of barley; Borsippa
8	82662	Dar -/10/5	NC	Loan of silver
9	82663	Dar 10/7/35	C	Loan of dates; Borsippa
10	82664	Dar 5/12/24	C	Account of assets
11	82665		C	List of calendar dates; astronomical(?)
12	82666	Dar 21/9/16	C	Contract for *ilku* dues; Borsippa
13	82667	Dar 11/6/8	C	Contract for dates; Borsippa
14	82668	10/5/-	NC	Rental of a house
15	82669	Ner 16/-/acc	NC	Loan; Borsippa
16	82670		C	Account of leather straps
17	82671	Ner 18/1/2	C	Sale of a slave; Borsippa
18	82672	Disintegrated		
19	82673	Nbn 11/12/15	C	Sale of a slave; Borsippa
20	82674	5/7/18	C	Account of land parcels
21	82675	Dar 28?/6a/3	C	Receipt for silver; Borsippa
22	82676	Nbn 8/11/5	C	Sales receipt
23	82677	Dar 18/5/31	C	House rental; Borsippa
24	82678	Nbn 23/6/12	C	Loan
25	82679	Nbn 18/5/5 or 6	C	House sale; Borsippa
26	82680	Nbn -/4/5	NC	Loan of dates; Borsippa
27	82681	Nbn 23/5/15	NC	Loan of dates; Borsippa
28	82682	Dar 10/6/25	NC	House rental; Borsippa

94-7-17,

1	82683	Nazi-marrutaš -/-/10	C	Account of dates
2+ 3	82684+ 82685		F	Tribute list; *BSOAS* 30 495ff.
3	82685	Joined to 94-7-17, 2 (= BM 82684)		
4	82686	5/3/5	F	Deposition; Borsippa
5	82687		F	Account of dates or grain
6	82688	Šu-Sin -/šu-numun/1	NC	Legal text concerning real estate
7	82689	Ur III	C	List of loans of silver
8	82690	Ur III	C	Account of silver
9	82691	Kassite	C	Letter; *CT* 43 102
10	82692	Kassite	C	Letter; *CT* 43 59
11	82693	-/1/16	F	Contract(?) for dates
12	82694		F	Loan of silver
13	82695	Cam	F	Deposition; Borsippa
14	82696	Cyr -/-/7	F	Deposition
15	82697	Dar 10/5/6	NC	Contract for bales of straw; Borsippa
16	82698		F	Account
17	82699	Kassite	F	List of workmen
18	82700	Dar 22/-/7	NC	Contract for bricks
19	82701	Dar	NC	Loan
20	82702	Cam 6/12b/-	F	Sale of a house; Borsippa
21	82703	Dar -/12/28	NC	Receipt for rent; Murašu(?); stamp seals
22	82704	Šu-Sin -/itu 6/2	NC	Sale of a slave girl
23	82705	Disintegrated		
24	82706	Ur III	NC	Account of silver
25	82707	Kassite	C	Account of expenditures
26	82708	Ur III	C	Issues of salt, *ḫa-nam* and *ḫa-šu-a-mu-um*, zi-ga itu-1-a-kam
27	82709		F	Account of garments
28	82710		F	Sale(?) of a house

94-7-17,

29	82711	Bar 3/3/acc	NC	Receipt for money bag; Borsippa
30	82712	Nbn 26/8/4	F	Account of oxen(?); Borsippa
31	82713	Dar 10/12/4	F	Sale of land; Borsippa
32	93001	Kan 14/3/7	F	Exchange of property
33	82714	Cam 5/3/6	F	Deposition; Borsippa
34	82715	Dar -/-/28	F	Rental(?); Borsippa
35	82716	Dar 20/6/18	F	Transfer of *ilku* dues; Borsippa
36	82717	Nbn -/9/3	NC	House rental; Borsippa
37	82718		F	House sale
38	82719	Kassite	NC	List of orchards and other property
39	82720	Kassite	C	Letter from Eriba-Marduk
40	82721	Xer 15/8/1	NC	Receipt for beer
41	82722		F	Loan of dates
42	82723	Cam 12/6/2	F	Obverse destroyed; Borsippa
43	82724	Dar	F	House rental
44	82725	Nbk 1/-/-	F	Field rental
45	82726	20/-/-	F	Loan of dates
46	82727	Dar 28/4/9	NC	Loan; Borsippa
47	82728	Dar 26/4/9	NC	Loan of silver; Borsippa
48	82729	Nbn 24/6/-	F	Loan of silver
49	82730	Dar 2/2/20	F	Loan; Borsippa
50	82731	Nbn 23/5/5	F	Deposition; Borsippa
51	82732		F	Deposition
52	82733	Dar 29/5/13	F	Loan of silver; Borsippa
53	82734		F	Contract
54	82735	Dar	F	Loan
55	82736	Dar 23/7/29	F	Loan of silver
56A	82737	Dar 28/6/26	F	Contract for dates
56B	82738		F	Contract
57	82739	Disintegrated		
58	82740		F	House sale
59	82741	Dar 3/3/-	F	House rental; Borsippa
60	82742		F	Loan
61	82743	Dar 4/6b/11	F	Contract for dates; Borsippa
62	82744	Cam 15/10/7	NC	Contract; Bit-zariya
63	82745	Cam 27/-/1	NC	Contract for barley; Borsippa
64	82746	13/6/5 Cam	F	Contract
64A	82747		F	Account

94-7-17,

65	82748	Nbk 7/11/18	C	Memorandum concerning debts; Borsippa
66	82749	Dar 26/2/6	F	Sales contract
67	82750	Ibbi-Sin -/ezen-^{d}Nin-a-zu/2	C	Receipt for oil; seals
68	82751	Šu-Sin -/ezen-Šu-Sin/9	NC	Receipt for silver; seals
69	82752	Ur III	C	Receipt for flour and dates; unusual script and format
70	82753	Šu-Sin 3/kin-^{d}inanna/9	C	Interest-free loan of barley for three months
71	82754		C	Letter order; seals; *TCS* 1 106
72	82755	Šu-Sin 26 ba-zal/ne-ne-gar/4	C	Court case concerning a loan(?) of dates
73	82756	Ur III	C	Court case concerning a loan of silver
74	82757	Šu-Sin 7 ba-zal/zíz-a/9	C	Receipt for barley and dates; seals
75	82758	OB	F	Account of dates or grain
76	82759	Šu-Sin -/-/9	F	Receipt; seals
77	82760	Dar 14/1/16	C	Receipt for bed and bedding for gods; Borsippa
78	82761		NC	List of days in the month Abu
79	82762	Cam 10/8/acc	F	Loan of silver
80	82763		F	Receipt for barley
81	82764	Dar 2/11/2	F	Sale of a field
82	82765		C	Receipt for dates
83	82766	Dar 24/3/2	C	Deposition; Borsippa
84	82767	Cam 9/10/2	NC	Contract for iron work; Borsippa
85	82768	Dar 10/8/35	C	Contract for dates
86	82769	Dar 16/7/16	NC	Contract for flour; Borsippa
87	82770	Kan 23/5/9	NC	Contract; Borsippa
88	82771	Disintegrated		
89	82772	Nbk 27/4/1	F	List of herdsmen; Borsippa
90	82773	Nbn 10/8/16	NC	Account of dates
91	82774	Cam 5/6/5	NC	Loan of silver; Borsippa
92	82775	Cam 25/10/1	NC	Deposition; Borsippa
93	82776	Dar -/-/35	NC	Loan; Borsippa
94	82777	-/-/3	NC	Loan; Borsippa
95	82778	Nbn 4/7/14	F	Loan of silver; Borsippa
96	82779	Dar 20/7/3	C	Loan of silver; Borsippa

94-7-17,

97	82780	Dar 26/6/4	NC	Receipt for bricks; Borsippa
98	82781	1/5/28	NC	Account of *telitu* tax
99	82782	Šagarakti-Šuriaš 12/6/acc	C	Receipt for the remainder of *mandattu* for the 8th year (i.e. of Kudur-Enlil)
100	82783	Cyr 10/2/5	NC	loan of silver; Borsippa
101	82784	Dar 23/7/9	C	Receipt for repayment of dates
102	82785	Dar -/3/1	C	Account of cattle
103	82786	Nbk 23/9/9	C	Sale of a slave; Bit-salu
104	82787	15/6/4	NC	Loan of silver
105	82788		F	Contract
106	82789	Dar 19/12/30	C	Receipt for silver payment; Borsippa
107	82790	15/5/4	F	Promissory note
108	82791	Dar 16/3/17	C	Promissory note for figs, dates, pomegranates
109	82792	Dar -/-/25	NC	Contract for barley; Borsippa
110	82793	Npl 21/11/17	C	Loan of silver; Borsippa
111	82794	Dar 19/4/3	C	Loan of silver; Borsippa
112	82795	Dar 16/8/2	C	Receipt for dates
113	82796		F	Letter
114	82797		C	Receipt for barley payments
115	82798	Cam 13/5/1	F	Account of dates
116	82799		F	Sale of prebends
117	82800		F	Loan of silver
118	82801		F	Contract for barley
119	82802		F	Account of silver
120	82803	Cam 28/2/2	F	Contract for dates; Borsippa
121	82804	Dar 27/4/19	F	Receipt for barley and dates
122	82805		F	Account
123	82806		F	Contract for dates
124	82807		F	Contract for dates
125	82808		F	Receipt for dates
126	82809		F	Letter
127	82810		F	Economic; Borsippa
128	82811		F	Economic
129	82812		F	Economic
130	82813		F	Only personal names preserved
131	82814			Strip of clay with seal impression
132	82815			Strip of clay with seal impression
133	82816			Uninscribed object
134	82817			Uninscribed object

95-10-22,

1	82818	Amar-Suen -/-/4	C	Account of food deliveries to various temples (Ningirsu, Baba, etc.)
2	82819	Šulgi -/-/47	C	Account of food deliveries

83-1-21,

1	82838		F	Uninscribed clay showing impression of a metal vessel(?); cf. *UE* 10 pl.43 and 82-9-18, 7017 (= BM 67022) and 83-1-21, 2763 (= BM 101102)
2	82839		F	*Ḫḫ* IV
3	82840		F	Astronomical omens
4	82841		F	School exercise; lexical
5	82842		F	Akkadian synonym list
6	82843		F	*Ḫḫ* IV
7	82844		F	*Šumma alu*; dupl. *CT* 28 15
8	82845		F	Lexical
9	82846		F	*Ḫḫ* I
10	82847		F	Lexical
11	82848		F	School exercise with god list
12	82849		F	School exercise with god list
13	82850		F	Lexical
14	82851		F	Lexical
15	82852		F	*Ḫḫ* I
16	82853		F	School exercise; lexical
17	82854		F	School exercise with god list
18	82855		F	Copy of an OB legal(?) text
19	82856		F	Lexical; *Ḫḫ* I
20	82857		F	Lexical(?)
21	82858		F	Lexical
22+ 132	82859+ 82969		F	List of *erib biti*
23	82860		F	*Ḫḫ* V
24	82861		F	Topographical list
25	82862	OB	F	Field sale(?)
26	82863		F	God list

83-1-21,

27	82864	14/4/9	F	Account of barley provisions
28	82865		F	Star list
29	82866		F	*Ḫḫ* XV
30	82867		F	Account
31	82868		F	Account
32	82869		F	Astronomical
33	82870		F	Astronomical omens (Sin)
34	82871	Joined to AH 83-1-18, 2112 (= BM 76741)		
35	82872		F	*Ḫḫ* I and II
36	82873		F	*Ḫḫ* I
37	82874		F	*Ḫḫ* V
38	82875		F	Lexical
39	82876		F	*Ḫḫ* I
40	82877		F	*Ḫḫ* II
41	82878		F	*Ḫḫ* I and school exercise
42	82879		F	*Ḫḫ* I
43	82880		F	Lexical
44	82881		F	Receipt
45	82882	Dar -/3/12	F	Account of flour
46	82883	18/5/-	F	Account of oxen
47	82884	Cam 2/9/1	F	Receipt for barley
48	82885	Dar -/8/32	F	Letter; stamp seal
49	82886		F	Offering ledger
50	82887		F	School exercise; wedge decoration
51	82888		F	Topographical; TIN.TIR
52	82889		F	*Ḫḫ* I
53	82890		F	School exercise
54	82891		F	God list
55	82892		F	Lexical
56	82893		F	*Ḫḫ* I
57	82894	Joined to 82-9-18, 1403 (= BM 61429)		
58	82895		F	Lexical
59+ 90	82896+ 82927		F	Lexical
60	82897		F	Topographical; TIN.TIR.KI
61	82898		F	Omens
62	82899		F	Lexical(?)
63	82900		F	School exercise
64	82901		F	Lexical

83-1-21,

65	82902		F	Topographical; list
66	82903	OAkk	F	Sale of slaves; *CT* 50, 78
67	82904	OB	F	House sale
68	82905	OB	F	Lexical; fish; glosses
69	82906	OB	F	Field rental
70	82907		F	Incantations; Udug.hul; bilingual dupl. *CT* 16:15: IV-V
71	82908		F	Omens
72	82909		F	Lexical
73	82910		F	Astronomical omens(?)
74	82911		F	School exercise with lexical and literary extracts
75	82912		F	School exercise
76	82913		F	Lexical
77	82914		F	Bilingual
78	82915		F	Bilingual; *Utukki lemnuti*
79	82916		F	*Maqlu* II
80	82917		F	Bilingual; *Utukki lemnuti*(?)
81	82918	Joined to AH 83-1-18, 2073 (= BM 76702)		
82	82919	Joined to 82-9-18, 7485 (= BM 67488)		
83	82920	Joined to AH 83-1-18, 1571 (= BM 76206)		
84	82921		F	*Lu* IV
85	82922		F	Account of sheep
86	82923		F	Astrolabe A; *LBAT* 1499; *MDOG* 109, 27-34
87	82924		F	Account of silver
88	82925	Aş 27/3/5	F	Sale of a slave
89	82926	OB	F	Letter; late period
90	82927	Joined to 83-1-21, 59 (= BM 82896)		
91	82928	OB	F	Sumerian; *Inanna and Ebih*
92	82929		F	School exercise; wedge decoration
93	82930	OB	F	Sumerian literary
94	82931	Aş	F	Loan; seals
95	82932	OB	F	Letter
96	82933		F	Bilingual incantations; school exercise
97	82934	Joined to 82-9-18, 9804 (= BM 69804)		
98	82935	Joined to 82-9-18, 7485 (= BM 67488)		
99	82936		F	Bilingual incantation; school exercise
100+ 101+ 138	82937+ 82938+ 82975		F	Bilingual lament with musical annotations

83-1-21,

101	82938	Joined to 83-1-21, 100 (= BM 82937)		
102	82939		F	*Ḫḫ* II
103	82940		F	School exercise
104	82941		F	School exercise
105	82942		F	School exercise
106	82943		F	*Ḫḫ* XV
107	82944		F	Lexical
108	82945		F	School exercise
109	82946		F	Lexical
110	82947	OB	F	Concerning fields
111	82948		F	Liver omens
112	82949		F	Literary; *Duranki and Borsippa*
113	82950		F	Dupl. *SBH* p. 146, VIII
114	82951		F	Sumerian literary
115	82952	OB	F	Sumerian literary; *Instructions of Šuruppak*
116	82953		F	Prayer(?)
117	82954		F	Incantation to Ištar
118	82955	Joined to 82-9-18, 4361 (= BM 64382)		
119	82956		F	Literary; incantation; cf. 82-3-23, 1649 (= BM 50658)
120	82957		F	Literary; *Ludlul* II
121	82958		F	*Aḫutu* omens from horses
122	82959		F	Literary
123	82960	Nbn	F	Account of dues; mentions Belshazzar
124	82961		F	Calendar dates (for offerings due) for the Ziggurat of Bunene
125	82962	Joined to AH 83-1-18, 1571 (= BM 76206)		
126	82963		F	Ritual; *Mis pi*
127	82964		F	Incantation and ritual
128	82965		F	Account of wool
129	82966		F	Account of workmen(?)
130+ 2171	82967+ 99809		F	*Ṭup abni*
131	82968		F	Literary
132	82969	Joined to 83-1-21, 22 (= BM 82859)		
133	82970		F	Prayer
134	82971		F	Extispicy omens
135	82972		F	Sumerian literary

83-1-21,

136	82973	Joined to AH 83-1-18, 1571 (= BM 76206)		
137	82974		F	Contract
138	82975	Joined to 83-1-21, 100 (= BM 82937)		
139	82976	Joined to K.11151		
140	82977		F	Prayer mentioning Ištar of Agade; two columns
141	82978	Joined to AH 82-9-18, 2757 (= BM 62788)		
142	82979		F	Nabu ritual mentioning stars; part of colophon
143	82980	Joined to AH 83-1-18, 2055 (= BM 76684)		
144	82981		F	Literary
145	82982		F	Omens; *Šumma alu*(?)
146	82983		F	Bilingual
147	82984		F	Omens; cf. *Dreambook* 334
148	82985	Joined to 82-9-18, 5459 (= BM 65472)		
149	82986		F	Omens
150	82987	Joined to 82-9-18, 1620 (= BM 61649)		
151	82988	Joined to 82-9-18, 1620 (= BM 61649)		
152	82989	Joined to 82-7-14, 989 (= BM 56607)		
153	82990	Joined to AH 83-1-18, 1576 (= BM 76211)		
154	82991		F	*Lamaštu*
155	82992		F	Literary; Marduk prayer; Borsippa
156	82993	Joined to 82-5-22, 479 (= BM 54327)		
157	82994		F	Ritual against sorcery and to promote well-being
158	82995		F	Literary
159	82996	Joined to 82-9-18, 9804 (= BM 69804)		
160	82997		F	Bilingual, probably incantation
161	82998	Cyr 6/8/8	F	List of oxherds; Aramaic note
162	82999		F	School exercise; *Ḫḫ* I
163	83000		F	Royal inscription; cylinder
164	83001		F	Royal inscription; cylinder
165	83002	Joined to 82-9-18, 8839 (= BM 68840)		
166+ 173	83003+ 83010		F	Literary; Sumerian
167	83004		F	Lexical and literary extract
168	83005		F	Economic; design on reverse
169	83006	Joined to K.11151		
170	83007		F	Literary
171	83008		F	Sumerian

83-1-21,

172	83009	Joined to AH 83-1-18, 1386 (= BM 76023)		
173	83010	Joined to 83-1-21, 166 (= BM 83003)		
174	83011		F	Omens
175	83012		F	School exercise; wedge decoration
176+ 193	83013+ 83030		F	Literary
177	83014		F	Sumerian literary
178	83015		F	Sumerian litany
179	83016		F	School exercise; "bulla" with sign list
180	83017		F	School exercise; lexical
181	83018		F	Lexical
182	83019	Joined to AH 83-1-18, 2099 (= BM 76728)		
183	83020		F	Account
184	83021	Kassite(?)	F	Sumerian, *Emesal*
185	83022		F	Aramaic docket
186	83023		F	Bilingual incantation
187	83024	OB	F	Harvest document; seals
188	83025	Joined to AH 83-1-18, 1863 (= BM 76493)		
189	83026		F	Sumerian liturgical text; musical glosses
190+ 82-7-14,1029	83027+ 91110	Nbn	F	Royal inscription; *Nbn* 1; *VAB* 4 218ff.; cylinder
191	83028	3/1/12	C	Receipt for chaff; Aramaic docket
192	83029		F	Incantation(?)
193	83030	Joined to 83-1-21, 176 (= BM 83013)		
194	83031		F	School exercise
195	83032	Joined to AH 83-1-18, 5445 (= BM 65458)		
196	83033		F	Prayer
197	83034	Joined to 82-5-22, 479 (= BM 54327)		
198	83035		F	Sumerian literary (Enlil-bani)
199	83036		F	Lexical
200	83037	Joined to AH 83-1-18, 1944 (= BM 76573)		
201	83038		F	Literary
202	83039	Joined to 82-5-22, 479 (= BM 54327)		
203	83040		F	Lexical
204	83041		F	Account of provisions
205	83042	Joined to 82-9-18, 5445 (= BM 65458)		
206	83043	Joined to 82-9-18, 1576 (= BM 76211)		
207	83044	Joined to 82-9-18, 6876 (= BM 66882)		
208	83045	Joined to 82-9-18, 6876 (= BM 66882)		

83-1-21,

209	83046	Joined to 82-9-18, 6876 (= BM 66882)		
210	83047		F	Bilingual incantation; dupl. *CT* 17 18
211	83048	Joined to 82-9-18, 9804 (= BM 69804)		
212	83049		F	*Utukku lemnutu*
213	83050		F	Prayer
214	83051		F	*Ḫḫ* XVIII
215	83052		F	Prayer to *Il-biti*; clay ball
216	83053	-/5/18	F	Receipt for barley; Aramaic docket
217	83054		F	Receipt; Aramaic docket
218	83055		F	Sumerian
219	83056	11/10/-	F	Receipt for flour; clay stopper
220	83057		F	Account of dates or grain
221	83058	-/-/3	F	Sales receipt
222	83059	-/4/-	F	Receipt
223	83060	Cam	F	Account of sesame
224	83061	Cyr 16/-/-	F	Receipt for wool
225	83062	-/12/6	F	Account of tithes
226	83063		F	Receipt for dyes
227	83064	Nbn 9/-/7	F	Account; Sippar
228	83065		F	Contract
229	83066		F	Account of dates
230	83067	Cyr -/-/2	F	Account of dates
231	83068		F	Account
232	83069		F	Account of dates or grain
233	83070		F	List of workmen
234	83071		F	List of temple personnel
235	83072		F	Account of silver
236	83073	Nbn -/-/16	F	Loan of barley; Sippar
237	83074		F	Account of dates or grain
238	83075		F	Account
239	83076	Nbn 20/-/14	F	Receipt for dates
240	83077	OB	C	Administrative
241	83078	Nbn 22/10/acc	C	Receipt for a dead donkey
242	83079	Cyr 25/8/6	C	Receipt for sesame
243	83080	Nb(-) 11/8/1	F	Account of dates
244	83081		F	List of workmen
245	83082		F	Account
246	83083		F	*Ḫḫ* II; curious firing holes
247	83084	OB	F	Content not apparent; seals

83-1-21,

248	83085		F	Contract
249	83086	OB	F	Loan
250	83087		F	Account of oxen
251	83088	Npl -/9/9	F	Account of barley
252	83089	9/4/-	F	Account of fruit
253	83090		F	Account
254	83091		F	Account of provisions
255	83092	Dar 7/-/-	F	Receipt for sesame
256	83093	Nbn 27/11/7	F	Account of dates or grain
257	83094		F	Account of wool
258	83095	Dar 29/11/-	F	Receipt for dates or grain
259	83096	-/12/11	F	Receipt for dates
260	83097		F	Receipt
261	83098		F	Account
262	83099		F	Account of barley
263	83100	Dar -/8/2	F	Account of dates
264	83101	16/4/14	F	Account of bricks
265	83102		F	Account of wages(?)
266	83103		F	Account
267	83104		F	Account of fodder
268	83105	Nbk	F	Account
269	83106		F	Account of workmen(?)
270	83107		F	Account of dates
271	83108	Nbn 16/9/3	F	Account of silver
272	83109		F	Contract for dates
273	83110	Cyr	F	Account of house rentals
274	83111	Dar 29/6/28	F	Receipt for silver
275	83112		F	Account
276	83113	28/7/3	F	Account
277	83114		F	Account of sheep
278	83115	Cam 14/5/8	F	Receipt for dates
279	83116		F	Account of dates or grain
280	83117		F	Account
281	83118	Nbk 11/4/23	F	Receipt for barley
282	83119	Nbk 1/4/-	F	List of workmen
283	83120		F	School exercise
284	83121		F	Account of payments
285	83122		F	Loan
286	83123		F	Contract

83-1-21,

287	83124		F	Account of provisions
288	83125		F	Account of dates or grain
289	83126		F	Account of barley
290	83127		F	Account
291	83128	Cyr	F	Account of dues
292	83129		F	School exercise
293	83130		F	Account of barley
294	83131		F	List of workmen
295	83132		F	School exercise
296	83133	Nbn -/-/4	F	Account of oxen
297	83134	Ner 10/2/2	F	Receipt for purchase of bitumen
298	83135		F	Account of garments of gods
299	83136		F	Account
300	83137		F	Account
301	83138	Nbn 19/-/8	F	Receipt for dates or grain
302	83139		F	Account
303	83140		F	List of farm workers
304	83141	22/-/acc	F	Account of dates or grain
305	83142	Nbn 27/12/-	F	Account of dates
306	83143		F	Receipt
307	83144	Cyr 12/12/4	F	Sales receipt
308	83145		F	Contract
309	83146		F	List of contracts for dates or grain
310	83147	Cam -/-/4	F	Receipt for barley
311	83148		F	Account of dates or grain
312	83149		F	Account of silver
313	83150	Cyr -/-/acc	F	Account of silver
314	83151		F	Account
315	83152	Dar 29/7/-	F	Account of dates or grain
316	83153		F	Account of provisions
317	83154		F	Loan
318	83155		F	Receipt for barley
319	83156		F	Unfinished account
320	83157		F	Account of provisions for workmen
321	83158	Nbk 16/10/23	F	Account
322	83159		F	Account of garments
323	83160	Nbn 9/-/-	F	Receipt for gold
324	83161	Nbn 30/1/2	F	Letter order
325	83162		F	Account of garments of gods

83-1-21,

326	83163		F	Account of wool and barley
327	83164		F	Account of dates
328	83165	Dar -/-/13	F	Sales receipt
329	83166	Dar 21/4/-	F	Sales receipt
330	83167		F	Account of barley
331	83168		F	Account of dates or grain
332+ 385	83169+ 83222		F	Account of provisions for workmen
333	83170		F	Account of provisions for workmen
334	83171		F	Only personal names preserved
335	83172	Dar -/-/36	F	Account
336	83173		F	Account
337	83174		F	Account
338	83175	2/7/-	F	Account of wool
339	83176		F	Account of tithes
340	83177	Nbn	F	Account of dates or grain tithes
341	83178		F	Account
342	83179		F	Account of dates or grain
343	83180	Nbn	F	Account of purchase of bricks
344	83181		F	Account of ducks
345	83182		F	Copy of a royal(?) inscription
346	83183		F	Account of dates or grain
347	83184	Cam 9/9/1	F	Account of dates
348	83185	Cam 22/11/2	NC	Receipt for flour
349	83186	8/1/8	F	Account of barley
350	83187	Nbn 30/6/10	F	Account of fodder
351	83188	15/12/-	F	Receipt for silver
352	83189		F	List of workmen
353	83190		F	Receipt for metal vessels
354	83191		F	Account of animals
355	83192	Cyr 10/2/1	F	Receipt
356	83193		F	Legal
357	83194	Nbn -/-/15	F	Account of dates
358	83195		F	Land sale
359	83196		F	Account
360	83197	-/-/8	F	Account of barley
361	83198	Nbn	F	Account of dates or grain
362	83199		F	School exercise
363	83200	8/-/-	F	Account

83-1-21,

439	83276		F	Dates or grain ledger
440	83277		F	Account
441	83278		F	Account of wool and sesame
442	83279	Cam	F	Account of dates
443	83280	-/-/5	F	Receipt for wool
444	83281	Nbn 13/6/8	F	Receipt for bitumen(?)
445	83282		F	Contract for barley
446	83283	Cyr 28/6/7	F	Receipt for dates
447	83284		F	Ledger
448	83285	Nbn 4/2/6	F	Account of sheep and wool
449	83286		F	Only personal names preserved
450	83287		F	Account of barley
451	83288			Uninscribed object
452	83289			Uninscribed object
453	83290	Dar -/7/11	F	Account
454	83291	Nbn 2/11/-	F	Contract
455	83292	Cam 7/12/1	F	Contract for barley
456	83293	Cam 16/9/2	F	Contract for fodder
457	83294		F	Account
458	83295		F	Account of provisions
459	83296		F	Contract; stamp seal
460	83297		F	Account of sheep
461	83298	-/11/4	F	Receipt for dates
462	83299	Cam 10/10/-	F	Receipt for purchase of oxen
463	83300	-/9/3	F	Receipt for dates
464	83301	Nbn 2/-/10	F	Account of dates
465	83302	Cam 23/5/-	F	Receipt for income
466	83303		F	Account
467	83304	Nbk 10/-/30	F	Receipt for metal
468	83305		F	Account of dates or grain
469	83306	Nbn 2/9/5	F	Receipt for purchase of cress
470	83307	Nbn -/-/14	F	Account of barley
471	83308		F	Account
472	83309		F	Account of dates or grain
473	83310		F	Receipt for barley
474	83311	10/-/2	F	Account of silver
475	83312		F	Account of animals(?)
476	83313	Dar -/-/15	F	Receipt for dates
477	83314	Dar -/-/4	F	Receipt for sesame

83-1-21,

478	83315		F	Account
479	83316	Nbk 19/-/23	F	Receipt for wool
480	83317	Nbn 5/12/6	F	Letter; stamp seal
481	83318		F	Account of animals(?)
482	83319	15/6/24	F	Contract
483	83320		F	Account of dates or grain
484	83321		F	Account
485	83322	Nbn 7/1/6	F	Account of purchase of barley
486	83323	Nbn 10+/5/-	F	Receipt for dates or grain
487	83324	Cam -/-/5	F	Receipt for dates or grain; stamp seal
488	83325		F	List of slaves
489	83326	Nbn 23/3/-	F	Receipt for birds
490	83327		F	Contract for dates
491	83328	Dar 7/10/9	F	Account of wool
492	83329	Nbn -/-/7	F	Account of garments of gods
493	83330		F	Account of sheep
494	83331	Cyr 23/1/4	F	Account of dates or grain
495	83332	1/2/6	F	Jewelry of the gods
496	83333		F	Jewelry of the gods
497	83334	-/-/12	F	Receipt for jewelry
498	83335	Nbn 9/8/10	F	Account of dates
499	83336	20/10/-	F	Account of dates
500	83337		F	Disbursements to personnel
501	83338	Nbn 15/6/15	C	Receipt for silver
502	83339	Ner 12/9/2	C	Receipt for flour
503	83340		C	Receipt for dates
504	83341	Nbn 12/11/13	C	Receipt for sesame
505	83342	Nbn 2/8/1	C	Receipt for a sheep
506	83343		C	Receipt for dates or grain
507	83344		F	Account of provisions
508	83345	17/2/-	F	Account
509	83346	Am 10/12/1	F	Receipt
510	83347		F	Account
511	83348		F	Account of dates or grain
512	83349		F	Sale of a field; Borsippa
513	83350		F	Account
514	83351		F	Account of dates
515	83352	Dar -/1/-	F	Loan of silver object
516	83353	Dar 8/6/11	F	Contract; Sippar

83-1-21,

517	83354	-/2/18	F	Account
518	83355		F	Account of barley
519	83356	Cyr 9/12/5	F	Account of beer
520	83357		F	List of workmen(?)
521	83358	Dar 1/6/-	F	Account
522	83359		F	Account of barley
523	83360		F	Dates or grain ledger
524	83361		F	Grain ledger
525	83362		F	Account of utensils
526	83363		F	Account of dates or grain
527	83364		F	Account
528	83365		F	Account of bricks
529	83366		F	Contract for wool
530	83367	Dar 3/8/19	F	Receipt; Aramaic docket
531	83368		NC	Receipt for vats
532	83369		F	Account of dates or grain
533	83370		F	Animal(?) ledger
534	83371	Nbn 2/-/10	F	Receipt for sesame, garments and utensils
535	83372		F	Account of oxen
536	83373		F	Account
537	83374		F	Account
538	83375		F	Account
539	83376		F	Receipt for young birds
540	83377	Nbn 5/12/2	C	Receipt for wool
541	83378	Nbn 2/5/1	C	Receipt for barley provisions
542	83379		F	Letter; stamp seal
543	83380		F	Contract for dates
544	83381		NC	Receipt
545	83382	Nbn 22/-/-	F	Receipt for purchase of dates
546	83383	Nbn 26/-/-	NC	Receipt for dates
547	83384	Dar 8/9/24	NC	Receipt for sesame
548	83385		F	Letter
549	83386	7/-/-	F	Account of dates or grain
550	83387	Cam -/-/1	F	Account of barley
551	83388		F	Account of missing slaves
552	83389	Dar 21/8/-	F	Account of barley
553	83390		F	Account of dates or grain
554	83391	5/6/2	F	Account of dates or grain

83-1-21,

555	83392	Nbk 2/2/34	NC	Receipt for dates or grain
556	83393	29/-/6	F	Account of ducks
557	83394		F	Account of dates or grain
558	83395		F	Account of garments
559	83396	Nbn 15/-/3	F	Account of jewelry(?)
560	83397	Nbn -/2/-	F	Account
561	83398		F	Account of workmen(?)
562	83399		F	Account of dates or grain
563	83400		F	Account of dates or grain; drawing
564	83401	Dar -/-/12	F	Account of dates
565	83402		F	Account of sesame
566	83403		F	Account
567	83404		F	Account of barley
568	83405		F	List of workmen
569	83406		F	Account of sheep
570	83407	11/4/6	F	Contract for reeds
571	83408	28/7/5	F	Account of wool
572	83409	Nbn 25/3/10	C	Receipt for dates
573	83410		F	Account of dates or grain
574	83411		F	Account
575	83412		F	Contract for barley
576	83413	Dar 28/4/34	F	Animal ledger
577	83414		F	Account
578	83415		F	Account
579	83416	Nbn 28/10/-	F	Receipt for income
580	83417		F	Account
581	83418	Nbk 11/12/-	F	Receipt for silver
582	83419	Nbn 3/2/5	NC	Receipt for flour
583	83420		F	Account
584	83421		F	Account of barley
585	83422	Nbn -/12/-	F	Receipt for dates
586	83423	5/3/19	F	Animal ledger
587	83424	-/7/16	F	Receipt for iron objects
588	83425		F	Account
589	83426	Dar 21/9/-	F	Receipt
590	83427		F	Receipt
591	83428	Dar 13/3/28	F	Receipt for silver
592	83429		F	Account
593	83430		F	Account of barley

83-1-21,

594	83431	Nbn	F	Receipt for dates
595	83432		F	Only personal names preserved
596	83433		F	Receipt for gold jewelry
597	83434		F	Account of dates or grain
598	83435	Nbn 23/-/13	F	Account of bows
599	83436		F	Account of jewelry of gods
600	83437	Ner 25/6/3	F	Account of fodder
601	83438	Nbn 9/10/-	F	Contract for tithes
602	83439	15/8/31	C	Receipt
603	83440		F	School exercise
604	83441		F	School exercise
605	83442	[...]-uṣur 23/-/-	F	Receipt for dates or grain
606	83443		F	School exercise
607	83444		F	School exercise
608	83445		F	Receipt
609	83446	Nbn 20/1/-	F	Account of dates
610	83447		F	Account of silver
611	83448		F	Account of dates or grain
612	83449		F	Account of jewelry
613	83450		F	Contract for barley
614	83451		F	Account
615	83452		F	Sales receipt
616	83453	Dar 1/11/5	F	Receipt for wool
617	83454		F	Account of barley
618	83455	Nbk 5/2/37	F	Receipt for flour
619	83456	-/4/3	F	Receipt for wool
620	83457	Nbn 27/8/-	F	Receipt for dates or grain
621	83458	Nbk 19/2/-	F	Receipt for silver
622	83459	25/-/17	F	Account of silver(?)
623	83460		F	Account of silver
624	83461	Dar -/-/12	F	Account
625	83462	-/-/10	F	Account of silver
626	83463		F	Account of dates
627	85464		F	Deposition
628	83465		F	Disbursement to personnel
629	83466		F	Account of dates or grain
630	83467	13/11/36	F	Receipt for dates or grain
631	83468		F	Account of garments of gods
632	83469	9/5/acc	F	Account of tithes

83-1-21,

633	83470	5/4/3	F	Account of wool
634	83471	-/-/16	F	Contract for barley; Babylon
635	83472		F	Account of dates or grain
636	83473		F	Account of dates or grain
637	83474	Dar -/7/3	F	Purchase of wool
638	83475	11/1/13	F	Account of silver or gold
639	83476	Dar -/3/-	F	Account of dates or grain
640	83477	Nbn 13/8/16	F	Account of dates
641	83478	Nbn 6/3/12	F	Receipt for barley provisions
642	83479	-/-/12	F	Contract for wool; Sippar
643	83480	4/-/10	F	Receipt for garments of gods
644	83481	Cam 12/-/-	F	Receipt for provisions
645	83482	Nbn 3/-/-	F	Receipt for metal objects
646	83483	24/-/11	F	Account of dates or grain
647	83484	-/-/11	F	Contract for barley
648	83485		F	Deposition
649	83486		F	Economic
650	83487	Nbn -/10/6	F	Purchase of dates or grain
651	83488	Nbk 25/11/37	F	Receipt for bitumen
652	83489	-/8/3	F	Account of sheep
653	83490		F	Receipt for bronze vessel
654	83491	Nbk 3/7/26	F	Account of sesame
655	83492	Nbn 25/5/-	F	Receipt for bronze vessel
656	83493		F	Account of sesame
657	83494		F	Account of dates
658	83495		F	Account of barley and emmer
659	83496		F	Ledger
660	83497	27/9/11	F	Account of fodder
661	83498		F	Account of commodities
662	83499		F	Account
663	83500		F	Only personal names preserved
664	83501	Nbn -/11/10	F	Account of silver
665	83502		F	Account of dates or grain
666	83503	Cam 10/6/2	F	Account of flour
667	83504	Cam 20/9/5	F	Account of barley
668	83505	-/12/1	F	Account of dates
669	83506	Nbn 24/12/12	F	Account
670	83507		F	Account of purchases
671	83508	27/12/-	F	Account of barley

83-1-21,

672	83509	Dar -/2/26	F	Account of barley
673	83510	-/2/-	F	Receipt
674	83511	Nbn 30/7/9	F	Receipt for wool
675	83512	3/2/6	C	Sales receipt
676	83513		F	Adoption
677	83514	25/-/-	F	Contract
678	83515	Cyr 13/-/5	F	Promissory note
679	83516	Nbn -/5/-	F	Account of dates or grain
680	83517		F	Account
681	83518	N[bn] 9/9/25?	F	Account of dates or grain
682	83519		F	Account
683	83520		F	Account of silver for sheep
684	83521	-/-/8	F	Account of flour
685	83522	-/11/-	F	Receipt for dates
686	83523	-/12/8	F	Receipt for silver
687	83524		F	Account
688	83525	Nbn 29/6/-	F	Loan
689	83526	Cyr 2/9/acc	F	Receipt
690	83527	-/9/-	F	Letter; stamp seal
691	83528	11/6/11	F	Receipt for wool
692	83529		F	School exercise
693	83530		F	Account of dates
694	83531	Cam 30/7/3	F	Receipt
695	83532	Cyr 29/-/-	F	Receipt for silver
696	83533	Nbn 7/6/-	F	Contract
697	83534	Cyr -/6/5	F	Account of garments of gods
698	83535		F	List of workmen
699	83536	Dar 23/1/23	F	Receipt for wool
700	83537	Nbn 1/8/3	F	Sale of a prebend
701	83538	Nbk 20/12/30	F	House rental; Sippar
702	83539		F	List of workmen
703	83540	Cam -/-/acc	F	Account of boats
704	83541		F	Account of dates or grain
705	83542	Dar -/-/7	F	Account of dates
706	83543		F	Receipt for barley
707	83544	-/1/9	F	Account of flour
708	83545	12/-/10+	F	Account of garments(?)
709	83546	Nbk	F	Ledger
710	83547		F	Account

83-1-21,

711	83548		F	Letter; stamp seals
712	83549	Cyr 1/2/-	NC	Receipt
713	83550	Dar 26/-/-	F	Receipt for silver
714	83551	Dar 24/8/6	F	Contract
715	83552	10/1/2	F	Receipt for silver
716	83553	Nbk 25/-/-	F	Receipt for dates or grain
717	83554	Dar 20/8/2	F	Receipt for silver
718	83555	Nbn 8/12/14	F	Receipt for barley
719	83556		F	Account
720	83557		F	Receipt
721	83558	OB	F	Land sale or rental
722	83559	-/2/7	F	Account of oxen
723	83560	Dar -/-/10	F	Economic
724	83561		F	Account of barley
725	83562		F	Deposition concerning barley
726	83563	-/-/17	F	Account of sheep
727	83564		F	Contract
728	83565		F	Receipt for date tithes
729	83566	Nbn 10/-/12	F	Account of dates or grain
730	83567		F	Account
731	83568		F	Account
732	83569		F	Account of sheep offerings
733	83570		F	Account of dates or grain
734	83571		F	Account
735	83572		F	Purchase of sheep
736	83573	Dar 2/1/6	F	Receipt for dates or grain
737	83574	9/-/12	F	Receipt for wool
738	83575	Nbn 2/5/2	F	Receipt
739	83576	Ner 29/3/2	F	Animal ledger
740	83577	Nbk -/5/-	F	Account of sheep
741	83578		F	Account of birds
742	83579	Nbn 20/-/2	F	Receipt for barley
743	83580		F	Account of barley
744	83581		F	Account
745	83582		F	Account of dates or grain
746	83583		F	Account of barley
747	83584		F	Legal; concerning women
748	83585		F	Account of dates or grain
749	83586		F	Account of silver

83-1-21,

750	83587		F	Account of dates or grain
751	83588		F	Account of wool
752	83589	Nbn 12/2/-	F	Receipt for sheep and oxen
753	83590	2/1/40	F	Rental
754	83591	Nbn 16/5/8	C	Receipt for barley
755	83592		F	Prescription
756	83593		F	Account of barley
757	83594	25/7/16	C	Receipt for garments
758	83595	Nbn 2/2/2	C	Receipt for beer
759	83596	22/-/-	F	Land sale
760	83597	10/8/-	F	Account of dates or grain
761	83598	Cyr 15/9/acc	F	Receipt
762	83599		F	Letter; stamp seals
763	83600		F	Uninscribed bulla; stamp seals
764	83601	4/10/16	F	Receipt
765	83602	Nbn 17/2/-	NC	Receipt for oxen and sheep
766	83603		F	Account of dates and barley
767	83604	Cyr 28/3/8	F	Account of poles
768	83605	Ner -/-/1	F	Ledger
769	83606	Ner 23/6/3	F	Account of dates or grain
770	83607	Nbn 26/-/9	F	Receipt
771	83608		F	Account of dates or grain
772	83609	Nbn -/8/16	F	Account of dates or grain
773	83610		F	Account of barley
774	83611	Ner 14/7/2	F	Account of dates
775	83612		F	Account of barley
776	83613	Dar 27/11/-	F	Account of dates
777	83614	Nbn 20/-/7	F	Receipt for dates
778	83615	-/-/26	F	Receipt
779	83616		F	Grain or dates ledger
780	83617	Nbn 30/1/6	NC	Receipt
781	83618	Nbk 24/2/26	NC	Receipt for silver
782	83619	Bar 1/5/1	F	Receipt
783	83620		F	Account
784	83621	Cam -/-/2	F	Account of purchases
785	83622		F	School exercise with god list
786	83623	Nbn -/11/3	F	Account
787	83624	Cam 2/6/-	F	Account
788	83625		F	Account

83-1-21,

789	83626		F	Account of dates and grain
790	83627	23/-/-	F	Contract
791	83628		F	Purchase of sheep
792	83629	Ner 2/12/-	F	Sale of a slave girl
793	83630		F	Account of objects
794	83631		F	Account of garments(?) of gods
795	83632		F	Account
796	83633		F	Account of garments of gods
797	83634	Nbk	F	Account of dates or grain
798	83635		F	Account of garments of gods
799	83636	Cyr 6/8/7	F	Receipt
800	83637		F	Account of dates
801	83638		F	Account
802	83639		F	List of workmen
803	83640	Dar	F	Account of dates or grain
804	83641	Dar 28/2/-	F	Account of barley
805	83642	-/-/16	F	Purchase of oxen
806	83643		F	Account of barley
807	83644		F	Account of dates
808	83645		F	Account of barley
809	83646	Nbn 30/2/[...]+3	F	Account of dates or grain
810	83647	Nbn -/3/10+	F	Receipt
811	83648	27/5/16	C	Receipt for clay vessels
812	83649		F	Account of barley for shepherds
813	83650	Dar 11/7/23	F	Account of wool
814	83651		F	Account of barley
815	83652		F	Account of dates or grain
816	83653	Nbn 24/11/10	C	Receipt for oxen
817	83654		F	Account of barley
818	83655		F	Account of barley
819	83656	Nbn 28/12/9	F	Contract for barley
820	83657		F	Contract
821	83658	-/-/12	F	Account of dates
822	83659	Cam -/-/2	F	Account of garments of gods
823	83660		F	Account of dates
824	83661	-/-/16	F	Purchase of oxen
825	83662	4/-/2	F	Contract for dates; Sippar
826	83663	Nbn -/5/-	F	Contract for dates; Sippar
827	83664	Nbn 10/1/-	F	Account of dates and barley

83-1-21,

828	83665		F	Letter; stamp seals
829	83666	13/9/10	F	Contract for barley
830	83667		F	Letter
831	83668	24/-/14	F	Receipt for wool and dyes
832	83669	Cyr -/10/-	F	Account of grain
833	83670	Nbn 30/6/9	F	Purchase of sesame
834	83671	Nbn 24/4/16	F	Account of bricks
835	83672	Dar	F	Letter
836	83673		F	Account
837	83674	2/2/8	F	Receipt
838	83675		F	Account of dates or grain
839	83676	-/-/acc	F	Contract for barley; Sippar
840	83677	Nbn 25/8/8	F	Receipt
841	83678		F	Contract
842	83679		F	Account of garments of gods
843	83680		F	Account
844	83681	Nbn 8/11/6	F	Contract; URU *ku-rap-su*
845	83682		F	Account of jewelry
846	83683	1/9/-	F	Sale of oxen
847	83684	Lm -/2/acc	F	Sale of oxen
848	83685		F	Sumerian
849	83686	Nbn -/5/17	F	Account of barley
850	83687		F	Account of dates or grain
851	83688		F	Account of bitumen
852	83689		F	Account of dates or grain
853	83690	14/3/3	NC	Receipt for provisions
854	83691	Nbn 7/9/13	NC	Receipt for tithes
855	83692		F	List of people
856	83693	Nbk 22/9/26	C	Receipt for date tithes
857	83694	Nbn 10/5/12	F	Receipt for tools
858	83695	Am 2/10/1	F	Account of dates or grain
859	83696	Cam 21/2/4	F	Receipt for an ox
860	83697	Nbk 9/2/36	NC	Receipt for an iron object
861	83698	Nbn 5/2/4	NC	Sale of an ox
862	83699	Nbn 24/5/2	C	Receipt for barley
863	83700		F	Letter(?)
864	83701		F	Account of oxen and grain or dates

83-1-21,

865	83702	Nbn -/-/7	F	List of workmen
866	83703	9/1/11	F	Receipt for dates and grain
867	83704	27/5/20	F	Contract
868	83705		F	Account
869	83706	-/10/30	F	Purchase of wool
870	83707	Nbn -/-/3	F	Receipt for barley
871	83708	Nbn 8/1/7	F	Receipt for wool
872	83709	-/-/5	F	Receipt
873	83710	Cam 10/-/2	NC	Receipt for barley
874	83711		NC	Receipt for dates
875	83712	Nbn 13/6/12	F	Receipt
876	83713	Nbn 2/-/-	F	Receipt for furniture
877	83714	Nbn 15/2/-	F	Account of silver
878	83715		F	Account
879	83716	Nbn 11/2/10	F	Receipt for gold vessel
880	83717	Npl -/2/10	F	Account of oxen
881	83718		F	Account of barley
882	83719	OB	F	Sumerian literature
883+ 884	83720+ 83721	Nbk 30/2/20	F	Account of sheep
884	83721	Joined to 83-1-21, 883 (= BM 83720)		
885	83722		F	Account
886	83723	Dar	F	Account of barley
887	83724	5/-/-	F	Contract
888	83725	-/9/7	F	Receipt for dates
889	83726	-/-/7	F	Contract
890	83727		F	Account of dates
891	83728		F	Account of flour
892	83729	3/-/16	F	Receipt for wool
893	83730	-/-/5	F	Contract for wool(?)
894	83731		F	Account of barley
895	83732		F	Account
896	83733		F	Account of dates and barley
897	83734	Dar	F	Receipt
898	83735		F	Receipt for silver
899	83736	Ner 10+/6/-	F	Account of dates or grain
900	83737	15/12/-	F	Account of jewelry

83-1-21,

901	83738	-/12b/3	F	Purchase of bitumen(?)
902	83739		F	Account of dates or grain
903	83740	Nbn 10+/12b/-	F	Contract; Sippar
904	83741	Nbn	F	Account of bitumen
905	83742		F	Ledger
906	83743	Dar 8/10/28	F	Letter(?); stamp seals
907	83744	Nbk	F	Offering ledger
908	83745	Nbn 23/12/1	F	Receipt for dates
909	83746		F	Account of barley
910	83747		F	Account of dates or grain
911	83748		F	Account of dates or grain
912	83749	-/-/5	F	Contract for dates; Sippar
913	83750		F	Account of barley
914	83751	Cyr 10/8/-	F	Account of hired men
915	83752		F	Account of dates or grain
916	83753	-/12/-	F	Sale of a boat
917	83754	Nbk 30/5/-	F	Account of silver
918	83755		F	Account of dates or grain
919	83756	Nbk	F	Account of dates or grain
920	83757		F	Account of dates or grain
921	83758		F	Account
922	83759	Cam	F	Account of silver
923	83760		F	Dates or grain ledger
924	83761	Nbn 8/-/-	F	Receipt for sesame
925	83762		F	Account
926	83763	Nb(-) -/10/7	F	Account of dates
927	83764	Nbn 27/4/-	F	Account of supplies for workmen
928	83765	Nbn -/2/-	F	Receipt for dates
929	83766	Nbk 10/10/35	F	Receipt for dates or grain
930	83767	10/5/27	F	Receipt for silver
931	83768		F	School exercise
932	83769	10+/7/23	F	Receipt for dates
933	83770	28/-/-	F	Contract
934	83771	1/2/31	F	Receipt for rental of a boat
935	83772		F	Account of sesame tithes
936	83773		F	List of workmen
937	83774		F	List of workmen

83-1-21,

938	83775		F	Account of wages(?)
939	83776		F	Account of wool for garments of gods
940	83777		F	Receipt; Aramaic docket
941	83778		F	Account of dates or grain
942	83779	Xer -/1/-	F	Account of garments
943	83780	Nbk -/2/14	F	Account of dates or grain provisions
944	83781	Nb(-)	F	Receipt for reeds
945	83782	Nbn	F	Purchase of oxen
946	83783	28/9/6	F	Account of flour
947	83784	Nbk 13/5/-	F	Account of dates
948	83785	Dar -/12/-	F	Garments of gods
949	83786		F	Account of dates or grain
950	83787		F	Account
951	83788	Dar 7/10/15	F	Receipt for silver
952	83789	Am -/-/1	F	Account of dates and grain
953	83790	Nbn 22/9/2	F	Account of dates
954	83791	Nbn -/-/acc	F	Receipt for wool(?)
955	83792		F	Receipt for silver
956	83793	Nbk -/1/20+	F	Receipt for dates or grain
957	83794	-/1/42	F	Receipt
958	83795	Nbn -/5/-	F	Receipt for dates or grain
959	83796		F	Account
960	83797		F	Account of sheep
961	83798	Cam	F	Account of bitumen
962	83799		F	Account
963	83800	Nbk 28/4/15	F	Receipt for bronze
964	83801	-/-/3	F	Account of garments of gods
965	83802	Dar	F	Account of dates
966	83803		F	Account of garments of gods
967	83804		F	Account of dates
968	83805		F	Account of purchases
969	83806		F	Account
970	83807	22/3/-	F	Account of sheep
971	83808		F	Account of dates or grain
972	83809		F	Account of dates or grain
973	83810	-/6/-	F	Receipt for silver
974	83811		F	Account of iron

83-1-21,

975	83812		F	Offering list
976	83813		F	Account
977	83814	Cyr	F	Account of dates or grain
978	83815		F	Receipt for sale
979	83816	-/-/15	F	Account of sheep
980	83817	Nbk -/-/31	F	Account
981	83818	Nbn 8/8/-	F	Account
982	83819	Cyr 23/1/3	F	Rental of a boat
983	83820		F	Account
984	83821		F	School exercise
985	83822	Dar -/-/31	F	Account of barley
986	83823		F	Account of dates
987	83824		F	Account of oil
988	83825	Cyr 10/8/7	F	Receipt
989	83826		F	Account of aromatics
990	83827	Nbn 18/5/10	F	Account of dates or grain
991	83828	-/1/5	F	Account of barley
992	83829		F	Account of dates or grain
993	83830		F	Account of dates or grain
994	83831	Nbn 24/7/5	NC	Receipt for gold
995	83832	Nbn 1/12b/3	NC	Receipt for sesame
996	83833	Nbn 15/9/-	F	Account of dates
997	83834	Cam 1/8/1	F	Receipt for barley and sesame
998	83835	Nbn -/6/15	F	Receipt for barley; stamp seal
999	83836	Nbk -/-/8	F	Receipt for iron
1000	83837		F	List of provisions
1001	83838		F	Receipt for bronze
1002	83839	-/-/8	F	Receipt for barley
1003	83840	Nbn 2/7/15	NC	Receipt for dates
1004	83841	Nb(-) 4/2/11	F	Receipt for garments
1005	83842	13/9/-	F	List of workmen
1006	83843		F	Only personal names preserved
1007	83844	Cam 7/-/6	F	Contract for birds
1008	83845	Cyr 15/2/3	F	Receipt for barley
1009	83846	5/10/31	F	Receipt for a garment (?)
1010	83847	Dar 27/12/-	F	Receipt for barley

83-1-21,

1011	83848	Cyr -/4/7	F	Account of sheep
1012	83849		F	Ledger
1013	83850		F	Account of provisions for workmen
1014	83851		F	Account of barley and dates
1015	83852	4/3/2	F	Receipt for silver
1016	83853	-/-/22	F	Account
1017	83854		F	Account of dates
1018	83855		F	Account of barley
1019	83856		F	Account of dates
1020	83857		F	Receipt
1021	83858	10/10/-	F	Account of dates or grain
1022	83859		F	Contract; stamp seals
1023	83860	Dar 5/9/10	F	Account of dates
1024	83861		F	Literary(?)
1025	83862		F	Account
1026	83863		F	Account of wool(?) for workmen
1027	83864	Cam 27/-/-	F	Account of barley
1028	83865		F	Account of dates or grain
1029	83866	Ner 18/6/acc	F	Receipt for dates
1030	83867		F	Account of garments
1031	83868		F	Account of barley
1032	83869	Nbn 15/-/-	F	Receipt for sheep
1033	83870	Ner -/7/1	F	Receipt
1034	83871		F	Account
1035	83872	-/-/2	F	Receipt for barley
1036	83873	-/-/6	F	Exchange; Sippar
1037	83874	Cyr 24/1/-	F	Receipt for dates and sesame
1038	83875	Nbn 8/2/3	F	Receipt
1039	83876	Cyr -/-/6	F	Account of workmen
1040	83877	Dar 26/2/-	F	Account of wool
1041	83878		F	Legal
1042	83879	Nbn 6/5/13	F	Receipt for dates or grain
1043	83880		F	Account of dates or grain
1044	83881		F	Account
1045	83882		F	Account of provisions for workmen
1046	83883		F	Contract
1047	83884		F	Account

83-1-21,

1048	83885	Cyr -/-/6	F	Account of silver
1049	83886	Nb(-) -/2/-	F	Promissory note
1050	83887	Ner 10/1/-	F	Receipt for flour
1051	83888	9/-/11	F	Receipt for bronze
1052	83889	Nbn -/3/-	F	Receipt for dates or grain
1053	83890		F	Account of dates or grain
1054	83891	16/9/6	F	Account of sheep
1055	83892		F	School exercise
1056	83893	Nbn -/5/17	F	Receipt for flour
1057	83894		F	Account
1058	83895		F	Contract for barley
1059	83896		F	Account of sheep
1060	83897		F	Contract for oxen and barley
1061	83898		F	Account of dates or grain
1062	83899		F	Account of dates or grain
1063	83900		F	Account of purchases
1064	83901		F	Contract
1065	83902	Dar -/8/-	F	Account
1066	83903		F	Account
1067	83904	12/-/5	F	Account of garments of gods
1068	83905	Cam 28/4/5	F	Receipt for dates
1069	83906	18/9/acc	F	Receipt for gold
1070	83907		F	Loan
1071	83908	8/-/-	F	Contract
1072	83909		F	Contract
1073	83910		F	Account
1074	83911	-/-/19	F	Account of provisions for workmen
1075	83912	Dar 6/2/10	F	Receipt
1076	83913		F	Receipt for dates or grain and tools
1077	83914	Nbk 23/-/-	F	Receipt for silver
1078	83915		F	List of workmen(?)
1079	83916		F	Ledger
1080	83917		F	Account of dates or grain
1081	83918		F	Receipt for wool
1082	83919		F	Account of silver
1083	83920	5/-/2	F	Contract for dates
1084	83921		F	Account of dates or grain

83-1-21,

1085	83922	Nbk 6/-/-	F	Receipt for bitumen(?)
1086	83923		F	Account of dates
1087	83924	Ner 8/11/-	F	Loan
1088	83925		F	Dates or grain ledger
1089	83926		F	Account of provisions for farmers
1090	83927		F	Account
1091	83928		F	Account of silver
1092	83929		F	Account of dates or grain
1093	83930	Dar 26/3/5	F	Receipt for silver
1094	83931		F	Receipt for sheep
1095	83932		F	List of offerings
1096	83933	Nbn 11/8/3	F	Receipt for barley
1097	83934	Dar 1/-/20	F	Receipt for sesame
1098	83935		F	Offering ledger
1099	83936	Am -/-/1	F	Legal
1100	83937		F	Purchase of dates
1101	83938		F	School exercise
1102	83939		F	Account of dates or grain
1103	83940		F	Account of sheep(?)
1104	83941		F	Sumerian
1105	83942		F	Account of dates or grain
1106	83943	-/-/2	F	Loan
1107	83944	Nbn 26/-/12	F	Account of barley and dates
1108	83945	Dar 9/8/5	F	Letter; stamp seals
1109	83946	Nbn 9/-/-	F	Receipt for wool
1110	83947	Nbn 23/12/9	F	Receipt for silver
1111	83948	Ner -/-/3	F	Ledger
1112	83949		F	Account of goats
1113	83950	2/8/7	F	Account of sheep
1114	83951		F	Account of dates
1115	83952		F	Account of garments of gods
1116	83953		F	Account of sesame
1117	83954		F	Barley ledger
1118	83955	Ad -/3/35?	F	Receipt for silver; seals
1119	83956		F	Account of dates or grain
1120	83957	Nbn 24/-/3	F	Contract; Sippar
1121	83958	27/-/-	F	Receipt for provisions
1122	83959	Nb(-) 6/8/11	F	Receipt for silver

83-1-21,

1123	83960		F	Account of wool(?)
1124	83961		F	Account of bricks(?)
1125	83962	OB	F	Field rental
1126	83963	Nbn 25/3/8	NC	Receipt for barley
1127	83964	OB	F	Lexical
1128	83965		F	Account of dates or grain
1129	83966	Nbn 19/8/8	NC	Receipt for wool
1130	83967		F	Broken inscription; bulla; seal
1131	83968	Nbn 22/5/-	F	Contract
1132	83969	Dar 12/-/2	F	Exchange of dates
1133	83970		F	Account of silver
1134	83971	Nbn -/-/11	F	Account of dates or grain
1135	83972		F	Account of tools
1136	83973		F	Account of garments
1137	83974	Nb(-) 20/7/1	F	Receipt
1138	83975		F	Account
1139	83976		F	Account of dates or grain
1148	83977		F	Account of sheep
1141	83978	Nbn 26/4/16	F	Receipt for sheep, wool and grain
1142	83979		F	Account of bricks(?)
1143	83980		F	Account
1144	83981		F	Account
1145	83982	OB	F	Letter
1146	83983		F	Account of sheep(?)
1147	83984	Nbn 23/12/2	NC	Receipt for dues
1148	83985	Nbn 2/1/-	F	Account of garments
1149	83986		F	Account of barley and dates
1150	83987	2/-/-	F	Account of garments
1151	83988		F	Letter
1152	83989	Dar 25/6/-	F	Account of dates
1153	83990	6/-/2	F	Account
1154	83991	Dar -/2/36	F	Letter
1155	83992		F	Receipt for purchase of dates or grain
1156	83993	Cam 5/3/-	F	Receipt for barley
1157	83994	Ner -/3/-	F	Land sale
1158	83995	Cam -/3/-	F	Account of dates, barley, and flour
1159	83996	Nbn 28/9/12	F	Receipt for barley
1160	83997		F	Receipt for barley for flour
1161	83998		F	Contract

83-1-21,

1162	83999		F	Account
1163	84000		F	Ledger
1164	84001	16/2/17	F	Account of dates or grain
1165	84002	Nbn 21/11/-	F	Sales of a boat load of barley
1166	84003	8/3/4	F	Account of sheep
1167	84004	16/6/21	F	Receipt for iron object
1168	84005	Dar 9/7/3	F	Account of oxen
1169	84006	14/12/-	F	Contract for sale
1170	84007		F	Account of dates or grain
1171	84008		F	Account of barley
1172	84009	-/1/1	F	Account of dates or grain
1173	84010		F	Account of provisions
1174	84011		F	Ledger
1175	84012	Nbn 6/3/-	F	Contract
1176	84013	Cyr 23/7/2	C	Receipt for sesame
1177	84014	Cyr 2/12/5	NC	Receipt for bronze
1178	84015		F	School exercise
1179	84016		F	Account
1180	84017	Nbn 17/10/-	F	Account of provisions
1181	84018	10/12/40	F	Receipt for metal for tithes
1182	84019		F	Contract
1183	84020	Nbn 28/-/11	C	Receipt for sesame
1184	84021		F	Account of aromatics
1185	84022		F	Account of dates or grain
1186	84023		F	Account of dates and sesame
1187	84024		F	Deposition
1188	84025		F	Account of sheep
1189	84026		F	Account of sheep(?)
1190	84027		F	Account of dates or grain
1191	84028	Dar 1/4/23	F	Account of sheep
1192	84029		F	Letter
1193	84030	Dar 4/7/2	F	Account
1194	84031	Nbn	F	Contract for barley
1195	84032		F	Account
1196	84033	Nbn 25/7/-	F	Account of wool
1197	84034	Cam 24/5/2	NC	Receipt for wool for garments
1198	84035	Nbn 8/9/-	F	Receipt for flour
1199	84036	Nbn 16/2/3	C	Receipt for a gold dipper; drawing on reverse

83-1-21,

1200	84037	Nbn 6/7/8	C	Receipt for sheep
1201	84038	Nbn -/11/2	C	Receipt for an ox
1202	84039		F	Personal names; names and countries
1203	84040		F	Receipt
1204	84041	Ner	F	Ledger; Gilušu
1205	84042		F	Account of garments of gods
1206	84043		F	Account of dates or grain for hired men
1207	84044		F	Account of barley and flour
1208	84045	Cyr -/9/6	F	Account of oil
1209	84046	Dar	F	Account of metal vessels
1210	84047	OB	F	Field sale or rental; seals
1211	84048		F	Account of dates
1212	84049		F	Account of dates or grain
1213	84050		F	Account of ships
1214	84051	Nbn	F	Account of dates or grain
1215	84052	Nbn 7/2/9	NC	Receipt for flour
1216	84053		F	One line; mentions wool; stamp seal
1217	84054	Cam -/-/2	NC	Account of garments
1218	84055		F	Account of sesame and barley
1219	84056	Nbn -/-/-	F	Account of dates
1220	84057	Nbn 18/8/15	F	Receipt for oxen
1221	84058		F	Account of sheep(?)
1222	84059	Nbn 4/3/3	F	Contract; Aramaic docket; Sippar
1223	84060		F	Account of animal and bird fodder
1224	84061	Dar 13/-/-	F	Receipt for purchase of sesame
1225	84062	Nbk -/6/-	NC	Receipt for barley
1226	84063		F	Account
1227	84064	-/-/25	F	Account of sheep
1228	84065	Nbk 14/-/16	NC	Receipt for bricks
1229	84066		F	Contract for barley and dates
1230	84067		F	Land sale
1231	84068	Cam 28/-/-	F	Account of sesame
1232	84069	Nbk 29/-/41	F	Receipt for tithe
1233	84070		F	Account
1234	84071	30/2/-	F	Receipt for dates or grain
1235	84072		F	Account of garments
1236	84073		F	Account of dates or grain
1237	84074	Cam 29/6/3	F	Receipt
1238	84075		F	Receipt for purchase of wool

83-1-21,

1239	84076		F	Account of dates or grain
1240	84077	Nbn -/-/7	F	Receipt for purchase of provisions
1241	84078	4/1/-	F	Receipt for barley
1242	84079	Dar	F	Account of garments(?)
1243	84080	-/5/38	F	Receipt for sesame
1244	84081	12/10/-	NC	Letter
1245	84082		F	Account of dates or grain
1246	84083	Cam 5/12/6	F	Loan
1247	84084	22/-/6	F	Account of seed
1248	84085		F	Account of dates
1249	84086		F	Account
1250	84087	Nbn 4/8/-	F	Receipt for metal vessel; drawing
1251	84088	-/10/15	F	Receipt for birds
1252	84089		F	Account of barley
1253	84090		F	Ledger
1254	84091	Nb[k] -/12b/36	F	Receipt for dates
1255	84092	6/-/8	F	Receipt; Sippar
1256	84093		F	Account of birds
1257	84094		F	Account of provisions(?) for workmen
1258	84095		F	Account of dates or grain
1259	84096	Cam 28/-/2	F	Receipt for dates or grain
1260	84097		F	Account of hired men
1261	84098	Nbn 5/5/3	F	Account of dates or grain
1262	84099	Dar -/-/4	F	Contract; Sippar
1263	84100		F	Account of barley
1264	84101	Dar -/9/-	F	Loan; Aramaic docket
1265	84102	Nbk 16/9/24	NC	Receipt for oil
1266	84103	-/-/2	F	Account of dates
1267	84104		F	Ledger
1268	84105	Dar 9/-/11	F	Promissory note
1269	84106		F	Account of jewelry
1270	84107	Dar -/8/24	F	Letter; stamp seals
1271	84108	Nbk -/7/31	F	Receipt for bitumen
1272	84109	OB	F	Loan of barley; seals
1273	84110	Ner 17/8/acc	F	Account of hired men
1274	84111		F	Rental(?)
1275	84112	Dar 30/5/27	F	Purchase of sesame
1276	84113	3/2/-	F	Account of workmen
1277	84114	5/1/14	F	Receipt

83-1-21,

1278	84115		F	Account of silver
1279	84116	Dar -/-/27	F	Contract
1280	84117	Nbn -/4/-	F	Account of jewelry
1281	84118		F	Receipt for tools
1282	84119	Sd 22/4/-	F	Administrative; round type; seals
1283	84120	23/5/-	F	Account of dates or grain
1284	84121	Nbk -/12/29	F	Sale of land
1285	84122	27/3/-	F	Receipt for tithes
1286	84123	Cyr 10/12/5	F	Receipt for fodder
1287	84124	Cyr 11/9/-	F	Account of dates
1288	84125	Nbn 13/1/-	F	Sales receipt
1289	84126	Cam 6/10/1	F	Sales contract; Sippar
1290+ 1484+ 1485	84127+ 84321+ 84322	Sel -/4/8	F	Marriage document; stamp seals
1291	84128		F	Legal
1292	84129		F	Legal; dowry(?); stamp seals
1293	84130	11/7/-	F	Legal; stamp seals
1294	84131	Art	F	Legal; stamp seals
1295	84132	2/2/12	F	Barley ledger
1296	84133		F	Account
1297	84134	Cam -/-/3	F	Account of bricks(?)
1298	84135	Nbk -/3/16	F	Account
1299	84136		F	Account of barley
1300	84137	Nbn -/4/-	F	Receipt for dates or grain
1301	84138		F	Prescriptions(?)
1302	84139	Cyr 6/6/-	F	Receipt
1303	84140	Nb(-) -/2/6	F	Receipt for garments
1304	84141		F	Receipt
1305	84142	Nbn -/-/9	F	Ledger
1306	84143	Nbn 6/-/acc	F	Account of barley
1307	84144		F	Account of wool
1308	84145	Nbn -/10/15	F	Receipt for sesame
1309	84146		F	Sale of land
1310	84147		F	Sumerian
1311	84148	Cam 29/6/-	F	Receipt for sesame
1312	84149	Ner 7/-/acc	F	Receipt for garments
1313	84150		F	Account of purchase of sheep
1314	84151	Nbn 28/-/-	F	Receipt for garments

83-1-21,

1315	84152		F	Account of barley
1316	84153	Npl -/1/18	F	Account of iron
1317	84154	Npl 19/-/5	F	Receipt for oxen
1318	84155		F	Account of sheep(?)
1319	84156	-/3/9	F	Account of silver
1320	84157		F	Account of dates or grain
1321	84158	Dar -/1/2	F	Contract
1322	84159	Dar -/-/7	F	Contract
1323	84160		F	Account of dates or grain
1324	84161		F	Contract
1325	84162	Nbn 1/8/3	NC	Receipt
1326	84163		F	Account; only personal names preserved
1327	84164		F	Account of dates or grain
1328	84165	8/-/6	F	Account
1329	84166	Nbn -/1/8	F	Account of dates or grain
1330	84167		F	List of workmen
1331	84168		F	Account of barley
1332	84169		F	List of slaves
1333	84170		F	Account of fodder
1334	84171	Nbn 9/-/-	F	Receipt for sesame tithes
1335	84172		F	Account of barley
1336	84173		F	Account of barley
1337	84174		F	Animal ledger
1338	84175		F	Account of dates or grain
1339	84176	-/-/acc	F	Contract; Sippar
1340	84177		F	Sale of land
1341	84178		F	Contract for dates
1342	84179	Nbn 15/9/-	F	Receipt for baskets
1343	84180	-/6b/-	F	Receipt for sesame
1344	84181	Cam 10/-/4	F	Account of garments of gods
1345	84182	Nbn 1/10/9	F	Receipt for sesame
1346	84183	Nb(-)	F	Receipt for sale of oxen
1347	84184	Nbn 16/8/11	F	Receipt for silver
1348	84185	2/-/-	F	Account of barley
1349	84186		F	Offering list
1350	84187	-/-/6	F	Contract for dates or grain; Sippar
1351	84188	Nbk -/-/-	F	Account of dates or grain
1352	84189		F	Account of hired men

83-1-21,

1353	84190		F	Account of silver(?)
1354	84191	Nbn 14/6/-	F	Receipt for metal for tools
1355	84192		F	Receipt
1356	84193		F	Account of sheep
1357	84194	Dar 4/-/3	F	Letter; stamp seal
1358	84195	Nbn 28/7/6	F	Contract for barley
1359	84196	12/8/-	F	Account of dates or grain
1360	84197		C	Account of oxen
1361	84198	Nbk 12/9/22	F	Account of jewelry
1362	84199		F	Account of dates or grain
1363	84200	-/-/8	F	Account
1364	84201		F	Account of silver
1365	84202		F	Account of silver
1366	84203	Nbk -/-/6	F	Account of dates or grain; Sippar
1367	84204	Nbn 5/-/-	F	Receipt for barley
1368	84205		F	Account of emmer
1369	84206	Nbn 4/-/12	F	Account of dates or grain
1370	84207		F	Account of wool(?)
1371	84208		F	Account of dues
1372	84209	Nbn 5/11/-	F	Contract
1373	84210		F	Account of dates or grain
1374	84211	22/11/-	F	Receipt for dates or grain
1375	84212	Ner 10/8/3	F	Account of dates
1376	84213		F	Account
1377	84214	Nbn 3/5/1	NC	Account of wool
1378	84215	Nbn 30/6/4	NC	Receipt for dates
1379	84216	Cam 6/-/1	F	Animal ledger
1380	84217	6/-/15	F	Receipt for silver for wages
1381	84218		F	Account
1382	84219	Nbn	F	Purchase of sheep
1383	84220	Cam 29/3/-	F	Receipt for dates or grain
1384	84221		F	Account
1385	84222	Ner	F	Account of dates or grain
1386	84223	15/6/-	F	Account of birds
1387	84224		F	Receipt for goats' wool
1388	84225		F	Receipt for purchase of dye
1389	84226	Nbn 14/10/acc	F	Receipt
1390	84227		F	Account of fig trees
1391	84228	28/1/15	F	Account of dates and barley

83-1-21,

1392	84229	Nbn 6/1/17	F	Account of sheep
1393	84230	-/-/13	F	Account of dates or grain; Sippar
1394	84231	2/-/8	F	Account
1395	84232		F	Account of dates
1396	84233	Dar 12/-/2	F	Account of barley fodder
1397	84234	Nb(-) -/7/15	F	Receipt for purchase of bricks
1398	84235		F	Account of dates or grain provisions
1399	84236		F	Account of dates or grain
1400	84237		F	Ledger
1401	84238	Cyr 8/5/-	F	Receipt for sesame
1402	84239		F	Account of dates
1403	84240		F	Account of dates or grain
1404	84241	Nbn 5/11/-	F	Receipt for tools
1405	84242	-/6/-	F	Receipt for supplies
1406	84243	11/-/11	F	Receipt
1407	84244		F	Account of dyes
1408	84245		F	Letter
1409	84246		F	Account
1410	84247		F	Account
1411	84248		F	Account
1412	84249		F	Dates or grain ledger
1413	84250	Cyr -/-/2	F	Account of dates or grain
1414	84251	Dar 11/-/21	F	Receipt
1415	84252	16/-/6	F	Receipt for sheep
1416	84253		F	Account of garments
1417	84254		F	Account of wool for garments
1418	84255	OB	F	Letter(?)
1419	84256	Nbn 6/3/1	F	Account of wool for garments
1420	84257		F	Ritual(?)
1421	84258	Nbk 29/5/40+	F	Purchase of sesame
1422	84259	Ner 20/2/3	F	Receipt
1423	84260	Nbn 25/5/acc	F	Receipt for metal for tools
1424	84261		F	Account of oil
1425	84262	Cam	F	Receipt for dates
1426	84263		F	Receipt for barley provisions
1427	84264	Nbn 23/-/8	F	Account of jewelry
1428	84265	2/-/10	F	Contract for barley
1429	84266		F	Ledger
1430	84267	-/-/8	F	Contract; Sippar

83-1-21,

1431	84268		F	*Ṭup abni*
1432	84269		F	Account of animals
1433	84270	8/-/12	F	Contract for dates and sesame
1434	84271		F	Account
1435	84272	Nbn -/-/1	F	Account
1436	84273		F	Deposition
1437	84274	26/-/-	F	Receipt for dates
1438	84275		F	Literary(?)
1439	84276	18/2/2	F	Account of barley
1440	84277		F	Account of dates or grain
1441	84278		F	Account of dates or grain
1442	84279	6/1/8	F	Receipt for barley fodder
1443	84280		F	Account of barley
1444	84281	Nbn -/9/1	F	Account of barley
1445	84282	29/-/-	F	Receipt for provisions
1446	84283	Cyr -/-/3	F	Account of garments
1447	84284		F	Purchase of a *šappatu*; stamp seal
1448	84285		F	Receipt for a sheep tithe
1449	84286		F	Lexical
1450	84287	Ner -/2/-	F	Receipt for garments
1451	84288		F	List of workmen
1452	84289	Cyr 10/7/2	F	Receipt for dates or grain
1453	84290		F	Deposition
1454	84291	-/12b/12	NC	Receipt for silver
1455	84292		F	Account
1456	84293		F	Account of sheep
1457	84294		F	Receipt for barley; stamp seals
1458	84295		F	Account of barley provisions
1459	84296		F	Account of dates or grain
1460	84297		F	Ledger
1461	84298	19/-/-	F	Receipt for vessels
1462	84299	Nbk 26/4/-	F	Receipt
1463	84300	Nbn -/7/-	F	Receipt for wool
1464	84301	Cam 30/7/-	F	Receipt for purchase
1465	84302	Nbn 30/6/9	F	Receipt for iron for tools
1466	84303		F	List of workmen
1467	84304	Nb(-) 23/12/3	F	Barley ledger
1468	84305	-/5/13	F	Receipt for dates or grain
1469	84306		F	Account of barley

83-1-21,

1470	84307	OB	F	Administrative; silver; round type; late period
1471	84308	Nbn	F	Receipt for dates or grain
1472	84309		F	List of workmen
1473	84310		F	Sale of land
1474	84311		F	Account
1475	84312	20/-/-	F	Receipt for barley
1476	84313		F	Account of beer vats
1477	84314	Cam 28/-/1	F	Receipt for iron for tools
1478	84315		F	Receipt for sesame
1479	84316	-/3/-	F	Receipt for barley
1480	84317	-/-/15	F	Receipt for dates
1481	84318		F	Ledger
1482	84319		F	Account of wool(?)
1483	84320		F	Letter
1484	84321	Joined to 83-1-21, 1290 (= BM 84127)		
1485	84322	Joined to 83-1-21, 1290 (= BM 84127)		
1486	84323	Art -/-/26	F	Loan; stamp seals
1487	84324		F	Account of bricks(?)
1488	84325		F	Account of silver
1489	84326	1/8/3	F	Promissory note
1490	84327	Nbn 10/-/-	F	Receipt for iron for tools
1491	84328		F	Receipt for gold; circle on reverse
1492	84329	Nbk -/-/20	F	Account of barley
1493	84330	Nbk	F	Ledger of animals
1494	84331		F	Account of dates or grain
1495	84332		F	Account of dates or grain
1496	84333		F	Account
1497	84334	Cyr 13/6/-	F	Receipt for iron for tools
1498	84335		F	School exercise
1499	84336		F	Barley ledger; Sippar
1500	84337	18/3/6	F	Receipt for sesame
1501	84338		F	Only personal names preserved
1502	84339	Dar 18/1/8	F	Receipt
1503	84340	-/-/3	F	Purchase of emmer
1504	84341		F	Account of garments of gods
1505	84342		F	Account of dates or grain
1506	84343		F	Letter; stamp seal
1507	84344	-/12/14	F	Account

83-1-21,

1508	84345		F	Account
1509	84346		F	Contract
1510	84347		F	Ledger
1511	84348	Nbk 19/8/+6	F	Receipt for silver
1512	84349	9/8/-	F	Receipt for sesame
1513	84350		F	Account of dates
1514	84351	Nbn 2/2/16	F	Receipt
1515	84352	Nbk -/9/24	F	Account
1516	84353	16/8/31	F	Account of animals(?)
1517	84354		F	Contract
1518	84355		F	Account
1519	84356	Cam 25/-/3	F	Purchase of sesame
1520	84357	-/12/-	F	List of workers
1521	84358	Cam 6/8/-	F	Receipt
1522	84359		F	Account
1523	84360	Cam	F	Account of dates or grain
1524	84361		F	Purchase of garments
1525	84362		F	Account of workmen
1526	84363		F	"Work of the *Zazakku* office"; dates; bulla
1527	84364		F	Account of wool
1528	84365	Nbn -/-/3	F	Account of sheep
1529	84366		F	Account of household goods
1530	84367	20/-/-	F	Account of dates or grain
1531	84368	7/3/8	F	Contract
1532	84369		F	Literary
1533	84370		F	Purchase of oxen
1534	84371		F	Receipt for dates
1535	84372		F	Account
1536	84373	10/9/6	F	Sales receipt
1537	84374	Nbn 12/7/-	F	Receipt for wool
1538	84375	28/12/-	F	Boat rental
1539	84376		F	Ledger
1540	84377		F	Account
1541	84378	Cyr 13/8/-	F	Receipt for barley
1542	84379		F	Contract for dates
1543	84380		F	Account of dates or grain
1544	84381	Cyr 18/12b/6	F	Account of garments of gods
1545	84382	7/2/4	F	Contract

83-1-21,

1546	84383		F	Dates or grain ledger
1547	84384	6/2/-	F	Receipt for dates or grain
1548	84385	20/-/11	F	Receipt for dates
1549	84386	Dar 1/11/5	F	Contract
1550	84387		F	Account
1551	84388		F	School exercise
1552	84389	Am -/2/2	F	Receipt for sheep
1553	84390	Nbn	F	Account of fodder
1554	84391	Nbn 3/2/11	F	Receipt for dyes
1555	84392		F	Account of dates or grain
1556	84393	Cyr -/-/2	F	Receipt for barley; stamp seal
1557	84394		F	Dates or grain ledger
1558	84395		F	Account of emmer
1559	84396		F	Account of silver
1560	84397	Npl 8/5/18	NC	Account of garments
1561	84398	Nbn 16/-/3	F	Receipt for barley; Sippar
1562	84399		F	Account of tools
1563	84400		F	Account of dates
1564	84401		F	Account of wool(?)
1565	84402	Nbn	F	Account of silver
1566	84403		F	Account of date or grain provisions
1567	84404		F	Account
1568	84405		F	Account of workmen(?)
1569	84406		F	Only personal names preserved
1570	84407		F	Account of garments of gods
1571	84408		F	Account of jewelry
1572+ 1573	84409+ 84410		F	Ledger
1573	84410	Joined to 83-1-21, 1572 (= BM 84409)		
1574	84411	11/21/-	F	Account
1575	84412	Nbn -/1/-	F	Account of wool
1576	84413	Nbn	F	Promissory note for barley
1577	84414	Cam 6/12/-	F	Receipt for dates
1578	84415	Cyr	F	Field sale
1579	84416		F	Ledger
1580	84417	Nbn 27/8/7	F	Account
1581	84418		F	List of workmen
1582	84419		F	Account
1583	84420	Nbn 2/11/3	F	Account of dates

83-1-21,

1584	84421		F	Account
1585	84422	Cyr 17/-/-	F	Receipt for dates
1586	84423		F	Contract
1587	84424	Lm -/-/acc	F	Account of house rentals
1588	84425	28/5/-	F	Account of provisions
1589	84426		F	Receipt for silver
1590	84427	Am 26/2/2	F	Receipt for dates or grain
1591	84428	11-/-/14	F	Account of barley for flour
1592	84429	Cyr 24/8/5	F	Receipt for a slave girl
1593	84430	Dar 21/4/8	F	Account of sheep
1594	84431		F	Receipt for dates or grain
1595	84432		F	Letter; stamp seal
1596	84433	Nbn 16/2/4	F	Account of silver
1597	84434	-/1/2	F	Account of dates
1598	84435		F	Receipt for silver
1599	84436		F	School exercise
1600	84437	-/6/-	F	Receipt for donkeys
1601	84438		F	Account of barley
1602	84439	-/-/5	F	Purchase of dates
1603	84440		F	Account of silver
1604	84441	-/2/-	F	Receipt for dates or grain
1605	84442		F	Dates or grain ledger
1606	84443		F	Purchase of sheep
1607	84444	2/-/43	F	Purchase of horses
1608	84445	Nbn 16/9/16	F	Receipt for silver; drawing
1609	84446	Cam 15/5/-	F	Receipt for metal objects; drawing
1610	84447		F	Account of dates or grain
1611	84448		F	Account of barley and dates
1612	84449		F	Bricks ledger
1613	84450	Dar -/-/5	F	Account of dates or grain
1614	84451		F	Account of precious metal
1615	84452		F	Receipt for barley
1616	84453		F	Contract for provisions
1617	84454		F	Contract for barley and beer
1618	84455		F	Account
1619	84456	Dar -/-/19	F	Contract for dates
1620	84457	Dar 12/2/8	F	Receipt for dates
1621	84458	5/7/-	F	Account
1622	84459		F	Account

83-1-21,

1623	84460	2/9/-	F	Receipt for silver
1624	84461		F	Account of sheep
1625	84462		F	Receipt for seals and gold
1626	84463		F	Account
1627	84464	Ner? 5/8/2	F	Account
1628	84465	Nbn 14/6/-	F	Account
1629	84466	Dar 10/3/35	F	Receipt for garments
1630	84467	Nbn 11/1/7	F	Offering list; oxen
1631	84468		F	Account of provisions
1632	84469	Nbk 20/1/26	F	Receipt for silver
1633	84470	Nbn 9/4/4	C	Receipt for wool
1634	84471	Nbn 10/8/-	F	Account of dates
1635	84472	Nbk 6/8/-	F	Account of barley provisions
1636	84473		F	Account of barley
1637	84474		F	Account
1638	84475	-/1/-	F	Account of wool(?)
1639	84476		F	Account
1640	84477		F	Account
1641	84478		F	Receipt for dates
1642	84479		F	Account of barley
1643	84480	2/11/acc	F	Receipt for metal objects
1644	84481	Nbn 27/2/12	F	Purchase of birds
1645	84482	Npl -/2/11	F	Account of oxen
1646	84483		F	Uninscribed bulla; stamp seal
1647	84484	25/-/-	F	Account of dates or grain
1648	84485		F	Account of dates or grain
1649	84486	Nbn 3/5/9	F	Receipt for provisions
1650	84487	OB	F	Sumerian literature
1651	84488		F	Purchase of oxen
1652	84489	26/2/2	F	Receipt for silver(?)
1653	84490	Nbn	F	Account of garments
1654	84491		F	Contract for barley
1655	84492		F	Account of bitumen
1656	84493	Nbn 8/9/4	F	Purchase of sheep
1657	84494		F	Receipt for silver
1658	84495		F	Account of dates or grain
1659	84496		F	Contract
1660	84497	Nbn -/1/6	F	Loan
1661	84498		F	Receipt for sesame

83-1-21,

1662	84499		F	Account
1663	84500		F	Account of garments of gods
1664	84501		F	Account of dates or grain and wool
1665	84502	Dar 16/6/16	F	Contract
1666	84503		F	Account
1667	84504		F	Account of dates or grain
1668	84505	-/-/5	F	Promissory note for barley
1669	84506		F	Account of provisions for workmen
1670	84507	Nbn 20/5/-	F	Account of dates or grain
1671	84508		F	Account of barley
1672	84509		F	Account of garments
1673	84510		F	Account of dates or grain
1674	84511	Nbn 29/11/4	F	Letter; stamp seal
1675	84512	-/-/40	F	Receipt
1676	84513		F	Account of silver
1677	84514	Cam 13/5/4	F	Contract for donkeys
1678	84515		F	Only personal names preserved
1679	84516		F	Receipt for silver vessels
1680	84517	Nbn	F	Receipt for vessels
1681	84518	Cam 6/6b/acc	F	Receipt for barley
1682	84519	21/6/17	F	Account
1683	84520		F	Account
1684	84521	Dar -/-/14	F	Receipt for silver
1685	84522	3/11/10+	F	Receipt for iron for tools
1686	84523	Dar -/2/-	F	Receipt
1687	84524	Cam 28/3/2	F	Receipt
1688	84525	Ner -/2/2	F	Account of sheep
	84526-84909 (= 51-9-2 collection)			Clay sealings
1689	84910		F	Account
1690	84911		F	Letter
1691	84912		F	Letter; *CT* 22, 26
1692	84913		F	Letter
1693	84914		F	Letter; *CT* 22, 180
1694	84915		F	Letter; *CT* 22, 18
1695	84916		F	Letter; *CT* 22, 198
1696	84917		F	Letter
1697	84918		F	Letter
1698	84919		F	Letter

83-1-21,

1699	84920		F	Letter; *CT* 22, 146
1700	84921		F	Letter; *CT* 22, 94
1701	84922		F	Letter; *CT* 22, 28
1702	84923	Joined to 82-9-18, 38 (= BM 60075)		
1703	84924		F	Letter
1704	84925		F	Letter
1705	84926		F	Letter
1706	84927		F	Letter
1707	84928		F	Letter; *CT* 22, 39
1708	84929		F	Letter
1709	84930		F	Letter; *CT* 22, 120
1710	84931		F	Letter
1711+ 1747	84932+ 84968		C	Letter; *CT* 22, 58
1712	84933		F	Letter
1713	84934		F	Letter
1714	84935		F	Letter
1715+ 1739	84936+ 84960		NC	Letter; *CT* 22, 19
1716	84937		F	Letter
1717	84938		F	Letter
1718	84939		F	Letter
1719	84940		F	Letter; *CT* 22, 5
1720	84941		F	Letter; *CT* 22, 47
1721	84942		F	Letter
1722	84943		C	Letter; *CT* 22, 225
1723	84944		F	Letter
1724	84945		F	Letter; *CT* 22, 107
1725	84946		F	Letter
1726	84947		F	Letter
1727	84948		F	Letter; *CT* 22, 170
1728	84949		F	Letter
1729	84950		F	Letter; *CT* 22, 119
1730	84951		F	Letter
1731	84952		F	Letter; *CT* 22, 178
1732	84953		F	Letter
1733	84954		F	Letter; *CT* 22, 125
1734	84955		F	Letter; *CT* 22, 106
1735	84956		F	Letter; *CT* 22, 197

83-1-21,

1736	84957		F	List of workmen
1737	84958		F	Letter; *CT* 22, 231
1738	84959		F	Letter
1739	84960	Joined to 83-1-21, 1715 (= BM 84936)		
1740	84961		F	Letter
1741	84962		F	Letter
1742	84963		F	Letter; *CT* 22, 37
1743	84964		F	Letter
1744	84965		F	Letter; *CT* 22, 199
1745	84966	Joined to 82-9-18, 4153 (= BM 64184)		
1746	84967		F	Letter
1747	84968	Joined to 83-1-21, 1711 (= BM 84932)		
1748	84969		F	Letter; *CT* 22, 169
1749	84970		F	Letter; *CT* 22, 242
1750	84971		F	Letter
1751	84972		F	Letter
1752+ 1766	84973+ 84987		NC	Letter; *CT* 22, 12
1753	84974		F	Letter
1754	84975		F	Letter
1755	84976		F	Letter; *CT* 22, 134
1756	84977		F	Aramaic docket
1757	84978		F	Letter
1758	84979		F	Letter
1759	84980		F	Letter
1760	84981		F	Letter
1761	84982		F	Letter
1762	84983		F	Letter
1763	84984		F	Letter
1764	84985		F	Letter
1765	84986		F	Letter; *CT* 22, 122
1766	84987	Joined to 83-1-21, 1752 (= BM 84973)		
1767	84988		F	Letter
1768	84989		F	Letter
1769	84990		F	Letter
1770	84991		F	Letter; *CT* 22, 163
1771	84992		F	Letter; *CT* 22, 135
1772	84993		F	Letter
1773	84994		F	Letter

83-1-21,

1774	84995		F	Letter; *CT* 22, 220
1775	84996		F	Receipt for dates; Aramaic docket
1776	84997		F	Contract for sheep; Aramaic docket
1777	84998		F	Letter
1778	84999	OB	F	Letter
1779	93043		F	*Aa* I/6; *CT* 12 16; *MSL* 14 224
1780	93044	Joined to 82-9-18, 4154 (= BM 93038); also registered as 82-9-18, 4155		
1781	93045		F	*Aa*; *CT* 12 17; *MSL* 14 518
1782	93046		F	Literary; Topography
1783	93047	Joined to 82-9-18, 5948 (= BM 65956)		
1784	93048	Joined to 82-7-14, 2292 (= BM 92632)		
1785	93049		F	Literary
1786	93050		F	Prayer to a goddess
1787	93051		F	*En el* IV; *CT* 13 20
1788	93052		F	*Gilgameš*; dupl. *LKU* 39; *CT* 46 21
1789	93053	Joined to AH 83-1-18, 2013 (= BM 76642)		
1790	93054		F	Apodoses of "historical" omens
1791	93055		F	*Atrahasis*(?); *AfO* 27 76
1792	93056		F	*Aa* VI/4; *CT* 12 23; *MSL* 14 441
1793	93057		F	*Aa* V/2; *CT* 12 21; *MSL* 14 415
1794	93058		F	*Aa* V/1; *CT* 12 21; *MSL* 14 407
1795	93059		F	*Aa* V/1; *CT* 12 21; *MSL* 14 407
1796	93060		F	*Aa*; *CT* 12 21; *MSL* 14 518
1797	93061		F	*Aa* V/1; *CT* 12 21; *MSL* 14 407
1798	93062		F	*Aa* V/1; *CT* 12 21; *MSL* 14 407
1799	93063		F	*Aa* VI/4; *CT* 12 23; *MSL* 14 441
1800	93064		F	*Aa* VI/4; *CT* 12 23; *MSL* 14 441
After 1800	7 boxes of unnumbered fragments			
1801	99439	Nbn 14/10/16	F	Receipt for barley
1802	99440		F	Account of jewelry of gods
1803	99441	Nb(-) -/8/8	F	Receipt for silver
1804	99442		F	Account
1805	99443		F	Account of barley, beer and other commodities
1806	99444		F	Receipt for grain or dates
1807	99445		F	Ledger
1808	99446	22/8/-	F	Account
1809	99447	-/3/23	F	Receipt
1810	99448	-/1/4	F	Receipt for silver

83-1-21,

1811	99449		F	Account
1812	99450		F	Account of barley
1813	99451		F	Receipt for silver
1814	99452	Nbn 10/-/-	F	Receipt for silver
1815	99453	-/-/19	F	Account
1816	99454	Nbk 9/7/-	F	Receipt for ducks
1817	99455	OB	F	Letter
1818	99456	30/-/9	F	Receipt for wool
1819	99457		F	Account of dates or grain
1820	99458	Cyr -/6b/-	F	Dates ledger
1821	99459	Nbn -/11/-	F	Receipt for sesame
1822	99460	29/10/14	F	Dates ledger
1823	99461	Cyr 27/10/-	F	Account of barley
1824	99462	Cam 22/1/-	F	Account of garments of gods
1825	99463	Nbn 20/4/14	F	Account of work done
1826	99464	Nbk	F	Animal ledger
1827	99465	Cyr 1/6/6	F	Receipt for silver
1828	99466	Nbn 10+/10/-	F	Receipt for dates
1829	99467	Nbn 1/11/6	F	Account of provisions
1830	99468		F	Account
1831	99469	Cyr -/6/-	F	Deposition; Sippar
1832	99470		F	Account of dates or grain provisions
1833	99471	Cyr 15/6/2	F	Receipt
1834	99472		F	Receipt for dates
1835	99473	Cam -/-/2	F	Receipt for dates and barley; Sippar
1836	99474	Dar 5/-/-	F	Account of garments of gods
1837	99475	Nb(-) 20/-/10	F	Contract
1838	99476		F	Sheep ledger
1839	99477	Cam 28/-/-	F	Receipt for silver
1840	99478	Nbk 10/-/-	F	Receipt for silver
1841	99479	25/3/15	F	Receipt for silver for fodder
1842	99480		F	Account of iron
1843	99481	Nbn 5/3/15	F	Account of barley and dates
1844	99482	Cam -/12/acc	F	Receipt for tools
1845	99483	Cam 26/-/4	F	Contract
1846	99484		F	Ledger
1847	99485	-/8/-	F	Measurement of land
1848	99486		F	Receipt for provisions
1849	99487		F	School exercise

83-1-21,

1850	99488		F	Accounts
1851	99489		F	Account of wool
1852	99490	Ner 21/12b/3	F	Sale of an ox
1853	99491		F	School exercise
1854	99492	Dar	F	Memorandum
1855	99493	Nbk 17/-/-	F	Receipt for iron tools
1856	99494		F	Account of garments of gods
1857	99495		F	Account of barley
1858	99496	28/4/-	F	Account of income
1859	99497	Nbn 10/4/-	F	Account of sheep
1860	99498		F	Letter; seals
1861	99499	-/-/5	F	Contract
1862	99500	4/8/5	F	Receipt for dates or grain
1863	99501	Cam -/-/acc	F	Sales receipt
1864	99502	10+/2/4	F	Receipt for silver(?)
1865	99503		F	Account of silver
1866	99504		F	Account
1867	99505		F	Account of provisions(?)
1868	99506	Nbn 15/2/-	F	Receipt for dates
1869	99507		F	Receipt for dates or grain
1870	99508	-/1/-	F	Account of dates or grain
1871	99509	Cyr 11/28/-	F	Account of dates
1872	99510	Nbn -/6/12	F	Loan; Sippar
1873	99511	25/-/-	F	Receipt for wine
1874	99512		F	Account of garments of gods
1875	99513		F	Account of dates or grain
1876	99514		F	Accounts
1877	99515	Nbk -/24/25	F	Receipt for purchase of sheep(?)
1878	99516		F	Receipt for purchase of sesame and garlic
1879	99517		F	School exercise; turns wrong way
1880	99518	Nbk -/9/-	F	Ledger
1881	99519	Nbk 3/10/-	NC	Receipt for bronze
1882	99520	Npl 1/8/5	C	Receipt for barley
1883	99521		NC	Receipt for plates
1884	99522	Ner 25/9/-	F	Dates ledger
1885	99523		F	Accounts
1886	99524		F	Letter; seal
1887	99525		F	Account of dates

83-1-21,

1888	99526		F	Accounts
1889	99527		F	Letter(?)
1890	99528		F	Receipt
1891	99529	5/5/3	F	Receipt
1892	99530	Nbk	F	Ledger
1893	99531		F	Account of barley
1894	99532		F	Account of wages(?)
1895	99533		F	Letter
1896	99534		F	Account of silver
1897	99535		F	Account of garments of gods
1898	99536		F	Ledger
1899	99537		F	Sales receipt
1900	99538	OB	F	Contract
1901	99539		F	School exercise
1902	99540	Cyr 11/9/5	NC	Letter
1903	99541		F	Account of dates or grain
1904	99542		F	Account of sheep
1905	99543	Xer -/3/-	F	Account of barley
1906	99544	Nbk 2/-/16	F	Receipt
1907	99545	Nbn -/8/3	F	Contract for purchase of sheep; Sippar
1908	99546	Nbn 29/4/-	F	Receipt for sesame
1909	99547	-/1/11	F	Account of dates or grain
1910	99548		F	Ledger
1911	99549		F	Account of dates
1912	99550		F	Account of barley fodder
1913	99551	Dar 19/-/-	F	Receipt for sesame
1914	99552	Nbn 7/-/13	F	Account of wages(?)
1915	99553	Nbn	F	Account of sheep
1916	99554		F	Contract
1917	99555	Dar -/-/22	F	Account of dates
1918	99556		F	Account of dates or grain
1919	99557		F	Account of barley
1920	99558		F	Accounts
1921	99559		F	Accounts
1922	99560		F	Purchases of sheep
1923	99561		F	Account of provisions
1924	99562	Nb(-) -/1/5	F	Account of silver
1925	99563		F	Account of flour
1926	99564	Am 1/8/acc	F	Receipt for bricks

83-1-21,

1927	99565	Nbn 21/8/5	F	Account of dates
1928	99566		F	Account of dates or grain
1929	99567	Nbn 1/12/-	F	Account of dates or grain
1930	99568		F	Accounts
1931	99569		F	Contract
1932	99570	9/-/16	F	Account of oxen
1933	99571	-/3/17	F	Receipt for silver
1934	99572	Nbn 29/-/-	F	Account of fodder
1935	99573		F	Contract
1936	99574	Ner 25/12/1	F	Receipt for flour for the *šalam biti*
1937	99575		F	Account of aromatics
1938	99576		F	Receipt for purchase of emmer
1939	99577		F	Account of garments of gods
1940	99578	Nbn 19/-/-	F	Receipt for bitumen
1941	99579	7/2/-	F	Account of workmen
1942	99580	Dar	F	Animal ledger
1943	99581	Nbn	F	Account of barley
1944	99582	OB	F	Sale or rental of *burubalum* land
1945	99583	Nbn 8/11/-	F	Account of rings
1946	99584	-/11/7	F	Receipt for sheep
1947	99585	Nbn 2/4/1	F	Receipt
1948	99586		F	Account of barley
1949	99587	Cyr 4/-/5	F	Contract; Sippar
1950	99588		F	Account of garments of gods
1951	99589		F	Letter(?)
1952	99590	Dar 10/1/-	F	Receipt for a sheep
1953	99591		F	Account of workmen
1954	99592	Nbk -/10/19	F	Contract for bricks; Babylon
1955	99593	Cam 7/-/-	F	Receipt for barley and sesame
1956	99594	Nbk	F	Contract for bricks
1957	99595		F	Account of workmen(?)
1958	99596	Nbn -/5/16	F	Receipt for bitumen
1959	99597		C	Personal name
1960	99598		F	Account of garments
1961	99599		F	Account of workmen(?)
1962	99600		F	Account of dates
1963	99601		F	Account of dates or grain
1964	99602		F	Receipt for wool
1965	99603		F	Account of garments

83-1-21,

1966	99604	15/5/-	F	Account of dates
1967	99605		F	Letter
1968	99606		F	Contract
1969	99607		F	Account of barley
1970	99608	Nbn 21/7/15	F	Account of dates
1971	99609		F	Account of barley
1972	99610	Dar -/1/-	F	Contract for oxen
1973	99611	Dar -/1/-	F	Account for the *šalam biti*
1974	99612		F	Astronomical(?)
1975	99613		F	Astronomical(?)
1976	99614		F	Only names preserved
1977	99615		F	Ritual, medical(?)
1978	99616		F	Account of garments
1979	99617		F	Extispicy
1980	99618	Disintegrated		
1981	99619		F	Omens(?)
1982	99620		F	Contract; nail mark
1983	99621		F	Economic(?)
1984	99622		F	Astronomical diary
1985	99623		F	Economic
1986	99624		F	Economic
1987	99625		F	Literary(?)
1988	99626		F	Economic
1989	99627		F	Astronomical
1990	99628		F	Economic
1991	99629		F	Astronomical
1992	99630		F	Literary(?)
1993	99631		F	Astronomical
1994	99632		F	School exercise
1995	99633		F	Mathematical
1996	99634		F	Astronomical diary
1997	99635		F	Astronomical
1998	99636		F	Astronomical(?)
1999	99637		F	Contract(?)
2000	99638		F	Astronomical(?)
2001	99639		F	Astronomical(?)
2002	99640		F	Astronomical diary
2003	99641	Disintegrated		
2004	99642	Joined to Sp. III 12 (= BM 35506)		

83-1-21,

2005	99643		F	Astronomical
2006	99644		F	Incantation
2007	99645		F	Astronomical
2008	99646		F	Astronomical
2009	99647		F	Astronomical
2010	99648		F	Astronomical
2011	99649		F	Astronomical
2012	99650		F	Astronomical
2013	99651		F	Lexical
2014	99652		F	Astronomical diary
2015	99653		F	Omens
2016	99654		F	Literary(?)
2017	99655		F	Mathematical
2018	99656		F	Astronomical
2019	99657		F	Contract(?)
2020	99658		F	Astronomical
2021	99659		F	Unidentified
2022	99660	Disintegrated		
2023	99661		F	Astronomical
2024	99662		F	Only personal names preserved
2025	99663		F	Astronomical
2026	99664	-/8/13	F	Contract
2027	99665		F	Omens
2028	99666		F	Bilingual; two columns
2029	99667		F	Astronomical omens
2030	99668		F	Astronomical
2031	99669		F	Literary
2032	99670	Disintegrated		
2033	99671		F	Astronomical; two columns
2034	99672		F	Astronomical
2035	99673		F	Accounts
2036	99674		F	Astronomical
2037	99675		F	Astronomical; two columns
2038	99676		F	Astronomical
2039	99677		F	*ašiputu* catalogue; dupl. *KAR* 44
2040	99678		F	Astronomical
2041	99679		F	Astronomical; two columns
2042	99680		F	Astronomical; two columns
2043	99681		F	Account of dates or grain

83-1-21,

2044	99682		F	Astronomical(?)
2045	99683		F	Astronomical(?)
2046	99684		F	Astronomical(?)
2047	99685		F	Literary(?)
2048	99686		F	Ritual
2049	99687		F	School exercise
2050	99688	Disintegrated		
2051	99689		F	Astronomical
2052	99690		F	Astronomical(?)
2053	99691		F	Astronomical
2054	99692		F	Astronomical; two columns
2055	99693		F	Astronomical
2056	99694		F	School exercise
2057	99695		F	Astronomical
2058	99696		F	Omens
2059	99697		F	Astronomical(?)
2060	99698		F	Ritual(?)
2061	99699		F	Astronomical diary
2062	99700		F	Contract(?)
2063	99701		F	Astronomical
2064	99702		F	Astronomical
2065	99703		F	Contract
2066	99704		F	Economic
2067	99705		F	Astronomical omens
2068	99706		F	Astronomical
2069	99707		F	Contract; seals
2070	99708		F	Astronomical
2071	99709		F	Astronomical
2072	99710		F	Astronomical
2073	99711		F	Astronomical colophon
2074	99712		F	Part of a drawing, or column rulings only
2075	99713		F	Astronomical
2076	99714		F	Astronomical
2077	99715		F	Astronomical; two columns
2078	99716		F	Account
2079	99717		F	Colophon
2080	99718		F	Astronomical

83-1-21,

2081	99719		F	Account of garments
2082	99720		F	Astronomical(?); two columns
2083	99721		F	Unidentified
2084	99722		F	Economic
2085	99723	Nbn -/6/-	F	Receipt
2086	99724		F	Unidentified
2087	99725		F	Unidentified
2088	99726		F	Omens
2089	99727		F	Astronomical
2090	99728		F	Economic
2091	99729		F	Astronomical(?)
2092	99730		F	Colophon
2093	99731		F	Account of dates
2094	99732		F	Unidentified
2095	99733		F	Unidentified
2096	99734		F	Astronomical
2097	99735		F	Astronomical
2098	99736		F	Economic
2099	99737		F	Astronomical
2100	99738	Dar	F	Receipt for silver
2101	99739		F	Literary
2102	99740		F	Astronomical
2103	99741		F	Astronomical omens
2104	99742		F	Astronomical
2105	99743		F	Unidentified
2106	99744		F	Literary(?)
2107	99745		F	Astronomical
2108	99746		F	Omens
2109	99747		F	Omens
2110	99748		F	Contract(?) for barley
2111	99749		F	Economic
2112	99750		F	Economic
2113	99751		F	Economic
2114	99752		F	Astronomical(?)
2115	99753		F	Astronomical
2116	99754		F	Astronomical(?)
2117	99755		F	Unidentified

83-1-21,

2118	99756		F	Account of barley
2119	99757		F	Sale of land
2120	99758		F	Ledger
2121	99759		F	Account of dates or grain
2122	99760		F	Account of barley
2123	99761		F	Account of silver
2124	99762	25/-/10+	F	Receipt for barley
2125	99763		F	Account of dates; deliberately erased
2126	99764		F	Accounts
2127	99765		F	Account of bitumen
2128	99766	19/3/-	F	Account of dates
2129	99767		F	Account of purchase of dates
2130	99768		F	Account of provisions
2131	99769	Nbn 3/6b/10	NC	Receipt for bronze vessels
2132	99770	Dar 23/11/4	F	Account of dates
2133	99771		F	Account of dates and barley
2134	99772		F	Account of dates and barley
2135	99773		F	Receipt for dates or barley
2136	99774		F	Accounts
2137	99775		F	Account of barley and dates
2138	99776	8/-/-	F	Receipt for barley
2139	99777	Cam 22/10/-	NC	Receipt for purchase of an ass
2140	99778		F	Account of commodities
2141	99779		F	Omens
2142	99780		F	Astronomical omens
2143	99781		F	Economic
2144	99782	Nbn 24/6/14	F	Receipt
2145	99783		F	Receipt for silver(?)
2146	99784	OB	F	Account; round type; late period
2147	99785	Disintegrated		
2148	99786		F	Accounts
2149	99787	Ner 4/7/-	F	Contract
2150	99788	Nb(-) 29/-/-	F	Account of provisions
2151	99789		F	Ledger
2152	99790		F	Receipt for purchase of dates
2153	99791		F	Receipt for metal objects
2154	99792		F	Account of dates or grain

83-1-21,

2155	99793	-/-/9	F	Account of wool
2156	99794		F	Account of dates or grain
2157	99795		F	Account of dates
2158	99796	Nbk 13/-/-	NC	Receipt for gold
2159	99797		F	Account of dates or grain
2160	99798		F	Account of wool(?)
2161	99799	Nbn -/3/3	NC	Receipt for a sheep
2162	99800	Nbk 28/8/25	NC	Receipt for silver
2163	99801	Nbk -/6/36	F	Account of animals
2164	99802		F	Account of provisions
2165	99803	Nbn 24/-/-	F	Account of workmen
2166	99804	Dar 10/-/20	F	Receipt for dates or grain
2167	99805		F	Account of silver
2168	99806	Cam 6/1/1	F	Receipt for purchase of a horse
2169	99807	OB	NC	Lexical terms concerning partnership money (kù-nam-tab-ba); round type; late period
2170	99808	Nbn 8/7/3	F	Account of oxen
2171	99809	Joined to 83-1-21, 130 (= BM 82967)		
2172	99810	Nbn 14/12/-	F	Receipt for date provisions
2173	99811		F	Literary
2174	99812		F	School exercise
2175	99813		F	School exercise
2176	99814		F	School exercise; personal names
2177	99815	Nbn 22/4/-	F	Account of dates or grain
2178	99816		F	Receipt
2179	99817	Dar -/12/-	F	Letter; seal
2180	99818	Nbk 7/11/-	F	Contract
2181	99819		F	Account of workmen
2182	99820		F	Account of wool
2183	99821		F	Account of flour
2184	99822		F	Accounts
2185	99823	Nbn 1/-/-	F	Receipt for wool
2186	99824		F	Letters
2187	99825		F	Account of seed
2188	99826		F	Receipt
2189	99827	-/-/6	F	Account of sheep

83-1-21,

2190	99828		F	Letter
2191	99829	Cyr 6/12/-	F	Contract for dates; Sippar
2192	99830		F	Account of workmen; two columns
2193	99831	Dar -/-/11	F	Account of garments of gods
2194	99832		F	Account of sheep
2195	99833		F	Only personal names preserved
2196	99834	Nbn 19/6/-	F	Account of oxen and silver
2197	99835		F	Account of dates
2198	99836		F	Accounts
2199	99837		F	Only personal names preserved
2200	99838	Nbn -/7/16	F	Account of dates
2201	99839	Dar -/3/27	F	Account of barley
2202	99840		F	Legal
2203	99841		F	Receipt for bird fodder
2204	99842		F	Accounts
2205	99843		F	Account of bricks(?)
2206	99844	-/1/23	F	Receipt for barley
2207	99845		F	Temple account
2208	99846		F	Account of barley
2209	99847		F	Account of rings
2210	99848		F	Contract(?)
2211	99849		F	Account of provisions
2212	99850	Nbn 22/2/10	F	Receipt for wool
2213	99851		F	Ledger
2214	99852	18/10/-	F	Account of silver
2215	99853		F	Accounts
2216	99854	Nbn -/2/16	F	Receipt for barley
2217	99855		F	Collection of transactions in columns
2218	99856	Nb(-) 3/1/11	F	Receipt for iron object
2219	99857	Nb(-) 4/-/3	F	Account of dates or grain
2220	99858	Nbn	F	Ledger
2221	99859	Nbk 4/	F	Account of workmen
2222	99860	Dar 24/-/-	F	Receipt for cassia
2223	99861	Nbn 24/-/-	F	Sales receipt
2224	99862		F	Omens
2225	99863		F	School exercise
2226	99864	Nbk 23/-/40	F	Account of dates

83-1-21,

2227	99865	Nbn 29/-/5	F	Account of dates
2228	99866		F	School exercise; personal names
2229	99867		F	Account of dates or grain
2230	99868	Cyr -/-/3	F	Accounts
2231	99869	Nbn -/10/4	F	Receipt
2232	99870		F	School exercise
2233	99871	Joined to 82-9-18, 9953 (= BM 69953)		
2234	99872		F	*Ḫḫ* II
2235	99873	Dar	F	Account of barley
2236	99874		F	Account of wool for textiles
2237	99875		F	Accounts
2238	99876	OB	F	Sumerian literature
2239	99877		F	Ledger
2240	99878	21/-/10	F	Account of figs
2241	99879	Cam -/1/3	F	Receipt
2242	99880		F	Account of workmen(?)
2243	99881		F	Account of provisions
2244	99882	Nbn -/5/11	NC	Receipt for seal rings
2245	99883		F	Account of dates or grain
2246	99884		F	Account of dates or grain
2247	99885		F	Only personal names preserved
2248	99886		F	Only personal names preserved
2249	99887	Nbk 22/-/-	F	Receipt for barley
2250	99888		F	Accounts
2251	99889	Cam 1/6/5	F	Account of silver
2252	99890		F	Accounts
2253	99891	Nbn 21/-/-	F	Account of wool
2254	99892	28/-/8	F	Account of dates or grain
2255	99893		F	Accounts
2256	99894	Nb(-) -/-/24	F	Animal ledger
2257	99895		F	Letter; seals
2258	99896	Cam 28/6/-	F	Receipt for wool
2259	99897		F	Letter
2260	99898	Cyr -/-/4	F	Receipt for silver
2261	99899	OB	F	Sumerian literature
2262	99900	Nbn 9/1/6	F	Receipt for silver
2263	99901		F	Contract for house rental

83-1-21,

2264	99902	Nbn	F	Dowry(?) list; mentions Nabonidus and Belshazzer
2265	99903		F	Accounts
2266	99904		F	Account of dates or grain
2267	99905	8/-/-	F	Letter; seal
2268	99906		F	School exercise
2269	99907		F	School exercise
2270	99908		F	School exercise
2271	99909		F	School exercise
2272	99910		F	Accounts
2273	99911		F	Account of barley
2274	99912		F	Accounts
2275	99913		F	Only personal names preserved
2276	99914		NC	Receipt
2277	99915		F	Ledger
2278	99916	14/-/-	F	Letter; seals
2279	99917	-/7/-	F	Letter
2280	99918		F	Receipt for silver
2281	99919	Dar 25/-/-	F	Receipt
2282	99920	-/-/acc	F	Account of silver
2283	99921		F	Account of barley
2284	99922	Nbn 21/6/-	F	Receipt for iron objects; drawing
2285	99923		F	Account of purchases
2286	99924		F	Account of dates or grain
2287	99925		F	Account of garments of gods
2288	99926		F	List of workmen(?)
2289	99927	26/-/12	F	Receipt for sesame
2290	99928		F	List of workmen(?); two columns
2291	99929	13/10/6	F	Account of sheep
2292	99930		F	School exercise
2293	99931	27/4/-	F	Audit of shepherds
2294	99932	Nbn 24/6/3	F	Receipt for metal(?)
2295	99933	Cam 12/8/-	F	Accounts
2296	99934	Nbk 16/3/1	F	Receipt
2297	99935	Nbk -/-/2	F	Receipt for silver
2298	99936		F	Seed ledger
2299	99937	Nb(-) -/3/7	F	Receipt for wool for garments

83-1-21,

2300	99938		F	Only personal names preserved
2301	99939		F	Account of silver purchases
2302	99940		F	Account of barley
2303	99941		F	Account of dates
2304	99942	Nb(-) -/10/6	F	Account of dates
2305	99943	Dar 20/7/-	F	Account of barley
2306	99944	Nb(-) -/9/7	F	Receipt for a sheep
2307	99945	Nbn 2/-/-	F	Account of dates
2308	99946		F	Only personal names preserved
2309	99947		F	Purchase receipt
2310	99948		F	Account of sheep(?)
2311	99949	Nbn 2/4/-	F	Receipt for purchase of an ox
2312	99950	-/-/21	F	Account of silver(?) for working
2313	99951		F	Account of garments of gods
2314	99952		F	Account of oil
2315	99953	Dar 25/11/-	F	Receipt for garlic
2316	99954	Nbn 9/-/-	F	Receipt for purchase; drawing on reverse
2316A	99954A	Nbn 10/2/11	F	Receipt for silver for temple paraphernalia
2317	99955		F	Account of sheep
2318	99956		F	List of workmen(?)
2319	99957	Cam	F	Account of dates and grain
2320	99958		F	Contract
2321	99959		F	Accounts
2322	99960		F	Contract
2323	99961		F	*En el* I
2324	99962	Dar -/1/-	F	Account of dates or grain
2325	99963		F	Account of gold for mountings
2326	99964	Cyr 15/2/3	C	Receipt for barley fodder
2327	99965		F	Accounts
2328	99966	23/-/-	F	Receipt
2329	99967	Dar 22/2/20+	F	Receipt for silver
2330	99968	Nbk	F	Receipt for reeds and building materials
2331	99969	Nbn -/-/acc	F	Account of wool
2332	99970		F	List of workmen(?) and children
2333	99971		F	Only personal names preserved

83-1-21,

2334	99972		F	Account of wheat
2335	99973	Cam -/5/-	F	Account of dates or grain
2336	99974		F	Accounts
2337	99975		F	Account of workmen
2338	99976		F	Receipt for wool
2339	99977	Nbn 25/-/4	F	Receipt for purchase
2340	99978		F	Account
2341	99979	8/-/15	F	Account of dates or grain
2342	99980		F	Accounts
2343	99981		F	Account by days
2344	99982		F	Account of oil
2345	99983		F	Contract
2346	99984	10+/12/6	F	Sales receipt
2347	99985		F	Receipt
2348	99986	Nbk -/-/20+	F	Account of garments
2349	99987		F	Account of oil by days
2350	99988		F	Account of shipments of bundles of reeds
2351	99989	8/5/14	C	Receipt for sheep
2352	99990	-/7/10	F	Receipt for wool
2353	99991		F	Measurements of land
2354	99992		F	Receipt for wool
2355	99993		F	Account of dates
2356	99994		F	Account of barley
2357	99995		F	Receipt for commodity measured in gur
2358	99996		F	Account of dates
2359	99997	9/-/22	F	Contract
2360	99998	-/-/9	F	Receipt for silver
2361	99999		F	Contract
2362	100701	-/10/-	F	Receipt for silver
2363	100702	Art 11/5/1	F	Receipt
2364	100703	14/5/18	F	Account of provisions
2365	100704		F	Account of wool
2366	100705	Npl 3/8/20	F	Account of barley
2367	100706	Cyr 1/12/-	F	Receipt for dates
2368	100707	4/-/22	F	Receipt for purchase of oxen
2369	100708	Cam -/8/-	F	Promissory note
2370	100709	5/-/16	F	Receipt for purchase of dates

83-1-21,

2371	100710	Nb(-) 10+/2/-	F	Receipt for an ox
2372	100711		F	Account of dates
2373	100712	Nbk -/-/15	F	Accounts
2374	100713	8/-/15	F	Receipt for barley
2375	100714	-/9/26	F	Receipt for barley
2376	100715		F	Accounts
2377	100716		F	Only personal names preserved
2378	100717		F	Accounts
2379	100718	-/12/20+	F	Account of silver
2380	100719	Nbn	F	Deposition
2381	100720		F	Account of garments of gods
2382	100721		F	Accounts
2383	100722		F	Account of wool and dates
2384	100723	Nb(-) 10/3/1	F	Receipt for bitumen
2385	100724		F	Account of dates or grain
2386	100725		F	Ledger
2387	100726	23/-/-	F	Account of sheep
2388	100727	Nbn 22/8/-	F	Account of dates
2389	100728	Nbn 5/-/15	F	Receipt for silver
2390	100729		F	Ledger
2391	100730	2/-/-	F	Account of silver
2392	100731	Nb(-) 20/6/-	F	Account of wool
2393	100732		F	Account
2394	100733		F	Account of garments of gods
2395	100734		F	Account of provisions
2396	100735	-/-/13	F	Account of jewelry of gods
2397	100736		C	Account of animals
2398	100737		F	Contract
2399	100738	25/-/-	F	Account of dates
2400	100739		F	Letter; seal
2401	100740	22/-/-	F	Accounts
2402	100741		F	Accounts
2403	100742	-/-/5	F	Contract
2404	100743		F	Account of dates or grain
2405	100744		F	Ledger
2406	100745	Art -/-/10	F	Concerning gates
2407	100746		F	Account of purchase of dates
2408	100747	Cam 9/11/-	F	Receipt for barley
2409	100748		F	Ledger

83-1-21,

2410	100749		F	Account of dates or grain
2411	100750	Nbn -/12/10	F	Account of dates or grain
2412	100751		F	Contract
2413	100752		F	Account of gold and silver of gods
2414	100753		F	Accounts
2415	100754		F	Account of oxen
2416	100755		F	Account of sheep
2417	100756	Nbk 16/-/-	F	Receipt for barley
2418	100757		F	Account of hired men
2419	100758	20+/4/20	F	Receipt for dates or grain
2420	100759		F	Only personal names preserved
2421	100760		F	Accounts
2422	100761		F	Accounts
2423	100762	Nbn 2/-/4	F	Receipt for silver tithe
2424	100763		F	Account of provisions(?)
2425	100764	-/2/17	F	Account of garments of gods
2426	100765	Nbn -/-/4	F	Account of silver
2427	100766		F	Receipt for silver jewelry; drawing
2428	100767		F	List of hired men
2429	100768	OB	F	Field rental; seals
2430	100769	-/-/10	F	Account of measurements of fields(?)
2431	100770	Nbn 6/5/10	F	Receipt for barley
2432	100771		F	Account of dates or grain
2433	100772	-/9/30	F	Letter; seal
2434	100773		F	Account of dates or grain
2435	100774	OB	F	Sale contract; oath by [Hammura]pi(?)
2436	100775	-/-/4	F	Receipt for garments(?) of gods
2437	100776	Nbn 5/10/11	F	Account of barley
2438	100777		F	Receipt
2439	100778		F	List of hired men
2440	100779		F	Only personal names preserved
2441	100780		F	Receipt
2442	100781		F	Ledger
2443	100782		F	Contract
2444	100783		F	Accounts
2445	100784	Nbn 6/8/-	F	Account of barley
2446	100785	18/-/7	F	Accounts
2447	100786	-/2/-	F	Receipt
2448	100787		F	List of workmen

83-1-21,

2449	100788		F	Account of dates or grain
2450	100789	Nbn -/2/-	F	Account of sheep
2451	100790	2/1/-	F	Account of oxen
2452	100791		F	Only personal names preserved
2453	100792		F	Account of garments of gods
2454	100793		F	Account of dates
2455	100794	12/11/7	F	Receipt for dates
2456	100795	Dar 23/5/-	F	Contract; Babylon
2457	100796		F	Account of provisions(?)
2458	100797		F	List of workmen(?)
2459	100798	-/-/16	F	Receipt for barley
2460	100799	-/-/8	F	Receipt
2461	100800	29/2/-	F	Contract
2462	100801		F	Ledger
2463	100802		F	Account of fodder
2464	100803	Ner -/8/3	F	Contract for barley
2465	100804	-/11/9	F	Receipt for wool
2466	100805	Dar 2/-/12	F	Contract
2467	100806	Cam 5/2/-	F	Receipt for hides
2468	100807	Nbn	F	Receipt for iron for objects
2469	100808		F	Account of oxen
2470	100809		F	Account of silver for objects
2471	100810	Nb(-) -/9/-	F	Account of dates or grain
2472	100811		F	Account of dates or grain
2473	100812	Nb(k) -/11/37	F	Contract for barley; Sippar
2474	100813		NC	List of men's names; two columns
2475	100814		F	Contract
2476	100815	Dar 11/-/-	F	Receipt
2477	100816	-/11/7	F	Receipt for sesame
2478	100817	Nbk 24/2/4	F	Receipt for income
2479	100818	Nbk 30/4/36	F	Receipt for barley
2480	100819		F	Account of wool
2481	100820		F	Accounts
2482	100821		F	Account of dates or grain
2483	100822		F	Contract for barley
2484	100823	Nbk 1/1/-	F	Receipt
2485	100824		F	Ledger
2486	100825		F	School exercise
2487	100826		F	Accounts

83-1-21,

2488	100827		F	Receipt for dates or grain
2489	100828	Cyr 28/-/-	F	Receipt for iron objects
2490	100829		F	Economic
2491	100830		F	Account of dates or grain
2492	100831		F	Account of flour provisions
2493	100832	Nbn 3/12/1	F	Contract for seed
2494	100833	Nb(-) -/2/12	F	Receipt for jewelry
2495	100834	Dar 28/-/-	F	Receipt for dates
2496	100835	20/-/1	F	Receipt for barley
2497	100836		F	Account of barley
2498	100837	Dar	F	Account of dates or grain
2499	100838		F	Account of bitumen
2500	100839		F	Receipt for dates or grain
2501	100840		F	Legal(?)
2502	100841	9/10/15	F	Receipt for bronze for objects
2503	100842		F	Contract for sale of a boat
2504	100843		F	Contract
2505	100844		F	Account of sheep
2506	100845		F	Receipt for sheep
2507	100846		F	Contract for wheat
2508	100847	Cam -/-/7	F	Receipt for barley
2509	100848		F	Account of various commodities
2510	100849	Cam 21/9/-	F	Receipt for purchase of a garment
2511	100850	-/-/3	F	Receipt for dates
2512	100851	11/-/9	F	Receipt for barley
2513	100852	Nbn 19/-/-	F	Receipt for spades
2514	100853	Cam 25/-/3	F	Receipt for purchase of sesame
2515	100854	Nbn	F	Account of dates or grain
2516	100855		F	Account of sheep
2517	100856	Nbn 10+/3/-	F	Account of sesame provisions
2518	100857		F	Account of sheep
2519	100858		F	Account of dates or grain
2520	100859		F	Accounts
2521	100860		F	Account of wool(?)
2522	100861	-/1/-	F	Account of sheep(?)
2523	100862		F	Account of wool(?)
2524	100863		F	Account of provisions(?)
2525	100864		F	Contract
2526	100865		F	Account of garments of gods

83-1-21,

2527	100866		F	Ledger
2528	100867		F	Account of barley provisions
2529	100868		F	Contract
2530	100869	Nbn 11/6/-	F	Receipt for silver
2531	100870		F	Account of oxen
2532	100871	-/1/-	F	Receipt for purchase of oil
2533	100872	Cyr -/-/1	F	Account of salt
2534	100873		F	Account of garments of gods
2535	100874	Nbk 7/3/43	F	Receipt for garments
2536	100875		F	Only personal names preserved
2537	100876	16/9/2	F	Receipt for dates
2538	100877	Nb(-) 16/10/2	F	Receipt for dates
2539	100878	-/-/4	F	Account of dates
2540	100879		F	Account of dates or grain
2541	100880		F	Receipt for dates or grain
2542	100881		F	Account of dates and sesame
2543	100882		F	Account of silver
2544	100883		F	List of workmen(?)
2545	100884		F	Only personal names preserved
2546	100885		F	List of workmen
2547	100886	Nbn 9/8/-	F	Account of dates
2548	100887	Cam -/7/1	F	Sales receipt
2549	100888		F	Accounts
2550	100889		F	Account of provisions(?)
2551	100890		F	Account of provisions(?)
2552	100891		F	Account of provisions(?)
2553	100892	Nb(-) -/-/9	F	Contract for barley
2554	100893	Nbn	F	Receipt for linen
2555	100894	Nbn 20/10/-	F	Loan of silver
2556	100895	21/4/20	F	Receipt for dates or grain
2557	100896		F	Receipt for dates or grain
2558	100897		F	Account of dates or grain
2559	100898	-/-/5	F	Accounts
2560	100899		F	Receipt for gold for rings for Šamaš
2561	100900	Dar 14/6/3	F	Account of dates
2562	100901		F	Literary
2563	100902	Nb(-) 25/5/7	F	Receipt for silver
2564	100903		F	Omens
2565	100904	Dar -/6b/-	F	Account of dates

83-1-21,

2566	100905		F	Contract for dyes; Sippar
2567	100906		F	School exercise
2568	100907	17/-/5	F	Receipt for gold jewelry
2569	100908	Nbn 27/7/13	F	Accounts
2570	100909		F	List of measurements
2571	100910	Nbn 24/9/5	F	Sales receipt
2572	100911	25/4/20	F	Receipt
2573	100912		F	Account of garments(?)
2574	100913		F	Only personal names preserved
2575	100914		F	Receipt for oxen
2576	100915		F	Contract
2577	100916		F	Only personal names preserved
2578	100917		F	Account of silver
2579	100918		F	Accounts of various purchases
2580	100919	Nbn -/8/15	F	Contract
2581	100920		F	Accounts
2582	100921	Dar 13/11/1	F	Receipt for purchase of a slave
2583	100922		F	Account of dates or grain
2584	100923	25/11/-	F	Letter; seal
2585	100924	Nb(-) -/1/-	F	Contract for dates
2586	100925		F	List of workmen
2587	100926	Nb(-)	F	Contract
2588	100927		F	Receipt for sesame
2589	100928		F	Lexical
2590	100929	Cyr 22/12b/6	F	Receipt for silver
2591	100930	Nbn 24/3/-	F	Audit of farmers
2592	100931		F	Contract for dates
2593	100932		F	Dates or grain ledger
2594	100933		F	Only personal names preserved
2595	100934		F	Only personal names preserved
2596	100935	-/12/-	F	Receipt for carded wool
2597	100936		F	Ledger
2598	100937	Nbn 5/-/6	F	Receipt for oxen
2599	100938	Dar 8/-/-	F	Receipt for sheep
2600	100939	Nbn 14/9/-	F	Receipt for purchases
2601	100940	-/2/27	F	Receipt for dates or grain
2602	100941	Nbk 6/5/25	F	Account of dates
2603	100942		F	Account of provisions
2604	100943		F	Account of dates or grain

83-1-21,

2605	100944		F	Account of sesame
2606	100945	Cyr 27/1/5	F	Receipt for tithes
2607	100946	Nbn -/9/4	F	Receipt for silver; drawing
2608	100947		F	Account of sesame
2609	100948	Dar -/-/13	F	Account of dates
2610	100949	Nbk 10/7/35	F	Receipt for oil
2611	100950	Dar	F	Receipt for sale of sheep
2612	100951	Ner 23/9/-	F	Receipt for dates
2613	100952		F	Accounts
2614	100953		F	Account of dates
2615	100954		F	Account of garments of gods
2616	100955	-/-/11	F	Contract
2617	100956	Nbn	F	Account of dates or grain
2618	100957		F	Ledger
2619	100958	-/2/1	F	Receipt for silver
2620	100959		F	Account of dates or grain
2621	100960		F	Receipt for purchase of garments
2622	100961	Dar 8/12/4	F	Receipt
2623	100962		F	Contract for dates
2624	100963	Nbn	F	Receipt for animals
2625	100964	7/2/-	F	Receipt for wool
2626	100965	Nbn	F	Account of wool
2627	100966	Nbn -/9/-	F	Account of dates
2628	100967		F	Contract
2629	100968	16/6/-	F	Account of dates
2630	100969		F	Account of silver
2631	100970	7/9/39	F	Receipt for wool
2632	100971		F	Account of garments of gods
2633	100972		F	Accounts
2634	100973		F	Account of dates
2635	100974		F	Account of dates or grain
2636	100975		F	Receipt for purchase of dates
2637	100976	-/12/4	F	Receipt
2638	100977		F	Contract; seals
2639	100978	-/3/2	F	Account of sheep
2640	100979	-/-/6	F	Receipt
2641	100980	2/5/25	F	Receipt for iron
2642	100981	14/10/-	F	Contract for dates or grain
2643	100982		F	Accounts

83-1-21,

2644	100983		F	Legal
2645	100984		F	Account of silver; turns wrong way
2646	100985		F	Account of bricks
2647	100986	Nbn 16/1/-	F	Receipt for dates or grain
2648	100987		F	Account of silver for purchases
2649	100988		F	List of workmen
2650	100989	OB	F	Witnesses only
2651	100990	Cyr 23/5/9	F	Contract
2652	100991		F	Receipt for purchase of sheep
2653	100992		F	Letter; seal
2654	100993	29/6/-	F	Account of barley
2655	100994	-/-/15	F	Account of provisions
2656	100995	Nbn 12/12/-	F	Receipt for sheep
2657	100996	-/1/-	F	Receipt for flour
2658	100997	Nbn 10/3/6	F	Receipt for silver
2659	100998	Nbn 13/9/13	F	Account of dates
2660	100999	4/1/-	F	Account of animals
2661	101000		F	Account of oxen
2662	101001		F	Account of dates
2663	101002	Dar 5/-/21	F	Accounts
2664	101003		F	List of workmen
2665	101004	Dar	F	Accounts
2666	101005		F	Contract
2667	101006		F	Letter
2668	101007		F	Dates or grain ledger
2669	101008		F	Account of silver
2670	101009	Nbn -/-/12	F	Account of farmers
2671	101010		F	Receipt for barley
2672	101011		F	Account of silver
2673	101012		F	Lexical; kù-nam-tab-ba
2674	101013		F	Receipt
2675	101014	Nbn 3/9/14	F	Receipt for dates
2676	101015	9/5/-	F	Fruit ledger
2677	101016	Dar 18/1/3	F	Contract
2678	101017		F	Account of silver for reeds
2679	101018		F	Letter(?)
2680	101019		F	Account of aromatics
2681	101020		F	Ledger
2682	101021		F	Accounts

83-1-21,

2683	101022		F	Contract for dates; Sippar
2684	101023		F	Account of dates or grain
2685	101024	Nbn 12/2/9	F	Receipt for purchase of stone
2686	101025	-/-/2	F	Receipt for dates or grain
2687	101026	Nbn 11/10/-	F	Account of dates
2688	101027	Dar 6/4/25	F	Receipt for wool
2689	101028		F	Account of dates or grain
2690	101029	Cam	F	Receipt; drawing
2691	101030		F	Account of silver
2692	101031		F	List of workmen
2693	101032		F	Receipt for dates or grain
2694	101033		F	Account of dates or grain
2695	101034		F	Ledger
2696	101035		F	Account of sheep
2697	101036	Dar -/10/26	F	Account of dates
2698	101037		F	Accounts
2699	101038		F	Account of barley
2700	101039	Nbn 27/3/9	NC	Receipt for tools
2701	101040		F	Account of barley
2702	101041	OB	F	Contract concerning slaves; seals
2703	101042		F	Accounts
2704	101043		F	Economic
2705	101044	Nbn -/-/2	F	Account of animals
2706	101045	OB	F	Administrative; sheep; seals
2707	101046		F	Account of dates or grain provisions
2708	101047	19/4/-	F	Account of animals
2709	101048	Nbn -/1/16	F	Account
2710	101049		F	Accounts
2711	101050	Nbk -/5/-	F	Contract for dates
2712	101051	13/8/-	F	Contract
2713	101052	Dar 12/1/-	F	Receipt for dates; drawing
2714	101053	1/3/30	F	Account of dates
2715	101054		F	Accounts
2716	101055		F	Accounts of barley and linen
2717	101056	6/7/22	F	Account of provisions(?) for workmen
2718	101057	-/-/12	F	Receipt for purchase of wool
2719	101058	Nbn 7/7/-	F	Account of barley
2720	101059		F	Account of silver
2721	101060	Nbn -/2/13	F	Account of garments of gods

83-1-21,

2722	101061	-/-/14	F	Account of dates
2723	101062		F	Account of jewelry
2724	101063		F	Account of wool
2725	101064		F	Ledger
2726	101065		F	Contract
2727	101066	Nb(-) -/3/-	F	Account of jewelry of gods
2728	101067	17/-/-	F	Receipt
2729	101068	Nbn 1/3/-	F	Account of sheep
2730	101069		F	Account of garments of gods
2731	101070	9/-/13	F	Contract
2732	101071	Nbn 7/1/10+	F	Receipt; drawing
2733	101072	-/-/19	F	Accounts
2734	101073		F	Account of provisions for workmen
2735	101074	Nbk 19/12/7	F	Receipt for dates or grain
2736	101075	-/-/2	F	Account of barley
2737	101076		F	Accounts
2738	101077		F	Account of oxen
2739	101078		F	Account of sheep
2740	101079		F	Account of provisions
2741	101080	-/9/10	F	Account of animals
2742	101081		F	Account of oxen
2743	101082	Nbn 22/-/-	F	Accounts
2744	101083		F	Ledger
2745	101084		F	Accounts
2746	101085		F	Account of dates or grain
2747	101086	22/-/10+	F	Account of sheep
2748	101087		F	Account of dates or grain
2749	101088		F	Account by days
2750	101089	OB	F	Administrative; sheep; seals
2751	101090		F	School exercise
2752	101091		F	Account of wool
2753	101092	Nbn	F	Accounts
2754	101093		F	Account of dates or grain
2755	101094	Nbk 5/8/26	F	Receipt for a bird
2756	101095	1/6/-	F	Account of garments
2757	101096		F	*Ḫḫ* I
2758	101097		F	Receipt for flour
2759	101098	Cam -/-/1	F	Account of dates
2760	101099	-/5/16	F	Account of dates

83-1-21,

2761	101100	Cyr 20/7/acc	F	Receipt for sheep
2762	101101		F	Ledger
2763	101102		F	Uninscribed clay showing impression of a metal vessel; cf. *UE* 10 pl. 43 and 82-9-18, 7017 (= BM 67022) and 83-1-21, 1 (= BM 82838)
2764	101103		F	Account of workmen
2765	101104		F	Receipt
2766	101105		F	Ledger
2767	101106		F	Account of dates
2768	101107		F	School exercise
2769	101108	Nbn 23/12/-	F	Account of sheep
2770	101109		F	School exercise
2771	101110	Dar 5/6/-	F	Account of barley
2772	101111		F	Account of provisions(?)
2773	101112		F	Accounts
2774	101113	Cam 4/6/1	F	Receipt
2775	101114		F	Account of provisions for workmen
2776	101115	Nbn 7/10/12	F	Receipt for materials
2777	101116		F	Accounts
2778	101117	Cam 17/9/-	F	Account of sheep
2779	101118		F	Account of dates or grain
2780	101119	Nbn -/-/3	F	Account of dates
2781	101120	Dar 9/8/5	F	Sales receipt
2782	101121		F	Ledger
2783	101122	12/-/7	F	Account of garments
2784	101123		F	Account of dates or grain provisions
2785	101124		F	Accounts
2786	101125	Nbn 25/12/2	C	Receipt for flour
2787	101126	16/12/-	F	Account of wages for hired men
2788	101127		F	Account of workmen
2789	101128	Dar -/1/21	F	Receipt for wool
2790	101129		F	Receipt for sheep
2791	101130	Nbn 14/10/15	F	Receipt for dates
2792	101131	Nbn -/-/1	F	Account of beer
2793	101132	Nbn 13/9/1	F	Receipt for sesame
2794	101133		F	Account of garments of gods
2795	101134		F	Accounts
2796	101135	Dar -/12/-	F	Receipt for wool(?); turns wrong way
2797	101136	Nbn 4/1/7	F	Receipt for iron; drawing

83-1-21,

2798	101137	Dar 10/2/-	F	Receipt for purchase of dates
2799	101138		F	School exercise
2800	101139		F	Deposition
2801	101140		F	Account of dates
2802	101141	Nbn -/-/9	F	Account of wool, garments and commodities
2803	101142	Nbk 12/4/-	F	Account of wages(?)
2804	101143		F	*Ḫḫ* I
2805	101144	Ner	F	Account of dates or grain
2806	101145	Dar -/4/25	F	Sales receipt
2807	101146		F	School exercise
2808	101147		F	School exercise
2809	101148		F	School exercise
2810	101149	Nbk 12/-/5	F	Receipt for oxen
2811	101150		F	Receipt for dates or grain
2812	101151	Dar 1/1/21	F	Receipt for silver
2813	101152		F	Account of dates
2814	101153	7/2/13	F	Receipt for gold vessels
2815	101154	Nbk 8/1/30	F	Receipt for dates or grain
2816	101155		F	Receipt for dates
2817	101156	Cam 4/9/-	F	Receipt for barley
2818	101157		F	Account of dates
2819	101158		F	List of workmen
2820	101159		F	Contract; seal
2821	101160	13/4/-	F	Account of wool
2822	101161		F	Receipt
2823	101162	Nbn	F	Account of oil
2824	101163	2/4/-	F	Account of sheep
2825	101164	10/4/-	F	Account of silver
2826	101165		F	Account of oxen
2827	101166		F	Account of dates or grain provisions
2828	101167		F	Accounts
2829	101168	Nb(-) 15/4/16	F	Receipt for barley
2830	101169		F	Account of garments of gods
2831	101170		F	Account of oxen
2832	101171		F	Accounts
2833	101172		F	Ledger
2834	101173		F	Account of dates
2835	101174		F	Account of dates or grain

83-1-21,

2836	101175		F	Account of barley
2837	101176		F	Account of fodder
2838	101177		F	Account of wool
2839	101178		F	Account of fruit
2840	101179		F	Accounts
2841	101180		F	Accounts
2842	101181		F	School exercise
2843	101182		F	Account of dates or grain
2844	101183	23/6/-	F	Accounts
2845	101184		F	Account of dates
2846	101185		F	School exercise
2847	101186		F	Account of dates
2848	101187	Nbn 7/1/-	F	Account of barley
2849	101188	Nbn 28/5/10	F	Deposition
2850	101189	Nbk 6/7/35	F	Account of dates or barley provisions
2851	101190		F	List of workmen
2852	101191		F	Account of dates
2853	101192		F	Account of barley
2854	101193	Nbn 12/9/8	F	Receipt for purchase of garments
2855	101194	-/-/1	F	Account of dates
2856	101195	Nbn 11/3/5	F	Account of dates or grain
2857	101196		F	Account of dates or grain provisions
2858	101197		F	Accounts
2859	101198	Nbn	F	Account of dates or grain
2860	101199	Dar 15/-/27	F	Letter; seals
2861	101200		F	*Ḫḫ* I
2862	101201		F	List of workmen
2863	101202		F	Account of dates or grain
2864	101203		F	Contract
2865	101204		F	Receipt for dates or grain
2866	101205	Cyr	F	Account of fodder
2867	101206		F	List of workmen; Aramaic docket
2868	101207		F	Account of dates
2869	101208	8/9/-	F	Receipt for wool
2870	101209		F	Account of bricks(?)
2871	101210	Nbn 9/-/14	F	Receipt for emmer
2872	101211		F	Account of oxen
2873	101212	Nbn 19/-/-	F	Receipt for purchase of flour
2874	101213		F	Accounts

83-1-21,

2875	101214	Nbn -/12/6	F	Receipt for dates or grain
2876	101215		F	Account of wool(?)
2877	101216	Nb(-) 5/-/-	F	Receipt for purchases of hides
2878	101217	-/5/-	F	Account of bread
2879	101218	Nbn	F	Receipt for boat rental
2880	101219		F	School exercise; phrases
2881	101220		F	Account of barley
2882	101221		F	Contract
2883	101222		F	Receipt for dates
2884	101223		F	Literary
2885	101224		F	Accounts
2886	101225	-/12/-	F	Receipt
2887	101226	1/6/1	F	Receipt for fleece
2888	101227	-/-/19	F	Receipt; Aramaic docket
2889	101228		F	Ledger
2890	101229		F	Dates or grain ledger
2891	101230	Nb(-) -/-/3	F	Account of barley
2892	101231	Nbn 5/5/14	F	Receipt
2893	101232		F	Field sale
2894	101233		F	Accounts
2895	101234		F	Legal(?)
2896	101235		F	Loan
2897	101236		F	Account of dates
2898	101237		F	Accounts
2899	101238		F	Animal ledger
2900	101239		F	Accounts
2901	101240		F	Account of provisions(?)
2902	101241		F	Account of workmen
2903	101242		F	Dates or grain ledger
2904	101243		F	Receipt
2905	101244		F	Account of dates or grain
2906	101245		F	Account of sheep
2907	101246	Dar 17/2/9	F	Receipt for barley for flour
2908	101247		F	School exercise
2909	101248	Cyr -/1/3	F	Account of aromatics
2910	101249	Dar 15/-/27	F	Letter; seals
2911	101250	15/1/-	F	Account of barley
2912	101251		F	Account of garments
2913	101252	10/11/-	F	Account of dates

83-1-21,

2914	101253		F	Accounts
2915	101254	Nbk 19/7/37	F	Account of bricks
2916	101255		F	Accounts
2917	101256	Nb(-) 20/-/6	F	Receipt for emmer
2918	101257	Nbn 8/-/-	F	Receipt for dates
2919	101258		F	Contract
2920	101259		F	School exercise
2921	101260	Nbn -/-/5	F	Account of oxen
2922	101261		F	Receipt
2923	101262	Nbn 17/-/10	F	Account of dates and cassia
2924	101263		F	Account of dates
2925	101264		F	Receipt for barley
2926	101265	Cyr 20+/1/8	F	Receipt for sesame
2927	101266		F	Account of dates or grain
2928	101267	Cam 24/-/1	F	Account of barley
2929	101268	Nbn 19/-/12+	F	Receipt for dates
2930	101269		F	List of workmen
2931	101270	-/-/27	F	Receipt for gold; seals
2932	101271	-/9/2	F	Receipt
2933	101272		F	Account of silver
2934	101273	Cam 6/6/-	F	Contract
2935	101274	11/2/11	F	Account of oxen
2936	101275		F	Accounts
2937	101276	Nbn 15/12/-	F	Receipt for dates
2938	101277		F	Account of silver
2939	101278		F	Letter(?)
2940	101279		F	Account of foremen and workmen
2941	101280		F	Accounts
2942	101281	Nbn 11/-/10	F	Accounts
2943	101282	Ner -/2/-	F	Receipt for barley
2944	101283		F	Receipt for dates
2945	101284		F	Account of dates
2946	101285		F	Account of sheep
2947	101286	Nbn 6/2/9	F	Receipt for garments of gods
2948	101287	Nbn 7/-/-	F	Receipt for silver
2949	101288		F	Account of silver
2950	101289		F	Account of oxen
2951	101290		F	Account of silver
2952	101291	-/10/11	F	Receipt for emmer

83-1-21,

2953	101292		F	Accounts
2954	101293		F	Account of silver
2955	101294	Nbn -/1/5	F	Account of oxen
2956	101295	Dar 16/6/7	F	Account of barley
2957	101296		F	Account of silver
2958	101297	Nbn 16/1/-	NC	Receipt for income
2959	101298	25/12/18	F	Receipt for flour; seal
2960	101299	Ner 1/7/acc	F	Receipt for wool
2961	101300	Nbn 10/6/17	F	Receipt
2962	101301	Nbn 4/12/1	F	Receipt for purchase of garments
2963	101302		F	Account of wool
2964	101303	Nbn -/7/-	F	Receipt
2965	101304		F	Account of hired men
2966	101305	Nbn	F	Account of barley
2967	101306		F	List of workmen
2968	101307		F	Account of gold
2969	101308		F	Accounts
2970	101309		F	Receipt for sesame
2971	101310	6/-/3	F	Receipt; drawing
2972	101311	Nbn 11/8/5	F	Receipt for jewelry(?) of gods
2973	101312	Cyr 17/-/-	F	Receipt for garments
2974	101313	Nbk 14/9/20	NC	Receipt for birds
2975	101314	Cyr 6/-/1	NC	Receipt for barley; seal
2976	101315	3/-/16	F	Account of dates
2977	101316	-/8/21	F	Account of dates
2978	101317	(Dar) -/10/30	F	Receipt for tools
2979	101318	Dar	F	Legal
2980	101319	Cam 4/7/acc	NC	Receipt for barley
2981	101320	Nbn -/-/2	F	Account of barley
2982	101321	Dar 14/1/9	F	Receipt for silver
2983	101322	-/-/15	F	Receipt
2984	101323		F	School exercise
2985	101324	-/-/29	F	Receipt for iron
2986	101325	Dar	F	Account of flour
2987	101326		F	Accounts
2988	101327	Nbn 29/-/10	F	Receipt for flour
2989	101328	Nbn -/-/16	F	Account of hired men
2990	101329	-/11/20+	F	Receipt for aromatics
2991	101330		F	Account of provisions(?)

83-1-21,

2992	101331		F	Accounts
2993	101332		F	Accounts
2994	101333		F	Accounts
2995	101334		F	Deposition
2996	101335		F	Contract for boat rental
2997	101336		F	Account of emmer
2998	101337		C	Letter
2999	101338	Nbn 16/-/6	F	Receipt for birds
3000	101339		C	School exercise
3001	101340		F	Account of garments
3002	101341	Cyr 5/12/7	F	Receipt for silver
3003	101342	15/2/43	C	Receipt for oil
3004	101343		F	Legal
3005	101344	Cam 22/12/-	F	Contract
3006	101345	-/10/-	F	Receipt for barley
3007	101346		F	Receipt for silver
3008	101347	13/7/1	F	Account of dates
3009	101348		F	Account of oxen
3010	101349		F	Grain ledger
3011	101350		F	Account of provisions(?)
3012	101351		F	Account of garments of gods
3013	101352	-/-/2	F	Accounts
3014	101353		F	Accounts
3015	101354		F	Account of barley
3016	101355	Nbn 14/7/11	F	Receipt for silver
3017	101356	15/3/10	F	Account of dates or grain
3018	101357		F	Account of dates or grain
3019	101358		F	Contract
3020	101359		F	Accounts
3021	101360		F	Account of barley
3022	101361		F	Account of provisions
3023	101362	Nbk -/9/18	F	Account of dates
3024	101363	Nbn 6/7/12	F	Receipt for dates or grain
3025	101364	Nbn 16/-/10	F	Accounts
3026	101365		F	Account of dates or grain
3027	101366		F	*Lu* IV 155ff.; dupl. *MSL* 12 p. 133
3028	101367	Nbk 10/-/34	F	Contract for dates
3029	101368		F	Account of dates or grain
3030	101369	17/11/13	F	Accounts

83-1-21,

3031	101370	-/-/26	F	Account of dates or grain; seal
3032	101371		F	Account of dates or grain
3033	101372		F	List of workmen
3034	101373		F	Receipt for dates or grain
3035	101374		F	Account of garments(?) of gods
3036	101375		F	Account of silver
3037	101376	26/-/11	F	Account of dates
3038	101377		F	Contract for seed
3039	101378		F	Ledger
3040	101379		F	Only personal names preserved
3041	101380	-/-/35	F	Account of provisions
3042	101381		F	Account of silver
3043	101382		F	Contract(?) for barley
3044	101383	Nbn 19/9/4	F	Receipt for barley
3045	101384		F	Account of provisions
3046	101385		F	Receipt for silver
3047	101386		F	Accounts; only personal names preserved
3048	101387	Dar 12/8/3	F	Receipt for dates
3049	101388	Nbk 8/3/-	F	Receipt for purchase of barley
3050	101389		F	Account of dates
3051	101390	Nbn -/-/9	F	Account of dates
3052	101391	Dar 3/6/7	NC	Receipt for dates
3053	101392		F	Account of animal offerings
3054	101393	Nbn 7/1/14	F	Account of offerings
3055	101394		F	Accounts
3056	101395		F	Account of wool(?)
3057	101396		F	Only personal names preserved
3058	101397		F	Contract(?)
3059	101398		F	Account of wool(?)
3060	101399		F	Date or grain ledger
3061	101400		F	Account of wool(?)
3062	101401		F	Sale of sheep
3063	101402		F	Lexical
3064	101403	Nbn 13/-/-	F	Account of copper vessels
3065	101404		F	Account of shares
3066	101405	OB	F	Letter
3067	101406		F	Account of utensils
3068	101407	-/-/7	F	Account of dates or grain

83-1-21,

3069	101408		F	Marriage contract
3070	101409		F	Astronomical
3071	101410		F	Account of date or grain provisions
3072	101411	5/4/-	F	Receipt for garments
3073	101412	Dar	F	Account of date tithes
3074	101413		F	Accounts
3075	101414		NC	Receipt for dates or grain
3076	101415	Xer	F	Receipt
3077	101416	27/10/15	F	Receipt for wool
3078	101417		F	Account of dates or grain
3079	101418	Dar	F	Rental of a field
3080	101419		F	Account of flour
3081	101420	Nbn -/-/9	F	Receipt for silver
3082	101421		F	Account of offerings
3083	101422		F	Account of silver(?)
3084	101423	-/-/16	F	Account of barley
3085	101424		F	Account of dates
3086	101425		F	Account of dates or grain
3087	101426	9/4/-	F	Receipt for garments of gods
3088	101427	Cyr -/5/2	F	Receipt for iron
3089	101428		F	Account of barley provisions
3090	101429		F	Account of sheep offerings
3091	101430	26/12/-	F	Receipt
3092	101431	Nbn 5/-/3	F	Account
3093	101432	-/11/-	F	Receipt for sheep
3094	101433	Nbn 22/6/-	F	Account of provisions for workmen
3095	101434		F	Account of sheep offerings
3096	101435	Cyr 5/8/9	F	Rental of a house
3097	101436		F	Ledger
3098	101437		F	Accounts
3099	101438		F	Account of dates and barley
3100	101439	Nbn 25/4/-	F	Account
3101	101440		F	Account of garments of gods
3102	101441		F	Ledger
3103	101442		F	Account of dates or grain
3104	101443		F	Only personal names preserved
3105	101444	17/11/13	F	Account of workmen
3106	101445		F	Accounts
3107	101446	Cam 9/7/1	NC	Receipt for dates

83-1-21,

3108	101447	Am 9/7/acc	F	Receipt for salt
3109	101448		F	Account of dates or grain
3110	101449		F	Receipt for dates or grain
3111	101450	Dar 27/3/21	F	Receipt
3112	101451		F	God list
3113	101452	Cam -/6/3	F	Receipt for sale of a house(?)
3114	101453	Nbn 2/11/-	F	Receipt for silver
3115	101454		F	Ritual(?) involving stones
3116	101455	Nbn 10/12/8	F	Receipt for barley flour
3117	101456		F	Incantation
3118	101457		F	Account of garments of gods
3119	101458		F	Accounts
3120	101459	Si -/-/7	F	Contract
3121	101460		F	Account of dates or grain
3122	101461		F	Account of dates or grain
3123	101462		F	Account of barley; erased
3124	101463	-/6/15	F	Barley ledger
3125	101464	( )-uṣur	F	Receipt
3126	101465		F	Account; only personal names preserved
3127	101466		F	Contract
3128	101467	Nbk 3/1/42	F	Receipt for garments
3129	101468		F	School exercise
3130	101469	9/-/-	NC	Receipt for iron for tools
3131	101470		F	Account of barley
3132	101471		F	Account of workmen
3133	101472		F	Account of dates or grain
3134	101473	Nbk 2/6/10+	F	Account of bricks
3135	101474	Sd -/10/mu gibil [...]	C	Loan; seals
3136	101475	-/1/-	F	Account of sheep
3137	101476		F	School exercise; *Ḫḫ* I
3138	101477		F	School exercise; personal names
3139	101478		F	School exercise
3140	101479	Nbn 8/7/6	F	Receipt for purchase of fodder
3141	101480		F	School exercise
3142	101481	Dar	F	Accounts
3143	101482	Dar 20+/1/-	F	Contract for barley
3144	101483		F	School exercise
3145	101484	Nbk 1/4/36	F	Receipt for provisions

83-1-21,

3146	101485		F	Economic
3147	101486		F	Account of dates
3148	101487		F	Account of date or grain provisions
3149	101488	Dar -/-/26	F	Receipt for wool
3150	101489	Cyr 15/7/9	F	Receipt for barley
3151	101490		F	Account of dates or grain
3152	101491	-/-/3	F	Offering ledger
3153	101492		F	Account of garments of gods
3154	101493	Nbk -/10/34	F	Receipt for bitumen
3155	101494		F	Receipt for silver
3156	101495		F	Contract
3157	101496		F	Account of sesame; drawing
3158	101497		F	Account of flour
3159	101498		F	Sale of land; Sippar
3160	101499		F	Account of barley and emmer
3161	101500	-/-/43	F	Contract
3162	101501	Dar -/-/3	F	Receipt for dates
3163	101502		F	Only personal names preserved
3164	101503	Dar 4/12/acc	F	Account of *telitu* tax
3165	101504	Nbn 12/12/-	F	Contract; Aramaic docket
3166	101505		F	Account of dates or grain
3167	101506		F	Account of barley
3168	101507		F	Dates or grain ledger
3169	101508		F	Accounts
3170	101509	Nbk 11/-/19	F	Receipt for gold
3171	101510	Ner -/-/1	F	Account of dates
3172	101511	Nbn -/-/-	F	Audit account
3173	101512		F	Contract
3174	101513		F	Receipt
3175	101514		F	Economic
3176	101515	Dar -/-/3	F	Account of dates
3177	101516	Nbn -/-/7	F	Receipt for dates or grain
3178	101517	Dar 21/3/35	F	Contract
3179	101518		F	Contract
3180	101519	Nbk	F	Account of workmen
3181	101520	Dar 23/3/27	F	Receipt for copper
3182	101521	Cam 6/10/-	F	Contract for barley
3183	101522		F	Account of dates or grain
3184	101523		F	Receipt; Aramaic docket

83-1-21,

3185	101524	Nbk 9/12/-	F	Receipt for barley
3186	101525		F	Receipt for sheep
3187	101526	Nbn -/6/-	F	Contract; Sippar
3188	101527		F	Account of dates or grain
3189	101528	Nbn 3/-/-	F	Receipt for purchase of barley
3190	101529	-/1/16	F	Account of dates or grain
3191	101530		F	Receipt for garments
3192	101531	Nbn 1/8/2	F	Receipt for dates or grain
3193	101532	Cam 29/-/1	F	Receipt for iron
3194	101533		F	Receipt for barley tithe
3195	101534		F	Account of dates or grain
3196	101535	Nbk 24/5/30	F	Account of sheep
3197	101536		F	Accounts
3198	101537		F	Ledger
3199	101538		F	Economic
3200	101539	Nbk -/3/-	F	Contract
3201	101540		F	Receipt for loan payment
3202	101541	Cyr	F	Legal document; Babylon
3203	101542	Cam 21/6/-	F	Receipt for dates
3204	101543	Nbn 28/-/-	F	Receipt for barley
3205	101544	Cam -/-/1	F	Account of dates
3206	101545		F	Loan(?)
3207	101546	9/12/20	F	Receipt for birds; drawing
3208	101547	Nbn 5/3/-	F	Account of dates
3209	101548		C	Receipt for workmen
3210	101549	Cam 20+/7/7	F	Receipt for purchase of beer
3211	101550		F	Dates or grain ledger
3212	101551		F	Account of garments of gods
3213	101552	Nb(-) -/12b/12	F	Account of dates
3214	101553		F	Account of dates or grain
3215	101554		F	Account of provisions for workmen
3216	101555	14/-/13	F	Accounts
3217	101556		F	Account of dates or grain
3218	101557		F	Account of workmen
3219	101558		F	School exercise; literary extract
3220	101559		F	Account of barley
3221	101560		F	Letter order
3222	101561		F	Accounts
3223	101562	Nbn 16/2/6	F	Contract for barley

83-1-21,

3224	101563	Cam	F	Accounts
3225	101564		F	Accounts
3226	101565	Nbn 18/2/-	F	Dialogue legal text
3227	101566		F	Account of animals(?)
3228	101567	OB	F	Field rental
3229	101568	Dar 28/12/-	F	Receipt for silver
3230	101569		F	Medical; probably same tablet as 83-1-21, 3599 (= BM 101938)
3231	101570	OB	F	School text(?)
3232	101571		F	Accounts
3233	101572		F	Account of workmen
3234	101573	Nbk 18/-/-	F	House rentals
3235	101574		F	Account of silver payments
3236	101575	16/6/1	F	Receipt for sheep
3237	101576		F	Astronomical
3238	101577		F	Account of dates or grain
3239	101578		F	Account of dates or grain
3240	101579		NC	Memorandum concerning wood
3241	101580		F	School exercise
3242	101581		F	Account of barley
3243	101582		F	Account of dates or grain
3244	101583	(-)-uşur -/10/23	F	Receipt for sesame
3245	101584	OB	F	Contract; seals
3246	101585		F	Ledger
3247	101586		F	Account of garments of gods
3248	101587		F	Accounts
3249	101588		F	Account of dates or grain
3250	101589	-/-/1	F	Letter order
3251	101590	Nbn -/-/12	F	Account of provisions for workmen
3252	101591		F	Yearly accounts
3253	101592		F	Accounts
3254	101593	Aş 28/1/16	F	Memorandum; round type
3255	101594		F	Account of dates or grain
3256	101595		F	Accounts
3257	101596	Nbn 5/5/-	F	Account of dates
3258	101597		F	Only personal names preserved
3259	101598		F	Account of barley
3260	101599	-/-/35	F	Receipt for barley fodder
3261	101600	Nbn -/-/13	F	Account of dates

83-1-21,

3262	101601		F	Account of sesame provisions
3263	101602		F	Accounts
3264	101603		F	Letter(?)
3265	101604		F	Account of dates or grain
3266	101605		F	Contract
3267	101606		F	Accounts of provisions(?)
3268	101607		F	Accounts
3269	101608		F	Account of dates
3270	101609		F	Account of dates
3271	101610		F	Account of *telitu* tax
3272	101611		F	Receipt for purchase of sheep
3273	101612	Dar	F	Accounts
3274	101613		F	Accounts
3275	101614		F	Contract
3276	101615	Nbk -/-/25	F	Receipt for barley fodder
3277	101616		F	Account of garments
3278	101617	Art	F	Letter
3279	101618	OB	F	Sumerian literary(?)
3280	101619	-/1/16	F	Receipt for metal for objects
3281	101620	Nb(-) 21/-/1	F	Account of sheep
3282	101621		F	Accounts
3283	101622		F	Account of barley
3284	101623	Nbk 21/8/-	F	Account of dates or grain
3285	101624		F	Account of provisions(?)
3286	101625	Cyr 23/-/3	NC	Receipt for iron
3287	101626	Nbn 16/12/-	F	Receipt
3288	101627		F	Ledger
3289	101628	20/2/26	F	Receipt for dates
3290	101629	19/-/14	F	Receipt for dates
3291	101630	(-)-uṣur 23/-/-	F	Receipt for metal(?)
3292	101631		F	Account of garments
3293	101632	Cam 18/4/-	F	Account of dates or grain
3294	101633	-/1/-	F	Receipt for dates or grain
3295	101634		F	Contract(?)
3296	101635		F	Account of expenditures of silver
3297	101636	Nbn 20+/1/-	F	Receipt for copper
3298	101637	Nbn -/-/13	F	Accounts
3299	101638		F	Account of craftsmen
3300	101639	Nbn 23/1/9	F	Receipt for dates

83-1-21,

3301	101640		F	Ledger
3302	101641	Nbk 25/8/24	F	Accounts
3303	101642	Cyr 10/8/2	F	Receipt for date tithes
3304	101643		F	Contract
3305	101644		F	Receipt for barley flour
3306	101645	Cam 26/6/1	F	Account of dates; drawing
3307	101646	Cyr 26/-/-	F	Contract for barley
3308	101647	Nbn 1/9/-	F	Contract for dates
3309	101648		F	Contract
3310	101649	Nbn 14/3/-	F	Account
3311	101650	Nbn	F	Account of dates or grain
3312	101651		F	Contract for emmer
3313	101652	Nb(-) -/6/5	F	Receipt for a sheep
3314	101653	Cyr 12/-/-	F	Receipt for metal
3315	101654	24/12/24	F	Account of dates
3316	101655		F	Account of dates
3317	101656		F	Accounts
3318	101657	Cam -/9/4	F	Account of dates
3319	101658		F	Account of animals(?)
3320	101659		F	Account of dates or grain
3321	101660	18/-/-	F	Account of dates or grain
3322	101661	-/-/acc	F	Account of barley
3323	101662		F	Account of provisions
3324	101663	10+/6/-	F	Contract; Sippar
3325	101664		F	Account of dates or grain
3326	101665		F	Receipt for date provisions
3327	101666	Nbn 23/3/-	F	Receipt; drawing
3328	101667		F	Receipt for date provisions; drawing
3329	101668	-/-/10	F	Accounts
3330	101669		F	Account of provisions
3331	101670		F	Accounts
3332	101671	Nb(-) 10+/10/12	F	Receipt for wool(?)
3333	101672	-/12/-	F	Receipt for barley
3334	101673	Cam -/8/4	F	Account of dates or grain
3335	101674	25/-/23	F	Receipt
3336	101675	20/2/26	F	Receipt for sheep
3337	101676	Nb(-) 15/2/11	F	Receipt for sesame
3338	101677	Cam 30/6/3	F	Letter
3339	101678	-/-/34	F	Account of wool

83-1-21,

3340	101679	Nbn -/12/16	F	Receipt for metal
3341	101680		F	Contract for barley
3342	101681	Nbn 3/6/-	F	Receipt for silver(?)
3343	101682	Nbn 23/4/-	F	Loan of silver
3344	101683	Dar 2/-/6	F	Receipt
3345	101684		F	Contract for barley
3346	101685	Nbn -/-/acc	F	Accounts
3347	101686	-/6/10	F	Receipt for silver for provisions
3348	101687	-/-/17	F	Receipt for blue wool
3349	101688		F	Account of barley
3350	101689	13/-/7	F	Account of jewelry of gods
3351	101690		F	Account of barley for provisions
3352	101691	Nbn -/4/7	F	Receipt for iron for working
3353	101692	Cam 4/2/-	F	Receipt for purchase of salt and provisions
3354	101693	2/7/6	NC	Receipt for garments
3355	101694	Npl 4/9/15	NC	Receipt for oil
3356	101695		F	Account of dates or grain
3357	101696		F	Accounts
3358	101697		F	Contract for dates
3359	101698		F	School exercise
3360	101699	Nbk	F	Ledger
3361	101700		F	Account of sesame
3362	101701		F	Account of workmen
3363	101702	-/16/16	F	Account of dates
3364	101703		F	Dates or grain ledger
3365	101704	Cam 30/-/1	F	Receipt for dates
3366	101705	Nbk -/7/20+	F	Receipt for dates or grain
3367	101706		F	Account of dates or grain
3368	101707		F	Contract
3369	101708		F	Account of provisions
3370	101709		F	Ledger; only personal names preserved
3371	101710	OB	F	List of loans of silver; round type
3372	101711	Nbn 25/2/-	F	Contract for sheep
3373	101712		F	Accounts
3374	101713	Cam 26/-/-	F	Receipt for purchase of sheep
3375	101714		F	Contract
3376	101715	12/-/5	F	Contract for barley
3377	101716		F	Account of oxen and sheep

83-1-21,

3378	101717	Nbn 1/-/2	NC	Receipt for barley
3379	101718		F	Economic
3380	101719	Nbn	F	Account of temple paraphernalia
3381	101720		F	Account of barley
3382	101721		F	School exercise
3383	101722		F	Account of workmen
3384	101723	Nbn	F	Accounts
3385	101724	OB	F	Summaries of real-estate transactions; unusual format
3386	101725		F	Contract
3387	101726	Nbn 20/8/9	F	Receipt for wool
3388	101727		F	Account of dates or grain
3389	101728		F	Account of dates or grain
3390	101729		F	Account of dates
3391	101730		F	Contract
3392	101731		F	Account of bricks(?)
3393	101732		F	Receipt for jewelry
3394	101733		F	Only personal names preserved
3395	101734		F	*Ḫulbazizi* incantations
3396	101735	Nbk 10/3/36	F	Receipt
3397	101736		F	Astronomical
3398	101737		F	School exercise; oxen sales
3399	101738		F	Account of workmen
3400	101739		F	Contract
3401	101740	Nbn 9/-/6	F	Receipt for cattle
3402	101741	Cam 20/12/5	F	Receipt for temple paraphernalia
3403	101742	Nbn 17/1/-	F	Account of barley
3404	101743	Cam 24/-/-	F	Account of dates or grain
3405	101744		F	Account of fodder
3406	101745	Dar 12/2/6	F	Receipt for silver
3407	101746		F	Receipt for iron objects
3408	101747	Nbn -/1/-	F	Contract for barley
3409	101748	Nbn 26/1/16	F	Receipt for iron objects
3410	101749		F	Contract(?)
3411	101750		F	Only personal names preserved
3412	101751		F	Account of sheep
3413	101752	Cyr 15/-/2	F	Receipt for dates
3414	101753	-/4/8	F	Receipt for dates or grain
3415	101754	Dar 15/-/-	F	House(?) rental

83-1-21,

3416	101755		F	Account of sheep
3417	101756		F	Dates or grain ledger
3418	101757		F	Only personal names preserved
3419	101758	Nbn 23/5/-	F	Receipt for iron
3420	101759		F	Accounts
3421	101760		F	Ledger
3422	101761		F	Account of dates or grain
3423	101762		F	Economic
3424	101763	Nbn 9/2/-	F	Receipt for jewelry
3425	101764		F	School exercise
3426	101765		F	School exercise
3427	101766		F	Account of barley
3428	101767		F	Account of provisions(?)
3429	101768	Nbk -/12/-	F	Receipt
3430	101769	Nbk -/5/31	F	Receipt for metal(?)
3431	101770		F	School exercise
3432	101771		F	School exercise
3433	101772		F	School exercise
3434	101773		F	Account of dates or grain
3435	101774	Nb(-) 10+/6/-	F	Receipt for dates
3436	101775		F	Contract
3437	101776	Nbn 24/8/-	F	Receipt for blue wool
3438	101777		C	Medical prescriptions
3439	101778	7/8/-	C	Tag; three seals
3440	101779	4/3/36	C	Receipt for silver
3441	101780		NC	Astronomical
3442	101781	Dar 15/3/16	C	Letter
3443	101782		C	Bulla with impression of tablet inscribed *ḫe-pí eš-šu*, etc.
3444	101783		C	Bulla; seal
3445	101784		F	Accounts
3446	101785		F	Astronomical
3447	101786		F	School exercise
3448	101787	Xer 11/11/4	F	Legal
3449	101788		F	Bulla; seal
3450	101789		F	Bulla; five seals
3451	101790		F	Bulla; seal
3452	101791	Dar	F	Receipt for dates or grain
3453	101792		F	Accounts

83-1-21,

3454	101793		F	Account of garments of gods
3455	101794	Nbn 13/6/-	F	Account of barley
3456	101795		F	Ledger
3457	101796		F	Receipt for dates or grain
3458	101797	Nbk -/-/17	F	Account of dates or grain
3459	101798	OB	F	Harvest loan(?); seals
3460	101799		F	Letter
3461	101800	Dar -/12/20	F	Account of barley
3462	101801		F	Account of silver
3463	101802		F	Accounts
3464	101803	-/2/-	F	Receipt for barley
3465	101804		F	Receipt for sesame
3466	101805	Ner 6/1/2	F	Receipt of metal tools
3467	101806		F	Account of jewelry
3468	101807		F	Account of provisions(?)
3469	101808	-/-/18	F	Account of wool for garments
3470	101809		F	Account of barley provisions
3471	101810		F	Receipt for silver for provisions
3472	101811	3/-/-	F	Receipt for provisions
3473	101812		F	Account of workmen(?)
3474	101813		F	Account of barley
3475	101814	Nbn 12/12/8	F	Account of dates
3476	101815		F	Account of dates
3477	101816	1/9/-	F	Account of dates
3478	101817	Dar 8/3/35	F	Receipt for dates or grain
3479	101818		F	Account by days
3480	101819	4/-/-	F	Receipt for silver; drawing
3481	101820	Nb(-) -/-/14	F	Account of barley fodder
3482	101821	Nbn 30/1/6	F	Receipt for oil
3483	101822		F	Account of dates or grain
3484	101823		F	Account of silver
3485	101824		F	Contract
3486	101825	14/7/-	F	Receipt for oxen
3487	101826	Nbk 14/8/-	F	Contract
3488	101827		F	Account of dates or grain
3489	101828	Ner 6/7/-	F	Account of workmen
3490	101829		F	Account of provisions(?) for workmen
3491	101830		F	Contract
3492	101831		F	Account of dates or grain provisions(?)

83-1-21,

3493	101832	Ner 18/1/-	F	House sale
3494	101833		F	Account of dates and wool(?)
3495	101834		F	Account of purchases(?)
3496	101835	13/-/-	F	Receipt
3497	101836	21/11/14	F	Receipt for barley
3498	101837		F	Letter; seal
3499	101838		F	School exercise
3500	101839		F	Contract
3501	101840		F	Contract
3502	101841	OB	F	Sale contract
3503	101842	Nbn 8/2/8	F	Receipt
3504	101843		F	Account
3505	101844		F	Account of dates
3506	101845		F	Account of workmen
3507	101846	28/7/38	F	Receipt for sesame
3508	101847	-/2/-	F	Account of blue wool
3509	101848	12/-/-	F	Receipt for sheep
3510	101849	Dar 6/6/-	F	Loan of silver
3511	101850	Nbn 6/12b/3	F	Receipt for purchase of oxen
3512	101851		F	Account of workmen
3513	101852	Nbn 30/10/-	F	Receipt for purchase of oxen
3514	101853		F	Account of house rentals
3515	101854	24/5/-	F	Account of garments of gods
3516	101855	Dar 15/12/-	F	Accounts
3517	101856	Nbn 2/11/3	F	Receipt
3518	101857	Nbk -/-/9	F	Offering ledger
3519	101858		F	Account of dates or grain
3520	101859		F	Ledger
3521	101860	20/-/36	F	Ledger
3522	101861		F	Account of provisions(?)
3523	101862		F	Account of dates or grain
3524	101863		F	Account
3525	101864		F	Account of animals(?)
3526	101865	12/10/-	F	Account of dates
3527	101866	Nbk -/12/28	F	Receipt for iron
3528	101867	-/-/40	F	Contract; Sippar
3529	101868	Nbn -/8/2	F	Receipt
3530	101869		F	Dates or grain ledger
3531	101870		F	Ledger

83-1-21,

3532	101871		F	Only personal names preserved
3533	101872	Nbn 26/6/-	F	Receipt for iron tools
3534	101873		F	Dates or grain ledger
3535	101874		F	Account of barley
3536	101875		F	Account of dates or grain provisions(?)
3537	101876	(-)-uṣur	F	Account of dates or grain
3538	101877		F	Account of dates or grain
3539	101878	Nbn -/-/6	F	Account of dates or grain
3540	101879	Dar 1/5/-	F	Account of barley
3541	101880	-/-/6	F	Account of dates
3542	101881		F	Receipt for barley provisions
3543	101882		F	Account of dates
3544	101883		F	Ledger
3545	101884	Nbn -/7/-	F	Account
3546	101885		F	Account
3547	101886		F	Dates or grain ledger
3548	101887		F	Ledger
3549	101888	-/3/-	F	Animal ledger; Sippar
3550	101889		F	Legal(?)
3551	101890	Nbn 19/2/10	F	Audit account
3552	101891		F	Ledger
3553	101892	Cam -/-/6	F	Receipt
3554	101893		F	Account of dates and emmer for provisions
3555	101894		F	Receipt for dates
3556	101895		F	Contract for dates
3557	101896		F	Account of dates or grain
3558	101897		F	Only personal names preserved
3559	101898	OB	F	Contract(?)
3560	101899	Nbn 7/10/-	F	Account of dates or grain
3561	101900		F	Ledger
3562	101901		F	Receipt for sheep
3563	101902		F	Account of dates or grain
3564	101903		F	Account
3565	101904		F	School exercise
3566	101905		F	Account of blue wool
3567	101906		F	Account
3568	101907	Nbk	F	Receipt for barley
3569	101908	27/2/1	F	Account of dates or grain tithe

83-1-21,

3570	101909		F	Account of sale of sheep and oxen
3571	101910		F	Account of animals
3572	101911		F	Account of barley
3573	101912		F	Only personal names preserved
3574	101913		F	Legal; inquiry concerning some priests
3575	101914		F	Account of sheep
3576	101915		F	Account
3577	101916	-/5/21	F	Receipt for bread
3578	101917		F	Account of barley
3579	101918	Dar -/4/27	F	Account of sale of sheep
3580	101919	Dar	F	Account of dates
3581	101920		F	Ledger
3582	101921		F	Account of barley
3583	101922		F	Letter(?)
3584	101923		F	Account of dates or grain
3585	101924		F	Receipt
3586	101925		F	Only personal names preserved
3587	101926		F	Ledger
3588	101927		F	Account of dates or grain
3589	101928		F	Only personal names preserved
3590	101929	Cam 29/-/-	F	Receipt for dates
3591	101930		F	Account of provisions(?)
3592	101931		F	Astronomical
3593	101932	Nbk -/-/20	F	Account of dates or grain
3594	101933	21/-/32	F	Receipt for dates
3595	101934		F	Account
3596	101935		F	Receipt for sheep
3597	101936		F	Account of dates
3598	101937	13/1/26	F	Receipt for a sheep
3599	101938		F	Medical; probably same tablet as 83-1-21, 3230 (= BM 101569)
3600	101939		F	Account of silver purchases
3601	101940		F	Account of dates
3602	101941		F	Account of provisions(?)
3603	101942	Ner 5/4/2	F	Contract for seed
3604	101943	Nbn 22/-/6	F	Account of silver
3605	101944		F	Receipt for barley
3606	101945	-/-/4	F	Contract

GENERAL INDEX

INDEX TO OLD BABYLONIAN TABLETS

SUPPLEMENTARY BIBLIOGRAPHY TO VOLUMES VI AND VII

82-5-22, 217	54096	*Nbk* 339
82-5-22, 221	54100	*Cyr* 379
82-5-22, 222	54101	*Cyr* 380
82-5-22, 224	54103	*Nbk* 241
82-5-22, 225	54104	*Cyr* 384
82-5-22, 226	54105	*Nbk* 6
82-5-22, 232	54111	*Nbk* 351
82-5-22, 233	54112	*Nbk* 324
82-5-22, 287	54166	*Nbk* 121
82-5-22, 288	54167	*Nbk* 432
82-5-22, 289	54168	*Nbk* 202
82-5-22, 291	54170	*Nbk* 161
82-5-22, 292	54171	*Nbk* 347
82-5-22, 294	54173	*Nbk* 335
82-5-22, 295	54174	*Nbk* 371
82-5-22, 296	54175	*Nbk* 364
82-5-22, 297	54176	*Nbk* 79
82-5-22, 298	54177	*Am* 3
82-5-22, 303	54181	*Nbn* 6
82-5-22, 304	54182	*Nbn* 206
82-5-22, 305	54183	*Nbn* 962
82-5-22, 306	54184	*Nbn* 230
82-5-22, 307	54185	*Cyr* 25
82-5-22, 361	54210	*Ner* 17
82-5-22, 371	54220	*Am* 23
82-5-22, 395	54244	*Ner* 62
82-5-22, 410	54259	*Ner* 61
82-7-14, 2	55647	*Npl* 15
82-7-14, 216	55858	*Am* 1
82-9-18, 1	60037	*Dar* 293
82-9-18, 3	60039	*Cam* 39
82-9-18, 4	60040	*Cam* 433
82-9-18, 5	60041	*Dar* 218
82-9-18, 7	60043	*Nbk* 209
82-9-18, 9	60045	*Nbn* 506
82-9-18, 10	60046	*Cyr* 151
82-9-18, 11	60047	*Nbn* 365
82-9-18, 12	60048	*Cyr* 13
82-9-18, 13	60049	*Nbk* 323
82-9-18, 15	60051	*Cam* 420
82-9-18, 16	60052	*Cam* 181

82-9-18, 17	60053	*Cam* 114
82-9-18, 19	60055	*Nbn* 984
82-9-18, 21	60057	*Nbn* 397
82-9-18, 22	60058	*Cyr* 153
82-9-18, 25	60061	*Nbn* 202
82-9-18, 27	60063	*Nbn* 1087
82-9-18, 28	60064	*Nbn* 1045
82-9-18, 29	60065	*Cam* 271
82-9-18, 30	60066	*Nbk* 167
82-9-18, 31	60067	*Cam* 30
82-9-18, 32A	60068	*Nbn* 491
82-9-18, 33	60070	*Nbn* 833
82-9-18, 35	60072	*Dar* 518
82-9-18, 36	60073	*Nbn* 200
82-9-18, 37	60074	*Cyr* 250
82-9-18, 40	60077	*Nbn* 1082
82-9-18, 41	60078	*Cyr* 286
82-9-18, 42	60079	*Nbn* 1041
82-9-18, 43	60080	*Cyr* 187
82-9-18, 44	60081	*Nbk* 114
82-9-18, 45	60082	*Nbn* 168
82-9-18, 46	60083	*Nbk* 460
82-9-18, 47	60084	*Nbk* 126
82-9-18, 48	60085	*Nbn* 416
82-9-18, 49	60086	*Nbn* 1042
82-9-18, 51	60088	*Nbn* 1058
82-9-18, 52	60089	*Nbn* 360
82-9-18, 53	60090	*Nbn* 714
82-9-18, 54	60091	*Nbn* 207
82-9-18, 55	60092	*Nbn* 1092
82-9-18, 56	60093	*Nbn* 135
82-9-18, 57	60094	*Nbn* 759
82-9-18, 58	60095	*Nbn* 234
82-9-18, 59	60096	*Cyr* 20
82-9-18, 60	60097	*Nbn* 822
82-9-18, 66	60103	*Nbn* 972
82-9-18, 67	60104	*Cyr* 84
82-9-18, 69	60106	*Nbn* 192
82-9-18, 70	60107	*Nbn* 1126
82-9-18, 73	60110	*Dar* 444
82-9-18, 74	60111	*Nbn* 1095
82-9-18, 76	60113	*Nbn* 1076
82-9-18, 78	60115	*Nbn* 277
82-9-18, 79	60116	*Nbn* 483
82-9-18, 80	60117	*Dar* 233
82-9-18, 85	60122	*Dar* 460
82-9-18, 87	60124	*Cyr* 357
82-9-18, 88	60125	*Nbn* 550
82-9-18, 89	60126	*Dar* 231
82-9-18, 90	60127	*Nbn* 1043
82-9-18, 92	60129	*Nbn* 1002

82-9-18, 95	60132	*Nbn* 1052
82-9-18, 97	60134	*Cyr* 205
82-9-18, 101	60138	*Cam* 59
82-9-18, 102	60139	*Nbn* 306
82-9-18, 104	60141	*Cam* 69
82-9-18, 106	60143	*Cam* 242
82-9-18, 108	60145	*Cyr* 348
82-9-18, 112	60149	*Nbn* 358
82-9-18, 114	60151	*Dar* 564
82-9-18, 115	60152	*Nbk* 74
82-9-18, 116	60153	*Cyr* 26
82-9-18, 120	60157	*Nbn* 1129
82-9-18, 137	60174	*Cyr* 365
82-9-18, 139	60176	*Cyr* 110
82-9-18, 142	60179	*Cam* 353
82-9-18, 146	60183	*Dar* 352
82-9-18, 147	60184	*Nbn* 826
82-9-18, 153	60190	*Cyr* 88
82-9-18, 157	60194	*Nbn* 1074
82-9-18, 159	60196	*Nbk* 128
82-9-18, 164	60201	*Nbn* 670
82-9-18, 165	60202	*Nbn* 513
82-9-18, 170	60206	*Cam* 262
82-9-18, 177	60213	*Dar* 513
82-9-18, 185	60221	*Nbk* 385
82-9-18, 188	60223	*Nbn* 998
82-9-18, 193	60228	*Nbk* 123
82-9-18, 194	60229	*Nbn* 1084
82-9-18, 195	60230	*Nbn* 303
82-9-18, 197	60232	*Cam* 367
82-9-18, 198	60233	*Nbn* 771
82-9-18, 199	60234	*Cyr* 113
82-9-18, 200	60235	*Nbn* 895
82-9-18, 201	60236	*Dar* 416
82-9-18, 205	60240	*Dar* 211
82-9-18, 207	60242	*Dar* 500
82-9-18, 208	60243	*Nbk* 412
82-9-18, 210	60245	*Cam* 259
82-9-18, 212	60247	*Nbn* 384
82-9-18, 214	60249	*Cam* 416
82-9-18, 215	60250	*Nbn* 1106
82-9-18, 216	60251	*Nbn* 1021
82-9-18, 218	60253	*Nbk* 240
82-9-18, 219	60254	*Dar* 432
82-9-18, 223	60258	*Nbn* 770
82-9-18, 224	60259	*Cyr* 170
82-9-18, 226	60261	*Nbn* 641
82-9-18, 227	60262	*Nbn* 739
82-9-18, 231	60266	*Cam* 206
82-9-18, 232	60267	*Nbn* 1081
82-9-18, 233	60268	*Cyr* 218

82-9-18, 234	60269	*Nbn* 1069
82-9-18, 237	60272	*Nbk* 178
82-9-18, 239	60274	*Cyr* 14
82-9-18, 241	60276	*Cam* 204
82-9-18, 243	60278	*Cyr* 206
82-9-18, 248	60283	*Nbn* 690
82-9-18, 249	60284	*Cam* 277
82-9-18, 252	60287	*Nbk* 16
82-9-18, 253	60288	*Nbn* 590
82-9-18, 254	60289	*Nbn* 269
82-9-18, 256	60291	*Nbn* 1133
82-9-18, 260	60295	*Nbk* 130
82-9-18, 261	60296	*Nbn* 705
82-9-18, 262	60297	*Nbn* 672
82-9-18, 263	60298	*Nbn* 488
82-9-18, 264	60299	*Cyr* 9
82-9-18, 268	60302	*Dar* 277
82-9-18, 269	60303	*Cam* 79
82-9-18, 270	60304	*Nbn* 469
82-9-18, 272	60306	*Cyr* 94
82-9-18, 278	60311	*Dar* 574
82-9-18, 279	60312	*Nbk* 341
82-9-18, 282	60314	*Cyr* 18
82-9-18, 283	60315	*Nbk* 113
82-9-18, 286	60318	*Nbn* 411
82-9-18, 287	60319	*Cam* 364
82-9-18, 290	60322	*Nbn* 894
82-9-18, 291	60323	*Nbn* 527
82-9-18, 293	60325	*Nbn* 482
82-9-18, 295	60327	*Nbn* 366
82-9-18, 296	60328	*Nbn* 795
82-9-18, 300	60332	*Cam* 107
82-9-18, 301	60333	*Cam* 268
82-9-18, 303	60335	*Cyr* 28
82-9-18, 304	60336	*Nbn* 747
82-9-18, 305	60337	*Nbn* 1023
82-9-18, 306	60338	*Cam* 63
82-9-18, 307	60339	*Nbn* 799
82-9-18, 310	60342	*Cyr* 289
82-9-18, 311	60343	*Cam* 155
82-9-18, 314	60346	*Dar* 517
82-9-18, 315	60347	*Nbn* 408
82-9-18, 316	60348	*Nbn* 754
82-9-18, 318	60350	*Nbn* 510
82-9-18, 319	60351	*Nbn* 1061
82-9-18, 320	60352	*Nbn* 330
82-9-18, 326	60358	*Nbn* 363
82-9-18, 327	60359	*Cam* 374
82-9-18, 329	60361	*Cam* 202
82-9-18, 330	60362	*Dar* 248
82-9-18, 331	60363	*Nbn* 1075

82-9-18, 332	60364	*Nbn* 1000
82-9-18, 336	60368	*Cam* 354
82-9-18, 337	60369	*Cam* 129
82-9-18, 338	60370	*Cyr* 256
82-9-18, 339	60371	*Nbn* 726
82-9-18, 340	60372	*Cam* 426
82-9-18, 342	60374	*Nbn* 454
82-9-18, 343	60375	*Cam* 311
82-9-18, 344	60376	*Nbn* 399
82-9-18, 346	60378	*Nbn* 925
82-9-18, 349	60381	*Nbn* 662
82-9-18, 350	60382	*Cam* 139
82-9-18, 351	60383	*Nbk* 150
82-9-18, 352	60384	*Dar* 479
82-9-18, 353	60385	*Cam* 32
82-9-18, 355	60387	*Nbn* 402
82-9-18, 356	60388	*Nbn* 409
82-9-18, 359	60391	*Nbn* 494
82-9-18, 360	60392	*Cam* 22
82-9-18, 361	60393	*Cyr* 339
82-9-18, 364	60396	*Nbn* 350
82-9-18, 366	60398	*Nbn* 422
82-9-18, 368	60400	*Nbn* 561
82-9-18, 370	60402	*Nbk* 75
82-9-18, 373	60405	*Nbn* 913
82-9-18, 374	60406	*Cam* 87
82-9-18, 376	60408	*Nbn* 702
82-9-18, 378	60410	*Nbk* 15
82-9-18, 379	60411	*Dar* 562
82-9-18, 380	60412	*Nbn* 423
82-9-18, 381	60413	*Cyr* 301
82-9-18, 385	60417	*Nbn* 848
82-9-18, 386	60418	*Cam* 237
82-9-18, 387	60419	*Nbn* 539
82-9-18, 388	60420	*Nbn* 421
82-9-18, 390	60422	*Cyr* 247
82-9-18, 392	60424	*Dar* 90
82-9-18, 393	60425	*Nbk* 174
82-9-18, 394	60426	*Nbn* 322
82-9-18, 396	60428	*Nbn* 563
82-9-18, 397	60429	*Cyr* 167
82-9-18, 398	60430	*Cam* 154
82-9-18, 400	60432	*Nbn* 467
82-9-18, 401	60433	*Cam* 158
82-9-18, 402	60434	*Nbn* 719
82-9-18, 404	60436	*Cyr* 21
82-9-18, 405	60437	*Cyr* 136
82-9-18, 406	60438	*Cam* 102
82-9-18, 407	60439	*Nbn* 689
82-9-18, 408	60440	*Nbn* 318
82-9-18, 409	60441	*Cyr* 138

82-9-18, 410	60442	*Nbk* 348
82-9-18, 411	60443	*Nbn* 846
82-9-18, 412	60444	*Cyr* 54
82-9-18, 414	60446	*Nbn* 768
82-9-18, 415	60447	*Nbn* 301
82-9-18, 416	60448	*Nbn* 866
82-9-18, 417	60449	*Nbk* 73
82-9-18, 418	60450	*Nbn* 630
82-9-18, 419	60451	*Nbn* 651
82-9-18, 424	60455	*Nbk* 132
82-9-18, 425	60456	*Nbn* 342
82-9-18, 429	60459	*Nbn* 828
82-9-18, 430	60460	*Cyr* 360
82-9-18, 431	60461	*Nbn* 865
82-9-18, 433	60463	*Nbn* 659
82-9-18, 439	60463	*Cyr* 166
82-9-18, 434	60464	*Nbn* 558
82-9-18, 435	60465	*Cam* 404
82-9-18, 436	60466	*Cam* 248
82-9-18, 437	60467	*Cam* 385
82-9-18, 438	60468	*Nbn* 1037
82-9-18, 442	60472	*Cyr* 210
82-9-18, 444	60473	*Nbn* 987
82-9-18, 446	60474	*Cyr* 99
82-9-18, 447	60475	*Cam* 255
82-9-18, 450	60476	*Cam* 421
82-9-18, 452	60478	*Cyr* 176
82-9-18, 455	60481	*Nbn* 486
82-9-18, 458	60484	*Nbn* 753
82-9-18, 462	60487	*Cam* 288
82-9-18, 463	60488	*Cyr* 185
82-9-18, 464	60489	*Nbn* 1050
82-9-18, 465	60490	*Nbn* 1096
82-9-18, 466	60491	*Nbn* 978
82-9-18, 467	60492	*Nbn* 789
82-9-18, 468	60493	*Cam* 283
82-9-18, 469	60494	*Nbk* 237
82-9-18, 470	60495	*Cyr* 298
82-9-18, 471	60496	*Dar* 471
82-9-18, 472	60497	*Nbn* 485
82-9-18, 473	60498	*Cam* 20
82-9-18, 475	60500	*Nbk* 181
82-9-18, 477	60502	*Nbn* 975
82-9-18, 478A	60503	*Nbn* 698
82-9-18, 479	60505	*Nbn* 857
82-9-18, 480	60506	*Nbn* 1108
82-9-18, 481	60507	*Nbn* 472
82-9-18, 482	60508	*Nbk* 415
82-9-18, 483	60509	*Nbk* 447
82-9-18, 484	60510	*Cyr* 251